>**business**research**methods**

The McGraw-Hill/Irwin Series in Operations and Decision Sciences

>businessresearchmethods

Pamela S. Schindler
Wittenberg University

thirteenedition

McGraw Hill Education

BUSINESS RESEARCH METHODS, THIRTEEN EDITION

Published by McGraw-Hill/Irwin, a business unit of The McGraw-Hill Companies, Inc., 1221 Avenue of the Americas, New York, NY, 10020. Copyright © 2019 by The McGraw-Hill Companies, Inc. All rights reserved. Printed in the United States of America. Previous editions © 2014, 2011, 2008, and 2006. No part of this publication may be reproduced or distributed in any form or by any means, or stored in a database or retrieval system, without the prior written consent of The McGraw-Hill Companies, Inc., including, but not limited to, in any network or other electronic storage or transmission, or broadcast for distance learning.

Some ancillaries, including electronic and print components, may not be available to customers outside the United States.

This book is printed on acid-free paper.

1 2 3 4 5 6 7 8 9 LWI 21 20 19 18

Bound:
ISBN 978-1-259-91893-3
MHID 1-259-91893-9

Looseleaf:
ISBN 978-1-260-21009-5
MHID 1-260-21009-X

Portfolio Manager: *Noelle Bathurst*
Product Developer: *Ryan McAndrews*
Executive Marketing Manager: *Harper Christopher*
Content Project Managers: *Erika Jordan and Angela Norris*
Buyer: *Susan K. Culbertson*
Design: *David Hash*
Content Licensing Specialist: *Melissa Homer*
Cover Image: *©scanrail/Getty Images*
Compositor: *MPS Limited*

All credits appearing on page or at the end of the book are considered to be an extension of the copyright page.

Library of Congress Cataloging-in-Publication Data

Schindler, Pamela S., author.
  Business research methods / Pamela S. Schindler, Wittenberg University.
  Thirteen edition. | New York, NY : McGraw-Hill/Irwin, [2019] |
  Earlier editions were co-authored with Donald R. Cooper.
  LCCN 2017055982 | ISBN 9781259918933 (alk. paper)
  LCSH: Industrial management–Research.
  LCC HD30.4 .E47 2018 | DDC 658.0072/1–dc23
  LC record available at https://lccn.loc.gov/2017055982

The Internet addresses listed in the text were accurate at the time of publication. The inclusion of a website does not indicate an endorsement by the authors or McGraw-Hill, and McGraw-Hill does not guarantee the accuracy of the information presented at these sites.

To my soulmate and husband, Bill, for his sound counsel and unwavering support.

Pamela S. Schindler

Walkthrough

Addressing a Revolution in Student Learning.

A transformation is taking place in many of our classrooms. During the last decade, more and more of our students have transformed to visual—from verbal—learners. Visual learners need pictures, diagrams, and graphs to clarify and reinforce what the text relates.

Integrated research process exhibits reveal a rich and complex process in a visual way.

31 fully integrated research process exhibits link concepts within stand alone chapters.

Each exhibit in this series shares symbols, shapes, and colors with others in the series. Exhibit 1-3 is the overview exhibit of the research process.

Subsequent exhibits (like this one for measurement instrument development) show more detail in a part of this process.

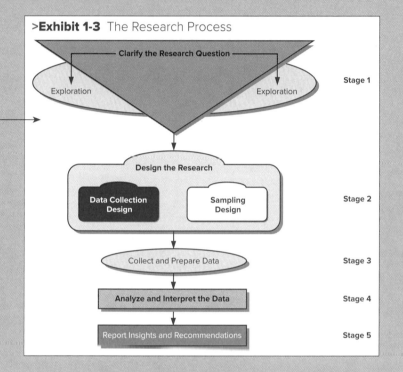

>**Exhibit 1-3** The Research Process

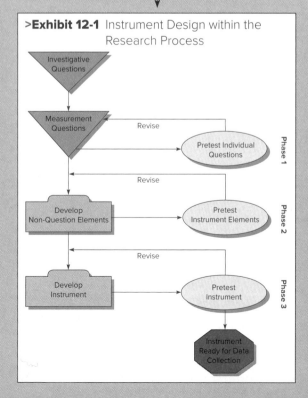

>**Exhibit 12-1** Instrument Design within the Research Process

Responsive to industry changes.

Understand what is happening behind the scenes during a project.

Research reports are increasingly oral and all about storytelling.

Clean data is critical to effective analysis.

All researchers need qualitative skills.

The research question is the basis of effective research.

You can't learn research without understanding the fundamentals.

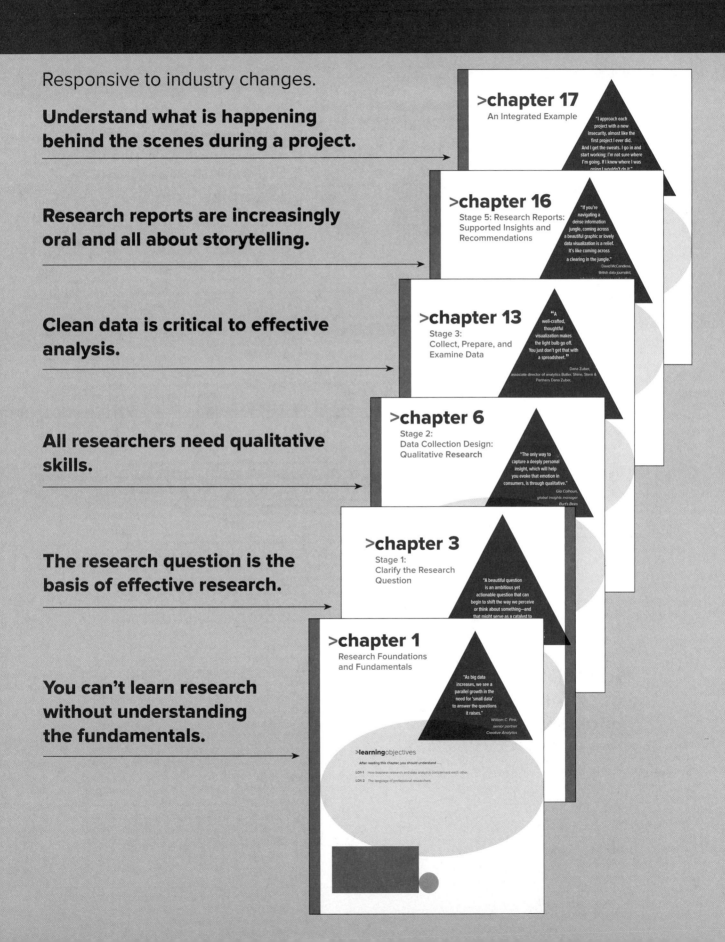

>**snap**shot

Internet Brings Prediction Research into 21st Century

Managers often must make decisions about the future. These decisions offer high uncertainty. Research is designed to reduce the risk, but simply asking people to predict their own behavior, attitude, or reaction hasn't worked well; we are notoriously poor at the task. For example, in 1985 when individuals were asked to predict their acceptance of Coke's planned reformulation, they predicted incredibly wrong and it cost Coca-Cola millions.

Historically, researchers have used the consensus prediction of experts (Delphi technique) to correct for the individual's poor predictive capabilities. However, not all situations offer a logical panel of experts. James Surowiecki, in his *The Wisdom of Crowds*, describes how a group of diverse individuals is able to make decisions and predictions better than isolated individuals or experts. MIT researchers explain that people's heightened connectivity due to the Internet has brought about the "emergence of surprising new forms of collective intelligence." As social animals, people are getting good at noticing what others are doing, sensing why they might be doing it, and predicting what they will do. In a PEW Research study, collectively Americans predicted 37 percent of Americans were obese, a fairly good predictor of the actual 31 percent who were so diagnosed.

Marcus Thomas (MT) needed a research method that was fast and that would overcome client skepticism about the inaccuracy of self-reported anticipated versus actual behaviors for its financial client. It chose to use a prediction market. "A prediction market is like an online stock investing game," explained Jennifer Hirt-Marchand, associate partner and strategic insights executive for MT. "Traders 'invest' virtual dollars in ideas, products, assets, etc. to be tested. Based on the investments they make, traders can win greater incentives if they invest in the winning idea than an incentive they might earn by completing a survey alone. This 'skin in the game' is a critical component of the methodology, as it fosters engagement and thoughtfulness on the part of the traders. Its strength is that it doesn't rely on asking individuals to make predictions about *what they would do* in the future but rather what they think *other people* would do."

Using the services of a sample provider, an online survey was sent to general population panelists. Likely participants self-identified based on having an understanding of finance with regard to estate planning, personal finances and investing, vacation planning, health care, etc. A thousand participants, known as *traders*, were recruited from this group. While panel participants are compensated by the sample company for their regular participation in research projects, panelists selected for this project could earn additional compensation based on the accuracy

©Ridofranz/Getty Images

of their predictions. Those payouts would be determined by the number of traders who invested in the "winning" group, as well as the amount each trader invested in that group.

Through a continuation of the online survey, the selected traders were first presented a written description of the new financial service (each had previously agreed to a nondisclosure agreement, as the product was in development). Then each was provided six consumer profiles (called vignettes) one at a time. Each vignette—developed based on consumer segmentation from prior research and extensive secondary research—represented a possible purchaser group. It included a narrative, describing the group as people, along with photographs bringing each group to life. Traders were each given $1,000 in virtual money to invest in one or more vignette groups—the ones they thought would be most likely to purchase the new financial service. In addition, through open-ended questions, each trader was asked to explain the reasons why they believed each vignette group would or would not purchase.

Using this methodology, Marcus Thomas identified three segments based on the best-choice vignettes, including one that seemed unlikely at the outset. It also revealed one vignette that represented the likely group at which the product line failed to rank higher among those interested in the new financial service. Marcus Thomas used these messaging insights to reach the prime segments with ads developed based on this research.

Some of the world's leading brands and companies rely on Cleveland-based Marcus Thomas to refine their brands and drive customer behavior toward their products and services.

www.marcusthomasllc.com

If a topic deals with a sensitive subject, researchers may start the topic with **buffer questions**, designed to build rapport and put the participant at ease. These are broad, neutral questions on the topic that don't require a participant to take a stand on the sensitive issue. For example, "In the last 30 days, have you personally used a streaming service to watch a movie?" before asking "Should anyone be able to access movies with graphic sexual content with streaming services?" In tests, sensitive questions that followed buffer questions have been shown to extract markedly different responses compared with when participants are directly asked a sensitive question without buffers.

Facilitate Topic and Measurement Question Sequencing

The design of measurement instruments is influenced by the need to relate each question to the others in the instrument. Often, the content of one question (called a **branched question**) assumes other questions have been asked and answered in a certain way. In computer-based instruments or computer-assisted instruments, such branching is handled by internal coding of the initial question. The PicProfile indicates a typical branch question; it reveals the elimination of alternatives not chosen in one question when asking the second question, thus shortening the participant's time.

Instructions also are a primary tool to facilitate sequencing Three types of sequencing result in **skip directions**. These instructions indicate where the participant or interviewer should go within the instrument—a question, topic or section— given one or a series of responses. These instructions can be embedded in the instrument (paper or computer-based) or provided to the interviewer. Computer-based instruments and computer-assisted interviewing make skipping fairly easy; once a pre-programmed response is entered, the computer automatically skips the participant ahead. The first type is a question-to-question skip: a question screens for experience or knowledge, and the participant is judged unable to answer the next question without it:

Example: In the last two weeks, have you used (product)? ❑ Yes ❑ No (If No, skip to Q3)

> 2. Which of the following attributes do you like about the automobile you just saw? (Select all that apply.)
>   ☑ Overall appeal
>   ☑ Headroom
>   ❑ Design
>   ❑ Color
>   ☑ Height from the ground
>   ❑ Other _____
>   ❑ None of the above
>   [Next Question]

> 3. For those items that you selected, how important is each? (Provide one answer for each attribute.)

	Extremely Important	Neither important nor unimportant		Not at all Important	Don't know
a) Overall appeal	○	○	○	○	○
b) Height from the ground	○	○	○	○	○
c) Headroom	○	○	○	○	○

>**pic**profile

One of the attractions of using a web survey is the ease with which participants follow branching questions immediately customized to their response patterns. In this survey, participants were shown several pictures of a prototype vehicle. Those who responded to question 2 by selecting one or more of the attributes in the checklist question were sequenced to a version of question 3 that related only to their particular responses to question 2. Note also that in question 3 the researcher chose not to force an answer, allowing the participant to indicate he or she had no opinion ("Don't know") on the issue of level of importance.

A Closeup offers a more in-depth example.

>**close**up

Who's Really Taking Your Surveys?

Early in panel development, panelists were offered $100 to $150 to join and participate in qualitative studies. Historically, these participants participated in longer engagements (on-line qualitative, ethnography studies or face to face in-depth interviews). As random digit dialing became less productive for recruiting respondents and the internet became more widely used, researchers started using panels—also called communities—to recruit participants for quantitative research. Quantitative respondents who are engaged for much shorter periods are more likely to be paid $1 to $10 per survey completed.

The professional respondent—one who takes repeated surveys—was once considered a deterrent to quality research. "As researchers," explained Jessica Broome, PhD, principal of Jessica Broome Research, "we wanted to keep the 'cheaters' and 'repeaters' out of our studies, believing they biased results." As decision cycles shorten, the demand for better and more timely information means attracting and retaining qualified participants. During the last three decades, increasingly this means researchers turn to panels, and by design, these participants are asked to participate in numerous studies.

"We wanted to know 'Who are these people willing to take repeated surveys?'" explained Broome. "And given that some surveys are overly long and others poorly designed, 'Why do they do this?'" Broome teamed with Kerry Hecht, Director of Research Services, Recollective, a division of Ramius Corporation, to find out what motivates panel members and what makes them likely to reduce the quality of the information they provide.

The Qualitative Study

Broome and Hecht designed a multistage study that drew participants from multiple panel providers, including Critical Mix, Schlesinger Associates, and Swagbucks. "We started with a 5-day online qualitative community study with 20 people to explore what got them started as a survey panelist and what kept them going," explained Hecht. "While money is a motivator in keeping panelists engaged, they also shared the influences of intrinsic motivators like fun, feeling useful, contributing to important decisions, and participation being more interesting than time spent on social media."

For any particular study, panelists are often screened exclusively on demographics. "Because participants derive intrinsic benefits, panelists will sometimes fudge on screening information in an attempt to be included in a study," shared Broome. When a panelist doesn't meet the desired demographic parameters, they are told "You don't qualify" but are rarely told why. "But once they are included," explained Broome, "participants

claim honesty drives their responses, they think lying on survey questions would undermine the study."

"Often panelists expressed feeling abused, misled, and disrespected. For example, when they are told about survey length, they often felt deceived when a promised 15-minute survey took 45 minutes, or when the survey was not only long, but boring," explained Broome. Increasingly, panelists in quantitative studies are tech-savvy. "They understand what current technology should permit a survey company to do—like eliminate the need to ask demographic questions repeatedly in the same survey process or use earlier answers to filter later questions," claimed Hecht. "They basically think researchers can make the experience so much better." "The research industry needs their insights, but can treat panelists with disdain," claimed Broome.

The Quantitative Study

Broome and Hecht followed their qualitative exploration study with Phase 2, a mobile-optimized quantitative study of 1,499 participants, also drawn from various panel providers and fielded by Propeller Insights. Each panelist took a topical survey that included a creativity assessment. Additionally, half the group (750) took a VARK assessment. VARK assesses visual, aural, audio, read/write, and kinesthetic learning preferences through a series of learning scenario questions. Creativity was assessed through a battery of 38 statements requiring agreement or disagreement, as well as a checklist of 54 descriptors. "We discovered that participants didn't favor any one of the learning approaches, nor were they outliers on the creativity assessment," shared Broome.

>**close**up**cont'd**

Broome and Hecht's Phase 2 research revealed factors essential for reducing respondent drop outs: Don't ask screening questions within a survey once a participant has answered a detailed screener to qualify; merge the data. Participants don't care that different companies do different aspects of the research; they want researchers to avoid duplication. Don't ask essentially the same question in different ways; once is enough. Use previous question responses to determine later questions asked; panelists are willing to share their thoughts, behaviors, and lives but don't want their time wasted. Respondents have different preferences and styles; let them respond as they wish—with text or video, exclusively on a mobile device or a computer. "They shared lots of ideas for making surveys more engaging and interesting," claimed Hecht, "including, adding music or video, getting rid of grid questions, and reducing survey time to 15 minutes or less."

Using information extracted from an open question and analyzed with OdinText, Phase 2 research also revealed that "most participants were a member of one or two panels but struggled to remain engaged with their panels," shared Hecht. "Participants appreciate feeling like a valued part of a full process, not just an interchangeable cog in a wheel. They like to participate in studies that are interesting to them and about products or services that are relevant to their daily lives—knowledge is a

powerful motivator." Many also cited meeting interesting people and hearing different viewpoints as motivation. "They also love learning the results of studies they participate in and understanding why we as researchers do what we do or ask what we ask," shared Broome.

Recently, a SurveyMonkey study also found panelists gave thoughtful, consistent answers over time. It released results of a 1,000-person international panel assessment study, using three surveys with the same respondents, one in each of three sequential months, which checked for quality-reducing behaviors like straight lining (repeatedly choosing the same answer choice in matrix questions), poor open response validity (responding with nonhelpful, gibberish answers), and whether they were unfocused or not paying attention. Of the panelists, 97 percent, 97 percent, and 94 percent or more passed each of these tests, respectively, with no difference between men and women. And in terms of response reliability, over the three waves of surveys, in 23 indicators SurveyMonkey tracked, only three items showed significantly significant change among U.S. participants, time-to-complete, choice of the "other" response, and attitude about "moral acceptability of alcohol use."

Sources: jessicabroomeresearch.com; recollective.com; surveymonkey.com

---

a particular software training strategy, we infer that others will also. The basic idea of taking a sample is that by selecting some cases in a population, we may draw conclusions about the entire target population.

There are several compelling reasons for using a **sample** (a subset of the target population) rather than a **census** (all cases within a population), including (1) lower cost, (2) greater speed of data collection, (3) availability of population cases, and (4) greater accuracy of results. The advantages of taking a sample over census are less compelling when two conditions exist: (1) a census is feasible due to a small target population and (2) a census is necessary when the cases are quite different from each other.[1] When the population is small and variable, any sample we draw may not be representative of the population from which it is drawn. The resulting values we calculate from the sample are incorrect as estimates of the population values.

promotions, training experiences, project assignments, project leadership, new customers captured, and so on. Sophisticated businesses track these KPIs through digitized, perpetually maintained **dashboards**—a data visualization tool that shows current and a period of prior status on each metric, usually on one screen. Even small businesses can dashboard KPIs create with the software tools available.

Identifying opportunity-based management dilemmas is more time consuming and difficult. It requires monitoring obscure developments in a variety of industries, as well as emerging trends in your own industry. Those companies looking for opportunities are trying to be first movers; they want to capitalize on an environmental trend that others haven't recognized. Jeff Bezos, chief executive officer (CEO) of Amazon, is always seeking these kinds of dilemmas: customers getting frustrated at not finding the solutions they sought at stores, companies needing a more reliable delivery option, readers wanting to take more books with them when they travel than luggage space permits, etc. The search for opportunity-based management dilemmas is full of risk, but when the approach pays off, it often pays big.

However, choosing one dilemma on which to focus may be difficult. Solving different dilemmas offers different rewards. One approach is to estimate the payoff of solving a dilemma, using this value to prioritize. This is more easily done for problems (e.g., estimating the cost of reducing customer returns) than for opportunities. Ultimately, to choose incorrectly puts a company or business on an unproductive path. As a manager, only practice makes you proficient at this task. For new managers, or for established managers facing new responsibilities, developing several management dilemma-to-research question hierarchies, each starting with a different dilemma, will assist in the choice process. To develop these, much exploratory research is used, tapping into published secondary sources and mining company data.

Exploration

Seeking existing information is often used not only to identify dilemmas (e.g., identify industry standard to compare to company performance), but also to ask the right questions and better understand decision options. Historic company data are increasingly being used in exploration as better tools to tap into digital data warehouses have become available.[1] Much of this information may not be in searchable databases; it may be in written reports, where accessibility is an issue. At this stage, it always pays the

We are attracted to experiments at an early age due to our unlimited curiosity. A great researcher fosters curiosity as an important skill.

31

Images are worth more than 1,000 words; they serve as visual cues to anchor concepts in memory.

Using learning aids to cement concepts.

Discussion questions tie to learning objectives and come in four types.

Relating questions to newsworthy businesses makes them more relevant to students.

→

>discussionquestions

Terms in Review

1 How does qualitative research differ from quantitative research?

2 What is data saturation, and how does it influence qualitative research?

3 What is the nature of data collected in qualitative research?

4 Why do senior executives feel more comfortable relying on quantitative data than qualitative data? How might a qualitative research company lessen the senior-level executive's skepticism?

5 Distinguish among structured, semistructured, and unstructured interviews.

Making Research Decisions

6 Assume you are a manufacturer of small kitchen electrics, like Hamilton Beach/Proctor Silex, and you want to determine if some innovative designs with unusual shapes and colors developed for the European market could be successfully marketed in the U.S. market. What qualitative research would you recommend, and why?

7 NCR Corporation, known as a world leader in ATMs, point-of-sale (POS) retail checkout scanners, and check-in kiosks at airports, announced in June 2009 that it would move its world headquarters from Dayton (OH) to Duluth (GA), a suburb of Atlanta, after more than 125 years. An employer of 1,200 mostly high-salaried, professional workers in Dayton, NCR was enticed to move by Georgia's offer of more than $56.9 million in tax credits; its fast-growing, educated 25- to 34-year-old population cohort; international offices for 10 European state governments; and the busiest international airport (Atlanta) in the world.

a. What qualitative research might NCR have done to reach this decision?

b. NCR will use its move to Georgia to downsize its world headquarters workforce. What qualitative research could help NCR determine which of its 1,200 employees will be offered positions in Duluth?

From Concept to Practice

8 Use Exhibit 6-6 to develop the recruitment screener for the research you described in your answer to question 5.

9 Conduct a focus group among students in your class on one of the following topics:

a. The department's problems offering requirements and electives essential for meeting your graduation expectations.

b. Entertainment sponsored by your university to bring the community on campus.

From the Headlines

10 Lately airlines have been having a rough time, in terms of legal actions and PR issues, with consumers openly expressing outrage at being bumped from—or forcibly removed from—flights. Design a qualitative study to reveal the suppressed (as opposed to surface) issues that are contributing to this rage.

a. What are some of the surface issues?

b. Who will you want to participate and how will you recruit them?

c. What qualitative method(s) will you choose. Be specific about any exercises you will incorporate.

>keyterms

3-D graph 456	facts 446	pictograph 456
actionable insights 434	findings nondisclosure 461	pie graph 451
analogy 447	geograph 456	predispositions 450
anchoring bias 438	graph 450	report framework 443
area graph 451	infographic 459	report structure 439
audience analysis 437	information 434	right to quality 460
audience-centric planning 436	insight 434	scope 441
auditory learners 445	jargon 458	statistics 446
bar graph 454	kinesthetic learners 445	story 447
confirmation bias 438	language level 458	survivorship bias 438
conformity bias 438	limitations 442	table 449
data 434	line graph 451	technical report 440
		ony/expert opinion 447
		458
		ze 444
		learners 445
		pace 457

Key terms are a valuable refresher, in each chapter and in the glossary.

←

>glossary

3-D graphic a presentation technique that permits a graphical comparison of three or more variables; types include column, ribbon, wireframe, and surface line.

a priori contrasts a special class of tests used in conjunction with the *F* test that is specifically designed to test the hypotheses of the experiment or study (in comparison to post hoc or unplanned tests).

acquiescence bias a tendency for participants to agree with an item or statement within a measurement question that asks for levels of agreement/disagreement; occurs when they have less knowledge on a topic; more a problem for less educated or less informed participants.

action research a methodology with brainstorming followed by sequential trial-and-error to discover the most effective solution to a problem; succeeding solutions are tried until the desired results are achieved; used with complex problems about which little is known.

actionable insights insights aligned with key business goals and strategic initiatives that are novel, unusual, or unexpected and that lead to recommendations for specific decisions.

administrative question a measurement question that identifies the participant, interviewer, interview location, and conditions; generates nominal data.

after-only design preexperimental design that takes one measurement of DV after manipulation of the IV.

alternative hypothesis (H_a) an assumption that a difference exists between the sample parameter and the population statistic to which it is compared; the logical opposite of the null

attitude a learned, stable predisposition to respond to oneself, other persons, objects, or issues in a consistently favorable or unfavorable way.

attitude scaling process of assessing a person's disposition (from extremely favorable disposition to an extremely unfavorable one) toward an *object* or its *properties* using a number that represents a person's score on an attitudinal continuum range.

audience analysis an analysis of the expected audience for a research report.

audience-centric planning a research report orientation whose focus is on gaining the audience's embrace of data insights and recommendations; the resulting presentation is persuasive and tells a story employing statistics.

auditory learners audience members who learn through listening; represent about 20 to 30 percent of the audience; implies the need to include stories and examples in research presentations.

authority figure a projective technique (imagination exercise) in which participants are asked to imagine that the brand or product is an authority figure and to describe the attributes of the figure.

automatic interaction detection (AID) a data partitioning procedure that searches up to 300 variables for the single best predictor of a dependent variable.

balanced rating scale has an equal number of categories above and below the midpoint or an equal number of favorable/ unfavorable response choices.

Glossary reinforces the language of research.

←

Summated Rating Questions

The **Likert scale**, developed by Rensis Likert (pronounced Lick-ert), is the most frequently used variation of the summated rating question. Questions based on **summated rating scales** consist of statements that express either a favorable or an unfavorable attitude toward the object of interest. The participant is asked to agree or disagree with each statement. Each response is given a numerical score to reflect its degree of attitudinal favorableness, and the scores may be summed to measure the participant's overall attitude. Summation is *not* necessary and in some instances may actually be misleading, as our caution below clearly shows.

In Exhibit 11-8, the participant chooses one of five levels of agreement. This is the traditional Likert scale because it meets Likert's rules for construction and testing. The numbers indicate the value to be assigned to each possible answer, with 1 the least favorable impression of Internet superiority and 5 the most favorable. Likert scales may also use 7 and 9 scale points. Technically, such question is a Likert-type question as its construction is less rigorous than the process Likert created. However, the advantages of the 7- and 9- point scales are a better approximation of a normal response curve and extraction of more variability among respondents.

Conscientious researchers are careful that each item meets an empirical test for discriminating ability between favorable and unfavorable attitudes. Originally, creating a Likert scale involved a procedure known as *item analysis*. Exhibit 11-9 provides the steps for selecting Likert statements (items) for the scale using item analysis. The values for each choice are normally not part of the measurement instrument, but they are shown in Exhibit 11-10 to illustrate the scoring system.

>Exhibit 11-9   How to Perform an Likert Item Analysis

Item analysis assesses each item (statement) in a Likert scale based on how well it discriminates between those people whose total score is high and those whose total score is low.

Step 1	Collect a large number of statements that meet the following criteria
	• Each statement is relevant to the attitude being studied.
	• Each statement reflects a favorable or unfavorable position on that attitude.
Step 2	Select people similar to study participants (participant stand-ins) to read each statement.
Step 3	Participant stand-ins indicate their level of their agreement with each statement, using a 5-point scale. A scale value of 1 indicates a strongly unfavorable attitude (strongly disagree). A value of 5 indicates a strongly favorable attitude (strongly agree). The other intensities (2 [disagree], 3 [neither agree nor disagree], 4 [agree]) are mid-range attitudes (see Exhibit 11-3).
	• To ensure consistent results, the assigned numerical values are reversed if the statement is worded negatively. The number 1 is always strongly unfavorable and 5 is always strongly favorable.
Step 4	Add each participant stand-in's responses to secure a total score.
Step 5	Array these total scores from highest to lowest; then and select some portion—generally defined as the top and bottom 10 to 25 percent of the distribution—to represent the highest and lowest total scores.
	• The two extreme groups represent people with the most favorable and least favorable attitudes toward the attitude being studied. These extremes are the two criterion groups by which individual Likert statements (items) are evaluated.
	• Discard the middle group's scores (50 to 80 percent of participant stand-ins), as they are not highly discriminatory on the attitude.
Step 6	Calculate the mean scores for each scale item among the low scorers and high scorers.
Step 7	Test the mean scores for statistical significance by computing a t value for each statement.
Step 8	Rank order the statements by their t values from highest to lowest.
Step 9	Select 20-25 statements (items) with the highest t values (statistically significant difference between mean scores) to include in the final Likert scale

Researchers have found that a larger number of items for each attitude object improves the reliability of the Likert scale. As an approximate indicator of a statement's discrimination power, one authority suggests using only those statements whose t value is 1.75 or greater, provided there are 25 or more participant stand-ins in each group. See Exhibit 11-5 for an example.

Source: Allen L. Edwards, *Techniques of Attitude Scale Construction* (New York: Appleton-Century-Crofts, 1957), pp. 152–54.

Observation Environment

Observation studies can be designed for the field or laboratory. In business research, field studies may take place at a customer's home, the shopping environment, an employee work area (plant, office, distribution center), a supplier's location, and more. Field studies, offering a natural setting, are most likely to obtain unaltered behavior, especially when the observer isn't directly involved.

Laboratory studies are most likely to provide data protection. When specialized equipment is needed for observation (e.g., eye-tracking cameras, heart rate monitors, galvanic skin response machines, etc) laboratory settings are often the choice. We've had some success with employing eye-tracking via a subject's laptop and tablet cameras. Laboratory settings are obviously more expensive, usually involve smaller sample sizes, and pose more difficulties in recruiting subjects. Laboratory observations can be part of an experimental design.

>snapshot

Observation and Police Cameras

If you read or watch the news, you'll know that urban areas have had a sharp increase in questioned—if not questionable—police actions with regard to excessive use of force, and bystander videos have played an increasing role in judging police actions. In 2015, the U.S. Supreme Court, in *Graham v. Connor*, held that an officer's actions, however, "must be judged from the perspective of a reasonable officer rather than with the 2020 vision of hindsight." In an article in *The Atlantic*, Seth W Stoughton, a law professor and former police officer, and Geoffrey Alpert, a professor of criminology both at the University of South Carolina, along with Jeff Noble, a police consultant based in Orange County, California, write, "The aversion to what officers derisively refer to as 'second-guessing' [makes] officers less receptive to a critique of their actions [and] makes them reluctant to provide their own complete and honest critiques." Yet nationwide, we've seen a demand for police to change and for police decisions to be more transparent, resulting in a clamoring for use of police body and cruiser cameras.

Do you believe you get a true picture of an incident when you see a body-mounted or dash-mounted video? Stoughton, who also consults with law enforcement agencies, has choreographed a series of videos to demonstrate the answer to this question. His use parallels an observation study based on respondents watching video footage of mock police incidents. Using a series of chest-mounted or dash-mounted cameras and bystander videos, he shows just how difficult it is to arrive at an accurate conclusion when using only a police-cruiser or body-cam video.

Chest-mounted cameras during interactions or pursuits often create jerky movements and wildly distorted images. Stoughton calls this "deceptive intensity"; it creates the impression that the officer is under attack when he might not be. In an interception incident video, using a dash-mounted camera involving a fleeing suspect and Taser use by an officer, accuracy is related to vantage point. The body camera doesn't reveal the use of a Taser or the absence of a gun, while video shot by a bystander does. "When video allows us to look through someone's eyes, we

©Aaron Roeth Photography

tend to adopt an interpretation that favors that person," explains Stoughton, a psychological phenomenon known as "camera perspective bias." Stoughton's research also reveals that the degree to which the viewer trusts or distrusts the police influences his or her video interpretation. So while the bystander might not know any facts leading up to the incident, his or her camera has its own bias. He concludes video evidence interpretation depends, therefore, on perspective as well as bias.

So in observation research, should we consider the camera as an accurate, unbiased observer? See for yourself. Check out the videos on Connect.

"How-to" exhibits and Appendices help students DO research.

Connect resources enrich and engage.

Cases, video, sample projects, templates, appendices, and more.

It's serious business to revise a book that has been a world-wide leading text for more than three decades, one that's published in eight international editions and is published in eight languages. The process of text writing and the speed with which revisions are developed don't often permit a complete overhaul. But for this edition, given major changes in how students and professors use text material and how professors are teaching, as well as major changes in the research industry, a fresh approach was necessary. To address major industry changes and both professor and student needs, my McGraw-Hill team and I came up with a process and plan to deliver what students are seeking while giving professors what they need. The approach involved the following:

- Reflect changes in student learning and teacher pedagogy:
  - Separate
  - Streamline and simplify
  - Clarify
- Reflect the current state of the research industry:
  - Rethink everything
  - Collaborate

Reflect Educational Changes

A deep dive into educational articles, as well as comments from our reviewers and numerous teaching colleagues and students, present a picture of some major changes in student learning and professors' use of textbooks.

- An increasing percentage of students don't buy books; some professors don't require this of them based on the way text material is or is not used in the course.
- Students often enter classrooms without a foundation for that day's discussion or activities.
- Professors see students disengaging from important tasks of the learning process: self-preparation and self-learning.
- Some professors—even educational institutions—are choosing to craft their own books, drawing only those chapters from one or multiple textbooks that are critical for their instructional approach.
- Customized books omit topics and tools deemed unnecessary for a given course based on its number of credit hours or the chosen pedagogy. Students revealed that omitted material often leaves them with voids affecting their understanding.

- Professors want chapters that stand alone, so they may order chapters however they choose to teach the material.
- Many professors want chapters to focus on the essential material of the topic of each chapter, not have that material spread intermittently throughout the book.
- Professors want any text-embedded examples to enhance clarity of a concept.
- Students want unnecessary material eliminated; to them, "unnecessary" means background and history of a concept, not practical examples.
- Students believe that in a course like business research, they should be able to DO research after they learn, not just be able to describe it.
- Students are expected to apply what is learned in their research methods course in more advanced classes; their research methods text needs to serve as a reference manual.

This revision accomplishes the above in the following ways:

- *Separate*. This edition:
  - Eliminated elements that artificially tie chapters together.
  - Reinvented the use of elements that share cross-chapter features.
- *Streamline and simplify*.
  - At the book level, this edition:
    - Changed the number and order of chapters.
    - Addressed writing and reading level by choosing more widely accepted vocabulary, rather than jargon, to describe and explain; shortening sentences; and employing a more approachable journalist style.
  - At the chapter level, this edition:
    - Moved some material from one chapter to another where it had a more logical fit.
    - Reorganized material in each chapter to make it flow more logically (always putting A before B),
    - Removed from every chapter material that might be "nice to know" but wasn't "critical to know."
    - Assessed the value of every exhibit and example and made appropriate changes.
    - Removed multiple terms for the same concept.
    - Held the list of Key Terms to research-specific terms.

- *Clarify*.
  - Students are often frustrated with textbooks; books define concepts using other concepts students don't fully understand. This edition redefines dozens of key terms to remedy this problem.
  - Students want examples to be relevant to them. This edition chose business research projects to profile by choosing behaviors, issues, or brands students might know or embrace.
  - Students want to understand; a definition alone doesn't achieve this. In this edition, any concept important enough to include has more than a definition.
  - Students prefer one term for a single concept; they find multiple terms aggravating and confusing. This edition uses one term for one concept, with alternatives relegated to the glossary.
  - Students want the key terms list for each chapter to be comprehensive but to exclude terms that aren't critical. After conferring with researchers and professors, several concepts were removed from the key terms lists and the glossary, while others—having achieved more common use in the industry—were added.
  - Students want, and need, to be able to DO research. This edition delivers:
    - One chapter for basic foundational concepts.
    - One chapter with everything needed to craft measurement questions.
    - One chapter with everything needed to develop a measurement instrument.
    - One chapter each for each of the data collection methods.
    - One chapter for preparing data for subsequent detailed analysis.
    - One chapter for reporting research.
    - "How-to" guides for difficult tasks and helpful tips for other tasks in exhibits and in several new appendices (*Better Tables, Better Reports, Sample Computer-Based Questions and Guidelines for Mobile Q.*).
    - A new chapter, *An Integrated Example*, that provides an insider's view of a research project from management dilemma to research report.
  - Students need visual cues to process and retain information:
    - This edition provides 66 new photo visual cues to help them remember material.
    - This text uses a series of exhibits linked to the research process; these use common shapes

and colors. Every exhibit in the 31-exhibit process series of exhibits has been subtly or substantially redesigned; the series includes two new exhibits.
    - Concepts are now strongly linked to the five stages in the primary research process model.
  - Students and faculty alike want ways to assess student understanding of material. This edition offers a new resource: *Connect. Connect* provides students computer-based assessment exercises, which encourage practice and provide instant feedback on mastery of material. Use of *Connect* improves understanding and recall. *Connect* provides instructors student- and class-level analytics to improve subject, class, and course decisions.

Reflect the Research Industry

As in prior editions, the use of various interim *GreenBook Research Industry Trends (GRIT)* reports guided the research for this revision. The 2016 GRIT Report is based on the largest study of research suppliers and users ever conducted.

- *Rethink*. This edition:
  - Makes a clear distinction between research and data analytics.
  - Removed topics that are no longer relevant.
  - Reduced coverage of topics showing waning importance.
  - Enhanced coverage of topics the industry has embraced.
  - Redesigned exhibits to reflect industry changes; of the more than 200 exhibits in this edition, 31 are completely new, and an additional 55 have been updated or redesigned.

- *Collaborate*. In an industry that is changing very quickly, any revision depends on people on the front lines of research. Hundreds of emails and conversations, numerous books and articles, and almost 100 webinars and presentations have influenced this edition.
  - Of the 56 Snapshots, PicProfiles, and Closeups featured in this edition, 79 percent are new (32) or updated (12). Topics in these rich research stories cover cyber security, prediction markets, sentiment analysis, why data analytics isn't delivering results, programmatic ad buying, millennials and housing, the art of asking questions, using interviews to define the management question, learning from Pixar to tell research stories, automated secondary data searchers, agile research, performance management research, who's taking surveys, digital

transformation, use of smartphones, eye tracking, observation with body cameras, experiments in employee health, use of robots, experimental labs, gaming, packaging redesign, question banks, survey engagement, infographic reports, coding word data, data insights, finding best practices, presentation venues, and much more.

- Discussion questions, especially those labeled *From the Headlines*, cover Chipotle's reputation, BMW and electric cars, Uber software that excludes neighborhoods and buildings, shifting jobs to robots, airline safety, Delta's reorganization of LAX, Dolby's experiments with theater light and sound, Mercedes-Benz and self-driving cars, Walmart and Nabisco's Oreo O's cereal, Kohl's department store and Apple Pay, performance-enhancing drugs in the workplace, Toyota and public confidence, and more.

Keep the Features Adopters Love

- *Critical Core Content.* The materials adopters have loved for decades are still the core of this edition. In an attempt to make the book more flexible to current instructional methodologies, we haven't abandoned what made the book an industry leader.

- *Strong Learning Objectives and Summaries.* Every chapter has new learning objectives. The summaries are comprehensive, knowing sometimes these are the only material a student has time to read before class.

- *Multipurpose Discussion Questions.* These can serve as review for students, as testing exercises, or as options for vibrant class discussions because many reflect real-business situations.

- *Versatile Appendices.* End-of-chapter and end-of-text appendices for information that, given the differing skills and knowledge of their students, professors may want to emphasize or exclude. New appendices relate to building *Better Tables* and offering tips on *Better Reports*; to address mobile and other types of computer-delivered measurement instruments, there is the appendix *Sample Computer-Based Questions and Guidelines for Mobile Q.* We retained end-of-chapter appendices related to *More Effective Measurement Questions* and *Calculate Sample Size.*

  Professors sometimes use writing a proposal as an end-of-term project or testing exercise. As a result, Appendix A has been rewritten with three exercises in mind: writing a formal proposal, creating an RFP, and assessing a proposal submitted in response to an RFP. Other end-of book appendices offer a professional focus group discussion guide (B), cover nonparametric statistics (C), and provide statistical tables (D).

Use the Cloud

We offer a comprehensive set of teaching and learning resources for *Business Research Methods* for faculty in Instructor Resources within Connect and for students at www.mhhe.com/Schindler13e. You'll find the following:

- *Written Cases.* Cases offer an opportunity to tell research stories in more depth and detail. You'll also find cases about hospital services, lotteries, data mining, fundraising, new promotions, and website design, among other topics, featuring organizations like Akron Children's Hospital, Kelley Blue Book, Starbucks, Yahoo!, the American Red Cross, and more.

- *Video Cases and Supplements.* New to this edition is a video supplement about an experiment in observation using body cameras; it should be ideal for discussing error in observation research. Additionally, several short segments drawn from a two-hour metaphor elicitation technique (MET) interview should be invaluable in teaching students to conduct almost any type of individual depth interview and to explain the concept of researcher–participant rapport. Four of our video cases were written and produced especially to match the research process model and feature noted companies: Lexus, Starbucks, Wirthlin Worldwide (now Harris Interactive), Robert Wood Johnson Foundation, GMMB, Visa, Bank One, Team One Advertising, U.S. Tennis Association, Vigilante New York, and the Taylor Group.

- *Data Files.* If your course doesn't involve a project where students collect their own data, use one of the cases here that contain data.

- *Sample Student Project.* Visualization of the finished deliverable is crucial to creating a strong research report, or critique this one.

- *Appendices.* You'll find helpful appendices within Connect: *Bibliographic Database Searches, Advanced Bibliographic Searches, Complex Experimental Designs, Test Markets,* and *Pretesting Options and Discoveries.*

- *Articles, Samples, and Templates.* Students often need to see how professionals do research to really understand the research process. You'll find a sample EyeTrackShop report, a Nielsen report of using U.S. Census data, an Excel template for generating sample data displays, and more.

- *Multivariate Analysis: An Overview* is a chapter for the benefit of graduate students who use *Business Research Methods.*

- *Instructor's Manual* (instructors only).
  - *Web Exercises.* Due to the ever-changing nature of web URLs, you'll find these exercises here.

- *Written and Video Case Discussion Guides.*
- *Additional Business Research Examples* for discussion.
- *Test Bank* (instructors only).

Collaborators

Research industry collaborators are the lifeblood of this textbook writer. The following people collaborated directly on this edition or connected me with those who did: Andy Peytchev, Research Triangle Institute; Bella Tumini, Suja; Betty Adamou, Research Through Gaming Ltd.; Cassandra McNeill, GutCheck; Colin McHattie, iTracks; Dan Weber, iTracks; Daniel Enson, Toluna; David Harris, Insight and Measurement; Denise D'Andrea, Focus Vision; Edwige Winans, Marcus Thomas LLC; Elaine Arkin, research consultant; Eric Lipp, Open Doors Organization; Ilan Hertz, SiSense; Jane Boutelle, Digsite; Jennifer Hirt-Marchand, Marcus Thomas LLC; Jessica Broome, Jessica Broome Research; Justin Ohanessian, Sticky; Kerry Hecht, Ramius; Lance Jones, Keynote Systems; Lenard Murphy, GreenBook; Lisa Whestone, Gutcheck; Malgorzata Kolling, OdinText; Mark Bunger, Forrester Research; Matt Marta, GutCheck; Monika Wingate, Digsite; Nicola Petty, Statistics Learning Centre; Patricio Pagani, InfoTools; Pete Cape, SSI; Rob Ramirez, Schlesinger Associates; Robert W. Kahle, author; Tom H.C. Anderson, Anderson Analytics and OdinText; Sean Case, Research for Good; Seth Stoughton, University of South Carolina;Stuart Schear, Robert Wood Johnson Foundation; and Zoe Downing, Focus Vision.

The following are just a few of the people who offered me ideas for new concepts, Snapshots, PicProfiles, and CloseUps for this edition: Andrew McAfee, MIT; Carlo Ratti, Senseable City Lab, MIT; David Kiron, MIT-Sloan; Didier Bonnet, Capgemini Consulting; George Westerman, MIT Sloan; Glenn Kelman, author; John Cendroski, TIAA; Julia Smith, AIG; Kevin Lonnie, KL Communications; Lenard Murphy, GreenBook; Martin Lindstrom, author; Michael Benisch, Rocket Fuel Inc.; Michelle Shail, TIAA; Nick Drew, Fresh Intelligence; Pamela Kirk Prentice, MIT-Sloan; Ray Poynter, NewMR; Richard Cassidy, AlertLogic; Sam Ransbotham, MIT-Sloan; Warren Berger, researcher and author; and William Pink, Millward Brown.

And to all those research collaborators who have suggested ideas, collaborated on cases or past Snapshots, Closeups, or PicProfiles, and continue to discuss the research industry with me, I'm grateful. These individuals include: Rachel Sockut, Innerscope; Erica Cenci, Brady PR for OpinionLab; Olescia Hanson, The Container Store; Cynthia Clark, 1to1 Magazine; Betty Adamou, Research Through Gaming Ltd.; Debra Semans, Polaris Marketing Research; Keith Chrzan, Maritz Research Inc.; Michael Kemery, Maritz Research Inc.; Christian Bauer,

Daimler AG; Kai Blask, TNS Infratest; Melinda Gardner, Novation; Keith Phillips, SSI; Nels Wroe; SHL; Ephraim (Jeff) Bander, Eye Track-Shop; Ron Sellers, Grey Matter Research & Consulting; Guadalupe Pagalday, Qualvu.com; Sandra Klaunzler, TNS Infratest; Steve August, Revelation; Kathy Miller, GMI (Global Market Insite Inc.); Takayuki Nozoe, NTT Communications Corporation; Janeen Hazel, Luth Research; Christine Stricker, *RealtyTrac*; Stephanie Blakely, The Prosper Foundation; Jennifer Frighetto, Nielsen; Andy Pitched, Research Triangle Institute (RTI International); Jeffrey C. Adler, Centric DC Marketing Research; Josh Mendelsohn, Chadwick Martin Bailey Inc.; Ruth Stan, SIS International Research; Sharon Starr, IPC Inc.; Keith Crosley, Proofpoint; Christopher Schultheiss, SuperLetter.com; Hy Mariampolski, QualiData Research Inc; Julie Grabarkewitz and Paul Herrera, American Heart Association; Holly Ripans, American Red Cross; Mike Bordner and Ajay Gupta, Bank One; Laurie Laurant Smith, Arielle Burgess, Jill Grech, David Lockwood, and Arthur Miller, Campbell-Ewald; Francie Turk, Consumer Connections; Tom Krouse, Donatos Pizza; Annie Burns and Aimee Seagal, GMMB; Laura Light and Steve Struhl, Harris Interactive; Emil Vicale, Herobuilders.com; Adrian Chiu, NetConversions; Colette Courtion, Starbucks; Mark Miller, Team One Advertising; Rebecca Conway, The Taylor Research Group; Scott Staniar, United States Tennis Association; Danny Robinson, Vigilante; Maury Giles, Wirthlin Worldwide; and Ken Mallon, Yahoo!.

To our faculty reviewers, your insights, aggravations, challenges, frustrations, suggestions, and disagreements were very helpful. These encouraged me to examine every word, every sentence, and every concept and see better, clearer ways to engage students in the subject we all love. Reviewers for this edition's revision are: Ahmed Al-Asfour, Ogala Lakota College; Zara Ambadar, Carlow University; Don Ashley, Wayland Baptist University; Kristopher Blanchard, Upper Iowa University; Cristanna Cook, Husson University; Charlene Dunfee, Capella University; Ernesto Gonzalez, Florida National University; Wendy Gradwohl, Wittenburg University; Pam Houston, Ogala Lakota College; Yan Jin, Elizabeth City State University; Abdullah Khan, Clafin University; Tracy Kramer, North Greenville University; Rex Moody, Angelo State University; Jason Patalinghug, University of New Haven; Glen Philbrick, United Tribes Technical College; Denel Pierre, Shorter University; Pushkala Raman, Texas Woman's University; Charles Richardson, Clafin University; Marcel Robles, Eastern Kentucky University; Angela Sandberg, Shorter University; Brian Satterlee, Liberty University; Jonathan Schultz, Amberton University; Stefano Tijerina, Husson University; Greg Turner, Clafin University; Sam VanHoose, Wayland Baptist University; Greg Warren, Wilmington University; Beyonka Wider, Claflin University; and Ron Zargarian, University of Indianapolis

Prior edition reviewers included: Scott Bailey, Troy University; Scott Baker, Champlain College; Robert Balik, Western Michigan University-Kalamazoo; John A. Ballard, College of Mount St. Joseph; Jayanta Bandyopadhyay, Central Michigan University; Larry Banks, University of Phoenix; Caroll M. Belew, New Mexico Highlands University; Kay Braguglia, Hampton University; Jim Brodzinski, College of Mount St. Joseph; Taggert Brooks, University of Wisconsin-La Crosse; Cheryl O'Meara Brown, University of West Georgia; L. Jay Burks, Lincoln University; Marcia Carter, University of Southern New Hampshire; Raul Chavez, Eastern Mennonite University; Darrell Cousert, University of Indianapolis; David Dorsett, Florida Institute of Technology; Michael P. Dumler, Illinois State University; Kathy Dye, Thomas More College; Don English, Texas A&M University-Commerce; Antonnia Espiritu, Hawaii Pacific University; Hamid Falatoon, University of Redlands; Judson Faurer, Metropolitan State College of Denver; Eve Fogarty, New Hampshire College; Bob Folden, Texas A&M University-Commerce; Gary Grudintski, San Diego State University; John Hanke, Eastern Washington University; Alan G. Heffner, Silver Lake College; Ron E. Holm, Cardinal Stritch University (Director of Distance Learning); Lee H. Igel, New York University; Burt Kaliski, New Hampshire College; Jane Legacy, Southern New Hampshire University; Andrew Luna, State University of West Georgia; Andrew Lynch, Southern New Hampshire University; Iraj Mahdvi, National University; Warren Matthews, LeTourmeau University; Erika Matulich, University of Tampa; Judith McKnew, Clemson University; Rosemarie Reynolds, Embry Riddle Aero University-Daytona; Randi L. Sims, Nova Southeastern University; Gary Stark, Northern Michigan University; Bruce Strom, University of Indianapolis; Cecelia Tempomi, Southwest Texas State University; Gary Tucker, Northwestern Oklahoma State University; Marjolijn Vandervelde, Davenport University; Charles Warren, Salem State College; Dennis G. Weis, Alliant International University; Robert Wheatley, Troy University; Bill Wresch, University of Wisconsin-Oshkosh; and Robert Wright, University of Illinois at Springfield; and Ken Zula, Keystone College.

This revision incorporates the feedback of dozens of students who identified areas of confusion so that this edition could make concepts more understandable, who participated in search tests, who worked on numerous research projects demonstrating where the book needed to include more information, and who provided reminders with their questions and actions that some aspects of the research process operate below their learning radar.

Through this 13th edition, I hope you and your students discover, or rediscover, how stimulating, challenging, fascinating, and sometimes frustrating this world of research-supported decision making can be.

Pamela Schindler

Many thanks to my McGraw-Hill team; without your assistance this revision wouldn't have happened so smoothly: Chuck Synovec, Director; Noelle Bathurst, Portfolio Manager; Ryan McAndrews, Product Developer; Erika Jordan, Core Project Manager; Harper Christopher, Executive Marketing Manager; David W. Hash, Designer; Daryl Horrocks, Program Manager; Sue Nodine, copyeditor; Elizabeth Kelly, proofreader; and Angela Norris, Senior Assessment Project Manager.

>detailedchangestothisedition

In its 13th edition, all chapters within *Business Research Methods* have been evaluated for currency and accuracy. Revisions were made to accommodate new information and trends in the industry, changing teaching pedagogy, and information about what teachers and students are looking for in their textbooks.

- The book's chapter structure is slimmer and has been changed to reflect how teachers are teaching research and using the book; the book now has 17 chapters.
  - A foundations chapter replaces the first three chapters.
  - The chapters on data preparation and examination have merged.
  - A *Research Reports* chapter now merges information on oral and written reports, with emphasis on oral reports to better reflect industry practice.
  - A new Chapter 17, *An Integrated Example*, now provides an insider's perspective of a research project. This example applies text practices and theory to one example from management dilemma to research report.
- Material has been reorganized to tie better to the modified research process model; there are now five parts, each part a match to a stage in the model. Part I, contains three chapters and establishes the foundations for what follows. Part II contains five chapters, all focused on research design and its various methodologies. Part III contains four chapters, all related to data collection and preparation. Part IV contains two chapters related to data analysis. Part V contains one chapter on research reporting. The part structure was designed to better reflect the research process as it is currently managed.
- Ethical issues are discussed, with their possible solutions, in every chapter, rather than in a stand-alone chapter, to reflect how teachers are using this material.
- Every section and every word has been examined for concept clarity and better student understanding; whole sections and whole chapters and appendices have been reconceived and rewritten.
- An emphasis has been placed on indicating solutions for problems or possible error sources, not just indicating or describing the errors/problems.
- Based on student feedback, an emphasis has been placed on providing sufficient information to "do" research, not just learn about research. Exhibits have been added to reflect *how* to execute a particular

practice, facilitating the experiential approach to teaching and learning business research methods.

- For clarity and to match a chapter's new structure, numerous Exhibits are new (38), have been revised significantly (34), or have been slightly modified (8).
- Continuing examples no longer weave throughout the text; chapters can now be assigned in different order to fit any teaching pedagogy.
- Images (58) have been added or replaced, giving a visual cue for new Snapshots, PicProfiles, or new embedded examples.
- To reflect industry practices, the series of exhibits that reflect the research process and that are used as conceptual "thought flowcharts"—especially valuable for visual learners—have been reenvisioned and redesigned; new exhibits have been added to this process series.
- The *Cases* section contains an updated case-by-chapter-suggested-use chart.
- Continuing to provide rich examples from the research industry, 30 new Snapshots, five new PicProfiles, and two new Closeups have been added; two Closeups have been updated.
- Several new chapter-level appendices have been added to this edition: *Better Reports* (Chapter 16), *Better Tables* (Chapter 13), *Sample Computer-Based Questions and Guidelines for Mobile Q* (Chapter 11), and *Sources of Measurement Questions* (Chapter 11).
- The Glossary has been updated; 77 new terms reflect changes in industry practices and 27 additional terms were upgraded to key term status.
- The *Instructor's Manual* contains additional research examples for discussion or testing.
- *McGraw-Hill Connect®* has been added to the book's resources; *Connect* provides opportunities for both formative and summative assessment by providing students regular and consistent feedback, encouraging practice, and enabling them to move closer to mastery by improving understanding and recall. Instructors are provided student and class analytics, to improve teaching decision making. Assignable material within Connect for this edition includes multiple choice questions for homework for each chapter and test bank questions for online testing.
- SmartBook®, also assignable in Connect, is a digital version of our textbook that actively tailors that content to an individual student's needs. It helps a student focus on the things they don't know, helps them retain key concepts, is accessible on the go, and tracks student progress.

- Student Resources/Faculty Resources within Connect contain new materials (sources, videos, examples) and video showcasing an observation experiment using body cameras.
- *Test Bank* has been updated to reflect changes in content and organization.
- *PowerPoint* slide decks have been updated to reflect changes in content and organization.

For Each of the Chapters   A detailed listing of chapter-by-chapter changes is provided here for your convenience.

- **Chapter 1**   This chapter was completely rewritten and has a new focus: the fundamentals or critical concepts students need to understand the remainder of the book. It combines material from 12e Chapters 1 and 3, with elements from Chapter 2. The following elements are new to this edition: chapter-opening quote (William Pink), the learning objectives and summary, a PicProfile on emerging trends based on the latest GRIT report, three new Snapshots (*Big vs. Small Data*, *Research on Cyber Security*, and *Identifying and Defining Constructs*), two revised exhibits, multiple images as visual cues, new embedded examples related to Hobby Lobby and Siemens AG, one new key term (data blending), four new photos serving as visual cues, and new discussion questions. Several sections have been pulled and others moved to chapters with a better fit. Six snapshots and three exhibits have moved to the IM.

- **Chapter 2**   Previously Chapter 4, this chapter features a restricted and simplified research process exhibit and a new structure based on five stages of the research process, with material on proposing research moving to Chapter 3. The following elements are new to this edition: chapter-opening quote (Brad Smith, Microsoft), learning objectives and summary, three new sections (identifying and prioritizing dilemmas, research project timeframe, and ethical issues and responsibilities) and five restructured sections, a PicProfile on emerging trends in research design, a Snapshot (*Research and Programmatic Algorithms*), a revised snapshot on outsourcing research, a new exhibit on Gantt chart of research project, four new images, five new key terms [key performance indicators (KPIs), dashboards, findings, insights, recommendations], and a new From-the-Headlines discussion question. The What is Good Research and Ethical Issues sections moved to this chapter from Chapters 1 and 3, respectively. Detailed management-research question hierarchy section was moved to Chapter 3. CPM chart was moved from Chapter 6.

- **Chapter 3**   Previously Chapter 5, this chapter is restructured and focuses on stage 1 of the research process: the management-research question hierarchy and exploration to include valuing and budgeting research. The following elements are new to this edition: chapter-opening quote (Warren Berger, author), learning objectives and summary, eight new sections, one modified and four new exhibits, three new Snapshots (*Housing and Millennials*, *The Art of Asking the Right Question*, *Using Interviews to Refine the Management Question*), eight key terms relocated from other chapters, and six new images as visual cues. The section on data mining was dropped to reinforce Chapter 1's emphasis on research and data mining as different courses. Several key terms have moved to other chapters to reflect relocation of certain material. Several Snapshots have moved to the IM.

- **Chapter 4**   Previously Chapter 6, the emphasis of this chapter has changed to research design once the research question(s) and investigative questions have been determined and the decisions involved in research design, including those involved in sampling design, have been made. The following elements are new to this edition: chapter-opening quote (Nick Drew, Fresh Intelligence), learning objectives and summary, a new section (sampling design), two new Snapshots (*TIAA Performance Management Overhaul*, *AIG and Research Design*), a new CloseUp (*How Agile Research Helped Prove the Value in a Packaging Redesign*), two modified exhibits, embedded example on productivity and morale, five new images as visual cues, one new key term (single-methodology design), and modified discussion questions—including a new From-the-Headlines discussion question. Detailed sections on causation moved to Chapter 8, and focus groups moved to Chapter 6. Two Snapshots moved to the IM.

- **Chapter 5**   Previously Chapter 14, this chapter has a different structure based on the six steps of sampling design. The following elements are new to this edition: chapter-opening quote (Gerald Earl Gillum, American rapper and producer), learning objectives and summary, three new sections (sampling design, selection and recruiting protocols, and ethical issues and their solutions), one new snapshot (*Who's Taking Your Surveys*), one revised PicProfile on mixed access sampling, four new exhibits, four revised or modified exhibits, four new images as visual cues, and anew From-the-Headlines discussion question. Two key terms were moved here (case, target population).

- **Chapter 6**   Previously Chapter 7, the following elements are new to this edition: chapter-opening quote (Gia Calhoun, Burt's Bees), learning objectives and summary, two new sections (qualitative sampling design, including incentivizing participants and interviewers as consultants, and ethical issues and their solutions) and one enhanced section (creative exercises), three new Snapshots (*Digital Transformation Revealed Using IDIs, IDIs Help Restructure Maritz Travel, Qualitative Research in the Era of Smartphones*), two revised exhibits, three new images as visual cues, and seven new key terms (data saturation, collage, completion/fill in the blank, role playing, creative innovation roleplay, storytelling, write a letter). Four Snapshots and PicProfiles moved to the IM.

- **Chapter 7** Previously Chapter 8, this chapter has been reorganized to follow the observation research design steps. The following elements are new to this edition: chapter-opening quote (Katie Hafner, author), learning objectives and summary, two new sections (sampling design, ethical issues and their solutions), two new Snapshots [*Visual Content Gets Sticky, Observation and Police Cameras* (with video on the website)], three revised or modified exhibits, six new images as visual cues, two new key terms (memory decay, selective filtering), and a new From-the-Headlines discussion question. Several Snapshots and a PicProfile have moved to the IM.

- **Chapter 8** Previously Chapter 9, this chapter has been reorganized, with evaluation of experiments moving toward the end of the chapter. The following elements are new to this edition: chapter-opening quote (Jeff Bezos, CEO, Amazon), learning objectives and summary, a new section (ethical issues and their solutions), a relocated section on causation (including two exhibits), four snapshots (*Experiments in Improving Employee Health, Robotic Experiments, Zeotap Experiments with Mercedes-Benz, MIT SENSEable City Lab*), two revised exhibits, four new images as visual cues, 14 new key terms (debriefing, after-only design, group time series design, history, instrumentation, maturation, nonequivalent control group design, one group pretest-posttest design, posttest-only control group design, selection, separate sample pretest-posttest design, static group comparison design, regression toward the mean, testing), and a From-the-Headlines discussion question. Four Snapshots moved to IM.

- **Chapter 9** Previously Chapter 10, this chapter has been reorganized. The following elements are new to this edition: chapter-opening quote (David Goldberg, CEO, SurveyMonkey), learning objectives and summary, four new sections (classification of data collection designs, telephone survey trends, evaluation of survey design, and ethical issues and their solutions), two new Snapshots (*Internet Brings Prediction*

Research into 21st Century, Research Embraces the Smartphone), two new PicProfiles on emerging trends in survey research and declining response rates, two new and three revised exhibits, four new images as visual cues, updated statistics, three new key terms (acquiescence bias, probe, social desirability bias), and a From-the-Headlines discussion question. Two additional exhibits moved to this chapter (informed consent and IRB process).

- **Chapter 10** Previously Chapter 11, The following elements are new to this edition: chapter-opening quote (David McCandless, author), one new exhibit, two revised exhibits, one new Snapshot (*The Emotional Face of Research*), four images as visual cues, and a From-the-Headlines discussion question.

- **Chapter 11** Previously Chapter 12, this chapter is reorganized and rewritten to focus on measurement questions, rather than the scales on which they are based, in order to work better with the chapter on measurement instruments. The following elements are new to this edition: chapter-opening quote (David F. Harris, president, Insight and Measurement), learning objectives and summary, two new sections (instrument design, prepare the preliminary analysis plan) and one revised section (data entry), a new Snapshot (*Toluna and Voss Measure Water*) and a new PicProfile about Urban Dictionary, four new and three revised or modified exhibits, two additional exhibits moved from other chapters, some material on coding moved from another chapter, five new images as visual cues, five new key terms (attitude scaling, checklist, error of strictness, interview guide, scaling) and 17 key terms moved here from other chapters, modified discussion questions (including a From-the-Headlines question), and two new appendices (sample computer-based questions by scale type, sources of measurement questions).

- **Chapter 12** Previously Chapter 13, this chapter has a new structure to work better with the chapter on Measurement Questions, with a stronger link to the preliminary analysis plan. The following elements are new to this edition: chapter-opening quote (Kristin Luck, research consultant), learning objectives and summary, three new sections (instrument design, physical design, nonquestion elements), one new Snapshot (*New Vehicle Survey*), five new and three revised exhibits, four new images as visual cues, 15 new key terms (assimilation effect, behavior cycle, behavior frequency, behavior time frame, completion estimate, contrast effect, filter question, instrument coverage, instrument scope, interview guide, measurement instrument, rapport, skip directions, skip logic diagram, social desirability bias), revised discussion questions, and a new From-the-Headline question. The Invoke PicProfile was moved to the IM.

- **Chapter 13** As a merger of 12e Chapters 15 and 16, this chapter has a new structure and new content. The following elements are new to this edition: chapter-opening quote (Dana Zuber, director of analytics for Butler, Shine, Stern & Partners), learning objectives and summary, one new section (collect the data) and a revised section (coding), six revised and three new exhibits, two new Snapshots (*How Might You Code Word Data*, *The Difference Between Data and Insight*), updated statistics, 17 new key terms (coding scheme, context units, cross-tabulation, data collection, data validation, inter-rater reliability, intra-rater reliability, listwise deletion, data missing at random (MAR), data missing but not missing at random (NMAR), data missing completely at random (MCAR), pairwise deletion, predictive replacement, recoding, recording units, sampling units, survey activation), revised discussion questions, and new chapter appendix (Better Tables). Four Snapshots, a CloseUp, and a PicProfile were moved to the IM.

- **Chapter 14** Previously Chapter 17, the following elements are new to this edition: one revised and one new exhibit, and three new images as visual cues.

- **Chapter 15** Previously Chapter 18, the following elements are new to this edition: chapter-opening quote (Jeff Bezos, CEO, Amazon), one new Snapshot, and three new images as visual cues. One exhibit (grammar and style proofreader results) was moved to the IM.

- **Chapter 16** As a merger of Chapters 19 and 20, this chapter has a new structure emphasizing the oral presentation. The following elements are new to this edition: chapter-opening quote (David McCandless, British data journalist, information designer, and author), learning objectives and summary, four new sections (audience-centric planning, visualization specifically for the oral report, infographics, ethical considerations in reporting), a new Snapshot (*Hitting the Wall is a Good Thing*), a new CloseUp (*Storytelling from Pixar Applied to Research*), five new and 10 revised exhibits, an infographic image, 21 new key terms (predispositions, confirmation bias, anchoring bias, conformity bias, survivorship bias, loss-aversion bias, visualize, data clarity, actionable insights, audience-centric planning, data-centric planning, desired audience effect, graph, information, insights, limitations, report framework, report structure, table, tone, geography), revised discussion questions, and a new chapter appendix—*Better Reports*—with five new exhibits and five existing exhibits from prior chapters. Two items (constructing a story and overcoming the jitters) were moved to the IM.

- **Chapter 17** This new chapter, *An Integrated Example*, provides an insider's perspective of a research project. This example applies text practices and theory to one example from management dilemma to research report. The companies, Visionary Insights and BrainSavvy, might be fictional, but the research profiled in the example is very real. This chapter can be used throughout the course to review (or test) various concepts, or at the end of the course as the basis for a lively discussion or final exam.

There is a wealth of information, samples, templates, and more within Connect for instructors, and at www.mhhe.com/Schindler13e for students.

Written Cases. Cases offer an opportunity to tell research stories in more depth and detail. You'll find a new case, *Marcus Thomas LLC Tests Hypothesis for Troy-Bilt Creative Development*, complete with its online questionnaire, at the Online Learning Center. You'll also find cases about hospital services, lotteries, data mining, fundraising, new promotions, and website design, among other topics, featuring organizations like Akron Children's Hospital, Kelley Blue Book, Starbucks, Yahoo!, the American Red Cross, and more.

Video Cases. We are pleased to continue to make available a first in video supplements: several short segments drawn from a two-hour metaphor elicitation technique (MET) interview. These segments should be invaluable in teaching students to conduct almost any type of individual depth interview and to explain the concept of researcher–participant rapport. Four of our video cases were written and produced especially to match the research process model in this text and feature noted companies: Lexus, Starbucks, Wirthlin Worldwide (now Harris Interactive), Robert Wood Johnson Foundation, GMMB, Visa, Bank One, Team One Advertising, U.S. Tennis Association, Vigilante New York, and the Taylor Group.

Web Exercises. It is appropriate to do web searches as part of a research methods course, so each chapter offers one or more exercises to stimulate your students to hone their searching skills. Due to the ever-changing nature of web URLs, however, we offer these exercises in the *Instructor's Manual*.

Articles, Samples, and Templates. Students often need to see how professionals do things to really understand, so you'll find a sample EyeTrackShop report, a Nielsen report of using U.S. Census data, an Excel template for generating sample data displays, and more.

Sample Student Project. Visualization of the finished deliverable is crucial to creating a strong research report.

 **McGraw-Hill Connect®** is a highly reliable, easy-to-use homework and learning management solution that utilizes learning science and award-winning adaptive tools to improve student results.

Homework and Adaptive Learning

- Connect's assignments help students contextualize what they've learned through application, so they can better understand the material and think critically.

- Connect will create a personalized study path customized to individual student needs through SmartBook®.

- SmartBook helps students study more efficiently by delivering an interactive reading experience through adaptive highlighting and review.

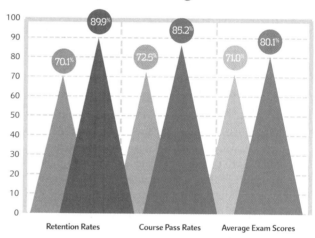

Connect's Impact on Retention Rates, Pass Rates, and Average Exam Scores

Over **7 billion questions** have been answered, making McGraw-Hill Education products more intelligent, reliable, and precise.

Using **Connect** improves retention rates by **19.8** percentage points, passing rates by **12.7** percentage points, and exam scores by **9.1** percentage points.

73% of instructors who use **Connect** require it; instructor satisfaction **increases** by 28% when **Connect** is required.

Quality Content and Learning Resources

- Connect content is authored by the world's best subject matter experts, and is available to your class through a simple and intuitive interface.

- The Connect eBook makes it easy for students to access their reading material on smartphones and tablets. They can study on the go and don't need internet access to use the eBook as a reference, with full functionality.

- Multimedia content such as videos, simulations, and games drive student engagement and critical thinking skills.

Robust Analytics and Reporting

©Hero Images/Getty Images

- Connect Insight® generates easy-to-read reports on individual students, the class as a whole, and on specific assignments.

- The Connect Insight dashboard delivers data on performance, study behavior, and effort. Instructors can quickly identify students who struggle and focus on material that the class has yet to master.

- Connect automatically grades assignments and quizzes, providing easy-to-read reports on individual and class performance.

Impact on Final Course Grade Distribution

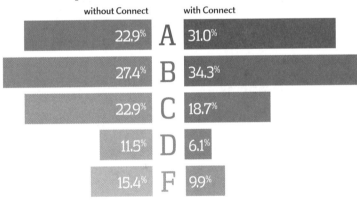

without Connect		with Connect
22.9%	A	31.0%
27.4%	B	34.3%
22.9%	C	18.7%
11.5%	D	6.1%
15.4%	F	9.9%

More students earn **As** and **Bs** when they use **Connect**.

Trusted Service and Support

- Connect integrates with your LMS to provide single sign-on and automatic syncing of grades. Integration with Blackboard®, D2L®, and Canvas also provides automatic syncing of the course calendar and assignment-level linking.

- Connect offers comprehensive service, support, and training throughout every phase of your implementation.

- If you're looking for some guidance on how to use Connect, or want to learn tips and tricks from super users, you can find tutorials as you work. Our Digital Faculty Consultants and Student Ambassadors offer insight into how to achieve the results you want with Connect.

www.mheducation.com/connect

>briefcontents

>contents

>part III
Measurement   225

>part VII
Research Project Overview

17 An Integrated Example

>case index

>appendices

>part I

Building the Foundation for Research

>chapter 1

Research Foundations and Fundamentals

"As big data increases, we see a parallel growth in the need for 'small data' to answer the questions it raises."

William C. Pink,
senior partner
Creative Analytics

>learningobjectives

After reading this chapter, you should understand . . .

LO1-1 How business research and data analytics complement each other.

LO1-2 The language of professional researchers.

>The Role and Process of Research

Every manager in the course of his or her career, regardless of his or her field, will make thousands of decisions of various types: strategic, tactical, and procedural. Each decision starts with a problem or opportunity—a dilemma. A strategic decision determines the general approach; a tactical one, a method for executing the strategic decision; and a procedural one, the specifics for executing the tactical decision. For example, brick-and-mortar retailers have been having significant difficulties as more people have embraced smartphones. Increasingly, people are bypassing stores to shop online (dilemma). Hobby Lobby, however, is thriving. This retailer chooses to serve the crafting market (strategic) and emphasizes supplying the needs of painters, photographers, jewelry makers, quilters, floral designers, and interior decorators (strategic). To serve photographers, it carries matting boards, tools for cutting such board, and frames, but not cameras (tactical). It might identify each new product for its photography area by reviewing an in-person, profit-based pitch (procedural). The company is family-owned (strategic). It makes its decisions guided by values emphasizing strengthening family (strategic). As a result, its brick-and-mortar stores are open fewer hours (tactical), and its full-time people are paid three times the minimum wage (tactical).[1] Researchers also make these kinds of decisions, deciding, for example, to use a communication study (strategic) and choosing a mobile survey (tactical) with participants recruited by posting an invitation on a company's Facebook page (procedural). Today, the pressure on managers to justify their decisions, in an effort to guarantee a return on the investment of the resources (people, money, time, equipment, facilities) that each decision requires, is enormous. The journey from dilemma to decision uses information as fuel.

Companies have always collected data. Each organization is not equally adept, however, at using those data to develop meaningful information and insights useful for making good decisions. Over the last decade, some organizations have used newly available tools (faster computing power, better data analytic software) to tap into data it has already collected, data that have been languishing in departmental silos or company data warehouses. What once was a pool of data has become a veritable ocean of data. Some firms are drowning. Others are barely staying afloat. Still others are grasping the opportunity to use this ocean of data as a foundation for their strategic direction and gain competitive advantage.[2] Those companies that have been successful have found fuel for their decisions. But fuel comes in different grades; think regular gasoline verses rocket fuel. Using only historic data to make a current decision is one approach to decision making; enriching that fuel mixture by collecting new data specific to a given dilemma, is another.

The field you are about to study is in the midst of upheaval and disruption.[3] For almost a century, researchers have been viewed by managers as technical support. These specialists were brought in on projects when technical expertise in research methodology and data analysis were needed. But, within the last few years, that has been changing. New technology, new and better computing tools (artificial intelligence, virtual reality, better mobile equipment, Internet of Things), and even a new computing environment (the cloud) are adding to industry chaos. In the midst of this sea change in business, new pressures are being put on the researcher. It is no longer acceptable to merely add to the data pool; business managers need clearly communicated insights from each new data addition. Researchers are now expected to not only be technologically competent, but to have an understanding of how businesses and organizations work. And managers, who once delegated research projects to specialists, are expected to be conversant with research methodologies and tools. Welcome to the new world of research, where researchers are data storytellers and insight providers, critical to helping provide strategic and tactical direction.

Research versus Data Analytics

Facing each new dilemma, it is the manager's decision whether he or she has sufficient information—drawn from data previously collected, either internal or external to the firm—or needs more information to make an appropriate decision. Managers draw on data from existing internal data sources (called a *decision support system*) when engaging in data analytics. For example, Amazon, in an attempt to increase our order, mines its data to provide us with a list of products that others—who bought what we

>snapshot

Analytics Under-delivers Compared to its Hype

According to the latest report from *MIT/Sloan Management Review* and SAS, data analytics is not living up to its hype. The report classifies analytic users on three levels of maturity: analytical innovators (who apply analytics strategically), analytical practitioners (who apply analytics operationally), and the analytically challenged (who rely more on management experience than analytics to make decisions). Analytical innovators—those benefiting the most from the application of analytics (both the extraction of insights and their dissemination to affect organizational actions)—have, rather than growing in the last four years, basically remained stagnant. They propose several reasons for this, including a lack of senior management commitment and a focus on operational rather than strategic use of data.

Some examples of analytical innovators, however, give us role models for the practice. Bank of England (BoE) is an analytic innovator; to fulfill its regulatory role in the British economy, it is aggregating datasets, both microeconomic and macroeconomic, for the first time. BoE has "hired a chief data officer, created a data lab, established an advanced analytics group and formed a bank-wide data community." General Electric, also an analytic innovator, created a new business unit, as well as a huge software division, to manage a cloud-based platform that aggregates and analyzes sensor data from industrial machines. "GE's strategy for data and analytics has become tightly linked to its corporate strategy, a tremendous corporate shift for what was once a traditional manufacturing conglomerate."

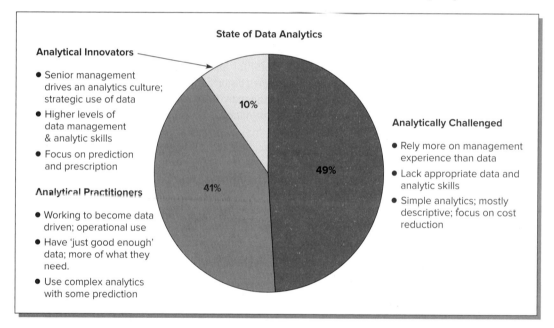

State of Data Analytics

Analytical Innovators

- Senior management drives an analytics culture; strategic use of data
- Higher levels of data management & analytic skills
- Focus on prediction and prescription

Analytical Practitioners

- Working to become data driven; operational use
- Have 'just good enough' data; more of what they need.
- Use complex analytics with some prediction

Analytically Challenged

- Rely more on management experience than data
- Lack appropriate data and analytic skills
- Simple analytics; mostly descriptive; focus on cost reduction

10%   41%   49%

Source: Sam Ransbotham, David Kiron, and Pamela Kirk Prentice, "Beyond the Hype: The Hard Work Behind Analytic Success," *MIT/Sloan Management Review*, April 2016, downloaded April 29, 2016 (http://marketing.mitsmr.com/PDF/57381-MITSMR-SAS-Analytics2016.pdf?utm_source=WhatCounts%2c+Publicaster+Edition&utm_medium=email&utm_campaign=darpt16&utm_content=Download+the+Report+%28PDF%29&cid=1).

are ordering—also bought. Such data is often referred to as *big data* due to the extensive size of many of these databases. Exhibit 1-1 provides some ideas for sources.

When existing data is mined, it may be used for a purpose other than that for which it was originally intended. In its mobility division, Siemens AG, the engineering powerhouse with almost 350,000 employees in 200 countries,[4] builds systems into its trains. These systems generate more than 1 billion data points[5] per train per year. They are used to track that train's performance and maintenance activity and to learn from any train malfunctions or accidents. Collecting train data to understand and improve that train's performance employs repetitive, ongoing observation research. However, drawing insights from data accumulated from European and U.S. trains to help design new rolling stock for China and Russia employs data analytics.

In another example, customer relationship management (CRM) software may initially be used to facilitate the sales process and improve the effectiveness of sales appeals to various customer groups.

>**Exhibit 1-1** Where Business Collects Information

Type of Data	Where/How	Data Source
Transactional	Online and in-store purchases	Customer
	Online, phone, in-store inquiries	Potential customer, customer
	Warehouse and shipping manifests	Logistic partners, employee
	Machine performance	Machine data log
Observational	Online Web visits and in-store shopping trips	Customer, employee
	Competitor interactions	Customer
	Click-through paths on Web	Potential customer, customer
	In-store customer service interactions	Customer, employee
	Stock price valuations	Investors
	Biometric measures (e.g., neuromarketing, fMRI, PET, eye tracking)	Potential customer, customer, employee
Conversational (Touch points)	Surveys, online and in-store intercepts	Potential customer, customer, employee
	Call center interactions	Customer, employee
	In-store customer service interactions	Customer, employee
	Web chat interactions	Customer, employee
	In-store checkout	Customer, employee
	Candidate interviews	Potential employee
	Performance reviews	Employee
	Exit interviews	Employee
	Annual stockholder meetings	Investor
	Financial performance presentations	Financial analyst, institutional investor
	Listening tours	Customer, supplier, logistic partner, employee, decision influencer
	Twitter posts	Customer, employee, competitor, trade associations, distributor
	Facebook posts (company site)	Customer, employee, trade associations, distributor
	Blog activity	Customer, employee, competitor, trade associations, distributor
	Other social media posts or discussions	Customer, employee, competitor, trade associations, distributor
Internet Analytics	Keyword searches	Potential customer, customer
	Click analysis	Potential customer, customer
	Google+	Potential customer, customer

Our interviews and research for this edition revealed several sources of research data. This table is adapted from that research and author experience as well as from material by Cynthia Clark, "5 Ways to Learn What Customers Aren't Telling You," *1to1 Magazine*, March 5, 2012, accessed March 8, 2012 (http://www.1to1media.com/view.aspx?docid=33464); and "Harness the Conversation: Business in Today's Social World," *Cvent*, accessed March 8, 2012 (http://www.cvent.com/en/sem/business-in-todays-social-worldsurvey-ebook.shtml).

Additionally, a call center is designed to answer questions, provide technical support, or funnel prospects into the sales process; many calls to a call center are recorded to improve performance. Using data analytics, a firm might mine these two datasets to extract insights that help design a new customer landing page for the firm's website. Businesses are getting better at **data blending**,[6] combining data from separate data files (e.g., financial, human resources [HR], CRM, inventory management, and manufacturing) into a new composite data file, and then querying that composite data file to help make decisions. While the information that comes from data blending has an important role in decision making, it is not the same as research.

Assume for the moment that you are the manager of a full-service restaurant. You are experiencing significant turnover in your server pool, and some long-time customers have commented that the friendly atmosphere, which has historically drawn them to your door, is changing. Where will you begin to try to solve this problem? Your *business intelligence system* is designed to provide ongoing information about events and trends in the technological, economic, political-legal, demographic, cultural/social, and competitive arenas (see Exhibit 1-2). It reveals that wait-staff turnover is high in your industry, regulations on restaurant operations have become more stringent, and some area competitors are experimenting with increasing wait-staff wages while eliminating tips. You also review your firm's financial records and HR records to determine pay, tips, pre-hire experience, and work hours of those who left and compare that information with those who stayed. Is this sufficient information, or is this a problem for which additional research should be used?

>**snap**shot

Big versus Small Data

In his book, *Small Data: The Tiny Clues That Uncover Huge Trends*, author Martin Lindstrom talks about the importance of knowing why. Lindstrom isn't an advocate of only using big data, indicating big data lacks insight because it focuses on analysis rather than emotional connection. His book focuses on what he's learned as he has visited or lived in more than 2,000 homes throughout the world and how those ethnographic observations paid big dividends. In a Knowledge@Wharton interview, Lindstrom described financially troubled Danish toymaker Lego. In 2002, Lego had ventured away from its core small blocks, instead emphasizing movies, theme parks, apparel, and large building blocks (based on big data about Millennials) only to discover—via interviews and ethnographic observations in homes across Europe—that it was taking away the major reason children play with the toy: the sense of accomplishment. In explanation, Lindstrom writes, "children attain social currency among their peers by playing and achieving a level of mastery at their chosen skill." Lego refocused on the small blocks based on its collection of small data. These actions brought Lego back from near bankruptcy. "You have to remember that Big Data is all about analyzing the past, but it has nothing to do with the future. Small Data, . . . seemingly

©Cr-Management GmbH & Co. KG/Getty Images

insignificant observations you identify in consumers' homes, is . . . the emotional DNA we leave behind."

Sources: Martin Lindstrom, *Small Data: The Tiny Clues That Uncover Huge Trends*, *St. Martin's Press* (February 23, 2016), pp 1-2; and "Why Small Data Is the New Big Data," Knowledge@Wharton, March 24, 2016. Downloaded March 25, 2016 (http://adage.com/article/special-report-4as-conference/tipping-point-j/303268/?utm _source=daily_email&utm_medium=newsletter&utm_campaign=adage&ttl =1459463433).

>**Exhibit 1-2** Some Sources of Business Intelligence

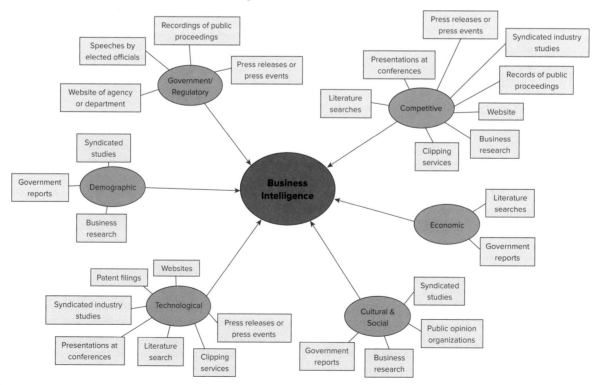

Perhaps you are the head of your state's department of transportation, charged with determining which roads and bridges will be resurfaced or replaced in the next fiscal year. You have data on which roads and bridges handle the most traffic, as well as those roads/bridges representing the greatest economic disaster if closed. However, the state's manager of public information has expressed concern about the potential for public outcry if work is once again directed to more affluent regions of the state. The manager suggests using new research to assist in making your decision because the decision is one with numerous operational, financial, and public relations ramifications. Should you authorize new research?

The Research Process

A deep dive into historical data rarely illuminates the 'why' behind actions. And the whys change over time; what was true a year ago might not be true today. To fulfill this new role of insight provider, you'll need an understanding of both the process and the tools used by a researcher. **Business research** is defined as a *systematic inquiry* that provides information to guide a specified managerial decision. More specifically, it is a set of processes that include planning, acquiring, analyzing, and reporting relevant data, information, and insights to decision makers in ways that mobilize the organization to take appropriate actions. These actions are designed to maximize performance and help accomplish organizational goals. Typically, the overall process is divided into the following stages:

1. Clarify the research question.
2. Design the research.
3. Collect and prepare the data.
4. Analyze and interpret the data.
5. Report insights and recommendations.

Exhibit 1-3 provides a graphic of the process that we will develop in this text. At times, a manager may start his or her journey at the beginning and proceed stage-by-stage to its culmination. At other times, a

>**Exhibit 1-3** The Research Process

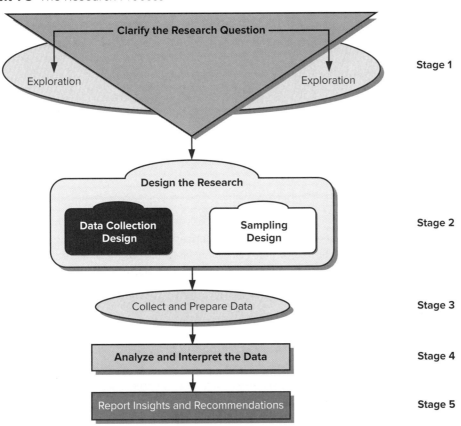

Research on Cyber Security

How does research keep an organization secure from criminal "bad actors" in the cyber security arena? It's used to spot the threat before it happens, to understand an organization's vulnerabilities, to spot the attack venues, and more.

Over the last decade, cyber attacks have become more frequent, more sophisticated, more complex, and easier for the bad actors, all at the same time. New digital tools make it possible for these criminals to do tasks that just recently would require sophisticated programming expertise. Today, they can purchase whatever tools they need from criminal networks using Bitcoin, a digital currency that makes tracking the purchase and finding the criminal very difficult. As Richard Cassidy, cyber security evangelist with Alert Logic, one of the nation's leading managed security providers, explains, "Companies are vulnerable from three types of bad actors. Not all pose the same degree of damage." *Hacktivists* have a political or social agenda, and garnering media attention is their goal; *cyber criminals* may also want the media attention, but they seek monetary gain from the data they capture; *advanced persistent threats* (APTs) are the most dangerous and spend significant time, money, and resources prior to crafting a target-specific attack and do so for significant monetary gain and/or damage to the target.

From research, Alert Logic discovered that passwords (49.9 percent) and email addresses (45.5 percent) remain the prize target of bad actors, along with usernames (37.7 percent) and names (29.4 percent). Using this stolen information in combination with information readily available on company websites and social media sites like LinkedIn, a bad actor can obtain access to servers, databases, web domains, and more.

Attacks via phishing emails and software application plug-ins are the chief avenues of access to deliver malware. A phishing email is disguised to appear as though from a trusted source—for example, another employee or your boss.

©solarseven/Shutterstock

A plug-in is a software component that adds a specific feature to an existing computer program. Employees today bring their own mobile devices to work and often use software that hasn't been rigorously evaluated for inappropriate plug-ins. Through these portals, malware (malicious software such as viruses, worms, Trojan horses, and spyware) can be injected into an organization's system.

"Bad actors often try out their approach before launching the real attack," claimed Cassidy. So catching them in this preliminary test should be the goal. The problem is that it takes an organization, on average, 205 days to identify that it has been compromised, and by then, the purpose of the attack has been accomplished.

www.alertlogic.com

Source: Richard Cassidy, "Behind The Scenes: Cybercrime Threat Landscape," Brighttalk webcast, April 27, 2016, downloaded May 26, 2016 (https://www.brighttalk.com/webcast/11587/201299?autoclick=true&utm_medium=web&utm_source=brighttalk-promoted&utm_campaign=player-page-feed&utm_content=promoted).

manager may need only a portion of the process, given information that is available from a variety of other sources. Research is often characterized by much smaller datasets than big data. Once the research is presented, the manager has one very important decision: How shall he or she resolve the management problem?

Research and the Scientific Method

Intelligent, curious people who have a driving need to seek answers are at the heart of great research. The foundation of the business research process is the **scientific method**. The essential tenets of the scientific method are:

- Clearly defined concepts, constructs, variables, methods, and procedures.
- Empirically testable hypotheses: a way exists to gather evidence that directly supports/refutes any hypothesis.

- Direct observation of phenomena (facts).
- Conclusions drawn from statistical evidence rather than inferred justification (educated guesses).
- The self-correcting process: ability to replicate and reassess validity of conclusions.

>The Language of Research

So where do we start to understand the preceding material? We start with the language of research. When we do research, we seek to know "what is" in order to understand, explain, or predict phenomena. We might want to answer the question "What will be the department employees' reaction to a new flexible work schedule?" or "Why did the stock market price surge higher when all normal indicators suggested it would go down?" When dealing with such questions, we must agree on definitions. Which *employees* of the department: clerical or professional? What *reaction*? What are *normal indicators*? These questions require the use of concepts, constructs, operational definitions, and variables.

Concepts

Concepts are used to understand and communicate information. The success of research hinges on (1) how clearly we conceptualize and (2) how well others understand the concepts we use. We design hypotheses using concepts. We devise measurement scales using concepts by which to test these hypotheses. We gather and analyze data using measurement concepts.

A **concept** is a generally accepted collection of meanings or characteristics associated with certain events, objects, conditions, situations, or behaviors:

- Concepts are created when we classify and categorize events, objects, conditions, situations, or behaviors—identifying common characteristics beyond any single observation.
- Concepts are acquired through personal experience or the experience of others.
- Concepts use words as labels to designate them; these words are derived from our experiences.
- Concepts have progressive levels of abstraction—that is, the degree to which the concept does or does not have something objective to refer to. At one extreme are objective concepts; at the other, abstractions. *Table* is an objective concept. We have images of tables in our mind. *Personality* is an abstract concept as it is much more difficult to visualize.

Think of a movie ticket as a concept. What comes to mind is not a single example, but your collected memories of all movie tickets from which you define a set of specific and definable characteristics (material, movie title use, perforation, multiple parts, screen location, etc.). For another example, assume you see a man passing and identify that he is running rather than walking, skipping, crawling, or hopping. Each movement represents a different concept. We also use concepts to identify that the moving object is an adult male rather than a truck or a horse.

Ordinary concepts make up the bulk of communication in research. *Ordinary*, however, does not mean *unambiguous*. We might, for example, ask research participants for an estimate of their family's total income. *Income* may seem to be a simple, unambiguous concept, but we will receive varying answers and confusing data unless we restrict or narrow the concept by specifying:

- Time period, such as weekly, monthly, or annually.
- Before or after income taxes are deducted.
- For head of household only or for all household members.
- For salary and wages only or also including tips, bonuses, dividends, interest, and capital gains.
- To include or not include in-kind income (e.g., free rent, employee discounts, vacations, or food stamps).

We run into difficulty when trying to deal with less ordinary phenomena or advance new ideas. One way to handle this problem is to borrow a concept from another language or from another field. Assume we are researching a brand logo's design strength. We can borrow the term *gestalt* from German, which translates as form or shape and means an organized whole more than the sum of its parts.[7] Or we might use the physics concept of *gravitation* to explain why people shop where they do or the geographic concept of *distance* to describe degree of variability between the attitudes of employees on a new work schedule.

Sometimes we need to make a word cover a different concept or develop new labels for a concept. When we adopt new meanings or develop new labels, we begin to develop a specialized language or jargon. While jargon contributes to efficiency of communication among specialists or a particular group, it excludes everyone else. Jargon is often avoided in business research for this reason unless the sample is very narrowly defined.

Constructs

When research requires us to work with abstract concepts, we define one or more constructs. A **construct** is an abstract idea specifically invented for a given research and/or theory-building purpose. We build constructs by combining simpler, more concrete concepts, especially when the idea or image we intend to convey is not subject to direct observation. Consider this example: Heather is a human resource analyst at CadSoft, an architectural software company that employs technical writers to write product manuals, and she is analyzing task attributes of a job in need of redesign.

Exhibit 1-4 illustrates some of the concepts and constructs Heather is dealing with. The concepts at the bottom of the exhibit (format accuracy, manuscript errors, and keyboarding speed) define a construct that Heather calls "presentation quality." Presentation quality is not directly observable. It is an invented construct, used to communicate the combination of meanings presented by the three objective, measurable concepts that Heather has discovered are related empirically. She is able to observe keyboarding speed, for example, by timing a person's entry of a paragraph.

Concepts at the next higher level of abstraction in Exhibit 1-4 are vocabulary, syntax, and spelling. Heather also finds them to be related. They form a construct that she calls "language skill." She has chosen this label because the three concepts together define the language requirement in the job description. Language skill is placed at a higher level of abstraction in the exhibit because two of the concepts it comprises, vocabulary and syntax, are more difficult to observe and their measures are more complex.

>**Exhibit 1-4** Constructs Composed of Concepts in a Job Redesign

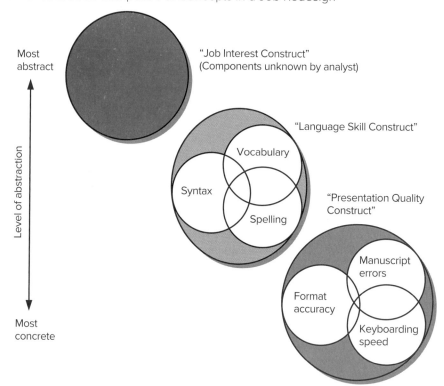

Heather has not yet defined the last construct, "job interest." It is the least observable and the most difficult to measure. It will likely be composed of numerous concepts—many of which will be quite abstract. Highly abstract constructs can be inferred only from the data; these are presumed to exist but must await further testing and definition. Heather will have the beginning of a **conceptual scheme** if research shows the concepts and constructs in this example to be interrelated and if their connections can be supported. In graphic form, the conceptual scheme depicts the relationships among the knowledge and skill requirements necessary to clarify the job redesign effort.

Operational Definitions

Confusion about the meaning of constructs or concepts can destroy a research study's value without the knowledge of the researcher or its sponsor. Definitions are one way to reduce this danger.

Researchers distinguish between dictionary definitions and operational definitions. In the more familiar dictionary definition, a concept is defined with a synonym. For example, a customer is defined as a patron; a patron, in turn, is defined as a customer or client of an establishment; a client is defined as one who employs the services of any organization or a patron of any shop.[8] These circular definitions may be adequate for general communication but not for research. In research, we measure concepts and constructs, and this requires more rigorous operational definitions.

An **operational definition** is a definition stated in terms of specific criteria for measurement or testing. We must be able to count, measure, or in some other way gather the information through our senses. Whether the object to be defined is physical (e.g., a can of soup) or highly abstract (e.g., achievement motivation), the definition must specify the characteristics and how they are to be observed. The specifications and procedures must be so clear that any competent person using them would classify the object in the same way.

To do this, you need operational definitions. Operational definitions may vary, depending on your purpose and the way you choose to measure them. College undergraduates are grouped by *class*. No one has much trouble understanding such terms as *senior*, *junior*, *sophomore*, and so forth. But the task may not be that simple if you must determine which students comprise each class. Here are two different situations involving a survey among students where we want to classify their answers by their class level. Each uses a different definition of the same concept:

1. You ask them to report their class status and you record it. In this case, class is freshman, sophomore, junior, or senior; you accept the answer each respondent gives as correct. The operational definition for class: how the student themselves classify their class.

2. You ask them to define their class by registrar guidelines. The operational definition for class: semester hours of credit completed by the end of the prior spring semester and recorded in each student's record in the registrar's office:

   - Freshman   Fewer than 30 hours' credit
   - Sophomore   30 to 59 hours' credit
   - Junior   60 to 89 hours' credit
   - Senior   90 or more hours' credit

These examples deal with relatively concrete concepts, but operational definitions are even more critical for constructs. Suppose one tries to measure a construct called "socialization." Are we referring to someone's level of activity on Facebook and other social media, whether they like to entertain, or whether they can converse with others? We would probably develop questions on access, posts, sharing, likes, etc., in the first instance; the number of times and the types of entertaining they do for the second; and the number, types of language used, and types of reactions received for the third as we grapple with the operational definition. We may use a measurement approach already developed and validated by other researchers or create our own. The measurement approach chosen operationally defines the construct.

We may need to provide operational definitions for only a few critical concepts or constructs, but these will almost always be the definitions used to develop the relationships found in hypotheses and theories.

Identifying and Defining Constructs

When you read in the business press or attend a business presentation, you are exposed to many constructs. If you don't struggle to define these, you miss out on a lot of what the article is telling you. Let's see how good you are at spotting these.

During the most recent *Ad Age Digital Conference*, in a panel discussion on major issues advertisers and marketers know they have but aren't ready to confront—the elephants in the room—Lou Paskalis, senior vice president of enterprise media at Bank of America shared, "We're optimizing advertising and people want storytelling. People are ad blocking because they don't like what we are doing." What are the constructs in this statement? What might be the operational definition of these constructs? What is(are) the management problem(s) confronting advertisers and their agencies?

The panel also revealed there are challenges beyond digital advertising's oft-cited viewability, ad blocking, and transparency (which refers to kickbacks and rebates from media to advertising

agencies). "The [industry trade associations] can't agree on what transparency is and, clearly, they are not speaking the same language. And that leads to a lack of trust," shared Ron Amram, vice president of media at Heineken USA. What are the constructs and operational definitions for these constructs? What is the management problem(s) confronting advertisers and advertising media?

Paskalis also shared, "We need to go back to what [the advertising] business is about. We need to ask, 'Is this compelling?' Clients need to step up and pay full value for things that are great, but we need to stop commoditizing everything." What are the constructs and the operational definitions for these constructs? What is the management problem revealed for advertisers and advertising agencies?

Source: George Slefo, "Digital Conference: Marketers Chime in on Elephants in the Room, Known and Unknown," *Ad Age*, April 05, 2016, downloaded April 6, 2016 (http://adage.com/article/special-report-digital-conference/marketers-chime-elephants-digital/303413/?utm_source=daily_email&utm_medium=newsletter&utm_campaign=adage&ttl=1460499287).

Variables

A **variable** is a measurable symbol of an event, act, characteristic, trait, or attribute.[9] In practice, one or more variables are used as a substitute for a concept or construct. As researchers are interested in relationships among concepts and constructs, researchers are interested in relationships among variables. Variables come in various types: independent, dependent, moderating, and extraneous (including control, confounding, and intervening). We'll expand this list when we get into the concept of measurement.

Independent and Dependent Variables

The **dependent variable (DV)** is of primary interest to the researcher; it is measured, predicted, or otherwise monitored and is expected to be affected by manipulation of an **independent variable (IV)**, another variable of primary interest. In each relationship, there is at least one independent variable (IV) and one dependent variable (DV). As one writer notes:

> Researchers hypothesize relationships of independence and dependence: They invent them, and then they try by reality testing to see if the relationships actually work out that way.[10]

The assignment of the variable type (dependent vs. independent) depends on the assumed relationship the researcher is studying. If you were interested in studying the impact of the length of the working week on productivity, you would make the length of working week the IV. If you were focusing on the relationship between age of the worker and productivity, then age would be the IV. Exhibit 1-5 lists some terms that have become synonyms for *independent variable* and *dependent variable*. Although it is easy to establish whether an IV influences a DV, it is much harder to show that the relationship between an IV and DV is a causal relationship.

Exhibit 1-6 summarizes the many variable types, while Exhibit 1-7 graphically shows their relationship to each other using an example. Researchers recognize that there are often several independent variables that might be studied and that they are probably at least somewhat related and, therefore, not

>**Exhibit 1-5** Independent and Dependent Variables: Synonyms

Independent Variable	Dependent Variable
Predictor	Criterion
Presumed cause	Presumed effect
Stimulus	Response
Predicted from ...	Predicted to ...
Antecedent	Consequence
Manipulated	Measured outcome

independent among themselves. When we study simple relationships, all other variables are considered unimportant and are ignored by the researcher. But for more complex relationships, researchers must identify and measure those variables.

In Exhibit 1-7a, a causal relationship is illustrated by an arrow pointing from the independent variable to the dependent variable.

Moderating Variables

A **moderating variable (MV)** is a second independent variable believed to have a *significant* contributory effect on the original IV–DV relationship. For example, one might hypothesize that in an office situation:

> The introduction of a four-day working week (IV) will lead to higher productivity (DV), especially among younger workers (MV).

In Exhibit 1-7a, the arrow pointing from the moderating variable to the arrow between the IV and DV shows the difference between an IV directly affecting the DV and an MV affecting the relationship between an IV and the DV. In this case, the researcher hypothesizes that a different relationship between the four-day week and productivity might result from age differences among the workers. Hence, after introduction of a four-day working week, the productivity gain for younger workers is compared with that for older workers. For example, let's assume that the productivity of younger workers is 12 percentage points higher than that for older workers before the introduction of the four-day working week. Assume that the productivity of all workers having a four-day working week is six percentage points higher than for those of workers having a five-day working week. If the productivity of a younger worker having a four-day working week is only 18 percentage points higher than the productivity of an older worker, there is no moderating effect (12 + 6 = 18), because the 18 percentage points are the sum of the main effects and the moderating effect should show a surplus. However, if the productivity of younger workers was 25 percentage points higher, then the moderating effect of a worker's age would be obvious.

Other Extraneous Variables

An almost infinite number of **extraneous variables (EVs)** exist that might conceivably affect a given relationship. Taking the example of the effect of the four-day working week again, one would normally

>**Exhibit 1-6** A Summary of Variable Types

Variable Type	Symbol	Presumed Effect on IV-DV Relationship	Action Needed
Dependent	DV	Concept/construct of interest	Measure
Independent	IV	Primary variable believed to have significant effect on DV	Manipulate
Moderating	MV	Alternative IV; possible *significant* contributory effect on IV-DV	Measure
Control	CV	Might influence the IV-DV, but effect is not at the core of the problem studied	Ignore; effect is randomized
Confounding	CFV	Alternative IV; unknown effect on IV-DV	Measure
Intervening	IVV	Theoretically might affect; effect can't be determined	Infer effect from IV and MV on DV

>Exhibit 1-7 Relationships among Types of Variables

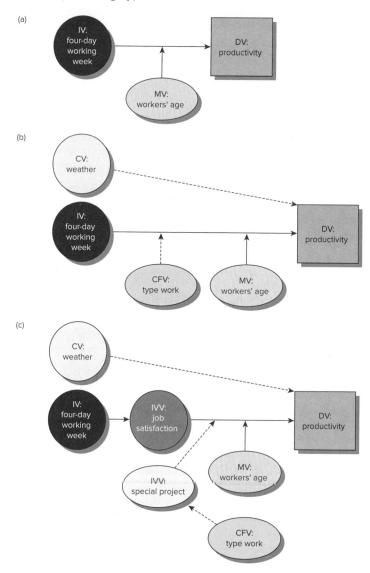

think that weather conditions, the imposition of a local sales tax, the election of a new mayor, and thousands of similar events and conditions would have little effect on work-week length and productivity. Most can safely be ignored because their impact occurs in such a random fashion as to have little effect. Others might influence the DV, but their effect is not at the core of the problem we investigate. **Control variables (CV)** are extraneous variables that we measure to determine whether they influence our results, as we want to make sure our results are not biased by excluding them. In Exhibit 1-7b, weather is shown as a CV; the broken line indicates that we included it in our research hypothesis because it might influence the DV, but we consider it irrelevant for the investigation of our research problem.

Extraneous variables can also be **confounding variables (CFVs)** to our hypothesized IV–DV relationship, similar to moderating variables. You may consider that the kind of work being done might have an effect on the impact of workweek length on productivity; productivity gains might not be universal across all types of work. This might lead you to introducing *type of work* as a confounding variable (CFV). In our example, we would study the effect of the four-day working week within groups (e.g., office workers vs. manufacturing workers vs. distribution plant workers). In Exhibit 1-7b, we included the type of work as a CFV, with a broken line.

>snapshot

Radio Chips versus Retinal Scans: Which Theory Offers the Best Protection?

When the first confirmed case of bovine spongiform encephalopathy (BSE—known as "mad cow" disease) was discovered in a Washington state dairy cow in December 2003, numerous countries banned U.S. beef imports, bringing the $3.2 billion export industry to a standstill. That year, the U.S. Department of Agriculture (USDA) performed random tests on approximately 0.03 percent of all slaughtered cattle, about 20,000 cows of the nearly 40 million head of cattle slaughtered annually. In comparison, western European countries tested 10 million cows and Japan tested each of its 1.2 million slaughtered cows.

Theories are essential to a researcher's quest to explain and predict phenomena while creating business opportunities and informing public policy. One USDA theory is that the best way to identify sources of cattle-born disease is to monitor a cow from birth to slaughter. Thus, the USDA wanted a national livestock database. After evaluating the options, the USDA proposed another theory: Cows tagged with radio frequency identification devices (RFID) would create the most accurate database.

About the size of a quarter, the RFID tag is stapled to the base of the animal's ear. It is programmed with a numeric code that is scanned by a stationary or handheld device when a cow reaches a new location in the production process. As cows move from farm to feeding lot to slaughterhouse, each animal's origin and location can be updated in the national database.

But RFID tags can be damaged, dislodged, or tampered with. Slaughterhouses need additional safeguards to be certain these devices don't end up in the meat. "All you need is one chip in someone's burger and you've got a problem," says Brian Bolton, vice president of marketing for Optibrand. This Colorado company offers a different theory for the best identification and tracking: A camera that records the unique vascular patterns in a cow's retina at each stage of the beef production chain is the most reliable. With retinal scanning, Bolton says, "the tracking technology is contained in the handheld reader. It takes a tiny picture of a cow's retina and then links it to that animal's computerized record." Meatpacker Swift & Co., the nation's third-largest beef processor, has been using Optibrand's devices for several years. Retinal scan wands also read RFID tags, access global positioning receivers, and stamp each scan with a location record. However, retinal scanning is not always practical because scans must be taken about an inch from an animal's eye.

In addition to RFID and retinal scanning, beef producers and processors implement other tracking systems, thus implementing their own theories. Some use implantable computer chips and others use DNA matching systems. While still preferring RFID technology, the USDA's director of national animal identification, John F. Wiemers, concedes, "We think there's room for all these technologies."

Which tracking theory do you favor? What are the most important variables you would consider in justifying your decision?

www.usda.gov; www.optibrand.com; www.jbsswift.com

Intervening Variables

The variables mentioned with regard to causal relationships are concrete and clearly measurable—that is, they can be seen, counted, or observed in some way. Sometimes, however, one may not be completely satisfied by the explanations they give. Thus, while we may recognize that a four-day workweek results in higher productivity, we might think that this is not the whole story—that workweek length affects some other variable that, in turn, results in higher productivity. The **intervening variable (IVV)** is a factor that theoretically affects the DV but cannot be observed or has not been measured; its effect must be inferred from the effects of the independent and moderating variables on the observed phenomenon.[11] In our example, one might view the intervening variable (IVV) to be job satisfaction, giving a hypothesis such as:

The introduction of a four-day working week (IV) will lead to higher productivity (DV) by increasing job satisfaction (IVV).

Here we assume that a four-day work week increases *job satisfaction*; similarly, we can assume that the introduction of *special project* work might influence productivity. Exhibit 1-7c illustrates how theoretical constructs, which are not directly observed, fit into our model.

Hypotheses, Theories, and Models

Hypotheses, theories, and models serve researchers in different ways but are related.

- A **hypothesis** is an unsubstantiated assumption about the relationship between concepts and constructs; it drives the research.
- A **theory** is comprised of data-tested, supported hypotheses; it is derived from research.
- A **model** is a visualization of a theory; it is used for clarification and to enhance understanding.

Hypotheses

At the core of any good research, then, is a carefully constructed hypothesis. A hypothesis can be phrased as a declarative statement (descriptive) or a question about the relationship between two or more concepts or constructs that may be judged as true or false. It is always conjecture and formulated for empirical testing/measurement.

Descriptive format	Question format
American cities are experiencing budget difficulties due to a decline in manufacturing.	Are American cities experiencing budget difficulties due to a decline in manufacturing?

Because if drives the research, crafting a hypothesis serves several important functions:

- It encourages researchers to think about the likely relationships to be found.
- It encourages researchers to think about the relevant facts (those needed to support or reject the hypothesis) and those facts that are not relevant.
- It suggests which research design is likely to be most appropriate.
- It is useful for testing statistical significance.
- It provides a framework for organizing the conclusions that result from the research.

To consider specifically the role of the hypothesis in determining the direction of the research, suppose we use this example:

Husbands and wives agree on their respective roles in vehicle purchase decisions.

The hypothesis specifies who shall be studied (married couples), in what context they shall be studied (their vehicle purchase decision making), and what shall be studied (their individual perceptions of their roles). This hypothesis suggests that the best research design is a communication-based study, either a survey or interview. We have at this time no other practical means to ascertain perceptions of people except to ask about them in one way or another. In addition, we are interested only in the roles that are assumed in the vehicle purchase decision. The study should not, therefore, seek information about roles husbands and wives might assume in other purchase decisions—say, electronics or furniture or movies. A study based on this hypothesis might reveal that husbands and wives disagree on their perceptions of roles, but the differences may be explained in terms of some factor(s) other than gender (i.e., mechanical knowledge, passion for cars, age, social class, religion, personality, etc.).

Types of Hypotheses There are numerous types of hypotheses. A **descriptive hypothesis** states the existence, size, form, or distribution of some concept/construct. For example, "The life expectancy of airplane Model 707 exceeds 16 years."

A **relational hypothesis** describes a relationship between two or more concepts/constructs. Each relationship describes a correlational or causal relationship. With **causal hypotheses** one variable being studied is assumed to cause a specific effect on other variables studied. With **correlational hypotheses** the variables being studied occur together, but there is no assumption of causation. For example:

- Women older than 50 (concept) purchase (concept) more or less of our product (concept) than those younger than 25 (concept). [correlational (neutral) relationship]
- Students who attend class regularly (construct) earn higher grades (concept) than those who do not attend regularly (construct). [correlational (positive) relationship]

- U.S. brand cars (concept) are perceived by American consumers (construct) to be of lesser quality (construct) than foreign brand cars (concept). [correlational (negative) relationship]

In the first example we hypothesize that the two groups purchase different levels of our product. In the second, there may be other factors that influence grades; it might be the amount of studying. In the last example, we hypothesize that "country of origin" (concept) influences "perceived quality" (construct), but we don't know what factors cause "perceived quality." Correlational hypotheses are often made when we believe there are more basic causal forces that affect the concepts/constructs (e.g., maybe a lack of product recalls causes high perceived quality) or when we do not have enough evidence to claim a stronger linkage.

Causal hypotheses not only predict the cause (cause means roughly to "help make happen") but also the effect. Here are three examples of causal hypotheses:

- An increase in the price of salvaged copper wire (concept/cause) leads to an increase in scavenging in abandoned homes (construct/effect).

- Exposure to a company's message concerning recent injuries (concept/cause) leads to more favorable attitudes among employees toward safety (construct/effect).

- Loyalty to a particular grocery store (construct/cause) leads to purchasing that store's private brands (concept/effect).

In proposing or interpreting causal hypotheses, the researcher must consider the *direction* of influence. One would assume the price of copper wire influences scavenging rather than the reverse. Once would also assume that the measure of attitude follows the release of the information about on-the-job injuries. Sometimes our ability to identify the direction of influence depends on the research design. Store loyalty and purchasing of store brands appear to be interdependent. Loyalty to a store may increase the probability of someone buying the store's private brands, but satisfaction with the store's private brand may also lead to greater store loyalty.

Reasoning and Hypotheses   Every day we reason with varying degrees of success. **Reasoning—** gathering facts consistent with the problem, proposing and eliminating rival hypotheses, measuring outcomes, developing crucial empirical tests, and deriving the conclusion—is pivotal to much of a researcher's success. Two types of reasoning are of great importance to research in forming and testing hypotheses: induction and deduction.

Induction   Researchers use induction to craft hypotheses. In **induction**, you start by drawing a conclusion from one or more particular facts or pieces of evidence. The conclusion explains the facts, and the facts support the conclusion. To illustrate, suppose your firm spends $10 million on a regional promotional campaign and sales do not increase; these are facts. Under such circumstances, we ask, "Why didn't sales increase?"

One likely answer to this question is that the promotional campaign was poorly executed (conclusion). This conclusion is an induction because we know from experience that regional sales should go up during a promotional event. Also we know from experience that if the promotion is poorly executed, sales will not increase. The nature of induction, however, is that the conclusion is only a hypothesis. It is *one* explanation, but there are others that fit the facts just as well. For example, each of the following hypotheses might explain why sales did not increase:

- A strike by the employees of our trucking firm prevented stock from arriving at retailers; regional retailers did not have sufficient stock to fulfill customer orders during the promotional period.

- A competitor lowered its price during the promotional period; customers bought their brand rather than ours.

- A category-five hurricane closed all our retail locations in the region for the 10 days during the promotion.

In this example, we see the essential nature of inductive reasoning. The inductive conclusion is an inferential leap beyond the evidence presented—that is, although one conclusion explains the fact of no sales increase, other conclusions also might explain the fact. It may even be that none of the conclusions we advanced correctly explain the failure of sales to increase.

Researchers often use observation when evaluating a customer's use of a product. Apply deductive reasoning to this image. Develop your own conclusions concerning what will happen next.

©Erik Isakson/Blend Images

For another example, let's consider the situation of Tracy Nelson, a salesperson at the Square Box Company. Tracy has one of the poorest sales records in the company. Her unsatisfactory performance prompts us to ask the question, "Why is she performing so poorly?" From our knowledge of Tracy's sales practices, the nature of box selling, and the market, we might conclude (hypothesize):

- Tracy makes too few sales calls per day to build a good sales record.
- Tracy's territory does not have the market potential of other territories.
- Tracy's sales-generating skills are so poorly developed that she is not able to close sales effectively.
- Tracy does not have authority to lower prices and her territory has been the scene of intense price-cutting by competitive manufacturers, causing her to lose many sales to competitors.
- Some people just cannot sell boxes, and Tracy is one of those people.

Each of the above hypotheses has some chance of being true, but we would probably have more confidence in some than in others. All require further confirmation before they gain our confidence. Confirmation comes with more evidence. The task of research is largely to (1) determine the nature of the evidence needed to confirm or reject hypotheses and (2) design methods by which to discover and measure this other evidence.

Deduction   Researchers use deduction to plan research and draw insights from data that will test hypotheses. **Deduction** is a form of reasoning that starts with one or more true premises and the conclusion flows from the premises given. For a deduction to be correct and sound, it must be both true and valid:

- Premises (reasons) given for the conclusion must agree with the real world (true).
- The conclusion must necessarily follow from the premises (valid).

A deduction is valid if it is impossible for the conclusion to be false if the premises are true. For example, consider the following simple deduction:

- All employees at BankChoice can be trusted to observe the ethical code. (Premise 1)
- Sara is an employee of BankChoice. (Premise 2)
- Sara can be trusted to observe the ethical code. (Conclusion)

If we believe that Sara can be trusted, we might think this is a sound deduction. But this conclusion cannot be a sound deduction unless the form of the argument is valid and the premises are true. In this case, the form is valid, and premise 2 can be confirmed easily. However, trillions of dollars each year in confirmed global employee theft[12] will challenge premise 1. If one premise fails the acceptance test, then the conclusion is not a sound deduction. It should be apparent that a conclusion that results from deduction is, in a sense, already "contained in" its premises.[13]

Combining Induction and Deduction Induction and deduction are used together in research reasoning. John Dewey, psychologist and educational reformer, describes this process as the "double movement of reflective thought."[14] Induction occurs when we observe a fact and ask, "Why is this?" In answer to this question, we advance a tentative explanation (hypothesis). The hypothesis is plausible if it explains the fact (event or condition) that prompted the question. Deduction is the process by which we test whether the hypothesis is capable of explaining the fact. The process is illustrated in Exhibit 1-8:

1. You promote a product but sales don't increase. (Fact 1)
2. You ask the question "Why didn't sales increase?" (Induction)
3. You propose a hypothesis to answer the question: The promotion was poorly executed. (Hypothesis)
4. You use this hypothesis to conclude (deduce) that sales will not increase during a poorly executed promotion. You know from experience that ineffective promotion will not increase sales. (Deduction 1)

This example, an exercise in circular reasoning, points out that one must be able to deduce the initiating fact from the hypothesis advanced to explain that fact. A second critical point is also illustrated in Exhibit 1-8. To test a hypothesis, one must be able to deduce from it other facts that can then be investigated. This is what research is all about. We must deduce other specific facts or events from the hypothesis and then gather information to see if the deductions are true. In this example:

5. We deduce that a well-executed promotion will result in increased sales. (Deduction 2)
6. We run an effective promotion, and sales increase. (Fact 2)

How would the double movement of reflective thought work when applied to the Tracy Nelson problem? The process is illustrated in Exhibit 1-9. The initial observation (fact 1) leads to hypothesis 1 that Tracy is lazy. We deduce several other facts from the hypothesis. These are shown as fact 2 and fact 3. We use research to find out if fact 2 and fact 3 are true. If they are found to be true, they confirm our hypothesis. If they are found to be false, our hypothesis is not confirmed, and we must look for another explanation.

In most research, the process may be more complicated than these examples suggest. For instance, we often develop multiple hypotheses by which to explain the manager's problem. Then we design a study to test all the hypotheses at once. Not only is this more efficient, but it is also a good way to reduce the attachment (and potential bias) of the researcher to any given hypothesis.

>**Exhibit 1-8** Why Didn't Sales Increase

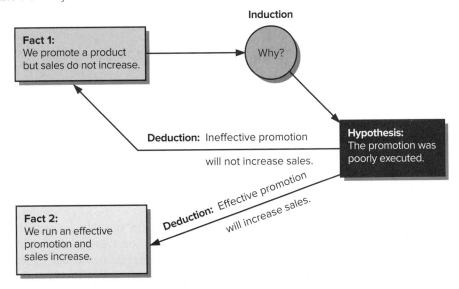

>**Exhibit 1-9** Why Is Tracy Nelson's Performance So Poor?

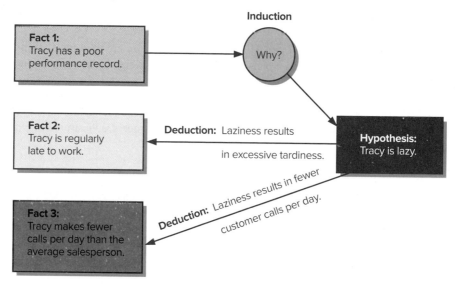

The steps that follow represent one approach to assessing the validity of conclusions about observable events.[15] These steps are particularly appropriate for business researchers whose conclusions result from empirical data. The researcher:

1. Encounters a curiosity, doubt, barrier, suspicion, or obstacle.

2. Struggles to state the problem—asks questions, contemplates existing knowledge, gathers facts and moves from an emotional to an intellectual confrontation with the problem.

3. Proposes a *hypothesis* (one plausible explanation) to explain the facts that are believed to be logically related to the problem.

4. *Deduces* outcomes or consequences of that hypothesis—attempts to discover what happens if the results are in the opposite direction of that predicted or if the results support the expectations.

5. Formulates several rival *hypotheses*.

6. Devises and conducts a crucial empirical test with various possible outcomes, each of which selectively excludes one or more hypotheses.

7. Draws a *conclusion* (an *inductive* inference) based on acceptance or rejection of the hypotheses.

8. Feeds information back into the original problem, modifying it according to the strength of the evidence.

What Is a Strong Hypothesis? A strong hypothesis should fulfill three conditions:

• Adequate for its purpose.

• Testable.

• Better than its rivals.

The conditions for developing a strong hypothesis are detailed more fully in Exhibit 1-10.

Theories

We have many theories and use them continually to explain or predict what goes on around us. To the degree that our theories are sound (empirically supported) and fit the situation, we are successful in our explanations and predictions. For example, it is midday and you note that outside the natural light is dimming, dark clouds are moving rapidly in from the west, the breeze is freshening, the barometric pressure is falling, and the air temperature is cooling but above 50 degrees. Would your understanding

>**Exhibit 1-10** Checklist for Developing a Strong Hypothesis

Criteria	Interpretation
Adequate for Its Purpose	1. Does the hypothesis reveal the original problem condition?
	2. Does the hypothesis clearly identify facts that are relevant and those that are not?
	3. Does the hypothesis clearly state the condition, size, or distribution of some variable in terms of values meaningful to the research problem (descriptive)?
	4. Does the hypothesis explain facts that gave rise to the need for explanation (explanatory)?
	5. Does the hypothesis suggest which form of research design is likely to be most appropriate?
	6. Does the hypothesis provide a framework for organizing the conclusions that result?
Testable	1. Does the hypothesis use acceptable techniques?
	2. Does the hypothesis require an explanation that is plausible given known physical or psychological laws?
	3. Does the hypothesis reveal consequences or derivatives that can be deduced for testing purposes?
	4. Is the hypothesis simple, requiring few conditions or assumptions?
Better Than Its Rivals	1. Does the hypothesis explain more facts than its rivals?
	2. Does the hypothesis explain a greater variety or scope of facts than its rivals?
	3. Is the hypothesis one that informed judges would accept as being the most likely?

of the relationship among these concepts/constructs (your weather theory) lead you to predict that it will rain?

A *theory* is an empirically supported description of the relationships among concepts, constructs, and hypotheses that are advanced to explain or predict phenomena. A theory, therefore, is comprised of data-tested, supported hypotheses; it is derived from research. Our ability to make rational decisions is based on our ability to develop theory. But a caution: No theory can ever be considered final because it is subject to challenge by new data.

In marketing, for example, the product life cycle theory describes the stages that a product category goes through in the marketplace.[16] It was developed based on observing thousands of product introductions and their success path over time. The generalized product life cycle has four stages: introduction, growth, maturity, and decline. In each stage, many concepts, constructs, and hypotheses describe the influences that change revenue and profit. Definitions are used for communicating the claims of the theory. In the growth stage of this theory, for example, companies in the category spend heavily on promotion to create product awareness (construct). In the early period of this stage these expenditures may be made to fuel *primary demand* (construct), improving product category awareness (construct) rather than brand awareness (construct). In this stage, sales (concept) increase rapidly because many customers (concept) are trying the product; and those who are satisfied and purchase again—*repeat purchasers* (concept)—are swelling the ranks. According to product lifecycle theory, if a given company is unable to attract repeat purchasers, this may mean death for its particular brand (hypothesis), even though the product category may endure. This theory has endured for more than 50 years.

Models

If you are an architect, a client might hire you to design their dream home. You might build them a physical model so that they could better visualize your design. Such models, while time-consuming to create, often save time and money during the construction process by avoiding costly onsite design changes.

>Exhibit 1-11 Model of the Traditional Product Life Cycle Theory

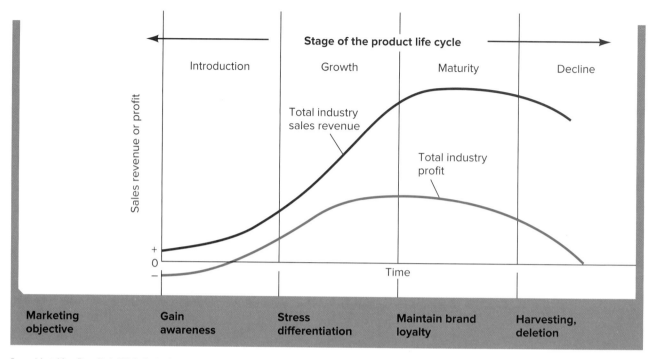

Source: Adapted from Roger Kerin, Eric Berkowitz, Steven Hartley, and William Rudelius, *Marketing*, 7th ed. (Burr Ridge, IL: McGraw-Hill, 2003), p. 295.

A *model*, therefore, is a representation of a theory or system that is constructed to study some aspect of that system or the system as a whole. A research model's purpose is to increase our understanding, prediction, and control of the complexities of the environment. While theory's role is explanation or prediction, a model's role is representation. Models allow researchers and managers to characterize present or future conditions: the effect of a raise on employee engagement, the effect of higher interest on bond purchase rates, the effect of advertising on purchase, the effect of scheduled maintenance on manufacturing defects. Exhibit 1-11 provides the model for the product life-cycle theory. Models are an important means of advancing theories and aiding decision makers.

>summary

LO1-1   Managers make thousands of decisions (strategic, tactical, and procedural) that use data as fuel. Business research and data analytics complement each other, but they are not synonymous. Data analytics needs data, some of which are provided by research. Managers often draw on data from existing internal data sources (called a decision support system) when engaging in data analytics. When these data are mined, they may be used for a purpose other than that for which they were originally collected. Collecting data to understand and improve performance employs ongoing observation or communication research. However, using such data for a different purpose employs data analytics. Businesses are getting better at data blending—combining data from separate datasets into a new actionable dataset and then querying that composite data to help make decisions. While the information that comes from data blending has a role in decision making, it is not the same as research.

Business research is a systematic inquiry that provides information to guide decisions. More specifically, it is a process of determining, acquiring, analyzing and synthesizing, and disseminating relevant data, information, and insights to decision makers in ways that mobilize the organization to take appropriate actions that, in turn, maximize performance and help achieve organizational goals. The research process is a model for the development and interpretation of research studies. Several subprocesses or stages are included in the process, including (1) clarify the research, (2) design the research, (3) collect and prepare the data, (4) analyze and interpret the data, and (5) report insights and recommendations. Despite variations, the idea of a sequence is useful for developing a project and for keeping the project orderly as it unfolds. The research process is based on the tenets of the scientific method: clearly defined concepts, constructs, methods, and procedures; empirically testable hypotheses; direct observation of phenomena; conclusions drawn from statistical evidence rather than inferred justification (educated guesses); and the self-correcting process (ability to replicate and reassess validity of conclusions). Although the scientific method consists of neither sequential nor independent stages, the problem-solving process that it reveals provides insight into the way research is conducted.

LO1-2 Understanding the language of professional researchers is crucial to doing great research. Researchers use concepts, constructs, operational definitions, and variables to form hypotheses. A concept is a generally accepted collection of meanings or characters associated with an event, object, condition, situation, or behavior. When we work with more abstract phenomena, we invent constructs. When we are trying to understand the relationships between concepts and constructs, we often form a conceptual scheme or map. Each concept or construct needs an operational definition, its specific criteria for measurement. Variables serve as measurable substitutes for concepts and constructs in research. There are many different types: independent, dependent, moderating, and extraneous (including control, confounding, and intervening).

Hypotheses are the core of good research and are crafted as descriptive statements or questions. Each hypothesis is an unsubstantiated assumption about a relationship between two or more concepts or constructs; it drives the research study. Hypotheses are either descriptive or relational. Relational hypotheses are either correlational or causal. The research process is grounded in reasoning. The reasoning process is used for the development and testing of various hypotheses largely through the double movement of reflective thinking. Reflective thinking consists of sequencing induction and deduction in order to explain inductively (by hypothesis) a puzzling condition. In turn, the hypothesis is used in a deduction of further facts that can be sought to confirm or deny the truth of the hypothesis. Hypotheses are often crafted using inductive reasoning and then tested using deductive reasoning. Induction starts by drawing a conclusion from one or more facts or pieces of evidence. Deduction starts by proposing one or more true premises and draws a conclusion based on those premises. A theory is a data-supported description of the relationships between concepts and constructs in hypotheses; it is derived from research. Its role is prediction. A model is the visualization (representation) of a theory; it is used for clarification and to enhance understanding. Models allow researchers and managers to characterize present or future conditions.

>**key**terms

>discussionquestions

Terms in Review

1 What is business research?

2 Distinguish among the following sets of items, and suggest the significance of each in a research context:

   a Concept and construct.

   b Deduction and induction.

   c Operational definition and dictionary definition.

   d Concept and variable.

   e Hypothesis and theory.

3 Describe the characteristics of the scientific method.

4 Below are some terms commonly found in a management setting. Are they concepts or constructs? Give two different operational definitions for each.

   a First-line supervisor.

   b Employee morale.

   c Assembly line.

   d Overdue account.

   e Leadership.

   f Union democracy.

   g Ethical standards.

5 In your company's management development program, there was a heated discussion between some people who claimed, "Theory is impractical and thus no good," and others who claimed, "Good theory is the most practical approach to problems." What position would you take and why?

6 An automobile manufacturer observes the demand for its brand increasing as per capita income increases. Sales increases also follow low interest rates, which ease credit conditions. Buyer purchase behavior is seen to be dependent on age and gender. Other factors influencing sales appear to fluctuate almost randomly (competitor advertising, competitor dealer discounts, introductions of new competitive models).

   a If sales and per capita income are positively related, classify all variables as dependent, independent, moderating, extraneous, or intervening.

   b Comment on the utility of a model based on the hypothesis.

Making Research Decisions

7 You observe the following condition: "Our female sales representatives have lower customer defections than do our male sales representatives."

   a Propose the concepts and constructs you might use to study this phenomenon.

   b How might any of these concepts and/or constructs be related to explanatory hypotheses?

8 You are the office manager of a large firm. Your company prides itself on its high-quality customer service. Lately, complaints have surfaced that an increased number of incoming calls are being misrouted or dropped. Yesterday, when passing by the main reception area, you noticed the receptionist fiddling with his hearing aid. In the process, a call came in and would have gone unanswered if not for your intervention. This particular receptionist had earned an unsatisfactory review three months earlier for tardiness. Your inclination is to urge this 20-year employee to retire or to fire him, if retirement is rejected, but you know the individual is well liked and seen as a fixture in the company.

   a Pose several hypotheses that might account for dropped or misrouted incoming calls.

   b Using the double movement of reflective thought, show how you would test these hypotheses.

From Concept to Practice

9 Using Exhibits 1-8 an 1-9 as your guides, graph the inductions and deductions in the following statements. If there are gaps, supply what is needed to make them complete arguments.

   a Repeated studies indicate that economic conditions vary with—and lag 6 to 12 months behind—the changes in the national money supply. Therefore, we may conclude the money supply is the basic economic variable.

   b Research studies show that heavy smokers have a higher rate of lung cancer than do nonsmokers; therefore, heavy smoking causes lung cancer.

   c Show me a person who goes to church regularly, and I will show you a reliable worker.

From the Headlines

10 Chipotle Mexican Grill continues to suffer from perception issues after a string of outbreaks, including *E.coli,* worried customers about the safety of eating at the fast casual chain. Chipotle's strategy for getting customers back into its restaurants was to give away free tacos, burritos, and chips. And while its customer survey scores are improving, Chipotle is still operating at a loss. What concepts, constructs, and operational definitions should any future research deal with?

>cases*

Campbell-Ewald: R-E-S-P-E-C-T Spells Loyalty

Open Doors: Extending Hospitality to Travelers with Disabilities

HeroBuilders.com

*You will find a description of each case in the Case Abstracts section of this textbook. Check the Case Index to determine whether a case provides data, the research instrument, video, or other supplementary material. Cases and case supplements are available in Connect.

>chapter 2

The Research Process:
An Overview

"Today individuals increasingly keep their emails and documents on remote servers in data centers— in short, in the cloud. But the transition to the cloud does not alter people's expectations of privacy."

Brad Smith,
President and Chief Legal Officer, Microsoft

>learningobjectives

After reading this chapter, you should understand . . .

LO2-1 The standards of good research.

LO2-2 What is happening within each stage of the research process.

LO2-3 Research process pitfalls and their solutions.

LO2-4 Ethical issues at each stage in the process.

>What Is Good Research?

Business research has inherent value only to the extent that it helps a manager make a better decision to achieve organizational goals than a decision made with the information he already has. Interesting information about consumers, employees, competitors, equipment, facilities, locations, or the environment might be pleasant to have, but it has limited value if the information cannot be applied to making the best decision in a critical situation. As we explore the research process, we need quality standards that will distinguish good research from poor research and that provide a manager limited insight. These six standards are summarized here and linked to researcher responsibilities in Exhibit 2-1.

1. *Purpose clearly defined.* The purpose of business research—the problem involved or the decision to be made—should be clearly defined in writing. This statement of the decision problem should include its scope, limitations, and the precise meanings of all concepts, and variables significant to the research.

2. *Research design thoroughly planned and executed.* The procedural design of the research, and its choice among competing designs, should be clearly described and justified. Procedures should be detailed and carefully followed to yield results that are as objective as possible. Researchers must avoid personal bias in selecting research and sampling designs and collecting and recording data.

3. *High ethical standards applied.* Researchers often have significant latitude in designing and executing projects. They face ethical dilemmas at each stage of the process and must be prepared to address these issues. A research design must include safeguards against causing mental or physical harm, exploitation, invasion of privacy, and/or loss of dignity to participants, as well as ensuring the adequate training and safety of data collectors. Procedures for ensuring data integrity are critical.

4. *Adequate analysis for decision maker's needs.* The analysis of the data should use appropriate techniques, be classified in ways that assist the researcher in reaching pertinent insights and conclusions, and clearly reveal the findings and procedures that have led to those conclusions. Insights should be limited to those for which the data provide an adequate basis. When statistical methods are used, the probability of error should be estimated, and the criteria of statistical significance applied; these should be revealed. The validity and reliability of data should be checked carefully.

5. *Limitations frankly revealed.* While few research designs are perfect, the researcher should report, with complete frankness, flaws in research design or design execution and estimate their effect on the findings. Some of the imperfections may have little effect on the validity and reliability of the data; others may invalidate them entirely. As a decision maker, you should question the value of research about which no limitations are reported.

6. *Findings reported unambiguously; insights and conclusions justified.* Except when confidentiality is imposed, research reports should reveal candidly the sources of data and the means by which data were obtained. Researchers should report procedural details to make it possible to estimate the validity and reliability of the data and increase confidence in the research itself, as well as any recommendations based on the research. Good researchers always specify the conditions under which their conclusions seem to be valid. Presentation of insights and conclusions should be comprehensive, easily understood by the audience, and organized so that the relevant decision maker can readily locate critical information.

>The Research Process

Organizations usually treat the **research process** as a sequential process involving several clearly defined stages: clarify the research question, design the research, collect and prepare data, analyze and interpret data, and report insights and recommendations. Recycling, circumventing, and skipping occur among

>**Exhibit 2-1** Actions That Deliver Effective Research

Category	Option
Purpose clearly defined	• Researcher distinguishes among symptom of organization's problem, the manager's perception of the problem, and the research problem. • Researcher includes the scope and limitations within the statement of the research problem. • Researcher operationally defines all concepts, constructs, and variables.
Research design thoroughly planned and executed	• Researcher provides a justification for the choice of a research design and the rejection of alternative designs. • Researcher details procedures within the chosen design and carefully executes them. • Researcher avoids personal bias in selecting research designs. • Researcher defines exploratory procedures. • Researcher defines target population and describes the sample unit along with the procedures for the selection. • Researcher defines and follows procedures for data collection.
High ethical standards applied	• Researcher designs safeguards to protect study participants, organizations, clients, and researchers. • Researcher recommendations do not exceed the scope of the study. • Researcher ensures the study's methodology and limitations sections reflect researcher's restraint and concern for accuracy. • Research protects confidentiality of subjects and sources, as necessary.
Adequate analysis for decision maker's needs	• Researcher follows analytical procedures acceptable for the data collected and the decision maker's needs. • Researcher connects findings to the research instrument. • Researcher connects insights and conclusions to the data collected, not exceeding the scope of the data. • Researcher checks for data validity and reliability.
Limitations frankly revealed	• Researcher reveals the study's limitations by comparing desired with actual procedure. • Researcher reveals the sample's limitations by comparing its characteristics with target population. • Researcher reveals the impact of limitations on findings, insights, and conclusions.
Findings reported unambiguously; insights and conclusions justified	• Researcher clearly presents findings in words, tables, and graphs. • Researcher logically organizes findings, insights, and conclusions to help the manager reach a decision. • Researcher summarizes conclusions. • Researcher provides a detailed table of contents in any written report to facilitate quick access to desired information.

steps. Some steps are begun out of sequence, some are carried out simultaneously, and some are omitted. Despite these variations, the idea of a sequence is useful for developing a project and for keeping the project orderly as it unfolds. Exhibit 2-2 models the research process we will develop in this text.

>Stage 1: Clarify the Research Question

The purpose of this stage in the research process is to determine whether research should be conducted. During this stage, managers must answer the following questions:

1. What is/are the management dilemma(s) and which should be the focus?
2. What do we know that might help define and solve the dilemma?
3. What information do we need to make a decision?
4. Would knowing this information improve the decision(s) we must make to resolve the dilemma?
5. Where will the funding come from for any proposed research?

>**Exhibit 2-2** The Research Process, with Ethical Responsibilities

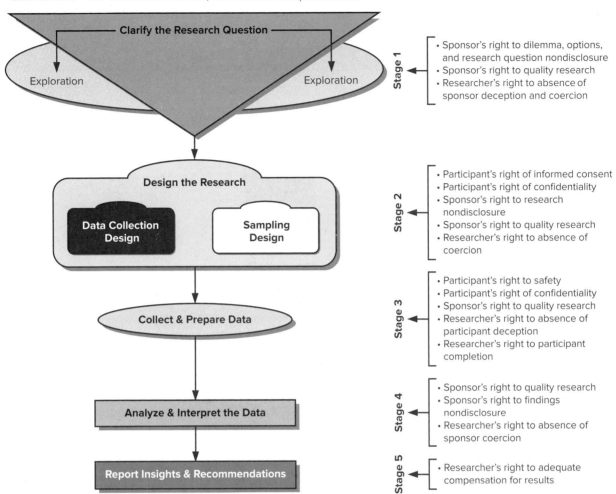

Identify and Prioritize Dilemmas

Managers don't have unlimited resources, so they have to focus these where they believe they will accomplish the most. This stage begins at the most general level with the **management dilemma(s)**, a symptom of an actual problem, such as:

- Rising costs.
- Increasing tenant move-outs from an apartment complex.
- Declining sales.
- Increasing employee turnover in a restaurant.
- A larger number of product defects during the manufacture of an automobile.
- An increasing number of letters and phone complaints about post-purchase delivery service.

The management dilemma can also be triggered by an early signal of an opportunity or growing evidence that a fad may be gaining staying power, such as:

- The discovery of an expensive chemical compound that would increase the efficacy of a drug.
- The shift in job hunting to digital job boards.
- The rise in penetration of smart phone usage.
- Increasing numbers of firms mining data to develop digital dashboards.

New Moms and Moms-to-be offer Video Insights

Doing research with mothers of infants and small children or expectant mothers can be problematic. These women between 21–40 have lots of distractions and their time availability is often at odd hours. Marcus Thomas LLC (it describes itself as an idea agency) and QualVu (a FocusVision company that helps its clients find truth) collaborated to help a durable baby goods producer better understand a mother's choices.

Specifically, the study objectives were to "gain insight into the mother's perceptions of specific products, uncover their path to purchase, [understand] purchase motivations, and [share their] experiences at key retailers (Target, Walmart, and Babies 'R' Us)," explained Jennifer Hirt-Marchand, associate partner, strategic insights executive with Marcus Thomas. Qualitative research would allow Marcus Thomas a deeper understanding of their subjects, so they opted for video diaries, and QualVU offered the platform.

Recruited participants needed to have a baby or be pregnant and have access to a computer and high-speed Internet access. Those who didn't already have a video camera were provided one (that they could keep at the end of the study). "We knew from secondary research provided by Forrester Research that women in the age group were active on social networks and accustomed to sharing their personal stories online, using both text and video," shared Edwige Winans, associate research director at Marcus Thomas. As moderator, Winans prerecorded "discussion points" and posted them to the QualVu platform, where participants accessed them. "What we tried to achieve was a semblance of a relationship with the participant, using the video." The participants answered various questions by uploading video diaries to the site over a four-day period. The participants actually have "conversations with themselves," explained Winans. "Their diaries provide really candid responses." Participants answer different discussion topics each day; the methodology allows participants to answer the questions on their own schedule. Videos are monitored

©Hero/Corbis/Glow Images

while the study is ongoing, and the moderator uses follow-up emails to prompt or redirect participants for further clarification, if necessary.

Over the course of the study, 21 compensated participants responded to eight topics with uploaded diaries on each topic (a typical video diary study is 7 to 10 topics). QualVu researchers watched the videos, identifying trends in comments, and provided a video report. "The client was especially interested in comments on retailer in-store merchandising elements," shared Winans. "But our most important task was to keep an open mind." Some of the most valuable insights came from secondary cues, like the participant's home environment, props the participant used in her diaries, and the product demonstrations she did in stores or in her home.

"A key consideration in recommending this methodology to our client was to ensure that technology was intuitive and natural to the participant and allow them to comfortably and confidently share their thoughts and perspectives," stated Hirt-Marchand. The client got just what it needed.

www.marcusthomasllc.com; www.focusvision.com

Identifying problem-oriented management dilemmas is rarely difficult, unless the organization fails to track its performance against prior performance and industry standards. These metrics are called **key performance indicators (KPIs)**. KPIs exit at the company, business unit, and individual employee levels. Company KPIs are driven by stockholder demands (sales, profits, growth, reputation), government regulations (safety, overtime, on-time performance), even employee unions (training, advancement). At the business unit, companies might track a variety of KPIs; for example, a production line might track manufacturing output, production defects, time frame of manufacturer, supply fulfillment, etc. For the office of human resources, KPIs might be employee turnover, employee engagement, applicants per open position, online training participation, safety training compliance scores, performance review ratings, etc. Even individual employees have KPIs, although we might not call them this; these include pay increases, promotions, training experiences, project assignments, project leadership, new customers captured, and so on. Sophisticated businesses track these KPIs through digitized, perpetually maintained **dashboards—** a data visualization tool that shows current and a period of prior status on each metric, usually on one screen. Even small businesses can dashboard KPIs create with the software tools available.

Identifying opportunity-based management dilemmas is more time consuming and difficult. It requires monitoring obscure developments in a variety of industries, as well as emerging trends in your own industry. Those companies looking for opportunities are trying to be first movers; they want to capitalize on an environmental trend that others haven't recognized. Jeff Bezos, chief executive officer (CEO) of Amazon, is always seeking these kinds of dilemmas: customers getting frustrated at not finding the solutions they sought at stores, companies needing a more reliable delivery option, readers wanting to take more books with them when they travel than luggage space permits, etc. The search for opportunity-based management dilemmas is full of risk, but when the approach pays off, it often pays big.

However, choosing one dilemma on which to focus may be difficult. Solving different dilemmas offers different rewards. One approach is to estimate the payoff of solving a dilemma, using this value to prioritize. This is more easily done for problems (e.g., estimating the cost of reducing customer returns) than for opportunities. Ultimately, to choose incorrectly puts a company or business on an unproductive path. As a manager, only practice makes you proficient at this task. For new managers, or for established managers facing new responsibilities, developing several management dilemma-to-research question hierarchies, each starting with a different dilemma, will assist in the choice process. To develop these, much exploratory research is used, tapping into published secondary sources and mining company data.

Exploration

Seeking existing information is often used not only to identify dilemmas (e.g., identify industry standard to compare to company performance), but also to ask the right questions and better understand decision options. Historic company data are increasingly being used in exploration as better tools to tap into digital data warehouses have become available.[1] Much of this information may not be in searchable databases; it may be in written reports, where accessibility is an issue. At this stage, it always pays the

We are attracted to experiments at an early age due to our unlimited curiosity. A great researcher fosters curiosity as an important skill.

©Blend/Image Source

researcher to search aggressively because the cost of exploration is far less than that of conducting new research. However, historic information and published information always have an inherent problem: it is a reflection of the past, not the present, and the situation or environment reflected in that past rarely matches the current situation.

Exploration is itself a type of research; it is usually highly unstructured. If you have a paper to write, you might start with a Google search using key words to search on a topic of interest. You are likely to get thousands of links but many won't directly relate to the information you seek. So you keep refining your search terms. And you try a different search engine, like Bing, to see if it gives you different results. Researchers might use Google or another search engine, but they are also likely to seek information in proprietary databases that general search engines can't access. The most important proprietary information source to a researcher might be company records, both written and digital.

During the process of exploration, the manager has, hopefully, defined plausible management actions (options) to address the dilemmas. Each of these options may be put into two groups: those that are feasible given company resources, and those that aren't currently feasible. Besides estimated payoff, managers use feasibility to prioritize management dilemmas and focus their attention. It is equally likely that we have raised numerous additional questions without answers, and thus identified what we don't know.

To move forward, the manager needs to frame a **research question**—the hypothesis that best states the objective of the research—and often specifies a choice between action options. The answer to this question must provide the manager with the desired information necessary to make a decision with respect to the management dilemma. Arriving at the research question usually involves additional exploration.

Value and Budget the Research

While identifying dilemmas and prioritizing them, exploration helped the manager determine the research question and what they know and don't know. Capturing the information you don't know (conducting a research project) always has a cost. So before a manager moves forward, he or she needs to estimate whether acquiring that information is worthwhile. Managers have prior experiences that frequently lead them to decisions without research. If that experience, when facing the newly chosen dilemma, would lead the manager to the same decision as new research, then the research has no value. However, if a decision is unlikely to be made without new research, then the research has value. The only way this estimate of value can be made is to consider plausible methods by which the information could be collected and from whom or what and to then determine the cost. Using this cost estimate, the manager determines a budget. If research has value, then the manager obtains the resources budgeted for the project. In most companies of any size, this is a competitive and political activity, pitting one manager's research proposal against another's. If the process is fair, the manager with the best justification will earn the budget he or she needs.

>Stage 2: Design the Research Project

The **research design** is the blueprint for collecting data that fulfills objectives and answers questions. This stage of the planning answers two questions:

- *Data collection design.* What data need to be collected, how, and in what format?
- *Sampling design.* From whom or what do the data need to be collected, and from how many?

Data

Data are collective units of information (e.g., production defects, purchases or returns, a person's attitudes, behaviors, motivations, attributes, photos, recorded comments, etc.) from a subject or case (people, events, machines, personnel records, etc.) measured by a data collector (person or a sensing device or machine, digital or mechanical) following consistent procedures. Data are of two classifications:

primary or secondary. **Primary data** are recorded directly; they are raw or unprocessed. For example, a researcher conducts a personal interview with a subject and digitally records the answers. Primary data are the focus of most business research studies. **Secondary data** contain at least one level of interpretation. For example, a researcher discovers a research report or article and uses the summarized graphical representation of the data contained within that report to extract data for his own research. Secondary data are often used during exploration and are helpful in the interpretation of new primary data on similar subjects.

We also describe data by its properties and group them into four types based on the type of measurement scale used to collect it: nominal, ordinal, interval, or ratio. **Nominal data** provide classification but no order, equal distance, or natural origin. When we ask people whether they prefer online training or classroom training, we group their data based on a classification system (online/classroom). In the classification, no group is more than or less than another. **Ordinal data** provide classification and order but no equal distance or natural origin. We can collect employees' home addresses then group them by whether they are within a two-mile radius of the business, two to five miles away from the plant, or beyond five miles; in the groups, we have classification and order (based on distance) but the distance represented by each group is not equal. **Interval data** reveal classification, order, equal distance, but no natural origin. If we give a person an attitude question and ask them to use a five-point scale of agreement (1 = strongly agree; 2 = agree; 3 = neither agree nor disagree; 4 = disagree; 5 = strongly disagree), we collect interval data. We assume that those who agree with a statement feel less strongly than someone else who chose "strongly agree." Because we anchored the words with numbers, we assume equal distance between word descriptors, but there is no natural origin. Finally, **ratio data** offer classification, order, equal distance, and natural origin. If we measure the number of defects produced by a machine in a 24-hour period, we get an actual number. That number can't be less than 0, its natural origin. We also know a machine that produces 10 defects a day produces a greater number of defects than a machine that produces only three defects a day; thus we also have classification and order. One defect is exactly one defect away from two defects; thus we have equal distance. Knowing statistically what we want to do with data often determines which of the four types we collect.

Category	Characteristics of Data	Basic Empirical Operation	Example
Nominal	Classification but no order, equal distance, or natural origin	Determination of equality	Gender (male, female)
Ordinal	Classification and order but no equal distance or natural origin	Determination of greater or lesser than	Doneness of meat (well, medium well, medium rare, rare)
Interval	Classification, order, equal distance, but no natural origin	Determination of equality of intervals or differences	Temperature in degrees
Ratio	Classification, order, equal distance, and natural origin	Determination of equality of ratios	Age in years

One writer suggests data also may be characterized by their abstractness, verifiability, elusiveness, and truthfulness (closeness to the phenomenon).[2]

- *Abstractness.* If what we measure is objective (e.g., someone's height) it is on one extreme of the abstractness continuum. We may not be able to observe and record some concepts and constructs directly, so we rely on variable substitutions. Someone's attitude about job satisfaction is at the opposite end of the abstract continuum.

- *Verifiability.* Data are processed by our senses. When sensory experiences consistently produce the same result, our data are said to be trustworthy because they have been verified.

- *Elusiveness.* Some data of interest occur at a speed that may make measurement during occurrence difficult. In these instances, we rely on video or audio recordings of events or people's memories. In other instances, the effects of an observable event may be quickly gone; in those instances, we also rely on people's memories. To capture elusive data, we need to measure as near to the event as possible.

- *Truthfulness.* If the data collected accurately reflect the phenomena being measured, they are considered truthful. Primary data collected at the time of the event being measured are considered the closest to truth.

Research and Programmatic Algorithms

At the American Advertising Federation's *D2 Digital Dialogue* conference Scott Franzer, associate director with OMG and responsible for P&G's programmatic digital ad buys, shared that P&G was experiencing "three to five times greater ROI through programmatic buying than . . . through traditional [digital ad buys]." Just a few years ago "the processes of ad buying and placement [of digital media ads] were handled by humans, and often conducted over the phone," explained Michael Benisch, director of artificial intelligence, Rocket Fuel Inc. But today's digital ads are bought via computer programmatically through an "astonishing range of complex calculations" that no human could do in the time available.

How does programmatic buying work? The consumer clicks on a content link. Behind the scenes, the publisher's computer profiles the consumer using previous contact history to determine which ads will appeal most to that consumer and earn the publisher the greatest advertising revenue. The publisher's computer sends out a bid, with information about the consumer's profile, through various ad exchanges to numerous advertisers. Each advertiser determines if it wants to bid on that consumer.

"Machine learning algorithms can decide exactly how much they want to bid for [each consumer's] attention—and in some cases they can even create the right ad and serve it on the fly," shared Benisch. All this happens in about 100 milliseconds.

Advertising research demonstrates that each consumer needs "to see an ad multiple times before the message [penetrates] to generate a response. And, for big-ticket, long purchase-cycle items like cars, it takes even more exposures over a longer time period. This is . . . why getting greater targeting capability through programmatic is important—to reach [the consumer] just often enough to make the sale, but not so often that [the seller annoys them and wastes money]." So, great results—a higher return on an advertising investment—is all about the algorithm and the data points it considers. "[The] more data points an algorithm [evaluates], . . . the more capable it is of learning from each bidding opportunity . . . , the smarter the system."

What role might research play in identifying powerful data points to create the smarter algorithm? Or is it all about following the click data?

www.pg.com

Consistency in collection produces verifiable data, but that does not guarantee its truthfulness. The Census Bureau, which manages the largest survey in the U.S.every 10 years, conducts a sample of follow-up interviews to determine that households have been counted and that the data are truthful— that they accurately reflect the household being measured.

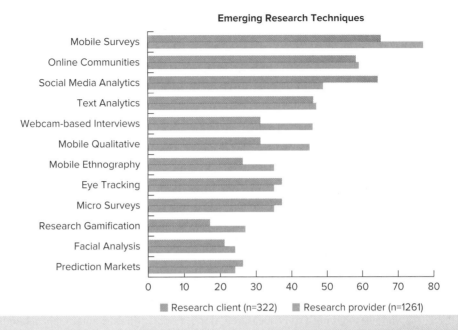

Emerging Research Techniques

Research client (n=322) ■ Research provider (n=1261)

>picprofile

According to the latest Greenbook Research Industry Trends (GRIT) report, the top four emerging techniques, among both research buyers and providers all involve Internet use. Mobile surveys continue to gain increasing acceptance by both research providers (77 percent) and managers (65 percent). The use of online communities made a big move over the last four years as a major source of samples. The gaining acceptance of social media analytics and better tools for text analytics explain their respective number 3 and number 4 positions. The interest in agile research has influenced a rise in the use of micro-surveys. As Gregg Archibald, managing partner with Gen2 Advisers, notes, "Big data, Automation, and AI are all seen as game-changers" for the research industry. What's next? "It's not just about the tools and processes of providing insights, it is about integrating disparate sources of knowledge for gaining a more complete understanding of people and issues." Read the report for yourself. It comes out every year free. **www.greenbook.org**

Data Collection Design

Selecting a data collection design is complicated by the availability of a large variety of methods, techniques, procedures, and protocols. For example, a researcher may decide on a survey, but she must choose it from a long list of research methodologies; other methodologies might be equally viable and the choice—of which will be used and which are rejected—must be justified. Once the method is chosen, the researcher faces other questions. Should the survey be administered via the Internet, via mobile device, or through a digitally recorded personal interview? Should all relevant data be collected at one time, or would multiple measurements over a period of time be a better choice? How will the questionnaire or interview guide be structured? What instructions will be provided? How will questions be worded? Should the responses be scaled or open-ended? How will reliability and validity be achieved? Will characteristics of the interviewer influence responses to the measurement questions? What kind of training should the data collectors receive? These questions represent only a few of the decisions that have to be made and justified when just one method is chosen.

Although selecting an appropriate design may be complicated by the widening range of options, the creative researcher actually benefits from this array. The numerous combinations spawned by the abundance of tools may be used to construct alternative perspectives on the same problem. By creating a design using diverse methodologies, researchers are able to achieve greater insight than if they followed the most frequently used method or the method receiving the most media attention. Although pursuing research on a single research problem from a multimethod, multistudy strategy is not currently the norm, such designs are getting increasing attention from researchers and winning industry awards for effectiveness.[3] One of the major trends in business is remote workforce collaboration; this is increasingly evident in the research process.[4] Collaborating to identify several plausible competing designs should be considered before settling on a final data collection design

Sampling Design

This subprocess answers the question: From whom or what (target population) does the data need to be collected, how, and from how many (cases)? The steps in this subprocess include:

- Define the target population.
- Define a case.
- Define the number of cases needed.
- Define the procedure for how each case will be recruited or selected.

The first step in planning the sampling design is to define the **target population**, those people, events, or records that possess the desired information to answer the research question. If a study's objective is to examine the attitudes of U.S. automobile assemblers about quality improvements, the population may be defined as "the entire adult population of auto assemblers employed by the auto industry in the United States." Using operational definitions for *adult* and *assembler* and the relevant job descriptions included under "assembly" and "auto industry in the United States" may further limit the population under study. The researcher may also restrict the research to specific companies or brands, vehicle types, or assembly processes.

Each unit in that target population is a **case**. Each case possesses the information on one or more variables that need to be measured. For example, using the automobile assembler study, each case is an employee. Each employee can be defined by his or her years on the job, his or her performance ratings, his or her skill set, the number of companies he or she has worked for, etc.

The number of cases we need depends on the size, variability, and accessibility of the target population. During sampling design we determine whether a sample or a census is desired. Taking a **census** requires that the researcher examines or counts every case in the target population. Using a **sample** requires examining a portion of the cases in the target population. When a target population is small, a census might be necessary; when it is large, a census might not be feasible or desired. For most business research, we use samples. We use statistical formulas for determining ideal sample sizes and types.

When researchers use a sample, they must determine a procedure for selecting which specific cases are most likely, collectively, to be representative. If our sample is drawn from records or events or machine performance data, statistical procedures to assure random selection are often employed. With people, however, accessibility may be a problem. Recruiting individuals to participate in research studies has become more difficult (higher decline rates) and more costly (higher incentives needed). As a result, researchers (1) employ sampling specialists to recruit participants or (2) use established communities of individuals who are more willing to participate in studies.[5] We still must employ consistent procedures for recruiting and keeping participants engaged; the mobile devices most individuals carry today have given researchers more options to accomplish these tasks.

>Stage 3: Collect and Prepare the Data

This stage contains two subprocesses: actual collection of the data and preparation of the data for analysis.

Collect the Data

Questionnaires, standardized tests, observation checklists, event notes, video or audio recordings, photographs, personal diaries, and instrument calibration logs are among the devices used to record primary data. Experiments, observation studies, online surveys, focus groups, photo ethnographic studies, and even research gaming are just a few of the methods used today. Increasingly, researchers combine more than one method to answer the research question(s)—for example, using a survey followed by sending a subject into a designated store to take video of what he or she is experiencing when making a choice

While intercept surveys are expensive due to the involvement of an interviewer and travel issues, if your target population is congregated—like at a concert or mall—it is sometimes the most efficient method to collect the data.

©wdstock/Getty Images

from a product array. Each research method used in a project requires varying degrees of scientific rigor, but each must follow consistent procedures to ensure the quality of the data. It is at this stage that the methods and the procedures specified during data collection design are executed.

Prepare the Data

Most data must be edited prior to analysis to ensure consistency across respondents, objects, or events and to locate and address errors and omissions. Data preparation processes address recording errors, improve legibility, and clarify unclear or unexpected responses. As data are processed by computer, the alphanumeric codes assigned to each data unit reduce responses to more manageable categories for storage and processing. These codes also assist with sorting, tabulating, and analyzing. Computers have made it possible to enter, merge, edit, and code data using fewer steps and at a faster speed, shortening the time frame of many research projects.

Processes for data preparation include more than code assignment. For example, a researcher may include early summarization of data to locate out-of-range answers and determine if coding is correct. The survey question requested *Yes* (code 1) or *No* (code 2) answers, but during data entry, some 3s were entered. Will you review the original mail survey for the correct answer or discard the data for this person on this question? What will you do if this question is so fundamental to the survey that, without it, you cannot correctly interpret other responses? Will you discard all of this person's answers? These types of issues are addressed during this stage.

>Stage 4: Analyze and Interpret the Data

Managers need information, not raw data. Researchers generate information by analyzing data. **Data analysis** involves reducing accumulated data by developing summaries (descriptive statistics of the variables), looking for patterns by looking for relationships among variables, and applying statistical techniques. For example, assume a researcher polls 2,000 people from prospects for a new generation of mobile phone (target population). Each respondent responds to four questions:

- Do you prefer the convenience of Pocket-Phone over existing mobile phones?

- Are there transmission problems with Pocket-Phone?

37

- Is Pocket-Phone better suited to worldwide transmission than your existing mobile phone?
- Would cost alone persuade you to purchase Pocket-Phone?

Each of these questions elicits a yes/no response, meaning their answers produce 8,000 pieces of raw data. Assume the researcher asked each respondent six demographic questions (age, gender, education, etc.); the raw data have more than tripled. If the researcher used a four-point scale rather than a yes/no response, the raw data increase again. Besides summarizing the data, data analysis also reduces the data. Reducing the original 8,000 data points produces eight statistics (for each question, the percentage of "yes" answers and percentage of "no" answers). If the researcher cross-tabulates the four answers by gender to look for patterns, he now has 16 statistics to interpret, as well as appropriate tests of significance to evaluate. Imagine if we ask one open-ended question (Describe an undesirable situation with your current phone?). A researcher would have to identify keywords, as well as sentiments, further expanding the data.

At the end of the data analysis process a researcher will often have reams of statistical information, but he or she must whittle this down to key **findings** (key patterns in the data). When the researcher interprets the findings in light of the manager's research questions, he or she develops **insights**. Insights determine whether the hypotheses and theories are supported or refuted. Increasingly, managers ask researchers to make **recommendations** (actions the manager should take that are empirically supported) based on their interpretations of the data.

>Stage 5: Report Insights and Recommendations

In this stage of the process, the researcher reports and transmits the findings, insights, and any recommendations to the manager. The researcher adjusts the type of reporting—and any style and organization of the report—to the target audience, the occasion, the method of presentation, and the purpose of the research. The results may be communicated via formal oral presentation, conference call, letter, detailed written report, top-line summary, infographic, or some combination of any or all of these methods. Reports are developed from the manager's or information user's perspective and from whether and how the information is to be shared within or outside the organization. The manager's foremost concern, solving the management dilemma, drives this stage.

A manager might receive a report but not take action. Inferior communication of results might be a primary reason. Managers don't always have the same statistical knowledge as a researcher, so careful choice of words, and providing explanations as needed, is important. Inaction after a project might also be caused by environmental factors beyond the researcher's control—a shift in business strategy, a change in a competitor's strategy, the disappearance of a dilemma, etc. For example, members of the Association of American Publishers wanted an ad campaign to encourage people to read more books. One finding from the $125,000 study, however, found that only 13 percent of Americans bought general-interest books in stores. When the time came to commit the $14 million to the ad campaign to raise book sales, member interest had faded and the project died.[6]

>The Research Project Time Frame

At its core, research is a time-based project, and project management tools can be used to depict sequential and simultaneous steps and estimate scheduling and timetables for each activity or phase of the research. Exhibit 2-3 shows the use of the *critical path method (CPM)* for a research project. The pathway from start to end that takes the longest time to complete is called the *critical path*. Any delay in an activity along this path will delay the end of the entire project. Researchers also use spreadsheets and *Gantt charts* (see Exhibit 2-4) to manage the various research activities. The most important lessons in using any planning tool are to make sure all tasks are included and that each task is tracked in terms of time so that time lost in one task is recaptured during another. Tracking project task timing is valuable in planning future research projects.

>**Exhibit 2-3** CPM Schedule of Research Design

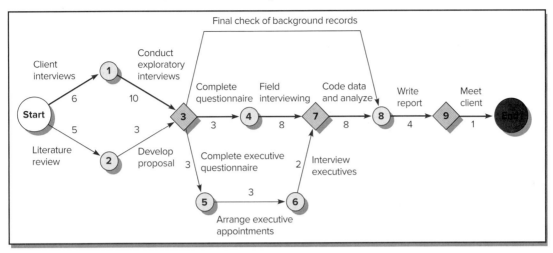

Milestones:

3 Proposal approval
7 Interviews completed
9 Final report completed

Critical Path:
S–1–3–4–7–8–9–E

Time to Completion:
40 working days

>**Exhibit 2-4** Gantt Chart of a Research Project

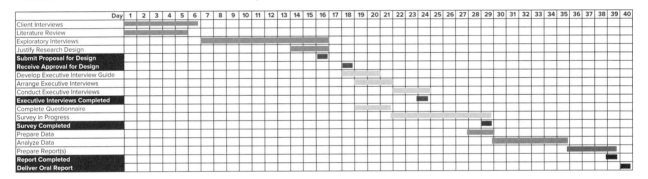

>Research Process Pitfalls and Solutions

Although it is desirable for research to be thoroughly grounded in management decision priorities, studies can wander off target or be less effective than they should be. Here are some pitfalls to watch for and how each can be addressed.

Ill-Defined Management Problems

Some research questions are so complex, value laden, and bound by constraints that they don't lend themselves to traditional forms of analysis. These questions or problems have characteristics that are virtually the opposite of well-defined problems. They have too many interrelated facets for measurement to handle with accuracy.[7] Or methods do not presently exist, or if the methods were to be invented, they still might not provide the data necessary to solve the problem.[8] One author describes the differences like this:

> To the extent that a problem situation evokes a high level of agreement over a specified community of problem solvers regarding the referents of the attributes in which it is given, the operations that are permitted, and the consequences of those operations, it may be termed unambiguous or well defined with respect to that community. On the other hand, to the extent that a problem evokes a highly variable set of responses concerning referents of attributes, permissible operations, and their consequences, it may be considered ill-defined or ambiguous with respect to that community.[9]

Spending sufficient time on exploration and problem definition may address this issue, but some ill-defined research questions are really unresearchable ones.

Unresearchable Questions

Not all questions are researchable. To be researchable, a question must (1) be one for which data collection and analysis can provide the answer, (2) be answerable with current data collection techniques, and (3) allow for some units within target population the to be accessible and willing to share the data. And some questions don't meet these criteria. There is little a researcher can do if a question can't be addressed with data. However, if he overcomes this first issue, then the researcher would need to develop new research designs and data collection procedures to address the last two issues.

Overembracing Data Analytics

If you have a researchable problem, the existence of big data can seduce a manager, seemingly eliminating the need for dilemma-specific research. Just because substantial data is available does not mean the modern management information system provides substantial knowledge. Each field in a database was originally created for a specific reason and drawn from a specific source. These decisions may or may not be compatible with the management dilemma facing the organization today. Data are also often found in unconnected silos, making extracting desired information difficult. While accessing such data is often a starting point in decision-based research, rarely will such activity answer all questions related to a particular research question. Researchers can avoid this problem by pointing out the lack of compatibility to the current dilemma of the source, time frame, and operational definitions of data variables on which the manager (or his or her superior) wants to rely.

The Manager's Hidden Agenda(s)

It is important to remember that all of a manager's motivations for seeking research are not always obvious to a researcher. Managers are often rewarded (higher pay, better office location, more status or prestige) for building empires of authority. In the ideal scenario for quality research, a manager expresses a genuine need for specific information on which to base a decision. Sometimes, research may be authorized even though a decision has been made; it's seen as a measure of protection for a manager in case he or she is criticized later. At other times, a research study is focused on a less-attractive action option; while not justified, such a study may win approval because it supports a manager's pet idea. Researchers facing hidden agendas often experience pressure to pursue research questions or specific research designs that, with analysis, seem inappropriate. Researchers avoid hidden agendas by asking the manager a lot of questions when clarifying the research question; the more questions asked, the more true motivations are revealed.

Favored-Technique Syndrome

Not all researchers are comfortable with every plausible methodology, so they stay within their comfort zone. These researchers recast any research question so that it is amenable to their favored methodology—a survey, for example. Avoiding this syndrome is as simple as demanding that the researcher justify his or her selection of a research design and rejection of all alternative designs.

Researcher Inexperience

Finally, lack of experience can create numerous pitfalls. Researchers may be tempted to rely too heavily on exploratory data to help define the research question or interpret the data in a new study. In

>**snap**shot

Is Your Research Leaving the Country?

Offshoring is defined as the movement of a process done at a company in one country to the same or another company in a different country. These processes in research often include IT (information technology), business, or knowledge processes. Researchers use offshoring to reduce costs, speed a research time frame, access hard-to-recruit research participants, or obtain specialized or proprietary methodologies.

There are significant risks associated with offshoring research services, as Gordon Morris, global insights manager for Sony Ericsson (London, UK), discovered. During a global research project for the Experia X10 Android phone, sensitive business plans were shared with the contracted researchers. As a result of offshoring of some research services, information about the phone launch leaked several months early. "We estimate the potential damage caused by the leak at approximately £100 milion," shared Morris. Leaks may be more likely to occur when offshoring is used because intellectual property standards,

safe computing standards, and contract laws vary from country to country. High employee turnover in some developing countries can also add to this risk.

A survey fielded by the Foundation for Transparency in Offshoring (FTO) among 850 U.S. and international research buyers and providers indicated that clients were more likely to think their projects did not involve offshoring than was actually true. Also, clients were much more likely than research services suppliers to think clients should be told about offshoring. "Very few buyers have sufficient information to assess the relative strengths and risks associated with offshoring," said Tom H. C. Anderson, FTO founder and chairman and managing partner of the research consultancy Anderson Analytics.

As Sonia Baldia, partner at Mayer Brown LLP and a legal expert on offshoring, explains, "Clients absolutely need to know about any offshore subcontracting and [its] location in order to risks and protect themselves."

www.offshoringtransparency.org

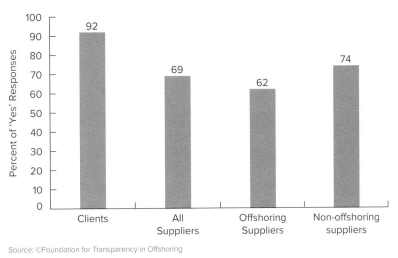

Q. Regardless of what your stance is on offshoring, do you believe research suppliers have an obligation to tell their clients that they offshore? (n=850)

Source: ©Foundation for Transparency in Offshoring

the absence of sufficient data, researchers sometimes substitute personal experiences to form their insights, thereby misdirecting conclusions. Researchers may be tempted to project the experiences from a limited sample to the population as a whole, thereby overstating the importance of a finding. Assigning a research project to a researcher with sufficient experience—or assigning a more seasoned researcher to oversee more novice researchers—goes a long way to avoiding the problems of inexperience. Managers today are pressured to do more of their own research; they need to be forthcoming when their knowledge and skill is insufficient to conduct a needed research project and recruit or hire the necessary expertise.

>Research Process Ethical Issues and Responsibilities

Research invades workers' and people's lives at some level, so appropriate behavior is always a concern. It also accesses proprietary and often sensitive records. Exhibit 2-2 links basic ethical rights to their appropriate stage(s) in the process.

Managers, researchers, and participants all have the responsibility to behave ethically. The ethical issues focus on deception, privacy, quality, notice, choice, access, security, respect, and bias. For the participant, his or her primary ethical responsibilities are truthfulness (researcher's right to absence of participant deception) and completion of research tasks (researcher's right to quality research).

For the manager, their ethical responsibilities are record accuracy (researcher's right to quality research), purpose transparency and truthfulness (researcher's right to absence of sponsor deception), discouraging falsification of research results (researcher's right to absence of sponsor coercion), and fulfilling contractual obligations (researcher's right to adequate compensation for results).

The researcher has the largest number of responsibilities because they must serve the needs of the participant as well as the manager. For the participant, these responsibilities include obtaining informed consent as required (participant's right of informed consent), accepting the subject's choice on whether to participate (participant's right to privacy), following appropriate safety procedures (participant's right to safety), and keeping participant identity confidential (participant's right to confidentiality). For the manager, these responsibilities include protecting manager confidentiality (sponsor's right of purpose nondisclosure and sponsor's right of sponsorship nondisclosure); following acceptable industry practices and procedures (sponsor's right to quality research); and protecting data, findings, insights, and recommendations (sponsor's right to findings nondisclosure).

>summary

LO2-1 What characterizes good research? Generally, one expects good research to be purposeful with a clearly defined focus and plausible goals; with defensible, ethical, and repeatable procedures; and with evidence of objectivity. The reporting of procedures—their strengths and weaknesses—should be complete and honest. Appropriate analytical techniques should be used; insights and conclusions drawn should be limited to those clearly justified by the findings; and reporting of findings, insights, and conclusions should be clearly presented and professional in tone, language, and appearance. Managers should always choose a researcher who has an established reputation for meeting these criteria.

LO2-2 The research process is a sequential process involving clearly defined stages: clarify the research question, design the research, collect and prepare data, analyze and interpret data, and report insights and recommendations. Stage 1: Clarify the Research Question starts

with a management dilemma, either a problem or an opportunity. Exploration reveals what managers know and don't know. Managers must prioritize dilemmas, choosing to focus on the one that is most important. It is also during this stage that managers justify that research will yield a better decision and develop a budget for a more formal study. Stage 2: Design the Research Project determines the sampling design and the data collection design. Sampling design determines the parameters of interest in a target population, whether a census or sample will be conducted, the procedures for selecting and recruiting each case, and the number of cases. Data collection design determines the type of data to be collected, either primary or secondary or some combination, the method, and the specific procedures for collecting it. Stage 3: Collect and Prepare the Data involves the actual data collection (including measurement instrument use and any training involved with using it), as well as the preparation of data (to include dealing with out-of-range and missing data). Stage 4: Analyze and Interpret Data involves data summarization; looking for patterns among variables; and applying statistical techniques with the purpose of discovering findings and insights and, ultimately, making recommendations in relation to the research question and management dilemma. Stage 5: Report the Results involves determining the audience(s), method, timing, and location to report the findings, insights, and recommendations.

LO2-3 Studies can wander off target or be less effective if the researcher experiences any of these pitfalls: ill-defined research question(s), unresearchable questions, overembracing data analytics, a manager's hidden agenda(s), application of favored-technique syndrome, or researcher inexperience. The ways to address these include a thorough exploration phase in Stage 1, avoiding questions where data aren't helpful, pointing out the lack of compatibility of stored data with the current dilemma,

thorough interviewing of the manager for his or her motivations, seeking a justification for any research design that includes why alternative designs were rejected, and seeking the researcher with sufficient experience.

LO2-4 Ethical research process issues focus on deception, privacy, quality, notice, choice, access, security, respect, and bias. A participant's primary ethical responsibilities are truthfulness and completion. A manager's responsibilities are accuracy, transparency, truthfulness, discouraging the falsification of results, and fulfilling contractual obligations. The researcher has the most ethical responsibilities,and these center around both participants and managers. For participants, a researcher is responsible for participants' safety and absence of harm, consent, privacy and confidentiality. For managers, a researcher is responsible for confidentiality, following acceptable industry standards for quality research, and protecting data, as well as its findings, insights, and recommendations.

>**key**terms

case 36	interval data 33	recommendations 38
census 36	key performance indicator (KPI) 30	research design 32
dashboard 31	management dilemma 29	research process 27
data 32	nominal data 33	research question(s) 32
data analysis 37	ordinal data 33	sample 36
findings 38	primary data 33	secondary data 33
insights 38	ratio data 33	target population 36

>**discussion**questions

Terms in Review

1 Distinguish between the following and identify the research use of each.

   a primary and secondary data

   b finding and insight

   c census and sample

   d management dilemma and research question

   e finding and insight

2 Kathy Lee Berggren, a professor of oral communication at Cornell University, indicates "a lot of my students really [only] scratch the surface with the type of research they're doing." According to Andy Guess, at Inside Higher Ed, "Just because students walk in the door as 'digital natives,' doesn't mean they're equipped to handle the heavy lifting of digital databases and proprietary search engines that

comprise the bulk of modern, online research techniques. Students erroneously think a Google search is research." As you evaluate the factors that guarantee good research, what actions do you propose to narrow the gap between students' research competence and what is required of a modern college graduate about to become a manager with research responsibilities?

Making Research Decisions

3 SupplyCo is a supplier to a number of firms in an industry. Several companies are involved in the manufacturing process—from processed parts to creation of the final product—with each firm adding some value to the product. SupplyCo provides materials and services to every part of the chain. By carefully study its customer data, SupplyCo discovers a plausible new model for manufacturing and distributing industry products that would increase the overall

efficiency of the industry, reduce costs of production, and result in greater sales and profits for some of the industry's participants (SupplyCo's customers). Implementing the model might hurt the sales and profits of some SupplyCo customers that did not have the manpower, plant or equipment, or financial resources to participate in the change. These companies might potentially go out of business, decreasing SupplyCo's sales and profits in the short term. SupplyCo is considering research to further study the new model. SupplyCo. had the data within its warehouse only because of its relationship with its customers.

   a Is it a betrayal to use the data in a manner that would cause some customers harm? Or does SupplyCo have a more powerful obligation to its stockholders and employees to aggressively research the new model?

   b What are the implications of your answers even if there is no violation of law, industry regulation, or company policy?

4 Based on an analysis of the last six months' sales, your boss notices that sales of beef products are declining in your chain's restaurants. As beef entrée sales decline, so do profits. Fearing beef sales have declined due to several newspaper stories reporting *E. coli* contamination discovered at area grocery stores, he suggests a survey of area restaurants to see if the situation is pervasive.

   a What do you think of this research suggestion?

   b How, if at all, could you improve on your boss's formulation of the research question?

5 You have received a business research report done by a consultant for your firm, a life insurance company. The study is a survey of customer satisfaction based on a sample of 600. You are asked to comment on its quality. What will you look for?

6 As area sales manager for a company manufacturing and marketing outboard engines, you have been assigned the responsibility of conducting a research study to estimate the sales potential of your products in the domestic (U.S. or Canadian) market. Discuss key issues and concerns arising from the fact that you, the manager, are also the researcher.

From Concept to Practice

7 Using Exhibit 2-2 and case examples from some research company's website, discover if favored-technique approaches to research design dominate a firms' activities.

8 Using Exhibit 2-2, find a case study of a research example in which a clear statement of the management dilemma leads to a precise and actionable research. (Hint: Visit research company websites; use a search engine to find examples.)

From the Headlines

9 Hearsay Social monitors how workers at large companies interact with outsiders on Facebook, LinkedIn, and other social media sites. Companies pay $100,000 or more for a digital dashboard that alerts supervisory managers if employees are violating privacy policies, regulatory compliance rules, or other company policies. If you were a large client, like Farmers Insurance, what information would you want to know?

10 Researchers recently reported in *Cell Metabolism* that a natural ingredient found in milk can protect mice against obesity even while they enjoyed diets that were high in fat. Mice given high doses of nicotinamide riboside along with their high-fat meals burned more fat. Their muscles worked better, providing them better endurance and making them better runners. If you worked for the National Milk Producers Federation, could you justify a research project to determine the value of a national ad campaign to promote the qualities of milk in a balanced diet and for avoiding obesity based on this information found during exploration? If not, develop an argument to justify a research study.

>cases*

Akron Children's Hospital	Lexus SC 430
Calling Up Attendance	Mastering Teacher Leadership
Covering Kids with Health Care	NCRCC: Teeing Up a New Strategic Direction
Donatos: Finding the New Pizza	Ohio Lottery: Innovative Research Design Drives Winning
Goodyear's Aquatred	Ramada Demonstrates Its *Personal Best*™
HeroBuilders.com	State Farm: Dangerous Intersections
Inquiring Minds Want to Know—NOW!	USTA: Come Out Swinging

*You will find a description of each case in the Case Abstracts section of this textbook. Check the Case Index to determine whether a case provides data, the research instrument, video, or other supplementary material. Cases and case supplements are available in Connect.

>chapter 3

Stage 1: Clarify the Research Question

> "A beautiful question is an ambitious yet actionable question that can begin to shift the way we perceive or think about something—and that might serve as a catalyst to bring about change."
>
> *Warren Berger,*
> *consultant and author,* A More Beautiful Question

>learningobjectives

After reading this chapter, you should understand . . .

LO3-1 The question hierarchy.

LO3-2 The purposes and process of exploration.

LO3-3 How internal and external exploration differ.

LO3-4 The process and goal of research valuation.

LO3-5 The process and justification needed to budget for research.

LO3-6 Ethical issues at this stage of the process.

>Stage 1 in the Research Process

Stage 1 uses exploratory research to accomplish the following tasks as depicted in Exhibit 3-1:

1. Define the management–research question hierarchy.
2. Define and execute the exploration strategy.
3. Value the research.
4. Justify and budget for research.

>The Question Hierarchy

A useful exercise to start Stage 1 of the research process (Exhibit 3-2) is to state the basic **management dilemma** (the problem or opportunity that requires a decision), then try to develop other questions by progressively breaking down the original question into more specific ones. You can think of the outcome of this process as the **management–research question hierarchy**.

The process takes the manager and his or her research collaborator through various brainstorming and exploratory research exercises to define the following:

- **Management question**—This is a restatement of the manager's dilemma(s) in question form. Think of it like a query about what should be done about the dilemma. Applying exploratory research to this question often reveals several options and information about whether an option might address the management dilemma.

- **Research questions**—These questions explore the various options and forms one or more hypotheses that best states the objective of the research; these questions focus the researcher's attention. Exploratory research helps identify the options and the hypotheses.

- **Investigative questions**—These are questions the researcher must answer to satisfactorily answer the research question; what the manager feels he or she needs to know to arrive at a conclusion about the management dilemma. Exploratory research will identify what information is known and what is unknown.

The final question in the hierarchy isn't addressed until Stage 2: Research Design.

- **Measurement questions**—These are questions that participants in research are asked or what specifically is observed in a research study.

This multistep process is presented in Exhibit 3-2 and in the example in Exhibit 3-3. The role of exploration in this process is depicted in Exhibit 3-4.

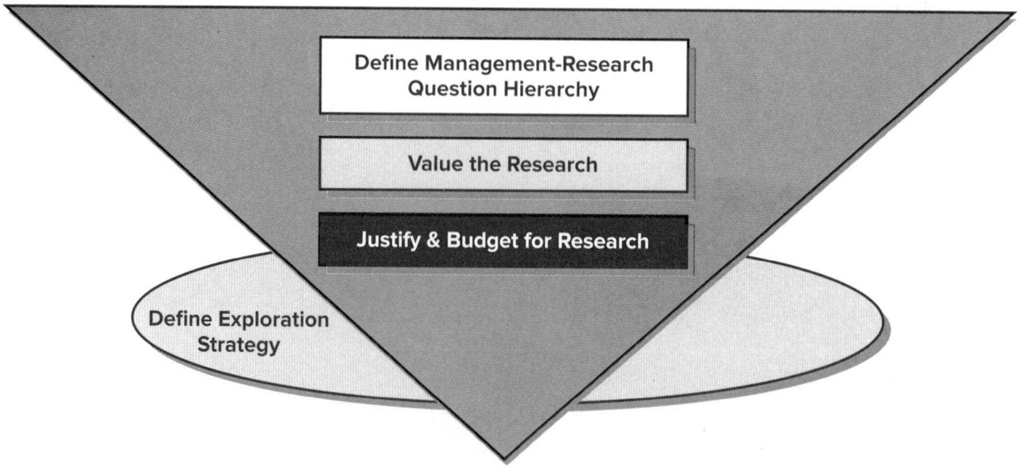

>**Exhibit 3-1** Tasks Associated with Stage 1 of Research Process

>**Exhibit 3-2** Management–Research Question Hierarchy

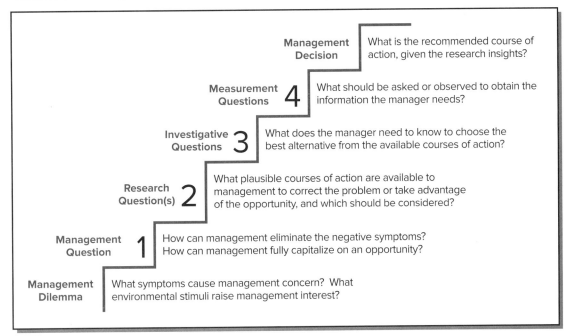

>**Exhibit 3-3** SalePro's Management–Research Question Hierarchy

Declining sales is one of the most common symptoms serving as a stimulus for a research project, especially a continuing pattern that is unexplained. SalePro, a large manufacturer of industrial goods, faces this situation. Exploration (1) reveals that sales, in fact, should not be declining in the South and Northeast. Environmental factors there are as favorable as in the growing regions. Subsequent exploration (2, 3) leads management to believe that the problem is in one of three areas: salesperson compensation, product formulation, or trade advertising. Further exploration (4) has SalePro management narrowing the focus of its research to alternative ways to alter the sales compensation system, which (5) leads to a survey of all sales personnel in the affected regions.

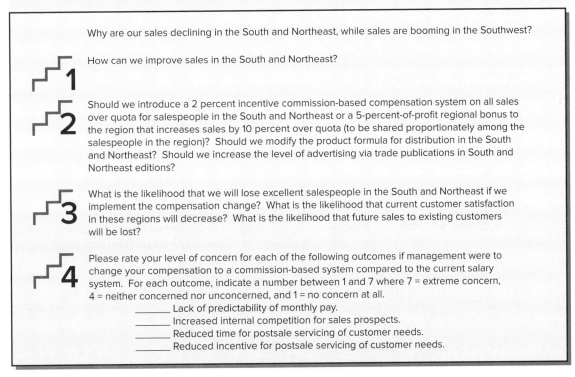

>**Exhibit 3-4** Formulating the Research Question, the Process

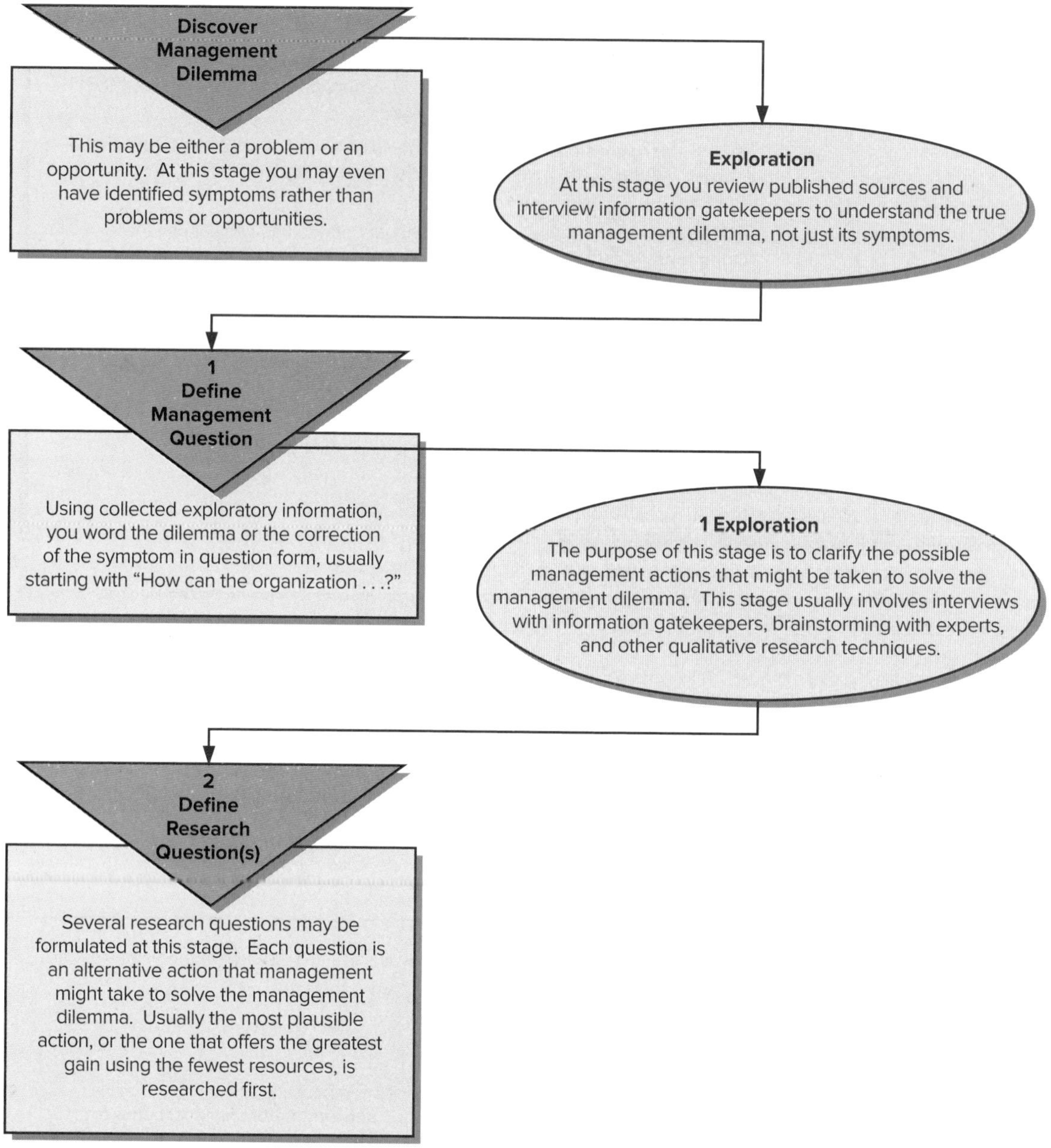

Discover Management Dilemma

This may be either a problem or an opportunity. At this stage you may even have identified symptoms rather than problems or opportunities.

Exploration
At this stage you review published sources and interview information gatekeepers to understand the true management dilemma, not just its symptoms.

1 Define Management Question

Using collected exploratory information, you word the dilemma or the correction of the symptom in question form, usually starting with "How can the organization . . .?"

1 Exploration
The purpose of this stage is to clarify the possible management actions that might be taken to solve the management dilemma. This stage usually involves interviews with information gatekeepers, brainstorming with experts, and other qualitative research techniques.

2 Define Research Question(s)

Several research questions may be formulated at this stage. Each question is an alternative action that management might take to solve the management dilemma. Usually the most plausible action, or the one that offers the greatest gain using the fewest resources, is researched first.

The Management Question

The *management question* restates the management dilemma in question form; the four types are detailed in Exhibit 3-5. Here's an example. A bank's president is concerned about low deposit growth, possibly the result of changes in their competitive environment. While lowered deposits directly affect profits, another part of the profit weakness is revealed in increasing customer complaints. The qualified researcher knows that the management question as originally stated is too broad to guide a definitive business research project. As a starting point, the broadly worded question "What can we do to increase profits?" might be fine, but the bank will want to refine its management question into these more specific subquestions:

- How can we improve deposits?
- How can we improve internal operations that currently result in customer complaints?

>**Exhibit 3-5** Types of Management Questions

Categories	General Question	Sample Management Questions
Evaluation of solutions (choices between concrete actions to solve problems or take advantage of opportunities)	• How can we achieve the objectives we have set?	• Should we reposition brand X as a therapeutic product from its current cosmetic positioning? • How can we improve our program for product repairs and servicing?
Choice of purpose (choice of objectives)	• What do we want to achieve?	• What goals should XYZ try to achieve in its next round of union negotiations? • What goals should we set for sales and profits in the next 5 years? • What goals should XYZ set for its return on its investment portfolio?
Troubleshooting (diagnosing ways an organization is failing to meet its goals)	• Why is our (blank) program not meeting its goals?	• Why does our department have the lowest sales-to–web page visit ratio? • Why does our recruiting program generate the lowest hire-to-offer ratio in the industry?
Control (monitoring or diagnosing ways an organization is failing to meet its goals)	• How well is our (blank) program meeting its goals?	• What is our product line's sales-to-promotion cost ratio?

This separation of the management question into two subquestions may not have occurred without a discussion between the researcher and the manager.

Assume the bank has done no formal business research in the past. It has little specific information about competitors or customers and has not analyzed its internal operations. To move forward in the management–research question hierarchy and define the research question, the client needs to collect some exploratory information:

- What factors are contributing to the bank's failure to achieve a stronger growth rate in deposits?
- How well is the bank doing regarding customer satisfaction and financial condition compared to industry norms and competitors?

Small-group discussions are conducted among employees and managers, and trade association data are acquired to compare financial and operating statistics from company annual reports and end-of-year division reports. From the results of these two exploratory activities, it is obvious that the bank's operations are not as progressive as its competitors', but it has its costs well in line. So the revised management question becomes "What should be done to make the bank more competitive?" The process of exploration will be critical in helping the bank identify its options.

In addition to solving problems, managers are likely to be looking for opportunities. So let's look at another case, TechByte. This company is interested in enhancing its position in a given technology that appears to hold potential for future growth. This interest or need might quickly elicit a number of questions:

- How fast might this technology develop?
- What are the likely applications of this technology?
- What companies now possess this technology, and which ones are likely to make a major effort to obtain the technology?
- How much will the new technology absorb in resources?
- What are the likely payoffs?

In the preceding exploration of opportunities, researchers would probably begin with specific literature, looking only for certain aspects, such as recent developments, predictions by informed individuals about the prospects of the technology, identification of those involved in the area, and accounts of successful ventures or failures by others in the field. After becoming familiar with the literature, researchers might seek interviews with scientists, engineers, and product developers who are well known in the field.

Housing and Millennials

Glenn Kelman, the CEO of Redfin, recently wrote a blog post around the provocative question, "What will America housing be like when all the cars leave?" He was alluding to several technical changes and changes in the behavior of Millennials. One research study shows that younger generations have not embraced the car-dependent, large-square-foot house in the suburbs that their parents and grandparents enjoy. Instead, these younger homebuyers are seeking smaller, urban spaces nearer to restaurants and entertainment options that are closer to work—or as Redfin's company suggests, houses with a great Walk Score. The success of such television shows as HGTV's *Small Space, Big Style* and *Property Virgins* also is testament to that conclusion.

A study by the Transportation Research Center at the University of California estimated that there are approximately eight parking spaces for every car—that inventory of parking not only includes where the owner resides, but also where he or she works, shops, eats, etc. That's approximately 2 billion spaces. Additionally, we have the technology for self-driving cars, and such cars will be constantly moving—not taking space in a garage or parking lot. According to Tesla CEO Elon Musk and Google, the reality of self-driving cars may be only two to five years away. Remember the battle between NYC and Uber? A research study of taxis and Uber rides showed that Uber serves the boroughs outside of Manhattan better than taxis (22 percent of Uber pickups

©Image Source/Getty Images

vs. 14 percent of taxi pickups), and many of Uber's strongholds were far from subways or a long transit trip away from Midtown.

So, in an environment of fewer or no cars per housing unit, of self-driving cars, of transportation seen as a service rather than an asset, will we need garages? If Millennials are eating out more, will they need elaborate kitchens? How large—or small—will houses need to be to satisfy this group? If you were a home builder serving any metro area, what would your management–research question hierarchy look like?

They would give special attention to those who represent the two extremes of opinion in regard to the prospects of the technology. If possible, they would talk with persons having information on particularly thorny problems in development and application. Of course, much of the information will be confidential and competitive. However, skillful investigation can uncover many useful indicators.

An unstructured exploration allows the researcher to develop and revise the management question and determine what is needed to secure answers to the proposed question.

The Research Question

One task of a researcher is to assist the manager in formulating a research question that fits the management dilemma. A *research question* best states the objective of the business research study. It is a more specific question from the manager's perspective that must be answered. It may be more than one question or just one. Incorrectly defining the research question is the fundamental weakness in the business research process. Time and money can be wasted studying an option that won't help the manager rectify the original dilemma.

Assume the bank's president has agreed to have the business research be guided by the following research question: Should the bank position itself as a modern, progressive institution (with appropriate changes in services and policies) or maintain its image as the oldest, most reliable institution in town?

Fine-Tuning the Research Question

The term *fine-tuning* might seem an odd choice for research, but it creates an image that most researchers come to recognize. Fine-tuning the question is precisely what a skillful practitioner must do after the exploration is complete. At this point, a clearer picture of the management and research questions begins to emerge. After the researcher does a preliminary review of the literature, a brief exploratory study, or both, the project begins to crystallize in one of two ways:

1. It is apparent that the question has been answered and the process is finished (no further research is needed).
2. A question different from the one originally addressed has appeared.

The research question does not have to be materially different, but it will have evolved in some fashion. This is not cause for discouragement. The refined research question(s) will have better focus and will move the business research forward with more clarity than the initially formulated question(s).

In addition to fine-tuning the original question, the researcher should address other research question–related activities in this phase to enhance the direction of the project:

1. Examine the variables to be studied. Are they satisfactorily defined? Have operational definitions been used where appropriate?
2. Review the research questions with the intent of breaking them down into specific second- and third-level questions.
3. If hypotheses (tentative explanations) are used, make sure they are appropriately stated.
4. Determine what evidence must be collected to answer the various questions and hypotheses.
5. Set the scope of the study by stating what is *not* a part of the research question. This will establish a boundary to separate contiguous problems from the primary objective.

Investigative Questions

Investigative questions represent the information that the decision maker needs to know; they are the questions the researcher must answer to satisfactorily arrive at a conclusion about the research question. To study the market, the researcher working on the bank project develops two major investigative questions. Each question has several subquestions. These questions provide insight into the lack of deposit growth:

1. What is the public's position regarding financial services and their use?
   a. What specific financial services are used?
   b. How attractive are various services?
   c. What bank-specific and environmental factors influence a person's use of a particular service?
2. What is the bank's competitive position?
   a. What are the geographic patterns of our customers and of our competitors' customers?
   b. What demographic differences are revealed among our customers and those of our competitors?
   c. What descriptive words or phrases does the public (both customers and noncustomers) associate with our bank? With our competitors?
   d. How aware is the public of our bank's promotional efforts?
   e. What opinion does the public hold of our bank and its competitors?
   f. How does growth in services compare among competing institutions?

Measurement Questions

Measurement questions are the actual questions that researchers use to collect data in a study. They could become questions on a survey or elements on an observation checklist. Measurement questions may or may not be defined during Stage 2: Research Design, but topics for such questions and even actual sample questions may be discovered during exploration.

The Art of Asking the Right Questions

A Generation X software engineer wanted a last family vacation before his oldest child headed off to college. The family chose Europe; first a quick stop to visit friends in London, then on to Paris. Among their criteria for Parisian lodging: a central location, access to laundry and kitchen facilities, and space for four for four nights. They rejected established hotels as too stuffy or too sleek. Their choice for booking accommodations: Airbnb.

Airbnb is an app and website that connects people seeking lodging with renters who have listed their personal houses, apartments, and guest rooms on either platform. The company boasts more than 1.5 million listings in 34,000 cities and more than 190 countries, as well as more than 40 million total guests. The idea for Airbnb came to two guys who didn't have jobs but did have an apartment for which they needed rent money. During a convention period in their hometown of San Francisco, when standard hotel rooms were at a premium or totally unavailable, they rented out the floor space and air mattresses to three desperate conventioneers. Some investors later, Airbnb was born.

Warren Berger, in his book *A More Beautiful Question: The Power of Inquiry to Spark Breakthrough Ideas*, notes that innovative ideas are the result of asking questions that challenge assumptions. In the case of Airbnb, that assumption would be that visitors to San Francisco would not want to stay in people's homes or apartments but would prefer to stay in recognized, established hotels. "It's one thing to see a problem and to question why the problem exists, and maybe even wonder whether there might be a better alternative," explains Berger. "It's another to keep asking those questions, even after experts have told you, in effect, 'You can't change this situation; there are good reasons why things are the way they are.'"

Berger suggests any question creates an unresolved tension in our minds, demonstrates what we don't know, organizes our thinking, and enables us to act in the face of uncertainty. But a *beautiful question* is phrased in such a way that it (1) reveals a problem or opportunity, (2) challenges existing assumptions, (3) shifts people's thinking, and (4) serves as a catalyst for change/action.

How might the creators of RedBull, Zipcar, Uber, the mobile phone, or the suitcase with wheels have phrased their beautiful question?

>The Exploration Strategy

To assist in the formation of the management–research question hierarchy, and later in the tasks related to valuing research and budgeting for research, an **exploration strategy** must answer these questions:

- *What information sources should be used?* These sources are designed to reveal information to help the manager understand the dilemma, identify courses of action (options), and clarify concepts, constructs, operational definitions, and variables needed to frame the research question and beyond

- *What methods will be used to extract information from these sources?* The methods detail how manager will communicate with or locate a desired source.

Exploration is loosely structured research but with a defined purpose. It involves some or all of the following: studying company records; tapping into company databases; exploring professional, scientific, and academic literature; and consulting experts, as well as those involved with the problem or its solution. Through exploration, researchers:

- Understand the management dilemma, management problem, and research question.
- Discover how others have addressed and/or solved problems similar to the current management dilemma or management question.
- Establish priorities for dilemmas and problems to be addressed.
- Identify action options and develop hypotheses.
- Gather background information on the topics in order to refine the research question.
- Identify information that should be gathered to formulate investigative questions.

>**Exhibit 3-6** Exploration Strategy Methods

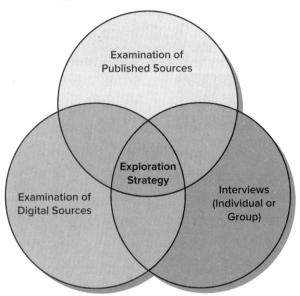

- Develop operational definitions for concepts, constructs, and variables.
- Provide the evidence for justifying and budgeting research.
- Set the foundation for the final research design.
- Exploration can also
  - Identify sources for and actual questions that might be used as measurement questions in any subsequent research.
  - Identify sources for actual sample frames that might be used in sampling design.

A thorough exploration strategy comprises subtasks (Exhibit 3-6): (1) examination of published sources, (2) examination of digital sources, and (3) interviews with knowledgeable people. The first two are discussed in extensive detail in the remainder of the chapter. The third is explored more thoroughly here.

Information Sources

In identifying sources, a good researcher will look at several classifications of information and use both internal and external sources within those classifications (see Exhibit 3-7). Some information has more value than others. Information sources are generally categorized into three levels (1) primary sources, (2) secondary sources, and (3) tertiary sources. As the source levels indicate, primary sources have more value than secondary sources, and secondary sources have more value than tertiary sources.

Primary sources are original works of research or raw data without interpretation or pronouncements that represent an official opinion or position. Included among the primary sources are memos; letters; complete interviews or speeches (in audio, video, or written transcript formats); laws; regulations; court decisions or standards; and most government data, including census, economic, and labor data. Other internal sources of primary data are inventory records, personnel records, purchasing requisition forms, statistical process control charts, and reports of earlier research. A researcher or manager seeking primary data can look internally or externally (e.g., the U.S. government offers extensive primary research useful for business).

Secondary sources are interpretations of primary data. Encyclopedias, textbooks, handbooks, magazine and newspaper articles, and most newscasts are considered secondary information sources. Indeed, many of the secondary reference materials businesses use fall into this category. Internally, dashboards of key performance indicators (KPIs) and investor annual reports would be examples of secondary

>**Exhibit 3-7** Exploration Strategy Sources

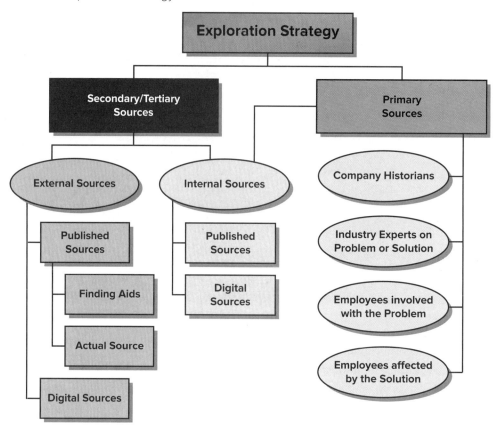

sources because they are compiled from a variety of primary sources. While to an outsider the annual report is viewed as a primary source, because it represents the official position of the corporation, to a researcher it represents secondary data. A firm searching for secondary sources can search either internally or externally.

Tertiary sources may be interpretations of a secondary source but generally are represented by indexes, bibliographies, and other finding aids (e.g., Internet search engines). These finding aids can be exceptionally valuable in providing direction for secondary searchers, as well as identifying people and events to explore.

When looking for sources, don't forget to look beyond a firm's immediate industry. Some of a researcher's best sources will be environmental, government, legal, and social sources, not only ones on business topics.

People as Sources

A strong search of published and digital sources will reveal the identity of people who can add valuable insight. Think of these individuals as information gatekeepers. They fall into four groups: (1) institutional memory guardians or company historians, (2) industry or problem experts, (3) company employees involved directly in the problem, and (4) company employees likely to be affected by any considered solution.

As the management dilemma is explored and the research question begins to formalize, those with long institutional memories are invaluable. These may or may not be current employees and may include those who have retired or left the company to pursue their careers elsewhere. What they offer is not only information about past decisions and effects of those decisions, but decision-making context. Very large and enduring organizations understand the value of historical context and may have an employee designated as a company historian. These individuals are responsible for company archives and are invaluable in helping a researcher because they may know others who should be interviewed. One study found that the person with the most historical context on a dilemma was a member of the janitorial staff, so keep an open mind about who might be valuable. If a name is mentioned repeatedly, that's a person who should be interviewed. Individual, face-to-face interviews are most productive here.

A second group of individuals to tap are industry or problem experts. These individuals can provide substantiation for trends, the identity of firms who have faced similar problems and identified solutions, background on management dilemmas in the broad sense, and more. For businesses involved in scientific breakthroughs, experts can provide valuable interpretations for the researcher or manager. Thanks to the Internet, professional communities often provide a rich source of industry experts. Another source is financial analysts. You might have noticed in the business press that reporters often reach out to experts to comment on breaking stories; you can do the same. Often industry/problem experts publish, so they are likely to be identified by some published sources or have their own Internet blogs. Keep your eyes open for names that repeat. These individuals might be inside or outside a company. Individual interviews are most productive here, but phone, video chat, or email might have to replace face-to-face interviews.

The third group comprises company employees directly involved in the current dilemma. Interview them about current conditions, likely contributing factors, and their perspective on action options. The employees you are looking for are those who hold extreme positions because you want breadth of ideas. When interviewing employees, individual or group interviews can be used, using informal or more formal techniques, such as focus groups, brainstorming sessions, online or mobile bulletin boards, etc.

The last group, although not necessary the least important, is company employees who would likely be directly affected by possible action decisions being considered. While at this stage of the research a manager might not want the solutions being considered to be fully known, most internal employee grapevines make it difficult to keep such considerations under wraps. Such individuals will likely have valuable perceptions of how likely actions would affect the work environment, work collaborations and relatonships, productivity, morale, etc. Again you are looking for employees who hold extreme perspectives because you want breadth of ideas. You can use individual or group interviews, informal or more formal techniques, such as focus groups, brainstorming sessions, online and mobile bulletin boards here as well.

Published Sources

In most cases, the external exploration strategy will begin with an examination of published sources, called a **literature search**—a review of books, as well as articles in journals or professional literature that relate to your management dilemma. A literature search requires the use of the library's online catalog and one or more bibliographic databases or indexes. This review should include high-quality, web-published materials.

In general, this literature search starts with the management dilemma or question and has four steps:

1. Consult encyclopedias, dictionaries, handbooks, and textbooks to identify key terms, people, companies, or events relevant to your management dilemma or management question.

2. Apply these key terms, names of people or companies, and events in searching indexes, bibliographies, and the web to identify specific secondary sources.

3. Locate and review specific secondary sources for relevance to the management dilemma.

4. Evaluate the value of each source and its content.

While many published sources now can be accessed digitally, many others cannot. A strong exploration of available published sources doesn't ignore nondigital sources just because they are more difficult to access.

External Sources

There are dozens of types of information sources, each with a special function. In this section we describe the information types used most by researchers in the exploratory phase, many of which help them find other valuable sources.

Using Interviews to Refine the Management Question

Exploratory research is unstructured. You don't know exactly what to ask or what you'll discover, only the focus of the discovery. Sometimes what you discover is enough to make a decision, and sometimes you discover that you need more information to move forward.

Tire brands offer lots of information to consumers to differentiate their brand from their competitors. But you and I, as tire purchasers, often need an interpreter to make sense of this information. We turn to our friendly, knowledgeable salesperson at our local tire store. What you might not know is that the salesperson is being offered competitive financial incentives to encourage them to recommend one brand versus another. These incentives might be in the form of cash or cash alternatives, points redeemable for merchandise, or travel experiences. One big problem with these incentives is that they are all pretty much the same; thus they can't accomplish the job of making one tire brand more attractive to the salesperson to sell.

One company wanted to identify the critical issues for salespersons—besides the amount of the incentive—when choosing one incentive offer over another and thereby recommending one brand. It chose a readily available tool, their marketing staff, to find out. The company gave the marketing team one week to visit tire stores and talk to salespeople and any other people who processed the paperwork for incentives. Their charge: determine how to solve the question of incentive program nondifferentiation. No formal interview guide was created. No interview training was provided.

Through their exploratory research, they learned the following:

- Incentives needed to be in cash, not merchandise or travel experiences.

©Tetra Images/Alamy

- Incentive-claims paperwork needed to be easy to process, not take hours or days to complete.
- Incentive claims needed to pay out quickly, even multiple times per week.
- Problematic incentive claims needed to be flagged quickly, the sales rep needed to be notified immediately, and the issue needed to be resolvable with one email or phone call.
- Superior performers—those that sell more of your brand than others—should be offered higher-level incentives.

The most popular program was a competitor's offer that involved immediately loading a reward card with incentive cash for each sale; it could be used by the salesperson like a reloadable debit card. As one salesperson told them, "People come to work to earn a living, not an inflatable boat."

Raw and Summarized Data In the United States, businesses are blessed with detailed, government-collected data from numerous agencies. Data.gov is a portal to downloadable data from numerous government agencies, including data on agriculture, climate, education, energy, finance, health, manufacturing, science and industry, consumer expenditures, and much more. Much of these data come from surveys, but some from censuses of various populations. Every 10 years, the U.S. government conducts the decennial census, one of the largest surveys conducted anywhere. It collects volumes of data on everything from household demographics to housing type. The 2010 Census contained the fewest questions in history and was also the most expensive.[1] Periodically, the Census Bureau updates population estimates with sample studies, as well as conducting numerous other studies on current topics of interest, including retail and food services, housing, capital expenditures, time use, wholesale trade, business dynamics, research and development, county business patterns, exports and imports, and more (more than 130 surveys each year). The Census Bureau also conducts the Economic Census, the "official 5-year measure of American business and the economy," a key data source for many business decisions.[2] Most of the summarized data are available through Census.gov. The Bureau of Labor

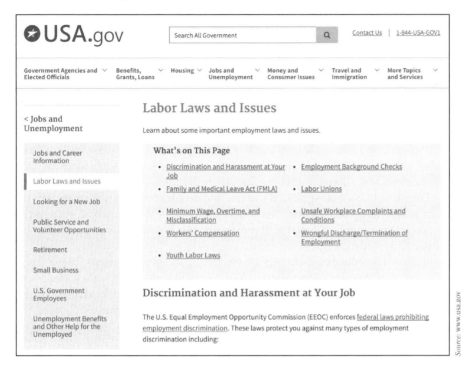

The U.S. government is the world's largest source of data and information used by managers of all business disciplines and of all types of organizations. Learning how to navigate this government portal is a critical skill for a researcher.

Statistics (www.bls.gov) provides data access and publishes numerous summaries in the area of inflation and prices, pay and benefits, spending and time use, unemployment, employment, and productivity.

Indexes and Bibliographies   **Indexes** and **bibliographies** are the mainstay of any search strategy because they help you identify and locate a single book or journal article from among the millions published. The single most important bibliography in any library is its online catalog. As with all other information types, there are many specialized indexes and bibliographies unique to business topics. These can be very useful in a literature search to find authors and titles of prior works on the topic of interest.

Skill in searching bibliographic databases is essential for the business researcher. For the novice or less skilled, we provide two how-to documents through Connect. The first, "Bibliographic Database Searches," reviews the process of searching. The second, "Advanced Searches," reveals the more advanced techniques of skilled searchers.

Dictionaries   In business, as in every field, there are many specialized **dictionaries** that define words, terms, or jargon unique to a discipline. Many of these specialized dictionaries include information on people, events, or organizations that shape the discipline. They are also an excellent place to find acronyms. A growing number of dictionaries and *glossaries* (terms in a specialized field, area, or topic plus their definitions) are now available on the web. Information from dictionaries and glossaries may be used to identify key terms for a search of an online or printed database.

Encyclopedias   Researchers use an **encyclopedia** to find background or historical information on a topic or to find names or terms that can enhance search results in other sources. For example, you might use an encyclopedia to find the date that Microsoft introduced Windows and then use that date to draw more information from an index to the time period. Encyclopedias are also helpful in identifying the experts in a field and the key writings on any topic. One example of an encyclopedia is the *Online TDM Encyclopedia* published by the Victoria Transportation Policy Institute.

The *Online TDM Encyclopedia* is a comprehensive source of information about innovative management solutions to transportation problems. The Encyclopedia provides detailed information on dozens of Transportation Demand Management (TDM) strategies, plus chapters on their planning, evaluation and implementation. It can help you view transportation problems from a new perspective, and expand the range of possible solutions to apply.[3]

Another example drawn from the area of finance is the *Encyclopedia of Private Equity and Venture Capital*, published by VC Experts Inc., a provider of expertise and opportunity in private equity and venture capital.[4]

Handbooks

A **handbook** is a collection of facts unique to a topic. Handbooks often includes statistics, directory information, a glossary of terms, and other data such as laws and regulations essential to a field. The best handbooks include source references for the facts they present. The *Statistical Abstract of the United States* is a valuable and frequently used handbook. It contains an extensive variety of facts, an excellent and detailed index, and a gateway to even more in-depth data for every table included. One handbook with which students and managers alike are familiar is the *Occupational Outlook Handbook* published by the U.S. Bureau of Labor Statistics. In it you can find details about many business occupations and whether each is expanding or declining.[5] Many handbooks are quite specialized, such as the one published by the Potato Association of America. It reveals not only consumption patterns, but also potato-growing and -processing statistics.[6]

One of the most important handbooks, especially in the business-to-business arena, is the *North American Industry Classification System, United States (NAICS)*. Jointly designed with Canada and Mexico to provide comparability in business statistics throughout North America, especially as new businesses and new business sectors develop, this classification system of all businesses replaced the Standard Industrial Classification in 1997.[7]

Directories

Directories are used for finding names and addresses as well as other data. Although many are available and useful in printed format, directories in digitized format that can be searched by certain characteristics or sorted and then downloaded are far more useful. Many are available free through the web, but the most comprehensive directories are proprietary (i.e., must be purchased). An especially useful directory is the *Encyclopedia of Associations* (called *Associations Unlimited* on the web), which provides a list of public and professional organizations plus their locations and contact numbers.[8] Several directories are available for firms seeking research services providers, including *GreenBook: A Guide for Buyers of Marketing Research Services,* and *BlueBook*, the member directory of Insights Association.[9]

Articles, Reports, Blogs, and Books

Media-published articles, whether in the professional, public, or academic press, are valuable sources for understanding the dilemma. We access these by searching various data-finding aids, such as those mentioned earlier, and through recommendations from our professional colleagues. Books are often maligned as an exploratory source, but they are valuable for putting a management dilemma in context, especially when they provide a detailed bibliography. In this era of self-publication, professional topic blogs are ubiquitous. Some of the things a researcher searches for in this category are prior research studies; reviews of studies, documents, or records; industry trend reports; and articles on problems and their solutions, as well as notable people and events. Some articles and reports are only available on the unindexed web, which means you need the resources of your local librarian for navigation or experience with portals that reveal such sites.

Presentations, Videos, and Webinars

Business professionals join organizations as a means of keeping current in their field and to develop professionally. As a result, these organizations often sponsor conferences at which noted professionals speak. The content of these presentations is often critical for providing evidence of possible dilemmas. Business professionals spend increasing amounts of time watching videos on business topics as a method of professional development, but also to familiarize themselves with what their counterparts are doing. These videos are the byproduct of professional presentations at conferences or webinars or produced as promotional materials (e.g., product demonstrations). Each has the ability to offer valuable information, so don't forget to search YouTube, SlideShare.net, and LinkedIn during exploration.

>snapshot

Secondary Data Sources Go Real Time

Two key trends in secondary data exploratory research are the incorporation of social media data and automation. Social media have been shown to provide significant influence on decision making in both the consumer and industrial spaces. Increasingly, researchers have spotted early signs of emerging trends using social media, before more formal research confirms such changes. Automation has to do with simplifying the capture and aggregation of all types of secondary data, including (but not exclusively) social media data; analyzing these data; and reporting them to critical decision makers through push emails, key information alerts, and sharable reports. Automation offers the researcher more efficient monitoring of secondary data, increased productivity by doing each task more quickly, and reductions in human error and omission, thereby increasing data quality.

Imagine you need information on automation in the workplace. You want to monitor what's being said and written on the topic of jobs being modified or eliminated due to automation of processes in preparation for preparing a research project for the retail industry. You find one relevant article on the topic in *McKinsey Quarterly*. It claims, "Very few occupations will be automated in their entirety in the near or medium term. Rather, certain *activities* are more likely to be automated, requiring entire business processes to be transformed, and jobs performed by people to be redefined, much like the bank teller's job was redefined with the advent of ATMs." Luckily, that article contains a bibliography, but the search for each article is time consuming and not altogether successful. And you need newer articles as technology advances are making automation easier. You also want to know what's being said in social media on the topic—not just in retail, but in other industries as well—including such venues as LinkedIn, Facebook, Twitter, and YouTube. You could manually search each of these sites, using keywords that relate to your topic, but it's really time consuming and you have a relatively short deadline.

What if you could set up an automated process in minutes that would collect everything said or written on your topic—every article, post, blog, forum, tweet, video—and you could add to that everything in the major retail and business, as well as the academic, press? And what if it updated every time something new was written or posted? And, what if it was collected in one digital place, with embedded links for easy access? Founded in 2005, Netvibes pioneered the first personalized dashboard publishing platform for the web. Today, Netvibes powers customized dashboards for more than 1,000 of the world's leading brands, interactive agencies, government organizations, non-profits and enterprises. Each dashboard aggregates information to a single computer screen. The owner of the dashboard specifies sources (media, people, etc.), as well as the keywords or tags, that guide the search widgets. As the owner reviews the aggregated information, he or she can add additional tags—for example, sentiments (positive, negative, etc.)—that can be tallied and graphed for use in reporting. The owner can also set profiles for alerts to be automatically sent to him by email when new information joins the dashboard. "All you really need to know is what data you want to listen to," shared Kim Terca, director UX and PR at Netvibes.

www.netvibes.com; www.gartner.com

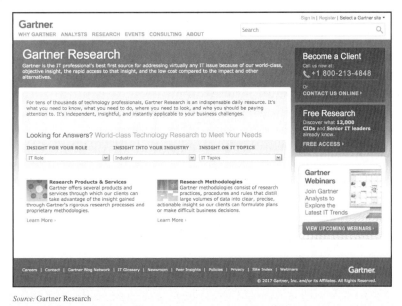

Source: Gartner Research

Evaluating External Sources

A researcher should conduct a **source evaluation** on any secondary source to evaluate the information's credibility. This is especially true of web sources where anyone can publish anything. Researchers should evaluate and select information sources based on five factors in Exhibit 3-8:

- *Purpose*—the explicit or hidden agenda of the information source.
- *Scope*—the breadth and depth of topic coverage, including time period, geographic limitations, and the criteria for information inclusion.
- *Authority*—the level of the data (primary, secondary, tertiary) and the credentials of the source author(s).
- *Audience*—the characteristics and background of the people or groups for whom the source was created.
- *Format*—how the information is presented and the degree of ease of locating specific information within the source.

>**Exhibit 3-8** Evaluating Websites as Information Sources

Evaluation Factor	Questions to Answer
Purpose	• Why does the site exist?
	• How evident is the purpose it is trying to convey?
	• Does it achieve its purpose?
	• How does its purpose affect the type and bias of information presented?
Authority	• What are the credentials of the author or institution or organization sponsoring the site?
	• Does the site give you a means of contacting anyone for further information?
	• Who links to this site?
	• If facts are supplied, where do they come from?
Scope	• How old is the information?
	• How often is it updated?
	• How much information is available?
	• Is it selective or comprehensive?
	• What are the criteria for inclusion?
	• If applicable, what geographic area or time period or language does it cover?
	• How does the information presented compare with that on similar sites?
	• Is it a series of links only (a metasite), or is there added value?
	• What is the nature of the added value?
	• What information did you expect to find that was missing?
	• Is the site self-contained, or does it link to other websites?
Audience	• Whom does the site cater to?
	• What level of knowledge or experience is assumed?
	• How does this intended audience affect the type and bias of the information?
Format	• How quickly can you find needed information?
	• How easy is the site to use? Is it intuitive?
	• Does it load quickly?
	• Is the design appealing?
	• Are there navigation buttons?
	• Is there a site map or search button?
	• Is there an easily identifiable Help button?
	• Is Help helpful?
	• Are pages in ASCII or graphic format?
	• Is the information downloadable into a spreadsheet or word processing program, if desired?

Internal Sources

Not all published sources are external to the firm; many are internal and include department or business unit reports, annual reports, research reports, memos, letters, email, etc. An organization's own internal historical data are often an underutilized source of information in the exploratory phase. Due to employee turnover, the manager may lack knowledge that such historical sources exist, or based on time or budget constraints and the lack of an organized archive, the researcher may choose to ignore such sources. Although digging through data archives can be as simplistic as sorting through a file containing employee service records or inventory shipping manifests, or rereading company reports and management-authored memos that have grown dusty with age, if these sources relate to the management dilemma or management question, they should never be totally ignored. Increasingly, managers and researchers are more likely to mine internal digital databases than paper ones during exploration, due to time pressures.

As computing power has increased and large-volume data storage become more common, accessing more recent data archives has become more likely, although not necessarily easier. A **data warehouse** is an electronic repository for data that organizes large volumes of data into categories or folders to facilitate retrieval, interpretation, and sorting by end users. The data warehouse provides an accessible archive to support dynamic organizational intelligence applications. The keywords here are *accessible* and *dynamic*. Data in a data warehouse must be continually updated (dynamic) to ensure that managers have access to data appropriate for real-time decisions. Today's cloud-based data warehouses have eliminated data silos for some businesses by housing data in a central repository where standard architecture and consistent data definitions are applied. These data are available to decision makers or cross-functional teams for direct analysis or through intermediate storage facilities, regardless of the manager's department or geographic location. However, such a system only works if it is constructed for integration and compatibility.

The more accessible the databases that comprise the data warehouse, the more likely a researcher will use such databases during exploration. Some data in a data warehouse were once primary data, collected for a specific purpose. Any patterns revealed will be used for purposes other than those originally intended. For example, in an archive of employee performance reports, we have a wealth of data about different classifications of workers, training, how often reviews are conducted, metrics used to evaluate performance, standards, etc. Initially the company generated these reports to determine pay scale, apply termination rules, determine if training were needed, etc.

Numerous companies build large consumer purchase behavior databases by collecting transaction data made via store-owned credit programs or frequent purchase loyalty identification programs not linked directly with payment plans. Studying such data can reveal the likely success of a new product introduction or the sales lift effect of a price incentive.

©stocknshares/Getty Images

When a researcher mines performance report archives, the search is for patterns (e.g., promotion, training, termination, etc.). Traditional database queries are often unidimensional and historical—for example, "How many IT employees were trained?" In contrast, advanced data mining uses artificial intelligence to discover patterns and trends in the data and to infer rules from these patterns. With the rules discovered from the data mining, a manager is able to support, review, and/or examine alternative courses of action for solving a management dilemma, alternatives that may later be studied further in the collection of new primary data.

Data-mining technology provides two capabilities for the researcher or manager seeking better understanding of the management dilemma: pattern discovery and prediction. Data-mining tools can be programmed to sweep regularly through databases and identify previously hidden patterns. An example of pattern discovery is the detection of stolen credit cards based on analysis of credit card transaction records. This pattern could be used to strengthen security protocols. Master-Card processes millions of transactions daily and uses pattern discovery to detect fraud in real time.[10] Other uses of pattern discovery include defining retail purchase patterns (used for inventory management and planning promotional efforts), identifying call center volume fluctuations (used to identify staff training needs and product defect detection), and locating abnormal data that could represent data-entry errors (used to evaluate the need for training, employee evaluation, or security).

During exploration, managers or researchers use data mining's predictive capabilities to identify possible action options to solve management dilemmas. Bank of America and Mellon Bank both use data mining's predictive capabilities to pinpoint marketing programs that attract high-margin, low-risk customers. Bank of America focuses on credit lines and retail lending; Mellon Bank focuses on its home equity line of credit.[11]

The process of digitally extracting information from databases has been done in some industries for years. It was State Farm Insurance's ability to mine its extensive nationwide database of accident locations and conditions at intersections that allowed it to identify high-risk intersections and then plan a primary data study to determine alternatives to modify such intersections. Functional areas of management and select industries are currently driving data-mining projects: marketing, customer service, administrative/financial analysis, sales, manual distribution, insurance, fraud detection, and network management.[12] However, two problems have limited the effectiveness of this method of exploration: Getting the data has been both difficult and expensive, and processing it into information has taken time—making it historical rather than predictive. While data warehouses offer great promise, businesses have a long way to go to achieve fully accessible and integrated data warehouses.

Evaluating Internal Sources

Internal sources should be evaluated on the following

- *Compatibility* with the current management dilemma, problem, and research question (the more compatible the data, the more valuable the data).
- *Timelessness* (the more the data hasn't been affected by time, the more valuable the data).
- *Recentness* (the more current the data, the more valuable the data).
- *Quality* of original research process (the more that standards of good research were applied in collecting the original data, the more valuable the data).
- *Author(s) experience* of the individual(s) compiling the source (the more experienced the individuals, the more valuable the data).

You should always try to identify the political and managerial situations in existence during the creation of internal sources, as these add valuable context for evaluating their value. For many businesses, the most valuable information will be embedded in the firm's current digital dashboards, as these data will tie directly to the firms current KPIs.

>Value the Research

By the time a researcher or manager arrives at this task, they know the research question. In a business situation, investing in research should increase the desired effect on KPIs in much the same way as any other investment of resources. These effects might include increased revenue, profits, applications, employee morale, and supplier loyalty or decreased expenses, injuries, defects, or employee turnover. One source suggests that the value of research be defined as "the difference between the result of decisions made with [new] information and the result that would be made without it."[13] While such a definition is simple, its actual application is more difficult.

Ideally, a manager needs to determine a research project's value prior to conducting the research. Most business research is designed to help choose between known alternative options. In such decisions we might use **option analysis** to determine the value of conducting research. We need several pieces of information, including two drawn from decision theory:

- *Two or more options*; these are actions a manager might take to address a management dilemma (e.g., replace a training program, change a product's design, realign the flow of an assembly line, contract with a different distribution company, etc.).

- *One or more decision variables*; these are projected quantifiable effects of any option being considered (e.g., the dollars projected for increased sales or profits from a new product introduction, the reduction of recruiting costs if employee turnover could be reduced, or a reduction in the number of on-the-job injuries.)

- *A decision rule*; this is the criteria the manager will use to make an unbiased decision among the options using the decision variable(s). For example: Choose the option that results in the fewest (criterion) on-the-job injuries (decision variable).

- *The estimated budget* needed for the research design to assess each option.

Plausible options, decision variables, and decision rules are often revealed during exploration. For example, low college student retention is plaguing colleges (management dilemma). Colleges are trying to increase their student retention rate (decision variable). They could identify different alternative programs that are used at other colleges that positively affected retention—peer mentoring, alumni mentoring, introductory course option for each major, freshman success program, etc. (options). Each of these programs has various elements—manpower, space, materials, etc.—and each element has a cost. A college could project various retention rate scenarios—best case, likely case, worst case scenarios—with each option. Their choice between options would be based on choosing the option that resulted in the highest student retention from one year to the next (decision rule).

If we can project the costs and outcomes of each option, how valuable would it be to know with certainty which one or combination of options would actually deliver the desired results (e.g., 10 percent higher student retention)? Because each management dilemma is unique, the resulting research question that will drive the research design will be unique. We can estimate the cost of a research project by first identifying alternative research designs—there is never just one way to conduct research. While any particular research design has unique properties, it also shares common properties with other similar designs. We use these commonalities to develop an estimate. Two approaches work: (1) consult research experts within or outside the firm, or (2) consult company records for actual costs of prior projects employing similar research designs. A seasoned researcher or a manager in a larger company that conducts hundreds of research projects each year might choose the latter approach because the information on costs for various research designs would be readily available.

If the best decision among available options *could* have been made without the benefit of research information, then the research has negative value (the cost of the research project, plus the opportunity cost of the time and dollars spent on that project). On the other hand, if the correct decision *could not* have been made without new research information, it has positive value. If a manager's assessment projects positive research value, he or she will recommend budgeting for research. Exhibit 3-9 models this subprocess.

Of course, it may not be possible to estimate a research's true value before conducting that research. In that scenario, we determine its value after the decision is made, an *ex post facto evaluation*. This type

>**Exhibit 3-9** Value the Research

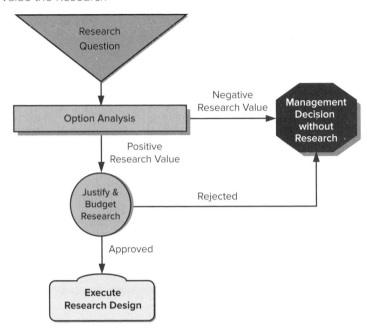

of evaluation comes too late to help a manager decide whether a current research decision should be made. The ex post facto evaluation process, however, adds to a manager's ability to make future research decisions.

>Justify and Budget for Research

Every decision in business—the purchase of a new machine, the hire of a new employee, the launch of an ad campaign, the issue of stock—needs an advocate. Organizations don't have unlimited resources. A manager who seeks to conduct research must be an advocate—not only to justify the costs to be spent on research, but also to identify the source of funds. A budget to conduct research is usually one of two types:

- *Task budget.* Dollars are drawn from the discretionary reserves of an organization or the budget of an in-house research operation to fund a research project. A discretionary reserve might be based on a fixed percentage of projected or prior year's sales. The process is a competitive process among managers; the best crafted argument should, but doesn't always, win approval, often due to internal politics.

- *Functional area budget.* Dollars drawn from a portion of the manager's business unit's operational funds and allocated to research activities. The manager has the authority to spend budget dollars as he or she desires. This process is also competitive because, internally, the manager has numerous goals and priorities. Government agencies, not-for-profits, and businesses alike frequently manage research budgeting this way.

Depending on the level of competition, firms may require a formal written proposal. If at this stage the manager may recognize that he has neither the skills or the resources to conduct research himself, a proposal for research is prepared to send to a sample of outside research organizations. You'll find this process and a sample proposal in Appendix A.

Without a persuasive argument for a sufficient budget, a research project might never be approved. A manager will be forced to make a decision with existing information.

Obtaining a budget for research is a competitive process. When competing for a portion of a finite pool of dollars, every research project needs an advocate. The stronger the argument of direct positive value, the more likely the manager will obtain necessary funds.

©Francisco Cruz/Purestock/Superstock

>Stage 1 Ethical Issues and Their Solutions

While a manager might have assigned a subordinate to conduct the exploration strategy, in many cases the person doing all Stage 1 tasks is the manager herself. Regardless of the organizational structure, the manager shares the heaviest weight in executing Stage 1 ethically. The primary issue involved is the manager's/researcher's right to quality research. Some actions that can guarantee these rights include full disclosure of facts (leading to the management dilemma), unfettered access to necessary internal sources (both people and records), clear identification of exploration's scope (to avoid wasting the researcher's time), absence of restrictions on secondary sources within that scope, encouragement to share all discoveries, and the absence of hidden agendas on discovered options (to avoid misstating the research question).

>summary

LO3-1 The manager starts the process of research question formation by focusing on the management dilemma. This problem/opportunity is translated into a management question and then into a research question—the major objective of any research study. In turn, the research question is further expanded into investigative questions. These questions represent what the manager needs to know in order to address the management question. The question hierarchy ends with measurement questions that are answered by respondents in a survey or answered about each case in an observational study; the topics may be revealed during this stage but are not refined until Stage 3: Design the Research.

LO3-2 Refining the research question is the ultimate objective of exploration. This phase of the process uses information to expand understanding of the management dilemma, look for ways others have addressed and/or solved problems similar to the management dilemma or management question, and gather background information on the topic to refine the research question. Exploration involves familiarization with the available literature, delving into company records, interviews (individuals and group) with experts and those involved with the problem or a possible solution. Exploration as a process uses a two-pronged approach, pursuing internal and external sources (often simultaneously) and pursuing people's perceptions of the problem or its solutions.

LO3-3 External sources are published works of three types: primary, secondary, and tertiary. Primary sources are original works of research or raw data without interpretation. Secondary sources are another's interpretation of primary research. Tertiary sources may be interpretations of secondary sources or, more commonly, finding aids. Researchers use several tools to identify information sources, including indexes and bibliographies, dictionaries, encyclopedias, handbooks, and directories. One of the hardest tasks in using secondary/tertiary published sources is evaluating the quality of the information. Five factors to consider when evaluating the quality of the source are purpose, scope, authority, audience, and format. External sources can also involve interviewing, through individual or group interviews, individuals who have knowledge of the problem or its solutions, or knowledge of research methodology. Extracting internal information often involves delving into company records or company databases. Some of these may be searchable, but others might not be digital, thus hampering easy searchability. The process of searching digital internal sources is referred to as data mining; its purpose is pattern discovery and predicting trends and behaviors.

LO3-4 The value of research can be defined as "the difference between the result of decisions made with [new] information and the result that would be made without it." In order to value research before it is conducted, researchers can use option analysis. This process needs four pieces of information: two or more options (actions the manager might take), one or more decision variables (quantifiable effects of any option), a decision rule (the criteria the manager will use to make an unbiased decision among options), and the estimated budget for the research design to assess each option. Plausible options, decision variables, and decision rules are often revealed during exploration. Estimating budgets for research

designs relies on prior experience or the consultation with experts. If the right decision can be made without new research, then research has no value. If, however, the correct decision cannot be made without new research, the research must be justified and budgeted.

LO3-5 Managers need to be advocates for necessary research. This means they need to identify a source of funds. Budgets for research generally fall into two categories: task and functional area. Task budgets draw funds from discretionary reserves or the operating budget of an in-house research operation. With a functional area budget, the manager uses a portion of the business unit's operating funds to cover the cost of the research. Both budgeting processes are competitive and, sometimes, political. The greater the level of competition for funds in task budgeting, the greater the likelihood that a formal written research proposal will be required. Without a persuasive argument of a sufficient budget, a research project might never be approved.

LO3-6 The primary ethical issue during this stage of the research process is the right to quality research. Actions that guarantee quality include full disclosure of facts (leading to the management dilemma), unfettered access to necessary internal sources (both people and records), clear identification of exploration's scope (to avoid wasting the researcher's time), absence of restrictions on secondary sources within that scope, encouragement to share all discoveries, and the absence of hidden agendas on discovered options (to avoid misstating the research question.

>**key**terms

>**discussion**questions

Terms in Review

1 Explain how each of the five evaluation factors for a secondary source influences its management decision-making value.

  a Purpose

  b Scope

  c Authority

  d Audience

  e Format

2 Define the distinctions among primary, secondary, and tertiary sources in a secondary search.

3 What problems of secondary data quality might researchers face? How can they deal with them?

Making Research Decisions

4 TJX Co., the parent company of T.J.Maxx and other retailers, announced in a Securities and Exchange Commission filing that more than 45 million credit and debit card numbers had been stolen from its IT systems. The company had taken some measures over a period of a few years to protect customer data through obfuscation and encryption. But TJX didn't apply these policies uniformly across its IT systems. As a result, it still had no idea of the extent of the damage caused by the data breach. If you were TJX, what internal sources could you use to evaluate the safety of your customer's personal data?

5 Confronted by low sales, the president of Oaks International Inc. asks a research company to study the activities of the customer relations department in the corporation. What are some of the important reasons that this research project may fail to make an adequate contribution to the solution of management problems?

6 You have been approached by the editor of *Gentlemen's Magazine* to carry out a research study. The magazine has been unsuccessful in attracting shoe manufacturers as advertisers because men's clothing stores are a small and dying segment of their business. *Gentlemen's Magazine* is distributed chiefly through men's clothing stores; the manufacturers reasoned that it was, therefore, not a good vehicle for their advertising. The editor believes that a survey of men's clothing stores in the United States will probably show that these stores are important outlets for

men's shoes and are not declining in importance as shoe outlets. Develop the management–research question hierarchy that will help you to develop a specific research proposal.

7 Develop the management–research question hierarchy for a management dilemma you face at work or with an organization to which you volunteer.

8 How might you use exploration using internal sources if you were a human resources officer or a supervising manager trying to increase compliance with safety policies?

9 When Oreo cookies turned 100, Nabisco celebrated with a limited-edition-flavor release called Birthday Cake Oreos, with the taste of Funfetti cake and rainbow sprinkles within the filling center. According to *Vanity Fair*, this Oreo is a very sweet smell and taste experience. Oreos are the number-one packaged cookie brand, selling more than $778.8 million each year. Oreo comes in more than 30 flavor versions, including original, Golden, Double Stuff, and Green Tea. If you were deciding whether to introduce a new Oreo as part of the celebration, how would you frame the question hierarchy?

From Concept to Practice

10 Develop the management-research question hierarchy (Exhibits 3-2, 3-3) citing the management dilemma, management question, and research question for each of the following:

  a The president of a home health care services firm.

  b The vice president of investor relations for an auto manufacturer.

  c The retail advertising manager of a major metropolitan newspaper.

  d The chief of police of a major city.

From the Headlines

11 At a BMW staff meeting, employees were told "We're in the midst of an electric assault," referring to electric cars introduced by Mercedes, Porsche, Jaguar, and most notably, Tesla. A fund manager at Union Investment parroted this sentiment, "BMW is falling behind in electrics." Develop an exhibit similar to Exhibit 3-4 for this management dilemma.

>cases*

A Gem of a Study

Akron Children's Hospital

Calling Up Attendance

Donatos: Finding the New Pizza

HeroBuilders.com

Inquiring Minds Want to Know—NOW!

Mastering Teacher Leadership

NCRCC: Teeing Up and New Strategic Direction

Ohio Lottery: Innovative Research Design Drives Winning

Ramada Demonstrates Its *Personal Best*™

State Farm: Dangerous Intersections

USTA: Come Out Swinging

*You will find a description of each case in the Case Abstracts section of this textbook. Check the Case Index to determine whether a case provides data, the research instrument, video, or other supplementary material. Cases and case supplements are available in Connect.

>additionalcontent

You'll find the following appendices available from Connect,

Appendix: Bibliographic Database Searches

Appendix: Advanced Searches

>part II

The Design of Business Research

>chapter 4

Stage 2: Research Design, An Overview

"Good research is about using the right platform for each piece of a study, for each activity or interaction."

Nick Drew,
VP Insights and Strategy,
Fresh Intelligence

>learningobjectives

After reading this chapter, you should understand . . .

LO4-1 The tasks that comprise research design.

LO4-2 The types of variable relationships.

LO4-3 The major descriptors of research designs.

>What Is Research Design?

At its most simplistic, **research design** is a blueprint for fulfilling research objectives. Regardless of the numerous definitions of research design,[1] they all have common properties. A design:

- Is a time-based, procedural plan for every research activity.
- Is always focused on the research question.
- Guides selection of sources of information (cases).
- Provides the framework for specifying the relationships among the study's variables.

The tasks covered by the term *research design* are wide-ranging, as depicted in Exhibit 4-1. Our objective here is not for you to acquire the details of research design in one reading, but for you to understand its scope and to get a glimpse of the available options for tailoring a design to an organization's particular research needs.

We finished Stage 1 of the research process by determining whether research would be justified given when we didn't know—our investigative questions. In detailing the design, a researcher must develop:

- The sampling design.
- The data collection design.
- The measurement instrument(s).

Some researchers choose to start the process of planning these three tasks with data collection design. Others prefer to start with sampling design. Either approach is appropriate.

>**Exhibit 4-1** Research Design in the Research Process

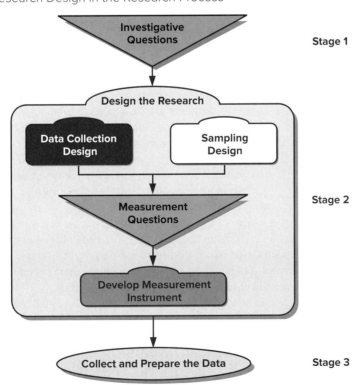

>Sampling Design

In **sampling design**, the task is to identify the sources of any information you did not find during exploration. The investigative questions you developed in Stage 1 are the focus of this process. Whatever sampling design you choose must answer two questions:

- Who or what should be measured?
- How do we access or recruit that source?

©Erik Isakson/Getty Images

While in business research, people don't always represent the target population of interest, we'll use an example here in which they would. Let's say that a firm is experiencing declining worker productivity that appears to parallel a decline in worker morale. The management question is, "What can be done to increase productivity?" During our Stage 1 exploration of secondary sources, we learn that worker morale often affects productivity and is itself affected by (1) a worker's perception of job uncertainty; and (2) on-the-job stress caused by perceptions (a) of the unfairness of a superior's expectations, (b) that there are insufficient resources to perform the job well, and (c) that worker efforts are unappreciated. We also find out that workers often feel they don't know what is going on in the firm outside their own responsibilities; this makes them feel isolated. We determine a list of investigative questions built around the research question of whether to implement an easily accessible, company-wide KPI dashboard to increase transparency of company performance with hopes of improving morale. Many of the investigative questions deal with what information items workers deem important; others deal with what causes worker stress, and how workers perceive the supportiveness of their work environment. Our exploratory study of performance evaluations revealed these records would give us little insight on the problem. Thus the workers themselves become our target population. If we had a small firm, we might ask all workers to participate in the research project. But if we have thousands of workers in numerous locations speaking a variety of languages, we might choose instead to conduct research using a presentative sample. Because these are our workers, we can encourage the chosen workers to participate by incentivizing them with paid time off work.

Once we determine a sample is our choice, we must choose a sample type based on what we plan to do with the information. It's costly to implement a digital dashboard, so we want to make sure it will have the desired effect before spending the money. Ideally, we want to predict all worker response with the evidence measured from just a sample of the workers, so we want a higher-order sample—a probability sample rather than a nonprobability sample. Depending on the variability of jobs within our worker structure, we might choose a specific type of probability sample—a stratified sample—to be sure to measure those attitudes among different classifications of workers. Using an employee roster, divided by job classification, to draw our sample will ensure its representativeness.

So knowing we will measure worker attitudes, perceptions, and feelings, in our sampling design we have made several sampling design decisions:

- We will draw a sample of workers from a company roster divided by job classifications.
- We will apply probability sampling procedures to that roster to extract a stratified sample based on job classification, identifying specific workers.
- We will recruit those specific workers to participate, compensating them for time off the job to encourage their participation.

>Data Collection Design

Data collection design involves a large number of decisions related to how, when, how often, and where data will be collected. In research we measure variables of interest. During data collection design we make numerous choices in order to accurately measure these variables and any relationships between these variables.

An Example

We'll use an example to discuss data collection design dimensions. For a bank, let's assume that it is considering building a new branch in an area of town where it is not yet established. The bank wants to stimulate savings based on the results of a formal study of existing savings activity at its current branches. If the manager hypothesized that savings activity is related to nearness of the branch bank to one's home, he might choose a location with a sizable population of homes. But buying land and constructing a branch is a significant investment of resources. The bank's board of directors will want to be sure that such an investment is empirically supported.

©YinYang/Getty Images

Assume the research question might be, "Is the distance from the account owner's residence to the branch related to saving activity?" Or using the hypothesis format, "Sixty percent of current savers live within a two-mile radius of the branch." In the first phase of the study, we use savings records to cross-tabulate the distance from the account owner's residence to his or her branch and account activity. It shows that differential rates of activity are related to an account owner's location. A cross-tabulation of home-to-branch distance to account size and gender of account owner also shows a relationship. Our task is to determine if the variables are independent (unrelated) or, if they are not, to determine the strength or magnitude of the relationships. Neither procedure tells us which variable is the cause. For example, we might be able to conclude that gender and distance are related to savings activity but not that gender is a causal factor in choice of branch.

Let's say the examination of account records reveals a concentration of near-to-their-branch savers. Their accounts were typically larger and more active than those of account holders who live at a distance. So we choose to add a second phase to our study: a survey of savers to provide information on stage in the family life cycle, attitudes toward savings, family income levels, and motivation for establishing the account. Correlation of this information with known savings data shows that women own larger accounts and that these women with larger accounts are non-working-widowed or working-single women who are older than the average account holder.

The correlation between nearness to the branch and the probability of having an account at the branch might suggest the question, "Why would people who live far from the branch have an account there?" The researcher might hypothesize that:

1. Distant savers (operationally defined as those with addresses more than two miles from the branch) have accounts at the branch because they once lived near the branch; they were "near" when the account decision was made.

2. Distant savers actually live near the branch, but the address on the account is outside the two-mile radius; they are "near," but the records are inaccurate.

3. Distant savers work near the branch; they are "near" by virtue of their work location.

4. Distant savers are not normally near the branch but responded to a promotion that encouraged savers to bank via computer; they are "near" by virtue of electronic banking.

When these hypotheses are tested, the researcher learns that a substantial portion of the distant savers can be accounted for by hypotheses 1 and 3. The conclusion: Location is closely related to saving at the branch.

Here are the data collection design decisions that were revealed:

- All design decisions are consistent with the hypothesis that savings activity is related to "nearness" of the branch to the account holder's home.
- We operationally defined the variable of interest (nearness) as "a home address within two miles of the branch where their account was opened."
- The board of directors will want statistical data to support a recommendation to build a new branch.
- Variables of interest include home location, a measure of *nearness*, the branch where participants opened their account, branch(es) where they do their saving, types of account activity (deposits, withdrawals, CDs, IRAs), frequency of account activity, attitudes toward saving, how account holders access their accounts (branch visits from home, work, or via Internet), and account holder demographics (age, gender, etc.).
- We cannot manipulate our primary variable of interest (*nearness*).
- While we would love to measure an causal relationship between nearness and saving activity, we will seek evidence of a strong correlational relationship.
- The research will be conducted in two phases: (1) an examination of savings records, followed by (2) a survey of savers.
  - The examination of savings records allows the researcher to track savings activity over the time the account has been open and link that activity to initial home address and any changes in home location during the life of the account.
  - A survey allows the researcher to collect more demographic data on the saver who opened the account, as well as attitudinal information about saving, motivational information about why the account was opened, and behavioral information about employment and location of employment.

Design Dimensions

All these decisions address dimensions important in data collection design. Exhibit 4-2 groups these dimensions.[2] A brief discussion of each dimension illustrates its nature and contribution to a researcher's design choices.

- Objective of the study.
- Researcher's ability to manipulate variables to be studied.
- The topical scope.
- Measurement emphasis of research techniques.
- Complexity of design.
- Method of data collection.
- Research environment.
- Time dimension.
- Participant's research awareness.

Objective of the Study

This is the most important dimension of any data collection design because it influences choices in all others. A **reporting study** provides a summation of data, often recasting data to achieve a deeper

>Exhibit 4-2 Dimensions of Data Collection Design

Dimensions	Data Collection Design Options
Objective of the study	• Reporting (who, what, when, where, how—in the past)
	• Descriptive (who, what, when, where, how—now)
	• Causal
	• Explanatory (why, how—now)
	• Predictive (what, why, in future)
Researcher's ability to manipulate variables being studied	• Experimental (ability to manipulate)
	• Ex post facto (no ability to manipulate)
The topical scope of the study	• Statisticalstudy (significant breadth, some depth)
	• Case study (little breadth, significant depth)
The measurement emphasis of research techniques	• Qualitative (emphasis on measures of meaning)
	• Quantitative (emphasis on measures of frequency)
Complexity of design	• Single methodology
	• Multiple methodologies
The method of data collection	• Monitoring
	• Communication study
The research environment	• Field setting
	• Laboratory research
	• Simulation
The time dimension	• Cross-sectional (one measurement at one point in time)
	• Longitudinal (many measurements in specified period of time)
The participants' research awareness	• No deviations perceived
	• Deviations perceived, not researcher related
	• Deviations perceived, researcher induced

understanding or to generate statistics for comparison. In a study of crime, for example, such a study might tally the number of employee thefts that take place in shopping malls versus free-standing stores. Businesses use reporting studies, but because they rely on existing data, they may not cover all the variables a researcher needs to measure. Phase 1 of the bank research is a reporting study.

A **descriptive study** attempts to determine *who, what, where, when,* or *how much.* Descriptive research on employee theft would measure the types of theft committed (clothing vs. electronics vs. housewares vs. money), how often, when (time of year, time of day, day of week), where (receiving dock, stockroom, sales floor, financial office), and by whom (gender, age, years of service, departmental assignment). Descriptive studies collect new data, which may be combined with existing data; such a study can be simple or complex. Phase 2 of our bank example is a descriptive study. These studies serve a variety of research objectives:

• Descriptions of phenomena or characteristics associated with a target population.

• Estimates of proportions of a population that have these characteristics.

• Discovery of associations among variables of interest.

A **causal-explanatory study** attempts to explain relationships among variables—to determine *how* one variable produces changes in another. For instance, such a study might try to explain why the crime rate is higher in mall A than in mall B or why male employees steal more than female employees. A **causal-predictive study** attempts to predict an effect on a dependent variable by manipulating another variable (independent) while holding all other variables constant. For example, researchers conducting a causal-predictive study might test whether installation of video surveillance cameras on the receiving dock and in stockrooms would reduce employee theft in mall stores. While causal inferences may be neither permanent nor universal, over time these inferences allow us to build knowledge of presumed causes. Such empirical conclusions provide us with successive approximations to the truth and the foundation of theories.

Researcher Ability to Manipulate Variables

With an **ex post facto design**, researchers have no ability to manipulate variables. Instead, the researcher studies participants who have been exposed to the independent variable and those who have not been so exposed and compare the results. In our bank research, we study savings account holders who live "near" to a branch and those who don't using an ex post facto design. It is important that the researchers using this design not influence the variables; to do so would introduce bias. The researcher is limited to holding factors constant by judicious selection of participants according to strict sampling procedures and by statistical manipulation of findings. Businesses use ex post facto data collection designs extensively.

In an **experiment**, the researcher must be able to control and/or manipulate the variables in the study. It is enough that the researcher can cause variables to be changed or held constant in keeping with the research objectives. Results from experiments provide the most powerful support possible for a hypothesis of causation. Banks can use experiments; for example, extending (or decreasing) the hours of ATM access to determine if ATM use would increase (decrease) compared to prior use.

The Topical Scope

Statistical studies attempt to capture a population's characteristics by making inferences from a sample's characteristics. They are designed for breadth rather than depth, extracting the same data from multiple cases. Hypotheses are tested quantitatively. Generalizations about findings are presented based on the representativeness of the sample and the validity of the design. In our bank research, our records study is statistical; our survey of savings account holders is statistical. Much of business research involves statistical studies.

Case studies place more emphasis on a full contextual analysis of one or a few events or conditions and their interrelationships. An emphasis on contextual detail provides valuable insight for problem solving, evaluation, and strategic or tactical change. This detail may be secured from multiple sources of information, allowing evidence to be verified and avoiding missing data. A single, well-designed case study can provide a major challenge to a hypothesis and provide a source of new hypotheses and constructs simultaneously.[3] Before the use of surveillance cameras, a business might have made assumptions about how employees followed or didn't follow safety procedures based on the infrequent observations of a manager; the eight-hour footage from a single camera (case) could challenge those assumptions. Businesses often use case studies. One often-used example is to study a firm that has achieved a solution to a similar problem as the one a manager faces. Such a case might be described as a *best-practice* case.

Measurement Emphasis

Business researchers use both qualitative and quantitative research, sometimes in the same study. **Qualitative research** use interpretive techniques to describe, decide, translate, and otherwise come to terms with the meaning of certain phenomenon. Qualitative research is often used during exploration, but it may also follow a statistical study to further understand what was measured. With the increasing use of mobile devices to conduct qualitative research involving larger samples, such studies may be sufficient on their own to guide a business decision. Qualitative research is dependent on the researcher for its rigor.

Quantitative research is interested in the quantity, frequency, or magnitude of a phenomenon; it is the basis of a statistical study. Quantitative research is dependent on the quality of the measurement instruments used for observation, surveys, and experimental tests. In our bank research, it is likely that our board of directors will be much happier with both phases being conducted quantitatively.

>**snap**shot

AIG AND Research Design

Following the financial crisis, AIG found itself under increasing scrutiny. It had an urgent need to demonstrate to shareholders that it could differentiate performance. When Julia Smith joined the HR team at AIG, she was told the performance management system was in peril. It was cumbersome, lacked manager ownership, and focused only on what employees were doing—without the effects of those actions—and provided little direction to employees on how to improve or enhance their performance.

AIG undertook a massive research project to determine what should replace its current system. It partnered with ThinkTank.net to conducted virtual focus groups, drawing participants from its more than 60,000 employees worldwide. AIG learned the ideal system needed to inspire employees to do their best, offer real-time feedback and constructive coaching, and reveal transformative development opportunities.

AIG recruited the expertise of noted expert in behavioral economics, as well as cognitive and social psychology, Danny Kahneman. And it interviewed hundreds of HR professionals about their performance appraisal systems to find best practices. The program that developed would evaluate 18 specific behaviors (e.g., able to anticipate problems, collaborative and helpful, open to new ways of doing things) using an online evaluation system in which both managers and employees have input; each behavior is needed to reinforce AIG values. The research taught AIG to frame the behaviors positively and to use everyday language rather than jargon. It also learned that the appraisal entry needed to be online, use simplistic scales, and be easy to complete by both manager and employee. It also needed to generate a consistent, computer-generated report on each employee. This report needed to show the employee not only his or her behavior achievement in comparison with others with the same type of job, but also how he or she compares with employees throughout the company regardless of job type or level. The research revealed the need to share the report with employees before any manager discussion and to prepare a discussion guide for managers and employees to use when they discussed the report.

AIG put its best ideas into a new program focused on two primary goals—reward collaboration and teamwork—while

©John Lund/Drew Kelly/Blend Images LLC

discouraging inter-employee competition. It then launched a pilot with 3,000 employees to test the new program and surveyed participants after the pilot. After tweaking the program, it went company-wide in 2016. Employees find the new program fair (96 percent), accurate (92 percent), and helpful to improving performance (92 percent), with 86 percent of employees indicating their relationship with their manager improving. Volunteer employees are featured in video clips focused on each of the 18 behaviors to encourage their fellow employees. That's what buy-in looks like.

AIG.com; ThinkTank.net

Complexity of Design

A **single-methodology design** would employ only one method—a survey, for example. However, business research is often complex, including more than one data collection methodology. A **multiple-methodology design** might include an array of methods—for example, a series of personal interviews, followed by a series of focus groups, followed by a survey. One of the most common multiple-methodology studies is the *two-stage design*, which employs qualitative research techniques to further understand the management problem and frame the research question, followed by a quantitative statistical study to collect data related to the measurement questions. Our bank study is using a multiple-methodology design employing observation of records and a survey of account holders.

For a business, the data collection design complexity choice is often influenced by the action option(s) the manager is considering and how much each would cost to implement; the more expensive the options being considered, the more likely that business might want to know with some statistical certainty that any hypothesis it formed is correct. This might lead the business to invest more in research. A business considering a major shift in its overall business strategy, for example, could lead to a more complex and more expensive data collection design. Our bank considering building a new branch is in just such a situation.

Method of Data Collection

In a **monitoring study** the researcher inspects the activities of a subject or the nature of some material or activity and records the information from observations; the researcher does not attempt to elicit responses from anyone. Traffic counts at an intersection, license plates recorded in a restaurant parking lot, a search of the library collection, an observation of the actions of a group of decision makers, the study of records of accidents by State Farm to identify dangerous intersections—all are examples of monitoring. These observations can be made in person or through digital or mechanical means. Our bank research employs monitoring in phase 1.

In a **communication study**, the researcher questions the participants and collects their responses by personal or impersonal means. The collected data may result from (1) interview, telephone, or web conversations; (2) self-administered or self-reported instruments sent through the mail, left in a convenient location (e.g., hotel room), or transmitted electronically or by other means; or (3) instruments presented before and/or after a treatment or stimulus condition in an *experiment*. We use the term *communication* because collecting data by questioning encompasses more than the survey method. Our bank research employs a communication study in phase 2.

Research Environment

Designs also differ as to whether measurement occurs under staged or manipulated conditions **(laboratory conditions)** or under actual environmental conditions **(field conditions)**. Laboratory conditions might be used in highly sensitive situations where you want the research to remain confidential (e.g., a taste test of a new menu item for Wendy's that, if known by competitors, would reveal too soon a possible new strategic direction). It is assumed when you collect data using field conditions that participants are not as likely to alter their actual behavior, behaviors of which they may not be fully aware. But it is also likely that you will not observe as many participants using field conditions. We are using visual ethnography more in business research, where, for example, we ask participants to take video of a shopping trip using their smartphone, then upload the video to a researcher. Setting up a fake store (laboratory), and asking participants to "shop" that store while we video them, is an alternative design, but it would be extremely costly. Some field conditions might put a participant or researcher at risk (e.g., observing how a participant handles a contrived, unsafe work environment or sending an interviewer into a crime-infested area to do interviews); in such cases, an alternative design would be explored. When we intercept customers in a mall or store to conduct a survey, we are using field conditions. The second phase of the bank study will likely communicate with the savings account holders in their homes, a field study.

Both field and laboratory conditions may use *simulations*—a replica of a system or process. As computer programming advances, some businesses are using mathematical models to simulate characteristics under various conditions and relationships (e.g., performance of an airplane engine design on its ability to deflect birds); others are using virtual reality (e.g., to determine the strength of a package design[4]). Role-playing and other behavioral activities may also be viewed as simulations. One behavioral role-play simulation in retail involves *mystery shoppers* where a researcher poses as a potential customer to record and evaluate the sales person's knowledge, customer service approach, and procedural skills.

>**snap**shot

TIAA Performance Management Overhaul

It doesn't take much effort to find a business press article that encourages the elimination of rating-based performance management (PM) systems. TIAA is a *Fortune* 100 financial institution with 12,800 employees that manages investment accounts for more than 5 million people employed in 16,000 institutions. It decided to approach anecdotal employee dissatisfaction with their PM processes more deliberately, designing a multi-stage, multi-year research project.

Quality	People	Character
• Provide exceptional service • Establish strategic priorities • Drive continuous Improvement	• Communicate Openly • Foster collaboration • Develop self and others	• Build trust • Take ownership • Make sound decisions

"Asking the right question to start the research process was critical," shared Michelle Shail, manager of talent management at TIAA. "Should we eliminate formal reviews and/or ratings?" was the wrong question, even though it was, in part, the annual review ratings that caused the dissatisfaction among employees. TIAA discovered that the right question was actually two questions: "How can we develop a PM process that will drive desired business outcomes?" and "What PM process will best fit our culture?"

Their first step was to conduct quantitative and qualitative-analyses of employee survey data from the prior five years. It partnered with i4CP to develop insights, connections, and guidance. Based on employee survey feedback, TIAA discovered that many employees found that the current PM process didn't help them improve their performance—one of its key goals. TIAA tallied time spent in the PM process and discovered the 71,800 hours was mostly spent on compliance documentation, not conversations between manager and employee. Additionally, employees were concerned about eliminating the rating system because it was integrated into their compensation system.

TIAA conducted direct benchmarking interviews with human resources (HR) professionals in more than 35 companies to help design a possible new system. Based on the HR interviews, TIAA learned that any great PM system contained three elements: (1) individual goal setting aligned with organizational goals, (2) coaching and feedback from both managers and peers, and (3) reviews that truly differentiated performance and transparently linked compensation with performance. "Every organizational culture is different. Ours is very focused on developing detailed documentation. Yet we discovered that employees and

their managers wanted PM information condensed and put in snippets."

TIAA designed a new PM system that focused on increasing coaching and feedback; incorporated accountability not only for business results, but also individual behaviors; simplified documentation; and increased management capability. To test-components of the new program, TIAA launched three different pilots (research studies). The first pilot tested the "Get Feedback" tool for peer evaluations—research had revealed that employees wanted to control who evaluated them and who had access to that evaluation.

The second pilot evaluated the critical behaviors list. It learned that nine key competencies or behaviors were critical to achieving company goals. They grouped the desired behaviors into three categories quality, people, and character.

The third pilot evaluated replacing the formal mid-year review with two brief check-in conversations, which were flexible in terms of timing but focused on employee goals and behaviors to accomplish those goals. They used focus groups to determine if the check-in interviews of the new process were taking place between employees and their managers and whether these provided the desired personal development feedback. They used discussions with 49 volunteer employee ambassadors, who were both passionate about the new process as well as strong performers, for additional feedback and to get critical buy-in among employees.

While it's early yet to determine if this new PM program will be successful, one thing it is doing is saving time—one to three hours per year for every employee and 5 to 18 hours for every manager.

www.tiaa.org; www.talentmgt.com; i4cp.com

Time Dimension

Longitudinal studies are repeated measures of the same variable over a specified period. The advantage of a longitudinal study is that it can track changes over time or involve participants in a variety of activities. Longitudinal studies can study the same people over time (e.g., via panel) or use different participants for each subsequent measurement (e.g., via cohort groups: the financial service industry might study the needs of aging baby boomers by sampling 40- to 45-year-olds in 1995, 50- to 55-year-olds in 2005, and 60-to 65-year-olds in 2015). Some types of information once collected cannot be collected a second time from the same person without the risk of injecting bias because participant awareness has been enhanced by introduction to a stimulus. The longitudinal study of public awareness of an advertising campaign over a six-month period would require different samples for each measurement. While longitudinal research is important, the constraints of budget and shortened decision-making time often impose the need for cross-sectional studies. Phase 1 of the bank research is a longitudinal study.

Cross-sectional studies are carried out once and represent a snapshot at one point in time. The advantages of a cross-sectional study are that it can be accomplished more quickly, at a lower cost, and error sources caused by changes over time are minimized. Discovering past attitudes, history, and future expectations can be discovered through a cross-sectional study; however, interpreting such data requires care. In the bank study, the survey is a cross-sectional study.

Participants' Research Awareness

The usefulness of a design may be reduced when a participant perceives that research is being conducted. This awareness influences the outcomes of the research in subtle ways or more dramatically as we learned from the pivotal Hawthorne studies of the late 1920s.[5] Although there is no widespread evidence of attempts by participants or respondents to please researchers through successful hypothesis guessing or evidence of the prevalence of sabotage, when participants believe that something out of the ordinary is happening, they may behave less naturally. There are three levels of perception:[6]

- Participants perceive no deviations from everyday routines.
- Participants perceive deviations, but as unrelated to the researcher.
- Participants perceive deviations as researcher-induced.

In *mystery shopper* research, if a retail sales associate knows she is being observed and evaluated—with consequences in future compensation, scheduling, or work assignment—she is likely to change her performance. In all research environments and control situations, researchers need to be vigilant to effects that may alter their conclusions. Participants' awareness concerns serve as a reminder of the value of classifying one's study, to examine validation strengths and weaknesses, and to be prepared to qualify results accordingly. In phase 1 of the bank research, the account holders would be unaware. In phase 2, they would be aware.

>Design the Measurement Instrument

When you get to this task, the sample design and data collection design choices are completed and the researcher knows the variables to be measured. The activities included in this task are

- Determine the appropriate measurement approach for each data collection task in the design.
- Craft the specific measurement questions or elements of an observation checklist.
- Determine the order of questions or elements.
- Determine the necessity of introductions, definitions, instructions, and conclusions for participants; develop these non-question elements.
- Craft the measurement instrument(s).
- Determine the necessity of training for data collectors.
- Craft any training guides and activities.

A **measurement instrument** is a tool for collecting data on a study's variables. There are many different types: survey questionnaires, interview guides, group discussion guides, and observation checklists, to name a few. Both qualitative and quantitative studies need measurement instruments. Also during this task, individual questions and whole instruments are tested, either with a sample of participants or their surrogates, with other researchers, or both. Tests determine wording problems, question order problems, the need for clarifying definitions or instructions, and more. These tests are always conducted as the instrument will actually be used, face-to-face or phone or personal interview, Internet chat, mobile survey, field observation, etc. In the bank study, we'll need a record's checklist for the observation study and a survey for bank savers.

>**close**up

How Agile Research Helped Prove the Value in a Packaging Redesign

Founded in 2010, rapidly growing San Diego-based organic juice company Suja offers a line of non-GMO, cold-pressured, preservative- and gluten-free juices and smoothies through 14,000 natural, grocery, box, and mass-market retailers. "One recent study showed while 4% of households actually consume organic foods," shared Suja's brand manager Bella Tumini, "many more are interested. Suja is trying to democratize organic for the 44% who are trying to incorporate organic foods into their diet."

In order to stay competitive and stand out to consumers, companies that offer organic and/or juice products must innovate constantly. Without a research budget, Suja considered their research approach as "scrappy," using secondary research to identify trends and turning to their own head of innovation—a Culinary Institute-trained chef—to develop juices to match these trends. Innovation ideas were vetted using mostly the opinions of employees, as well as those of their family and friends. Additionally, the team used do-it-yourself (DIY) surveys, drawing participants from their social media followers, leaving room for biased results. The team lacked the time and research expertise necessary for survey creation, data analysis, and report building. "Having the DIY tools without the people wasn't helpful because we're such a small team," explained Tumini.

By using this "gut" process, Suja was able to innovate-quickly—often taking just six weeks from idea to distribution. "That speed allowed us to stay ahead of the competition and establish Suja as a leader in the category," explained Tumini. And while the Suja team has launched well over 100 products since inception, almost half of those have been discontinued. In order to pivot quickly based on product performance, the marketing team employs a flexible approach when it comes to testing and launching different products, especially being a team of three people with a tight budget.

In just four years, the company grew from 300 to 14,000 stores in which Suja products are sold. Yet many brands have entered the category, making it harder on consumers to make a choice at the shelf. As such, the marketing team sought to decrease the amount of time spent at the shelf by differentiating Suja's product labels from competitors. Before moving forward with a redesign of the leading product line's packaging, the team had to be sure the update would enhance the brand's performance while appealing to both of their consumer segments.

The Suja team decided to partner with GutCheck, a provider of online agile market research, in order to ensure a packaging and brand update would be worth the risk. GutCheck offers several online agile research solutions that are fast, adaptable, and iterative (giving clients the option for more waves or stages

of research, if needed). "By automating certain steps in the research process that don't add value, research strategists are able to focus on what matters: research design, data collection, analysis, and delivering reports within days, instead of months," shared Matt Marta, CEO, GutCheck. The Suja team was attracted by the speed and iterative nature of GutCheck's research for the redesign of its Suja Essentials package.

Together, the Suja marketing team and GutCheck research team designed the multiphase research to answer the key question, "Are consumers more or less likely to buy the new packaging versus the current one?" Phase I (five days from recruit to report) employed an Instant Research Group. An Instant Research Group is an online qualitative discussion where respondents—recruited from global panel providers—answer open-ended questions and follow-up inquiries posted by a trained moderator over the course of several days. This methodology allows for quick consumer feedback and gives respondents the ability to interact with others in the group. To avoid bias, all participants first answer each question themselves. Then, on the next screen, they see all participants' responses and can react to and comment on each other's responses. This encourages conversations and sparks ideas among respondents. This phase was exploratory and included 30 participants who evaluated four package designs based on key metrics: likes, dislikes, overall appeal, purchase intent, believability, and uniqueness.

Primary findings showed that the product claims were believable based on the presence of certification labels, which added

Courtesy of GutCheck and Suja

trust in the brand. Respondents also liked that the bottle color matched the juice color. Verbatims indicated the new designs were perceived as clean, stylish, modern, and unique—all what the Suja team wanted.

These qualitative findings were used to further optimize the new package concept. Phase 2, the test of the refined design against the existing design, utilized an Agile Screen (five days from recruit to report), which is an online quantitative survey designed to provide quick consumer feedback based on a set of key metrics, including purchase intent, uniqueness, believability, quality, and product function for this particular project. This methodology helps clients reduce the ideas or concepts that merit further attention. For this phase, a sample size of 200 respondents was used. Sample size is an important component of statistical significance. "In order for our results to be considered representative and projected to the broader population, we suggest a minimum sample size of 200. As the sample size drops below 200, the margin of error widens and the results in the survey have a higher risk of not encapsulating the true mean of the population," explained Laura Jett, research manager at GutCheck. Participants for both research phases were screened based on demographic and attitudinal/behavioral requirements, including household shopping responsibility and type of stores

frequently visited; the sample needed to include shoppers from both natural and conventional consumer segments to ensure neither segment would be alienated by the packaging update.

With only 45 days to implement a design prior to the start of Suja's primary selling season, the short five-day-recruit-to-report time frame was critical. Within days, it was clear the new packaging outperformed the current (at time of study) design by nearly a two-to-one ratio, giving the Suja team confidence to move forward with the redesign. After taking into account all consumer feedback, the Suja team made updates to the packaging, which led to the final design, now available in stores.

Most importantly, the research results proved to both the marketing team and the key stakeholders that the packaging redesign was not only worth the investment, but that the new packaging would likely increase purchases. Having the results so fast allowed the team to launch the new product line in time for their peak buying season.

"The Suja Essentials product line is our number-one revenue-driver and makes up the largest percentage of our portfolio; because of the risk involved in updating its packaging, this was one of the most important studies we've done as a company," said Tumini.

www.sujajuice.com; www.gutcheckit.com

>summary

LO4-1 Research design is a time-based plan for the execution of all research activities. It has three tasks: sampling design, data collection design, and development of the measurement instrument. Each of these stages is integrated, although they are tackled separately. Some researchers choose to start with sampling design, while others choose to start with data collection design; either starting point is appropriate. Sampling design answers who or what is the source of measurement and how we access or recruit that source.

LO4-2 Data collection design involves the measurement of variables and the search for relationships between those variables. Data collection design involves a large number of decisions related to how, when, how often, and where data will be collected. Design

of the measurement instrument involves translating investigative questions into measurement questions that are appropriate for the chosen data collection design. Researchers not only craft instruments, but also test them to reveal problems for both the participant and any data gatherers.

LO4-3 A number of different design dimensions influence data collection design: objective of the study, the researcher's ability to manipulate variables in the study, the topical scope, the measurement emphasis, the complexity of design, the method of data collection, the research environment, the time dimension, and whether participants are research aware. Each of these dimensions represent multiple options to the researcher.

>**key**terms

case study 76

causal-explanatory study 75

causal-predictive study 75

communication study 78

cross-sectional study 80

data collection design 73

descriptive study 75

ex post facto design 76

experiment 76

field conditions 78

laboratory conditions 78

longitudinal study 79

measurement instrument 80

monitoring study 78

multiple-methodology design 77

qualitative research 76

quantitative research 76

reporting study 74

research design 71

sampling design 72

single-methodology design 77

statistical study 76

>**discussion**questions

Terms in Review

1 Distinguish between the following:

  a. Exploratory and formal studies.

  b. Experimental and ex post facto research designs.

  c. Descriptive and causal studies.

Making Research Decisions

2 You have been asked to determine how hospitals prepare and train volunteers. Because you know relatively little about this subject, how will you find out? Be as specific as possible.

3 You are the administrative assistant for a division chief in a large holding company that owns several hotels and theme parks. You and the division chief have just come from the CEO's office, where you were informed that the guest complaints related to housekeeping and employee attitude are increasing. Your onsite managers have mentioned some tension among the workers but have not considered it unusual. The CEO and your division chief instruct you to investigate. Suggest at least three different types of research that might be appropriate in this situation.

4 Kraft split off its global snack business, naming it Mondelez International. The name came from a massive name suggestion program from Kraft employees, involving more than 1, 700 names by more than 1, 000 Kraft employees over a five-month process. The name plays on the connotation of "delicious world." How would you design this process to ensure that viable names were produced?

5 P&G recently moved its IAMS pet food division from Vandalia (OH) to Mason (OH). The move affected 240 workers, who were offered positions to join the 2, 000 workers already occupying the pet food division headquarters in Mason. A company statement indicated, "We're doing this to increase productivity, collaboration, and access to P&G's resources/expertise." P&G also told employees that it was beginning a separate, multi-month study on how to increase collaboration and efficiencies with the 250 employees still working in its pet food research and development (R&D) complex located in Lewisburg (OH). What research might be included in the multi-month study to determine the future of the Lewisburg R&D facility and its employees?

From Concept to Practice

6 Using the eight design descriptors (Exhibit 4-2), describe a study to determine why enrollment in your major at your university is increasing (decreasing).

7 Use the eight design descriptors in Exhibit 4-2 to profile the research described in the chapter Snapshots.

From the Headlines

8 Uber is facing a large number of lawsuits, among them a charge of technology theft from Google, installation of software that blanks out the availability of Uber rides near government buildings or when government-employed riders call, discrimination in the workplace, etc. Using an Internet search on this topic, design a study to determine the effect on ridership of the charge you examined.

>cases*

A Gem of a Study

Calling Up Attendance

Campbell-Ewald Pumps Awareness into the American Heart Association

Covering Kids with Health Care

Donatos: Finding the New Pizza

Goodyear's Aquatred

Inquiring Minds Want to Know—NOW!

Ohio Lottery: Innovative Research Design Drives Winning

Open Doors: Extending Hospitality to Travelers with Disabilities

Proofpoint: Capitalizing on a Reporter's Love of Statistics

Ramada Demonstrates Its *Personal Best*™

Starbucks, Bank One, and Visa Launch

Starbucks Card Duetto Visa

State Farm: Dangerous Intersections

Volkswagen's Beetle

* You will find a description of each case in the Case Abstracts section of this textbook. Check the Case Index to determine whether a case provides data, the research instrument, video, or other supplementary material. Cases and case supplements are available in Connect.

>chapter 5

Stage 2:
Sampling Design

> "When you sample something, you're using the crutch of borrowing chords and melodies from a song that's already great, that's already stood the test of time, that's already special."
>
> *Gerald Earl Gillum (G-Eazy),*
> *American rapper and record producer*

>learningobjectives

After reading this chapter, you should understand . . .

LO5-1 The six tasks that comprise sampling design.

LO5-2 The premises on which sampling theory is based.

LO5-3 The characteristics of accuracy and precision for measuring sample validity.

LO5-4 The two categories of sampling methods and the variety of sampling techniques within each category.

LO5-5 The various sampling techniques and when each is used.

LO5-6 The ethical issues related to sampling design.

>Sampling Design

This subprocess of research design answers the question: From whom or what (target population) does the data need to be collected and how and from how many (cases)? The steps in this subprocess (Exhibit 5-1) include:

1. Define the **target population** and a **case** (describe those entities—collectively and individually—that possess the desired information about the chosen variables and its parameters).

2. Define the **population parameters** of interest (summary descriptors—proportion, mean, variance—of study variables) in the population.

3. Identify and evaluate the **sample frame** (list of cases within the target population) or create one.

4. Define the number of cases needed (choose between a census or sample; choose the size of any sample).

5. Define the appropriate sampling method (the type of sample to be used).

6. Define the sampling selection and recruitment protocols (choose standardized procedures or custom-design ones).

>**Exhibit 5-1** Sampling Design in the Research Process

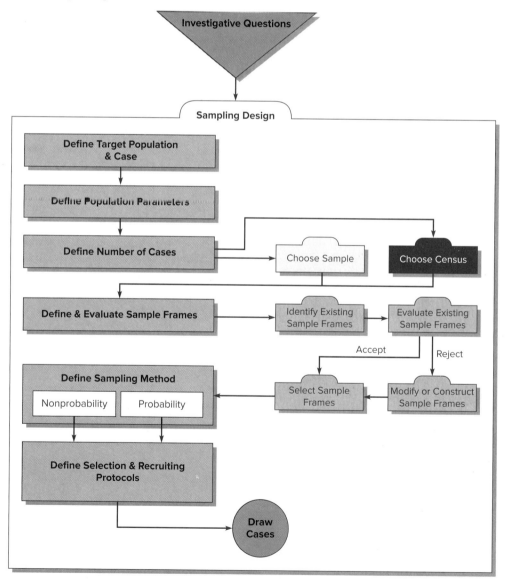

If a study's objective is to understand data security breaches, then the target population might be "any event where data were accessed by an unauthorized source." Using operational definitions for "accessed" and "unauthorized source" would be critical. IT experts indicate exploratory data breaches by hackers are often so well hidden that they may not be discovered for months, if at all, until a major breach occurs. Would these exploratory breaches also be part of the target population? For each data breach (case), the population parameters of interest might be whether data were accessed but not modified, what modifications occurred, whether data were permanently lost, the method of access, etc. The sample frame would be the list of every such data breach within a specified period of time (e.g., five years). The number of cases we need depends on the size, variability, and accessibility of the target population. Depending on the number of breaches a company experienced, using a census (evaluating all instances of unauthorized access) might be feasible. If the number of breaches is very large, and exploration showed that one method of access and type of breach was common (limited variability), then using a sample (examining only a portion of unauthorized access records) might be chosen. In this instance, a researcher would need special forensic computing skills, thus using a sample might also be more desirable due to time constraints on a limited pool of researchers.

>Define the Target Population and Case

In business, a *target population* can be any of the following (Exhibit 5-2), with a *case* being a single element drawn from that target population:

- People (individuals or groups: e.g., employees, customers, suppliers).
- Organizations or institutions (companies, trade associations, professional online communities, unions).
- Events and happenings (e.g., trade association meetings, presentations to financial analysts, industry conventions, employee picnics).
- Objects or artifacts (e.g., products, machines, production waste or byproducts, tools, maps, process models, ads).
- Settings and environments (e.g., warehouses, stores, factories, distribution facilities).
- Texts (e.g., annual reports, productivity records, social media posts, emails, memos, reports).

>**Exhibit 5-2** Common Types of Target Populations in Business Research

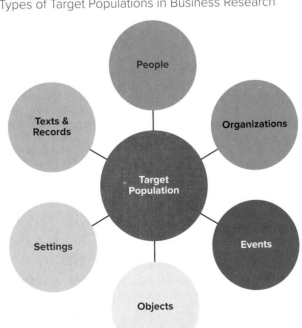

Ford Reenergizes by Changing Its Sampling Design

In the midst of the financial crisis in the automobile industry, Ford's James Farley decided his research was excluding a very important target population: dealers. With dealers controlling 75 percent of advertising expenditures for the auto giant, Farley thought excluding them as research participants was suicidal. So he recruited 30 of the most influential dealers to fly to Detroit to provide information and critique the creative proposals of the Ford ad agency, Team Detroit.

Farmington Hills (MI) full-service research firm Morpace put the dealers through an intensive group interview experience. The dealers were soon challenged with questions. "Which incentives work and which don't?" "What does the Ford brand mean to you?" "What is wrong with Ford's advertising?" In subsequent sessions, the dealers were asked to critique ad slogans and branding strategies and recommend those that best captured the Ford experience. The dealers left the 72-hour marathon session enthusiastic about the direction Ford was taking and with significant buy-in for the next ad campaign. Farley's

©Joe Raedle/Staff/Getty Images

actions gave voice to its dealers with its altered research sampling design.

www.ford.com; www.morpace.com; www.teamdetroit.com

The definition of the target population may be apparent from the management problem or the research question(s), as it was in our data breach study, but often it is not so obvious. Sometimes there is more than one option for the target population. The researcher will choose one or more options that will provide him or her with the most answers to the investigative questions.

In the discussion that follows, we will use a dining study on a college campus: The researchers at Metro University (Metro U) are exploring the feasibility of creating a dining club whose facilities would be available on a membership basis. To launch this venture, they will need to make a substantial investment. Research will allow them to reduce many risks. Thus, the research question is: Would a membership dining club be a viable enterprise? Some investigative questions that flow from the research question include:

1. Who would patronize the club, and on what basis?

2. How many would join the club under various membership and fee arrangements?

3. How much would the average member spend per month?

4. What days would be most popular?

5. What menu and service formats would be most desirable?

6. What lunch times would be most popular?

7. Given the proposed price levels, how often per month would each member have lunch or dinner?

8. What percent of the people in the population say they would join the club, based on the projected rates and services?

Is the target population for the dining club study at Metro University defined as "full-time day students on the main campus of Metro U"? Or should the population include "all persons employed at Metro U"? Or should townspeople who live in the neighborhood be included? Without knowing the likely patron for the new venture, it is not obvious which of these is the appropriate target population. Assume the Metro University Dining Club is to be solely for the students and employees on the main campus. The researchers might define the population as "currently-enrolled students and employees (full- and part-time) of Metro U, main campus, and their families." Thus, any single student or employee would be a likely case.

>Define the Population Parameters

Population parameters are summary descriptors (e.g., incidence proportion, mean, variance, etc.) of variables of interest in the population. **Sample statistics** are descriptors of those same relevant variables computed from sample data. Sample statistics are used as estimators of population parameters. The sample statistics are the basis of our inferences about the population. Exhibit 5-3 indicates population parameters for the Metro U dining study.

©Wavebreak Media/Getty Images

Depending on how measurement questions are phrased, each will collect a different level of data. Each different level of data also generates different sample statistics. Thus, choosing the parameters of interest will actually dictate your sample type and its size. Data have different properties depending on how they were collected. Exhibit 5-4 reviews the data types and these properties.

When the variables of interest in the study are measured on interval or ratio scales, we use the sample mean to estimate the population mean and the sample standard deviation to estimate the population standard deviation. When the variables of interest are measured on nominal or ordinal scales, we use the sample proportion of incidence (p) to estimate the population proportion and the pq to estimate the population variance where $q = (1 - p)$. The **population proportion of incidence** "is equal to the number of cases in the population belonging to the category of interest, divided by the total number of cases in the population."[1] Proportion measures are necessary for nominal data and are widely used for other measures as well. The most frequent proportion measure is the percentage. In the Metro U study, examples of nominal data are the proportion of a population that expresses interest in joining the club (e.g., 30 percent; therefore p is equal to 0.3 and q, those not interested,

>**Exhibit 5-3** Example Population Parameters in the Metro U Dining Study

Population Parameter of Interest	Data Level and Measurement Scale
Frequency of eating on or near campus at a restaurant within the last 30 days	• Ratio data (actual number of eating experiences) • Ordinal data (less than 5 times per month, greater than 5 but fewer than 10 times per month, greater than 10 times per month)
Proportion of student/employees expressing interest in the dining club	• Nominal data (interested, not interested)
Proportion of students/employees spending money per person per visit	• Interval data ($5–9.99, $10–14.99, $15–19.99, $20–24.99, $25–29.99)

>**Exhibit 5-4** Data Types and Characteristics

Data Type	Data Characteristics	Example
Nominal	Classification	Respondent type (faculty, staff, student)
Ordinal	Classification and Order	Preferred doneness of steak (well done, medium well, medium rare, rare)
Interval	Classification, order, & distance	How rated last restaurant experience (scale of 1-10; l=very poor, 10=exceptional)
Ratio	Classification, order, distance & natural origin	Average $ amount spent per person for last dinner in restaurant.

equals 0.7) or the proportion of married students who report they now eat in restaurants at least five times a month.

There may also be important subgroups in the population about whom we would like to make estimates. For example, we might want to draw conclusions about the extent of dining club use that could be expected from married faculty versus single students, residential students versus commuter students, and so forth. Such questions have a strong impact on the nature of the sampling frame we accept (we would want the list organized by these subgroups, or within the list each characteristic of each case would need to be noted), the design of the sample, and its size.

>Define the Sampling Frame

The *sampling frame* is the list of cases in the target population from which the sample is actually drawn. Ideally, it is a complete and correct list of population members only. As a practical matter, however, the sampling frame often differs from the desired population. For the dining club study, the Metro U directory would be the logical first choice as a sampling frame. Published directories are usually accurate when published in the fall, but suppose the study is being done in the spring. The directory may contain errors and omissions because some people will have withdrawn or left since the directory was published, while others will have enrolled or been hired. Usually university directories don't mention the families of students or employees. Just how much inaccuracy one can tolerate in choosing a sampling frame is a

With the growing number of people in cell-phone-only households, the printed phone directory has become obsolete as a sample frame for household research. Specialized business directories are still viable options for business-to-business research.

©Olly/Shutterstock

matter of judgment. You might use the directory anyway, ignoring the fact that it is not a fully accurate list. However, if the directory is a year old, the amount of error might be unacceptable. One way to make the sampling frame for the Metro U study more representative of the population would be to secure a supplemental list of the new students and employees as well as a list of the withdrawals and terminations from Metro U's registrar and human resources databases. You could then craft your own sample frame by adding and deleting information from the original directory. Or, if their privacy policies permit, you might just request a current listing from each of these offices and combine these lists to create your sampling frame.

A greater distortion would be introduced if a branch campus population were included in the Metro U directory. This would be an example of a too-inclusive frame—that is, a frame that includes many cases other than the ones in which we are interested. A university directory that includes faculty and staff retirees is another example of a too-inclusive sampling frame.

Often you have to accept a sampling frame that includes people or cases beyond those in whom you are interested. You may have to use a telephone directory to draw a sample of business telephone numbers. Fortunately, this is easily resolved. You draw a sample from the larger population and then use a screening procedure to eliminate those who are not members of the group you wish to study.

The Metro U dining club survey is an example of a sampling frame problem that is readily solved. Often one finds this task much more of a challenge. Suppose you need to sample the members of an ethnic group, say, Asians residing in Little Rock, Arkansas. There is probably no list of this population. Although you may use the general city directory, sampling from this too-inclusive frame would be costly and inefficient because Asians represent only a small fraction of Little Rock's population. The screening task would be monumental. Because ethnic groups frequently cluster in certain neighborhoods, you might identify these areas of concentration and then use a city directory, which is organized by street address, to draw the sample.

It is not until we begin talking about sampling frames and sampling methods that international research starts to deviate. International researchers often face far more difficulty in locating or building sample frames. Countries differ in how each defines its population; this affects census and relevant population counts.[2] Some countries purposefully over sample to facilitate the analysis of issues of particular national interest; this means we need to be cautious in interpreting published aggregate national figures.[3] These distinctions and difficulties may lead the researcher to choose nonprobability techniques or different probability techniques than they would choose if doing such research in the United States or other developed countries. In a study that is fielded in numerous countries at the same time, researchers may use different sampling methodologies, resulting in hybrid studies that will need care to be combined. It is common practice to weight sample data in cross-national studies to develop sample data that are representative.[4] Choice of sampling methods is often dictated by culture as much as by communication and technology infrastructure. Just as all advertising campaigns would not be appropriate in all parts of the world, all sampling techniques would not be appropriate in all subcultures. The discussion in this text focuses more on domestic than international research. It is easier to learn the principles of research in an environment that you know versus one in which many students can only speculate. Ethnic and cultural sensitivity should influence every decision of researchers, whether they do research domestically or internationally.

>Define the Number of Cases

The ultimate test of a sampling design is how well any cases we measure represent the characteristics of the target population the design purports to represent.

Sample versus Census

Most people intuitively understand the idea of why drawing a sample works. One taste from a drink tells us whether it is sweet or sour; we don't need to drink the whole glass. If we select a few ads from a magazine, we assume our selection reflects the characteristics of the full set. If some members of our staff favor

>**close**up

Who's Really Taking Your Surveys?

Early in panel development, panelists were offered $100 to $150 to join and participate in qualitative studies. Historically, these participants participated in longer engagements (online qualitative, ethnography studies or face to face in-depth interviews). As random digit dialing became less productive for recruiting respondents and the Internet became more widely used, researchers started using panels—also called communities—to recruit participants for quantitative research. Quantitative respondents who are engaged for much shorter periods are more likely to be paid $1 to $10 per survey completed.

The professional respondent—one who takes repeated surveys—was once considered a deterrent to quality research. "As researchers, " explained Jessica Broome, PhD, principal of Jessica Broome Research, "we wanted to keep the 'cheaters' and 'repeaters' out of our studies, believing they biased results." As decision cycles shorten, the demand for better and more timely information means attracting and retaining qualified participants. During the last three decades, increasingly this means researchers turn to panels, and by design, these participants are asked to participate in numerous studies.

"We wanted to know 'Who are these people willing to take repeated surveys?'" explained Broome. "And given that some surveys are overly long and others poorly designed, 'Why do they do this?'" Broome teamed with Korry Hecht, Director of Research Services, Recollective, a division of Ramius Corporation, to find out what motivates panel respondents and if their motivations are likely to reduce the quality of the information they provide.

The Qualitative Study

Broome and Hecht designed a multistage study that drew participants from multiple panel providers, including Critical Mix, Schlesinger Associates, and Swagbucks. "We started with a 5-day online qualitative community study with 20 people to explore what got them started as a survey panelist and what kept them going," explained Hecht. "While money is a motivator in keeping panelists engaged, they also shared the influences of intrinsic motivators like fun, feeling useful, contributing to important decisions, and participation being more interesting than time spent on social media."

For any particular study, panelists are often screened exclusively on demographics. "Because participants derive intrinsic benefits, panelists will sometimes fudge on screening information in an attempt to be included in a study, " shared Broome. When a panelist doesn't meet the desired demographic parameters, they are told "You don't qualify" but are rarely told why. "But once they are included, " explained Broome, "participants

claim honesty drives their responses; they think lying on survey questions would undermine the study."

"Often panelists expressed feeling abused, misled, and disrespected. For example, when they are told about survey length, they often felt deceived when a promised 15-minute survey took 45 minutes, or when the survey was not only long, but boring," explained Broome. Increasingly, panelists in quantitative studies are tech-savvy. "They understand what current technology should permit a survey company to do—like eliminate the need to ask demographic questions repeatedly in the same survey process or use earlier answers to filter later questions, " claimed Hecht. "They basically think researchers can make the experience so much better." "The research industry needs their insights, but can treat panelists with disdain," claimed Broome.

The Quantitative Study

Broome and Hecht followed their qualitative exploration study with Phase 2, a mobile-optimized quantitative study of 1,499 participants, also drawn from various panel providers and fielded by Propeller Insights. Each panelist took a topical survey that included a creativity assessment. Additionally, half the group (750) took a VARK assessment. VARK assesses visual, aural/audio, read/write, and kinesthetic learning preferences through a series of learning scenario questions. Creativity was assessed through a battery of 38 statements requiring agreement or disagreement, as well as a checklist of 54 descriptors. "We discovered that participants didn't favor any one of the learning approaches, nor were they outliers on the creativity assessment," shared Broome.

>**close**up**cont'd**

Broome and Hecht's Phase 2 research revealed factors essential for reducing participant discontinuation: Don't ask screening questions within a survey once a participant has answered a detailed screener to qualify; merge the data. Participants don't care that different companies do different aspects of the research; they want researchers to avoid duplication. Don't ask essentially the same question in different ways; once is enough. Use previous question responses to determine later questions asked; panelists are willing to share their thoughts, behaviors, and lives but don't want their time wasted. Participants have different preferences and styles; let them respond as they wish—with text or video, exclusively on a mobile device or a computer. "They shared lots of ideas for making surveys more engaging and interesting," claimed Hecht, "including, adding music or video, getting rid of grid questions, and reducing survey time to 15 minutes or less."

Using information extracted from an open question and analyzed with OdinText, Phase 2 research also revealed that "most participants were a member of one or two panels but struggled to remain engaged with their panels," shared Hecht. "Participants appreciate feeling like a valued part of a full process, not just an interchangeable cog in a wheel. They like to participate in studies that are interesting to them and about products or services that are relevant to their daily lives—knowledge is a powerful motivator." Many also cited meeting interesting people and hearing different viewpoints as motivation. "They also love learning the results of studies they participate in and understanding why we as researchers do what we do or ask what we ask," shared Broome.

Recently, a SurveyMonkey study also found panelists gave thoughtful, consistent answers over time. It released results of a 1,000-person international panel assessment study, using three surveys with the same respondents, one in each of three sequential months, which checked for quality-reducing behaviors like straight lining (repeatedly choosing the same answer choice in matrix questions), poor open response validity (responding with nonhelpful, gibberish answers), and whether they were unfocused or not paying attention. Of the panelists, 97 percent, 97 percent, and 94 percent or more passed each of these tests, respectively, with no difference between men and women. And in terms of response reliability, over the three waves of surveys, in 23 indicators SurveyMonkey tracked, only three items showed significantly significant change among U.S. participants: time-to-complete, choice of the "other" response, and attitude about "moral acceptability of alcohol use."

jessicabroomeresearch.com; recollective.com; surveymonkey.com

a particular software training strategy, we infer that others will also. The basic idea of taking a sample is that by selecting some cases in a population, we may draw conclusions about the entire target population.

There are several compelling reasons for using a **sample** (a subset of the target population) rather than a **census** (all cases within a population), including (1) lower cost, (2) greater speed of data collection, (3) availability of population cases, and (4) greater accuracy of results. The advantages of taking a sample over a census are less compelling when two conditions exist: (1) a census is feasible due to a small target population and (2) a census is necessary when the cases are quite different from each other.[5] When the population is small and variable, any sample we draw may not be representative of the population from which it is drawn. The resulting values we calculate from the sample are incorrect as estimates of the population values.

Lower Cost

The economic advantages of taking a sample rather than a census are massive. Consider the cost of taking a census. The 2020 U.S. Census of the Population is expected to cost as much as $30 billion, barring any natural disasters and using 2010 costs as a barometer; the Census Bureau's own estimate is $22 billion.[6] By any reasonable standard, continuing to take a census of the population every 10 years is unsustainable. Is it any wonder that researchers in all types of organizations ask, "Why should we spend thousands of dollars interviewing thousands of employees in our company if we can find out what we need to know by asking only a few hundred?"

Greater Speed of Data Collection

Due to the smaller number of cases in a sample, using a sample drawn from a target population will always take less time than conducting a census.

>**Exhibit 5-5** Sources of Error

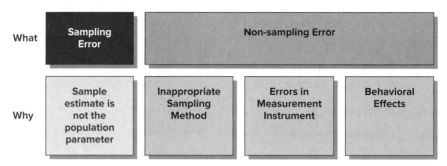

Availability of Population Cases

Some situations require using a sample. Safety is a compelling appeal for most vehicles. Yet we must have evidence to make safety claims. Therefore, we crash-test cars to evaluate bumper strength or efficiency of airbags to prevent injury. In testing for such evidence, we destroy the cars we test. A census would require complete destruction of all cars manufactured. Drawing a sample is also the only process possible if the population is infinite.

Better Quality Results

W. Edwards Deming, who developed the sampling techniques used by the U.S. Census Bureau and the Bureau of Labor Statistics, argues that the quality of a study is often better with a sample than with a census. He suggests samples possess "the possibility of better interviewing (testing), more thorough investigation of missing, wrong, or suspicious information, better supervision, and better processing than is possible with complete coverage."[7] Error related to research comes from two sources: errors related to the sample itself (**sampling error**, or estimates of a variable drawn from a sample differ from true value of a population parameter) and error not related to the sample but to all other decisions made in the research design (**nonsampling error**). As Exhibit 5-5 depicts, and research supports, nonsampling error often exceeds sampling error.[8] For a sample to be valid, it must offer both accuracy and precision. The U.S. Bureau of the Census, while mandated to take a census of the population every 10 years, shows its confidence in sampling by taking sample surveys to check the accuracy of its census. The U.S. Bureau of the Census knows that in a census, segments of the population are seriously undercounted.

Accuracy

Accuracy is the degree to which bias is absent from the sample. When the sample is drawn properly, the measure of behavior, attitudes, or knowledge (the measurement variables) of some cases will be less than (thus, underestimate) the measure of those same variables drawn from the population. Also, the measure of the behavior, attitudes, or knowledge of other cases will be more than the population values (thus, overestimate them). Variations in these sample values offset each other, resulting in a sample value that is close to the population value. Thus an accurate (unbiased) sample is one in which the underestimators offset the overestimators. For these offsetting effects to occur, however, there must be enough cases in the sample, and they must be drawn in a way that favors neither overestimation nor underestimation. Only when the population is small, accessible, and highly variable is accuracy likely to be greater with a census than a sample.

For example, assume in the Metro U study you measured likelihood to join the dining club. Hypothetically, you could measure via sample or census. In a hypothetical census, 32 percent of the population (currently enrolled students and current employees) said they would join. However, 52 percent of a sample made that choice. With both results for comparison, you would know that your sample was not representative because it significantly overestimated the population value of 32 percent. Without the census information, you might not know that you have significant error. Unfortunately, in most studies taking a census is not feasible, so we need an estimate of the amount of error.[9]

Systematic variance has been defined as "the variation in measures due to some known or unknown influences that 'cause' the scores to lean in one direction more than another."[10] Homes on the corner of the block, for example, are often larger and more valuable than those within the block. Thus, a sample that selects only corner homes will cause us to overestimate home values in the area.

Increasing the sample size can reduce systematic variance as a cause of error. However, even the larger size won't reduce error if the sample frame from which you draw your cases is biased. The classic example of a sample with systematic variance was the Literary Digest presidential election poll in 1936, in which more than 2 million people participated. The poll predicted Alfred Landon would defeat Franklin Roosevelt for the presidency of the United States. Your memory is correct; we've never had a president named Alfred Landon. The poll drew its sample from telephone owners, who were in the middle and upper classes—at the time, the bastion of the Republican Party—while Roosevelt appealed to the much larger working class, whose members could not afford to own phones and typically voted for the Democratic Party candidate.

Precision

A second criterion of a valid sample is precision of estimate. Researchers accept that no sample will fully represent its population in all respects. However, to interpret the findings of research, we need a measure of how closely the sample estimate represents the population parameter on any variable of interest. The numerical descriptors that describe samples may be expected to differ from those that describe populations because of random fluctuations inherent in the sampling process. Sampling error reflects the influence of chance in drawing the sample cases. Sampling error is what is left after all known sources of systematic variance have been accounted for. In theory, sampling error consists of random fluctuations only, although some unknown systematic variance may be included when too many or too few cases possess a particular characteristic.

Precision is measured by the standard error of estimate, a type of standard deviation measurement; the smaller the standard error of estimate, the higher is the precision of the sample. The ideal sample produces a small standard error of estimate. However, not all types of sample design provide estimates of precision, and samples of the same size can produce different amounts of error.

Sample Size

So assume you have chosen a sample rather than a census. Much folklore surrounds the question: How many cases should comprise your sample. The most pervasive myths are (1) a sample must be large or it is not representative and (2) a sample should bear some proportional relationship to the size of the population from which it is drawn. With nonprobability samples, researchers use subgroups, rules of thumb, and budget considerations to settle on a sample size. In probability sampling, how large a sample should be is a function of the variation in the population parameters under study and the estimating precision needed by the researcher. Some principles that influence sample size include:

- The greater the dispersion or variance within the population, the larger the sample must be to provide estimation precision.
- The greater the desired precision of the estimate, the larger the sample must be.
- The narrower or smaller the error range, the larger the sample must be.
- The higher the desired confidence level in the estimate, the larger the sample must be.
- The greater the number of subgroups of interest within a sample, the greater the sample size must be, as each subgroup must meet minimum sample size requirements.

Cost considerations influence decisions about the size and type of sample and the data collection methods. Probability sample surveys incur list costs for sample frames, callback costs, and a variety of other costs that are unnecessary when nonprobability samples are used. As research has budgetary constraints, this may encourage a researcher to use a nonprobability sample. When the data collection method is changed, the amount and type of data that can be obtained also change. Note the effect of a $2,000 budget on hypothetical sampling considerations:[11]

- Simple random sampling: $25 per interview; 80 completed interviews.
- Telephone interviews: $10 per participant; 200 completed interviews.
- Self-administered questionnaire: $12 per participant; 167 completed instruments.
- Geographic cluster sampling: $20 per interview; 100 completed interviews.

The investment required to open the dining club at Metro U justifies the more careful probability approach which means the researcher needs a quality sample frame. See the chapter appendix, Calculate the Sample Size.

If a census is chosen, then the researcher need not determine sample method or size. For most business research, however, we use samples. The remainder of the chapter will focus on sampling designs using samples.

>Define the Sampling Method

The researcher faces a basic choice in **sampling method:** a probability sample or nonprobability sample. Any discussion of the relative merits of probability versus nonprobability sampling clearly shows the technical superiority of the former. Yet businesses often use nonprobability methods.

Key to the difference between nonprobability and probability samples is the term *random*. In the dictionary, *random* is defined as "without pattern"or as "haphazard." In sampling, random means something else entirely. **Probability sampling** is based on the concept of random selection—a controlled procedure that assures that each case is given a known nonzero chance of selection. This procedure is never haphazard. Only probability samples provide estimates of precision. When a researcher is making a decision that will influence the expenditure of thousands, if not millions, of dollars, an estimate of precision is critical. Under such conditions, we can have substantial confidence that the sample is representative of the population from which it is drawn. In addition, with probability sample designs, we can estimate an error range within which the population parameter is expected to fall. Thus, we can reduce not only the chance for sampling error, but also estimate the range of probable sampling error present. Also, only probability samples offer the opportunity to generalize the findings to the population of interest from the sample population. Although exploratory research does not necessarily demand this, explanatory, descriptive, and causal studies do.

Alternatively, **nonprobability sampling** is arbitrary and subjective; when we choose subjectively, we usually do so with a pattern or scheme in mind (e.g., only talking with department heads or only talking with women). Each member of the target population does not have a known nonzero chance of being included. Allowing data collectors to use their judgment in drawing records or choosing participants is arbitrary. Early Internet samples had all the drawbacks of nonprobability samples. Those individuals who frequented the Internet were not representative of most target populations, because far more young, technically-savvy men frequented the Internet than did any other demographic group. As Internet access has reached saturation, with some estimates near 88 percent in the United States, this concern is diminished.[12] Such samples now closely approximate non-Internet samples. Of increasing concern, however, is what the Bureau of the Census labels the "great digital divide"—low-income and ethnic subgroups' underrepresentation in their use of technology compared to the general population.[13] Additionally, many Internet samples were, and still are, drawn substantially from panels or communities. These are composed of individuals who have self-selected to become part of a pool of individuals interested in participating in online research. There is much discussion among professional researchers about whether Internet samples should be treated as probability or nonprobability samples. Some admit that any sample drawn from a panel is more appropriately treated as a nonprobability sample; others vehemently disagree, citing the success of such well-known panels as Nielsen Media's People Meter panels for radio audience assessment.[14] As you study the differences here, you should draw your own conclusion.

>**Exhibit 5-6** Types of Sampling Designs

Case Selection	Representation Basis	
	Probability	**Nonprobability**
Unrestricted	Simple random	Convenience
Restricted	Complex random	Purposive
	• Systematic	• Judgment
	• Cluster	• Quota
	• Stratified	• Snowball
	• Double	

With a probability sample, a researcher can make probability-based confidence estimates of various parameters that cannot be made with nonprobability samples. Choosing a probability sampling technique has several consequences. A researcher must follow appropriate procedures so that:

• Interviewers or others cannot modify the selections made.

• Only the selected cases from the original sampling frame are included.

• Substitutions are excluded except as clearly specified and controlled according to predetermined protocols.

Despite all due care, the actual sample drawn will not match perfectly the probability sample that is originally planned. Some people will refuse to participate, and others will be difficult, if not impossible, to find. Thus, no matter how careful we are in replacing those who refuse or are never located, sampling error is likely to rise.

With personnel records available at Metro U and a population that is geographically concentrated, a probability sampling method is possible in the dining club study. University directories are generally available, and the costs of using a simple random sample would not be great here. Then, too, because the researchers are thinking of a major investment in the dining club, they would like to be highly confident they have a representative sample.

The researcher makes several decisions when choosing a design that uses a sample. These are represented in Exhibit 5-6. The sampling decisions flow from the management question, the research question, and the specific investigative questions that evolve from the research question. These decisions are influenced by requirements of the project and its objectives, level of risk the researcher can tolerate, budget, time, available resources, and culture.

>Probability Sampling

Simple Random Sampling

The unrestricted, simple random sample is the purest form of probability sampling. Because all probability samples must provide a known nonzero probability of selection for each population element, the **simple random sample** is considered a special case in which each population element has a known and equal chance of selection.

$$\text{Probability of selection} = \frac{\text{Sample size}}{\text{Population size}}$$

The Metro U dining club study has a population of 20,000. If the sample size is 300, the probability of selection is 1.5 percent (300/20,000 = 0.015). In this section, we use the simple random sample to build a foundation for understanding sampling procedures and choosing probability samples. The simple random sample is easy to implement with automatic dialing (random dialing) and with computerized voice response systems. However, it requires a list of population elements, can be time-consuming and expensive, and can require larger sample sizes than other probability methods. Exhibit 5-7 provides an overview of the steps involved in choosing a random sample.

>**Exhibit 5-7** How to Choose a Random Sample

Selecting a *random sample* is accomplished with the aid of computer software, a table of random numbers, or a calculator with a random number generator. Drawing slips out of a hat or Ping-Pong balls from a drum serves as an alternative *if every case in the sampling frame has an equal chance of selection*. Mixing the slips (or balls) and returning them between every selection ensures that every case is just as likely to be selected as any other.

A table of random numbers (such as Appendix D, Exhibit D-10) is a practical solution when no software program is available. Random number tables contain digits that have no systematic organization. Whether you look at rows, columns, or diagonals, you will find neither sequence nor order. Exhibit C-1 in Appendix C is arranged into 10 columns of five-digit strings, but this is solely for readability.

Assume the researchers want a sample of 10 from a population of 95 cases. How will the researcher begin?

1   *Assign each case within the sampling frame a unique number* from 01 to 95.

2   *Identify a random start from the random number table*. Drop a pencil point-first onto the table with closed eyes. Let's say the pencil dot lands on the eighth column from the left and 10 numbers down from the top of Exhibit C-1, marking the five digits 05067.

3   *Determine how the digits in the random number table will be assigned to the sampling frame* to choose the specified sample size (researchers agree to read the first two digits in this column downward until 10 are selected).

4   *Select the sample cases from the sampling frame* (05, 27, 69, 94, 18, 61, 36, 85, 71, and 83) using the above process. (The digit 94 appeared twice and the second instance was omitted; 00 was omitted because the sampling frame started with 01.)

Other approaches to selecting digits are endless: horizontally right to left, bottom to top, diagonally across columns, and so forth. Computer selection of a simple random sample will be more efficient for larger projects.

Complex Probability Sampling

The limitations of simple random sampling have led to the development of alternative designs that are superior to the simple random design in statistical and/or economic efficiency.

A more efficient sample in a statistical sense is one that provides a given precision (standard error of the mean or proportion) with a smaller sample size. A sample that is economically more efficient is one that provides a desired precision at a lower dollar cost. We achieve this with designs that enable us to lower the costs of data collecting, usually through reduced travel expense and interviewer time.

In the discussion that follows, four alternative probability sampling approaches are considered: (1) systematic sampling, (2) stratified random sampling, (3) cluster sampling, and (4) double sampling.

Systematic Sampling

A versatile form of probability sampling is **systematic sampling**. In this approach, every kth element in the population is sampled, beginning with a random start of any case in the range of 1 to k. The kth case, or **skip interval**, is determined by dividing the sample size into the population size to obtain the skip pattern applied to the sampling frame. This assumes that the sample frame is an accurate list of the population; if not, the number of cases in the sample frame is substituted for population size.

$$k = \text{Skip interval} = \frac{\text{Population size}}{\text{Sample size}}$$

The major advantage of systematic sampling is its simplicity and flexibility. It is easier to instruct field interviewers to choose the dwelling unit listed on every kth line of a listing sheet than it is to use a random numbers table. With systematic sampling, there is no need to number the entries in a large personnel file before drawing a sample. To draw a systematic sample, do the following:

- Identify, list, and number the cases in the population.
- Identify the skip interval (k).
- Identify the random start.
- Draw a sample by choosing every kth entry.

Invoices or customer accounts can be sampled by using the last digit or a combination of digits of an invoice or customer account number. Time sampling is also easily accomplished.

Systematic sampling can introduce subtle biases. A concern with systematic sampling is the possible *periodicity* in the population that parallels the sampling ratio. In sampling restaurant sales of dessert by drawing days of the year, a skip interval of 7 would bias results, no matter which day provides the random start. A less obvious case might involve a survey in an area of apartment buildings where the typical pattern is eight apartments per building. A skip interval of 8 could easily over sample some types of apartments and under sample others.

Another difficulty may arise when there is a *monotonic trend* in the population cases. That is, the population list varies from the smallest to the largest case or vice versa. Even a chronological list may have this effect if a measure has trended in one direction over time. Whether a systematic sample drawn under these conditions provides a biased estimate of the population mean or proportion depends on the initial random draw. Assume that a list of 2,000 commercial banks is created, arrayed from the largest to the smallest, from which a sample of 50 must be drawn for analysis. A skip interval of 40 (2,000 divided by 50) beginning with a random start at 16 would exclude the 15 largest banks and give a small-size bias to the findings.

The only protection against these subtle biases is constant vigilance by the researcher. Some ways to avoid such bias include:

- Randomize the target population before drawing the sample (e.g., order the banks by name rather than size).
- Change the random start several times in the sampling process.
- Replicate a selection of different samples.

Although systematic sampling has some theoretical problems, from a practical point of view it is usually treated as equivalent to a simple random sample. When similar cases are grouped within the sampling frame, systematic sampling is statistically more efficient than a simple random sample. This might occur if the listed cases are ordered chronologically, by size, by class, and so on. Under these conditions, the sample approaches a proportionate stratified sample. The effect of this ordering is more pronounced on the results of cluster samples than for other samples and may call for a proportionate stratified sampling formula.[15]

Stratified Random Sampling

Most populations can be segregated into several mutually exclusive subpopulations, or strata. The process by which the sample is constrained to include cases from each of the segments is called **stratified random sampling.** University students can be divided by their class level, school or major, gender, and so forth. After a population is divided into the appropriate strata, a simple random sample can be taken within each stratum. The results from the study can then be weighted (based on the proportion of the strata to the population) and combined into appropriate population estimates.

There are three reasons a researcher chooses a stratified random sample: (1) to increase a sample's statistical efficiency, (2) to provide adequate data for analyzing the various subpopulations or strata, and (3) to enable different research methods and procedures to be used in different strata.[16]

Stratification is usually more efficient statistically than simple random sampling and at worst it is equal to it. With the ideal stratification, each stratum is homogeneous internally (cases are similar) and heterogeneous with other strata (cases of one stratum are not similar to cases within another stratum). This might occur in a sample that includes members of several distinct ethnic groups. In this instance, stratification makes a pronounced improvement in statistical efficiency.

Stratification is also useful when the researcher wants to study the characteristics of certain population subgroups. Thus, if one wishes to draw some conclusions about activities in the different classes of a student body, stratified sampling would be used. Similarly, if a restaurant were interested in testing menu changes to attract younger patrons while retaining its older, loyal customers, stratified sampling using age and prior patronage as descriptors would be appropriate. Stratification is also called for when different methods of data collection are applied in different parts of the population, a research design that is becoming increasingly common. This might occur when we survey company employees at the

>closeup

Keynote Systems Tests the Power of Search

Twice yearly Keynote Systems evaluates the performance of five search engines, including market leader Google, AOL Search, Yahoo! Search, Ask.com, and MSN Search. Keynote, a "worldwide leader in services that improve online business performance and communications technologies," uses an online panel to perform "interactive Web site tests to assess user experience," profiling not only how people use search engines, but why they search as they do. Keynote allocates participants and experimental treatments as in Exhibit CU-1: 2,000 people are randomly drawn from more than 160,000 panel members and invited to participate via e-mail. They are assigned randomly to five groups of 400; each group is assigned a particular search engine. Whether participants have any experience with that particular engine is not a criterion for assignment. Each group is assigned a series of search tasks, starting with a general task—Think about anything you would like to search for; go and search that—to more specific tasks—find a local establishment, a product, an image, and a news item. Each search engine–allocated group essentially performs the same series of tasks. From their activities, Keynote generates 250,000 metrics (including time involved in the search, whether the search was successful, etc.). It matches these metrics to survey data used to measure satisfaction, perceived difficulty, and specific frustrations. From this combined data it develops several indices.

"One of the things we noted from a series of such tests was that Google repeatedly received rave reviews, even in instances where performance measures told a different story," shares senior research consultant Lance Jones. With almost 60 percent market share, Google has strong recognition and tends to set the bar in search site design. Is its brand that powerful that it can influence attitudes even in the face of conflicting performance experience? If the brand is not a factor, which search engine would produce the most satisfying and useful results, the best sponsored results, and the best presentation and design? Keynote wanted to design an experiment that would show the power of the search engine brand. To do that, it needed to remove brand identity from the search results. Its solution was to design a generic-appearing search engine website and results format page, feeding actual search results into its generic format.

For the brand power test (Exhibit CU-2) 2,000 participants were again divided into five groups and assigned one search engine. This time, however, half the participants were assigned to a branded group ($n = 200$) and would see the results with a text line "Results brought to you by Yahoo/Google/Ask, etc."; the other half ($n = 200$) would see the same results but without the brand notation line ($n = 200$). All five search engines were tested using the tasks performed in the standard twice-annual test, but all the results seen by participants were actually generated using the assigned search engine, then fed into the generic results presentation. "The results pages were delivered live and participants would have perceived no difference in elapsed time, as the results were delivered within milliseconds of what the standard search would have delivered," explained Jones. The test produced 1,600 queries that generated 12 distinct metrics.

Source: Lance Jones, senior research consultant.

>**Exhibit CU-1** Participant Allocation in Search Engine Test

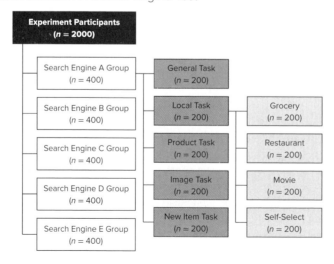

>**close**up**cont'd**

>**Exhibit CU-2** Participant Allocation in Brand Power Test

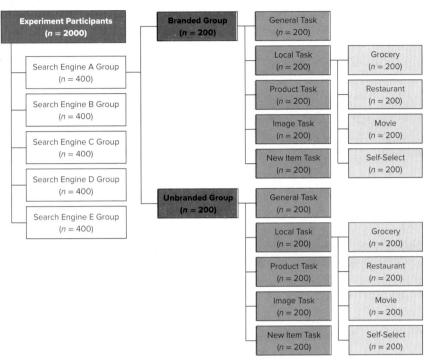

Is a brand powerful? Here are some sample results for Google; keep in mind that the branded group and the unbranded group saw the exact same results pages. On the unbranded group, the calculated Google results satisfaction score was 732 (on a 1,000-point scale), while the branded group delivered an 800; Google's sponsored results satisfaction was 763 (unbranded) compared to 809 (branded); full design satisfaction was 753 (unbranded) compared to 806 (branded). Evaluate the design of this sample.

www.keynote.com

home office with one method but must use a different approach with employees scattered throughout the country or the world.

If data are available on which to base a stratification decision, how shall we go about it?[17] The ideal stratification would be based on the primary variable under study. If the major concern were to learn how often per month patrons would use the Metro U dining club, then the researcher would stratify on the expected number of use occasions. The only difficulty with this idea is that if we knew this information, we would not need to conduct the study. We must, therefore, pick a variable for stratifying that we believe will correlate with the frequency of club use per month, something like days at work or class schedule as an indication of when a sample case might be near campus at mealtimes.

Researchers often have several important variables about which they want to draw conclusions. A reasonable approach is to seek some basis for stratification that correlates well with the major variables. It might be a single variable (class level), or it might be a compound variable (class by gender). In any event, we will have done a good stratifying job if the stratification base maximizes the difference among strata means and minimizes the within-stratum variances for the variables of major concern.

The more strata used, the closer you come to maximizing inter-strata differences (differences between strata) and minimizing intrastratum variances (differences within a given stratum). You must base the decision partially on the number of subpopulation groups about which you wish to draw separate conclusions. Costs of stratification also enter the decision. The more strata you have, the higher the cost of the research project due to the cost associated with more detailed sampling. There is little to be gained in estimating population values when the number of strata exceeds six.[18]

The size of the strata samples is calculated with two pieces of information: (1) how large the total sample should be and (2) how the total sample should be allocated among strata. In deciding how to allocate a total sample among various strata, there are proportionate and disproportionate options.

Proportionate versus Disproportionate Sampling In **proportionate stratified sampling**, each stratum is proportionate to the stratum's share of the total population. This approach is more popular than any of the other stratified sampling procedures. Some reasons for this include:

- It has higher statistical efficiency than a simple random sample.
- It is much easier to carry out than other stratifying methods.
- It provides a self-weighting sample; the population mean or proportion can be estimated simply by calculating the mean or proportion of all sample cases, eliminating the weighting of responses.

On the other hand, proportionate stratified samples often gain little in statistical efficiency if the strata measures and their variances are similar for the major variables under study.

Any stratification that departs from the proportionate relationship is **disproportionate stratified sampling**. There are several disproportionate allocation schemes. One type is a judgmentally determined disproportion based on the idea that each stratum is large enough to secure adequate confidence levels and error range estimates for individual strata. The following table shows the relationship between proportionate and disproportionate stratified sampling.

Stratum	Population	Proportionate Sample	Disproportionate Sample
Male	45%	45%	35%
Female	55	55	65

A researcher makes decisions regarding disproportionate sampling, however, by considering how a sample will be allocated among strata. One author states,

In a given stratum, take a larger sample if the stratum is larger than other strata; the stratum is more variable internally; and sampling is cheaper in the stratum.[19]

If one uses these suggestions as a guide, it is possible to develop an optimal stratification scheme. When there is no difference in intra-stratum variances and when the costs of sampling among strata are equal, the optimal design is a proportionate stratified sample.

While disproportionate stratified sampling is theoretically superior, there is some question as to whether it has wide applicability in a practical sense. If the differences in sampling costs or variances among strata are large, then disproportionate sampling is desirable. It has been suggested that "differences of several-fold are required to make disproportionate sampling worthwhile.[20]

The process for drawing a stratified sample is:

- Determine the variables to use for stratification.
- Determine the proportions of the stratification variables in the population.
- Select proportionate or disproportionate stratification based on project information needs and risks.
- Divide the sampling frame into separate frames for each stratum.
- Randomize the case listing within each stratum's sampling frame.
- Follow random or systematic procedures to draw the sample from each stratum.

Cluster Sampling

In a simple random sample, each population element is selected individually. The population can also be divided into groups of elements with some groups randomly selected for study. This is **cluster sampling.** Cluster sampling differs from stratified sampling in several ways, as indicated in Exhibit 5-8.

>**Exhibit 5-8** Comparison of Stratified and Cluster Sampling

Stratified Sampling	Cluster Sampling
1. We divide the population into a few subgroups.	1. We divide the population into *many* subgroups.
• Each subgroup has *many* cases in it.	• Each subgroup has *few* cases in it.
• Subgroups are selected according to some criterion that is related to the variables under study.	• Subgroups are selected according to some criterion of ease or availability in data collection.
2. We try to secure *homogeneity* within subgroups.	2. We try to secure *heterogeneity* within subgroups.
3. We try to secure *heterogeneity* between subgroups.	3. We try to secure *homogeneity* between subgroups.
4. We randomly choose *cases* from within each subgroup.	4. We randomly choose several *subgroups* that we then typically study in depth.

Two conditions foster the use of cluster sampling: (1) the need for more economic efficiency than can be provided by simple random sampling and (2) the frequent unavailability of a practical sampling frame listing individual cases.

Statistical efficiency for cluster samples is usually lower than for simple random samples chiefly because clusters often don't meet the need for heterogeneity and, instead, are homogeneous. For example, families in the same block (a typical cluster) are often similar in social class, income level, ethnic origin, and so forth. Although statistical efficiency in most cluster sampling may be low, economic efficiency is often great enough to overcome this weakness. The criterion, then, is the net relative efficiency resulting from the trade-off between economic and statistical factors. It may take 690 interviews with a cluster design to give the same precision as 424 simple random interviews. But if it costs only $5 per interview in the cluster situation and $10 in the simple random case, the cluster sample is more attractive ($3,450 versus $4,240).

Area Sampling Much research involves populations that can be identified with some geographic area. When this occurs, it is possible to use **area sampling**, the most important form of cluster sampling. This method overcomes the problems of both high sampling cost and the unavailability of a practical

A low-cost, frequently used method, the area cluster sample may use geographic sample units (e.g., city blocks).

©Tetra Images/Alamy

sampling frame for individual cases. Area sampling methods have been applied to national populations, county populations, and even smaller areas where there are well-defined political or natural boundaries.

Suppose you want to survey the adult residents of a city. You would seldom be able to secure a listing of such individuals. It would be simple, however, to get a detailed city map that shows the blocks of the city. If you take a sample of these blocks, you are also taking a sample of the adult residents of the city.

Design   In designing cluster samples, including area samples, we must answer several questions:

1. How homogeneous are the resulting clusters?
2. Shall we seek equal-size or unequal-size clusters?
3. How large a cluster shall we take?
4. Shall we use a single-stage or multistage cluster?
5. How large a sample is needed?[1]

1. When clusters are homogeneous, this contributes to low statistical efficiency. Sometimes one can improve this efficiency by constructing clusters to increase intracluster variance. In the dining club study, researchers might have chosen a course as a cluster, choosing to sample all students in that course if it enrolled students of all four class years. Or maybe they could choose a departmental office that had faculty, staff, and administrative positions as well as student workers. In area sampling to increase intra-cluster variance, researchers could combine into a single cluster adjoining blocks that contain different income groups or social classes.

2. A cluster sample may be composed of clusters of equal or unequal size. The theory of clustering is that the means of sample clusters are unbiased estimates of the population mean. This is more often true when clusters are naturally equal, such as households in city blocks. While one can deal with clusters of unequal size, it may be desirable to reduce or counteract the effects of unequal size. There are several approaches to this:

- Combine small clusters and split large clusters until each approximates an average size.
- Stratify clusters by size and choose clusters from each stratum.
- Stratify clusters by size and then subsample, using varying sampling fractions to secure an overall sampling ratio.[21]

3. There is no *a priori* answer to the ideal cluster size question. Comparing the efficiency of differing cluster sizes requires that we discover the different costs for each size and estimate the different variances of the cluster means. Even with single-stage clusters (where the researchers interview or observe every element within a cluster), it is not clear which size (say, 5, 20, or 50) is superior. Some have found that in studies using single-stage area clusters, the optimal cluster size is no larger than the typical city block.[22]

4. Concerning single-stage or multistage cluster designs, for most large-scale area sampling, the tendency is to use multistage designs. Several situations justify drawing a sample within a cluster, in preference to the direct creation of smaller clusters and taking a census of that cluster using one-stage cluster sampling:[23]

- Natural clusters may exist as convenient sampling units yet, for economic reasons, may be larger than the desired size.
- We can avoid the cost of creating smaller clusters in the entire population and confine subsampling to only those large natural clusters.
- The sampling of naturally compact clusters may present practical difficulties. For example, independent interviewing of all members of a household may be impractical.

5. The answer to how many subjects must be interviewed or observed depends heavily on the specific cluster design, and the details can be complicated. Unequal clusters and multistage samples are the chief complications, and their statistical treatment is beyond the scope of this book.[24] Here we will treat only single-stage sampling with equal-size clusters (called *simple cluster sampling*). It is analogous to simple random sampling. We can think of a population as consisting of 20,000 clusters of one student each, or 2,000 clusters of 10 students each, and so on. Assuming the same specifications for precision and confidence, we should expect that the calculation of a probability sample size would be the same for both clusters.

Double Sampling

It may be more convenient or economical to collect some information by sample and then use this information as the basis for selecting a subsample for further study. This procedure is called **double sampling**, (also called *sequential sampling* or *multiphase sampling*) It is usually found with stratified and/or cluster designs. The calculation procedures are described in more advanced texts.

Double sampling can be illustrated by the dining club example. You might use an email survey or another inexpensive survey method to discover who would be interested in joining such a club and the degree of their interest. You might then stratify the interested respondents by degree of interest and subsample among them for intensive interviewing on expected consumption patterns, reactions to various services, and so on. Whether it is more desirable to gather such information by one-stage or two-stage sampling depends largely on the relative costs of the two methods.

Because of the wide range of sampling designs available, it is often difficult to select an approach that meets the needs of the research question and helps to contain the costs of the project. To help with these choices, Exhibit 5-9 may be used to compare the various advantages and disadvantages of probability

>**Exhibit 5-9** Comparison of Probability Sampling Designs

Type	Description	Advantages	Disadvantages
Simple Random Cost: *High* Use: Moderate	Each population case has an equal chance of being selected into the sample. Sample drawn using random number table/generator.	Easy to implement with automatic dialing (random-digit dialing) and with computerized voice response systems.	Requires a listing of population cases. Takes more time to implement. Uses larger sample sizes. Produces larger errors.
Systematic Cost: *Moderate* Use: Moderate	Using a random start, selects a population case and following the sampling skip interval selects every kth case.	Simple to design. Easier to use than the simple random. Easy to determine sampling distribution of mean or proportion.	Periodicity within the population may skew the sample and results. If the population list has a monotonic trend, a biased estimate will result based on the start point.
Stratified Cost: *High* Use: Moderate	Divides population into subpopulations or strata and draws a simple random sample from each stratum. Results may be weighted and combined.	Researcher controls sample size within strata. Increased statistical efficiency. Provides data to represent and analyze subgroups. Enables use of different methods in strata.	Increased error will result if subgroups are selected at different rates. Especially expensive if population strata must be created.
Cluster Cost: *Moderate* Use: High	Population is divided into internally heterogeneous subgroups. Some subgroups are randomly selected for further study.	Provides an unbiased estimate of population parameters if properly done. Economically more efficient than simple random. Lowest cost per sample, especially with geographic clusters. Easy to do without a population list.	Often lower statistical efficiency (more error) due to subgroups being homogeneous rather than heterogeneous.
Double (Sequential or multiphase) Cost: *Moderate* Use: *Moderate*	Process includes collecting data from any type sample. Based on the information found, a subsample is selected for further study.	May reduce costs if first stage results in enough data to stratify or cluster the population.	Increased costs if indiscriminately used.

sampling. Nonprobability sampling techniques are covered in the next section. They are used frequently and offer the researcher the benefit of low cost. However, they are not based on a theoretical framework and do not operate from statistical theory; consequently, they produce selection bias and nonrepresentative samples. Despite these weaknesses, their widespread use demands their mention here.

>Nonprobability Sampling

With a subjective approach like nonprobability sampling, the probability of selecting population cases is unknown. There are a variety of ways to choose persons or cases to include in the sample. Often we allow the choice of subjects to be made by field workers on the scene. When this occurs, there is greater opportunity for bias to enter the sample selection procedure and to distort the findings of the study. Also, we cannot estimate any range within which to expect the population parameter. Given the technical advantages of probability sampling over nonprobability sampling, why would anyone choose the latter? There are some practical reasons for using the less precise methods.

We may use nonprobability sampling procedures because they satisfactorily meet the sampling objectives. Although a random sample will give us a true cross section of the population, this may not be the objective of the research. If there is no desire or need to generalize to a population parameter, then there is much less concern about whether the sample fully reflects the population. Often researchers have more limited objectives. They may be looking only for the range of conditions or for examples of dramatic variations. This is especially true in exploratory research in which one may wish to contact only certain persons or cases that are clearly atypical.

Additional reasons for choosing nonprobability over probability sampling are cost and time. Probability sampling clearly calls for more planning and repeated callbacks to ensure that each selected case is contacted. These activities are expensive. Carefully controlled nonprobability sampling often seems to give acceptable results, so the investigator may not even consider probability sampling. While probability sampling may be superior in theory, there are breakdowns in its application. Even carefully stated random sampling procedures may be subject to careless application by the people involved. Thus, the ideal probability sampling may be only partially achieved because of the human element.

It is also possible that nonprobability sampling may be the only feasible alternative. The total population may not be available for study in certain cases. At the scene of a major event, it may be infeasible to attempt to construct a probability sample. A study of past correspondence between two companies must use an arbitrary sample because the full correspondence is normally not available.

In another sense, those who are included in a sample may select themselves. In mail surveys, those who respond may not represent a true cross section of those who receive the questionnaire. The receivers of the questionnaire decide for themselves whether they will participate. In web-based surveys those who volunteer don't always represent the appropriate cross section—that's why screening questions are used before admitting a participant to the sample. There is, however, some of this self-selection in almost all surveys because every respondent chooses whether to be interviewed.

Convenience

Nonprobability samples that are unrestricted are called **convenience samples**. They are the least reliable design but normally the cheapest and easiest sample to draw. Researchers or field workers have the freedom to choose whomever they find: thus, the name "convenience." Examples include informal pools of friends and neighbors, people responding to a newspaper's invitation for readers to state their positions on some public issue, a TV reporter's "person-on-the-street" intercept interviews, or the use of employees to evaluate the taste of a new snack food.

Although a convenience sample has no controls to ensure precision, it may still be a useful procedure. Often you will take such a sample to test ideas or even to gain ideas about a subject of interest. In the early stages of exploratory research, when you are seeking guidance, you might use this approach. The results may present evidence that is so overwhelming that a more sophisticated sampling procedure is unnecessary. In an interview with students concerning some issue of campus concern, you might talk to 25 students selected sequentially. You might discover that the responses are so overwhelmingly one-sided that there is no incentive to interview further.

Purposive Sampling

A nonprobability sample that uses certain criteria to select cases is called *purposive sampling*. There are two major types—judgment sampling and quota sampling.

Judgment sampling occurs when a researcher selects sample members to conform to some criterion. In a study of labor problems, you may want to talk only with those who have experienced on-the-job discrimination. Another example of judgment sampling occurs when election results are predicted from only a few selected precincts that have been chosen because of their predictive record in past elections.

When used in the early stages of an exploratory study, a judgment sample is appropriate. When one wishes to select a biased group for screening purposes, this sampling method is also a good choice. Companies often try out new product ideas on their employees. The rationale is that one would expect the firm's employees to be more favorably disposed toward a new product idea than the public. If the product does not pass this group, it does not have prospects for success in the general market.

Quota sampling is the second type of purposive sampling. We use it to improve representativeness. The logic behind quota sampling is that certain relevant characteristics describe the dimensions of the population. If a nonprobability sample has the same distribution on these characteristics, then it is likely to be representative of the population regarding other variables on which we have no control. Suppose the student body of Metro U is 55 percent female and 45 percent male. The sampling quota would call for sampling students at a 55 to 45 percent ratio.

In most quota samples, researchers specify more than one control dimension. Each should meet two tests: it should (1) have a distribution in the population that we can estimate and (2) be pertinent to the topic studied. We may believe that responses to a question should vary depending on the gender of the respondent. If so, we should seek proportional responses from both men and women. We may also feel that undergraduates differ from graduate students, so this would be a dimension. Other dimensions, such as the student's academic discipline, ethnic group, religious affiliation, and social group affiliation, also may be chosen. Only a few of these controls can be used. To illustrate, suppose we consider the following:

- *Gender:* Two categories—male, female.
- *Class level:* Two categories—graduate, undergraduate.
- *College:* Six categories—arts and science, agriculture, architecture, business, engineering, other.
- *Religion:* Four categories—Protestant, Catholic, Jewish, other.
- *Fraternal affiliation:* Two categories—member, nonmember.
- *Family social-economic class:* Three categories—upper, middle, lower.

In an extreme case, we might ask an interviewer to find a male undergraduate business student who is Catholic, a fraternity member, and from an upper-class home. All combinations of these six factors would call for 288 such cells to consider. This type of control is known as *precision control*. It gives greater assurance that a sample will be representative of the population. However, it is costly and too difficult to carry out with more than three variables.

When we wish to use more than three control dimensions, we should depend on *frequency* control. With this form of control, the overall percentage of those with each characteristic in the sample should match the percentage holding the same characteristic in the population. No attempt is made to find a combination of specific characteristics in a single person. In frequency control, we would probably find that the following sample array is an adequate reflection of the population:

	Population	Sample
Male	65%	67%
Married	15	14
Undergraduate	70	72
Campus resident	30	28
Greek member	25	23
Protestant	39	42

Quota sampling has several weaknesses. First, the idea that quotas on some variables assume a representativeness on others is argument by analogy. It gives no assurance that the sample is representative of the variables being studied. Often, the data used to provide controls might be outdated or inaccurate. There is also a practical limit on the number of simultaneous controls that can be applied to ensure precision. Finally, the choice of subjects is left to field workers to make on a judgmental basis. They may choose only friendly looking people, people who are convenient to them, and so forth.

Despite the problems with quota sampling, it is widely used by opinion pollsters and business researchers. Probability sampling is usually much more costly and time-consuming. Advocates of quota sampling argue that although there is some danger of systematic bias, the risks are usually not that great. Where predictive validity has been checked (e.g., in election polls), quota sampling has been generally satisfactory.

Snowball

This design has found a niche in recent years in applications where respondents are difficult to identify and are best located through referral networks. It is also especially appropriate for some qualitative studies. In the initial stage of **snowball sampling**, individuals are discovered and may or may not be selected through probability methods. This group is then used to refer the researcher to others who possess similar characteristics and who, in turn, identify others. Similar to a reverse search for bibliographic sources, the "snowball" gathers subjects as it rolls along. Various techniques are available for selecting a nonprobability snowball with provisions for error identification and statistical testing. Let's consider a brief example.

The high end of the U.S. audio market is composed of several small firms that produce ultra-expensive components used in recording and playback of live performances. A risky new technology for improving digital signal processing is being contemplated by one firm. Through its contacts with a select group of recording engineers and electronics designers, the first-stage sample may be identified for interviewing. Subsequent interviewees are likely to reveal critical information for product development and marketing.

Variations on snowball sampling have been used to study drug cultures, teenage gang activities, power elites, community relations, insider trading, and other applications where respondents are difficult to identify and contact.

>Define the Selection and Recruiting Protocols

Whether the researcher chooses a census or sample, selection and recruiting answers the following questions:

- How will the researcher select cases (from a sample frame or without a sample frame)?
- How will each desired case/gatekeeper be contacted?
- How will the case/gatekeeper be convinced to participate?
- What follow-up procedures will be used to guarantee the case/gatekeeper completes the research?

The sampling methodology often has specific protocols for drawing cases (e.g., the simple random sample, the stratified sample, etc.); we've given you these in the earlier section. If the chosen method doesn't have such a protocol—as with nonprobability samples—you must create one. Will the data

Percent of U.S. Households Accessible by Phone Method of Sampling Invitation

Landline and Cell Phone	Cell Phone Only
39.4%	50.4%
Landline Phone Only	**Neither Cell nor Landline**
6.5%	3.3%

>**pic**profile

Mixed-access sampling means that multiple methods are used to invite participants to a research study—phone, email, mobile or wireless, addressed based/mail, etc. According to the CDC, approximately 97% of possible participants are reachable by phone, while on 87% are reachable online. Mixed-access sampling reduces non-coverage error and nonresponse error. Once a participant is recruited, regardless of the means, he or she may complete the study by a different mode (e.g., recruited by phone but take a survey online). Sample recruitment is increasingly done by mixed access.

www.surveysampling.com, www.pewresarch.org, www.cdc.gov

collector have the latitude to choose anyone to participate, or will they need to follow specific guidelines? In the Metro U study, if we use registrar and personnel lists for accuracy, systematic or stratified sampling protocols would be appropriate.

Research shows that participants are research weary. This means you may face difficulties gaining compliance and cooperation. Most researchers will tell you participants need to feel that they are part of something bigger than themselves in order to give of their time and expertise. They also may need to be offered an incentive for sharing their ideas and experiences. In the Metro U study, we could compel faculty to participate due to their employment, but it might backfire. It would be better to encourage participation as a means for the university to address financial issues (as they are plaguing many colleges). For students, we will need some other means of enticement.

Some individuals actually enjoy participating in research, feeling they have much to contribute when they are knowledgeable about the topic. These individuals often volunteer for research panels or join communities of like-minded individuals. They have volunteered, so recruiting them is not difficult; keeping them engaged so that they follow through during a multi-activity research study is more problematic. To keep research participants engaged, researchers need to have procedures in place (e.g, follow-up emails or phone calls) to keep in touch with participants. For this group, an inducement to concluding a research project is the promise to share some or all of the results; this often works when the participant/gatekeeper is a business manager or professional. Finally, a charitable gift in the participant's name is gaining favor as an incentive; this might work for faculty in the Metro U study. Food incentives often work for students. And both students and faculty would likely respond to money as an incentive.

We often use email or phone to contact potential cases or gatekeepers. The PicProfile in this chapter offers an example done by email. When your target population is a person, they will often inquire about why they were chosen. If the research sponsor is willing, researchers might divulge the sample frame, or at least its essence to the potential case as a means to recruit them (e.g., "You have posted on our Facebook in the last two weeks" or "You have a Plenti loyalty card"). In the Metro U study, email contacts would be appropriate for both students and faculty.

Research for Good: Using Charity as an Incentive

If you could feed a hungry child or prevent the euthanasia of a dog by taking a survey, would you?

Researchers have been using online panels to draw samples for Web, email, and mobile surveys for the last decade. Most of these panels are developed using three sources: advertising networks (sample providers advertise via the web, e-mail, and other media to attract individuals who are willing to participate in surveys), loyalty programs (a sponsor company uses its own list of individuals who are part of its loyalty efforts and recruit them to take surveys), and social media (sample providers use Facebook, Twitter, and numerous other social media to recruit participants). Sampling firms under the current model employing these sources often incentivize their participants with money, Internet currency or points, or prizes. Unfortunately, one of the drawbacks is a small pool of individuals—even though in the millions—from which thousands of firms are drawing their participants.

The founding partners of Research for Good (RFG) were concerned that people receiving a personal incentive to give their opinion tend to only represent a particular segment of the population. Also, there was the ongoing industry concern about the development of "professional respondents"—when volunteer participants are recruited by hundreds of sampling companies in roughly the same three ways to meet an ever-growing demand for survey participants. RFG was also concerned about social responsibility. So, it developed an incentivized sampling model that uses charitable donations to attract uniquely different respondents. Its SaySo for Good panel draws on the 90 percent of U.S. and Canadian adults who support at least one charity. When joining the panel, each participant chooses a charity to receive their survey incentive. The RFG database of charities includes every government-registered charity in both the U.S. and Canada. RFG delivers to the specified charity $1.00 or 25 percent of the budgeted cost of a per

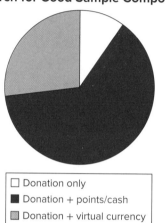

Research for Good Sample Composition

☐ Donation only
■ Donation + points/cash
▨ Donation + virtual currency

completed survey for each participant (i.e., if a completed survey is budgeted at $8.00 per participant, then the charity receives $2.00).

RFG has discovered that participants attracted by charity incentives are different—in both behavior and attitude—than those attracted to a research panel by other means. These survey takers tend to be cause-minded, are financial supporters or volunteers to charities, and are not likely to be motivated by typical cash or prize incentives. Their response rates are higher, as well as their completion rates. And they are infrequent survey takers, reducing the concern about "professional respondents." RFG now counts thousands of charity-incentivized members in its panel. "By attracting new participants, we will generate better data quality while we serve the greater good, " emphasized co-founder Sean Case. As a result, RFG now composes its samples by including this charity-incentive model.

www.researchforgood.com; www.saysoforgood.com

>Ethical Issues and Their Solutions

Ethical issues in relation to sampling fall into three broad categories: deception, incentives, and quality. Many studies in business require that the sponsor not be revealed (sponsor nondisclosure) and that the purpose be protected (purpose nondisclosure); participant deception is often the method to ensure the first, while a consent agreement is a means to the second. If the sponsor permits, after-research debriefing is one solution available for deception. Otherwise, getting informed consent to participate from each participant/gatekeeper is critical.

Incentives may be offered to participants, so a researcher must keep those promises as soon as possible. Quality is the responsibility of both the participant and the researcher. For the participant, truthfully answering screening questions to ensure they are the correct participant is critical and keeping their participation confidential (if that was a condition of participation). Quality is also dependent on researchers (1) using the best sample frame available and (2) conscientiously following selection protocols, whether these are industry standards or project specific.

>summary

LO5-1 Sampling design comprises six primary tasks:

    a. Define the target population and a case.

    b. Define the population parameters of interest.

    c. Identify and evaluate the sample frame or create one.

    d. Define the number of cases needed.

    e. Define the appropriate sampling method.

    f. Define the sampling selection and recruitment protocols.

LO5-2 An effective use of a sample versus a census is based on two premises: (1) enough similarity exists among the cases in a target population that a few of these cases will adequately represent the characteristics of the target population and (2) that although some elements in a sample underestimate a population parameter, others overestimate this value. The result of these tendencies is that a sample statistic is generally a good estimate of a population parameter.

LO5-3 A quality sample has both accuracy and precision. An accurate sample is one in which there is little or no bias or systematic variance. A sample with adequate precision is one that has a sampling error that is within acceptable limits for the study's purpose.

LO5-4 Many sampling techniques are available. They may be classified by their representation basis and element selection techniques.

Element Selection	Representation Basis	
	Probability	**Nonprobability**
Unrestricted	Simple random	Convenience
Restricted	Complex random	Purposive
	• Systematic	• Judgment
	• Cluster	• Quota
	• Stratified	• Snowball
	• Double	

Probability sampling is based on random selection—a controlled procedure that ensures that each population case is given a known nonzero chance of selection. The simplest type of probability approach is simple random sampling. In this design, each case within the target population has an equal chance of being included in a sample. In contrast, nonprobability selection is arbitrary. In unrestricted sampling, each sample case is drawn from the target population without defining criteria. In restricted sampling, the selection process follows more complex rules.

Complex sampling is used when conditions make simple random samples impractical or uneconomical. The four major types of complex random sampling

discussed in this chapter are systematic, stratified, cluster, and double sampling. Systematic sampling involves the selection of every kth element in the population, beginning with a random start between elements from 1 to k. Its simplicity in certain cases is its greatest value.

Stratified random sampling is based on dividing a population into subpopulations and then randomly sampling from each of these strata. This method usually results in a smaller total sample size than would a simple random design. Stratified samples may be proportionate or disproportionate.

In cluster sampling, we divide the population into convenient groups and then randomly choose the groups to study. It is typically less efficient from a statistical viewpoint than the simple random because of the high degree of homogeneity within the clusters. Its great advantage is its savings in cost—if the population is dispersed geographically—or in time. The most widely used form of clustering is area sampling, in which geographic areas are the selection elements.

At times, it may be more convenient or economical to collect some information by sample and then use it as a basis for selecting a subsample for further study. This procedure is called double sampling.

Nonprobability sampling also has some compelling practical advantages that account for its widespread use. Often probability sampling is not feasible because the population is not available. Then, too, frequent breakdowns in the application of probability sampling discount its technical advantages. You may find also that a true cross section is often not the aim of the researcher. Here the goal may be the discovery of the range or extent of conditions. Finally, nonprobability sampling is usually less expensive to conduct than is probability sampling.

Convenience samples are the simplest and least reliable forms of nonprobability sampling. Their primary virtue is low cost. One purposive sample is the judgmental sample, in which one is interested in studying only selected types of subjects. The other purposive sample is the quota sample. Subjects are selected to conform to certain predesignated control measures that secure a representative cross section of the population. Snowball sampling uses a referral approach to reach particularly hard-to-find respondents.

LO5-5 Ethical issues in sampling design relate to deception, compensation, and quality. These are addressed through informed consent; compensation fulfillment (including cash, charitable donations, food, etc); and quality procedures, including adequate participant screening, using the best sample frame available, and conscientiously following selection protocols, whether these are industry standards or project specific.

>**key**terms

>**discussion**questions

Terms in Review

1 Distinguish between:

   a Statistic and parameter.

   b Sample frame and target population.

   c Case and target population.

   d Simple random and complex random sampling.

   e Convenience and purposive sampling.

   f Sample precision and sample accuracy.

   g Nonsampling and sampling error.

   h Proportionate and disproportionate samples.

2 Under what conditions would you recommend:

   a A probability sample? a nonprobability sample?

   b A simple random sample? a cluster sample? a stratified sample?

   c A disproportionate stratified probability sample?

3 You plan to conduct a study using unrestricted sampling. What subjective decisions must you make?

4 Describe the differences between a probability sample and a nonprobability sample.

5 Why would a researcher use a quota purposive sample?

Making Research Decisions

6 Your task is to interview a representative sample of attendees for the large concert venue where you work. The new season schedule includes 200 live concerts featuring all types of musicians and musical groups. Because neither the number of attendees nor their descriptive characteristics are known in advance, you decide on nonprobability sampling. Based on past seating configurations, you can calculate the number of tickets that will be available for each of the 200 concerts. Thus, collectively, you will know the number of possible attendees for each type of music. From attendance research conducted at concerts held by the Glacier Symphony during the previous two years, you can obtain gender data on attendees by type of music. How would you conduct a reasonably reliable nonprobability sample?

7 Your large firm is about to change to a customer-centered organization structure, in which employees who have rarely had customer contact will now likely significantly influence customer satisfaction and retention. As part of the transition, your superior wants an accurate evaluation of the morale of the firm's large number of computer technicians. What type of sample would you draw if it was to be an unrestricted sample?

8 When Nike introduced its glow-in-the-dark Foamposite One Galaxy sneakers, fanatics lined up at distributors around the country. As crowds became restless, jockeying for position at the front of increasingly long lines for the limited-supply shoes, Footlocker canceled some events. It's been suggested that Nike should sell its limited-release introductions online rather than in stores to avoid putting its customers' safety in jeopardy. What sample group would you suggest Nike use to assess this suggestion?

From Concept to Practice

9 Using Exhibit 5-9 as your guide, for each sampling technique, describe the sample frame for a study of employers' skill needs in new hires using the industry in which you are currently working or wish to work.

From the Headlines

10 As populations age and young workers reject work requiring repetitive operations, factories around the world are turning to robots. It is estimated that the United States has 176 robots for every 10,000 workers, with South Korea (531) and Germany (301) leading the charge and China, with its investment in being a leading maker of robots, expected to advance quickly (90,000 robots installed by 2016, one-third of the world's total). You are a worldwide manufacturer of industrial equipment with 10 plants and more than 10,000 manufacturing employees and supervisors. Some of your plants are represented by unions. Create the sampling design to study robotics as a solution to a manufacturing worker shortage.

>cases*

Akron Children's Hospital

Calling Up Attendance

Campbell-Ewald Pumps Awareness into the American Heart Association

Campbell-Ewald: R-E-S-P-E-C-T Spells Loyalty

Can Research Rescue the Red Cross?

Goodyear's Aquatred

Inquiring Minds Want to Know—NOW!

Marcus Thomas LLC Tests Hypothesis for Troy-Bilt Creative Development

Ohio Lottery: Innovative Research Design Drives Winning

Pebble Beach Co.

Starbucks, Bank One, and Visa Launch Starbucks Card Duetto Visa

State Farm: Dangerous Intersections

The Catalyst for Women in Financial Services

USTA: Come Out Swinging

Volkswagen's Beetle

* You will find a description of each case in the Case Abstracts section of this textbook. Check the Case Index to determine whether a case provides data, the research instrument, video, or other supplementary material. Cases and case supplements are available in Connect.

Calculate the Sample Size

Basic Concepts for Sampling

In the Metro University Dining Club study, the university is exploring whether to develop a membership-only dining facility on campus. One set of measured questions deals with lunch behaviors for five different groups (faculty, students, staff, alumni, "friends" of the university. We explore probability sampling and the various concepts used to design the sampling process using this example.

Exhibit Ca-1 shows the Metro U dining club study population ($N = 20,000$) consisting of five subgroups based on their preferred lunch times. The values 1 through 5 represent the preferred lunch times of 11 a.m., 11:30 a.m., 12 noon, 12:30 p.m., and 1 p.m. The frequency of response (f) in

the population distribution, shown beside the population subgroup, is what would be found if a census of the elements was taken. Normally, population data are unavailable or are too costly to obtain. We are pretending omniscience for the sake of the example.

Point Estimates   Now assume we sample 10 elements from this population without knowledge of the population's characteristics. We use a sampling procedure from a statistical software program, a random number generator, or a table of random numbers. Our first sample ($n_1 = 10$) provides us with the frequencies shown below sample n_1 in Exhibit Ca-1. We also calculate a mean score, $X_1 = 3.0$, for this sample. This mean would place the average preferred

>**Exhibit Ca-1** Random Samples of Preferred Lunch Times

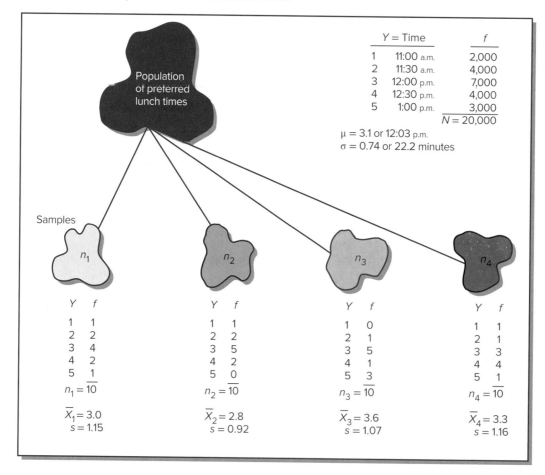

Y = Time		f
1	11:00 a.m.	2,000
2	11:30 a.m.	4,000
3	12:00 p.m.	7,000
4	12:30 p.m.	4,000
5	1:00 p.m.	3,000
		$N = 20,000$

$\mu = 3.1$ or 12:03 p.m.
$\sigma = 0.74$ or 22.2 minutes

Population of preferred lunch times

Samples

n_1

Y	f
1	1
2	2
3	4
4	2
5	1
$n_1 = 10$	

$\overline{X}_1 = 3.0$
$s = 1.15$

n_2

Y	f
1	1
2	2
3	5
4	2
5	0
$n_2 = 10$	

$\overline{X}_2 = 2.8$
$s = 0.92$

n_3

Y	f
1	0
2	1
3	5
4	1
5	3
$n_3 = 10$	

$\overline{X}_3 = 3.6$
$s = 1.07$

n_4

Y	f
1	1
2	1
3	3
4	4
5	1
$n_4 = 10$	

$\overline{X}_4 = 3.3$
$s = 1.16$

lunch time at 12 noon. The mean is a *point estimate* and our best predictor of the unknown population mean, μ (the arithmetic average of the population). Assume further that we return the first sample to the population and draw a second, third, and fourth sample by the same procedure. The frequencies, means, and standard deviations are as shown in the exhibit. As the data suggest, each sample shares some similarities with the population, but none is a perfect duplication because no sample perfectly replicates its population.

Interval Estimates   We cannot judge which estimate is the true mean (accurately reflects the population mean). However, we can estimate the interval in which the true μ will fall by using any of the samples. This is accomplished by using a formula that computes the *standard error of the mean*:

$$\sigma_{\bar{X}} = \frac{\sigma}{\sqrt{n}}$$

where

$\sigma_{\bar{X}}$ = standard error of the mean or the standard deviation of all possible $\bar{X}$s

σ = population standard deviation

n = sample size

The standard error of the mean measures the standard deviation of the distribution of sample means. It varies directly with the standard deviation of the population from which it is drawn (see Exhibit Ca-2): If the standard deviation is reduced by 50 percent, the standard error will also be reduced by 50 percent. It also varies inversely with the square root of the sample size. If the square root of the sample size is doubled, the standard error is cut by one-half, provided the standard deviation remains constant.

Let's now examine what happens when we apply sample data (n_1) from Exhibit Ca-1 to the formula. The sample standard deviation from sample n will be used as an unbiased estimator of the population standard deviation:

$$\sigma_{\bar{X}} = \frac{s}{\sqrt{n}}$$

where

s = standard deviation of the sample, n_1
n_1 = 10
$\bar{X}_1$ = 3.0
s_1 = 1.15

Substituting into the equation:

$$\sigma_{\bar{X}} = \frac{s}{\sqrt{n}} = \frac{1.15}{\sqrt{10}} = 0.36$$

Estimating the Population Mean

How does this improve our prediction of μ from X? The standard error creates the interval range that brackets the point estimate. In this example, μ is predicted to be 3.0 or 12 noon (the mean of n_1) ±0.36. This range may be visualized on a continuum (see diagram at bottom of next page).

We would expect to find the true μ between 2.64 and 3.36—between 11:49 a.m. and 12:11 p.m. (if 2 = 11:30 a.m. and 0.64 = (30 minutes) = 19.2 minutes, then 2.64 = 11:30 a.m. + 19.2 minutes, or 11:49 a.m.). Since we assume omniscience for this illustration, we know the population average value is 3.1. Further, because standard errors have characteristics like other standard scores, we have 68 percent confidence in this estimate—that is, one standard error encompasses ±1 Z or 68 percent of the area under the

>**Exhibit Ca-2** Effects on Standard Error of Mean of Increasing Precision

	Reducing the Standard Deviation by 50%	Quadrupling the Sample
$\sigma_{\bar{X}} = \frac{s}{\sqrt{n}}$	$\sigma_{\bar{X}} = \frac{0.74}{\sqrt{10}} = 0.234$	$\sigma_{\bar{X}} = \frac{0.8}{\sqrt{25}} = 0.16$
	$\sigma_{\bar{X}} = \frac{0.37}{\sqrt{10}} = 0.117$	$\sigma_{\bar{X}} = \frac{0.8}{\sqrt{100}} = 0.08$

where

$\sigma_{\bar{X}}$ = standard error of the mean

$\sigma_{\bar{X}}$ = standard deviation of the sample

n = sample size

Note: A 400 percent increase in sample size (from 25 to 100) would yield only a 200 percent increase in precision (from 0.16 to 0.08). Researchers are often asked to increase precision, but the question should be, at what cost? Each of those additional sample elements adds both time and cost to the study.

>**Exhibit Ca-3** Confidence Levels and the Normal Curve

95%

68%

$-1.96\sigma_{\overline{X}}$ $-1\sigma_{\overline{X}}$ 0 $+1\sigma_{\overline{X}}$ $+1.96\sigma_{\overline{X}}$

>**Exhibit Ca-4** Standard Errors Associated with Areas under the Normal Curve

Standard Error (Z)	Percent of Area*	Approximate Degree of Confidence
1.00	68.27	68%
1.65	90.10	90
1.96	95.00	95
3.00	99.73	99

*Includes both tails in a normal distribution.

normal curve (see Exhibit Ca-3). Recall that the area under the curve also represents the confidence estimates that we make about our results. The combination of the interval range and the degree of confidence creates the *confidence interval*. To improve confidence to 95 percent, multiply the standard error of 0.36 by ± 1.96 (Z), because 1.96 Z covers 95 percent of the area under the curve (see Exhibit Ca-4). Now, with 95 percent confidence, the interval in which we would find the true mean increases to ± 0.70 (from 2.3 to 3.7 or from 11:39 a.m. to 12:21 p.m.).

Parenthetically, if we compute the standard deviation of the distribution of sample means in Exhibit Ca-1, [3.0, 2.8, 3.6, 3.3], we will discover it to be 0.35. Compare this to the standard error from the original calculation (0.36). The result is consistent with the second definition of the standard error: the standard deviation of the distribution of sample means (n_1, n_2, n_3, and n_4). Now let's return to the dining club example and apply some of these concepts to the researchers' problem.

If the researchers were to interview all the students and employees in the defined population, asking them, "How many times per month would you eat at the club?" they would get a distribution something like that shown in part A of Exhibit Ca-5. The responses would range from zero to as many as 30 lunches per month with a μ and σ.

However, they cannot take a census, so μ and σ remain unknown. By sampling, the researchers find the mean to be 10.0 and the standard deviation to be 4.1 eating experiences (how often they would eat at the club per month). In part C of Exhibit Ca-5, three observations about this sample distribution are consistent with our earlier illustration. First, it is shown as a histogram; it represents a frequency distribution of empirical data, while the smooth curve of part A is a theoretical distribution. Second, the sample distribution (part C) is similar in appearance but is not a perfect duplication of the population distribution (part A). Third, the mean of the sample differs from the mean of the population.

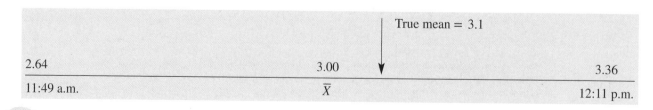

>**Exhibit Ca-5** A Comparison of Population Distribution, Sample Distribution, and Distribution of Sample Means of Metro U Dining Club Study

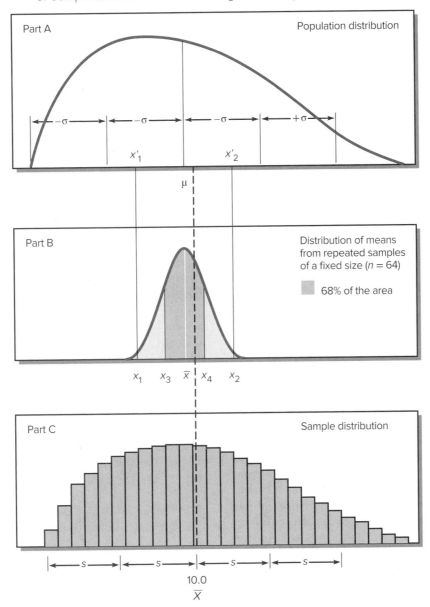

Note: The distributions in these figures are not to scale, but this fact is not critical to our understanding of the dispersion relationship depicted.

If the researchers could draw repeated samples as we did earlier, they could plot the mean of each sample to secure the solid line distribution found in part B. According to the *central limit theorem,* for sufficiently large samples ($n = 30$), the sample means will be distributed around the population mean approximately in a normal distribution. Even if the population is not normally distributed, the distribution of sample means will be normal if there is a large enough set of samples.

Estimating the Interval for the Metro U Dining Club Sample Any sample mean will fall within the range of the distribution extremes shown in part B of Exhibit Ca-5. We also know that about 68 percent of the sample means in this distribution will fall between x_3 and x_4 and 95 percent will fall between x_1 and x_2.

If we project points x_1 and x_2 up to the population distribution (part A of Exhibit Ca-5) at points $x'1$ and $x'2$, we see the interval where any given mean of a random sample of 64 is likely to fall 95 percent of the time. Because we will not know the population mean from which to measure the standard error, we infer that there is also a 95 percent chance that the population mean is within two standard errors of the sample mean (10.0). This inference enables us to find the sample mean, mark off an interval around it, and state a confidence likelihood that the population mean is within this bracket.

Because the researchers are considering an investment in this project, they would want some assurance that the population mean is close to the figure reported in any sample they take. To find out how close the population mean is to the sample mean, they must calculate the standard error of the mean and estimate an interval range within which the population mean is likely to be.

Given a sample size of 64, they still need a value for the standard error. Almost never will one have the value for the standard deviation of the population (σ), so we must use a proxy figure. The best proxy for σ is the standard deviation of the sample (s). Here the standard deviation ($s = 4.1$) was obtained from a pilot sample:

$$\sigma_{\bar{X}} = \frac{s}{\sqrt{n}} = \frac{4.1}{\sqrt{64}} = 0.51$$

If one standard error of the mean is equal to 0.51 visit, then 1.96 standard errors (95 percent) are equal to 1.0 visit. The students can estimate with 95 percent confidence that the population mean of expected visits is within 10.0 ± 1.0 visit, or from 9.0 to 11.0 mean visits per month.

Changing Confidence Intervals

The preceding estimate may not be satisfactory in two ways. First, it may not represent the degree of confidence the researchers want in the interval estimate, considering their financial risk. They might want a higher degree of confidence than the 95 percent level used here. By referring to a table of areas under the normal curve, they can find various other combinations of probability. Exhibit Ca-6 summarizes some of those more commonly used. Thus, if the students want a greater confidence in the probability of including the population mean in the interval range, they can move to a higher

standard error, say, $X \pm 3\sigma_{\bar{X}}$. Now the population mean lies somewhere between $10.0 \pm 3 (0.51)$ or from 8.47 to 11.53. With 99.73 percent confidence, we can say this interval will include the population mean.

We might wish to have an estimate that will hold for a much smaller range, for example, 10.0 ± 0.2. To secure this smaller interval range, we must either (1) accept a lower level of confidence in the results or (2) take a sample large enough to provide this smaller interval with the higher desired confidence level.

If one standard error is equal to 0.51 visit, then 0.2 visit would be equal to 0.39 standard error ($0.2/0.51 = 0.39$). Referring to a table of areas under the normal curve (book Appendix C, Exhibit C-1), we find that there is a 30.3 percent chance that the true population mean lies within ± 0.39 standard error of 10.0. With a sample of 64, the sample mean would be subject to so much error variance that only 30 percent of the time could the researchers expect to find the population mean between 9.8 and 10.2. This is such a low level of confidence that the researchers would normally move to the second alternative; they would increase the sample size until they could secure the desired interval estimate and degree of confidence.

Calculating the Sample Size for Questions Involving Means

Before we compute the desired sample size for the Metro U dining club study, let's review the information we will need:

1. The *precision* desired and how to quantify it:
   a. The *confidence level* we want with our estimate.
   b. The *size of the interval estimate.*
2. The expected *dispersion in the population* for the investigative question used.
3. Whether a finite population adjustment is needed.

The researchers have selected two investigative question constructs as critical—"frequency of patronage" and "interest in joining"—because they believe both to be crucial to making the correct decision on the Metro U dining club opportunity. The first requires a point estimate, the second

>**Exhibit Ca-6** Estimates Associated with Various Confidence Levels in the Metro U Dining Club Study

Approximate Degree of Confidence	Interval Range of Dining Visits per Month
68%	μ is between 9.48 and 10.52 visits
90%	μ is between 9.14 and 10.86 visits
95%	μ is between 8.98 and 11.02 visits
99%	μ is between 8.44 and 11.56 visits

>**Exhibit Ca-7** Metro U Sampling Design Decision on "Meal Frequency" and "Joining"
Constructs

	Metro U Decisions	
Sampling Issues	**"Meal Frequency" (interval, ratio data)**	**"Joining" (nominal, ordinal data)**
1. The precision desired and how to quantify it:	95% confidence (Z = 1.96)	95% confidence (Z = 1.96)
• The confidence researcher wants in the estimate (selected based on risk)	±0.5 meal per month	±0.10 (10 percent)
• The size of the interval estimate the researcher will accept (based on risk)		
2. The expected range in the population for the question used to measure precision: **Measure of Central Tendency**	0 to 30 meals 10	0 to 100% 30%
• Sample mean		
• Sample proportion of population with the given attribute being measured		
Measure of Dispersion	4.1	$pq = 0.30(0.70) = 0.21$
• Standard deviation		
• Measure of sample dispersion		
3. Whether a finite population adjustment should be used	No	No
4. Estimate of standard deviation of population:	0.5/1.96 = 0.255	0.10/1.96 = 0.051
• Standard error of mean		
• Standard error of the proportion		
5. Sample size calculation	See formula (p. 120)	See formula (p. 121)
6. Calculated sample size	$n = 259*$	$n = 81$

*Because both investigative questions were of interest, the researcher would use the larger of the two sample sizes calculated, $n = 259$ for the study.

a proportion. By way of review, decisions needed and decisions made by Metro U researchers are summarized in Exhibit Ca-7.

Precision With reference to precision, the 95 percent confidence level is often used, but more or less confidence may be needed in light of the risks of any given project. Similarly, the size of the interval estimate for predicting the population parameter from the sample data should be decided. When a smaller interval is selected, the researcher is saying that precision is vital, largely because inherent risks are high. For example, on a 5-point measurement scale, one-tenth of a point is a very high degree of precision in comparison to a 1-point interval. Given that a patron could eat up to 30 meals per month at the dining club (30 days times 1 meal per day), anything less than one meal per day would be asking for a high degree of precision in the Metro U study. The high risk of the Metro U study warrants the 0.5 meal precision selected.

Population Dispersion The next factor that affects the size of the sample for a given level of precision is the population dispersion. The smaller the possible dispersion, the smaller will be the sample needed to give a representative picture of population members. If the population's number of meals ranges from 18 to 25, a smaller sample will give us an accurate estimate of the population's average meal consumption. However, with a population dispersion ranging from 0 to 30 meals consumed, a larger sample is needed for the same degree of confidence in the estimates. Since the true population dispersion of estimated meals per month eaten at Metro U dining club is unknowable, the standard deviation of the sample is used as a proxy figure. Typically, this figure is based on any of the following:

• Previous research on the topic.

• A pilot test or pretest of the data instrument among a sample drawn from the population.

- A rule of thumb (one-sixth of the range based on six standard deviations within 99.73 percent confidence).

If the range is from 0 to 30 meals, the rule-of-thumb method produces a standard deviation of 5 meals. The researchers want more precision than the rule-of-thumb method provides, so they take a pilot sample of 25 and find the standard deviation to be 4.1 meals.

Population Size A final factor affecting the size of a random sample is the size of the population. When the size of the sample exceeds 5 percent of the population, the finite limits of the population constrain the sample size needed. A correction factor is available in that event.

The sample size is computed for the first construct, meal frequency, as follows:

$$\sigma_{\bar{X}} = \frac{s}{\sqrt{n}}$$

$$\sqrt{n} = \frac{s}{\sigma_{\bar{X}}}$$

$$n = \frac{s^2}{\sigma_{\bar{X}}}$$

$$n = \frac{(4.1)^2}{(0.255)^2}$$

$$n = 258.5 \text{ or } 259$$

where

$$\sigma_x = 0.255 \ (0.51/1.96)$$

If the researchers are willing to accept a larger interval range (±1 meal), and thus a larger amount of risk, then they can reduce the sample size to $n = 65$.

Calculating the Sample Size for Questions Involving Proportions

The second key question concerning the dining club study was, what percentage of the population says it would join the dining club, based on the projected rates and services? In business, we often deal with proportion data. An example is a CNN poll that projects the percentage of people who expect to vote for or against a proposition or a candidate. This is usually reported with a margin of error of ±5 percent.

In the Metro U study, a pretest answers this question using the same general procedure as before. But instead of the arithmetic mean, with proportions, it is p (the proportion of the population that has a given attribute)[1]—in this case, interest in joining the dining club. And instead of the standard deviation, dispersion is measured in terms of $p \times q$ (in which q is the proportion of the population not having the attribute), and $q = (1 - p)$. The measure of

dispersion of the sample statistic also changes from the standard error of the mean to the standard error of the proportion σ_p.

We calculate a sample size based on these data by making the same two subjective decisions—deciding on an acceptable interval estimate and the degree of confidence. Assume that from a pilot test, 30 percent of the students and employees say they will join the dining club. We decide to estimate the true proportion in the population within 10 percentage points of this figure ($p = 0.30 \pm 0.10$). Assume further that we want to be 95 percent confident that the population parameter is within ±0.10 of the sample proportion. The calculation of the sample size proceeds as before:

±0.10 = desired interval range within which the population proportion is expected (subjective decision)

$1.96\sigma_p$ = 95 percent confidence level for estimating the interval within which to expect the population proportion (subjective decision)

$\sigma_p = 0.051$ = standard error of the proportion (0.10/1.96)

pq = measure of sample dispersion (used here as an estimate of the population dispersion)

n = sample size

$$\sigma_p = \sqrt{\frac{pq}{n}}$$

$$n = \frac{pq}{\sigma_p^2}$$

$$n = \frac{0.3 \times 0.7}{(0.051)^2}$$

$$n = 81$$

The sample size of 81 persons is based on an infinite population assumption. If the sample size is less than 5 percent of the population, there is little to be gained by using a finite population adjustment. The students interpreted the data found with a sample of 81 chosen randomly from the population as: We can be 95 percent confident that 30 percent of the respondents would say they would join the dining club with a margin of error of ±10 percent.

Previously, the researchers used pilot testing to generate the variance estimate for the calculation. Suppose this is not an option. Proportions data have a feature concerning the variance that is not found with interval or ratio data. The pq ratio can never exceed 0.25. For example, if $p = 0.5$, then $q = 0.5$, and their product is 0.25. If either p or q is greater than 0.5, then their product is smaller than 0.25 ($0.4 \times 0.6 = 0.24$, and so on). When we have no information regarding the probable p value, we can assume that $p = 0.5$ and solve for the sample size:

$$n = \frac{pq}{\sigma_p^2}$$

$$n = \frac{(0.50)(0.50)}{(0.51)^2}$$

$$n = \frac{0.25}{(0.51)^2}$$

$$n = 96$$

where

pq = measure of dispersion
n = sample size
σp = standard error of the proportion

If we use this maximum variance estimate in the dining club example, we find the sample size needs to be 96 persons in order to have an adequate sample for the question about joining the club.

When there are several investigative questions of strong interest, researchers calculate the sample size for each such variable—as we did in the Metro U study for "meal frequency" and "joining." The researcher then chooses the calculation that generates the largest sample. This ensures that all data will be collected with the necessary level of precision.

>chapter 6

Stage 2:
Data Collection Design:
Qualitative **Research**

"The only way to capture a deeply personal insight, which will help you evoke that emotion in consumers, is through qualitative."

Gia Calhoun,
global insights manager
Burt's Bees

>**learning**objectives

After reading this chapter, you should understand . . .

LO6-1   The nature of qualitative research and its distinctions from quantitative research.

LO6-2   The types of business decisions that use qualitative methods.

LO6-3   The variety of qualitative research methods.

LO6-4   The importance and responsibility of the interviewer.

LO6-5   Ethical issues related to qualitative research.

Qualitative research methodologies have roots in a variety of disciplines, including anthropology, sociology, psychology, linguistics, communication, economics, and semiotics. Possibly because of these origins, qualitative methods have not enjoyed the unqualified endorsement of upper management. Some senior managers maintain that qualitative data are too subjective and susceptible to human error and bias in data collection and interpretation. The fact that results cannot be generalized from a qualitative study to a larger target population is considered a fundamental weakness. Thus some senior managers believe a qualitative study provides an unstable foundation for expensive and critical business decisions. Increasingly, however, managers are turning to these techniques because quantitative techniques take too long and fall short of providing true insights needed to make those ever-more-expensive business decisions.[1]

Historically, qualitative methodologies have been available much longer—some as early as the 19th century—than the quantitative tools managers rely on so heavily. While qualitative research currently accounts for about 20 percent of research expenditures by businesses, new technology is helping to rapidly expand the insights drawn from such methods [e.g., social media analysis (*netnography*), ethnography (observation of human cultures), crowdsourcing (tasking a group of people with a problem or task, usually via the Internet, the availability of online communities and virtual groups, and most notably the smartphone].[2] Some believe that the use of qualitative research by business is on the verge of massive expansion.[3] Even the most recent GreenBook Research Industry Trends report cites several qualitative methods in its top 12 emerging research techniques (Exhibit 6-1).

Researchers deal with the issue of management's concern over the trustworthiness of qualitative data by employing exacting protocols when using qualitative methodology:[4]

- Carefully using literature searches to build probing questions.

- Thoroughly justifying the methodology or combination of methodologies chosen.

- Executing the chosen methodology in its natural setting (field study) rather than a highly controlled setting (laboratory).

- Choosing sample participants for relevance to the breadth of the issue rather than how well they represent the target population.

- Developing and including questions that reveal the exceptions to a rule or theory.

- Carefully structuring the data analysis.

- Comparing data across multiple sources and different contexts.

- Conducting peer-researcher debriefing on results for added clarity, additional insights, and reduced bias.

>**Exhibit 6-1** Emerging Qualitative Research Techniques

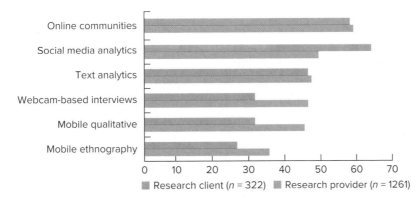

Source: This graph was developed from data presented in Leonard F. Murphy, "GRIT Report," Greenbook, June 2016, p. 5, downloaded June 30, 2016 (https://www.greenbook.org/images/GRIT/2016_grit/GRIT_Report_2016_Edition.pdf).

>What Is Qualitative Research?

Qualitative research includes an "array of interpretive techniques which seek to describe, decode, translate, and otherwise come to terms with the meaning, not the frequency, of certain more or less naturally occurring phenomena in the social world."[5] These techniques include individual depth interviews (IDIs) and group interviews, as well as multiple-method approaches involving interviews and observation techniques (e.g., case studies, ethnography, grounded theory, action research). Qualitative research can be conducted *asynchronously* (from multiple participants at different times) or *synchronously* (from all participants at the same time). Qualitative research can be conducted as a cross-sectional study (e.g., one interaction per participant during the research period) or as a longitudinal study (e.g., multiple interactions per participant during the research period).

If the manager needs to know only what happened, or how often things happened, **quantitative research** methodologies would serve the purpose. But to understand the different meanings that people place on their experiences often requires research techniques that delve more deeply into people's hidden interpretations, understandings, and motivations. Qualitative research is designed to tell the researcher how (process) and why (meaning) things happen as they do. Judith Langer, a noted qualitative researcher, indicates that qualitative research is ideal if you want to extract feelings, emotions, motivations, perceptions, people's "language," or self-described behavior.[6] Exhibit 6-2 offers some examples of appropriate uses of qualitative research in business.

Qualitative research is based on "researcher immersion in the phenomenon to be studied, data which provide a detailed description of events, situations and interaction between people and things,

>Exhibit 6-2 Some Business Uses for Qualitative Research

Decision Arena	Questions to Be Answered
Job analysis	• Does the current assignment of tasks generate the most productivity? • Does the advancement through different job levels incorporate the necessary training to foster the strongest performance?
Advertising concept development	• What images should we use to connect with our target customers' motivations?
Productivity enhancement	• What actions could we take to boost worker productivity without generating worker discontent?
New product development	• What would our current market think of a proposed product idea? • We need new products, but what should they be to take advantage of our existing customer-perceived strengths? • Which products will create the greatest synergy with our existing products in terms of ROI and distribution partner growth?
Benefits management	• Should our compensation plan be more flexible and customizable? • How do employees perceive wellness-prevention programs as compared to corrective health programs in terms of value?
Retail design	• How do consumers prefer to shop in our store? Do they shop with a defined purpose, or are they affected by other motives?
Process understanding	• What steps are involved in cleaning a wood floor? How is our product perceived or involved in this process?
Market segmentation	• Why does one demographic or lifestyle group use our product more than another? • Who are our customers and how do they use our product to support their lifestyle? • What is the influence of culture on product choice?
Union representation	• How do various departments perceive the current effort to unionize our plant? Where and what are the elements of discontent?
Sales analysis	• Why have once-loyal customers stopped buying our service?

Digital Transformation Revealed Using IDIs

Businesses in the midst of digital transformation use digital advances, as well as improve their use of traditional technologies, to change customer relationships, internal processes, and business models. The MIT Center for Digital Business and Capgemini Consulting set out to investigate whether and how large, traditional companies ($1 billion or more in annual sales) around the world—as opposed to high-tech companies or digital startups—are managing and benefiting from this digital transformation.

They conducted a multiyear study using in-depth interviews with 157 executives (half business leaders and half IT leaders) in 50 companies in 15 countries. Interviews focused on how four digital technologies—analytics, mobile, social media, and embedded devices—are being used in the enterprise.

The study revealed companies follow three different strategies to address three key areas of transformation (customer experience, operational processes and business models): *substitution* (e.g., using smartphones rather than PCs for email), *extension* (a significant improvement—e.g., using tablets rather than paper for processing orders), or *breakthrough* (fundamentally redefining a process or function—e.g., using embedded devices and analytics to create fully automated factories). *Substitution* dominates across the technologies except in the use of social media. Embedded devices are still an emerging technology; less than one-fourth of companies are using these.

The interviews revealed that "very few businesses are gaining the full value of technologically-enabled change, even with technologies they already own." Some have improved process efficiency and improved financial data for strategic decisions, but not learned how to use the information in negotiating with suppliers. Others have gathered detailed information on buyer

©Mutlu Kurtbas/Getty Images

behavior, but lack the analytical capabilities to tap the power of the data they have collected. Still others haven't begun the transformation process.

Slow progress in digital transformation is caused by lack of impetus at the top; lack of a clear business case for some technologies within some industries; regulatory, privacy, and security concerns; missing skills, especially in analytics; organizational culture related to changes in jobs due to automation, information empowerment, and labor relations; or a poor information technology base. Digital transformation successes reveal where the IT team has a deep understanding of underlying business processes and acts as internal process consultants; they energize the digital transformation.

Why did the researchers choose to use IDIs to collect this data?

ebusiness.mit.edu; capgemini.com

[thus] providing depth and detail.[7] Qualitative research—sometimes labeled *interpretive research* because it seeks to develop understanding through detailed description—contributes to building theory but rarely tests it.

Qualitative data were once exclusively about texts. Today, detailed descriptions of events, situations, and interactions—verbal, visual, and audio—constitute the data. Data may be contained within transcriptions of interviews or video focus groups, as well as in notes taken during those interactions. By definition, qualitative techniques generate reams of words and images that need to be coded and analyzed by humans for meaning. While computer software is increasingly used for the coding process in qualitative research, at the heart of the qualitative process is the researcher—and his or her experience—framing and interpreting the data.[8]

In qualitative research, the researcher and manager (research sponsor) often have significant involvement in collecting and interpreting the data. The researcher may serve as a participant or a catalyst, as a participant observer, or as an interviewer. The manager may observe (in some cases via webcast of interviews directly to the sponsor's desktop computer), influence interview questions, and add interpretations and insights during the debriefing process. The qualitative researcher uses content analysis of written or recorded materials drawn from personal expressions by participants, behavioral observations, and debriefing of data collectors, as well as the study of artifacts and trace evidence from the physical environment of the participant interaction.

Qualitative studies with their smaller sample sizes offer an opportunity for faster turnaround of findings. While speed should never be the primary reason for choosing a methodology, qualitative data may be especially useful to support low-risk decisions that must be made quickly. Both group and individual interviewing, the mainstay techniques of qualitative research, can be conducted in highly secure environments. In this era of data security, protecting research from the eyes of competitors is critically important. Qualitative techniques are suitable to research in all business disciplines.

>Qualitative Research Design

Exhibit 6-3 reveals several key distinctions that affect the research design when qualitative research is used:

- *The level of question development in the management–research question hierarchy prior to the commencing of qualitative research and how it affects development of the measurement instrument.* In qualitative studies, the researcher starts with broader investigative questions and has the ability to modify the measurement questions asked or the observations made—while the study is in progress—to gain a deeper understanding.

>**Exhibit 6-3** Qualitative Research Design within the Research Process

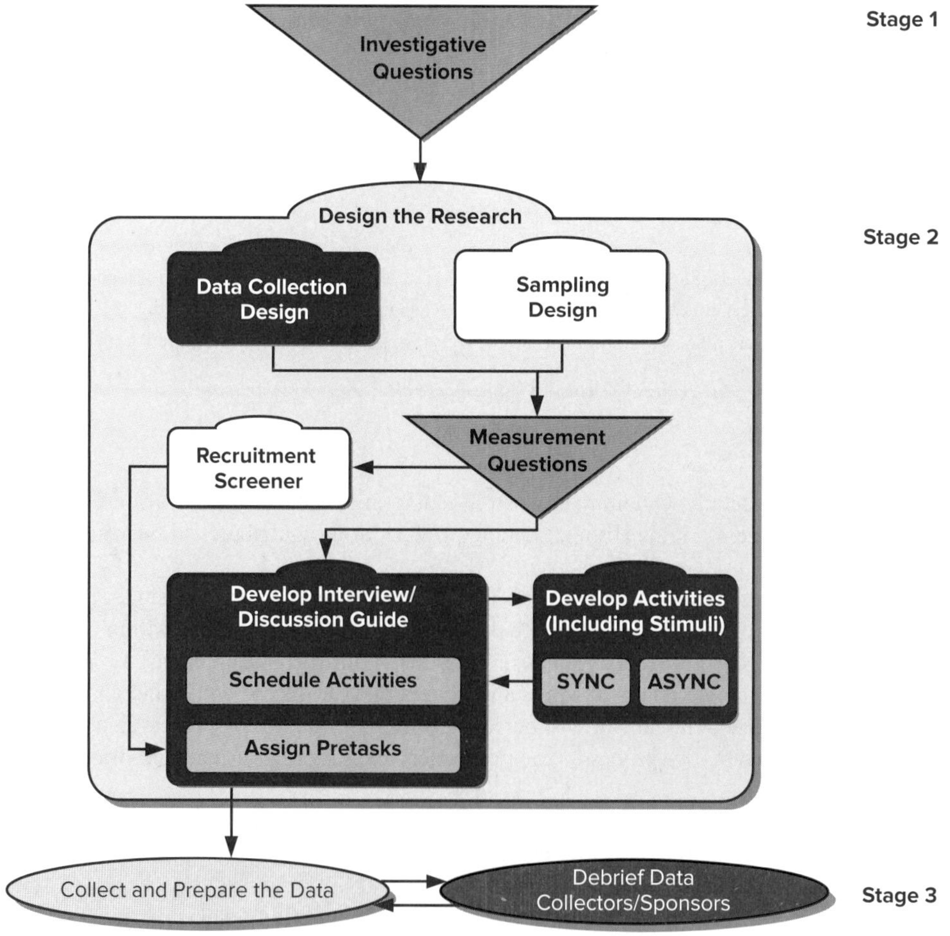

- *The preparation of the participant prior to the research experience.* In qualitative studies participants involved in an interview-based design are not only thoroughly prescreened but often prepared with pre-study exercises before the research starts (**pretasking**), sensitizing them to the research topic if not its objective. Participants are recruited in large part due to their ability to communicate their innermost thoughts and feelings; this requires some forethought on the part of the participant. The integration of data and insights that come from data collectors and sponsors as part of the data collection and preparation processes (debriefing).

- *The integration of data and insights from the data collectors and manager-sponsors during data collection and preparation.* In a qualitative study, multiple sources add to the insights, especially debriefing of data collectors, manager-sponsors, and others observing participant interviews.

Key to the preceding is a fundamental difference in qualitative research: The researcher is the center; he or she is responsible for guiding the process to extract the desired insights. In quantitative research, the researcher is mostly invisible to the participant. In any quantitative study, any and all of these distinctions would inject unacceptable bias, reducing the value of the data. But in qualitative research, they are the essence of discovering the insights that are sought. Exhibit 6-4 reveals the distinctions between qualitative and quantitative designs.

>Qualitative Sampling Design

Unlike in quantitative design, the qualitative researcher, while identifying the desired characteristics of a sample case, may not predetermine the project's sample size. The researcher seeks **data saturation**—the point at which no new information is forthcoming and no new insights seem feasible.[9] That said, sample sizes for qualitative research vary by technique but are generally far smaller than quantitative statistical studies. Of course, there are always exceptions to the rule of smaller sample sizes. AT&T conducted a qualitative study to develop its 800 Reasons ad campaign for using its long-distance service, using thousands of structured interviews with business professionals in dozens of cities over several weeks. These interviews provided numerous reasons why businesses used the AT&T 800 service, and each of these "reasons" became the focus of a television and/or magazine ad in the multi-ad campaign.[10]

Qualitative research employs **nonprobability sampling**. In the arbitrary and subjective procedure for selecting sample cases, not only is little attempt made to generate a representative sample, the researcher often seeks a nonrepresentative one in order to extract the most, and most significant insights. Several types of nonprobability sampling are common to qualitative research:

- *Purposive sampling.* Researchers choose participants for their unique characteristics or their experiences, attitudes, or perceptions; as conceptual or theoretical categories of participants develop during the interviewing process, researchers seek new participants to challenge emerging patterns. Today, this often includes drawing participants from existing communities or panels.

- *Snowball sampling.* Participants refer researchers to others who have characteristics, experiences, or attitudes similar to or different from their own.

- *Convenience sampling.* Researchers select any readily available individuals as participants.

Recruiting top-quality participants is one of the most important jobs of the qualitative researcher. Without the right people, they won't achieve deep meaning. Researchers want people who:[11]

- Share common characteristics, so they can be comfortable with each other.
- Have a range of life experiences.
- Hold different perspectives on issues.
- Can articulate their ideas, experiences, feelings, attitudes, and beliefs.
- Want to share their ideas/experiences.
- Want to hear the ideas/experiences of others.
- Like to collaborate to solve problems.

>Exhibit 6-4 Qualitative versus Quantitative Research

	Qualitative	Quantitative
Focus of research	• Understand and interpret	• Describe, explain, and predict
Researcher involvement	• High—researcher is participant or catalyst	• Limited; controlled to prevent bias
Research purpose	• In-depth understanding; theory building	• Describe or predict; build and test theory
Sampling design	• Nonprobability; purposive, convenience, snowball	• Probability
Sample size	• Small to medium	• Medium to large
Research design	• May evolve or adjust during the course of the project • Often uses multiple methods simultaneously or sequentially • Consistency is not expected • Involves either cross-sectional or longitudinal approach	• Determined before commencing the project • Uses single method or mixed methods • Consistency is critical • Involves either a cross-sectional or a longitudinal approach
Engagement exercises, including projective techniques	• Frequently used	• Rarely used
Participant preparation	• Pretasking is common	• No preparation desired to avoid biasing the participant
Data type and preparation	• Verbal, video, or pictorial descriptions • Reduced to verbal codes	• Verbal descriptions • Reduced to numerical codes for computerized analysis
Data analysis	• Human analysis following computer or human coding; primarily nonquantitative • Analysis is ongoing during the project • Distinctions between facts and judgments less clear—researcher to seek the contextual framework of the phenomenon being measured • Involves debriefing of data collectors/moderators/research sponsors/observers for greater insights	• Computerized analysis—statistical and mathematical methods dominate • Analysis may be ongoing during the project • Maintains clear distinction between facts and judgments
Insights and meaning	• Determined by type and quantity of free-response questions, involvement activities; adjustable during the process • Probing is expected and used • Insights are formed and tested during the process	• Limited by the quality of the measurement instrument • Limited opportunity to probe participants during data collection, with limited ability to re-interview participants • Insights follow data collection and data entry, with limited ability to re-interview participants
Research sponsor involvement	• May participate by observing research in real time or via taped interviews, or conducting interviews or observations	• Rarely has either direct or indirect contact with participant
Feedback turnaround	• Smaller sample sizes make some data collection faster for shorter possible turnaround • Insights are developed as the research progresses, shortening data analysis	• Larger sample sizes lengthen data collection; Internet methodologies can shorten turnaround but inappropriate for some studies • Insight development follows data collection and entry, lengthening research time frame; software permits some tallying of responses as data collection progresses
Data security	• More absolute given use of restricted access facilities and smaller sample sizes	• Act of research in progress is often known by competitors, employees, etc. • Insights may be gleaned by competitors/employees for some visible, field-based studies

Source: This exhibit was developed from material extracted from Judith Langer, *The Mirrored Window: Focus Groups from a Moderator's Point of View* (Ithaca, NY: Paramount Market Publishing, 2001); Hy Mariampolski, *Qualitative Market Research: A Comprehensive Guide* (Thousand Oaks, CA: Sage Publications, 2001); David Carson, Audrey Gilmore, Chad Perry, and Kjell Gronhaug, *Qualitative Marketing Research* (Thousand Oaks, CA: Sage Publications, 2001); and Norman K. Denzin and Ynonna S. Lincoln, editors, *The SAGE Handbook Qualitative Research,* 4th ed. (Thousand Oaks, CA: Sage Publications, April 27, 2011).

Increasingly, we are using online communities and panels to find participants because both the time and effort we need from them is significant. But we also use organization members when the research topic is general or relevant to a particular group. For example, we might recruit from the members of a church to interview prospects on laundry product purchases (general topic), or recruit those who belong to a social club to evaluate restaurants (topic relevant to a particular group). When the desired participants are difficult to access (e.g., doctors, lawyers, scientists, etc.), researchers are likely to use the services of a sample recruiter who will call and email prospects until a sample group is formed. Recruiting can sometimes take as long as the actual qualitative study.

Much of qualitative research involves the deliberate preparation of the participant called *pretasking*. Finding people who are willing to participate at this level of engagement is critical. This step is important due to the desire to extract detail and meaning from the participant. A variety of creative and mental exercises draw participants' understanding of their own thought processes and ideas to the surface. Some pretasking exercises include:

- *In-home product use* (with instructions to use the product or medium—e.g., a magazine—repeatedly over the preparation period before the interview).
- *Collecting and supplying visual stimuli* (e.g., family photos of areas or rooms in their homes that they hate to clean or have trouble decorating, or a favorite item of clothing).
- *Preparing a visual collage* (e.g., take pictures over several weeks, with a one-time-use camera, of their children's favorite outfits for different purposes or situations, or cutting pictures out of magazines that reflect how they feel when dealing with a particular supervisor).
- *Preparing detailed diaries of behavior and perceptions* (e.g., a record of their step-by-step experience preparing a travel proposal).
- *Drawing a picture of an experience* (e.g., what they felt like when they last shopped in a particular store).
- *Writing a dialog of a hypothetical experience* (e.g., how a conversation between the participant and a sales associate would progress when a complaint was not resolved).[12]

There is a growing awareness among participants that their information has value, and that they should be compensated in some way for sharing information about themselves.[13] The more time involved, the more exercises required, the more rare the participant, the more follow-up contacts desired—all increase the participation incentive. Thus, researchers have to be prepared to incentivize individuals for participating in qualitative research; this might not always be in the form of cash, but could also be in terms of discounts, customer perks, time off from the job, etc. Artem Patakov of CEO of Noom Inc., the behavioral modification organization designed to improve heath care, says firms increasingly need a privacy philosophy that includes not just a commitment to protect participant privacy, control of data, and participant choice to participate in data collection, but also a policy to fairly compensate participants for sharing information.[14]

>Qualitative Data Collection Design

Interviews

The **interview** is the primary data collection technique for gathering data in qualitative methodologies. Interview techniques vary based on the number of participants involved in the interview, the level of structure, the proximity of the interviewer to the participant, and the number of interviews conducted during the research time frame. An interview can be conducted individually or in groups. Exhibit 6-5 compares the individual and the group interview as a research methodology. Both have a distinct place in qualitative research.

Interviewing requires a trained interviewer (called a **moderator** for group interviews) or the skills gained from experience. These skills include making respondents comfortable, probing for detail without making the respondent feel harassed, remaining neutral while encouraging the participant to talk openly, listening carefully, following a participant's train of thought, and extracting insights from hours

>**Exhibit 6-5** A Comparison of Individual Depth Interviews and Group Interviews

Individual Interview	Group Interview
Research Objective	
• Explore life of individual in depth	• Orient the researcher to a field of inquiry and the language of the field
• Create case histories through repeated interviews over time	• Explore a range of attitudes, opinions, and behaviors
• Test a survey	• Observe a process of consensus and disagreement
	• Add contextual detail to quantitative findings
Topic concerns	
• Detailed individual experiences, choices, biographies	• Issues of public interest or common concern
• Sensitive issues that might provoke anxiety if discussed in a group	• Issues where little is known or of a hypothetical nature
Participants	
• Time-pressed participants or those difficult to recruit (e.g., doctors)	• Participants whose backgrounds are similar or not so dissimilar as to generate conflict or discomfort
• Participants with sufficient language skills (e.g., those older than seven)	• Participants who can articulate their ideas
• Participants whose distinctions would inhibit participation	• Participants who offer a range of positions on issues

of detailed descriptive dialogue. Skilled interviewers learn to use their personal similarities with or differences from their interviewee to mine for information; similarities are used to convey sympathy and understanding, while differences are used to demonstrate eagerness to understand and empathize. Unlike quantitative research, where we are interested in the data collector following a prescribed procedure, in qualitative research the interviewer needs flexibility to extract meaning. This usually means the interviewer has a fuller understanding of the dilemma and how the insights will be used. The skilled interviewer must be a "quick-study," someone who can grasp an understanding of an issue without necessarily having prior experience with the topic or being a technical expert.

The researcher chooses either an **unstructured interview** (no specific questions or order of topics to be discussed, with each interview customized to each participant; generally starts with a participant narrative—their story related to the topic of the research) or a **semistructured interview** (generally starts with a few specific questions and then follows the individual's tangents of thought with interviewer probes) or a **structured interview** (often uses a detailed interview guide similar to a questionnaire to guide the question order and the specific way the questions are asked, but the questions generally remain open-ended). In mobile or Internet-based interviews, the moderator's questions may be pretaped, especially if the interviews are asynchronous. Structured interviews permit more direct comparability of responses; question variability has been eliminated and thus answer variability is assumed to be real. Structured interviews are the choice when activities (such as video, photos, collaging, etc.) are used. In the structured interview, the interviewer's neutrality is enhanced.

The unstructured and semistructured interviews used in qualitative research are distinct from the structured interview in several ways. They:

• Rely on developing a dialog between interviewer and participant.

• Require more interviewer creativity.

• Use the skill of the interviewer to extract more and a greater variety of data.

• Use interviewer experience and skill to achieve greater clarity and elaboration of answers.

Interviews conducted face-to-face in specialized facilities offer the obvious benefit of being able to observe and record nonverbal as well as verbal behavior. An interview, however, can be conducted by mobile phone or via the Internet. In these instances, the participant must willingly use his or her own device's camera to allow the interviewer such observation. Phone and online interviews offer the opportunity to conduct more interviews within the same time frame and draw participants from a wider geographic area. These approaches also save the travel expenses of moving trained interviewers to participants, as well as the travel fees associated with bringing participants to a neutral site. Using interviewers who are fresher and more comfortable in conducting an interview—often from their home or office—should increase the quality of the interview. Also, depending on the group from which participants are drawn, there may be insufficient numbers to conduct group interviews in any one location, forcing the use of mobile or online techniques to supplement the sample.

Interviewers as Consultants

As data collectors, interviewers have unique responsibilities in qualitative research due to their specialized skill set. The interviewer, in his or her role as a collaborative consultant:[15]

- Recommends method and level of structure.
- Proposes the criteria for drawing the sample participants.
- Writes the recruitment screener and may recruit participants.
- Controls the interview, but also plans—and may manage—the locations and facilities for the study.
- Develops the various pretasking exercises.
- Prepares the interview or discussion guide (recommends topics, question wording, question order).
- Prepares instructions.
- Prepares any research stimuli (e.g., activities, tools used within activities) to be used during the interview.
- Debriefs the manager-sponsor and others observing the research.
- Supervises the transcription process.
- Helps analyze the data and draw insights.
- Prepares or directs the preparation of the client report, including extracting video or audio clips for the oral report.

Within this list of responsibilities, two deserve special attention: the recruitment screener and the interview/discussion guide. The interviewer is often responsible for generating the screening questions used to recruit participants for the qualitative research. This preinterview uses a device similar to a questionnaire, called a **recruitment screener**. Exhibit 6-6 provides the various elements necessary for a comprehensive recruitment screener. Each question is designed to reassure the researcher that the person who has the necessary information and experiences, as well as the social and language skills to relate the desired information, is invited to participate. Data gathered during the recruitment process are incorporated into the data analysis phase of the research, as recruitment data provide additional context for participants' expressions.

The interviewer needs to be able to extract information from a willing participant who often is not consciously aware that he or she possesses the information desired. Thus the actual interviewer generates the **interview** or **discussion guide**, the list of topics to be discussed (unstructured interview) or the questions to be asked (semistructured) and in what order (structured), as well as any preparatory pretasks or during-research activities. In building this interview/discussion guide, many interviewers employ a hierarchical questioning funnel, depicted in Exhibit 6-7. Broader questions start the interview, designed to put participants at ease and give them a sense that they have a lot to contribute, followed by increasingly more specific questions to draw out detail.

>**Exhibit 6-6** What Is Included in the Recruitment Screener?

For best effect, qualitative research takes creative, articulate, expressive individuals. Finding appropriate participants is the task of the researcher. Here are some common elements addressed at this phase of the research.

Category	Option
Heading	Include project name, date of interviews, identity of screener.
Screening requirements	Specify conditions that must be met to extend a prospect an offer to participate; may include quotas for various demographic, lifestyle, attitudinal, or usage questions.
identity information	Include name of prospect, address, phone, email.
Introduction	Describe purpose of study in a motivational way. Completely "blind" studies do not motivate participation.
Security questions	Reveal possible participant overparticipation or conflicts of interest; similar information on spouse or immediate family members.
Demographic questions	Determine match for age, gender, ethnicity or race, income, geography, employment status, or occupation.
Product/brand usage/ purchase questions	Establish frequency of use, purchase, loyalty, etc.
Lifestyle questions	Establish the participant's daily life experiences, as well as those of the person with whom the participant shares his or her life.
Attitudinal and knowledge questions	Look for breadth in perceptions, attitudes, opinions, knowledge.
Articulation and creative questions	Seek evidence that participant can articulate his or her ideas and form and express opinions; scenarios might include problem–solution questions or ask participant to confront an unusual challenge. ("What could you do with a brick?")
Offer or termination	Invite participation, discuss compensation and pretasking, set up interview, or indicate that the person is not right for the current study but may be right for future studies.

>**Exhibit 6-7** Interview Question Funnel

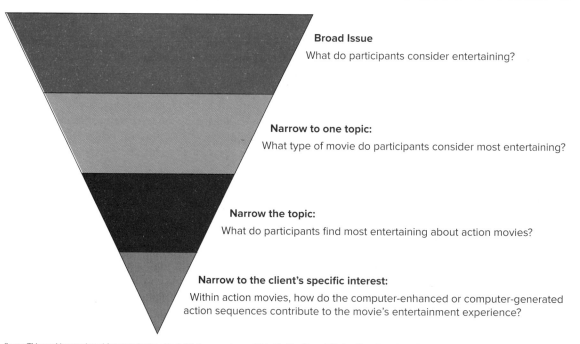

Broad Issue
What do participants consider entertaining?

Narrow to one topic:
What type of movie do participants consider most entertaining?

Narrow the topic:
What do participants find most entertaining about action movies?

Narrow to the client's specific interest:
Within action movies, how do the computer-enhanced or computer-generated action sequences contribute to the movie's entertainment experience?

Source: This graphic was adapted from one developed by Judith Langer and was published in *The Mirrored Window: Focus Group from a Moderator's Point of View* (Ithaca, NY: Paramount Market Publishing, 2001). www.paramountbooks.com.

Creative Exercises

Creative exercises or activities are common within a qualitative interview. Because researchers are often looking for hidden or suppressed meanings, projective techniques can be used. **Projective techniques** are "exercises or activities that are purposely ambiguous and unstructured in nature so that beliefs, feelings, attitudes, and motivations, which may otherwise be hard for consumers to articulate, can be uncovered."[16] These techniques allow the participant to project their feelings and ideas onto another—often hypothetical—individual. Some examples of these activities include:[17]

- **Word or picture association** Participants are asked to match images, experiences, emotions, products and services, even people and places, to whatever is being studied. *"Tell me what you think of when you think of Kellogg's Special K cereal."*
- **Completion/fill in the blank** Participants are given an incomplete sentence, story, argument, or conversation and asked to finish it. *"Complete this sentence: People who buy over the Internet . . ."*
- **Collage** Participants are asked to collect images (e.g., from personal photos, magazines, or the Internet) and use these to express their feelings or the feelings of others like them on a topic.
- **Cartoons or empty balloons** Participants are asked to write the dialog for a cartoonlike picture. *"What will the employee say when she sees her production supervisor approach her?"*
- **Thematic Apperception Test** Participants are confronted with a picture (usually a photograph or drawing) and asked to describe how the person in the picture feels and thinks.
- **Component sorts** Participants are presented with flash cards containing component features and asked to create new combinations.
- **Sensory sorts** Participants are presented with scents, textures, and sounds, usually verbalized on cards, and asked to arrange them by one or more criteria.
- **Laddering or benefit chain** Participants are asked to link functional features to their physical and psychological benefits, both real and ideal.
- **Write a letter** Participants are asked to write a letter to a person empowered to make things happen (e.g., CEO, HR director, parent, etc.).
- **Storytelling** A scenario is described and participants are asked to tell a story related to the scenario.
- **Projective drawing** Participants are asked to draw a concept or create a model, and then asked to explain it.
- **Third-party projection** Participants are asked to describe what others feel, believe, think, or do.
- **Role-playing** Participants are asked to assume a role within the organization and respond to a situation as they think that individual would.
  - **Creative innovation role-play** Participants assume an innovation position (e.g., scientist), create something (e.g., new product, package), and then explain it.
- **Imagination exercises** Participants are asked to relate the properties of one thing/person/brand to another. *"If Crest toothpaste were a college, what type of college would it be?"*
  - **Imaginary universe** Participants are asked to assume that the brand and its users populate an entire universe; they then describe the features of this new world.
  - **Visitor from another planet** Participants are asked to assume that they are aliens and are confronting the situation for the first time; they then describe their reactions, questions, and attitudes about the situation.
  - **Personification** Participants are asked to imagine inanimate objects with the traits, characteristics and features, and personalities of humans. *"If brand X were a person, what type of person would brand X be?"*
  - **Authority figure** Participants are asked to imagine that the brand or product is an authority figure and to describe the attributes of the figure.
  - **Ambiguities and paradoxes** Participants are asked to imagine a brand as something else (e.g., Tide dog food or Marlboro cereal), describing its attributes and position in the category.

©Tom H. C. Anderson (OdinText Inc.)

>picprofile

When Anderson Analytics wanted to help its research participants delve into their deepest thoughts on a research topic, they used projective techniques that employed a colorful cast of characters. Participants choose one from the cast that most closely represents them or another they are trying to describe. They then attributed attitudes, feelings, emotions, and perceptions to the character. "The added bonus of the characters is that some of the characters elicit similar responses [across research projects], so we have some idea on benchmarking," shared Anderson Analytics managing partner Tom Anderson. "For instance the heavier male character with the guitar is often thought of as an outsider, 'poser' wanting desperately to fit in, generally not well liked." **www.odintext.com**

Exercises often draw out less verbal members of a group. Projective techniques can dissipate tension caused by sensitive topics or can be useful when a change of focus in the interview is imminent. A well-trained interviewer is required if the research demands that one or more of these techniques be included within an individual depth interview or group interview. These techniques are also time-consuming to apply, lengthening the time frame of the individual or group interview. With online interviews, participants are asked to develop these techniques on their own time, to shorten the time spent with the interviewer. These techniques lengthen data analysis time, but enrich the data obtained.

Individual Depth Interviews

An **individual depth interview (IDI)** is an interaction between an individual interviewer and a single participant. Individual depth interviews generally take between 20 minutes (telephone interviews) and two hours (prescheduled, face-to-face interviews) to complete, depending on the issues or topics of interest and the contact method used. Some techniques such as *life histories* may take as long as five hours. Participants are usually paid to share their insights and ideas; $1 per minute is the budgeting rule of thumb for general consumers, but much higher rates are demanded by participants representing highly skilled professionals.[18]

Interviewees are often provided with advance materials via mail, fax, or the Internet. Recently, advances in technology have encouraged the use of detailed visual and auditory aids during interviews, creating the methodology known as **computer-assisted personal interviews (CAPIs)**. CAPIs often use a structured or semistructured individual depth interview.

Several unstructured individual depth interviews are common in business research, including oral histories, cultural interviews, life histories, critical incident technique, and sequential (or chronologic) interviewing. Exhibit 6-8 describes these techniques and provides examples.

>**Exhibit 6-8** Qualitative Methods That Use IDIs

Types	How Research Is Conducted	How Research Is Used
Oral history (narrative)	Ask participants to relate their personal experiences and feelings related to historical events or past behavior.	To develop products [e.g., books: *September 11, 2001: Stories from 55 Broad Street* by Eddie T. Deerfield and Thomas T. Noland Jr. (editors); *An Album of Memories: Personal Histories from the Greatest Generation* by Tom Brokaw].
Cultural interviews	Ask a participant to relate his or her experiences with a culture or subculture, including the knowledge passed on by prior generations and the knowledge participants have or plan to pass on to future generations.	To determine product positioning or advertising creation (e.g., how people use baking soda leads to positioning the product as not just a baking ingredient but also a deodorizer, toothpaste substitute, etc.).
Life histories	Extract from a single participant memories and experiences from childhood to the present day regarding a product or service category, brand, or firm. Participants are encouraged to share how the significant people in their lives talked about or were involved with the organization, how their attitudes or preferences have changed over their lives with respect to the organization, and how their perceptions and preferences have been altered by their various life experiences.	To determine positioning for company prior to an identity or name change (e.g., Frosted Flakes and Tony the Tiger—ad spots where adults feel they must appear in disguise because they eat a "child's cereal").
Critical incident technique	The participant describes: • What led up to the incident. • Exactly what he or she did or did not do that was especially effective or ineffective. • The outcome or result of this action and why this action was effective or what more effective action might have been expected.	To evaluate manufacturing processes, personal sales and telemarketing sales programs, compensation or incentive programs, or other management-related incidents.
Convergent interviewing (convergent and divergent interviewing)	Experts serve as participants in a sequential series of IDIs; researcher refines the questions with each interview in order to converge on the central issues or themes in a topic area.	To develop appropriate questions for all types of research (in exploratory research).
Sequential interviewing (chronologic interviewing)	Approach the participant with questions formed around an anticipated series of activities that did or might have happened, in order to have the participant recall the detail of his or her own experience.	To determine store design, advertising development, and product design; it is used to extract details related to shopping behavior, advertising consumption behavior, and product use behavior.
Ethnography	Interviewer and participant collaborate in a field-setting participant observation and unstructured interview.	To determine product redesign, advertising development, positioning, distribution selection; to discover reactions and attitudes of striking employees.
Grounded theory	Using a structured interview, each subsequent interview is adjusted based on the findings and interpretations from each previous interview, with the purpose to develop general concepts or theories with which to analyze the data.	To determine product design or redesign and advertising and promotion development.

Source: This exhibit was developed from Hy Mariampolski, *Qualitative Market Research: A Comprehensive Guide* (Thousand Oaks, CA: Sage Publications, 2001), p. 53; David Carson, Audrey Gilmore, Chad Perry, and Kjell Gronhaug, *Qualitative Marketing Research* (Thousand Oaks, CA: Sage Publications, 2001), pp. 84–89 and 152–157; Anselm Strauss and Julia Corbin, *Basics of Qualitative Research: Techniques and Procedure for Producing Grounded Theory* (Thousand Oaks, CA: Sage Publications, 1998); and Norman K. Denzin and Ynonna S. Lincoln, editors, *The SAGE Handbook of Qualitative Research,* 4th ed. (Thousand Oaks, CA: Sage Publications, April 27, 2011).

IDIs Help Restructure Maritz Travel

For 50 years, Maritz Travel Company (MTC) has produced meetings, events, and incentive travel experiences. But it is really in the motivation business, helping its business clients educate, motivate, and inspire their employees to achieve business objectives. With the recent acquisition of Experient plus service expansions and aggressive growth goals, MTC hired Marcus Thomas LLC to answer the questions, "How should Maritz Travel Company be structured in order to build equity in the entire portfolio of brands while enhancing long-term value?" and "How can Maritz Travel Company optimize positioning and messaging for each of its audiences?" The complex nature of this business demanded a comprehensive research approach, outlining every detail from sample recruitment of some rare and hard-to-reach audiences to a detailed plan for analysis and deliverables.

After three weeks of extensive recruiting using client lists and target lists developed from trade publications, the research included 22 in-depth interviews with key purchase decision makers (meeting planners and association and trade show organizers with event budgets from $500,000 to $1,000,000) as well as influencers for each audience within key markets and industries. All participants were screened for prior awareness of Maritz Travel or Experient; this screening included competitors to keep participants blind to the research purpose until it was revealed during the interview. Interviews were conducted via in-person focus groups (90 minutes) or WebEx IDIs (45–60 minutes). "The online WebEx interview platform allows us to show imagery and other assets by sharing our screen, as well as view participants' non-verbal reactions on camera," explained Edwige Winans, associate research director at Marcus Thomas. Brand perceptions were captured using projective techniques, and buying journey experiences were captured using a pretask storytelling exercise. All interviews were recorded.

The comprehensive interview guide was designed to elicit the following:

1. Perceptions of Maritz Travel Company, Maritz Travel, Experient, and key competitors.
2. The equity of each brand.
3. The perceived value of three brand structure scenarios:
   - P&G model (*sub-brands* stand above the company brand).

©Ryan McVay/Getty Images

   - Marriott model (the *company* brand and the *sub-brands* are balanced).
   - Harley Davidson model (the *master* brand is leveraged at the expense of *sub-brands*).

4. Buying journey experiences.

"[Once MTC was revealed as the research sponsor], to test the different brand structures, specific hypothetical scenarios were worked into the discussions designed to capture respondent gut reactions. A change in brand structure clearly became imperative, as an alternate structure demonstrated the greatest potential for impact," revealed Stefanie Riediger, strategic planner at Marcus Thomas.

Upon completion of this research, a complete analysis of the gathered primary research in combination with provided company intelligence and secondary research, helped shape key conclusions and implications for MTC. Marcus Thomas analyzed responses according to their TRU approach: what was Truthful, Relevant, and Unique about each sub-brand within the house of brands. A final written and oral report outlined detailed findings and summarized conclusions, with strategic implications, recommendations, and next steps required to execute the brand strategy successfully.

Maritz Travel Company has made critical strategic business and communications decisions based on the research.

www.marcusthomasllc.com;www.maritzglobalevents.com

Managing the IDI

Participants for individual depth interviews are usually chosen not because their opinions are representative of the dominant opinion, but because their experiences and attitudes will reflect the full scope of the issue under study. Participants for individual depth interviews also need to be verbally articulate in order to provide the interviewer with the richness of desired detail. Primary Insights Inc. developed its *CUE* methodology to help marketers understand the performance cues that consumers use to judge a product. It uses purposive sampling to recruit individuals "with a specific interest in and aptitude for analytical thinking and discovering how things work." CUE combines in-home product use with a diary pretask, followed by individual depth interviews that extract what the participant saw, felt, heard, smelled, and sensed when interacting with the product. What evolves is a hierarchy of sensory cues that clients may use when modifying products to improve customer satisfaction.[19]

Individual depth interviews are usually recorded (audio and/or video) and transcribed to provide the researcher with the rich detail for which the methodology is used. Interviewers are also themselves debriefed to get their personal reactions to participant attitudes, insights, and the quality of the interview. Individual depth interviews use extensive amounts of interviewer time, in both conducting interviews and evaluating them, as well as facility time when premises are occupied for interviews. And while some respondents feel more comfortable discussing sensitive topics or sharing their own observations, behaviors, and attitudes with a single person, others are more forthcoming in group situations.

Group Interviews

A **group interview** is a data collection method using a single interviewer with more than one research participant. Driven by the belief that the data extracted will be richer because of the interaction, group interviews are one of the few research techniques in which the participants are encouraged to interact. Group interviews can be conducted in-person, on the phone or other mobile device, or via the Internet; the moderator works harder to keep participants engaged with each other in the latter two types of groups.

Group interviews can be described by the group's size or its composition. Group interviews vary widely in size: dyads (two people), triads (three people), minigroups (two to six people), small groups (focus groups—6 to 10 people—unarguably the most well known of group interview techniques), or supergroups (up to 20 people). Smaller groups are usually used when the target population is small, when the topic or concept list is extensive or technical, or when the research calls for greater intimacy. Dyads also are used when the special nature of a friendship or other relationship (e.g., spouses, superior–subordinate, siblings) is needed to stimulate frank discussion on a sensitive topic. Dyads and triads are also used frequently with young children who have lower levels of articulation or more limited attention spans and are thus more difficult to control in large groups. A supergroup is used when a wide range of ideas is needed in a short period of time and when the researcher is willing to sacrifice a significant amount of participant interaction for speed.

In terms of composition, groups can be **heterogeneous** (consisting of different individuals; variety of opinions, backgrounds, actions) or **homogeneous** (consisting of similar individuals; commonality of opinions, backgrounds, actions). Groups also can comprise **experts** (individuals exceptionally knowledgeable about the issues to be discussed) or **nonexperts** (those who have at least some desired information but at an unknown level).

A group interview's structure and process include moderator interaction with the group and probing of the group to clarify responses. As a result, the moderator may create bias in the results by sending verbal and nonverbal signals that some responses are more favorable than others. The moderator might also direct discussion down paths that are least likely to help the client. Only training, and subsequent experience, can overcome these potential weaknesses of group interviews. The skilled researcher helps the manager determine an appropriate number of group interviews to conduct. The number of groups is determined by

- The *scope* of the issue(s) being studied: The broader the issue(s), the more groups needed.
- The *number of a target population's distinct segments* of interest: The larger the number and the greater the distinctions, the more groups needed.
- The *number of new ideas or insights* desired: The larger the number, the more groups needed.
- The *level of detail* of information: The greater the level of detail, the more groups needed.

>**Exhibit 6-9** Factors Influencing Participant Contributions in Group Interviews

Positive/Facilitators	
Recognition/ego enhancement	Moderator's expressed appreciation for participant contributions that contribute to issue understanding; participant's open agreement with other participant comments.
Personal contribution	Participant's desire to be helpful and perception that his or her contributions are helpful.
Validation	Participant's need to have his or her feelings, attitudes, or ideas validated.
Catharsis/load-sharing	Participant's need to share something negative or bothersome with others.
Personal growth	Participant's desire to increase knowledge or understanding through new perspectives; participant's desire for new experiences.
Socialization	Participant's desire to meet new people and make new friends in a "safe" environment.
Expectations	Participant's accurate understanding of the purpose of the group discussion.
Extrinsic rewards	Participant's value perception of fee for participation.
Negative/Inhibitors	
Use of abstract terminology	Moderator or participant's use of terminology or unfamiliar jargon.
Ego threats	Participant's challenging another participant's knowledge of the subject.
Political correctness	Participant's withholding comments for fear that his or her contributions might be perceived as disrespectful of another's knowledge or opinions.
Ego defense	Participant's withholding a comment for fear that it will make him or her appear unintelligent or that the opinion will be unpopular with the group.
Memory decay	Participant's failure to remember incidents or details of incidents.
Embellishment	Participant's creative additions to memories of behaviors in order to participate fully or inflate status.
Inarticulation/rambling accounts	Participant's inability to express ideas quickly or concisely.
Confusion	Participant's lack of understanding of the issue under discussion.
Reticence	Participant's need to be invited to participate (rather than actively volunteering comments).
Time	Participant's concern about other obligations.
Dominating/monopolizing	Participant's attempting to take leadership or the spotlight, thus blocking contributions of others.

- The level of geographic or ethnic distinctions in attitudes or behavior: The greater these influences, the more groups needed.

- The *homogeneity of the groups:* The less homogeneity, the more groups needed.

The general rule is: Keep conducting group interviews until no new insights are gained. Often a limited number of groups will suffice, or sometimes the number might grow to 8 or even 12. It is often preferable, depending on the topic, to run separate group interviews for different subsets of the target population. For example, a study on nutritional advice may begin with separate consumer and physician groups to determine the best ways to provide the advice. This type of homogeneous grouping tends to promote more intense discussion and freer interaction.[20]

Researchers caution against forming groups solely on demographic descriptors; they favor "natural" groups (like families, co-workers, church members, etc.) where the participants share an affinity base.[21] For customer groups, however, consideration should be given to such factors as gender, ethnicity, employment status, and education because culture is a primary determinant of perception. In a recent exploratory study of discount shoppers, the attitudes about the economy and personal finances expressed by East Coast respondents and West Coast respondents diverged widely. The research sponsor was able to use information from group interviews to build a strategy tailored to each geographic area.[22]

Regardless of group composition, it is the moderator who sets the tone of the group. Homogenous groups often discover their similarities early and get along well. But with heterogeneous groups, the moderator must provide the ice-breaker activities that get the participants interacting with each other. As with individual depth interviews, the moderator is responsible for developing the recruitment screener and the group discussion guide. Exhibit 6-9 summarizes the facilitators and inhibitors of individual participation in group interviews. A closer look at one of the best known of group interviews, the focus group, may clarify these distinctions.

Focus Groups

The term *focus group* was first coined by R. K. Merton in his 1956 book, *The Focused Interview*. The **focus group** is a panel of people (typically made up of 6 to 10 participants), led by a trained moderator, who meet for 90 minutes to two hours. The facilitator or moderator uses group dynamics principles to focus or guide the group in an exchange of ideas, feelings, and experiences on a specific topic. You'll find a sample focus group discussion guide for an in-person focus group in Appendix B.

Focus groups are often unique in research due to the research sponsor's involvement in the process. Most facilities permit the sponsor to observe the group and its dynamics in real time, drawing his or her own insights from the conversations and nonverbal signals he or she observes. Many facilities also allow the client to supply the moderator with new topics or questions in real time that are generated by those observing. This option is generally not available in an IDI, other group interviews, or survey research.

Focus groups typically last about two hours but may run from one to three hours. Facilities usually provide for the group to be isolated from distractions. Thus, the famous, or infamous, mirrored window allows those who are interested to observe the group while they avoid interfering with the group dynamics. Some facilities allow for product preparation and testing, as well as other creative exercises.

Fewer and lengthier focus groups are becoming common, especially as we use online panels and communities to draw participants. As sessions become longer, activities are needed to bring out deeper feelings, knowledge, and motivations. Many of the projective techniques used in IDIs are also used in focus groups:[23]

Focus groups are often used as an exploratory technique but may be a primary methodology. In two such cases, a small college used focus groups to develop a plan to attract more freshmen applications, and a blood center used a focus group to improve blood donations.[24] Focus groups are especially valuable in the following scenarios:[25]

- Obtaining general background about a topic or issue.
- Generating research questions to be explored via quantitative methodologies.
- Interpreting previously obtained quantitative results.
- Stimulating new ideas for products and programs.
- Highlighting areas of opportunity for specific managers to pursue.
- Diagnosing problems that managers need to address.
- Generating impressions and perceptions of brands and product ideas.
- Generating a level of understanding about influences in the participant's world.

Groups best enable the exploration of surprise information and new ideas. Discussion guides can be modified as the research team moves on to the next focus group. Even within an existing focus group, an adept facilitator can build on the ideas and insights of previous groups, getting to a greater depth of understanding.

>**snap**shot

Qualitative Research in the Era of Smartphones

Qualitative research covers a wide range of techniques, but they share important qualities. Every technique is an attempt to elicit meaning. Every technique digs deep but uses a smaller sample size to deliver that depth. Every technique depends on communication, albeit in a variety of formats. Qualitative researchers have used the Internet for decades, but they have embraced the smartphone as penetration has improved. More than 77 percent of U.S. adults now own a smartphone, up from 35 percent just six years earlier; making penetration near 100 percent among younger adults. Internet broadband is now used by 88 percent of U.S. adults. Dan Weber, CEO of Canada-based itracks, has been taking notice. "We've seen increased adoption of online qualitative and specifically mobile qualitative methods with increased penetration of mobile devices," shared Weber. "Participants are communicating a strong preference for mobile-friendly research experiences."

itracks GO is a complete suite of online and mobile tools for the qualitative researcher, covering IDIs and group discussions. The newest version of this software has solved some problems that have plagued qualitative researchers. itracks has designed the itracks Board platform to engage with people who may have intermittent or limited access to broadband or WiFi Internet by coming up with a mobile solution that allows participants to respond to qualitative questions and post video responses without being connected to the Internet. When their device returns to an environment with broadband or WiFi Internet access, the responses, including videos, will be automatically posted. "Stability is no longer an issue regarding mobile research," shared Weber. "If you're conducting research using an Internet-based platform and the participant's daughter downloads a movie, you could lose them. itracks Board will accommodate intermittent disconnections to the Internet by uploading of responses and videos once Internet access is restored. Research conducted on smartphones now allows participation from any environment including backyards, stores, or in remote locations regardless of Internet capability."

In an era of incredible time pressure, itracks GO, as part of the software's back end, builds in participant calendar notices and reminders, as well as reminder notices to sponsoring managers. Those managers can observe from their office or home what the qualitative moderator sees and hears. In an era of global research, itracks GO provides its suite in almost any language (or can have a new language ready in fewer than seven days).

Qualitative researchers generally want to record participants whether in the midst of a group discussion, IDI, testing a new product in their home or in a store making a purchasing decision. Any projective techniques generate video. Video clips provide an extensive amount of additional information beyond word choice, including body language and tone of voice. These clips also provide additional context, which can be observed in the video's background. But uploading these high-quality, full-length videos was problematic until itracks designed a way to com-

Courtesy of itracks

press and fragment a single video into thousands of smaller clips that could upload quickly, then be reconnected just as quickly. It also incorporates marking software for tagging clip sentiments such as *positive, neutral,* or *negative* and offers "VideoVault" for storing and editing videos into video highlight reels. These highlight reels provide important validation support for research findings and insights in research reports.

Some qualitative subjects are highly sensitive. Weber noticed an uptick in researcher concern that subjects who had agreed to participate were dropping out of groups or IDIs; these participants were uncomfortable broadcasting their own image. itracks GO now includes an audio-based IDI tool that allows respondents to participate without being filmed and includes media shares and markup tools to enhance participant engagement.

Gen Y and Gen Z cohorts (born 1960–2000) are great texters, so itracks GO incorporates a text-based chat platform. Transcripts of these sessions can be instantly downloaded and later analyzed by text-analytic software, such as OdinText.

"Mobile is playing a critical role in Qual," claimed Weber. He expects that role will be even more important as our dependence on the smartphone continues to grow.

www.itracks.com

Telephone or online focus groups have proven effective in the following scenarios:

- When it is difficult to recruit desired participants—members of elite groups and hard-to-access individuals such as experts, professionals, physician specialists, high-level executives, and store owners.
- When target group members are rare, "low-incidence," or widely dispersed geographically—directors of a medical clinic, celebrities, early adopters, and rural practitioners.
- When issues are so sensitive that anonymity is needed but respondents must be from a wide geographic area—people suffering from a contagious disease, people using nonmainstream products, high-income individuals, competitors.
- When you want to conduct only a couple of focus groups but want nationwide representation.

Additionally, online focus groups work well when:

- Teens or young adults are the desired participants.
- Desired participants are technically employed segments of the market, those essentially comfortable with computer use.
- A computer-based application, such as software or a game, is the topic of group discussion.
- Visual stimuli are necessary to discuss the topics of interest.

Like telephone focus groups, videoconferencing and online focus groups offer significant savings over in-person focus groups. By reducing the travel time for the moderator and the manager, coordinating such groups can be accomplished in a shorter time and at a lower cost.

Group Interview Drawbacks and Their Solutions

However, given time constraints, group interviews permit spending only limited time extracting detail from each participant.[26] This problem is magnified when a group interview is structured to cover numerous questions or topics.

Another drawback of the group interview is the increased difficulty recruiting, arranging, and co-ordinating group discussions that require travel. But this aggravation—which can be subcontracted to a specialist research supplier—is deemed a small price to pay for the insights that often are revealed by group interaction.

Interviewers are tested by the challenge of managing the group's conversation while avoiding interjecting themselves into the group's process. It is also the moderator's job to control the extrovert or dominant personality and ensure meaningful contributions from all others, including the most introverted or private thinkers. When control is not maintained, some members' opinions may be suppressed and valuable insights lost. Sometimes an individual will be more honest with a neutral interviewer than with a group of peers. One example is a group of small-business owners being unwilling to divulge competitive strengths and weaknesses. A skilled researcher can anticipate which topics are more likely to obtain good results with an individual or a group interview.

Recording, Analyzing, and Reporting Group Interviews

In face-to-face settings, some moderators use large sheets of paper on the wall of the group room to record trends; others use a personal notepad. Facility managers produce both video- and audiotapes to enable a full analysis of the interview. The verbal portion of the group interview and moderator debriefing sessions are transcribed and added to moderator notes. These are analyzed across several focus group sessions using **content analysis**. This analytical process provides the research sponsor with a qualitative picture of the respondents' concerns, ideas, attitudes, and feelings. The preliminary profile of the content of a group interview is often done with computer software in content analysis. Such software searches for common phrasing and words, context, and patterns of expression on digitized transcripts.

Problems within Focus Groups

Founder and principal researcher Robert W. Kahle of Kahle Research Solutions Inc., in his book *Dominators, Cynics, and Wallflowers*, dissects typical focus group participants to illuminate ways to modify their problem behaviors. DOMINATORS are all-knowing, quick to answer, and choose a seat location in order to challenge the moderator for control. CYNICS display negative behaviors and deride the ideas of others. HOSTILES have an agenda of their own and seek corrective action; they are often angry and combative. INTOXICATEDS are under the influence of something, fidgety and incoherent. PROSELYTIZERS cannot accept that others hold opposing opinions and try to persuade others to their opinion. BLATHERERS offer long, off-topic answers and ignore moderator cues. JOKERS find every comment source material for a new joke, story, or comical facial expression. FOLLOWERS tend to repeat others' opinions. WALLFLOWERS withdraw both physically and verbally. Finally, CO-MODERATORS often engage participants before a discussion starts, ask questions of their own, and seek to befriend or support other participants.

©Spencer Grant/PhotoEdit/Getty Images

Why is each of these behaviors a problem and how would you handle each of these problem participants?

www.kahleresearch.com, www.paramountbooks.com

>Combining Qualitative Methodologies

In a researcher's search for meaning, he often combines the two primary qualitative methodologies of interview and observation. Two of these combinations, the case study and action research, deserve special mention as they are used frequently in business research.

Case Study[27]

The **case study**, also referred to as the *case history*, is a powerful research methodology that combines individual and (sometimes) group interviews with record analysis and observation. Researchers extract information from company brochures, annual reports, sales receipts, and newspaper and magazine articles, along with direct observation (usually done in the participant's "natural" setting), and combine it with interview data from participants. The objective is to obtain multiple perspectives of a single organization, situation, event, or process at a point in time or over a period of time. Case study methodology—or the written report from such a research project, often called a *case analysis* or *case write-up*—can be used to understand particular processes. For example, one study might evaluate new product development processes for similarities, especially the use of outside consultants, ideational techniques, and computer simulation. Another study might examine in detail the purchaser's response to a stimulus like a display. The results of the research could be used to experiment with modifications of the new product development process or with display selection and placement processes to generate higher-value transactions. The research problem is usually a how and why problem, resulting in a descriptive or explanatory study.

Researchers select the specific organizations or situations to profile because these examples offer critical, extreme, or unusual cases. Researchers most often choose multiple cases, rather than a single case, to study because of the opportunity for cross-case analysis. In studying multiple cases, a deeper understanding emerges. When multiple cases are chosen, it is because they offer similar results for predictable reasons (literal replication) or contrary results for predictable reasons (theoretical replication). While theoretical sampling seems to be common, a minimum of 4 cases with a maximum of 15 seems to be favored.

In the case study, interview participants are invited to tell the story of their experience, with those chosen representing different levels within the same organization or different perspectives of the same situation or process to permit depth of perspective. The flexibility of the case study approach and the emphasis on understanding the context of the case being studied allow for a richness of understanding sometimes labeled *thick description*.

During analysis, a single case analysis is always performed before any cross-case analysis is conducted. The emphasis is on what differences occur, why, and with what effect. Prescriptive inferences about best practices are concluded after completing case studies on several organizations or situations and are speculative in nature.

Business students are quite familiar with studying cases as a means of learning business principles. *In Search of Excellence,* a book by Tom Peters and Robert Waterman, was developed using case study methodology.[28] Other similar studies profiled in books written on Procter & Gamble and Disney have also used this methodology. In the business arena, such case studies have examined changes in new product development, sales processes, hiring practices, and training programs.

Action Research

Managers conduct research in order to gain insights to make decisions in specific scenarios. **Action research** is designed to address complex, practical problems about which little is known—thus no known heuristics exist. So the scenario is studied; a corrective action is determined, planned, and implemented; the results of the action are observed and recorded; and the action is assessed as effective or not. The process is repeated until a desired outcome is reached, but along the way much is learned about the processes and about the prescriptive actions being studied. Action researchers investigate the effects of applied solutions. Whatever theories are developed are validated through practical application.[29]

Suppose a restaurant that had never received a customer complaint earns its first challenge by a disgruntled diner. If no general rule existed about how to treat unhappy patrons, the organization could study the situation and come up with alternative actions. It might:

- Ignore the problem. (Its lack of experience would prevent it from knowing that negative word of mouth—negative buzz—would be the likely result.)
- Do whatever is necessary to replace the unsatisfactory meal within the shortest period of time.
- Accept the current circumstance as uncorrectable, apologize to the customer, and remedy the situation by picking up the table's full dining tab and offering the customer a free meal to get him or her back in the restaurant another day.

In action research, one of those alternatives would be chosen and implemented, and then the results recorded. Was the customer happy when he or she left? Did the customer return to dine another evening or never return again? Over the next three months, what was the customer's full revenue value? If the customer didn't return, the next time a disgruntled customer voiced dissatisfaction, a different action would be chosen, implemented, and then assessed in comparison to the first option's results.

>Merging Qualitative and Quantitative Methodologies

Triangulation is the term used to describe the combining of several qualitative methods or combining qualitative with quantitative methods. Because of the controversy described earlier, qualitative studies may be combined with quantitative ones to increase the perceived quality of the research, especially when a quantitative study follows a qualitative one and provides validation for the qualitative findings. Four strategies for combining methodologies are common in business research:[30]

1. Conducting qualitative and quantitative studies simultaneously.
2. Conducting multiple waves of quantitative studies, measuring changes in behavior and attitudes over time, while a qualitative study is ongoing.
3. Conducting a qualitative study prior to conducting a quantitative study. A second qualitative study then might follow the quantitative study, seeking more clarification.
4. Conducting a quantitative study before conducting a qualitative study.

An example of the first strategy would be the combination of a public opinion poll at the time focus groups are being held to discover ways to sway a particular public's opinion on a union election process. For the second strategy, we might collect life histories while multiple waves of questionnaires are measuring the response to differing training tactics. For the third, we could perform a qualitative study to identify peoples' behaviors and perceptions with respect to furniture shopping processes and interior decorating; then we could use that information to develop a quantitative study to measure the actual frequency of behaviors and attitudes. And, fourth, we might survey people's behavior and attitudes toward a change in company mission and find we need some IDIs to explain findings that are unclear.

Many researchers recognize that qualitative research compensates for the weaknesses of quantitative research and vice versa. These forward thinkers believe that the methodologies complement rather than rival each other.

>Ethical Issues and Their Solutions

As with any design, the participants, the research sponsors, and the researchers have responsibilities in the planning of qualitative research. These responsibilities are focused on privacy, confidentiality, quality, and safety. Qualitative studies often cover numerous activities over a span of days or weeks; participants have the responsibility of completion. They are also asked to share life experiences and anecdotes; they have a responsibility of truthfulness.

Managers often don't have the skill set to conduct qualitative research because many of the techniques require specialized educational background and training. Managers who want quality research have the responsibility of full disclosure and lack of coercion when hiring that expertise.

Because qualitative research often tackles sensitive subjects and probes for meaning, researchers have the responsibility to protect confidentiality of both participant and the manager sponsor, choose appropriate methods and activities within those methods, and train moderators/interviewers within those methods to ensure quality.

To address these concerns, researchers often go to extremes to make participants feel comfortable and keep them engaged. Participants are sharing their innermost thoughts and personal experiences with the researcher. One of the strengths of qualitative research is the ability to use a participant's voice, video, photos, collages, etc., as evidence to support researcher insights. During the process, the participants need to feel that their identity is protected. Thus researchers must deliver on the participants' right of privacy and the right of consent before using their image, words, and audio and video files. The researcher must also protect the insights gathered, sharing these only with the manager-sponsor. It is especially important in qualitative research to respect the data's limitations: not to project results of a small sample to a target population.

>summary

LO6-1 Qualitative research includes an array of interpretive techniques that seek to describe, decode, translate, and otherwise come to terms with the meaning, not the frequency, of certain more or less naturally occurring phenomena in the social world. Qualitative research methodologies differ from quantitative methodologies based on the focus of the research; its purpose; researcher involvement; sampling design; sample size; research design, including participant pretasking; data source, type, and preparation; methods of data analysis; level of insights and meaning extracted; research sponsor involvement; speed of the research; and data security. A qualitative methodology may be used alone to address organizational problems or in combination with other qualitative or quantitative methodologies.

LO6-2 Qualitative research is designed to tell the researcher how (process) and why (meaning) things happen as they do. It is appropriate for all business disciplines and is used extensively in marketing, HR, finance, and general management. In business planning and decision making, qualitative methodologies are used in job analysis, advertising concept development, productivity enhancement, new product development, retail design, process understanding, market segmentation, sales analysis, and union representation.

LO6-3 Qualitative methodologies used in decision making evolved from techniques used in anthropology, sociology, psychology, linguistics, communication, economics, and semiotics. Common among these methods are the individual depth interview (IDI) and the group interview, as well as observation combination methodologies (e.g., ethnography, action research, case analysis, and grounded theory). Within group interviews, the focus group is the most widely used methodology. Qualitative research often uses creative exercises to probe deeply into motivations, attitudes, opinions, feelings and experiences. These exercises can include projective techniques, which encourage the participant to share their own thoughts while projecting them on another. Among these techniques are word or picture association, completion, cartoons or empty balloons, the Thematic Apperception Test, imagination exercises, and sorting and writing exercises.

LO6-4 The interviewer is central to great qualitative research and should be chosen for his or her skills. The interviewer is not just a data collector, but a collaborative consultant on the project, with numerous contributions, including recommending method and level of structure; developing the criteria for sample participants, developing the recruitment screener, and recruiting participants; controlling the interview and managing special facilities, if necessary; developing pretasking exercises; preparing the interview/discussion guide; preparing instructions, research stimuli and tools; debriefing observers; supervising the transcription process; contributing to data analysis and insight formation; and preparing or directing the preparation of the research report, including extracting video or audio clips.

LO6-5 The ethical issues of qualitative research include confidentiality (both sponsor and participant), quality, and safety. The interviewer/data collector shares these responsibilities with the research designer. Due to the nature of the sensitive subjects sometimes discussed in qualitative research, protecting the participant is paramount. Obtaining informed consent is the best strategy for working with this issue, as well as adhering to strict privacy guidelines. Participants often agree to engage in projects that cover a period of days and sometimes weeks; they have the responsibility to complete research once it is started, as well as to share truthfully their life experiences, thought, attitudes, and opinions.

>keyterms

action research 143

authority figure 133

ambiguities and paradoxes 133

cartoons or empty balloons 133

case study (case history) 142

collage 133

completion/fill in the blank 133

component sorts 133

computer-assisted personal interview (CAPI) 134

content analysis 141

convergent interviewing 135

creative innovation role play 133

critical incident technique 135

cultural interviews 135

data saturation 127

ethnography 135

expert group 137

focus group 139

grounded theory 135

group interview 137

heterogeneous group 137

homogeneous group 137

imaginary universe 133

imagination exercises 133

individual depth interview (IDI) 134

interview 129

interview guide (discussion guide) 131

laddering or benefit chain 133

life histories 135

>discussionquestions

Terms in Review

1 How does qualitative research differ from quantitative research?

2 What is data saturation, and how does it influence qualitative research?

3 What is the nature of data collected in qualitative research?

4 Why do senior executives feel more comfortable relying on quantitative data than qualitative data? How might a qualitative research company lessen the senior-level executive's skepticism?

5 Distinguish among structured, semistructured, and unstructured interviews.

Making Research Decisions

6 Assume you are a manufacturer of small kitchen electrics, like Hamilton Beach/Proctor Silex, and you want to determine if some innovative designs with unusual shapes and colors developed for the European market could be successfully marketed in the U.S. market. What qualitative research would you recommend, and why?

7 NCR Corporation, known as a world leader in ATMs, point-of-sale (POS) retail checkout scanners, and check-in kiosks at airports, announced in June 2009 that it would move its world headquarters from Dayton (OH) to Duluth (GA), a suburb of Atlanta, after more than 125 years. An employer of 1,200 mostly high-salaried, professional workers in Dayton, NCR was enticed to move by Georgia's offer of more than $56.9 million in tax credits; its fast-growing, educated 25- to 34-year-old population cohort; international offices for 10 European state governments; and the busiest international airport (Atlanta) in the world.

a What qualitative research might NCR have done to reach this decision?

b NCR will use its move to Georgia to downsize its world headquarters workforce. What qualitative research could help NCR determine which of its 1,200 employees will be offered positions in Duluth?

From Concept to Practice

8 Use Exhibit 6-6 to develop the recruitment screener for the research you described in your answer to question 6.

9 Conduct a focus group among students in your class on one of the following topics:

a The department's problems offering requirements and electives essential for meeting your graduation expectations.

b Entertainment sponsored by your university to bring the community on campus.

From the Headlines

10 Lately, airlines have been having a rough time, in terms of legal actions and PR issues, with consumers openly expressing outrage at being bumped from—or forcibly removed from—flights. Design a qualitative study to reveal the suppressed (as opposed to surface) issues that are contributing to this rage.

a What are some of the surface issues?

b Who will you want to participate and how will you recruit them?

c What qualitative method(s) will you choose. Be specific about any exercises you will incorporate.

>cases*

Akron Children's Hospital

Covering Kids with Health Care

Lexus SC 430

NCRCC: Teeing Up a New Strategic Direction

Ohio Lottery: Innovative Research Design Drives Winning

Open Doors: Extending Hospitality to Travelers with Disabilities

Ramada Demonstrates Its *Personal Best*™

Starbucks, Bank One, and Visa Launch Starbucks Card Duetto Visa

USTA: Come Out Swinging

*You will find a description of each case in the Case Abstracts section of this textbook. Check the Case Index to determine whether a case provides data, the research instrument, video, or other supplementary material. Cases and case supplements are available in Connect.

chapter 7

Stage 2:
Data Collection
Design:
Observation Research

"No longer do companies study consumers' psyches only by asking people what they think about technology and how they use it. Now they conduct observational research, dispatching anthropologists to employ their ethnographic skills by interviewing, watching and videotaping consumers in their natural habitats."

Katie Hafner,
author

>**learning**objectives

After reading this chapter, you should understand . . .

LO7-1   When observation studies are most useful.

LO7-2   The distinctions between monitoring nonbehavioral and behavioral activities.

LO7-3   The strengths of the observation approach in research design.

LO7-4   The weaknesses of the observation approach in research design.

LO7-5   The three perspectives from which the observer–participant relationship may be viewed in observation studies.

LO7-6   The various designs of observation studies.

Research designs are classified by the *approach* used to gather primary data: Researchers can *monitor* (observe) or *communicate*. Behavioral scientists define observation research in terms of animal or human behavior, but this is too limiting for observation as a methodology in business research. We prefer that you define **observation** as a method that collects data through all our primary senses; it involves listening, reading, smelling, tasting, and touching.

It's important to remember that businesses are using research to identify paths to innovation. Structured communication studies sometimes stifle the very participants businesses hope to use to open doors to such innovation; they interrupt participants' natural thought processes and behaviors with questions that might seem irrelevant to the participant. During observations, participants engage in actual behaviors with processes, objects, environments, and people. Participants offer nonverbal cues about their feelings through body language and verbal cues through spontaneous comments. Trained observers often identify participant innovations and the motivations for those innovations (e.g., participants combine products or products and services to tackle a problem; they change processes to work more efficiently, save time, or reduce waste). Participants in communication studies have proven to be highly unreliable reporters of their own behavior, but observers work with actual actions, not memories. Observers can be trained not only in what is but in what might be feasible. Exhibit 7-1 describes the conditions under which observation is an appropriate method for data collection, contrasting those conditions with ones from the communication modes (e.g., interviews, surveys, etc.).

While it might appear that the communication approach dominates, observational research has never been more important to business. We monitor everything—from the movement of goods from factory floor to retail store to the performance of every part in a fast-moving train; from the performance of workers in emergency rooms to the shelf life of food in the refrigerators in homes; from the behavior of patrons in restaurants to the readers' eye movements on web pages. Where once organizations might

>**Exhibit 7-1** Selecting the Data Collection Method

have relied solely on human observation, then later enhanced that human observation with camera footage, today some observation increasingly relies on embedded sensors or software as collection methods. In the past few years, we've reached a tipping point where computerized sensors in devices—the Internet of Things (IoT)—are expanding our observation data at a rate that exceeds our ability to analyze it. And more changes in observational research are coming.

Much of what we know comes from observation. We notice co-workers' reactions to political intrigue, the sounds in the assembly area, the smell of perfume, the taste of office coffee, the smoothness of the vice president's marble desk, and a host of other stimuli. While such observation may be a basis for knowledge, the collection processes are often haphazard. Observation research, as scientific inquiry, is conducted specifically to answer a research question, must be systematically planned and executed, must use proper controls, and must provide a reliable and valid description of what happened. The versatility of observation makes it an indispensable primary method and a supplement for other methods. Exhibit 7-2 depicts the use of observation in the research process.

Sometimes, while observation is the right approach, we need to change the observation protocol to achieve our research objectives. One example might be how we use observation research to understand planes and catastrophic airline accidents. Currently, airlines collect critical plane operation data and minute-by-minute cockpit conversations with sensors and digital recording devices that store this

>**Exhibit 7-2** Observation and the Research Process

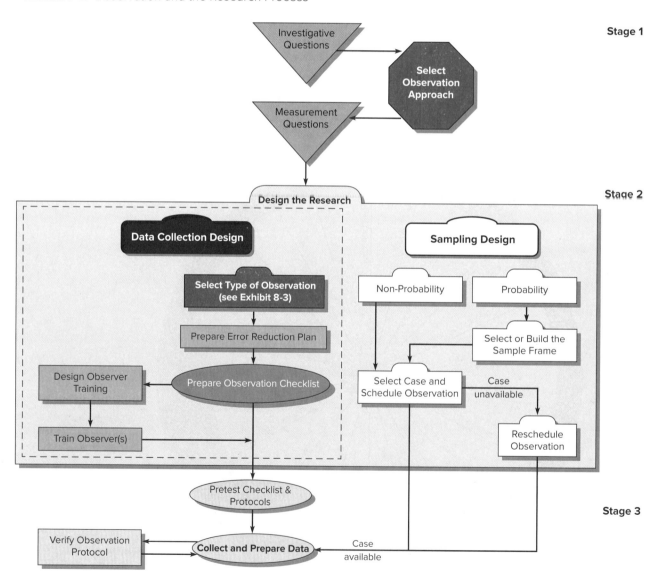

information in "black boxes" mounted in the plane. Once collected, we might analyze these data to schedule maintenance, understand part design or performance, or explain plane failure. But in one year, we lost hundreds of lives when three planes crashed and the black box—and its data—was not retrieved. Following one such accident, a CBS News story reported that current technology could capture such information in real time and store it on cloud servers. Such a method would allow the airline to know precisely what happened to a downed plane and when and where it happened. As with all research decisions, the cost of using this newer methodology (estimated at as much as $10,000 per year per plane) is a concern, but also to be considered is the coverage of ground-based radar (estimated at 30 percent of the world), the availability of satellite-based WiFi and GPS, and the high cost of black-box retrieval in water-based crashes. Are observation data captured via on-plane black boxes sufficient as an observation method to meet the research objectives?[1]

>Observation Research Design

Numerous factors influence research design, as summarized in Exhibit 7-3, including:

- Choice of sampling design
- Choices within data collection design:
  - Content of observation
  - Environment
  - Observational condition
  - Data collection protocols
  - Observer presence
  - Observer concealment

>**Exhibit 7-3** Factors Influencing Observation Research Design

	Factors	Options
Who/What	Sampling Designs	• Event sampling • Time sampling
What	Content of Types	• Factual • Inferential • Both
What	Types of Observation	• Nonbehavioral observation • Behavioral observation
When/where	Environment	• Field (natural setting) • Laboratory (artificial setting)
How	Data Collection Protocols	• Simple observation • Systematic observation
How	Observer presence	• Direct • Indirect
How	Observation concealment	• No Concealment • Concealment • Partial Concealment
How	Observer involvement	• No Involvement • Participant observation

>Sampling Design

What qualifies a case—a participant activity, record, object, event—to be observed? The answer is in the investigative questions. If a case possesses that information, it qualifies.

Acts or behaviors, time frames or people can represent target populations in observation. While some forms of observation can use probability sampling (e.g., analysis of records, video records of behaviors), many forms of observation must rely on nonprobability sampling.

Within these two broad categories, there are two types of sampling designs that are specially designed for observation: event sampling and time sampling.[2] In **event sampling**, the researcher records that a specific behavior or act occurs; the duration of the observation is determined by when the act begins and ends. In some instances, the researcher may also capture its antecedents—events and conditions immediately before the behavior of interest—and the consequences—what happens immediately after the event. For example, assume a machine malfunctions or stops; the event of interest is the stoppage itself. When did it occur, what was the machine producing, what or who stopped the machine (an internal device, a person operating the machine, etc.), who was operating the machine at the time it stopped, etc. While it is unlikely we could hire an observer to wait and watch for machines to malfunction, we can use records of such events. Either event or time sampling can be used when observing human behavior.

In **time sampling**, the choice of cases is based on some time interval. There are three types of time sampling: a time-point sample, continuous real-time samples, or a time-interval sample. For *time-point sampling*, recording occurs at fixed points for a specified length of time, the variable of interest is measured if it falls within that time frame from all cases. For example, a manager might be interested in how often her employees check their email during the day. With the assistance of her IT department, she monitors email access during three times: 2:00, 3:00, and 4:00 for 10 minutes each time. If employees access their email, she measures not only access, but duration of access (were they on email for 2 minutes, 7 minutes, or all 10 minutes). From this study, an assessment about the disruptiveness of email might be determined. Over a prolonged period, if the samples are drawn randomly, time sampling can give a good estimate of the pattern of activities.

With *continuous real-time sampling*, any and all behavior during the specified time of the behavior is recorded; behavior of the sampled case as well as behavior by others. For example, imagine you plan professional conferences for a living. You are interested in how attendees use breaks between conference sessions. You might record the spaces outside the conference sessions during breaks and study the various behaviors (do attendees exchange contact information, discuss on conference topics, make plans to meet for dinner or drinks; contact their office or make personal calls, work on tablets or desktops, enter restroom facilities; return to sessions or remain in break spaces, etc.) Any and all behaviors are captured, and you likely have anticipated some of these behaviors, so you can check off how often each occurs, even recording what men and women attendees do. In this study, we might assess the placement of refreshments, seating capacity in break spaces, and time frame allotted for breaks.

Time-interval sampling records every desired behavior in real time but counts the behavior only once during the interval for each case. In essence, you are interested in whether the behavior occurred, not how often or its many variations. So using our conference planner, she might record whether any man or woman used the restroom facilities or checked his or her phone, etc., during the break time; if just one did, for each activity, then that act would be verified as occurring during break times.

If we use people as sample cases, then their selection is often because of some prior behavior or characteristic. For example, an observation study might involve product use. We observe a person purchase an item in a store (e.g., box of cake mix) and recruit them for a home-use study. We arrange a time to watch them bake their cake. Do they follow directions precisely or make modifications; what tools (pans, spatulas, bowls) do they use in the preparation of cake batter; what additional products do they use to complete the cake (e.g., fruit preserves or spreads, icing, candies, sprinkles or decorations, candles); do they have difficulties or is the cake a masterpiece? From such a study, we might recommend changes in packaging directions, packaging design, or new products.

Sampling design must also answer the following: Who are the contacts to gain access to the sample cases? These are often intermediaries who help with introductions and serve as contacts to reach if conditions change or trouble develops. These intermediaries also provide access to desired records, recording devices, etc.

>Data Collection Design

The data collection design specifies the details of the observation. In essence it answer the questions of what, when, where, and how.

Content Type

Specific conditions, events, or activities that we want to observe determine the observational reporting system (and correspond to measurement questions). To specify the observation content, we should include both the major variables of interest and any other variables that may affect them. From this cataloging, we then select those items we plan to observe. For each variable chosen, we must provide an operational definition if there is any question of concept ambiguity or special meanings. Even if the concept is a common one, we must make certain that all observers agree on the measurement terms by which to record results. For example, we may agree that variable W will be reported by count, while variable Y will be counted and the effectiveness of its use judged qualitatively.

Observations may be either *facts* (overt actions, surface indicators, spontaneous utterances) or *inferences* (interpretations of facts). Let's use a salesperson's presentation as what is observed. Maybe the researcher is trying to determine the effectiveness of the current training program. What is measured may be defined as an act. Any of the following could be defined as an act for an observation study:

- A single expressed thought
- A physical movement
- A facial expression
- A motor skill
- An outcome

Although acts may be well defined, they often present difficulties for the observer. A single statement from a sales presentation may include several thoughts about product advantages, a rebuttal to an objection about a feature, or some remark about a competitor. The observer is hard-pressed to sort out each thought, decide whether it represents a separate unit of observation, and then record it quickly enough to follow continued statements.

Exhibit 7-4 shows how we could separate the factual and inferential components of an observation for the salesperson's presentation. This table is suggestive only. It does not include many other variables that might be of interest, including factual data on customer purchase history; company, industry, and general economic conditions; the order in which sales arguments are presented; and specific words used to describe certain product characteristics. The particular content of observation will also be affected by the nature of the observation setting.

>**Exhibit 7-4** Content of Observation: Fact versus Inference

Fact	Inference
Introduction/identification of salesperson and customer	Credibility of salesperson; qualified status of customer
Time and day of week	Convenience for the customer; welcoming attitude of the customer
Product presented	Customer interest in product
Selling points presented per product	Customer acceptance of selling points per product
Number of customer objections raised per product	Customer concerns about features and benefits
Salesperson's rebuttal of objection	Effectiveness of salesperson's rebuttal attempts
Salesperson's attempt to restore controls	Effectiveness of salesperson's control attempt; consequences for customer who prefers interaction
Length of interview	Customer's/salesperson's degree of enthusiasm for the interview
Environmental factors interfering with the interview	Level of distraction for the customer
Customer purchase decision	General evaluation of sales presentation skill

Types of Observation

Researchers using observation monitor behavioral activities and nonbehavioral conditions, which, as shown in Exhibit 7-5, can be classified roughly as follows:

Nonbehavioral Observation

- Record analysis
- Physical condition analysis
- Physical process analysis

Behavioral Observation

- Nonverbal analysis
- Linguistic analysis
- Extralinguistic analysis
- Spatial analysis

Nonbehavioral Observation

A prevalent form of observation research is **record analysis**. This may involve historical or current records and public or private records. These may be written, printed, sound-recorded, photographed, film, or videos. Historical statistical data may be the only sources used for a study. Analysis of current financial records and economic data also provide major data sources for business studies. Other examples of this type of observation are the content analysis of competitive advertising and the analysis of personnel records. The major problem associated with nonbehavioral observation is the lack of consistency of data recorded over time. If a business failed to use consistent operating definitions of concepts and constructs, it makes direct comparison difficult.

Physical condition analysis is typified by store audits of merchandise availability, studies of plant safety compliance, and analysis of inventory conditions. **Process analysis** (or *activity analysis*) includes time/motion studies of manufacturing processes and analysis of traffic flows in a distribution system, paperwork flows in an office, and money (digital and currency) flows in the banking system. Both of these types of observations can use observers to record overt actions and conditions or record analysis, or a combination.

>**Exhibit 7-5** Selecting an Observation Approach

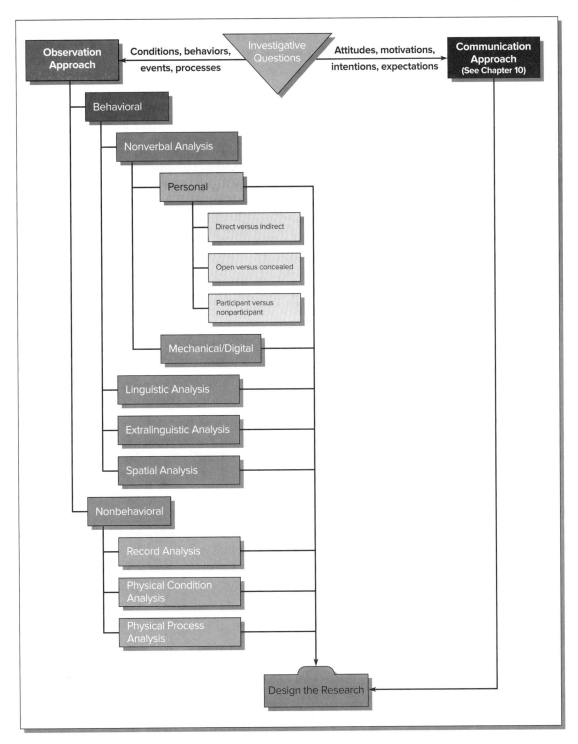

Behavioral Observation

The observational study of persons can be classified into four major categories.[3] **Nonverbal behavior,** the most prevalent of these, includes body movement, motor expressions, and even exchanged glances. At the level of gross body movement, one might study how a salesperson travels a territory. At a fine level, one can study the body movements of a worker assembling a product or time-sample the activity of a department's workforce to discover the share of time each worker spends in various ways. More abstractly, one can study body movement as an indicator of interest or boredom, anger or pleasure in a certain environment. Motor expressions such as facial movements can be observed as a sign of emotional state. Eyeblink rates are studied as indicators of interest in advertising messages. Exchanged glances are of interest in studies of interpersonal behavior.

>**snap**shot

Visual Content Gets Sticky

One emerging technology that is gathering interest among researchers and their clients is eye-tracking; more than 58 percent of researchers in the annual GRIT study indicate they are currently or plan to use the technology. Sticky, a leading visual optimization platform, provides a biometric solution that helps digital content developers measure and optimize the visual web. Participants, often members of client panels or Sticky's own panel called "The Crowd," are introduced to visual stimuli via the Internet via their laptop, desktop, or tablet. "Sticky measures facial expressions and eye movements in 3D, allowing for the most accurate tracking possible, even when people move, lighting changes, or the face is partially obstructed," shared Hans Lee, CEO of Sticky. "When measuring the impact of video and other content, the intensity of emotions defines message resonance—and therefore the likelihood that the content goes viral." Businesses curate a lot of content on the web. Each is intensely interested in what the eye sees and tracks and in having their content shared. "Earning attention leads to market success. With Sticky, a firm can measure the number of seconds a medium actually earns—an industry first," claimed Lee.

For example, Sticky's online eye-tracking methodology tested one of its own planned ads—Guessing Game—and revealed that while almost all of the ad's audience quickly saw the key visual and the headline message, the ad delivered only average brand recognition. Without brand recognition, an ad is unlikely to drive prospects to the company. (See the generated heat map in action on Connect.)

How your eye tracks through visual stimuli translates not only to engagement with an organization's social network sites, but also to message recall, website click-through, and ultimately, purchase. Sticky can aggregate survey data with its eye-tracking and facial coding data to understand a participant's level of emotional engagement with visual stimuli. The technology—once only available in specially equipped labs but now available no matter where a participant is located—is used in website design, package design, ad design, email communications, and emotion understanding.

www.sticky.ad

Courtesy of Sticky by Tobii Pro

>snapshotcont'd

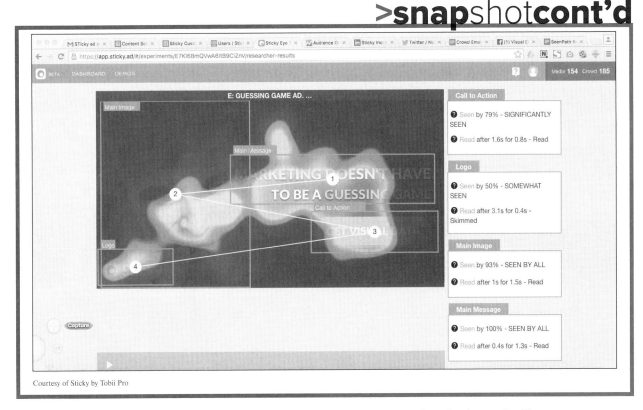

Courtesy of Sticky by Tobii Pro

Linguistic behavior is a second frequently used form of behavior observation. One simple type familiar to most students is the tally of "ahs" or other annoying sounds or words a professor makes or uses during a class. More serious applications are the study of an executive's presentation content when addressing financial analysts or the study of what, how, and how much information is conveyed in a training situation. A third form of linguistic behavior involves interaction processes that occur between two people or in small groups. In some observations, spontaneous utterances are as important as the overt acts of behavior measured.[4]

Verbal behavior also may be analyzed as **extralinguistic behaviors**. One author suggests there are four dimensions of extralinguistic activity:[5] (1) vocal, including pitch, loudness, and timbre; (2) temporal, including the rate of speaking, duration of utterance, and rhythm; (3) interaction, including the tendencies to interrupt, dominate, or inhibit; and (4) verbal stylistic, including vocabulary and pronunciation peculiarities, dialect, and characteristic expressions. These dimensions could add substantial insight to the linguistic content of the interactions between supervisors and subordinates or salespeople and customers.

A fourth type of behavior study involves **spatial relationships**, especially how a person relates physically to others. One form of this study, *proxemics*, concerns how people organize the territory about them and how they maintain discrete distances between themselves and others. A study of how salespeople physically approach customers and a study of the effects of crowding in a workplace are examples of this type of observation.

Often in a study, the researcher will be interested in two or more of these types of information. Such studies may require more than one observer. In these forms of behavior study, it is also important to consider the relationship between observers and participants.

If you observed this behavior, what would you record?

Observation Environment

Observation studies can be designed for the field or laboratory. In business research, field studies may take place at a customer's home, the shopping environment, an employee work area (plant, office, distribution center), a supplier's location, and more. Field studies, offering a natural setting, are most likely to obtain unaltered behavior, especially when the observer isn't directly involved.

Laboratory studies are most likely to provide data protection. When specialized equipment is needed for observation (e.g., eye-tracking cameras, heart rate monitors, galvanic skin response machines, etc) laboratory settings are often the choice. We've had some success with employing eye-tracking via a subject's laptop and tablet cameras. Laboratory settings are obviously more expensive, usually involve smaller sample sizes, and pose more difficulties in recruiting subjects. Laboratory observations can be part of an experimental design.

>**snap**shot

Observation and Police Cameras

If you read or watch the news, you'll know that urban areas have had a sharp increase in questioned—if not questionable—police actions with regard to excessive use of force, and bystander videos have played an increasing role in judging police actions. In 2015, the U.S. Supreme Court, in *Graham v. Connor,* held that an officer's actions, however, "must be judged from the perspective of a reasonable officer, rather than with the 20/20 vision of hindsight." In an article in *The Atlantic*, Seth W. Stoughton, a law professor and former police officer, and Geoffrey Alpert, a professor of criminology, both at the University of South Carolina; along with Jeff Noble, a police consultant based in Orange County, California, write, "The aversion to what officers derisively refer to as "'second-guessing' . . . [makes] officers less receptive to a critique of their actions . . . [and] makes them reluctant to provide their own complete and honest critiques." Yet nationwide, we've seen a demand for police to change and for police decisions to be more transparent, resulting in a clamoring for use of police body and cruiser cameras.

Do you believe you get a true picture of an incident when you see a body-mounted or dash-mounted video? Stoughton, who also consults with law enforcement agencies, has choreographed a series of videos to demonstrate the answer to this question. His use parallels an observation study based on respondents watching video footage of mock police incidents. Using a series of chest-mounted or dash-mounted cameras and bystander videos, he shows just how difficult it is to arrive at an accurate conclusion when using only a police-cruiser or body-cam video.

Chest-mounted cameras during interactions or pursuits often create jerky movements and wildly distorted images. Stoughton calls this "deceptive intensity"; it creates the impression that the officer is under attack when he might not be. In an interception incident video, using a dash-mounted camera involving a fleeing suspect and Taser use by an officer, accuracy is related to vantage point. The body camera doesn't reveal the use of a Taser or the absence of a gun, while video shot by a bystander does. "When video allows us to look through someone's eyes, we

©Aaron Roeth Photography

tend to adopt an interpretation that favors that person," explains Stoughton, a psychological phenomenon known as "camera perspective bias." Stoughton's research also reveals that the degree to which the viewer trusts or distrusts the police influences his or her video interpretation. So while the bystander might not know any facts leading up to the incident, his or her camera has its own bias. He concludes video evidence interpretation depends, therefore, on perspective as well as bias.

So in observation research, should we consider the camera as an accurate, unbiased observer? See for yourself. Check out the videos on Connect.

>**Exhibit 7-6** Classification of Observation Studies

Class	Purpose	Structure	Environment	Research Tool
1	Generate hypothesis	Completely unstructured	Natural setting	
2		Unstructured	Laboratory	
3		Structured	Natural setting	Observation checklist
4	Test hypothesis	Completely structured	Laboratory	Observation checklist

Data Collection Protocol

Observation is found in almost all research studies, at least at the exploratory stage. Such data collection is known as **simple observation**. Its data collection protocols (procedures used to record observations) are not standardized, as one would expect, because of the discovery nature of exploratory research. The decision to use observation as the major data collection method may be made as early as the moment the researcher moves from research questions to investigative questions—the specific questions the researcher must answer with collected data. If the study is to be something other than exploratory, **systematic observation** employs standardized procedures, trained observers, schedules for recording, and other devices for the observer that mirror the scientific procedures of other primary data methods. Systematic studies vary in the emphasis placed on recording and encoding observational information:

> At one end of the continuum are methods that are unstructured and open-ended. The observer tries to provide as complete and nonselective a description as possible. On the other end of the continuum are more structured and predefined methods that itemize, count, and categorize behavior. Here the investigator decides beforehand which behavior will be recorded and how frequently observations will be made. The investigator using structured observation is much more discriminating in choosing which behavior will be recorded and precisely how [it is] to be coded.[6]

One author classifies observation studies by the degree of structure in the environmental setting and the amount of structure imposed on the environment by the researcher,[7] as reflected in Exhibit 7-6. The researcher conducting a class 1, completely unstructured study would be in a natural or field setting endeavoring to adapt to the culture. A typical example would be an ethnographic study in which the researcher, as a participant-observer, becomes a part of the culture and describes in great detail everything surrounding the event or activity of interest. One researcher took a punch press job in a factory to describe the rituals that a small work group relied on to make their highly repetitive, monotonous work bearable.[8] With other purposes in mind, business researchers may use this type of study for hypothesis generation.

Class 4 studies—completely structured research—are at the opposite end of the continuum from completely unstructured field investigations. The research purpose of class 4 studies is to test hypotheses; therefore, a definitive plan for observing specific, operationalized behavior is known in advance. This requires a measuring instrument, called an **observation checklist**; think of this as similar to the interview discussion guide or the questionnaire but for observation studies. These are developed in much the same way—working from the measurement questions to determine what should be observed. For human observations—those following behaviors and processes—the checklist may contain maps of interior spaces and diagrams to show where behaviors, or deviations from current processes, occurred. Exhibit 7-7 shows the parallels between survey design and checklist development.

Checklists should possess a high degree of precision in defining relevant behavior or acts and have mutually exclusive and exhaustive categories. The coding is frequently predetermined, thereby simplifying data recording and analysis. The participant groups being observed must be comparable and the laboratory conditions identical. The classic example of a class 4 study was Bales's investigation into group interaction.[9] Many team-building, decision-making, and assessment center studies follow this structural pattern.

The two middle classes of observation studies emphasize the best characteristics of either researcher-imposed controls or the natural setting. In class 2, the researcher uses the facilities of a laboratory—videotape recording, two-way mirrors, props, and stage sets—to introduce more control into the environment while simultaneously reducing the time needed for observation. In contrast, a class 3 study takes advantage of a structured observation checklist in a natural setting.

>**Exhibit 7-7** Flowchart for Observation Checklist Creation

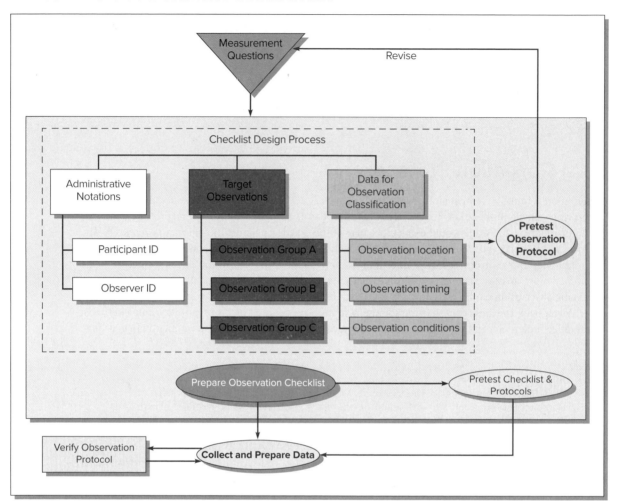

Data collection protocols must answer questions of when observations are to be made. Remember, observers collect with all their senses, so these decisions reflect not just what can be seen, but what can be heard, touched, smelled, etc. In terms of when, is the time of the observation important? Assume we are studying the out-of-stock conditions in a supermarket. The exact times of observation may be important. Inventory is shipped to the store on certain days only and at certain times, and buying peaks occur on various days and times. The likelihood of a given product being out of stock is a function of both time-related activities. Or assume we are observing worker break habits and patterns to determine how a space set aside for this purpose is redesigned. Would use patterns differ in the middle of shift verses closer to end of shift?

Protocols must also answer questions of how. If there are two or more observers, how will they divide the task? How will the results be recorded for later analysis? How will the observers deal with various situations that may occur—when expected actions do not take place or when someone challenges the observer in the setting?

Protocols must also answer questions of where. Within a spatial confine, where does the act take place? In a retail traffic pattern study, the proximity of a customer's pause space just inside the door before choosing a direction of movement to the entry door, a display, or directional sign might be recorded. Must the observation take place from a particular location within a larger venue? The location of the observer plus the location of the act observed (e.g., a sales approach observation within a store) can significantly influence the acts recorded. Observers face unlimited variations in conditions and must respond to these during the time frame of a study. When the plans are thorough and the observers well trained, observation research can be responsive. Fortunately, problems that do occur rarely occur simultaneously.

Observer Presence

Human observation studies present a clear opportunity for observer bias. Careful consideration must be made in determining the relationship between observer and participant. Consider these three choices:

- Whether the observation is direct or indirect.
- Whether the observer's presence is known or unknown to the participant.
- What role the observer plays.

Direct observation occurs when the observer is physically present and personally monitors and records what takes place. This approach is very flexible because it allows the observer to react to and report subtle aspects of events and behaviors as they occur. He or she is also free to shift places, change the focus of the observation, or concentrate on unexpected events if they occur. A weakness of this approach is that observers' perception circuits overload as events move quickly, and observers must later try to reconstruct what they were not able to record.

Indirect observation occurs when a recording is made by mechanical, photographic, or electronic means. For example, a special camera that takes one frame every second may be mounted in a department to study employee movement. The observer then extracts data from the images. Indirect observation is less flexible than direct observation but is also much less biasing and may be less erratic in accuracy. Another advantage of indirect observation is that the permanent record can be reanalyzed to include many different aspects of an event. Electronic recording devices, which have improved in quality and declined in cost, are used frequently in observation research.

Observer Concealment

Should the participant know of the observer's presence? Observers use **concealment** to shield themselves from the object of their observation. Often, technical means such as one-way mirrors, hidden

cameras, or microphones are used. When the observer is known, there is a risk of atypical activity by the participant (**reactivity response**). The initial entry of an observer into a situation often upsets the activity patterns of the participants, but this influence usually dissipates quickly, especially when participants are engaged in some absorbing activity or the presence of observers offers no potential threat to the participants' self-interest. Hidden observation is a form of spying, however, and the propriety of this action must be reviewed carefully. The potential bias from participant awareness of observers is always a matter of concern. It also raises ethical issues. Would participants have given their consent to be observed? After being deceived and having their privacy invaded, what further damage could come to the participants if the results became public? This issue needs to be addressed when concealment and covert participation are used.

Unobtrusive Measures

To minimize reactivity response, some researchers suggest using innovative observational procedures that can be both nonreactive and inconspicuously applied. Called **unobtrusive measures**, these approaches encourage creative and imaginative forms of indirect observation, archival searches, and variations on

©DreamPictures/Shannon Faulk/Getty Images

simple and contrived observation.[10] Of particular interest are measures involving indirect observation based on **physical traces** that include erosion (measures of wear) and accretion (measures of deposit).

Natural erosion measures are illustrated by using the frequency of replacement of vinyl floor tile in front of certain museum exhibits as an indicator of exhibit popularity. The study of wear and tear on book pages could be used is a measure of library book use. Counting the remaining brochures in a car dealer's display rack after a favorable magazine review could be used to suggest consumer interest. Physical traces also include natural accretion such as discovering the listenership of radio stations by observing car radio settings as autos are brought in for service. Another type of unobtrusive study involves estimating liquor and magazine consumption by collecting and analyzing family trash. One interesting study compared beer consumption reports acquired through interviews with the findings of sampled trash. The validity of interview data was questioned when the beer can count from trash supported a 77 percent consumption rate, not the 15 percent reported.[11]

By excavating landfills, one researcher who gained insight into human behavior and cultural patterns noted "people will describe their behavior to satisfy cultural expectations, like the mothers in Tucson who unanimously claimed they made their baby food from scratch, but whose garbage told a very different tale."[12]

Physical trace methods present a strong argument for use based on their ability to provide low-cost access to frequency, attendance, and incidence data without contamination from other methods or reactivity from participants. They are excellent "triangulation" devices for cross-validation. Thus, they work well as supplements to other methods. Designing an unobtrusive study can test a researcher's creativity, and one must be especially careful about inferences made from the findings. Erosion results may have occurred because of wear factors not considered, and accretion material may be the result of selective deposit or survival.

Partial Concealment

A modified approach involves partial concealment. The presence of the observer is not concealed, but the objectives and participant of interest are concealed. For example, a study of selling methods may be conducted by sending an observer with a salesperson who is making calls on customers. However, the observer's real purpose may be hidden from both the salesperson and the customer (e.g., the observer may pretend she is analyzing the display and layout characteristics of the company's merchandise in the stores they are visiting).

Observer Involvement

Should the observer enter the observation setting and act as both an observer and a participant—called **participant observation**? We have several situations where observers might be involved in the observation act: (1) The behavior we want to measure occurs infrequently, so we create a scenario to simulate the behavior within our research time frame; (2) the behavior we want to measure has many variations, and we need to measure each variation; and (3) the recruited observer is part of the process or behavior we need to measure, so excluding them is not practical. Sometimes he or she is known as an observer to some or all of the participants; at other times the observer's true role is concealed. In-home- and in-work-environment ethnography studies (immersion by the observer into the culture of the participant) are used in business; the participant is aware of the observation and has fully consented to the protocols that are used. Some examples are product use studies and work process studies.

Participant observation has two major problems: The observer's role may influence the way others act, and it places a dual role on the observer (recording can interfere with participation and participation can interfere with observation and recording). These problems are the major reason that business research avoids participant observation, when possible. Training can address both these problems, but also causes participant observation to be more costly or less reliable.

Observer Training and Supervision

The data collector/observer is a critical aspect of observation research. We want the best observers possible. What we look for in observers are:

- *Experience:* Ability to extract the most from an observation.
- *Concentration:* Ability to function in a setting full of distractions.
- *Detail-oriented:* Ability to remember details of an experience.
- *Unobtrusive presence:* Ability to blend with the setting and not be distinctive.

The observers should be thoroughly versed in the requirements of the specific study. Each observer should be informed of the outcomes sought and the precise content elements to be studied. Observer trials with the instrument and sample videotapes should be used until a high degree of reliability is apparent in their observations. If observation is at the surface level and involves a simple checklist or coding system, then experience is less important. Inexperience may even be an advantage if there is a risk that experienced observers may have preset convictions about the topic. Only intensive videotaped training relieves these problems.

When a study calls for multiple observers, there may be interpretative differences between observers. These must be reconciled. Training can address these differences. Another approach to dealing with problems related to variability between observers is to turn the problem into an opportunity—use teams. IDEO used a team comprised of a human factors expert, an engineer, and a designer to go into office buildings when it was working on an empathic design project for office-equipment supplier Steelcase. Each used their inherent differences in training and education to observe the same workers in their respective environments, but each brought back different data.[13]

Observers may be subject to **halo effects** (cognitive bias that influences the observer's impression of the person, object, event or act he or she is observing),[14] **observer drift** (gradual alterations over time in observation documentation),[15] and fatigue. If a halo effect bias is at work, an obviously attractive subject might get more positive inferential observations. In such an instance, an observer would use the global evaluation of beauty to make positive judgments on other traits, like friendliness, socially adeptness, efficiency, ability to maintain strong relationships, etc. Halos are like any other heuristic; they shorten our time to decision, but they may also be false, leading us to the wrong conclusion. Observers can have halos relating to gender, age, ethnicity, job performance, etc. Observer drift causes decay in reliability or validity of observations over time that affects the coding of categories; this is a serious problem if not caught early.[16] Both halo effects and observer drift can be addressed in training and by having supervisors verify that observation protocols are being strictly followed. Only multiple observers, rest periods during observation, and shortening the observation study time frame can address fatigue.

>Evaluation of the Observation Method

Strengths

Observation is the only method available to gather certain types of information. The study of records, mechanical processes, and young children, as well as other inarticulate participants, falls into this category. Another value of observation is that we can collect the original data at the time they occur. We need not depend on reports by others. Researchers can avoid **memory decay** (loss of detail about an event or prior behavior caused by passage of time or interfering events, such as learning)[17] and **selective filtering** or selective attention (due to sheer volume of information collected through our senses, we pay attention to only a small proportion of information we believe is critical).[18] Observation overcomes many of these deficiencies of questioning.

Designing the Observation Study

The design of a behavioral observation study follows the same pattern as other research. Once the researcher has specified the investigative questions, it is often apparent that the best way to conduct the study is through observation. Guidance for conducting a behavioral observation and translating the investigative question(s) into an observation checklist is the subject of this Closeup. We first review the procedural steps and then explain how to create a checklist.

Most studies that use behavioral observation follow a general sequence of steps that parallel the research process. (See Exhibit 7-2.) Here we adapt those steps to the terminology of the observation method:

- Define the content of the study.
- Develop a data collection plan that identifies the observational cases, sampling strategy, and acts (operationalized as a checklist or coding scheme).
- Secure and train observers.
- Collect the data.
- Analyze the data.

Assume you work for MarketViews, a specialty research firm hired to conduct a study for HomeExtravaganza, which has been experiencing declining repeat visits at its new superstore units. Preliminary results from a periodic survey indicate that customer confusion in the megastore is discouraging customers from returning, so an observation study is planned to see how employees and store design elements contribute to or solve the problem. The research questions might be:

- What do employees do to reduce or eliminate customer confusion?
- What do employees do that contributes to customer confusion?
- Which design elements diffuse customer confusion?
- Which design elements contribute to customer confusion?

Further assume that the survey indicates that customers who feel confused and cited this confusion as their reason for not returning had entered the store looking for a variety of merchandise, stocked in various locations throughout the vast store. They described their hopelessness as evolving from the experience of not knowing where to start the process of searching. Such customers showed no particular similarities or differences in terms of ethnic background, age, or education level. Some

had the assistance of greeters or floor assistance associates, while others did not.

The observation cases will be twofold: shoppers entering the store through the main entrance and employees serving as greeters or floor assistance associates. Customers who request assistance from the main-entrance greeter or who consult the directional location signs will be the primary target. If they approach a floor assistance associate, the employee will also become a case.

Survey research reveals some inconsistency by time of day and type of merchandise sought, so MarketViews plans to select cases during four primary day parts—early morning, midday, afternoon, and early evening—as well as at all three "directional locations," where signage describing the store and the shopper's current "You are here" location is noted.

A preliminary tour of the store helps identify the acts to record. During a subsequent meeting, it is decided that MarketViews will record the customer's seeking of assistance, either personal or signage; his or her consulting of the directional signage and its location; the customer's path to the desired merchandise; and whether a purchase is completed. The assistance acts of the floor assistance associate will also be recorded. These are determined to be assistance versus no assistance, providing the customer with copy of a directional map on which the associate marks the location of the merchandise and the path to get there, inquiry of other staff for location assistance, passing the customer to another floor assistance associate, accompanying the customer to the correct aisle, accompanying the customer to actual merchandise shelf location, and providing verbal assistance to selection of the appropriate product from the array of products provided.

It is determined that MarketViews will create and test an observation checklist, making any necessary changes after the test. The checklist developed is shown in Exhibit CU-1. The foremost concern is that either the customer or the associate will discover that he or she is being observed and will change behavior. Human observers will be used to trace the path of observational targets. By means of the store's security cameras, researchers will record customers flowing through the main entrance and past the greeter location and stopping at directional location signs. Counts of brochure store maps distributed from the directional signage locations and copysheet directional maps used by floor assistance associates will also be used as a measure of customers seeking directional assistance.

>**close**up**cont'd**

>**Exhibit CU-1** Sample Checklist for HomeExtravaganza Study

Time _____ Day: M T W Th F Sa Su Date _____ Store No. _____ Observer # _____

Target Customer Interception Location: ❏ Main Entry ❏ Directional Location Sign: ❏ #1
❏ #2
❏ #3

Target Shopper Characteristics: ❏ Male ❏ Female
❏ Child ❏ Child-teen+ ❏ Adult ❏ Senior

Shopper Companion(s): ❏ Alone ❏ With others: ❏ Other adult No. ____ M No. ____ F
❏ Child/children No. ____

Shopping Cart Used: ❏ No ❏ Yes

Greeter verbal interaction with target: ❏ No ❏ Yes Greeter No. _____
Action ❏ Point to directional sign
❏ Verbal directions

Floor Assistance Associate Interaction: ❏ No ❏ Yes Interception location: Aisle # _____ Crossway # _____
Associate # _____
Assistance given: ❏ No ❏ Yes Action: ❏ Verbal direction only
❏ Verbal direction plus pointing
❏ Store directional copy-map with marked mdse location
❏ Store directional copy-map with mdse location & path
❏ Inquire of other staff
❏ Pass customer to another FAA
❏ Accompany customer to aisle location
❏ Accompany customer to mdse shelf location
❏ Product selection assistance offered

Directional Sign Interaction: ❏ No ❏ Yes Sign location: ❏ #1
❏ #2
❏ #3

Purchase: ❏ No ❏ Yes: Item Sought Assistance for: ❏ No ❏ Yes

Customer Path:

A third strength is that we can secure information that most participants would ignore either because it is so common and expected or because it is not seen as relevant. For example, if you are researching buying activity in a store, there may be conditions important to the research study that the shopper does not notice or consider important, such as: What is the weather? What is the day of the week or the time of the day? How heavy is customer traffic? What is the level of promotional activity in competing stores? We can expect to learn only a few of the answers to these questions from most participants in a communication study.

The fourth advantage of observation is that it alone can capture the whole event as it occurs in its natural environment. Whereas the environment of an experiment may seem contrived to participants, and the number and types of questions limit the range of responses gathered from respondents in a survey or interview, observation is less restrictive than most primary collection methods. Also, the limitations on the length of data collection activities imposed by surveys or experiments are relaxed for observation. You may be interested in all the conditions surrounding a confrontation at a bargaining session between union and management representatives. These sessions may extend over time, and any effort to study the unfolding of the negotiation is facilitated by observation. Communication studies could seldom provide the insight of observation for many aspects of the negotiation process.

Finally, participants seem to accept an observational intrusion better than they respond to communication study. Observation is less demanding of participants and normally has a less biasing effect on their behavior than does communication. In addition, it is also possible to conduct disguised and unobtrusive observation studies much more easily than disguised communication studies.

Limitations

The observation method has some research limitations, yet any consideration of the merits of observation confirms its value when used with care and understanding.

Observation is a slow and expensive process that requires either human observers or costly surveillance equipment. The data collector may be needed at the scene of the event when it takes place, yet it is often impossible to predict where and when the event will occur. One way to guard against missing an event is to observe for prolonged periods until it does occur; in such situations, observer fatigue, boredom, and distracting events can reduce the accuracy and completeness of observation.

Reliable observations are restricted to information that can be learned by overt action or surface indicators. To go below the surface, the observer must make inferences. Two observers will probably agree on the nature of various surface events, but the inferences they draw from such data are much more variable.

Observation is more suited to subjective assessment and recording of data than to controls and quantification of events. When control is exercised through active intervention by the researchers, their participation may threaten the validity of what is being assessed. Even when the sampled number of cases is small, the observation records can be disproportionately large and difficult to analyze.

Observation is limited as a way to learn about the past. It is similarly limited as a method by which to learn what is going on in the present at some distant place.

Finally, it is difficult to gather information on intentions, attitudes, opinions, or preferences with observation.

>Ethical Issues and Their Solutions

When we conduct a communication-based study, we obtain consent from the participant. But when we conduct an observation using human cases, we conceal our presence and their participation. Yes, we can let them know they were a subject after the fact, but they might still feel violated. While it is not illegal to observe people in public places or in their work environment, their presence in such places does not remove their right for some privacy.

The right of quality research is not inherent in observation research, but it must be protected by developing an appropriate observation checklist and extensive observer training. The observer has a much more involved role in not only data collection, but also in data interpretation and developing insights. Pretesting the checklist and observation protocols, as well as supervising observers in their execution of observation protocols and debriefing observers following data collection, are valuable steps in assuring quality research.

Observation research frequently uses nonprobability sampling. In such instances, assuring quality also means not projecting small-sample, nonrespresentative results to a target population and drawing conclusions that can't be supported by the data collected. Using such research to form hypotheses rather than test hypotheses is appropriate. When a census or probability sample is used, observation can be used to test hypotheses.

>summary

LO7-1 Observation is one of the few options available for studying records, mechanical processes, lower animals, small children, and complex interactive processes. We can gather data as the event occurs and can come closer to capturing the whole event than with communication. On the other hand, we have to be present to catch the event or have some recording device on the scene to do the job.

LO7-2 Sampling design in observation includes choosing the target population (people, acts or events, behaviors, etc.) and the appropriate approach (probability vs. nonprobability). Two sampling methods are unique to observation: event and time sampling. Event sampling measures all factors involved with a single specified event, while time sampling chooses a time interval and records desired variables within that time frame. There are three types of time sampling (time point, continuous time, and time interval). In data collection design, we must address seven different factors: content type (facts or acts, inferences of those acts, or both), type of observation (nonbehavioral or behavioral), the environment (field or laboratory), data collection protocol (simple observation or systematic observation), observer presence (direct or indirect observation), observation concealment (full, partial, or none), and observer involvement (participant observation or none). The measurement instrument for observation research is the observation checklist.

LO7-3 Observation includes a variety of monitoring situations that cover nonbehavioral and behavioral activities. Both types may be conducted with human or digital/mechanical observers, but all require human coding and interpretation. Nonbehavioral observation includes record analysis, physical condition analysis, and physical process analysis. The most common nonbehavioral observation is record analysis. Lack of consistency in creating records can limit the effectiveness of record analysis. Behavioral observation includes nonverbal analysis, linguistic and extralinguistic analysis, and spatial analysis.

LO7-4 The strengths of observation as a data collection method include securing information about people or events that cannot be derived from communication approaches, avoiding memory decay and selective filtering by securing information as it occurs, securing information participants might ignore or not think to report, securing environmental context information, securing data in a less intrusive way, and being more flexible about data collection time periods.

LO7-5 Observation may be limited by any of the following: the difficulty of predicting when specific desired events or acts might occur, causing long periods of observation; slow nature of data collection; possible reactivity response if observation is known by participants; small sample size; high costs, especially when specialized equipment or facilities are used; recording demands of high-speed events; questionable reliability of inference for capturing attitudes, motivations, and cognitive processes; coding for disproportionately large records; reconciling variability between observers on facts and inferences from the same act or record; observer halo effects, drift, and fatigue; excessive responsibilities caused by the dual role required during participant observations; and lack of express consent and resulting violation of participant's right to privacy. Unobtrusive measures offer ways to reduce reactivity response in observation research, either to confirm the findings from other methods or operate as singular data sources. Most limitations may be addressed by digitally recording acts of interest, providing observer training, pretesting observation checklists and observation protocols, and verifying observation protocols during actual data collection.

LO7-6 The ethical issues are focused on the participant's right to privacy and the manager's right to quality research. The first might be addressed by debriefing participants after the research if observation was concealed. The right of quality is not inherent in observation research unless the researcher takes special care with the development of the observation checklist, develops checklist-specific training, pretests both the checklist and the observation protocols, and verifies those protocols during the observation research. Observation can be used to generate and test hypotheses, so knowing which is appropriate for a given study also protects research quality.

>**key**terms

>**discussion**questions

Terms in Review

1   Compare the advantages and disadvantages of the observation to the communication approach. Under what circumstances could you make a case for using observation?

2   What ethical risks are involved in observation? In the use of unobtrusive measures?

3   Based on present or past work experience, suggest management problems that could be resolved by using observation-based data.

4   Distinguish between the following:

   a   Nonverbal, linguistic, and extralinguistic analysis.

   b   Factual and inferential observation.

   c   Memory decay and selective filtering.

Making Research Decisions

5   The observer–participant relationship is an important consideration in the design of observation studies. What kind of relationship would you recommend in each of the following cases?

   a   Observations of professional conduct in the classroom by the student author of a course evaluation guide.

   b   Observation of retail shoppers by a researcher who is interested in determining customer purchase time by type of goods purchased.

   c   Observation of a focus group interview by a client.

   d   Effectiveness of individual farmworker organizers in their efforts to organize employees of grape growers.

6   Assume you are the manufacturer of modular office systems and furniture as well as office organization elements (desktop and wall organizers, filing systems, etc.). Your company has been asked to propose an observation study to examine the use of office space by white-collar and managerial workers for a large insurance company. This study will be part of a project to improve office efficiency and paperwork flow. It is expected to involve the redesign of office space and the purchase of new office furniture and organization elements.

   a   What are the varieties of information that might be observed?

   b   Select a limited number of content areas for study, and operationally define the observation acts that should be measured.

   c   Develop a checklist to be used by observers in the previous study. Determine how many observers you need, and assign two or three to a specific observation task.

   d   Compare the results of your group members' checklists for stability of recorded perceptions.

7   Amazon's Kindle (its electronic book, magazine, and newspaper reader) has been far more successful than its SONY competitor. This could be at least somewhat influenced by the "Oprah factor"; the Kindle was first introduced on the *Oprah* show and strongly endorsed by the mega-mogul. But the original Kindle had some physical problems—button placement and page-turn speed among them. Correcting these problems resulted in the Kindle2, released in 2009 to glowing reviews, and ultimately to the Kindle Fire. What observation research might have been used in the redesign of the original Kindle?

8   You wish to analyze the pedestrian traffic that passes a given store in a major shopping center. You are interested in determining how many shoppers pass by this store, and you

would like to classify these shoppers on various relevant dimensions. Any information you secure should be obtainable from observation alone.

a What other information might you find useful to observe?

b How would you decide what information to collect?

c Devise the operational definitions you would need.

d What would you say in your instructions to the observers you plan to use?

e How might you sample this shopper traffic?

9 Walmart got a very mixed reaction when it announced that after 30 years it was eliminating greeters from its overnight shift in more than 3,800 stores, redefining the role of day-shift greeters, and moving them further into the store and away from the door. What observation research would you have conducted to reach these decisions?

From Concept to Practice

10 Using Exhibit 7-5, identify the type of study described in each of the Snapshots featured in this chapter.

From the Headlines

11 In May 2017, LAX, the world's fourth-largest airport, relocated 15 airlines in a three-night (five hours per night) period in order to accommodate Delta's expansion. During the period, Delta operated more than 200 flights a day out of four terminals. In Terminal 2 and 3, everything moved. It relocated ticket counters, kiosks, computer systems, and more than 1,000 signs. The process was in the planning stages for 15 months. Delta picked up the tab for the move for all airlines involved. If you were Delta, what observation research would you have conducted during this massive endeavor to judge the effectiveness of the move planning?

>cases*

Akron Children's Hospital

Envirosell

Net Conversions Influence Kelley Blue Book

State Farm: Dangerous Intersections

*You will find a description of each case in the Case Abstracts section of this textbook. Check the Case Index to determine whether a case provides data, the research instrument, video, or other supplementary material. Cases and case supplements are available in Connect.

>**chapter 8**

Stage 2:
Data Collection Design:
Experiments

> "It's not
> an experiment
> if you know
> it's going to work."
>
> *Jeff Bezos, CEO,*
> *Amazon*

>**learning**objectives

After reading this chapter, you should understand . . .

LO8-1   How an experiment is different than other primary data collection methods.

LO8-2   The seven steps of a well-planned experiment.

LO8-3   Internal and external validity with experimental research designs.

LO8-4   The three types of experimental designs and the variations of each.

LO8-5   The advantages and disadvantages of the experimental method.

LO8-6   Ethical issues in experiments and their solutions.

> Experiments and Causation

Why do events occur under some conditions and not under others? **Experiments** are research studies designed to explain why something happens; in these studies the researcher proposes a **causal hypothesis** (a speculation that one variable causes a change in another variable). The researcher then manipulates the **independent variable (IV)** and observes whether the **dependent variable (DV)** is affected as hypothesized.

Causation Evidence

The essential element of **causation** is that A "produces" B or A "forces" B to occur. Thus, there is at least one independent variable (IV) and one dependent variable (DV) in a causal relationship. Empirically, we can never demonstrate with any certainty an A-B causality. Causation needs evidence to support an *inductive* conclusion; we cannot demonstrate a causal relationship *deductively*. As such, in a causal study we estimate the probability that A "produces" B based on what we observe and measure.

In testing a causal hypothesis, we seek three types of evidence:

1. Covariation between A and B
    *   Do we find A and B occur together in the way hypothesized?
    *   When A does not occur, is there also an absence of B?
    *   When there is more or less of A, does one also find more or less of B?
2. Time order of events moving in the hypothesized direction
    *   Does A occur before B?
3. No other possible causes of B
    *   Can one determine that C, D, and E do not covary with B in a way that suggests possible causal connections?

In addition to these three conditions, successful inference-making in causal designs must meet two other requirements. All factors, with the exception of the independent variable, must be held constant and not confounded with another variable that is not part of the study (**control**). Each case studied must have an equal chance for exposure to each level of the independent variable in the study (**random assignment** of cases to groups).

Causal Conclusion

The Mill's *method of agreement*,[1] illustrated in Exhibit 8-1, helps rule out some variables as irrelevant. If we can find Z and only Z in every case where we find C, and no others (A, B, D, or E) are consistently found with Z, then we can conclude that C and Z are causally related. In Exhibit 8-1, A, B, D, and E are unlikely to be causes of Z. However, there is an implicit assumption that there are no variables to consider other than A, B, C, D, and E. One can never accept this supposition with certainty because the

>**Exhibit 8-1** Mill's Method of Agreement

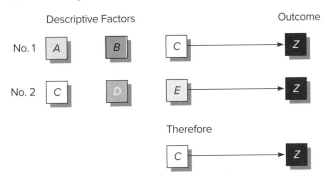

>**Exhibit 8-2** Mill's Method of Difference

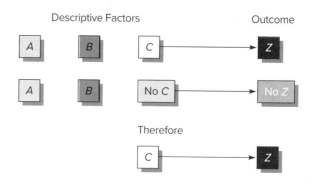

number of potential variables is infinite. In addition, while *C* may be the cause, it may instead function only in the presence of some other variable we haven't studied.

The *negative canon of agreement* states that where the absence of *C* is associated with the absence of *Z* there is evidence of a causal relationship between *C* and *Z*. Together with the *method of agreement*, this forms the basis for the *method of difference* (see Exhibit 8-2): "If there are two or more cases, and in one of them observation *Z* can be made, while in the other it cannot; and if variable *C* occurs when observation *Z* is made, and does not occur when observation *Z* is not made; then it can be asserted that there is a causal relationship between *C* and *Z*."[2]

There are three major types of relationships that can occur between two variables:[3]

- Symmetrical
- Reciprocal
- Asymmetrical

A **symmetrical relationship** is one in which two variables fluctuate together, but we assume the changes in neither variable are due to changes in the other. Symmetrical conditions are most often found when two variables are alternate indicators of another cause or independent variable. Assume a business sponsors a camping club for its workers and occasionally this club sponsors weekend camping events. The business experiences high absenteeism on Mondays following a camping club event among those who are members. If the relationship is symmetrical, a correlation between low work attendance and active participation in a company camping club would be dependent on another factor. Many research studies reveal symmetrical relationships.

A **reciprocal relationship** exists when two variables mutually influence or reinforce each other. This could occur if the reading of an advertisement leads to the use of a brand of product. The usage, in turn, sensitizes the person to notice and read more of the advertising of that particular brand. Many research studies reveal reciprocal relationships.

Research analysts often look for **asymmetrical relationships**. With these we hypothesize that changes in one variable (the independent variable—IV) are responsible for changes in another variable (the dependent variable—DV). For example, we hypothesize that participation in the company-sponsored camping club event (IV) is responsible for high absenteeism at work on the following Monday (DV). The identification of the IV and DV is often obvious (as in our absenteeism scenario), but sometimes the choice is not clear. In these latter cases, we evaluate independence and dependence on the basis of:

1. *The degree to which each variable may be altered.* The relatively unalterable variable is the independent variable (IV) (e.g., age, social status, camping club membership, present manufacturing technology).

2. *The time order between the variables.* The independent variable (IV) precedes the dependent variable (DV).

Exhibit 8-3 describes four types of asymmetrical relationships: stimulus-response, property-disposition, disposition-behavior, and property-behavior. Experiments usually involve stimulus-response relationships. Property-disposition relationships are often studied in business and social science research.

>**Exhibit 8-3** Four Types of Asymmetrical Causal Relationships

Relationship Type	Nature of Relationship	Examples
Stimulus-Response	An event or change results in a response from some object.	• A change in work rules leads to a higher level of worker output. • A change in government economic policy restricts corporate financial decisions. • A price increase results in fewer unit sales.
Property-Disposition	An existing property causes a disposition.	• Age and attitudes about saving. • Gender and attitudes toward social issues. • Social class and opinions about taxation.
Disposition-Behavior	A disposition causes a specific behavior.	• Opinions about a brand and its purchase. • Job satisfaction and work output. • Moral values and tax cheating.
Property-Behavior	An existing property causes a specific behavior.	• Stage of the family life cycle and purchases of furniture. • Social class and family savings patterns. • Age and sports participation.

Definitions: A *stimulus* is an event or force (e.g., drop in temperature, crash of stock market, product recall, or explosion in factory). A *response* is a decision or reaction. A property is an enduring characteristic of a participant that does not depend on circumstances for its activation (e.g., age, gender, family status, religious affiliation, ethnic group, or physical condition). A *disposition* is a tendency to respond in a certain way under certain circumstances (e.g., attitudes, opinions, habits, values, and drives). A *behavior* is an action (e.g., consumption practices, work performance, interpersonal acts, and other kinds of performance).

Although experimental methods neither ensure discovery of all relevant variables nor provide certain proof of causation, they help advance our understanding of causality by eliminating inadequate causal arguments.[4]

Causal inferences are going to be made. Although they may be neither permanent nor universal, these inferences allow us to build knowledge of presumed causes over time. Such empirical conclusions provide us with successive approximations to the truth.

One classic example of an experiment is the study of bystanders and thieves.[5] In this experiment, participants were asked to come to an office where they had an opportunity to see a person steal some money from a receptionist's desk. A confederate of the experimenter, of course, did the stealing. The major hypothesis concerned whether people observing a theft will be more likely to report it (1) if they are alone when they observe the crime or (2) if they are in the company of someone else.

The independent variable in our example was the state of either being alone when observing the theft or being in the company of another person. The dependent variable was whether the participants reported observing the crime. The "theft" had to occur before the "report of the crime," so the time order of events is upheld. The results suggested that bystanders were more likely to report the theft if they observed it alone rather than in another person's company. Researchers concluded it was based on this factor as there was no other variable to affect the reporting of the crime. All other variables were controlled.

Ex post facto research designs, in which a researcher interviews respondents or observes what is or what has been, also have the potential for discovering causality. The distinction between these methods and an experiment is that the researcher is required to accept the world as it is found, whereas an experiment allows the researcher to alter systematically the variables of interest and observe what changes follow.

Experiments in Improving Employee Health

If we could get overweight employees to lose weight and smokers to quit, employers would have lower health care costs. That's the motivation behind health-based incentives among employers. A recent experiment sheds light on which incentive approaches are more likely to work—and which aren't.

Mitesh Patel, a professor of medicine at the University of Pennsylvania's Perelman School of Medicine and a professor of health care management at Wharton, claims, "About 80% of large employers in the United States use some form of financial incentive for health promotion," but little research has been done to demonstrate effectiveness of these programs. Patel conducted a year-long experiment to test whether or not financial incentives delivered through premium adjustments (offering to lower an employee's contribution to their health insurance if health goals are met) work to help people lose weight.

In the experiment, "we offered people $550 if they could lose 5% of their weight over the course of the year. They would get that as a premium adjustment, dispersed across 26 payments" (each paycheck would increase by $21 each pay period). One group got the incentive starting the next year. Another group got the incentive immediately. A third group got cash incentives rather than the premium adjustment. And the control group got nothing. The employees in the control group essentially lost no weight, and neither did any of the employees assigned to the experimental groups.

Patel concluded from the research that the standard approach of using premium adjustments didn't work. He hypothesized that the reason is that the incentives are often hidden. "People tend to prefer immediate gratification; they want rewards now. It's really hard to get someone to lose weight and do something that's hard to do now for a reward that's next year." Behavioral economics studies recommend that incentives be immediate and noticeable to be effective.

©imtmphoto/Alamy

How would you diagram this experiment? What are the experimental variables? What are the dependent variables? What were the weaknesses and strengths of this experimental design?

Source: "Why Some Workplace Health Incentive Programs Don't Work-and Some Do," Knowledge@Wharton, April 4, 2016, downloaded April 6, 2016 (http://knowledge .wharton.upenn.edu/article/workplace-health-incentive-programs-dont-work/?utm _source=kw_newsletter&utm_medium=email&utm_campaign=2016-04-06).

> Conduct an Experiment[6]

In a well-executed experiment, researchers must complete a series of activities to carry out their craft successfully. Although the experiment is the premier scientific methodology for establishing causation, the resourcefulness and creativeness of the researcher are needed to make the experiment live up to its potential. The researcher must accomplish following to make the endeavor successful, as shown in Exhibit 8-4:

1. Select relevant variables.
2. Specify the treatment levels.
3. Control the experimental environment.
4. Choose the experimental design.
5. Select and assign the participants.
6. Pilot test, revise, and test again.
7. Analyze the data.

>**Exhibit 8-4** Experiments in the Research Process

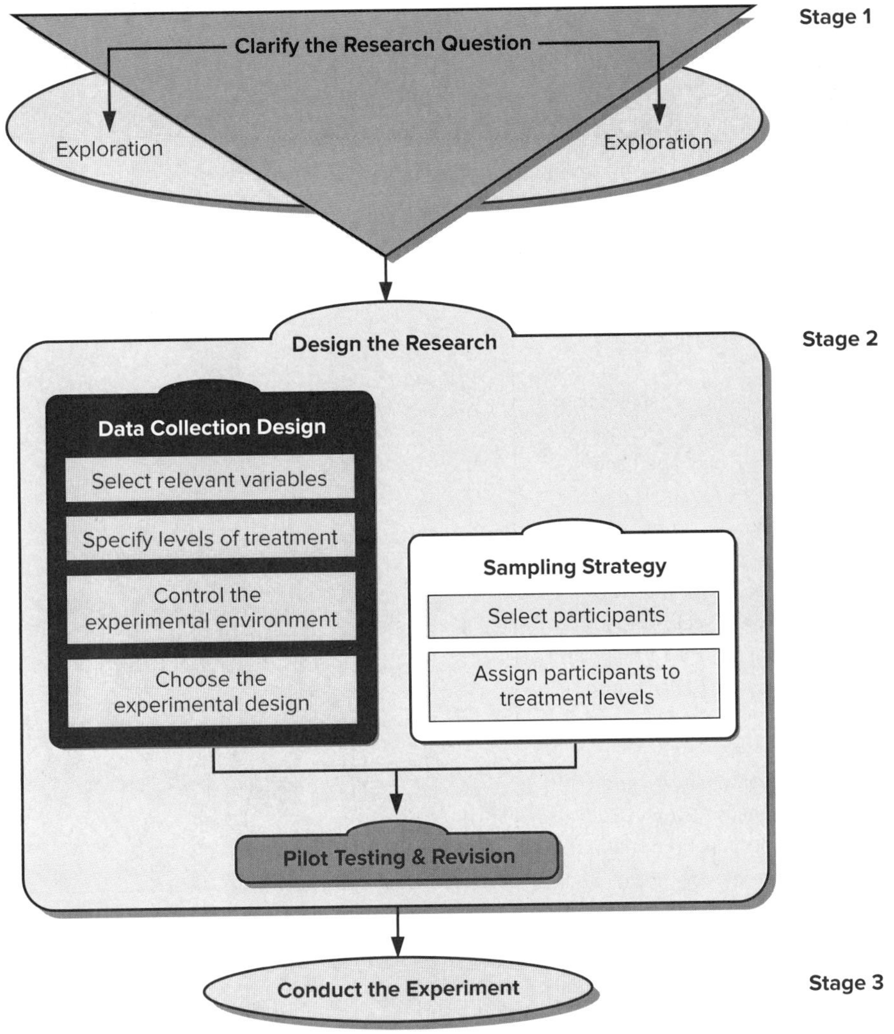

Select Relevant Variables

The researcher's task is to translate an amorphous management problem into the question or hypothesis that best states the objectives of the research. Consider the following research question as we work through the seven points listed above:

Does a sales presentation that describes product benefits in the introduction of the message lead to improved retention of product knowledge?

Because a hypothesis is a speculation about the outcome of the study, it might take this form:

Sales presentations in which the benefits module is placed in the introduction of a 12-minute message produce better retention of product knowledge than those where the benefits module is placed in the conclusion.

The researchers would need to select variables that best operationalize the concept's sales presentation, product benefits, retention, and product knowledge. The product's classification and the nature of the intended audience should also be defined. In addition, the term could be better operationalized statistically by means of a significance test. The number of variables in an experiment is constrained by the project budget, the time allocated, the availability of appropriate controls, and the number of participants being tested. For statistical reasons, there must be more participants than variables.[7]

Robotic Experiments

For decades, we've seen robots replacing humans on the manufacturing floor. Where repetitive tasks require highly precise maneuvers, robots seem to have worked well. The push toward a higher minimum wage—$15 is being implemented in some states and counties—is also increasing interest in robotics. Has artificial intelligence advanced enough that we might use robots in retail situations?

In robot-enthusiastic Japan, CBS correspondent Seth Doane spent a night in Henn na Hotel, a low-cost, futuristic facility near the city of Nagasaki, where everything from baggage handling to checking in to room service is handled by robots. The move toward human replacement in jobs was driven by economics. "For five-star hotels that are selling high-end service, human staff are essential. But for three- or four-star hotels, you need comfortable lodging, and a basic level of communication at a reasonable price," claimed Hideo Sawada, the manager at Henn'na Hotel. The robots have reduced labor costs by 70 percent compared to a hotel staffed by humans.

The founding partner of Peppers and Rogers Group, Don Peppers, warns that the trade-off of machines and humans should consider more than economics. "Even the most routine and repetitive tasks can still be improved, altered, upgraded, or modified into better, more efficient tasks, and machines will never suggest those kinds of changes. Human beings will."

Computers get exponentially more powerful at a lower cost each year. This makes cost-effective robotics more likely for many repetitive tasks. And the experiments continue. In one San Francisco store, Target is testing the use of a robot to spot inventory vacancies or out-of-place merchandise on shelves. In a Whole Foods store, if you drink tea, you can participate in an experiment where tea is ordered from and brewed by a robot. Wendy's and McDonald's are testing self-serve kiosks in some restaurants.

But inside Toyota Motor Corp.'s oldest plant, there's a corner where humans are forging crankshafts. "We cannot simply depend on the machines that only repeat the same task over and over again," Mitsuru Kawai, a senior managing officer at Toyota revealed in a *Bloomberg* article. "To be the master of the machine, you have to have the knowledge and the skills to teach the machine."

©Colin Anderson/Blend Images LLC

Sources: "A night in Japan's robot hotel," CBS News, July 22, 2015, downloaded May 23, 2016 (http://www.cbsnews.com/news/inside-japan-robot-hotel-hennna-where-staff-are-robots/); Craig Trudell, Yuki Hagiwara and Ma Jie, "Herald Toyota's Vision of Future," Bloomberg, April 7, 2014, downloaded May 23, 2016 (http://www.bloomberg.com/news/articles/2014-04-06/humans-replacing-robots-herald-toyota-s-vision-of-future); Judith Aquino, "Automate or Humanize? The Great Customer Service Debate," 1to1 Media, May 23, 2016, downloaded May 23, 2016 (http://www.1to1media.com/view.aspx?docid=35796&utm_content=title&utm_source=1to1weekly&utm_medium=email&utm_campaign=05232016); Larry Downes, "Happy birthday to Moore's Law," The Washington Post, April 16, 2015, downloaded May 29, 2016 (https://www.washingtonpost.com/news/innovations/wp/2015/04/16/happy-birthday-to-moores-law/); Matt McFarland, "Ex-McDonald's CEO says raising the minimum wage will help robots take jobs," Washington Post, May 25, 2016, downloaded May 29, 2016 (https://www.washingtonpost.com/news/innovations/wp/2016/05/25/ex-mc-donalds-ceo-says-raising-the-minimum-wage-will-help-robots-take-jobs/); Julie Vogtman and Agata Pelka, "Minimum Wage Update: State and Local Highlights," National Women's Law Center Blog, June 5, 2015, downloaded May 23, 2017 (https://nwlc.org/blog/minimum-wage-update-state-local-highlights/); Julie Vogtman, "The Fight for $15 is Winning for Women and Families," National Women's Law Center, April 2017, downloaded May 23, 2017 (https://nwlc.org/wp-content/uploads/2017/04/The-Fight-for-15-is-Winning.pdf).

The selection of measures for testing requires a thorough review of the available literature and instruments. In addition, measures must be adapted to the unique needs of the research situation without compromising their intended purpose or original meaning.

>**Exhibit 8-5** Experiment of Benefits Module Placement of within a Sales Presentation

Hypothesis: Sales presentations in which the benefits module is placed in the introduction of a 12-minute message produce better retention of product knowledge by the customer than those in which the benefits module is placed in the conclusion.

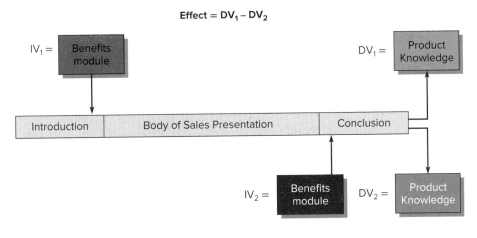

$$\text{Effect} = DV_1 - DV_2$$

Specify Treatment Levels

In an experiment, the researcher manipulates the independent variable, called the **experimental treatment**. The **treatment levels** of the independent variable are the arbitrary or natural groups the researcher chooses within the independent variable of an experiment. For example, if salary (IV) is hypothesized to have an effect on employees' exercising of stock purchase options (DV), salary might be divided into high, middle, and low ranges to represent three treatment levels of the independent variable.

The levels assigned to an independent variable should be based on simplicity and common sense. In the sales presentation example, the experimenter should not select 8 minutes and 10 minutes as the starting points to represent the two treatment levels if the average message about the product is 12 minutes long. Similarly, if the benefits module is placed in the first and second minutes of the presentation, observable differences may not occur because the levels are too close together. Thus, in the first trial, the researcher is likely to position the midpoint of the benefits module the same interval from the end of the introduction as from the end of the conclusion (see Exhibit 8-5).

Under an entirely different hypothesis, several levels of the independent variable may be needed to test order-of-presentation effects. Here we use only two. Alternatively, a **control group** could provide a base level for comparison. The control group is composed of participants who are not exposed to the independent variable(s), in contrast to those who receive the experimental treatment.

Control the Experimental Environment

At this stage, we are principally concerned with **environmental control**, holding constant the physical environment of the experiment. The introduction of the experiment to the participants and the instructions would likely be videotaped for consistency. The arrangement of the room, the time of administration, the experimenter's contact with the participants and so forth, must all be consistent across each administration of the experiment.

Other forms of control involve subjects and experimenters. When participants do not know if they are receiving the experimental treatment, the experiment is characterized as **blind**. When the experimenters do not know if they are giving the treatment to the experimental group or to the control group, the experiment is characterized as **double blind**. Both approaches control unwanted complications such as participants' reactions to expected conditions or experimenter influence.

Zeotap Experiments with Mercedes Benz

Data privacy and security regulations are very different throughout the world, so finding a model that allows a telecom to monetize its extensive customer data is an important task. Zeotap, a German startup that interfaces multiple telecom companies' data with advertisers wishing to target specific prospects, just completed an experiment with Mercedes-Benz.

When you purchase a mobile device, you provide your carrier with your name and address. They match this with your plan details, including the number of phones, your phone models, your plan details (voice, data), and your monthly plan cost. Over time, they add your actual usage, including how and where you use your various mobile devices. What Zeotap does is take anonymized, non–personally identifiable telecom data and targets mobile ads to segments of those consumers through its own platform and those of ad tech partners (like Zenith).

Because the E-class is an expensive sedan, Mercedes wanted to reach "individuals between the ages of 40 and 60 who spent 100 euros or more on their mobile bill each month, or

©Lars A. Niki

those who spent 100 euros or more and paid for more than one mobile line" and was able to do so with Zeotap's technology. How would you design and evaluate the experiment?

www.mercedes-benz.com; www.zeotap.comwww.zeotap.com

In our sales presentation experiment, extraneous variables have the potential for distorting the effect of the treatment on the dependent variable and must be controlled or eliminated. These might include differences in age, gender, race, dress, communications competence, and many other characteristics of the presenter, the message, or the situation.

Choose the Experimental Design

Experiments have their own unique designs. In conducting an experiment, the researcher uses his or her experience and knowledge to select one design that is best suited to the goals of the research. Judicious selection of the design improves the probability that the observed change in the dependent variable was caused by the manipulation of the independent variable and not by another factor. It simultaneously strengthens the generalizability of results beyond the experimental setting.

Select and Assign Cases

The participants or participants selected for the experiment should be representative of the target population to which the researcher wishes to generalize the study's results. In the sales presentation example, corporate buyers, purchasing managers, or others in a decision-making capacity would provide better generalizing power than, say, undergraduate college students if the product in question was targeted for industrial use rather than to the consumer.

The procedure for random sampling of experimental cases is similar in principle to the selection of participants for a survey or an observation study. The researcher first prepares a sampling frame and then assigns the participants for the experiment to groups using a randomization technique. However, if randomization is used, those assigned to the experimental group are likely to be similar to those assigned to the control group. **Random assignment** to the groups is required to make the groups as comparable as possible with respect to the dependent variable. Randomization does not guarantee that if a pretest of the groups was conducted before the treatment condition, the groups would be pronounced identical; but it is an assurance that those differences remaining are randomly distributed. In our example, we would need three randomly assigned groups—one for each of the two treatments (benefits module early, benefits module late) and one for the control group.

When it is not possible to randomly assign cases to groups, matching may be used. **Matching** employs a nonprobability quota sampling approach. The object of matching is to have each experimental and control case matched on every characteristic used in the research. This becomes more cumbersome as the number of variables and groups in the study increases. Because the characteristics of concern are only those that are correlated with the treatment condition or the dependent variable, they are easier to identify, control, and match.[8] In the sales presentation experiment, if a large part of the sample of participants was composed of businesswomen who had recently completed communications training, we would not want the characteristics of gender, business experience, and communication training to be disproportionately assigned to one group.

Some authorities suggest a **quota matrix** as the most efficient means of visualizing the matching process.[9] In Exhibit 8-6, one-third of the cases from each cell of the matrix would be assigned to each

>**Exhibit 8-6** Quota Matrix Example

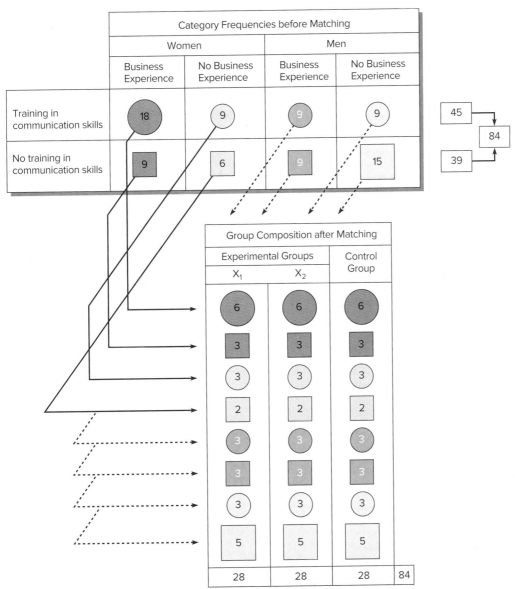

of the three groups. If matching does not alleviate the assignment problem, a combination of matching, randomization, and increasing the sample size would be used.

Pilot Test, Revise, and Pretest

The procedures for this stage are similar to those for other forms of primary data collection. Pilot testing is intended to reveal errors in the experiment's design and improper control of extraneous or environmental conditions. Pretesting the measurement instruments permits refinement before the final test. This is the researcher's best opportunity to revise scripts, look for control problems with laboratory conditions, and scan the environment for factors that might confound the results. In field experiments, researchers are sometimes caught off guard by events that have a dramatic effect on cases: the test marketing of a competitor's product announced before an experiment, or a reduction in force, reorganization, or merger before a crucial organizational change. The experiment should be timed so that subjects are not sensitized to the independent variable by factors in the environment.

>**snap**shot

MIT SENSEable City Lab

How might future work spaces be different than those of today or 10 years ago? According to Carlo Ratti, director of MIT's SENSEable City Lab, work, living, and recreational spaces of today will all be the work spaces of tomorrow. "Charles-Édouard LeCorbusier, [the father of modern architecture and instrumental in the present design of urban spaces], claimed cities had four functions: dwelling, work, recreation, and transportation. Some current researchers predict that cities will effectively disappear. But cities are not obsolete; they are thriving with the merger of the digital and physical worlds. And we are collecting data to understand that combination."

"In 1979 there were no cell phones. It's estimated that more than 7 billion connections on mobile devices will be made in 2016, with more than 50 billion connections by 2020. With sensors being embedded in all facets of our lives through the IoT, that number will only climb." SENSEable has done experiments on work, living, and leisure spaces in such diverse places as Dubai shopping centers, the Louvre museum in Paris, and the campus of MIT. MIT was one of the first campuses to be totally WiFi enabled (pre-2000), so it should be no surprise that MIT is monitoring where and when that WiFi network is accessed. It is also experimenting using its WiFi network to monitor when spaces are occupied and adjusting the heating/cooling environment on demand—what they call "local warming."

SENSEable's research reveals that work isn't stationary, it shifts to various spaces throughout the day. Thus, a space no longer has to have a single, dedicated use—a space that is empty when that use is no longer immediate. One European

©Blend Images LLC

furniture manufacturer is experimenting with modular furniture made up of a single-size pod that can adjust its height. When several pods are massed together, they can become desks, chairs, sofas, beds, and even a pub table with stools. Some cities are embracing this concept of flexible spaces by offering "co-working spaces" for individuals who work remotely but don't want to work from home. Starbucks may be attractive for some, but soon, such workers will have many different options.

senseable.mit.edu

Analyze the Data

If adequate planning and pretesting have occurred, the experimental data will take an order and structure uncommon to surveys and unstructured observational studies. It is not that data from experiments are easy to analyze; they are simply more conveniently arranged because of the levels of the treatment condition, pretests and posttests, and the group structure. The choice of statistical techniques is commensurately simplified. Researchers have several measurement and instrument options with experiments. Among these are:

- Observational checklists and coding schemes.
- Self-report instruments with open-ended or closed questions.
- Scaling techniques (e.g., Likert scales, semantic differentials, Q-sort).
- Physiological measures (e.g., galvanic skin response, EKG, voice pitch analysis, eye dilation).

> Validity in Experimentation

Even when an experiment is the ideal research design, it is not without problems. There is always a question about whether the results are true. Although there are several different types of validity (whether a measure accomplishes what it claims), here only the two major varieties are considered: **internal validity** (do the conclusions we draw about a demonstrated experimental relationship truly imply cause?) and **external validity** (does an observed causal relationship generalize across persons, settings, and times?).[10] Each type of validity has specific threats we need to guard against.

Internal Validity

Among the many threats to internal validity, we consider the following seven:

- **History**
- **Maturation**
- **Testing**
- **Instrumentation**
- **Selection**
- **Regression toward the mean**
- **Experimental mortality**

We'll use a design called a preexperiment to discuss several of these. Assume a company's management wishes to find the best way to educate its workers about the financial condition of the company before this year's labor negotiations. To assess the value of such an effort, managers design an experiment of employee knowledge of the company's finances (O_1). Then they present the educational campaign (X) to a sample of employees, after which they again measure their knowledge level (O_2). This design can be diagrammed as follows:

$$O_1 \qquad X \qquad O_2$$

Pretest   Manipulation   Posttest

In this design, we take a control measurement (O_1) of the dependent variable before introducing the manipulation to the independent variable (X). After the manipulation, we take an after-measurement (O_2) of the dependent variable. Then the difference between O_1 and O_2 is the change that the manipulation has caused. Between O_1 and O_2, however, many events could occur to confound the effects of the education effort.

History

During the time that an experiment is taking place, some events outside the company's control may occur that confuse the relationship being studied. A major corporation may experience a strike. A newspaper article about companies with financial problems might appear. A union meeting at which this topic is discussed might be held, or another occurrence could distort the effects of the company's education test.

Maturation

Changes also may occur within the participant that are a function of the passage of time and are not specific to any particular event. These are of special concern when the experiment covers a long time, but they may also be factors in tests that are as short as an hour or two. A participant can become hungry, bored, or tired in a short time, and this condition can affect response results. In our experiment, a participant could begin a course in finance or accounting at the local university, between O_1 and O_2.

Testing

The process of taking a test can affect the scores of a second test. The mere experience of taking the first test can have a learning effect that influences the results of the second test. So in our experiment, the act of testing financial knowledge can actually increase employee sensitivity to such information, especially to those answers they did not know.

Instrumentation

This threat to internal validity results from changes between observations in either the measuring instrument or the observer. Using different questions at each measurement is an obvious source of potential trouble, but using different observers or interviewers also threatens validity. There can even be an instrumentation problem if the same observer is used for all measurements. Observer experience, boredom, fatigue, and anticipation of results can all distort the results of separate observations. As we would likely measure financial knowledge with a survey or interview, if we change either the method or the instrument, we threaten the experiment's internal validity.

Selection

An important threat to internal validity is the assignment of participants to experimental and control groups. Validity considerations require that the groups be equivalent in every respect. If participants are randomly assigned to experimental and control groups, this selection problem can be largely overcome. Additionally, matching the members of the groups on key factors can enhance the equivalence of the groups. If we chose only participants from the financial or accounting departments for one group and only workers from the manufacturing floor for another, we would create internal validity problems for our experiment.

Regression toward the Mean

This factor operates especially when groups have been selected by their extreme scores. Suppose we measure the output of all workers in a department for a few days before an experiment and then conduct the experiment with only those workers whose productivity scores are in the top 25 percent and bottom 25 percent. No matter what is done between O_1 and O_2, there is a strong tendency for the average of the high scores at O_1 to decline at O_2 and for the low scores at O_1 to increase. This tendency results from imperfect measurement that, in effect, records some persons abnormally high and abnormally low at O_1. In the second measurement, members of both groups score more closely to their long-run mean scores.

Experimental Mortality

This occurs when the composition of the experimental groups changes during the test. Attrition is especially likely in the experimental group, and with each dropout, the group changes. Because members of the control group are not affected by the testing situation, they are less likely to withdraw. In a compensation incentive study, some employees might not like the change in compensation method and may withdraw from the test group; this action could distort the comparison with the control group that has continued working under the established system, perhaps without knowing a test is underway.

All the threats mentioned to this point are generally, but not always, dealt with adequately in experiments by random assignment. However, five additional threats to internal validity are independent of whether or not one randomizes.[11] The first three have the effect of equalizing experimental and control groups, something no researcher wants.

1. *Diffusion or imitation of treatment.* If people in the experimental and control groups talk, then those in the control group may learn of the treatment, eliminating the difference between the groups.

2. *Compensatory equalization.* Where the experimental treatment is much more desirable, there may be an administrative reluctance to deprive the control group members. Compensatory actions for the control groups may confound the experiment.

3. *Compensatory rivalry.* This may occur when members of the control group know they are in the control group. This may generate competitive pressures, causing the control group members to try harder.

4. *Resentful demoralization of the disadvantaged.* When the treatment is desirable and the experiment is obtrusive, control group members may become resentful of their deprivation and lower their cooperation and output.

5. *Local history.* The regular history effect already mentioned impacts both experimental and control groups alike. However, when one assigns all experimental persons to one group session and all control people to another, there is a chance for some idiosyncratic event to confound results. This problem can be handled by administering treatments to individuals or small groups that are randomly assigned to experimental or control sessions.

External Validity

Internal validity factors cause confusion about whether the experimental treatment (X) or extraneous factors are the source of observation differences. In contrast, external validity is concerned with the interaction of the experimental treatment with other factors and the resulting impact on the ability to generalize to (and across) times, settings, or persons. Among the major threats to external validity are the following interactive possibilities:

- Reactivity of testing on X
- Interaction of selection and X
- Other reactive factors

The Reactivity of Testing on X

The reactive effect refers to sensitizing participants via a pretest so that they respond to the experimental stimulus (X) in a different way. A before-measurement of a participant's knowledge about the ecology programs of a company will often sensitize the participant to various experimental communication efforts that might be made about the company. This before-measurement effect can be particularly significant in experiments where the IV is a change in attitude.

Interaction of Selection and X

The target population from which one selects cases may not be the same as the population to which one wishes to generalize results. Suppose you use a selected group of workers in one plant for a test of the piecework incentive system. The question may remain as to whether you can extrapolate those results to all production workers within the firm. Or consider a study in which you ask a cross section of a population to participate in an experiment but a substantial number refuse. If you conduct the experiment only with those who agree to participate (self-selection), can the results be generalized to the total population?

Other Reactive Factors

The experimental settings themselves may have a biasing effect on a participant's response to X. An artificial setting can obviously produce results that are not representative of larger populations. Suppose the workers who are given incentive pay are moved to a different work area to separate them from the control group. These new conditions alone could create a strong reactive condition.

If participants know they are participating in an experiment, there may be a tendency to role-play in a way that distorts the effects of *X*. Another reactive effect is the possible interaction between *X* and participant characteristics. An incentive pay proposal may be more effective with persons in one type of job, with a certain skill level, or with a certain personality trait (competitiveness).

Problems of external validity may not be as easily alleviated with careful design selections. External validity is largely a matter of generalization, which, in a logical sense, is an inductive process of extrapolating beyond the data collected. In generalizing, we estimate the factors that can be ignored and that will interact with the experimental variable. Assume that the closer two events are in time, space, and measurement, the more likely they are to follow the same laws.

As a rule of thumb in experimental design choices, we first seek internal validity. Researchers then try to secure as much external validity as is compatible with the internal validity requirements by making experimental conditions as similar as possible to conditions under which the results will apply.

> Experimental Research Designs

The many experimental designs vary widely in their power to control contamination of the relationship between independent and dependent variables. The most widely accepted designs are based on this characteristic of control: (1) preexperiments, (2) true experiments, and (3) field experiments (see Exhibit 8-7).

Preexperimental Designs

All three preexperimental designs are weak in their scientific measurement power—that is, they fail to control adequately the various threats to internal validity. This is especially true of the after-only study.

After-Only Design

This may be diagrammed as follows:

$$X \qquad\qquad O$$

Treatment or manipulation   Observation or measurement   (1)
of independent variable   of dependent variable

An example is an employee education campaign about the company's financial condition without a prior measurement of employee knowledge. Results would reveal only how much the employees know after the education campaign, but there is no way to judge the effectiveness of the campaign. How well do you think this design would meet the various threats to internal validity? The lack of a pretest and control group makes this design inadequate for establishing causality.

One-Group Pretest–Posttest Design

This is the design used earlier in the educational example. It meets the various threats to internal validity better than the after-only study, but it is still a weak design. How well does it control for history? Maturation? Testing effect? The others?

$$O \qquad X \qquad O$$

Pretest   Manipulation   Posttest   (2)

>**Exhibit 8-7** Key to Design Symbols

X	An *X* represents an experimental manipulation of the independent variable presented to a group.
O	An *O* is a measurement of the dependent variable.
R	An *R* indicates that the group members have been randomly assigned to a group.
E	An *E* represents the effect of the experiment and is presented as an equation.

The *X*s and *O*s in the diagram are read from left to right in temporal order.

$$O \quad X \quad O \quad O$$
$$\xrightarrow{\hspace{2cm}}$$
Time

When multiple *X*s and *O*s appear vertical to each other, this indicates that the stimuli and/or the observations take place simultaneously.

$$X \; \substack{O \\[4pt] | \\[4pt] O}$$
Time
q

Parallel rows that are not separated by dashed lines indicate that comparison groups have been equalized by the randomization process.

$$X \quad O$$
$$O$$

Those separated with a dashed line have not been so equalized.

$$O \quad X \quad O$$
$$----$$
$$O$$

Static Group Comparison Design

This design provides for two groups, one of which receives the experimental stimulus while the other serves as a control. In a field setting, imagine this scenario. A forest fire or other natural disaster is the experimental treatment, and psychological trauma (or property loss) suffered by the residents is the measured outcome. A pretest before the forest fire would be possible, but not on a large scale (as in the California fires). Moreover, timing of the pretest would be problematic. The control group, receiving the posttest, would consist of residents whose property was spared.

$$\frac{X \qquad O_1}{O_2} \tag{3}$$

The addition of a comparison group creates a substantial improvement over the other two designs. Its chief weakness is that there is no way to be certain that the two groups are equivalent.

True Experimental Designs

The major deficiency of the preexperimental designs is that they fail to provide comparison groups that are truly equivalent. The way to achieve equivalence is through matching and random assignment of cases. With randomly assigned groups, we can employ tests of statistical significance of the observed differences.

It is common to show an X for the test stimulus and a blank for the existence of a control situation. This is an oversimplification of what really occurs. More precisely, there is an X_1 and an X_2, and sometimes more. The X_1 identifies one specific independent variable, while X_2 is another independent variable that has been chosen, often arbitrarily, as the control case. Different levels of the same independent variable may also be used, with one level serving as the control.

Pretest–Posttest Control Group Design

This design consists of adding a control group to the one-group pretest–posttest design and assigning the participants to either of the groups by a random procedure (R). The diagram is:

$$R \quad O_1 \quad X \quad O_2$$
$$R \quad O_3 \qquad O_4$$

$$(4)$$

The effect of the experimental variable is:

$$E = (O_2 - O_1) - (O_4 - O_3)$$

In this design, the seven major internal validity problems are dealt with fairly well, although there are still some difficulties. Local history may occur in one group and not the other. Also, if communication exists between people in test and control groups, there can be rivalry and other internal validity problems.

Maturation, testing, and regression are handled well because one would expect them to be felt equally in experimental and control groups. Mortality, however, can be a problem if there are different dropout rates in the study groups. Selection is adequately dealt with by random assignment.

The record of this design is not as good on external validity, however. There is a chance for a reactive effect from testing. This might be a substantial influence in attitude change studies where pretests introduce unusual topics and content. Nor does this design ensure against reaction between selection and the experimental variable. Even random selection may be defeated by a high decline rate by participants. This would result in using a disproportionate share of people who are essentially volunteers and who may not be typical of the population. If this occurs, we will need to replicate the experiment several times with other groups under other conditions before we can be confident of external validity.

Posttest-Only Control Group Design

In this design, the pretest measurements are omitted. Pretests are well established in classical research design but are not really necessary when it is possible to randomize. The design is:

$$R \quad X \quad O_1$$
$$R \qquad O_2$$

$$(5)$$

The experimental effect is measured by the difference between O_1 and O_2:

$$E = (O_2 - O_1)$$

The simplicity of this design makes it more attractive than the pretest–posttest control group design. Internal validity threats from history, maturation, selection, and statistical regression are adequately controlled by random assignment. Because the participants are measured only once, the threats of testing and instrumentation are reduced, but different mortality rates between experimental and control groups continue to be a potential problem. The design reduces the external validity problem of testing interaction effect.

Field Experiments: Quasi- or Semi-Experiments[12]

Under field conditions, we often cannot control enough of the extraneous variables or the experimental treatment to use a true experimental design. Because the stimulus condition occurs in a natural environment, a field experiment is required.

A modern version of the bystander and thief field experiment, mentioned at the beginning of the chapter, involves the use of electronic article surveillance to prevent shrinkage due to shoplifting. In a proprietary study, a shopper came to the optical counter of an upscale mall store and asked to be shown special designer frames. The salesperson, a confederate of the experimenter, replied that she would get them from a case in the adjoining department and disappeared. The "thief" selected two pairs of sunglasses from an open display, deactivated the security tags at the counter, and walked out of the store.

Thirty-five percent of the participants (store customers) reported the theft upon the return of the salesperson. Sixty-three percent reported it when the salesperson asked about the shopper. Unlike previous studies, the presence of a second customer did not reduce the willingness to report a theft.

This study was not possible with a control group, a pretest, or randomization of customers; but the information gained was essential and justified a compromise of true experimental designs. We use the preexperimental designs previously discussed or quasi-experiments to deal with such conditions. In a quasi-experiment, we often cannot know when or to whom to expose the experimental treatment. Usually, however, we can decide when and whom to measure. A quasi-experiment is inferior to a true experimental design but is usually superior to preexperimental designs. In this section, we consider a few common quasi-experiments.

Nonequivalent Control Group Design

This is a strong and widely used quasi-experimental design. It differs from the pretest–posttest control group design because the test and control groups are not randomly assigned. The design is diagrammed as follows:

$$O_1 \quad X \quad O_2$$
$$\overline{O_3 \qquad\quad O_4}$$

(6)

There are two varieties. One is the *intact equivalent design*, in which the membership of the experimental and control groups is naturally assembled. For example, we may use different classes in a school, membership in similar clubs, or customers from similar stores. Ideally, the two groups are as alike as possible. This design is especially useful when any type of individual selection process would be reactive.

The second variation, the *self-selected experimental group design*, is weaker because volunteers are recruited to form the experimental group, while nonvolunteer participants are used for control. Such a design is likely when participants believe it would be in their interest to be a participant in an experiment—say, an experimental training program.

Comparison of pretest results ($O_1 - O_3$) is one indicator of the degree of equivalence between test and control groups. If the pretest results are significantly different, there is a real question about the groups' comparability. On the other hand, if pretest observations are similar between groups, there is more reason to believe internal validity of the experiment is good.

Separate Sample Pretest–Posttest Design

This design is most applicable when we cannot know when and to whom to introduce the treatment but we can decide when and whom to measure. The basic design is:

$$R \quad O_1 \quad (X)$$
$$R \qquad\quad X \quad O_2$$

(7)

A Job Enrichment Quasi-Experiment[13]

One theory of job attitudes holds that "hygiene" factors, which include working conditions, pay, security, status, interpersonal relationships, and company policy, can be a major source of dissatisfaction among workers but have little positive motivational power. This theory says that the positive motivator factors are intrinsic to the job; they include achievement, recognition for achievement, the work itself, responsibility, and growth or advancement.[a]

A study of the value of job enrichment as a builder of job satisfaction was carried out with laboratory technicians, or "experimental officers" (EOs), at British Chemical. The project was a multiple group time series quasi-experiment. The project is diagrammed at the end of this Closeup.

Two sections of the department acted as experimental groups, and two sections acted as control groups. It is not clear how these groups were chosen, but there was no mention of random assignment. One of the experimental groups and one of the control groups worked closely together, while the other two groups were separated geographically and were engaged in different research. Hygiene factors were held constant during the research, and the studies were kept confidential to avoid the tendency of participants to act in artificial ways.

A before-measurement was made using a job reaction survey instrument. This indicated the EOs typically had low morale, and many wrote of their frustrations. All EOs were asked to write monthly progress reports, and these were used to assess the quality of their work. The assessment was made against eight specifically defined criteria by a panel of three managers who were not members of the department. These assessors were never told which laboratory technicians were in the experimental group and which were in the control group.

The study extended over a year, with the treatments introduced in the experimental groups at the start of the 12-month study period. Changes were made to give experimental group EOs important chances for achievement; these changes also made the work more challenging. Recognition of achievement was given, authority over certain aspects was increased, new managerial responsibilities were assigned to the senior EOs, added advancements were given to others, and the opportunity for self-initiated work was provided. After about six months, these same changes were instituted with one of the control groups, while the remaining group continued for the entire period as a control. Several months of EO progress reports were available as a prior baseline for evaluation. The results of this project are shown in the exhibit below.

O O O X O O O O O O O O O O O O

O O O O O O O O X O O O O O O O

O O O O O O O O O O O O O O O O

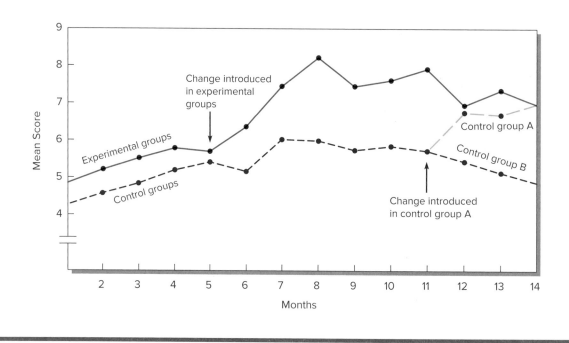

The bracketed treatment (X) is irrelevant to the purpose of the study but is shown to suggest that the experimenter cannot control the treatment.

This is not a strong design because several threats to internal validity are not handled adequately. History can confound the results but can be overcome by repeating the study at other times in other settings. In contrast, it is considered superior to true experiments in external validity. Its strength results from its being a field experiment in which the samples are usually drawn from the population to which we wish to generalize our findings.

We would find this design more appropriate if the population were large, if a before-measurement were reactive, or if there were no way to restrict the application of the treatment. Assume a company is planning an intense campaign to change its employees' attitudes toward energy conservation. It might draw two random samples of employees, one of which is interviewed about energy-use attitudes before the information campaign. After the campaign the other group is interviewed.

Group Time Series Design

A time series design introduces repeated observations before and after the treatment and allows participants to act as their own controls. The single treatment group design has before-after measurements as the only controls. There is also a multiple design with two or more comparison groups as well as the repeated measurements in each treatment group.

The time series format is especially useful where regularly kept records are a natural part of the environment and are unlikely to be reactive. The time series approach is also a good way to study unplanned events in an ex post facto manner. If the federal government were to suddenly begin price controls, we could still study the effects of this action later if we had regularly collected records for the period before and after the advent of price control.

The internal validity problem for this design is history. To reduce this risk, we keep a record of possible extraneous factors during the experiment and attempt to adjust the results to reflect their influence.

> An Evaluation of Experiments

Advantages

Causality cannot be proved with certainty, but the probability of one variable being linked to another can be established convincingly. The experiment comes closer than any primary data collection method to accomplishing this goal.

The foremost advantage is the researcher's ability to manipulate the independent variable. Consequently, the probability that changes in the dependent variable are a function of that manipulation increases. Also, a control group serves as a comparison to assess the existence and potency of the manipulation.

The second advantage of the experiment is that contamination from extraneous variables can be controlled more effectively than in other designs. This helps the researcher isolate experimental variables and evaluate their impact over time.

Third, the convenience and cost of experimentation are superior to other methods. These benefits allow the experimenter opportunistic scheduling of data collection and the flexibility to adjust variables and conditions that evoke extremes not observed under routine circumstances. In addition, the experimenter can assemble combinations of variables for testing rather than having to search for their fortuitous appearance in the study environment.

Fourth, **replication**—repeating an experiment with different participant groups and conditions—leads to the discovery of an average effect of the independent variable across people, situations, and times. Fifth, researchers can use naturally occurring events and, to some extent, **field experiments** (a study of the dependent variable in actual environmental conditions) to reduce participants' perceptions of the researcher as a source of intervention or deviation in their everyday lives.

Disadvantages

The artificiality of the laboratory is arguably the primary disadvantage of the experimental method. However, many participants' perceptions of a contrived environment can be improved by investment in the facility. Second, generalization from nonprobability samples can pose problems despite random assignment. The extent to which a study can be generalized from college students to managers or executives is open to question. And when an experiment is unsuccessfully disguised, volunteer participants are often those with the most interest in the topic. Third, despite the low costs of experimentation, many applications of experimentation far outrun the budgets for other primary data collection methods. Fourth, experimentation is most effectively targeted at problems of the present or immediate future. Experimental studies of the past are not feasible, and studies about intentions or predictions are difficult. Finally, management research is often concerned with the study of people. There are limits to the types of manipulation and controls that are ethical.

> Ethical Issues and Their Solutions

The major ethical issues involved with experiments are participant welfare, participant privacy, research quality, and sponsor and result nondisclosure. In laboratory experiments, participants are often pre-recruited, so privacy would not be an issue as informed consent is a normal protocol. However, in field settings where participants don't know they are part of an experiment, researchers do not have prior consent. This means that a participant's privacy is violated for the sake of protecting the research objective. Researchers deal with this by **debriefing** participants—sharing what details they can about the experiment—without damaging the continuing experiment.

In any experiment, when researchers manipulate one or more variables, participants are affected. In the classic experiment about bystanders reporting theft, the researcher can't know what emotional trauma the participant experienced just by being an observer to a crime. The researcher should always judge the value of the information and insights against any possible harm to a participant. If the researcher has significant concerns, he or she can arrange for trained personnel (e.g., psychologists, counselors, etc.) to deal with expected or likely repercussions.

Research quality is always of paramount importance, especially when determining causation is the objective. A researcher guarantees quality by carefully planning the design and execution of the experiment; this includes thorough training of any data collectors or parties executing the manipulation of variables.

Depending on the environment of the experiment, it may not be possible to keep the identity of the sponsor concealed. But a researcher can always protect the results. Even if debriefing a participant is required in the protocol, it is inappropriate for the researcher or data collector to discuss results or research objective.

>summary

LO8-1 Experiments are studies involving intervention by the researcher beyond that required for measurement. The usual intervention is to manipulate a variable (IV) and observe how it affects the variable being studied (DV).

LO8-2 Consideration of the following activities is essential for the execution of a well-planned experiment:

  a Select relevant variables for testing.

  b Specify the treatment levels.

  c Control the environmental and extraneous factors.

  d Choose an experimental design suited to the hypothesis.

  e Select and assign participants to groups.

  f Pilot test, revise, and conduct the final test.

  g Analyze the data.

LO8-3 We judge various types of experimental research designs by how well they meet the tests of internal and external validity. An experiment has high internal validity if one has confidence that the experimental treatment has been the source of change in the dependent variable. More specifically, a design's internal validity is judged by how well it meets seven threats. These are history, maturation, testing, instrumentation, selection, regression toward the mean, and experiment mortality.

External validity is high when the results of an experiment are judged to apply to some larger population. Such an experiment is said to have high external validity regarding that population. Three potential threats to external validity are testing reactivity, selection interaction, and other reactive factors.

LO8-4 Experimental research designs include (1) preexperiments, (2) true experiments, and (3) quasi-experiments. The main distinction among these types is the degree of control that the researcher can exercise over validity problems. Three preexperimental designs were presented in the chapter. These designs represent the crudest form of experimentation and are undertaken only when nothing stronger is possible. Their weakness is the lack of an equivalent comparison group; as a result, they fail to meet many internal validity criteria. They are the (1) after-only study, (2) one-group pretest–posttest design, and (3) static group comparison.

Two forms of the true experiment were also presented. Their central characteristic is that they provide a means by which we can ensure equivalence between experimental and control groups through random assignment to the groups. These designs are (1) pretest–posttest control group and (2) posttest-only control group.

The classical two-group experiment can be extended to multigroup designs in which different levels of the test variable are used as controls rather than the classical nontest control.

Between the extremes of preexperiments, with little or no control, and true experiments, with random assignment, there is a gray area in which we find quasi-experiments. These are useful designs when some variables can be controlled, but equivalent experimental and control groups usually cannot be established by random assignment. There are many quasi-experimental designs, but only three were covered in this chapter: (1) nonequivalent control group design, (2) separate sample pretest–posttest design, and (3) group time series design.

LO8-5 An evaluation of the experimental method reveals several advantages: (1) the ability to uncover causal relationships, (2) provisions for controlling extraneous and environmental variables, (3) convenience and low cost of creating test situations rather than searching for their appearance in business situations, (4) the ability to replicate findings and thus rule out idiosyncratic or isolated results, and (5) the ability to exploit naturally occurring events.

Some advantages of other methods that are liabilities for the experiment include (1) the artificial setting of the laboratory, (2) generalizability from nonprobability samples, (3) disproportionate costs in select business situations, (4) a focus restricted to the present and immediate future, and (5) ethical issues related to the manipulation and control of human participants.

LO8-6 The major ethical issues involved with experiments are participant welfare, participant privacy, research quality, and sponsor and result nondisclosure. Researchers deal with these responsibilities by obtaining participant consent when possible and debriefing the participant when warranted, by anticipating likely subject reactions and planning accordingly, by careful design and thoroughly following design protocols, and by keeping sponsor identity concealed and study results private.

>**key**terms

after-only design 184	external validity 181	quota matrix 179
asymmetrical relationship 172	field experiment 189	random assignment 171
blind 177	group time series design 189	reciprocal relationship 172
causal hypothesis 171	history 181	regression toward the mean 181
causation 171	independent variable (IV) 171	replication 189
control 171	instrumentation 181	selection 181
control group 177	internal validity 181	separate sample pretest–posttest design 187
debriefing 190	matching 179	static group comparison design 185
dependent variable (DV) 171	maturation 181	stimulus-response 173
disposition-behavior 173	nonequivalent control group design 187	symmetrical relationship 172
double blind 177	one-group pretest–posttest design 184	testing 181
environmental control 177	posttest-only control group design 186	treatment levels 177
experiment 171	pretest–posttest control group design 186	
experimental mortality 181	property-behavior 173	
experimental treatment 177	property-disposition 173	

>discussionquestions

Terms in Review

1   Distinguish between or among the following:

   a   Internal validity and external validity.

   b   Preexperimental design and quasi-experimental design.

   c   History and maturation.

   d   Random sampling, randomization, and matching.

   e   Environmental variables and extraneous variables.

2   Compare the advantages of experiments with the advantages of survey and observational methods.

3   Why would a noted business researcher say, "It is essential that we always keep in mind the model of the controlled experiment, even if in practice we have to deviate from an ideal model"?

4   What ethical problems do you see in conducting experiments with human participants?

5   What essential characteristics distinguish a true experiment from other research designs?

Making Research Decisions

6   A lighting company seeks to study the percentage of defective glass shells being manufactured. Theoretically, the percentage of defectives is dependent on temperature, humidity, and the level of artisan expertise. Complete historical data are available for the following variables on a daily basis for a year:

   a   Temperature (high, normal, low).

   b   Humidity (high, normal, low).

   c   Artisan expertise level (expert, average, mediocre).

Some experts feel that defectives also depend on production supervisors. However, data on supervisors in charge are available for only 242 of the 365 days. How should this study be conducted?

7   Much Internet advertising is priced based on click-through activity. A prospect is shown an ad on a host website based on search words he or she might have entered in a search engine such as Google or Bing. If the prospect clicks directly on the ad he or she sees on the host website to visit the advertiser's site, the ad is considered effective and the advertiser must pay the host website for the ad. But research reveals that while all prospects do not click on the ad they are shown on a host website, many do visit the advertiser's site. They simply key in the advertiser's URL directly into their browser or search engine. How would you design an experiment to determine if non-click-through ads displayed on your host website were actually effective in getting a prospect to an advertiser's website?

8   A pharmaceuticals manufacturer is testing a drug developed to treat cancer. During the final stages of development, the drug's effectiveness is being tested on individuals for different (1) dosage conditions and (2) age groups. One of the problems is patient mortality during experimentation. Justify your design recommendations through a comparison of alternatives and in terms of external and internal validity.

   a   Recommend the appropriate design for the experiment.

   b   Explain the use of control groups, blinds, and double blind studies if you recommend them.

9   You are asked to develop an experiment for a study of the effect that compensation has on the response rates secured from personal interview participants. This study will involve 300 people who will be assigned to one of the following conditions: (a) no compensation, (b) $10 compensation, and (c) $30 compensation. A number of sensitive issues will be explored concerning various social problems, and the 300 people will be drawn from the adult population. Describe your design. You may find the website Appendix *Complex Experimental Designs* valuable for this question.

10   What type of experimental design would you recommend in each of the following cases? Suggest in some detail how you would design each study:

   a   A test of three methods of compensation of factory workers. The methods are hourly wage, incentive pay, and weekly salary. The dependent variable is direct labor cost per unit of output.

   b   A study of the effects of various levels of advertising effort and price reduction on the sale of specific branded grocery products by a retail grocery chain.

   c   A study to determine whether it is true that the use of fast-paced music played over a store's public address system will speed the shopping rate of customers without an adverse effect on the amount spent per customer.

11   One of the hardest aspects of a merger is making the IT systems of the merging companies talk with each other. That problem grows in magnitude when you are talking about merging airlines, Continental and United Airlines. While the ticketing conversion worked well, the distinctness of the air traffic tracking systems made the conversion problematic. So when the company decided that United's system was more suitable for the merged airline, it needed to test it. How would you design an experiment to see if your tracking system could know where flights were, what their arrival times and departure times were, what the flight numbers were, and whether they deviated from their flight plan?

From Concept to Practice

12 Using Exhibit 8-7, diagram an experiment described in one of the Snapshots in this chapter using research design symbols.

From the Headlines

13 Dolby, the company that provides advanced sound and light systems in movie theaters, is operating in an environment where theater ticket sales are dropping 5 to 10 percent per year due to a better variety of entertainment options, shorter attention spans, and better in-home and device streaming. Dolby Cinema now does for the eyes what it once did for the ears. In its LA operations, Dolby conducts lab experiments measuring brain waves, galvanic skin response, and heart rate as volunteer participants experience a Dolby Cinema–enhanced movie. Diagram this experiment, and discuss its strengths and weaknesses.

>cases*

McDonald's Tests Catfish Sandwich   NetConversions Influences Kelley Blue Book

* You will find a description of each case in the Case Abstracts section of this textbook. Check the Case Index to determine whether a case provides data, the research instrument, video, or other supplementary material. Cases and case supplements are available in Connect.

>additionalcontent

Web appendices are available through Connect.

Appendix *Complex Experimental Designs*

Appendix *Test Markets*

>chapter 9

Stage 2:
Data Collection Design:
Survey Research

"We saw that our customers required help beyond the data sets they had and that they could benefit from a wider opinion. So we built SurveyMonkey Audience, and we've now got 4 million users who signed up to take surveys. Our clients can choose the demographic they want to hear from, and we can provide that sample."

David Goldberg, CEO,
Survey Monkey

>learningobjectives

After reading this chapter, you should understand . . .

LO9-1 The process for selecting the appropriate and optimal survey approach.

LO9-2 The major advantages and disadvantages of the three survey methods.

LO9-3 What factors affect participation in survey research.

LO9-4 The major sources of error in communication studies and how to minimize them.

LO9-5 Why an organization might outsource a communication study.

LO9-6 Ethical issues with survey research and their solutions.

Data collection designs can be classified by the approach used to gather primary data. We can collect data by observation of a target population or a sample drawn from it. Or we can use communication with some target populations about various topics, including participants' behaviors, opinions, attitudes, intentions, expectations, motivations, and knowledge. The **communication approach** involves surveying people, through the use of a questionnaire or a personal interview. Students often make the mistake of seeing survey research in business as the only appropriate data collection design. Rather, it should be seen as a strong complement to observation research. Exhibit 9-1 summarizes when each approach is most effective.

Several factors strongly influence our choice of the communication approach. The first is the nature of the investigative questions; we need information that observation cannot provide. Communication-based research can be used by all disciplines of business, which makes it a very versatile data collection method. Information about past events is often available only through communication. The second is the characteristics of the sample case—specifically, whether the case can articulate his or her ideas, thoughts, and experiences. The third is speed needed in decision making; communication is faster than observation. And the fourth is cost; some communication methods offer a low cost per case. Thus, the choice of communication versus observation may seem an obvious one. Exhibit 9-2 shows this choice within the research process.

>**Exhibit 9-1** Two Data Collection Design Approaches

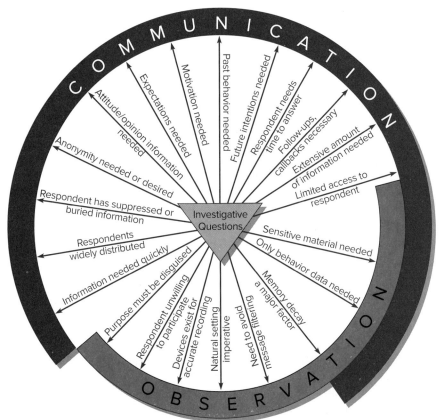

>Exhibit 9-2 Survey Research and the Research Process

> Data Collection Design: The Survey

The **survey** is a data collection design used to collect information during a structured interview—sometimes with a human interviewer and other times without. Questions are carefully chosen or crafted, sequenced, and precisely asked of each participant. The goal of a survey is to collect comparable data across all cases so that similarities and differences can be found. When combined with statistical probability sampling for selecting participants, survey findings and conclusions are projectable to large and diverse populations.

Once the sponsor or researcher has determined that the survey is the appropriate data collection approach, various means may be used to secure information from individuals. As noted in Exhibit 9-3, the three primary categories of surveys are the self-administered survey, survey via personal interview, and the phone survey. As noted in Exhibit 9-4, although there are commonalities among these approaches, several considerations are unique to each.

In the last 20 years, a quiet revolution has been underway in survey research. The computer and mobile survey has substantially replaced the paper-and-pencil survey, once the standard of the prior

>**snap**shot

Gamification in Survey Research

By 2020, Gartner Group estimates 100 million consumers will shop in augmented reality. According to author Gabe Zicherman, in *The Gamification Revolution*, businesses are experiencing success when they make behavior modification more game like. For those of you in Generation G, where gaming has been a primary form of entertainment, this might not be surprising. Gamification, however, is just starting to be recognized as a powerful force outside the entertainment industry.

Gamification, according to Gabe Zichermann, author of Gamification, the blog, and *Gamification in Marketing* and *Gamification by Design*, is the process of "using game thinking and game mechanics to engage audiences and solve problems." Gartner Group analyst Brian Burke indicates that gamification is destined to be used in such "non-game environments such as innovation, marketing, training, employee performance, health and social change."

Many survey participants consider the survey process boring. Some of the fundamental tenets of gamification, shared Betty Adamou, CEO and founder of Research Through Gaming Ltd (RTG) and also editor-in-chief of Game Access, a dedicated gamification blog, are engagement and rewards. RTG created a term for its gamified research participants: playspondents. "As our surveys become games, the people taking part aren't quite respondents but they're not quite game players either." RTG's fundamental research environment is the Playspondent Playhouse. Here a client can "rent a room to carry out [its] project, so when Avatars are made, they can be placed in a room with [the client's] questions, product images and quotas and [be] ready to go!"

The U.K.'s Department for Work and Pensions created an innovation game called Idea Street to generate ideas from its

Gamification is designed to more highly engage the participant in the survey, by evoking the fun, challenge, and competitive nature of gaming.

©Fuse/Getty Images

120,000 employees. Within the first 18 months, Idea Street had approximately 4,500 users who had generated 1,400 ideas. The collaboration element of the game generated 63 ideas that were implemented.

Neurological research supports gaming as a research technique as dopamine is released in the brain during gaming, and this pleasurable sensation serves as a reward for participation. The game world has conditioned players to seek its clearly articulated rewards. Many think research needs to be more involved in this trend.

www.researchthroughgaming.com; www.gartner.com; www.m2research.com

millennium. Today, people's embrace of the smartphone and mobile tablet (due not only to hardware advances, but also the increasing speed and reliability of data transfer), as well as broadband availability and widespread Internet access, have had profound influences on survey research in just the last few years. These factors have influenced not only the choice of survey approach, but have also had an immense influence on measurement instrument design. In addition, businesses are striving to capture more meaning through data analytics—especially social media analytics—as a means of gaining insights into people's behaviors. But researchers caution that data drawn from surveys—highly structured research—are very different than data drawn from social media. One CEO puts it this way:

> If social media is the temperature check, surveys are the taste test to validate that the meal is cooked properly. A good survey enables you to: (1) tune out the noise and zero in on the opinions and comments that are directly applicable to your most pressing questions, and (2) validate trends and shifts in preference that you may have suspected, but weren't certain about.[1]

>**Exhibit 9-3** Selecting a Survey Method

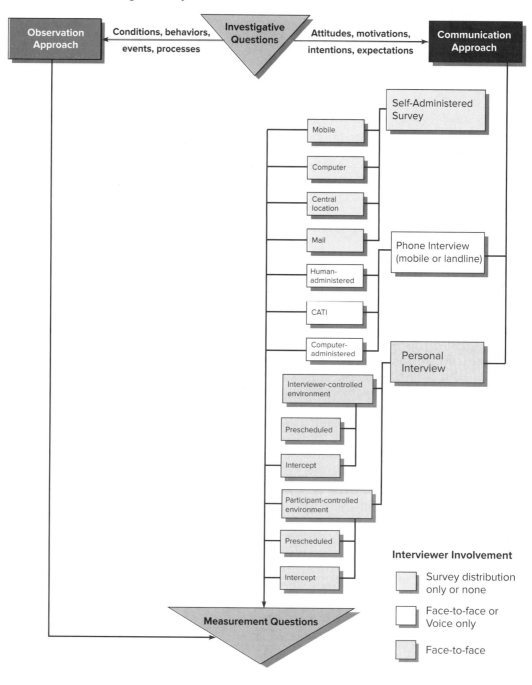

Whether it goes by the name of computer-assisted data collection (CADAC), computer-assisted survey information collection (CASIC), or computer-assisted interviewing (CAI), the computer's involvement in survey research is entrenched. Automation is the new buzzword in survey research, and it is influencing all levels of the process—from question formation, to data collection, to analysis, and report writing. Although less obvious in the public sector (the U.S. government is the largest survey researcher in the world, and paper-and-pencil approaches still hold prominence there), in business surveys with households and organizations, the computer's influence is far-reaching.

The choice of a survey method is not as complicated as it might first appear. By comparing your research objectives with the strengths and weaknesses of each method, a researcher can choose one that is suited to the project's needs. The summary of advantages and disadvantages of personal interviews, telephone interviews, and self-administered surveys presented in Exhibit 9-4 should be useful in making such a comparison.

When your investigative questions call for information from hard-to-reach or inaccessible participants, the telephone interview, mail survey, or computer-delivered survey should be considered. However, if data must be collected very quickly, the mail survey should be discarded because of lack of control over

>**Exhibit 9-4** Comparison of Survey Methods

	Self-Administered Survey	Telephone Survey	Survey via Personal Interview
Description	Questionnaires are: a. Sent via mobile device service provider (to phone, tablet) or delivered via messenger app. b. Mailed, faxed, or couriered with return mechanism generally included. c. Computer-delivered via intranet, Internet, or online service. d. People are intercepted in a central location for a computerized or paper survey.	People selected to be part of the sample are interviewed on the telephone by a trained interviewer.	People selected to be part of the sample are interviewed in person by a trained interviewer.
Advantages	• Allows contact with otherwise inaccessible participants (e.g., CEOs). • Incentives may be used to increase response rate. • Is often lowest-cost option. • Allows expanded geographic coverage without increase in costs (c). • Requires minimal staff (a,c). • Perceived as more anonymous (c). • Allows participants time to think about questions (c). • More complex instruments can be used (c). • Visual and audio stimuli can be used (a,c,d). • Offers participants upload capabilities (a, c). • Offers fast access to the computer-literate and tech savvy (a,c). • Allows rapid data collection (a,c,d). • Participant who cannot be reached by phone (voice) may be accessible (a,c,d). • Sample frame lists viable locations rather than prospective participants (b,d).	• Costs are lower than personal interview. • Allows expanded geographic coverage without dramatic increase in costs. • Uses fewer, more highly skilled interviewers. • Offers reduced interviewer bias. • Allows for fastest completion time. • Offers better access to hard-to-reach participants through repeated callbacks. • Can use computerized random dialing. • Allows CATI—computer-assisted telephone interviewing; responses can be entered directly into a computer file to reduce error and cost. • Interview may be closely supervised and recorded. • Visual and audio stimuli can be used if participant is on a smartphone or tablet.	• Interviewer can prescreen participant to ensure he or she fits the population profile. • Allows good cooperation from participants. • Interviewer can answer questions about survey, probe for answers, use follow-up questions, and gather information by observation. • Special visual aids and scoring devices can be used. • Illiterate and functionally illiterate participants can be reached. • Allows CAPI—computer-assisted personal interviewing; responses can be entered into a portable microcomputer to reduce error and cost.

>**Exhibit 9-4** Comparison of Survey Methods (cont'd)

	Self-Administered Survey	Telephone Survey	Survey via Personal Interview
Disadvantages	• Access is declining (a) as people switch from landlines to cell phones. • There is no probing for explanation (a). • Response rates are low in some modes. • Cannot be long or complex (a). • Accurate mailing lists are needed (b). • Often participants returning survey represent extremes of the population—skewed responses (b). • Allows for anxiety among some participants. • Directions/software instruction are needed for progression through the instrument (a,c). • Computer security (b) is a concern. • There is a need for low-distraction environment for survey completion (d).	• Response rate is lower than for personal interview. • Costs are higher if interviewing geographically dispersed sample. • Interview length must be limited • Is difficult to ask complex questions. • Directories are unreliable sample frames. • Some target groups are not available by phone. • Responses may be less complete. • Visual stimuli are available only if participant is on smartphone or tablet.	• High costs. • Need for highly trained interviewers. • Longer time frame for field data collection. • Difficult or costly if sample is geographically dispersed. • Follow-up is labor-intensive, costly. • Not all desired participants are available or accessible. • Participants may be unwilling to talk to researchers in their homes. • Some neighborhoods are difficult, dangerous to visit. • Questions may be altered or participant coached by interviewers.

the timeliness of returns. Alternatively, you may decide your objective requires extensive questioning and probing; then the survey via personal interview should be considered.

If none of the choices turns out to be a particularly good fit, it is possible to combine the best characteristics of two or more alternatives into a *hybrid* or *mixed-mode* survey. Although this decision incurs the costs of the combined survey methods, the flexibility of tailoring a method to your unique needs is often an acceptable trade-off.

While online and mobile surveys offer speed in data collection, real-time data entry, and a lower cost than one with post-collection data entry (paper-and-pencil surveys), they are not without problems. Not all customers will participate when invited, creating *nonresponse error*. Even though theoretically the online format offers unlimited space for questions, only a short survey is likely to encourage participation and full survey completion. Alerting participants to the importance of their participating in the survey by phone or email might improve the survey research design, but it would add significantly to the cost. Telephone and personal interviewing creates the possibility of injecting *interviewer bias* at an unknown level for at least part of the data in mixed-mode research designs.

Ultimately, all researchers are confronted by the practical realities of cost and deadlines. As Exhibit 9-4 suggests, on average, surveys via personal interview are the most expensive communication method and take the most field time unless a large field team is used. Telephone surveys are moderate in cost and offer the quickest option, especially when computer-assisted telephone interviewing (CATI) is used. Questionnaires administered by email or the Internet are the least expensive. When your desired sample is available via the Internet, the Internet survey may prove to be the least expensive communication method with the most rapid (simultaneous) data availability. The use of the computer to select participants and reduce coding and processing time will continue to improve the cost-to-performance profiles of this method in the future.

Most of the time, an optimal method will be apparent. However, managers' needs for information often exceed their internal resources. Such factors as specialized expertise, a large field team, unique facilities, or a rapid turnaround prompt managers to seek assistance from research vendors of survey-related services.

>snapshot

Internet Brings Prediction Research into 21st Century

Managers often must make decisions about the future. These decisions offer high uncertainty. Research is designed to reduce the risk, but simply asking people to predict their own behavior, attitude, or reaction hasn't worked well; we are notoriously poor at the task. For example, in 1985 when individuals were asked to predict their acceptance of Coke's planned reformulation, they predicted incredibly wrong and it cost Coca-Cola millions.

Historically, researchers have used the consensus prediction of experts (Delphi technique) to correct for the individual's poor predictive capabilities. However, not all situations offer a logical panel of experts. James Surowiecki, in his *The Wisdom of Crowds*, describes how a group of diverse individuals is able to make decisions and predictions better than isolated individuals or experts. MIT researchers explain that people's heightened connectivity due to the Internet has brought about the "emergence of surprising new forms of collective intelligence." As social animals, people are getting good at noticing what others are doing, sensing why they might be doing it, and predicting what they will do. In a PEW Research study, collectively Americans predicted 37 percent of Americans were obese, a fairly good predictor of the actual 31 percent who were so diagnosed.

Marcus Thomas (MT) needed a research method that was fast and that would overcome client skepticism about the inaccuracy of self-reported anticipated versus actual behaviors for its financial client. It chose to use a prediction market. "A prediction market is like an online stock investing game," explained Jennifer Hirt-Marchand, associate partner and strategic insights executive for MT. "Traders 'invest' virtual dollars in ideas, products, assets, etc. to be tested. Based on the investments they make, traders can win greater incentives if they invest in the winning idea than an incentive they might earn by completing a survey alone. This 'skin in the game' is a critical component of the methodology, as it fosters engagement and thoughtfulness on the part of the traders. Its strength is that is doesn't rely on asking individuals to make predictions about what *they* would do in the future but rather what they think *other people* would do."

Using the services of a sample provider, an online survey was sent to general population panelists. Likely participants self-identified based on having an understanding of finance with regard to estate planning, personal finances and investing, vacation planning, health care, etc. A thousand participants, known as *traders*, were recruited from this group. While panel participants are compensated by the sample company for their regular participation in research projects, panelists selected for this project could earn additional compensation based on the accuracy

©Ridofranz/Getty Images

of their predictions. Those payouts would be determined by the number of traders who invested in the "winning" group, as well as the amount each trader invested in that group.

Through a continuation of the online survey, the selected traders were first presented a written description of the new financial service (each had previously agreed to a nondisclosure agreement, as the product was in development). Then each was provided six consumer profiles (called vignettes) one at a time. Each vignette—developed based on consumer segmentation from prior research and extensive secondary research— represented a possible purchaser group. It included a narrative, describing the group as people, along with photographs bringing each group to life. Traders were each given $1,000 in virtual money to invest in one or more vignette groups—the ones they thought would be most likely to purchase the new financial service. In addition, through open-ended questions, each trader was asked to explain the reasons why they believed each vignette group would or would not purchase.

Using this methodology, Marcus Thomas identified three segments based on the best-choice vignettes—including one that seemed unlikely at the outset—for its financial client. The vignette that represented the client's core segment for its main product line failed to rank high in the prediction research for the new financial service. Media/engagement touchpoints and messaging insights to reach the three best-choice groups were developed based on this research.

Some of the world's leading consumer and industrial companies rely on Cleveland-based Marcus Thomas LLC to create or refine their brands and drive customers to seek out and buy their products and services.

www.marcusthomasllc.com

Self-Administered Survey

The **self-administered survey** is a highly structured interview experience designed to be completed without an interviewer. It is ubiquitous in modern living. You have experienced survey research in service evaluations of hotels, restaurants, car dealerships, and transportation providers. Often, a short questionnaire is left to be completed by the participant in a convenient location or is packaged with a product. User registrations, product information requests in magazines, warranty cards, and online surveys of employee motivation are examples of self-administered surveys. Self-administered surveys are delivered via email, the U.S. Postal Service, fax and courier service, phone, in person during intercept studies, or on pop-up screens when you land on certain web pages. Even experiments may include such surveys.

Nowhere in research has the computer revolution been felt more strongly than in the area of the self-administered survey. Computer-delivered self-administered questionnaires (also labeled **computer-assisted self-interviews, or CASIs**) use organizational intranets, the Internet, or online services via tablet and mobile devices to reach their participants. Participants may be targeted (as when BizRate, an online e-business rating service, sends an email to a registered e-purchaser to participate in a survey following the completion of their order) or self-selecting (as when a computer screen pop-up window offers a survey to an individual who clicks on a particular website or when a potential participant responds to a postcard or email inquiry looking for participants). The questionnaire and its managing software may reside on the computer or its network, on the cloud, or both. Computer delivered surveys are migrating quickly to the mobile phone and tablet. In fact, the mantra among researchers today is "mobile first."

Data from the Pew Research Center shows 88 percent of U.S. households use the Internet.[2] The digital divide between low- and high-income households is diminishing, with 79 percent of households below $30,000 annual income and 98 percent of households above $75,000 using the Internet. Roughly 73 percent of Americans access broadband service at home, with that number dropping to 54 percent for low-income households.[3] Researchers embrace online surveys, finding that online participants generally parallel participants reached by other methods. More than half of U.S. households are wireless-phone-only households,[4] and this number is higher for young Hispanics and African Americans. As the number of adults only reachable by cell phones has grown, the potential for bias in surveys that do not include both landline and cellphone interviews is growing.[5] See Exhibit 9-5.

Intercept surveys—at malls, conventions, state fairs, vacation destinations, even busy city street corners—may use a traditional paper-and-pencil questionnaire or a computer-delivered survey via a tablet, computer, or a kiosk. The respondent participates without interviewer assistance, usually in a predetermined environment, such as a room in a shopping mall. All modes have special problems and unique advantages (as shown in Exhibit 9-4).

Costs

Self-administered surveys of all types typically cost less than surveys via personal interview. This is true of mail surveys, as well as of both computer-delivered and intercept surveys. Telephone and mail costs are in the same general range, although in specific cases, either may be lower. The more geographically dispersed the sample, the more likely it is that self-administered surveys via computer or mail will be the low-cost method. A mail or computer-delivered study can cost less because it is often a one-person job. And computer-delivered studies (including those that employ interviewer-participant interaction) eliminate the cost of printing surveys, a significant cost of both mail studies and personal interviewing employing printed surveys. The most significant cost savings with computer-delivered surveys involve the much lower cost of pre- and post-notification (often done by mail or phone when other self-administered surveys are involved), the lower data entry costs (especially with self-administered computer-delivered surveys), as well as the lower per-participant survey delivery cost of very large studies.[6]

Sample Accessibility

One asset to using mail self-administered surveys is that researchers can contact participants who might otherwise be inaccessible. Some groups, such as corporate executives and physicians, are

>**Exhibit 9-5** The Web as a Survey Research Venue*

Web Advantages	Examples
Short turnaround of results; results are tallied as participants complete surveys.	• A soft-drink manufacturer got results from a web survey in just five days.
Ability to use visual stimuli.	• Florida's tourism office used eye movement tracking to enhance its website and improve its billboard and print ads.
	• One major advertising agency is conducting web research using virtual supermarket aisles that participants wander through, reacting to client products and promotions.
	• LiveWorld has developed a packaging study showing more than 75 images of labels and bottle designs.
Ability to do numerous surveys over time.	• A printer manufacturer did seven surveys in six months during the development of one of its latest products.
Ability to attract participants who wouldn't participate in another research project, including international participants.	• An agricultural equipment manufacturer did a study using two-way pagers provided free to farmers to query users about its equipment—participants were usually unavailable by phone or PC.
Participants feel anonymous.	• Anonymity was the necessary ingredient for a study on impotence conducted by a drug manufacturer.
Shortened turnaround from questionnaire draft to execution of survey.	• A Hewlett-Packard survey using Greenfield Online's Quick-Take took two weeks to write, launch, and field—not the standard three months using non-web venues.

Web Disadvantages (and emerging solutions)	Examples
Recruiting the right sample is costly and time-consuming; unlike phone and mail sample frames, no lists exist and must be built. (Firms like Toluna and Survey Samples Inc. now provide samples built from panels of Internet users who have indicated an interest in participating in online surveys.)	• TalkCity, working for Whitton Associates and Fusion5, set up a panel of 3,700 teens for a survey to test new packaging for a soft drink using phone calls, referrals, e-mail lists, banner ads, and website visits. It drew a sample of 600 for the research. It cost more than $50,000 to set up the list.
Converting surveys to the web can be expensive. (Firms like Qualtric Labs with its SurveyPro software and Apian with its Perseus software for wireless surveys and intranet surveys have made the process of going from paper to Internet much easier.)	• LiveWorld's teen study cost $50,000 to $100,000 to set up, plus additional fees with each focus group or survey. The total price tag was several hundred thousand dollars.
It takes technical as well as research skill to field a web survey. (Numerous firms now offer survey hosting services, e.g., SurveyMonkey.com.)	• A 10- to 15-minute survey can take up to five days of technical expertise to field and test.
While research is more compatible with numerous browsers, the technology isn't perfect. (Some survey hosting services use initial survey screen questions that identify the browser and system specifications and deliver the survey in the format most compatible with the participant's system.)	• A well-known business magazine did a study among a recruited sample only to have the survey abort on question 20 of a longer study.

difficult to reach in person or by phone, as gatekeepers (secretaries, office managers, and assistants) limit access. But researchers can often access these special participants by mail, email, or computer. When the researcher has no specific person to contact—say, in a study of corporations—the mail or computer-delivered survey may be routed to the appropriate participant. Additionally, the computer-delivered survey can often reach samples that are identified in no way other than their computer and Internet use, such as the users of a particular online game or those who have shopped with a particular online retailer.

Time Constraints

Although intercept studies still pressure participants for a relatively quick response, in most self-administered surveys, the participant can take, theoretically, as much time as they need to collect facts, talk with others, or consider replies at length than is possible in a survey employing the telephone or in a personal interview. Computer-delivered studies, especially those accessed via email links to the Internet, often have time limitations on both access and completion once started. And once started, computer-delivered studies usually cannot be interrupted by the participant to seek information not immediately known. One recent computer-delivered study sponsored by Procter & Gamble, however, asked of participants (who used skin moisturizers) the actual duration of time that the participant spent applying the product to various skin areas following a bath or shower. These questions came in the middle of a fairly lengthy survey. The participant was encouraged to discontinue the survey, time his or her moisturizer application following the next bath or shower, and return to the survey via a link and personal code with detailed responses.[7] Participants grow time weary, however, and most, except in rare instances, are unwilling to spend more than 5 to 10 minutes sharing their idea, thoughts, and experiences.

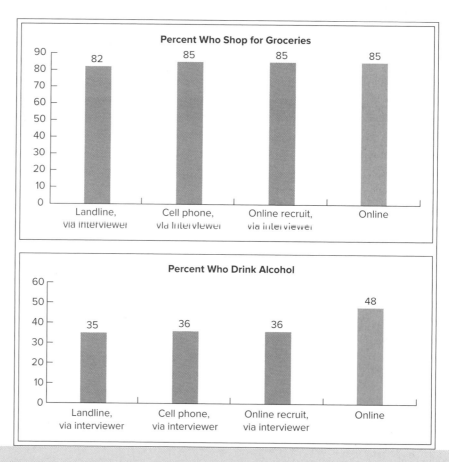

>**pic**profile

Anonymity

Mail surveys are typically perceived as more impersonal, providing more anonymity than the other communication modes, including other methods for distributing self-administered questionnaires. Computer-delivered surveys still enjoy that same perceived anonymity, although increased concerns about privacy may erode this perception in the future.[8]

Topic Coverage

A major limitation of self-administered surveys concerns the type and amount of information that can be secured. Researchers normally do not expect to obtain large amounts of information and cannot probe deeply into topics. Participants will generally refuse to cooperate with a long and/or complex mail, computer-delivered, or intercept questionnaire unless they perceive a personal benefit. Returned mail questionnaires with many questions left unanswered testify to this problem, but there are also many exceptions. One general rule of thumb is that the participant should be able to answer the questionnaire in no more than 10 minutes—similar to the guidelines proposed for telephone studies. On the other hand, one study of the general population delivered more than a 70 percent response to a questionnaire calling for 158 answers.[9] Several early studies of computer-delivered surveys show that participants indicate some level of enjoyment with the process, describing the surveys as interesting and amusing.[10] The novelty of the process, however, is expected to decline with experience, and recent declines in Web and e-mail survey response rates seem to be supporting this expectation.

Maximizing Participation in the Self-Administered Survey

To maximize the overall probability of response, attention must be given to each point of the survey process where the response may break down.[11] For example:

- The wrong address, email or postal, can result in nondelivery or nonreturn.
- The envelope, email, or fax invitation may look like junk mail and be discarded without being opened, or the subject line on email may give the impression of spam and not encourage that the email be opened.
- Lack of proper instructions for completion may lead to nonresponse.
- The wrong person may open the envelope or receive the fax or email and fail to call it to the attention of the right person.
- A participant may find no convincing explanation or inducement for completing the survey and thus discard it.
- A participant may temporarily set the questionnaire aside or park it in his or her email in-box and fail to complete it.
- The return address may be lost, so the questionnaire cannot be returned.

Thus, efforts should be directed toward maximizing the overall probability of response. One approach, the Total Design Method (TDM), suggests minimizing the burden on participants by designing questionnaires that:[12]

- Are easy to read.
- Offer clear response directions.
- Include personalized communication.
- Provide information about the survey via advance notification.
- Encourage participants to respond.[13]

Hundreds of methodological articles have been published on efforts to improve response rates. Few approaches consistently showed positive response rates.[14] However, several practical suggestions emerge from the conclusions that show promise to improve response rates:[15]

- A compelling appeal for participation.
- Preliminary or advance notification of the delivery of a self-administered questionnaire.

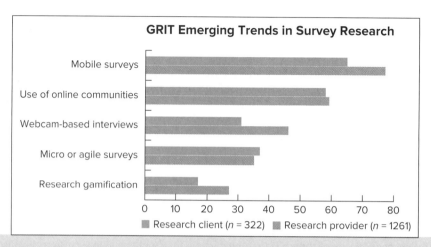

GRIT Emerging Trends in Survey Research

The GRIT survey each year studies trends in research methodology. The top-trending methodology for both managers and researchers was the mobile survey, And the use of online communities to conduct all types of research was number two overall. Several other trending methodologies show the influence of technology on survey research. **www.greenbook.org**

- Follow-ups or reminders after the delivery of a self-administered questionnaire.
- Clearly specified return directions and devices (e.g., upload URLs, postage-stamped envelopes).
- Monetary incentives for participation.

The following did not improve response rates:

- Deadline dates—although they did encourage sooner response.
- A promise of anonymity.

Self-Administered Survey Trends

Since our last edition, the major trends in self-administered surveys are being driven by technology and a demand for speed. Businesses are demanding that researchers deliver at the "speed of business." Managers can no longer wait weeks or months for research processes to go from research question to result delivery. The computer or web survey industry has delivered with its *agile research* methodology. Using panel members as participants, companies can field a computer or mobile survey from planning to result delivery within 7 to 10 days.

Especially with computer-delivered self-administered surveys, researchers are making survey research more engaging, using color, visual and audio stimuli, and even gaming attributes. And participants are responding with pictures, video, and detailed written responses.

Central location sampling is marrying the tablet and large-format smartphone (*phablet*) and taking advantage of GPS technology. At trade shows, in hospitals, at shopping malls and theme parks, and even on college campuses, participants use their own equipment or are provided with tablets in order to complete questionnaires while making a visit. Questions are asked of them based on their location.

Continuous tabulation of results allows managers and researchers alike more flexibility in adjusting measurement questions for subsequent surveys.

Companies are now using intranet capabilities to evaluate employee policies and behavior. Ease of access to electronic mail systems makes it possible for both large and small organizations to use computer surveys with both internal and external participant groups. Many techniques of traditional mail surveys can be easily adapted to computer-delivered questionnaires (e.g., follow-ups to nonparticipants are more easily executed and are less expensive).

Easy-to-use software for designing and fielding questionnaires, many with sophisticated, advanced features, is no longer a promise of the future—it's here. A short voyage on the Internet reveals organizations

Research Embraces the SmartPhone

According to a National Health Interview Survey, more than half of households in the United States are wireless-phone-only households. That number has grown 500 percent in the last decade. With landline phone coverage on the decline in many developed countries, researchers are using sampling techniques and survey design to address issues and take advantage of the opportunities that wireless phones offer.

According to Andy Peytchev, PhD, survey methodologist with Research Triangle Institute (RTI International) in North Carolina, multimethod phone studies, where some participants are reached via landlines and others via cell phones, are becoming the norm rather than the exception to achieve a national probability sample. Landline data can be weighted according to census population parameters. But not all problems can be fixed by weighting. "Youth landline responses versus youth cell phone responses, for example, are different. We don't know exactly why, just that they are different. You would have potential for undercoverage errors if you just used cell phones or landlines."

Cell phone surveys offer unique challenges. Many participants want to know why they are being contacted on their cell phone. So RTI International has changed its standard phone introduction. Interviewers inform cell phone participants that they know they are being contacted via their cell phone and why.

RTI International also offers cell phone respondents an incentive to continue the survey that is sufficient to show its appreciation and recognize the cost of cell phone charges. Cell phone surveys also require additional questions. RTI International trains its interviewers to inquire, "Are you driving right now?" If participants are driving, surveyors ask for an alternative time to contact the participant and then disconnect the call. Interviewers may also ask cell phone participants whether they are in a safe place.

Little research has been done on self-administered smartphone surveys, but Peytchev is interested in the opportunities. Smartphone surveys can include images—both those the participants take and share and those shared by the researcher. But Peytchev cautions, "Images can distort the meaning of the question. Everything you present to the participant is seen as information." And images collected from participants have to be analyzed and interpreted. Some RTI experiments have revealed that participants are reluctant to complete text-box responses and that if such a response device is included, cell phone participants are more likely to choose nonsense answers to avoid texting. This adds a new twist to survey research on the age-old issue of just what questions to ask.

www.rti.org; www.cdc.gov/nchs

using their sites to evaluate customer service processes, build sales-lead lists, evaluate planned promotions and product changes, determine supplier and customer needs, discover interest in job openings, evaluate employee attitudes, and more.

While web-, mobile-, and email-based self-administered surveys have certainly caught the lion's share of business attention in the last few years, the tried-and-true methods of telephone and personal interviews still have their strengths—and their advocates in the research community.

Survey via Telephone Interview

The **telephone survey** is still a workhorse of survey research. With the high level of telephone service penetration in the developed world, access to participants through low-cost, efficient means has made telephone interviewing a viable alternative for researchers. Pollsters working with political candidates use telephone surveys to assess the power of a speech or a debate during a hotly contested campaign. Numerous firms field phone *omnibus studies* each week. Individual questions in these studies are used to capture everything from people's feeling about the rise in gasoline prices to the power of a celebrity spokesperson in an advertising campaign or the latest teenage fashion trend.

Of the advantages that telephone interviewing offers, probably none ranks higher than its moderate cost. One study reports that sampling and data collection costs for telephone surveys can run from 45 to 64 percent lower than costs for comparable personal interviews.[16] Much of the savings comes from lower travel costs and administrative savings from training and supervision. When calls are made from a single location, the researcher may use fewer, yet more skilled, interviewers. Telephones are especially economical

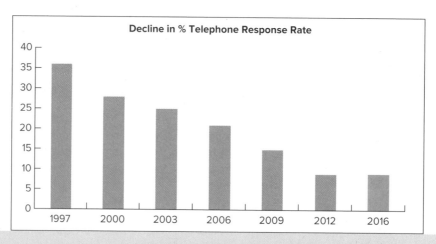

>picprofile

when callbacks to maintain precise sampling requirements are necessary and participants are widely scattered. Long-distance service options make it possible to interview nationally at a reasonable cost.

Telephone interviewing can be combined with immediate entry of the responses into a data file by means of terminals, personal computers, or voice data entry. This brings added savings in time and money. The **computer-assisted telephone interview (CATI)** is used in research organizations throughout the world. A CATI facility consists of acoustically isolated interviewing carrels organized around supervisory stations. The telephone interviewer in each carrel has a personal computer or terminal that is networked to the phone system and to the central data processing system. A software program that prompts the interviewer with introductory statements, qualifying questions, and precoded questionnaire items drives the survey. These materials appear on the interviewer's monitor. CATI works with a telephone number management system to select numbers, dial the sample, and enter responses. Research facilities that offer CATI often maintain 20 to 60 interviewer carrels and employ hundreds of interviewers, often speaking multiple languages in order to field international studies. Such facilities may operate 24/7, depending on the study, and complete tens of thousands of interviews per month.[17]

Another means of securing immediate response data is the **computer-administered telephone survey**. Unlike CATI, there is no human interviewer. A computer calls the phone number, conducts the interview, places data into a file for later tabulation, and terminates the contact. The questions are voice-synthesized, and the participant's answers and computer timing trigger continuation or disconnect. Several modes of computer-administered surveys exist, including *touch-tone data entry (TDE)*; *voice recognition (VR)*, which recognizes a limited vocabulary—usually yes/no responses; and *automatic speech recognition (ASR)* for recognizing and recording a wide range of verbal responses. CATI is often compared to the self-administered questionnaire and offers the advantage of enhanced participant privacy. One study showed that the noncontact rate for this electronic survey mode is similar to that for other telephone interviews when a random phone list is used. It also found that rejection of this mode of data collection affects the refusal rate (and thus nonresponse error) because people hang up more easily on a computer than on a human.[18]

The **noncontact rate** is the percent of potential contacts not reached (no answer, busy, answering machine or voice mail, and disconnects but not refusals) to all potential contacts. Behavioral norms might seem to work to the advantage of telephone interviewing; if someone hears the phone ring, doesn't it demand to be answered? But, while it is the caller who decides the purpose and length of the interview,[19] it is the targeted participant who determines the acceptance and termination of the call. Technology—notably, call-filtering systems in which the receiver can decide whether a call is answered based on caller identity as well as unknown numbers noted on smartphones—is expected to increase the noncontact rate associated with telephone surveys.

The **refusal rate** refers to the percentage of contacted potential participants who decline the interview. One study noted that "positive attitudes [about participating in surveys] are declining, while negative perceptions are increasing," which will increase refusal rates.[20] For the first time in 20 years, the well-regarded Pew Research Center notes that telephone response rates have held steady at 9 percent (a refusal rate of 91 percent).[21]

When compared to either personal interviews or mail self-administered surveys, the use of telephones provides a shorter time frame for the study, sometimes taking only a day or so for the fieldwork. When compared to personal interviewing, it is also likely that interviewer bias, especially bias caused by the physical appearance, body language, and actions of the interviewer, is reduced by using telephones.

There are also disadvantages to using the telephone for research. A skilled researcher will evaluate the use of a telephone survey to minimize the effect of these disadvantages:

- Inaccessible households (no telephone service or no/low contact rate).
- Inaccurate or nonfunctioning numbers.
- Limitation on interview length (fewer measurement questions).
- Limitations on use of visual stimuli or complex questions.
- Ease of interview termination.
- Less participant involvement.
- Distracting physical environment.

Inaccessible Households

Approximately 94 percent of all U.S. households have access to telephone service.[22] On the surface, this should make telephone surveys a prime methodology for survey research. However, several factors reduce such an enthusiastic embrace of the methodology. More households are using technology that restricts access. As cell-phone-only households increase, access decreases. Effective May 2004, federal wireless local-number portability legislation made it possible for subscribers to take their wired phone number to their wireless phone service (or the reverse) or to shift their wireless service between carriers without losing their wireless number. Thus, the guidelines for identifying the physical location of a phone by its number—and, in turn, the location of its owner—no longer apply.[23]

These causes of variations in participant availability by phone can be a source of error. A random dialing procedure is designed to reduce some of this bias. **Random dialing** normally requires choosing phone exchanges or exchange blocks and then generating random numbers within these blocks for calling.[24] Of course, just reaching a household doesn't guarantee its participation.

Inaccurate or Nonfunctioning Numbers

Several methods have been developed to overcome the deficiencies of directories; among them are techniques for choosing phone numbers by using random dialing or combinations of directories and random dialing.[25] However, increasing demand for multiple phone lines by both households and individuals has generated new phone area codes and local exchanges. This, too, increases the inaccuracy rate.

Limitation on Interview Length

A limit on interview length is another disadvantage of the telephone survey, but the degree of this limitation depends on the participant's interest in the topic. Ten minutes has generally been thought of as ideal, but interviews of 20 minutes or more are not uncommon. One telephone survey sponsored by Kraft lasted approximately 30 minutes. It was designed to judge the willingness of sample issue recipients to subscribe to a prototype magazine, *food&family*. The survey also measured the effectiveness of the sample issue of the magazine to deliver purchase intent for Kraft products featured in the recipes contained therein.[26] In another study, interviews ran for one and a half hours in a survey of long-distance services.[27]

Limitations on Use of Visual Stimuli or Complex Questions

The telephone survey limits the complexity of the survey and the use of complex scales or measurement techniques that is possible with personal interviewing, CASI, or computer-based surveys. For example, in personal interviews, participants are sometimes asked to sort or rank an array of cards containing different responses to a question. For participants who cannot visualize a scale or other measurement device that the interview is attempting to describe, one solution has been to employ a nine-point scale and to visualize it by using the telephone keypad.[28] The keypad is actually used to respond to questions using CATS. In telephone interviewing it is difficult to use maps, illustrations, and other visual aids. In some instances, however, interviewers have supplied these prior to a prescheduled interview via fax, email, or the Internet.

Ease of Interview Termination

Some studies suggest that the response rate in telephone studies is lower than that for comparable face-to-face interviews. One reason is that participants find it easier to terminate a phone interview. Telemarketing practices may also contribute. Public reaction to investigative reports of wrongdoing and unethical behavior within telemarketing activities places an added burden on the researcher, who must try to convince a participant that the phone interview is not a pretext for soliciting contributions (labeled *frugging*—fundraising under the guise of research) or selling products (labeled *sugging*—sales under the guise of research).

Lower Participant Engagement

Telephone surveys can result in less thorough responses, and persons interviewed by phone find the experience to be less rewarding than a personal interview or computer-based survey. Participants report less rapport with telephone interviewers than with personal interviewers. Given the growing costs and difficulties of personal interviews, it is likely that an even higher share of interviewer-involved surveys will be by telephone in the future. Thus, it behooves researchers using telephone surveys to attempt to improve the enjoyment of the interview. One authority suggests:

> We need to experiment with techniques to improve the enjoyment of the interview by the participant, maximize the overall completion rate, and minimize response error on specific measures. This work might fruitfully begin with efforts at translating into verbal messages the visual cues that fill the interaction in a face-to-face interview: the smiles, frowns, raising of eyebrows, eye contact, etc. All of these cues have informational content and are important parts of the personal interview setting. We can perhaps purposefully choose those cues that are most important to data quality and participant trust and discard the many that are extraneous to the survey interaction.[29]

Changes in the Physical Environment

Reliance on mobile phones raises serious questions about environmental influence on responses. What is the quality of data given at a busy intersection, in the midst of weekly shopping in a congested grocery aisle, or at the local high school basketball tournament? In some telephone surveys you might be asked where you are (e.g., in a store), what you are doing (e.g., driving), or whether you are in a safe location; interviewers will call you back if the environment is not conducive to taking a survey.

Telephone Survey Trends

How researchers deal with the continued increase in cell-phone-only households will be the most important trend to watch. Caller identification technology and technology that identifies computer-automated dialers and sends a disconnect signal in response are all expected to have an impact on the noncontact rate of phone interviews. But don't sell this tried-and-trusted survey method short; the institution of CATI, CATS, and random dialing shows that technology has been its savior in the past.

Privacy laws and the government-facilitated Do Not Call registry initiated in 2003 by the Federal Trade Commission and amended by the Do-Not-Call Improvement Act of 2007[30] pose a threat to

>**snap**shot

Voice Adds Depth to Survey

Do telephone surveys and interviews fit in today's computer- and mobile-survey dominant research landscape? Anderson Analytics, a Stamford (CT) business intelligence and marketing research company, recently teamed up with BigEars, a New Zealand–based company specializing in fully automated telephone surveys and interviews, to conduct a survey among college students about their cell phones. The hybrid study employed both an online survey and the automated telephone survey method.

BigEars operates much like a web-based survey tool. The difference is that the respondent answers over the phone, typically via an 800 number. "By eliminating the human interviewer from the call, we allow the caller to participate whenever it suits them, rather than when it suits us," shared Tom Anderson, managing partner of Anderson Analytics.

The survey results indicated that the main advantage of using telephone surveys is its ability to encourage longer and more robust responses to open-ended questions. According to Mark Forsyth, managing director of BigEars, "Talking isn't work."

Answers given to open-ended questions over the phone were 15 percent longer than answers typed in the parallel online survey. In addition, the voice recording offered opportunities for in-depth qualitative analysis; emotion and inflection in individual voice clips were used to examine the outliers in the study. "Being able to listen to the actual voices of participants, rather than simply coding or reading their responses, allows for a whole new dimension of analysis and confidence in the findings," said Tom Anderson.

"With this new hybrid methodology, if you want reaction to an event or transaction, such as a visit to a store, you can capture your data immediately, while it's fresh in the person's mind," said Jesse Chen, senior consultant and developer at Anderson Analytics. "Some people are more comfortable on the Web, and some are more comfortable on the phone—by catering to these differences you can broaden participation."

www.andersonanalytics.com; www.yourbigears.com

researchers. Although survey researchers are currently exempt from its restrictions, customer confusion about the distinction between research and telemarketing continues to cause complaints to legislators. When legislators get complaints, legislation is known to follow. The dissatisfaction with telemarketers is likely to cause an increase in the nonresponse rate. Telemarketers might be the catalyst, but legitimate research will suffer.

That participants don't connect with telephone researchers will continue to plague telephone survey research. How telephone interviewers increase engagement of participants bears watching. Here, the technology of the smartphone has the ability to increase the enjoyment factor and the quality of the data by using voice responses to open-ended rather than structured questions.

Survey via Personal Interview

A **survey via personal interview** is a quantitative study using an **individual depth interview (IDI)** between a trained interviewer and a single participant taking anywhere from 20 minutes to an hour or more. This **structured interview** uses a measurement instrument similar to a questionnaire which specifies the questions and the order of the questions. One unique quality that separates it from the self-administered survey is the interviewer's flexibility to **probe** the participant for clarification by asking prepared follow-up questions. It is the structured interview format that distinguishes the survey via personal interview from the qualitative IDI. Structured interviews permit more direct comparability of responses; question variability has been eliminated and thus answer variability is assumed to be real.

An interviewer's skills include making respondents comfortable, remaining neutral while encouraging the participant to talk openly, listening carefully and watching body language that notes confusion with the question or the response format, following a participant's train of thought, and probing for clarification without making the respondent feel harassed. In this quantitative approach, the researcher is interested in the interviewer following a prescribed procedure to avoid injecting bias into the results.

There are real advantages as well as clear limitations to surveys via personal interview. The greatest value lies in the depth of information and detail that can be secured. It far exceeds the information secured from either telephone surveys or self-administered studies via mail or computer (both intranet and Internet). Survey by personal interview can set up and control interviewing conditions. It can use special scoring devices and visual materials, as is done with a **computer-assisted personal interview (CAPI)**, where the interviewer has the ability to share his or her screen during the interview.

The interviewer can also do more things to improve the quality of the information received than is possible with another method. Interviewers can note conditions of the interview and gather supplemental information through observation. Interviewers can adjust the language level and tone of the interview as they observe problems and interview effects on the participant.

Interviews conducted face-to-face in specialized facilities offer the obvious benefit of being able to observe and record nonverbal as well as verbal behavior. A survey by personal interview can be conducted via the Internet as long as the participant and interviewer have the ability to see each other. It is the advance of this technology that has made it possible to address some of the strongest weaknesses of the format: high cost of the individual interview, long time frame to achieve sufficient sample size, restricted geographic coverage, and physical presence bias.

Cost

In terms of cost, a face-to-face survey via personal interview may cost anywhere from a few dollars to several hundred dollars for an interview with a hard-to-reach person. Costs are particularly high if the

study covers a wide geographic area or has stringent sampling requirements. An exception to this is the survey via **intercept interview** that selects participants in centralized locations such as retail malls, sports arenas, concerts, conventions, or office buildings Intercept interviews reduce costs associated with the need for several interviewers, training, and travel. Their cost-effectiveness, however, is offset when probability sampling is crucial to the study's outcome.

Costs have also risen rapidly due to changes in the social climate that have made personal interviewing more difficult. Many people today are reluctant to talk with strangers or to permit strangers to visit in their homes. Interviewers are reluctant to visit unfamiliar neighborhoods alone, especially for evening interviewing.

Time Frame of Data Collection

It takes longer to extract information from the same number of participants via personal interview than by other survey methods. Even when the study design has the participant coming to the interviewer, it takes longer to have a two-way conversation. Internet-based survey via personal interview can reduce the data collection time frame, but not by much, due to that two-way conversation format; its advantage is real-time data entry, which shortens the study time frame.

Geographic Coverage

Survey via personal interview via a face-to-face formats poses significant geographic limitations if the researcher wants to control costs, unless the target population is geographically concentrated (e.g, the employees in a plant, the shoppers in a given store, the patients in a doctor's office, etc.). When the target population is not geographically concentrated, a high cost of reaching participants often affects the representativeness of the sample. Technology, using Internet-based survey via personal interview, addresses both geographic coverage and its cost.

Physical Presence Bias

The physical presence of the interviewer is a plus in many ways, but survey via personal interview always has the potential of injecting bias. **Physical presence bias** is a participant's conscious or subconscious response to the interviewer, often based on the interviewer's looks, body language, language, ethnicity, etc. The bias might be caused by a reaction to the interviewer's gender, age, ethnicity, perceived social status or education level, or even weight. It can be either negative or positive, and how it affects their responses is unknown for any given study. Interviewer selection and training is our best solution to this battling this bias.

Interview Falsification

Results of surveys via personal interviews can be affected adversely by interviewers who alter the protocol to select participants, alter the questions asked, alter the order of questions, or falsify answers to individual questions or whole interviews. CAPI, with its use of computer-prompted questions, can address question order, but providing the question doesn't necessarily mean that a field interviewer might not alter the way it is asked. Field supervision of interviewers is possible to some extent, but interviewer hiring and training is the best defense against falsification.

> Error in Survey Research

As depicted in Exhibit 9-6, there are three major sources of error in communication research: measurement questions and survey instruments, interviewers, and participants. Researchers cannot help a business decision maker answer a research question if they (1) select or craft inappropriate questions, (2) ask them in an inappropriate order, or (3) use inappropriate transitions and instructions to elicit information.

Interviewer Error

From the introduction to the conclusion of the interview, there are many points where the interviewer's control of the process can affect the quality of the data. **Interviewer error**, a major source of sampling error and response bias, is caused by numerous actions:

- *Failure to secure full participant cooperation (sampling error).* The sample is likely to be biased if interviewers do not do a good job of enlisting participant cooperation.
- *Failure to record answers accurately and completely (data-entry error).* Error may result from an interview recording procedure that forces the interviewer to summarize or interpret participant answers or that provides insufficient space to record verbatim answers as provided by the participant.

>**Exhibit 9-6** Sources of Error in Survey Research

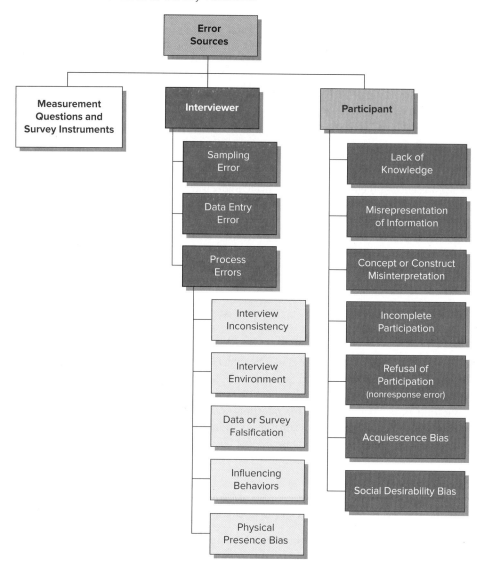

- *Failure to consistently execute interview procedures.* The precision of survey estimates will be reduced and there will be more error around estimates to the extent that interviewers are inconsistent in ways that influence the data.

- *Failure to establish appropriate interview environment.* Answers may be systematically inaccurate or biased when interviewers fail to appropriately train and motivate participants or fail to establish a suitable interpersonal setting.[31]

- *Falsification of individual answers or whole interviews.* Perhaps the most insidious form of interviewer error is cheating. Surveying is difficult work, often done by part-time employees, usually with only limited training and under little direct supervision. At times, falsification of an answer to an overlooked question is perceived as an easy solution to counterbalance the incomplete data. This easy, seemingly harmless, first step can be followed by more pervasive forgery. It is not known how much of this occurs, but it should be of constant concern to researchers as they develop their data collection design and to those organizations that outsource survey projects.

- *Inappropriate influencing behavior.* It is also obvious that an interviewer can distort the results of any survey by inappropriate suggestions, directions, or verbal probes; by word emphasis and question rephrasing; by tone of voice; or by body language, facial reaction to an answer, or other nonverbal signals. These activities, whether intentional or merely due to carelessness, are widespread. This problem was investigated using a simple questionnaire and participants who then reported on the interviewers. The conclusion was "The high frequency of deviations from instructed behavior is alarming."[32]

- *Physical presence bias.* Interviewers can influence participants in unperceived subtle ways. Older interviewers are often seen as authority figures by young participants, who modify their responses accordingly. Some research indicates that perceived social distance between interviewer and participant has a distorting effect, although the studies do not fully agree on just what this relationship is.[33]

In light of the numerous studies on the various aspects of interview bias, the safest course for researchers is to recognize the constant potential for response error, provide field supervision, and take greater care in data preparation.

Participant Error

Three broad conditions must be met by participants to have a successful survey:

- The participant must possess the information being targeted by the investigative questions.
- The participant must understand his or her role in the survey as the provider of accurate information.
- The participant must have adequate motivation to cooperate.

Thus, participants cause error in two ways: whether they respond (willingness versus refusal) and how they respond.

Participation-Based Errors

Three factors influence participation:[34]

- The participant must believe that the experience will be pleasant and satisfying.
- The participant must believe that answering the survey is an important and worthwhile use of his or her time.
- The participant must dismiss any mental reservations that he or she might have about participation.

Whether the experience will be pleasant and satisfying depends heavily on the interviewer in personal and telephone surveys and on the invitation in self-administered surveys. Typically, participants will cooperate with an interviewer whose behavior reveals confidence and who engages people on a personal level. Effective interviewers are differentiated not by demographic characteristics, but by these interpersonal skills. By confidence, we mean that most participants are immediately convinced they will want to participate in the study and cooperate fully with the interviewer. An engaging personal style is one in which the interviewer instantly establishes credibility by adapting to the individual needs of the participant. For the survey that does not employ human interpersonal influence, convincing the participant that the experience will be enjoyable is the task of a prior notification device or the study's written introduction.

For the participant to think that answering the survey is important and worthwhile, some explanation of the study's purpose is necessary, although the amount of disclosure will vary based on the sponsor's objectives. In personal or phone surveys the researcher will provide the interviewer with instructions for discovering what explanation is needed and supplying it. Usually, the interviewer states the purpose of the study, tells how the information will be used, and details what is expected of the participant. Participants should feel that their cooperation will be meaningful to themselves and to the survey results. When this is achieved, more participants will express their views willingly.

>**Exhibit 9-7** Factors Influencing Participant Motivation*

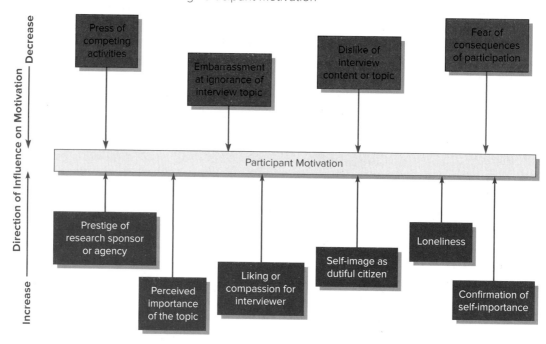

As depicted in Exhibit 9-7, the quality and quantity of information secured depend heavily on the ability and willingness of participants to cooperate. Potential participants often have reservations about being interviewed that must be overcome. They may suspect the interviewer has an illegitimate purpose. They may view the topic as too sensitive and thus the interview as potentially embarrassing or intrusive. Or they may feel inadequate or fear the questioning will belittle them. Previous encounters with businesses that have attempted to disguise their sales pitch or fundraising activities as a research survey can also erode participants' willingness to cooperate. In personal and phone interviews, participants often react more to their feelings about the interviewer than to the content of the questions.

At the core of a survey or interview is an interaction between two people or between a person and an organization. In the interaction, the participant is asked to provide information. While he or she has hope of some minimal personal reward—in the form of compensation for participation or enhanced status or knowledge—he or she has little hope of receiving any immediate or direct benefit from the data extracted. Thus, participant motivation is a responsibility of the researcher and the interviewer. Studies of reactions to many surveys show that participants can be motivated to participate in personal and phone interviews and, in fact, can even enjoy the experience. In one study, more than 90 percent of participants said the interview experience was interesting, and three-fourths reported they were willing to be interviewed again.[35] In intercept/self-administered studies, the interviewer's primary role is to encourage participation as the participant completes the questionnaire on his or her own.

In surveys, **nonresponse error** occurs when the responses of participants differ in some systematic way from the responses of nonparticipants. This occurs when the researcher (1) cannot locate the predesignated sample case or (2) is unsuccessful in encouraging that person to participate. This is an especially difficult problem when you are using a probability sample of subjects. By failing to respond or refusing to respond, participants create a nonrepresentative sample for the study overall or for a particular item or question in the study. Many studies have shown that better-educated individuals and those more interested in the topic participate in surveys. A high percentage of those who reply to a given survey have usually replied to others, while a large share of those who do not respond are habitual nonparticipants.[36]

Researchers are not without actions to avoid or diminish the error discussed above. Despite its challenges, communicating with research participants—and the use of the survey—is the principal method of business research.

Response-Based Errors

Response error is generated in two ways: when the participant fails to give a correct answer or fails to give the complete answer. The interviewer can do little about the participant's information level. Screening questions qualify participants when there is doubt about their ability to answer. The most appropriate applications for survey research are those where participants are uniquely qualified to provide the desired information. Questions can be used to inquire about characteristics of a participant, such as his or her household income, age, sexual preference, ethnicity, or family life-cycle stage. Questions can also be asked that reveal information exclusively internal to the participant. We include here items such as the participant's lifestyle, attitudes, opinions, expectations, knowledge, motivations, and intentions.

If we ask participants to report on events that they have not personally experienced, we need to assess the replies carefully. If our purpose is to learn what the participant understands to be the case, it is legitimate to accept the answers given. But if our intent is to learn what the event or situation actually was, we must recognize that the participant is reporting secondhand data and the accuracy of the information declines.

Participants also cause error by responding in such a way as to unconsciously or consciously misrepresent their actual behavior, attitudes, preferences, motivations, or intentions (*response bias*). Participants create response bias when they modify their responses to be socially acceptable or to save face or reputation with the interviewer (**social desirability bias**), and sometimes even in an attempt to appear rational and logical.

One major cause of response bias is **acquiescence bias**—the tendency to agree. On the participant's part, acquiescence may be a result of lower cognitive skills or knowledge related to a concept or construct, language difficulties, or perceived level of anonymity. However, researchers can contribute to acquiescence bias by the speed with which they ask questions (the faster questions are asked, the more acquiescence) and the placement of questions in an interview (the later the question, the more acquiescence).[37]

Sometimes participants may not have an opinion on the topic of concern. Under this circumstance, their proper response should be "don't know" or "have no opinion." Some research suggests that most participants who chose the don't-know response option actually possess the knowledge or opinion that the researcher seeks.[38] Participants may choose the option because they may want to shorten the time spent in the participation process, may be ambivalent or have conflicting opinions on the topic, may feel they have insufficient information to form a judgment—even though they actually have taken a position—don't believe that the response choices match their position, or don't possess the cognitive skills to understand the response options. If they choose the don't-know option for any of these reasons, studies suggest that probing for their true position will increase both reliability and validity of the data. However, forcing a participant to express some opinion he or she does not hold by withholding a don't-know option makes it difficult for researchers to know the reliability of the answers.

Participants may also interpret a question or concept differently from what was intended by the researcher. This occurs when the researcher uses words that are unfamiliar to the participant. Thus, the individual answers a question that is different from the one the researcher intended to ask.

Regardless of the reasons, each source of participant-initiated error diminishes the value of the data collected. It is difficult for a researcher to identify such occasions. Thus, communicated responses should be accepted for what they are—statements by individuals that reflect varying degrees of truth and accuracy.

> Outsourcing Survey Tasks

Commercial suppliers of research services vary from full-service operations to specialty consultants. When confidentiality is likely to affect competitive advantage, the manager or staff will sometimes prefer to bid only a phase of the project. Alternatively, the organization's staff members may possess such unique knowledge of a product or service that they must fulfill a part of the study themselves. Regardless, the exploratory work, design, sampling, data collection, or processing and analysis may be contracted separately or as a whole.

Research firms also offer special advantages that business managers do not typically maintain in-house. Centralized-location interviewing or computer-assisted telephone facilities may be particularly desirable for certain research needs. A professionally trained staff with considerable experience in similar management problems is another benefit. Data processing and statistical analysis capabilities are especially important for survey research. Other vendors have specially designed software for interviewing and data tabulation.[39] Panel suppliers provide another type of research service, with emphasis on longitudinal survey work. By using the same participants over time, a **panel** can track trends in attitudes toward issues or products, product adoption or consumption behavior, and a myriad of other research interests. Suppliers of panel participants can secure information from personal and telephone interviewing techniques as well as from the mail, the web, mobile, and mixed-mode surveys. Diaries are a common means of chronicling events of research interest by panel members. These are uploaded or mailed back to the research organization. Point-of-sale terminals and scanners aid electronic data collection for panel-type participant groups. And mechanical devices placed in the homes of panel members may be used to substantiate survey data. Yankelovich Partners, The Gallup Organization, SSI, and Harris Interactive all manage extensive panels.

Omnibus surveys (where the questions of more than one company are fielded in the same survey, but where the results are separated) or *syndicated research providers* (who collect data that are of interest to multiple companies and sell this data to interested parties willing to pay the fee) are other mechanisms for businesses to collect survey data. BDRC is an example of the omnibus survey; it fields the *Business Opinion Omnibus* to finance executives.[40] Gartner Research is an example of a syndicated researcher, serving IT and other industries.[41]

> Evaluation of Survey Research

The great strength of the survey as a primary data collection design is its versatility and its application to all business disciplines. Abstract information of all types can be gathered by questioning people. Additionally, a few well-chosen questions can yield information that would take much more time and effort to gather by other data collection approaches. A survey that uses the mobile phone, telephone, mail, a computer, email, or the Internet as the medium of communication can expand geographic coverage at a fraction of the cost and time of other methods. Surveys conducted using probability samples can provide results that can be projected to much larger populations.

But the bad news is that surveys posses numerous sources of possible error that make the results questionable if researchers haven't carefully crafted an error reduction plan.

> Ethical Issues and Their Solutions

The primary ethical issues involving surveys are deception, confidentiality, quality, and safety. Deception relates to three issues: amount of time required to complete the survey, sponsor and purpose concealment, and lying to achieve your research purpose. **Deception** occurs when participants are told only part of the truth or when truth is fully compromised. Survey research requires an estimate of time commitment for the participant. If researchers aren't careful in questionnaire design, surveys are often longer than they need to be. If a researcher fails to correctly estimate time, he or she may falsely gain a participant's cooperation. The solution is to adequately pretest the survey to determine a solid estimate of the time needed for completion. Underestimates of completion time also lead to higher drop-out rates that, for any given survey, cause poorer-quality data. In the broader sense, such underestimates discourage people from participating in surveys, increasing the likelihood of nonresponse error.

Business research must often be concealed to protect potential major decisions affecting resource allocations—for innovation, hiring or outsourcing, building or closing physical facilities, etc. Especially where an interviewer is involved, the latitude the format provides might jeopardize the research sponsor's right of nondisclosure. Temporary deception may also be employed to prevent biasing participant's answers. Where employees are the target population, concealment may be designed to protect their sense of job security, safety, or self-worth. Researchers have the responsibility to protect participants and sponsors and do so through careful interviewer training and professional development of the measurement instrument.

Lying to gain access to a desired participant, or to extract competitive business intelligence, is also part of the deception issue. These are unacceptable research practices. The solution involves using a different research approach or a different survey method with different recruitment protocols.

To protect participants from the consequences of deception, researchers should explain the benefits of the study (through introducing themselves or their company, explaining participants' rights and protections, and obtaining **informed consent**—a full disclosure of research procedures). Exhibit 9-8 offers suggestions for informed consent procedures in survey research. Researchers may also debrief participants following data collection, by explaining any deception, offering researcher contact information for any follow-up concerns participants may have, and revealing a hypothesis under study or offering to share some results.

Most developed countries have laws governing information privacy and data protection; some are far stricter than those in the U.S, so U.S. businesses must comply with the highest applicable standard. Data privacy, including data movement, has been the focus of such legislation since 2000.[42] Participants, therefore, have the **right to privacy**—to refuse to be interviewed or to refuse to answer any question within a survey process, to not admit researchers into their homes, to not answer their telephones or respond to email or web solicitations, to block their current location on their phone, etc. They also have the **right to confidentiality**—to protect their identity and specific responses from being attached to their identity. Researchers address these rights by prescreening participants to ensure willingness, prescheduling survey experiences, limiting time requirements, restricting access to participant identification, restricting access to completed data instruments, and revealing participant information only with signed consent. The sponsoring manager shares responsibility for protecting these rights.

>Exhibit 9-8 Informed Consent for Surveys

Content
Surveys conducted by the Indiana University Center for Survey Research contain the following informed-consent components in their introductions:

1. Introduce ourselves—interviewer's name and Indiana University Center for Survey Research.

2. Briefly describe the survey topic (e.g., barriers to health insurance).

3. Describe the geographic area we are interviewing (e.g., people in Indiana) or target sample (e.g., aerospace engineers).

4. Tell who the sponsor is (e.g., National Endowment for the Humanities).

5. Describe the purpose(s) of the research (e.g., satisfaction with services received/provided by a local agency).

6. Give a "good-faith" estimate of the time required to complete the interview.

7. Promise anonymity and confidentiality (when appropriate).

8. Tell the participant the participation is voluntary.

9. Tell the participant that item-nonresponse is acceptable.

10. Ask permission to begin.

Sample Introduction
Hello, I'm [fill in NAME] from the Center for Survey Research at Indiana University. We're surveying Indianapolis area residents to ask their opinions about some health issues. This study is sponsored by the National Institutes of Health and its results will be used to research the effect of community ties on attitudes toward medical practices. The survey takes about 40 minutes. Your participation is anonymous and voluntary, and all your answers will be kept completely confidential. If there are any questions that you don't feel you can answer, please let me know and we'll move to the next one. So, if I have your permission, I'll continue.

Sample Conclusion
The participant is given information on how to contact the principal investigator. For example: John Kennedy is the principal investigator for this study. Would you like Dr. Kennedy's address or telephone number in case you want to contact him about the study at any time?

>**Exhibit 9-9** Characteristics of the Institutional Review Board (IRB) Process*

Step	Process	Examples
Purpose	A committee is established to review and approve research involving human subjects.	Review minimizes potential research related risks and requires full disclosure so that participants can make informed decisions about whether or not to participate.
Applications	Determine the level of participant involvement in your study and select appropriate forms.	• Involves human subjects. • Does not involve human subjects. • Analyzes coded (secondary) data. • Analyzes biological specimens.
Initial Review	Center level review (previously exempt research).	• Research involving watching public behavior of children, in which the investigator does not take part in the activities, can be reviewed at the center level. • Research conducted in established or commonly accepted educational settings, involving normal educational practices, such as (1) research on regular and special education instructional strategies, or (2) research on the effectiveness of or the comparison among instructional techniques, curricula, or classroom management methods. (Surveys or interviews cannot be center level reviewed.)
	Expedited review.	Research on individual or group behavior characteristics (such as studies of perception, motivation, communication, cultural beliefs or practices, and social behavior) or research employing survey, interview, oral history, focus group, program evaluation, human factors evaluation or quality assurance methodologies when the research does not qualify for center level review.
	Full review.	Research involving physically intrusive procedures; where previous experience has been shown to create a potential of risk to subjects; that may result in a significant level of psychological or physical stress.
Prepare IRB Materials	An IRB submission form and research protocol.	Submissions are often accompanied by: • Informed-consent forms. • Completed informed consent form checklists. • Evidence of approval by cooperative IRBs at other sites. • Data collection instruments. • Certification of translation for consents or instruments to be used with non-English-speaking subjects. • Brochure/recruitment materials.
Continuing Review	Research approved for limited period of time (e.g., one year).	Beyond time period, research cannot continue without IRB approval: A continuation request is submitted.
Revision	The principal investigator submits in writing any changes he or she intends to make to the study to the IRB.	Revision to the research protocol (e.g., changes to the informed consent form, survey instruments used, or number and nature of subjects.
IRB Actions	Approve.	Approve as submitted.
	Pending.	(1) Researcher clarifies an aspect of the study, provides additional information, or discusses the potential risks and benefits of the study, or (2) makes minor changes to the informed consent document(s) or the research protocol.
	Disapprove.	Proposed research places the participants at risks that outweigh the benefit or value of the gained knowledge; study raises unacceptable ethical questions.

Quality relates to avoidance of error, which translates to strict adherence to questionnaire structure and instructions. It also relates to not asking unnecessary questions to achieve the research objective or making claims about data that cannot be supported by the survey protocols employed. Interviewers have the responsibility to not falsify survey completions. Researcher solutions to quality issues relate to interviewer training and to following appropriate industry standards for measurement—including selection and development of measurement scales and measurement instruments—and for data analysis.

Interviewers have the **right to safety**. Safety refers to not putting the interviewer in harm's way due to the environment where the interview takes place (e.g., night interview, high crime location) or the people they must interview. Researchers, who are insensitive to interviewers' fears of bodily harm, face potential legal consequences as well as research quality issues (falsified measurement instruments). The solution involves choosing a different interviewer or a different survey method.

Many businesses have government contracts and are subject to federal, state, and local laws, policies, and procedures that regulate research on human subjects. One of these, implemented in 1966 by the Department of Health and Human Services, is the Institutional Review Board (IRB) risk assessment. Many institutions require all research to comply with the guidelines of this process. Your university likely has its own IRB process. Exhibit 9-9 provides the highlights of an IRB process. A researcher's strict adherence to the IRB process can identify issues and prevent subsequent problems.

>summary

LO9-1   The communication approach involves surveying people, either with an interviewer or not, and recording their responses for analysis. Survey research is accomplished via personal interviews, telephone interviews, or self-administered surveys, with each method having its specific strengths and weaknesses. The optimal communication method is the one that is instrumental for answering your research question and dealing with the constraints imposed by time, budget, and human resources. The opportunity to combine several survey methodologies makes the use of mixed-mode surveys desirable in many projects.

LO9-2   The self-administered questionnaire can be delivered by the U.S. Postal Service, facsimile, a courier service, email, phone, web, or an intercept. Computer-delivered self-administered questionnaires use organizational intranets, the Internet, or online services to reach their participants. Participants may be targeted or self-selecting. Intercept studies may use a traditional questionnaire or a computerized instrument in environments where interviewer assistance is minimal.

Telephone interviewing remains popular because of the diffusion of telephone service in households and the low cost of this method compared with personal interviewing. Long-distance telephone interviewing has grown. There are also disadvantages to telephone interviewing. Many phone numbers are unlisted, and directory listings become obsolete quickly. There is also a limit on the length and depth of interviews conducted using the telephone.

The major advantages of personal interviewing are the ability to explore topics in great depth, achieve a high degree of interviewer control, and provide maximum interviewer flexibility for meeting unique situations. However,

this method is costly and time-consuming, and its flexibility can result in excessive interviewer bias.

LO9-3   Successful survey research requires that we seek information the participant can provide and that the participant understands his or her role and be motivated to play that role. Motivation, in particular, is a task for the researcher and/or his interviewer. Good rapport with the participant should be established quickly, and then the technical process of collecting data should begin. The latter often calls for skillful probing to supplement the answers volunteered by the participant. Simplicity of directions and instrument appearance are additional factors to consider in encouraging response in self-administered communication studies.

LO9-4   Two factors can cause bias in interviewing. One is nonresponse. It is a concern with all surveys. Some studies show that the first contact often secures less than 20 percent of the designated participants. Various methods are useful for increasing this representation, the most effective being making callbacks until an adequate number of completed interviews have been secured. The second factor is response error, which occurs when the participant fails to give a correct or complete answer. The interviewer also can contribute to response error. The interviewer can provide the main solution for both of these two types of errors.

LO9-5   Outsourcing survey services offers special advantages to managers. A professionally trained research staff, centralized-location interviewing, focus group facilities, and computer-assisted facilities are among them. Specialty firms offer software and computer-based assistance for telephone and personal interviewing as well as for mail and mixed modes. Panel suppliers produce data for longitudinal studies of all varieties.

LO9-6   The ethical issues involved with survey research relate to deception, confidentiality, privacy, quality, and safety. Deception occurs when participants are told only part of the truth or when truth is fully compromised. Deception is often involved to protect sponsor-purpose nondisclosure or sponsor identity or to prevent biasing participant answers. It should not be used to misrepresent the time required to participate in order to gain participant engagement. Researchers use informed consent and debriefing of participants to address the consequences of deception.

Privacy and confidentiality are heavily influenced by various federal, state, and local legislation, as well as by industry standards. Researchers address these rights by prescreening, prescheduling, limiting time requirements, restricting access to participant identity and data, and written consent to reveal.

Interviewers also have a right to safety, often choosing an alternative survey method or interviewer when safety issues are raised.

To address these issues, many businesses follow the Institutional Review Board procedures outlined by the U.S. federal government and required of businesses doing human research when they have government contracts.

>**key**terms

>**discussion**questions

Terms in Review

1 Distinguish among response error, interviewer error, and nonresponse error.

2 How do environmental factors affect response rates in personal interviews? How can we overcome these environmental problems?

3 Distinguish between social desirability bias and acquiescence bias.

Making Research Decisions

4 Assume you are planning to interview shoppers in a shopping mall about their views on increased food prices and what the federal government should do about them. In what different ways might you try to motivate shoppers to cooperate in your survey?

5 In recent years, in-home personal interviews have grown more costly and more difficult to complete. Suppose, however, you have a project in which you need to talk with people in their homes. What might you do to hold down costs and increase the response rate?

6 In the following situations, decide whether you would use a personal interview, telephone survey, or self-administered survey. Give your reasons.

   a A survey of the residents of a new subdivision on why they happened to select that area in which to live. You also wish to secure some information about what they like and do not like about life in the subdivision.

   b A poll of students at Metro University on their preferences among three candidates who are running for president of the student government.

c A survey of 58 wholesale grocery companies, scattered over the eastern United States, on their personnel management policies for warehouse personnel.

d A survey of financial officers of the *Fortune* 500 corporations to learn their predictions for the economic outlook in their industries in the next year.

e A survey of applicant requirements, job tasks, and performance expectations as part of a job analysis of student work-study jobs on a college campus of 2,000 students, where 1,500 are involved in the work-study program.

7 You decide to conduct a telephone survey of 40 families in the 721 phone-exchange block. You want an excellent representation of all subscribers in the exchange area. Explain how you will carry out this study.

8 You plan to conduct a mail survey of the traffic managers of 1,000 major manufacturing companies across the country. The study concerns their company policies regarding the payment of moving expenses for employees who are transferred. What might you do to improve the response rate of such a survey?

9 A major corporation agrees to sponsor an internal study on sexual harassment in the workplace. This is in response to concerns expressed by its female employees. How would you handle the following issues?

a The communication approach (self-administered, telephone, personal interview, and/or mixed).

b The purpose: fact finding, awareness, relationship building, and/or change.

c Participant motivation.

d Minimization of response and nonresponse error.

10 As competition for a scarcer dollar increases, an increasing number of companies are taking action by fostering customer-centric cultures that enhance satisfaction and drive bottom-line profitability. Research reveals that 96 percent of companies are leveraging voice-of-consumer (VoC) data in some way to improve business performance. Companies now expect to achieve substantial improvements in customer retention and top-line growth from these targeted customer programs. If you wanted to know what kind of VoC programs were being used and which were effective or ineffective, what method of survey would you design and why?

From Concept to Practice

11 Using Exhibit 9-2 as your guide, graph the communication study you designed in question 7 or 8.

From the Headlines

12 Mercedes-Benz has a self-driving car capable of 80 miles-per-hour speed. You have to keep your hands on the wheel in this E-class sedan to operate the self-driving feature, but the car reads and responds to speed limits and is capable of stopping or swerving to avoid obstructions in the 40–55 mph range, either physical or human. Any liability for use of the technology still resides with the driver. How would you use survey research to determine whether the public is ready for such a car?

>cases*

Akron Children's Hospital

Campbell-Ewald Pumps Awareness into the American Heart Association

Can Research Rescue the Red Cross?

Covering Kids with Health Care

Data Development

Donatos: Finding the New Pizza

Inquiring Minds Want to Know—NOW!

Lexus SC 430

Marcus Thomas LLC Tests Hypothesis for Troy-Bilt Creative Development

Mastering Teacher Leadership

NCRCC: Teeing Up and New Strategic Direction

Ohio Lottery: Innovative Research Design Drives Winning

Proofpoint: Capitalizing on a Reporter's Love of Statistics

Starbucks, Bank One, and Visa Launch Starbucks Duetto Visa

USTA: Come Out Swinging

* You will find a description of each case in the Case Abstracts section of this textbook. Check the Case Index to determine whether a case provides data, the research instrument, video, or other supplementary material. Cases and case supplements are available in Connect.

>part III

Measurement

>chapter 10

Stage 3: Measurement Foundations

> "Absolute figures in a connected world don't give us a whole picture. They are not as true as they could be. We need relative figures that are connected to other data, that can lead us to change our perspective."
>
> *David McCandless,*
> *author*
>
> Knowledge Is Beautiful: Impossible Ideas, Invisible Patterns, Hidden Connections—Visualized

>learningobjectives

After reading this chapter, you should understand. . .

LO10-1 The distinction among measuring objects, properties, and indicants of properties.

LO10-2 The similarities and differences among the four scale types used in measurement and when each is used.

LO10-3 The four major sources of measurement error.

LO10-4 The criteria for evaluating good measurement.

>The Nature of Measurement

To *measure* is to discover the extent, dimensions, quantity, or capacity of something, especially by comparison with a standard. So we can measure our height (in inches or centimeters), weight (in grams or pounds), accuracy of our eyesight (against a 20/20 scale), etc. You also can measure how well you like a song, the taste of food at a restaurant, or the personality of a friend.

The goal of measurement is to provide the highest-quality, lowest-error data for testing hypotheses, forming estimates or predictions, or describing. Researchers deduce from a hypothesis that certain conditions should exist. Then they measure for these conditions in the real world. If found, the data lend support to the hypothesis and a decision can be made relying on this hypothesis; if not, researchers conclude the hypothesis is faulty, and the manager looks for an alternative solution or action.

Businesses are interested in measuring *concepts* and *constructs*, but their "stand-ins"—variables—are what we actually measure. We assign an *operational definition* to each *variable* (possibly more than one for a construct) that defines it in terms of measurement criteria. The definition must specify adequately the empirical information needed and how it will be collected. In addition, it must have the proper scope or fit for the research problem. We review these terms in Exhibit 10-1.

Tasks of Measurement

Thus, **measurement** in research consists of assigning numbers to empirical events, objects or properties, or activities in compliance with a set of rules. This definition implies that measurement has three tasks:

1. Select variables to measure.
2. Develop a set of **mapping rules**: a scheme for assigning numbers or symbols to represent aspects of variable being measured.
3. Apply the mapping rule(s) to each observation of that event.[1]

>**Exhibit 10-1** Review of Key Terms

Concept: a bundle of meanings or characteristics associated with certain events, objects, conditions, situations, or behaviors.

Classifying and categorizing objects or events that have common characteristics beyond any single observation creates concepts. When you think of a movie ticket, what comes to mind is not a single example but your collected memories of tickets from which you abstract a set of specific and definable characteristics.

Construct: an image or idea specifically invented for a given research and/or theory-building purpose.

We build constructs by combining the simpler, more concrete concepts, especially when the idea or image we intend to convey is not subject to direct observation. Car styling is a construct.

Variable: an event, act, characteristic, trait, or attribute that can be measured and to which we assign numerals or values; a synonym for the construct or the property being studied.

Some variables, said to be dichotomous, have only two values, reflecting the presence or absence of a property: employed versus unemployed. Some variables are discrete; they measure categories, such as demographic variables of race and religion. At an auto show, "Chevrolet" is assigned a 5 and "Honda" is assigned a 6 when we measure it, with no option for a 5.5. Income, temperature, age, and a test score are examples of continuous variables. These variables may take on values within a given range or, in some cases, an infinite set. Your test score may range from 0 to 100, your age may be 23.5, and your present income could be $35,463.

Operational definition: a definition for a construct stated in terms of specific criteria for testing or measurement; refers to an empirical standard (we must be able to count, measure, or gather information about the standard through our senses).

Whether the object being defined is physical (e.g., a can of peaches) or highly abstract (e.g., an attitude toward work safety), the operational definition must specify the characteristics (variables) and how they are to be observed or counted. The specifications and procedures must be so clear that any competent person using them would classify the objects in the same way. For example: *A "can of peaches" is any container—metal, glass, plastic, or composite—that weighs at least 12 ounces and is purchased at a grocery, drug, convenience, or mass merchandiser within the Detroit, Michigan, Consolidated Metropolitan Statistical Area (CMSA).*

Assume you are studying people who attend an auto show where prototypes for new models are on display. You are interested in learning the male-to-female ratio among attendees. You observe those who enter the show area. If a person is female, you record an F; if male, an M. Some measurement theorists believe that because measurement involves quantification, that "numbers must be assigned to objects to represent the amounts or degrees of a property or the property by all objects."[2] So you could have assigned males a 1 and females a 2 and you would have a mapping rule that meets the needs of these purists. Data analysis software today, however, can handle all types of symbols and still count those symbols. Researchers might also want to measure the styling desirability of a new concept car at this show. They interview a sample of visitors and assign, with a different mapping rule, their opinions to the following measurement question:

What is your opinion of the styling of the concept CS?

Very desirable   5   4   3   2   1   Very undesirable

Exhibit 10-2 uses this example to illustrate the three tasks of measurement.

>**Exhibit 10-2** Tasks of Measurement

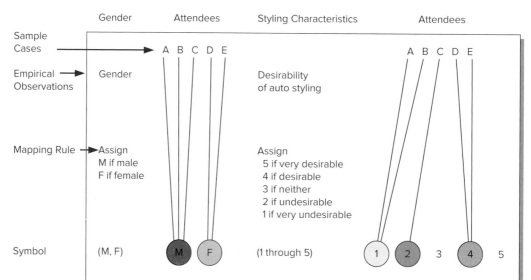

Attendees A, B, and C are male, and find the auto's styling to be undesirable.
Attendees D and E are female and find the auto's styling desirable.

What Is Measured

Variables measured in research may be classified as objects or as properties. **Objects** include both concepts and constructs. *Concepts* are the more concrete and tangible items of daily life, like furniture, laundry detergent, a person, or an automobile. *Constructs* are more abstract, like peer pressure, leadership, or lifestyle. **Properties** are the characteristics of an object. For example, if the object you are measuring is a person, their physical properties include its weight, height, vision, and posture, among others. Their psychological properties include attitudes and intelligence. Their social properties include leadership ability, class affiliation, and status. These and many other properties of an individual can be measured in a research study.

In a literal sense, researchers do not measure either objects or properties; they measure indicants of the properties or objects. Suppose you are analyzing members of a sales force of several hundred people to learn what contributes to sales success. Some properties you think might be influential are years of sales experience, and number of calls made per week. In contrast, it is not easy to measure properties of constructs "opinion leadership" or "persuasiveness." Because each property cannot be measured directly, the researcher must infer its presence or absence by observing some indicant or pointer measurement. When you begin to make such inferences, there is often disagreement about how to develop an operational definition for each indicant.

>Measurement Scales

A study's quality depends on what measures are selected or developed and how they fit the circumstances. In measuring, one devises some mapping rule and then translates the observation of property indicants using this rule. For each concept or construct, several types of measurement are possible; the appropriate choice depends on what you assume about the mapping rules. Each one has its own set of underlying assumptions about how the numerical symbols correspond to real-world observations.

Given the nature of the object or property, mapping rules follow one of four assumptions:

1. Numerical labels are used to classify, group, or sort responses. No order exists because the numbers have no arithmetic value.

2. Numerical labels provide order. One number is greater than, less than, or equal to another number.

3. Numerical labels provide order and the differences between numbers is greater than, less than, or equal to the difference between any other pair of numbers.

4. Numerical labels have arithmetic value because the number series has a unique origin indicated by the number zero. This is an absolute and meaningful zero point.

Combinations of these characteristics of classification, order, distance, and origin provide four widely used classifications of measurement scales:[3] (1) nominal, (2) ordinal, (3) interval, and (4) ratio. Suppose your professor asks a student volunteer to taste-test six candy bars. The student begins by evaluating each on a chocolate–not chocolate scale; this is a nominal measurement. Then the student ranks the candy bars from best to worst; this is an ordinal measurement. Next, the student uses a 7-point scale that has equal distance between points to rate the candy bars with regard to some criterion (e.g., crunchiness); this is an interval measurement. Finally, the student considers another taste dimension and assigns 100 points among the six candy bars; this is a ratio measurement. The characteristics of these measurement scales are summarized in Exhibit 10-3.

Deciding which type of scale is appropriate for your research needs should be seen as a part of the research process, as shown in Exhibit 10-4.

Nominal Scales

In business research, nominal data are widely used. With **nominal scales**, you are collecting information on a variable that naturally or by design can be grouped into two or more categories that are mutually exclusive and collectively exhaustive.

>**Exhibit 10-3** Summary of Measurement Scale Types

Type of Scale	Characteristics of Data	Empirical Operations
Nominal	Classification (mutually exclusive and collectively exhaustive categories), but no order, distance, or natural origin	• Count (frequency distribution); *mode* as central tendency; no measure of dispersion • Used with other variables to discern patterns, reveal relationships
Ordinal	Classification and order, but no distance or natural origin	• Determination of greater or lesser value • Count (frequency distribution); median as central tendency; nonparametric statistics
Interval	Classification, order, and distance, but no natural origin	• Determination of equality of intervals or differences • Count (frequency distribution); mean or median as measure of central tendency; measure of dispersion is standard deviation or interquartile range; parametric tests
Ratio	Classification, order, distance, and natural origin	• Determination of equality of ratios • Any of the above statistical operations, plus multiplication and division; mean as central tendency; coefficients of variation as measure of dispersion

The counting of members in each group is the only possible arithmetic operation when a nominal scale is employed. If we use numerical symbols within our mapping rule to identify categories, these numbers are recognized as labels only and have no quantitative value. Using nominal classifications one might classify participants in a study according to their expressed religious preferences. Two mapping rules are given in Exhibit 10-5. Mapping rule A given in the table is not a sound nominal scale because its categories are not mutually exclusive or collectively exhaustive. Mapping rule B meets the minimum requirements; it covers all the major religions and offers an "other" option. Nominal scales are the least powerful of the four data types. They suggest no order or distance relationship and have no arithmetic origin. The scale wastes any information a sample case might share about varying degrees of the property being measured.

Because the only quantification is the number count of cases in each category (the frequency distribution), the researcher is restricted to the use of the mode as the measure of central tendency.[4] The *mode* is the most frequently occurring value. You can conclude which category has the most members, but that is all. There is no generally used measure of *dispersion* for nominal scales. Dispersion describes how scores cluster or scatter in a distribution. By cross-tabulating nominal variables with other variables, you can begin to discern patterns in data.

Although nominal data are statistically weak, they are still useful. If no other scale can be used, one can almost always classify a set of properties into a set of equivalent classes. Nominal measures are especially valuable in exploratory work where the

>**Exhibit 10-4** Measurement: Move from Investigative to Measurement Questions

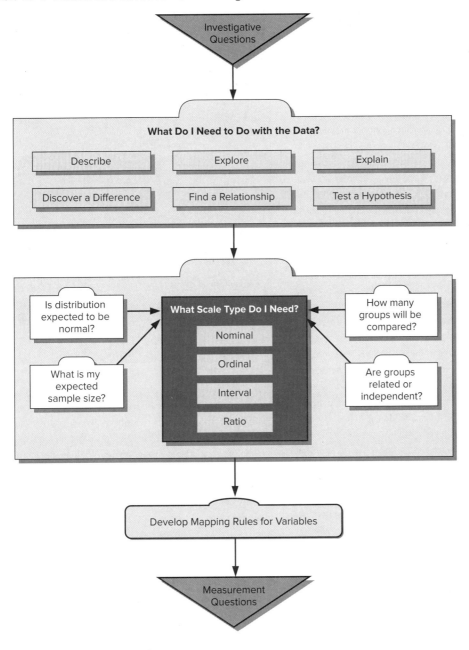

>**Exhibit 10-5** Evaluate Two Mapping Rules

Religious Preferences	
Mapping Rule A	**Mapping Rule B**
1 = Baptist	1 = Christian
2 = Catholic	2 = Muslim
3 = Protestant	3 = Hindu
4 = Scientology	4 = Buddhist
5 = Unitarian-Universalist	5 = Jewish
6 = Jewish	6 = Other
7 = Secular/nonreligious/agnostic/atheist	

The Emotional Face of Research

Creative testing methodologies for advertising nearly exclusively measure *rational* consumer response (e.g., brand recall, brand linkage, message understanding, purchase consideration and intent) and fail to incorporate well-thought-out measures of *emotional* response. Some of the world's leading consumer and industrial companies rely on Cleveland-based Marcus Thomas LLC to create or refine their brands and drive customers to seek out and buy their products and services. One such client, The Ohio Lottery, wanted a better way to assess the impact of its TV and radio advertising on consumers and understand their reactions to varying elements of style (e.g., story, characters, music, tone) to guide the development of future advertising executions. So, Marcus Thomas (MT) recommended a new methodology.

Marcus Thomas chose its 1,000 participants from a respondent panel of Ohio adults who had played the Lottery in the past 12 months. MT and the Lottery jointly chose 11 campaign executions (both TV and radio spots), representing a variety of genres and styles, and presented these to its sample. Previous research suggested that emotional response—the way people felt after seeing an advertisement—could be a better predictor of effectiveness than commonly used rational measures. So in an online, 15-minute survey, emotions were captured first, immediately after ad exposure. Respondents chose from photography of faces representing fundamental feelings (e.g., happiness, surprise, anger) to report how the one ad they saw/heard made them feel. Using responses to open-ended questions, participants also reported their moment-by-moment mood changes, and their reasons for those changes, while watching/listening to the spot a second time. Respondents also answered questions measuring rational response, including traditional questions of brand recall and linkage, likelihood to purchase, intention to purchase, etc. "Collecting feelings *immediately* after exposure and using photography *representing* emotions were critical in ensuring the capture of *pure* non-rationalized feelings," shared Edwige Winans, associate research director at Marcus Thomas, describing the methodology. Because there were many questions, the questionnaire used gamification techniques to enhance respondent experiences and maintain engagement.

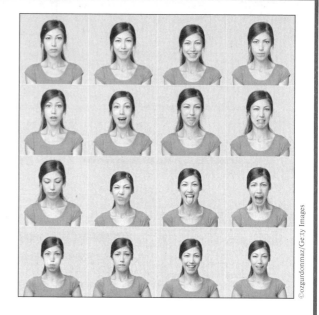

©ozgurdonmaz/Getty Images

Marcus Thomas, working with BrainJuicer, aggregated the emotional responses and created emotional journey maps for each ad. These responses provided insight into ad elements (characters, tone, colors, music, dialog, etc.) that affected respondent feelings. Additionally, the emotional responses were compared with the rational reactions, and these were compared to industry benchmarks for added context. The findings clearly identified elements that generated positive and negative emotions and pointed to neutral moments when consumers lacked emotional engagement—something no advertiser wants. What MT learned in the research has established modified creative guidelines for development of future Lottery ads. Insights were applied to creative executions (e.g., dialogue, music, sequence of events) to maximize consumer emotional engagement the following year, resulting in a sales increase of 4 percent, exceeding projections.

www.marcusthomasllc.com; www.system1group.com

objective is to uncover relationships rather than secure precise measurements. This type of scale is also widely used in survey and other research when data are classified by major subgroups of the population. Classifications such as participants' marital status, gender, political orientation, and exposure to a certain experience provide insight into important demographic data patterns.

Ordinal Scales

Ordinal scales include the characteristics of the nominal scale plus an indication of order. Ordinal data require conformity to a logical postulate, which states: If *a* is greater than *b* and *b* is greater than *c*, then *a* is greater than c.[5] The use of an ordinal scale implies a statement of "greater than" or "less than" (without stating how much greater or less) or "equal to". While ordinal measurement speaks of greater-than and less-than measurements, other descriptors may be used—"superior to," "happier than," "poorer than," or "more important than." Like a rubber yardstick, an ordinal scale can stretch varying amounts at different places along its length. Thus, the real difference between ranks 1 and 2 on a satisfaction scale may be more or less than the difference between ranks 2 and 3. An ordinal concept can be extended beyond the three cases used in the simple illustration of $a > b > c$. Any number of cases can be ranked.

Another extension of the ordinal concept occurs when there is more than one property of interest. We may ask a participant to rank varieties of carbonated soft drinks by flavor, color, carbonation, and a combination of these characteristics. We can secure the combined ranking either by asking the participant to base his or her ranking on the combination of properties or, after data collection, constructing a combination ranking of the individual rankings on each property.

Examples of ordinal data include attitude and preference scales. Because the numbers used with ordinal scales have only a rank meaning, the appropriate measure of central tendency is the median. The *median* is the midpoint of a distribution. A percentile or quartile reveals the dispersion.

Correlational analysis of ordinal data is restricted to various ordinal techniques. Measures of statistical significance are technically confined to a body of statistics known as *nonparametric methods,* synonymous with *distribution-free statistics.*[6]

Researchers differ about whether more powerful tests are appropriate for analyzing ordinal measures. Because nonparametric tests are abundant, simple to calculate, have good statistical power,[7] and do not require that the researcher accept the assumptions of parametric testing, we advise their use with nominal and ordinal data. It is understandable, however, that because parametric tests (such as the *t*-test or analysis of variance) are versatile, accepted, and understood, they will be used with ordinal data when researchers can demonstrate that those data approach the assumptions necessary for interval level analysis.

Interval Scales

Interval scales have the power of nominal and ordinal data plus one additional strength: They incorporate the concept of equality of interval (the scaled distance between 1 and 2 equals the distance between 2 and 3). Calendar time is such a scale. For example, the elapsed time between 3 and 6 a.m. equals the time between 4 and 7 a.m. One cannot say, however, that 6 a.m. is twice as late as 3 a.m., because "zero time" is an arbitrary zero point. Centigrade and Fahrenheit temperature scales are other examples of classical interval scales. Both have an arbitrarily determined zero point, not a unique origin.

Researchers treat many attitude scales as interval. When a scale is interval and the data are relatively symmetric with one mode, you use the arithmetic mean as the measure of central tendency. You can compute the average time of a TV promotional message or the average attitude value for different age groups in an insurance benefits study. The standard deviation is the measure of dispersion. The product-moment correlation, *t*-tests, *F*-tests, and other parametric tests are the statistical procedures of choice for interval data.[8]

When the distribution of scores computed from interval data leans in one direction or the other (skewed right or left), we often use the median as the measure of central tendency and the interquartile range as the measure of dispersion.[9]

Ratio Scales

Ratio scales incorporate all of the powers of the previous scales plus the provision for absolute zero or origin. Ratio data represent the actual amounts of a variable. Measures of physical dimensions such as weight, height, distance, and area are examples. In business research, we find ratio scales in many areas:

©Carles Campsolinas/Age fotostock

Measurement of TiVo Households: Skipped Ads vs. Most Watched

Doesn't it seem odd that some of the most popular shows on TV have the least watched ads? From TiVo research we discover that, "nearly all of the television shows that won 2009 Emmys showed higher levels of ad-skipping than the averages for their respective genres."[a] Sitcoms had a 66 percent level of ad-skipping in contrast to the 88 percent who fast-forwarded through "MadMen" ads and the 73 percent of the audiences who skipped over ads for all TV dramas.[b] According to Todd Juenger, TiVo's vice president for audience research and measurement, people who watch hit shows are more likely to skip ads because they are more involved in the show than other viewers.[c]

Madison Avenue media planners have long counseled companies to avoid buying ads in the fourth quarter of the Super Bowl, even understanding that part of the appeal of the Super Bowl is watching the ads. However, such advice is now being reassessed after the second championship in consecutive years was won in the final moments of play.[d] NBC's broadcast of commercials in the last quarter of Super Bowl XLIII had strong viewer numbers. Two of the most-watched ads on TiVo DVRs were the final ads in the game: Bud Light Lime beer and GoDaddy.com, the website registration firm. These ads were broadcast after the Arizona Cardinals touchdown and before the Pittsburgh Steelers reclaimed the lead and won. "There are two reasons a commercial gets a high rating [in a TiVo household]," Mr. Juenger said. "Either [the show] is rewound often and watched repeatedly or [the ad] happens to be in the middle of [compelling programming that is watched over and over]."[e]

Those who sat on the edge of their seats for the end of Super Bowl XLIII helped rank it as the second-most-watched Super Bowl. For those rewatching the end of the fourth quarter, suggest some hypotheses that explain ad-skipping. What measures would you use to test your hypotheses?

www.tivo.com

sales, profits, number of employees, shipping distances, return rates on investments, productivity rates, elapsed time before a customer service representative answer a phone inquiry, square feet of office space, etc.

Swatch's *BeatTime*—a proposed standard global time introduced at the 2000 Olympics is a ratio scale. It offers a standard time with its origin at 0 beats (12 midnight in Biel, Switzerland, at the new Biel Meridian timeline). A day is composed of 1,000 beats, with a "beat" worth 1 minute, 26.4 seconds.[10]

All statistical techniques mentioned up to this point are usable with ratio scales. Other manipulations carried out with real numbers may be done with ratio-scale values. Thus, multiplication and division can be used with ratio-scale data but not with the others mentioned. Geometric and harmonic means are measures of central tendency, and coefficients of variation may also be calculated for describing variability.

Recoding

Certain statistical techniques require that the measurement types be the same. To accommodate this, variables can be adjusted after collection, even as part of data preparation and examination, by **recoding** responses into a different scale type. This requires applying a new set of mapping rules to a variable to create a new scale type. While we can't upgrade a scale, we can reduce its power in recoding. For example, we might ask for a participant's after-tax income (ratio) and reduce this to ranges of income that match Census data (interval data) or some arbitrary income ranges (ordinal) during data exploration. Because a nominal variable does not have the characteristics of order, distance, or point of origin, we cannot create these artificially after the fact. Recoding a variable involves reducing the measure from the more powerful and robust level to a lesser one.[11] The loss of measurement power with this decision means that lesser-powered statistics are then used in data analysis, but fewer assumptions for their proper use are required.

In summary, higher levels of measurement generally yield more information. Because of the measurement precision at higher levels, more powerful and sensitive statistical procedures can be used. When one moves from a higher measurement level to a lower one, there is always a loss of information. Finally, when we collect information at higher levels, we can always convert, recode, or reduce the data to arrive at a lower level.

>Sources of Measurement Differences

The ideal research project should be designed and controlled for precise and unambiguous measurement of the variables. Because complete control is unattainable, error does occur. Much error is systematic (results from a bias), while the remainder is random (occurs erratically). One authority has pointed out several sources from which measured differences can come.[12]

Assume you are conducting an ex post facto study of corporate citizenship of a multinational manufacturer. The company produces family, personal, and household care products. The participants are residents of a major city. The study concerns the Prince Corporation, a large manufacturer with its headquarters and several major facilities located in the city. The objective of the study is to discover the public's opinions about the company's approach to health, social welfare, and the environment. You also want to know the origin of any generally held adverse opinions.

Ideally, any variation of scores among the participants would reflect true differences in their opinions about the company. Attitudes toward the firm as an employer, as an ecologically sensitive organization, or as a progressive corporate citizen would be accurately expressed. However, four major error sources may contaminate the results: (1) the participant, (2) the situation, (3) the measurer, and (4) the data collection instrument.

Error Sources

The Participant

Opinion differences that affect measurement come from relatively stable characteristics of the participant. Typical of these are employee status, ethnic group membership, social class, and nearness to manufacturing facilities. The skilled researcher will anticipate many of these dimensions, adjusting the design to eliminate, neutralize, or otherwise deal with them. However, even the skilled researcher may not be as aware of less obvious dimensions. The latter variety might be a traumatic experience a given participant had with the Prince Corporation, its programs, or its employees. Participants may be reluctant to express strong negative (or positive) feelings, may purposefully express attitudes that they perceive as different from those of others, or may have little knowledge about Prince but be reluctant to admit ignorance. This reluctance to admit ignorance of a topic can lead to an interview consisting of "guesses" or assumptions, which, in turn, create erroneous data.

Participants may also suffer from temporary factors like fatigue, boredom, anxiety, hunger, impatience, or general variations in mood or other distractions; these limit the ability to respond accurately and fully. Designing measurement scales that engage the participant for the duration of the measurement is crucial.

Situational Factors

Any condition that places a strain on the interview or measurement session can have serious effects on the interviewer–participant rapport. If another person is present, that person can distort responses by joining in, distracting, or merely being there. If the participants believe anonymity is not ensured, they may be reluctant to express certain feelings. Intercept interviews are unlikely to elicit as detailed a response, as in-home interviews.

Talent Analytics: The Frontier of HR Research

The biggest investment for most firms is their people. These firms would love to know whether they are attracting, recruiting, and developing the best people given their type of business and the market for talent for a given position. According to research by Bersin & Associates, "Initially, many [HR] assessments were used primarily for pre-hire selection; today, assessment providers offer strategic resources for global organizations that want to build their overall knowledge of their employees beyond hiring—for development, promotion, internal mobility and succession planning."

People intelligence, as defined by Bersin, is "the collected body of information on an individual over the course of that individual's affiliation with an organization—from pre-application through emeritus stages. It is comprised of data that, when analyzed, is useful both to the individual and to the organization as a whole for strategic talent and business decision making and performance improvement." Such people intelligence is gaining increasing interest as technology makes it possible to connect business outcomes more closely with the people who deliver them.

SHL offers a research process called Talent Analytics for this purpose. In its 2012 *Business Outcomes Study Report*, covering more than 66 business outcome studies, SHL demonstrated that great assessment tools and competitive benchmarking can attract better talent (people with the skills and attributes to better fit an organization and provide better bottom-line results), retain talent, enhance productivity, and reduce the negative effects of a rejected hire. Clients—like Time Warner, GlaxoSmithKline, Kellogg's, and Hilton Hotels—choose from more than 1,000 off-the-shelf, prepackaged assessment solutions delivered via a secure, user-friendly online platform.

The results of employing these measurement tools are impressive. An automotive parts retailer discovered sales associates who earned higher scores on an assessment designed to predict sales potential sold 21 percent more over their first three months on the job. An insurance company used talent analytics

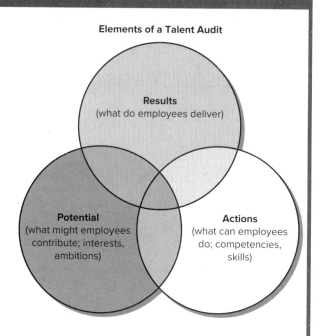

Elements of a Talent Audit

Results
(what do employees deliver)

Potential
(what might employees
contribute; interests,
ambitions)

Actions
(what can employees
do; competencies,
skills)

to reduce employee turnover by 40 percent. Restaurant managers earning high scores on the talent analytic metrics of problem solving and organizational fit were twice as likely to be great performers. A car manufacturer using talent analytics measuring dependability and safety demonstrated that high scorers were twice as likely to be rated by superiors as having high potential for advancement.

Bersin & Associates is a consultancy designed to improve a firm's enterprise learning and talent management strategies, processes, and systems. SHL is the result of a merger between SHL and PreVisor, two talent assessment pioneers. As the world's largest talent assessment firm, SHL performs more than 25 million scientifically proven selection and development assessments each year in more than 30 languages. You can learn more about talent analytics by visiting its website.

www.shl.com; www.bersin.com

The Measurer

The interviewer can distort responses by rewording, paraphrasing, or reordering questions. Stereotypes in appearance and action introduce bias. Inflections of voice and conscious or unconscious prompting with smiles, nods, and so forth, may encourage or discourage certain replies. Careless mechanical processing—recording of the wrong response (according to the mapping rule) or failure to record full replies—will obviously distort findings. In the data analysis stage, incorrect coding, careless tabulation, and faulty statistical calculation may introduce further errors.

The Instrument

A defective measurement instrument can cause distortion in two major ways. First, it can be too confusing and ambiguous. The use of jargon or complex words and syntax beyond participant comprehension is typical. Leading questions (that imply a desired answer), ambiguous meanings, mechanical defects (inadequate space for replies, response-choice omissions, or poor printing or screen design), and multiple questions (that ask two or more questions with options that answer only one) suggest the range of problems. Many of these problems are the direct result of operational definitions that are insufficient, resulting in an inappropriate scale being chosen or developed.

A more elusive type of instrument deficiency is one that doesn't cover the investigative questions. The Prince Corporation study might treat company image in areas of employment and ecology but omit the company management's civic leadership, its support of local education programs, its philanthropy, or its position on minority issues. Even if the general issues are studied, the questions may not cover enough aspects of each topic of concern. Although we might study the Prince Corporation's image as an employer in terms of salary and wage scales, promotion opportunities, and work stability, perhaps such topics as working conditions, company management relations with organized labor, and retirement and other benefit programs should also be included.

>The Characteristics of Good Measurement

What are the characteristics of a good measurement tool? An intuitive answer to this question is that the tool should be an accurate and both easy and efficient to use. There are three major criteria for evaluating a measurement tool: validity, reliability, and practicality.

- *Validity* is the extent to which a chosen or developed scale (our measurement questions) actually measure what we wish to measure (our investigative questions).
- *Reliability* has to do with the accuracy and precision of a measurement procedure.
- *Practicality* is concerned with a wide range of factors of economy, convenience, and interpretability in measurement.[13]

In the following sections, we discuss the nature of these qualities and how researchers can achieve them in their measurement procedures.

Validity[14]

Many forms of **validity** are mentioned in the research literature.[15] This text explored *external validity* (the data's ability to be generalized across persons, settings, and times) in the chapters on experiments and sampling design and will explore internal validity here and when we discuss data preparation. The text's discussion of **internal validity** is further limited to the ability of a research instrument to measure what it is purported to measure. Does the instrument really measure what its designer claims it does?

One widely accepted classification of internal validity consists of three major forms: (1) content validity, (2) criterion-related validity, and (3) construct validity (see Exhibit 10-6).[16]

Content Validity

The **content validity** of a measuring instrument is the extent to which it provides adequate coverage of the investigative questions guiding the study. If the instrument adequately covers the topics of interest, then content validity is good. To evaluate the content validity of an instrument, one must first agree on what elements constitute adequate coverage. In the Prince Corporation study, we must decide what knowledge and attitudes are relevant to the measurement of corporate public image and then decide which forms of these opinions are relevant positions on these topics.

A determination of content validity involves judgment. First, the researcher may determine it through a careful definition of the topics, the items to be scaled, and the scales to be used. This logical process is often intuitive and unique to each researcher.

>**Exhibit 10-6** Summary of Validity Estimates

Types	What Is Measured	Methods
Content	Degree to which the content of the items adequately represents the universe of all relevant items under study.	• Judgmental • Panel evaluation with content validity ratio
Criterion-related	Degree to which the predictor is adequate in capturing the relevant aspects of the criterion.	• Correlation
Concurrent	Description of the present; criterion data are available at the same time as predictor scores.	• Correlation
Predictive	Prediction of the future; criterion data are measured after the passage of time.	• Correlation
Construct	Answers the question, "What accounts for the variance in the measure?"; attempts to identify the underlying construct(s) being measured and determine how well the test represents it (them).	• Judgmental • Correlation of proposed test with established one • Convergent-discriminant techniques • Factor analysis • Multitrait-multimethod analysis

A second way is to use a panel of persons to judge how well the instrument covers the appropriate topics. The panel independently assesses measurement questions for an instrument as essential, useful but not essential, or not necessary. "Essential" evaluations on each item from each panelist are evaluated by a content validity ratio, and those meeting a statistical significance value are retained. In both informal judgments and this systematic process, content validity should be primarily concerned with inferences about measurement instrument construction rather than inferences about measurement instrument scores or values.[17]

It is important not to define content too narrowly. If you were to secure only superficial expressions of opinion in the Prince Corporation attitude survey, it would probably not have adequate content coverage.

Criterion-Related Validity

Criterion-related validity reflects the success of measures used for prediction or estimation. You may want to predict an outcome or estimate the existence of a current behavior or time perspective. An attitude scale that correctly forecasts the outcome of a purchase decision has predictive validity. An observational method that correctly categorizes families by current income class has concurrent validity. Although these examples appear to have simple and unambiguous validity criteria, there are difficulties in estimating validity. Consider the problem of estimating family income. There is a knowable true income for every family, but we may find the figure difficult to secure. Thus, while the criterion is conceptually clear, it may be unavailable.

A researcher may want to develop a preemployment test that will predict sales success. There may be several possible criteria, none of which individually tells the full story. Total sales per salesperson may not adequately reflect territory market potential, competitive conditions, or the different profitability rates of various products. One might rely on the sales manager's overall evaluation, but how unbiased and accurate are such impressions? The researcher must ensure that the validity criterion used is itself "valid." Any criterion measure must be judged in terms of four qualities: (1) relevance, (2) freedom from bias, (3) reliability, and (4) availability.[18]

A criterion is *relevant* if it is defined and scored in the terms we judge to be the proper measures of salesperson success. If you believe sales success is adequately measured by dollar sales volume achieved per year, then that is the relevant criterion. If you believe success should include attracting new accounts, then sales volume alone is not fully relevant. In making this decision, the researcher uses his judgment and exploratory research results to decide what partial criteria are appropriate indicants of salesperson success.

Freedom from bias is attained when the criterion gives each salesperson an equal opportunity to score well. The sales criterion would be biased if it did not show adjustments for differences in territory potential and competitive conditions.

A *reliable* criterion is stable or reproducible. An erratic criterion (using monthly sales, which are highly variable from month to month) can hardly be considered a reliable standard to judge performance on sales success. Finally, the information specified by the criterion must be *available*. If it is not available, how much will it cost and how difficult will it be to secure? The amount of money and effort that should be spent on development of a criterion depends on the importance of the problem for which research is being conducted.

Once there are measurements and criterion scores, they must be compared in some way. The usual approach is to correlate them. For example, you might correlate measurements of 40 new salespeople with first-year sales achievements adjusted to reflect differences in territorial selling conditions.

Construct Validity

In attempting to evaluate **construct validity**, we consider both the theory and the measuring instrument being used. If we were interested in measuring the effect of trust in cross-functional teams, the way in which "trust" was operationally defined would have to correspond to an empirically grounded theory on trust in teams. If a known measure of trust was available, we might correlate the results obtained using this measure with those derived from our new instrument. Such an approach would provide us with preliminary indications of *convergent* validity (the degree to which scores on one scale correlate with scores on other scales designed to assess the same construct).

Returning to our preceding example, another method of validating the trust construct would be to separate it from other constructs in the theory or related theories. To the extent that trust could be separated from bonding, reciprocity, and empathy, we would have completed the first steps toward *discriminant* validity (the degree to which scores on a scale *do not* correlate with scores on scales designed to measure different constructs).

The three forms of validity are interrelated, both theoretically and operationally. Predictive validity is important for a measurement designed to predict product success. In developing such a measurement you would probably first list the factors (constructs) that provide the basis for useful prediction. For example, you would advance a theory about the variables in product success—an area for construct validity. Finally, in developing the specific items for inclusion in the success prediction measure, you would be concerned with how well the specific measurement scales cover the full range of each construct (a matter of content validity). Looking at Exhibit 10-7, we can better understand the concepts of validity and reliability by using an archer's bow and target as an analogy.

Reliability

Reliability is concerned with the degree to which a measurement is free of random or unstable error. A measure is reliable to the degree that it supplies consistent results. The relationship between reliability and validity can be simply illustrated with the use of a bathroom scale. If the scale measures your weight correctly (using a concurrent criterion such as a scale known to be accurate), then it is both reliable and valid. If it consistently overweighs you by six pounds, then the scale is reliable but not valid. If the scale measures erratically from time to time, then it is not reliable and therefore cannot be valid. So if a measurement is not valid, it hardly matters if it is reliable—because it does not measure what the researcher needs to measure in order to solve the research problem. Reliability is a necessary contributor to validity but is not a sufficient condition for validity. In this context, reliability is not as valuable as validity, but it is much easier to assess.

Reliable instruments can be used with confidence that transient and situational factors are not interfering. Reliable instruments are robust; they work well at different times under different conditions. This distinction of time and condition is the basis for frequently used perspectives on reliability—stability, equivalence, and internal consistency (see Exhibit 10-8).

>**Exhibit 10-7** Understanding Validity and Reliability

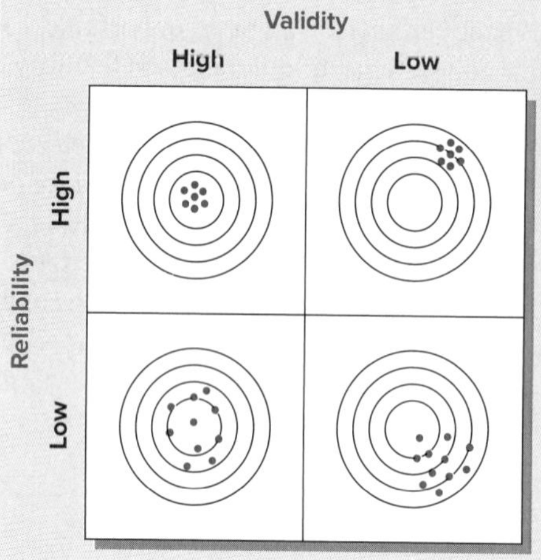

Let's use an archer's bow and target as an analogy.

High reliability means that repeated arrows shot from the same bow would hit the target in essentially the same place—although not necessarily the intended place (first row of the graphic). If we had a bow with high validity as well, then every arrow would hit the bull's-eye (upper left panel). If reliability is low or decreases for some reason, arrows would be more scattered (lacking similarity or closeness, like those shown in the second row).

High validity means that the bow would shoot true every time. It would not pull to the right or send an arrow careening into the woods. Arrows shot from a high-validity bow will be clustered around a central point (the bull's eye), even when they are dispersed by reduced reliability (lower left graphic). Low-validity shots are distorted, rather like a flawed bow pulling our arrows to the right (second column of the graphic). We wouldn't hit the bull's-eye we were aiming at because the low-validity bow—like the flawed data collection instrument—would not perform as planned. When low validity is compounded by low reliability, the pattern of arrows is not only off the bull's-eye but also dispersed (lower right graphic).

>**Exhibit 10-8** Summary of Reliability Estimates

Type	Coefficient	What Is Measured	Methods
Test–retest	Stability	Reliability of a test or instrument inferred from examinee scores; same test is administered twice to same subjects over an interval of less than six months.	Correlation
Parallel forms	Equivalence	Degree to which alternative forms of the same measure produce same or similar results; administered simultaneously or with a delay. Interrater estimates of the similarity of judges' observations or scores.	Correlation
Split-Half, KR20, Cronbach's Alpha	Internal consistency	Degree to which instrument items are homogeneous and reflect the same underlying construct(s).	Specialized correlational formulas

Stability

A measure is said to possess **stability** if you can secure consistent results with repeated measurements of the same person with the same instrument. An observation procedure is stable if it gives the same reading on a particular person when repeated one or more times. It is often possible to repeat observations on a subject and to compare them for consistency. When there is much time between measurements, there is a chance for situational factors to change, thereby affecting the observations. The change would be interpreted incorrectly as a drop in the reliability of the measurement process.

Stability measurement in survey situations is more difficult and less easily executed than in observational studies. Although you can observe a certain action repeatedly, you usually can resurvey only once. This leads to a test-retest arrangement—with comparisons between the two measures (tests) to learn how reliable they are. Some of the difficulties that can occur in the test–retest methodology and cause a downward bias in stability include:

- *Time delay between measurements*—leads to situational factor changes (a problem in both observation and survey reseearch).

- *Insufficient time between measurements*—permits the participant to recall previous answers and repeat them, resulting in biased reliability indicators.
- *Participant's discernment of a study's disguised purpose*—may introduce bias if the participant holds opinions related to the purpose but not assessed with current measurement questions.
- *Topic sensitivity*—occurs when the participant seeks to learn more about the topic or form new and different opinions before the retest.

A suggested remedy is to extend the interval between test and retest (from two weeks to a month). While this may help, the researcher must be alert to the chance that an outside factor will contaminate the measurement and distort the stability score. Consequently, stability measurement through the test-retest approach has limited applications. More interest has centered on equivalence.

Equivalence

A second perspective on reliability considers how much error may be introduced by different investigators (in observation) or different samples of items being studied (in surveys). Thus, while stability is concerned with personal and situational fluctuations from one time to another, **equivalence** is concerned with variations at one point in time among observers and samples of items. A good way to test for the equivalence of measurements by different observers is to compare their scoring of the same event. An example of this is the scoring of Olympic gymnastics by a panel of judges.

In studies where a consensus among experts or observers is required, the similarity of the judges' perceptions is sometimes questioned. How does a panel of supervisors render a judgment on merit raises, a new product's packaging, or future business trends? *Interrater reliability* may be used in these cases to correlate the observations or scores of the judges and render an index of how consistent their ratings are. In Olympic gymnastics, a judge's relative positioning of gymnasts (determined by establishing a rank order for each judge and comparing each judge's ordering for all gymnasts) is a means of measuring equivalence.

The major interest with equivalence is typically not how participants differ from item to item on a measurement instrument but how well a given set of items (measurement questions) will categorize individuals. There may be many differences in response between two samples of questions, but if a person is classified the same way by each measurement instrument, then the instruments have good equivalence.

©Image Source

One tests for item equivalence by using alternative or *parallel forms* of the same measurement administered to the same persons simultaneously. The results of the two measures are then correlated. Under this condition, the length of the testing process is likely to affect the subjects' responses through fatigue, and the inferred reliability of the parallel form will be reduced accordingly. Some measurement theorists recommend an interval between the two tests to compensate for this problem. This approach, called *delayed equivalent forms*, is a composite of test-retest and the equivalence method. As in test-retest, one would administer measure X followed by measure Y to half the participants and measure Y followed by measure X to the other half to prevent "order-of-presentation" effects.[19]

The researcher can include only a limited number of measurement questions in an instrument. This limitation implies that a sample of measurement questions from a content domain has been chosen and another sample producing a similar number will need to be drawn for the second instrument. It is frequently difficult to create this second set. Yet if the pool is initially large enough, the items may be randomly selected for each instrument. Even with more sophisticated procedures used by publishers of standardized tests, it is rare to find fully equivalent and interchangeable questions.[20]

Internal Consistency

A third approach to reliability uses only one administration of an instrument to assess the **internal consistency** or homogeneity among the items. The *split-half* technique can be used when the measurement instrument has many similar questions or statements to which the participant can respond. The instrument is administered and the results are separated by item into even and odd numbers or into randomly selected halves. When the two halves are correlated, if the results of the correlation are high, the instrument is said to be highly reliable in terms of internal consistency. The high correlation tells us there is similarity (or homogeneity) among the measures. The potential for incorrect inferences about high internal consistency exists when the test contains many items—which inflates the correlation index.

The Spearman-Brown correction formula is used to adjust for the effect of measurement length and to estimate reliability of the whole measurement instrument.[21]

Practicality

The scientific requirements of a project call for the measurement process to be reliable and valid, while the operational requirements call for it to be practical. **Practicality** has been defined as *economy, convenience, and interpretability*.[22] Although this definition refers to the development of educational and psychological tests, it is meaningful for business measurements as well.

Economy

Some trade-off usually occurs between the ideal research project and the budget. Data are not free, and instrument length is one area where economic pressures dominate. More items give more reliability, but in the interest of limiting the interview or observation time (and therefore costs), we hold down the number of measurement questions. The choice of data collection method is also often dictated by economic factors. The rising cost of personal interviewing first led to an increased use of telephone surveys and subsequently to the current rise in Internet and mobile surveys. In standardized tests, the cost of test materials alone can be such a significant expense that it encourages multiple reuse, such as when businesses use the same instrument to measure understanding of harassment policies. Add to this the need for fast and economical coding and tallying, and we see why computer scoring and scanning are attractive.

Convenience

A measuring device passes the convenience test if it is easy to administer. A questionnaire or a measurement instrument with a set of detailed but clear instructions, with examples, is easier to complete correctly than one that lacks these features. In a well-prepared study, it is not uncommon for the interviewer instructions to be several times longer than the interview questions. Naturally, the more complex the concepts and constructs, the greater is the need for clear and complete instructions. We can also make the instrument easier to administer by giving close attention to its design and layout. Although reliability and validity dominate our choices in design of scales here, administrative difficulty should play some role. A long completion time, complex instructions, participant's perceived difficulty with a survey, and their rated enjoyment of the process also influence design. Layout issues include crowding of material, poor reproductions of visual stimuli, and the carryover of items from one page to the next or the need to scroll the screen when taking a computer-based or mobile survey. Both design and layout decisions can make completion of the instrument more difficult.

Interpretability

This aspect of practicality is relevant when persons other than the instrument designer must interpret the results. It is usually, but not exclusively, an issue with standardized measurements. In such cases, the designer of the measurement instrument provides several key pieces of information to make interpretation possible:

- A statement of the functions the instrument was designed to measure and the procedures by which it was developed.
- Detailed instructions for administration.
- Scoring keys and instructions.
- Norms for appropriate reference groups.
- Evidence about reliability.
- Evidence regarding the intercorrelations of subscores.
- Evidence regarding the relationship of the test to other measures.
- Guides for instrument use.

>summary

LO10-1 Although people measure things casually in daily life, research measurement is more precise and controlled. In measurement, one settles for measuring properties of the objects rather than the objects themselves. An event is measured in terms of its duration. What happened during it, who was involved, where it occurred, and so forth, are all properties of the event. To be more precise, what are measured are indicants of the properties. Thus, for duration, one measures the number of hours and minutes recorded. For what happened, one uses some system to classify types of activities that occurred. Measurement typically uses some sort of scale to classify or quantify the data collected.

LO10-2 There are four scale types. In increasing order of power, they are nominal, ordinal, interval, and ratio. Nominal scales classify without indicating order, distance, or unique origin. Ordinal data show magnitude relationships of more than and less than but have no distance or unique origin. Interval scales offer classification, order, and distance but no unique origin. Ratio scales possess classification, order, distance, and unique origin.

LO10-3 Instruments may yield incorrect readings of an indicant for many reasons. These may be classified according to error sources: (a) the participant, (b) situational factors, (c) the measurer, and (d) the instrument.

LO10-4 Sound measurement must meet the tests of validity, reliability, and practicality. Validity reveals the degree to which an instrument measures what it is supposed to measure to assist the researcher in solving the research problem. Three forms of validity are used to evaluate measurement questions. Content validity exists to the degree that a measure provides an adequate reflection of the topic under study. Its determination is primarily judgmental and intuitive. Criterion-related validity relates to our ability to predict some outcome or estimate the existence of some current condition. Construct validity is the most complex and abstract. A measure has construct validity to the degree that it conforms to predicted correlations of other theoretical propositions.

A measure is reliable if it provides consistent results. Reliability is a partial contributor to validity, but a measurement tool may be reliable without being valid. Three forms of reliability are stability, equivalence, and internal consistency. A measure has practical value for the research if it is economical, convenient, and interpretable.

>**key**terms

>**discussion**questions

Terms in Review

1 What can we measure about the four objects listed below? Be as specific as possible.

  a Laundry detergent.

  b Employees.

  c Factory output.

  d Job satisfaction.

2 What are the essential differences among nominal, ordinal, interval, and ratio scales? How do these differences affect the statistical analysis techniques we can use?

3 What are the four major sources of measurement error? Illustrate by example how each of these might affect measurement results in a face-to-face interview situation.

4 Do you agree or disagree with the following statements? Explain.

  a Validity is more critical to measurement than reliability.

  b Content validity is the most difficult type of validity to determine.

  c A valid measurement is reliable, but a reliable measurement may not be valid.

  d Stability and equivalence are essentially the same thing.

Making Research Decisions

5 You have data from a corporation on the annual salary of each of its 200 employees.

  a Illustrate how the data can be presented as ratio, interval, ordinal, and nominal data.

  b Describe the successive loss of information as the presentation changes from ratio to nominal.

6 Below are listed some objects of varying degrees of abstraction. Suggest properties of each of these objects that can be measured by each of the four basic types of scales.

  a Store customers.

  b Voter attitudes.

  c Hardness of steel alloys.

  d Preference for a particular common stock.

  e Profitability of various divisions in a company.

7 You have been asked by the head of marketing to design an instrument by which your private, for-profit school can evaluate the quality and value of its various curricula and courses. How might you try to ensure that your instrument has:

  a Stability?

  b Equivalence?

  c Internal consistency?

  d Content validity?

  e Predictive validity?

  f Construct validity?

8 As part of its bankruptcy restructuring, General Motors (GM) launched an ad campaign that revealed glimmers of a streamlined GM: fewer brands (Cadillac, Buick, Chevrolet, GMC) and fewer models within each brand.

  a What research would you have done to determine which vehicle models GM should retain and which it should drop?

  b What would you have measured and with what type of measurement scale?

9 You have been asked to develop an index of student morale in your department.

  a What constructs or concepts might you employ?

  b Choose several of the major concepts, and specify their dimensions.

  c Select observable indicators that you might use to measure these dimensions.

  d How would you compile these various dimensions into a single index?

  e How would you judge the reliability and/or validity of these measurements?

10 After more than 75 years in the business, Walsworth Publishing's leadership was well aware of the efforts that go into juggling school work and the production of a high-quality school yearbook. They examined their communication and production processes and decided to implement the Information Builders' WebFOCUS-based reporting portal, an online dashboard. Each of the more than 4,000 schools had its own dashboard, and the volunteer student staff and faculty advisor could access the dashboard in real time. The online dashboard contained notices, progress toward deadlines, alerts about missing or corrupt content, and more. What should be the research measure(s) to determine the effectiveness of the new online dashboard process for improving efficiency and quality of each school's yearbook?

From Concept to Practice

11 Using Exhibit 10-3 and one of the case questionnaires from Connect match each question to its appropriate scale type. For each scale type not represented, develop a measurement question that would be of that scale type.

From the Headlines

12 Walmart recently asked Mondelez, owner of Oreos, to bring back a new-and-improved version of its 1990s cereal, Oreo O's. By studying social media comments, Walmart discovered a preference for cereal to address late-night snacking. What should Walmart measure during the initial 90-day relaunch, exclusive to its stores? At what level should it measure, and why?

>cases*

Campbell-Ewald: R-E-S-P-E-C-T Spells Loyalty

Data Development

Donatos: Finding the New Pizza

NCRCC: Teeing Up and New Strategic Direction

NetConversions Influences Kelley Blue Book

Ohio Lottery: Innovative Research Design Drives Winning

Pebble Beach Co.

Ramada Demonstrates Its *Personal Best*™

USTA: Come Out Swinging

Yahoo!: *Consumer Direct* Marries Purchase Metrics to Banner Ads

* You will find a description of each case in the Case Abstracts section of this textbook. Check the Case Index to determine whether a case provides data, the research instrument, video, or other supplementary material. Cases and case supplements are available in Connect.

>chapter 11

Stage 3: Measurement Questions

"We increase measurement error when we ask the wrong questions. The questions we ask need to be answerable, clear, unbiased, and easy to answer."

David F. Harris
president and author
Insight and Measurement
The Complete Guide to Writing Questionnaires: How to Get Better Information for Better Decisions

>learningobjectives

After reading this chapter, you should understand . . .

LO11-1   The role of a preliminary analysis plan in developing measurement questions.

LO11-2   The critical decisions involved in selecting an appropriate measurement scale for a measurement question.

LO11-3   The characteristics and use of various questions based on the categories of scales: rating, ranking, sorting, and other scales.

LO11-4   The factors that influence a specific measurement question.

>Instrument Design

The objective of instrument design process (Exhibit 11-1) is the **measurement instrument**—the compilation of measurement questions and nonquestion elements. It starts when the researcher assesses his information needs. It is a multiphase process.

In this chapter, we will explore Phase 1 of instrument design, the development of **measurement questions**—what the researcher will ask the participant or record about cases during a research study. Measurement questions can be written and designed in many ways. Even for a particular *variable*, there is always more than one way to ask the question. A **measurement scale** refers to the type of measurement question a researcher chooses to use to collect the data. To find or create just the right question, researchers often seek or draft multiple questions on a variable, each employing a different scale, then choose the one that gives them the appropriate measurement level for the analysis they want to perform. Conceptually, Phase 1 takes the researcher through the steps described in Exhibit 11-2. As earlier chapters discussed variables and measurement, we'll begin the discussion with the preliminary analysis plan.

>Prepare the Preliminary Analysis Plan

Central to the creation or selection of appropriate measurement questions is the **preliminary analysis plan**. It describes the procedures the researcher plans for the data he collects. These may include statistical summaries, cross-tabulations of variables to search for patterns, hypothesis tests, and measures of association, as well as graphical displays of data. The analytical procedures available to the researcher

>**Exhibit 11-1** Instrument Design in the Research Process

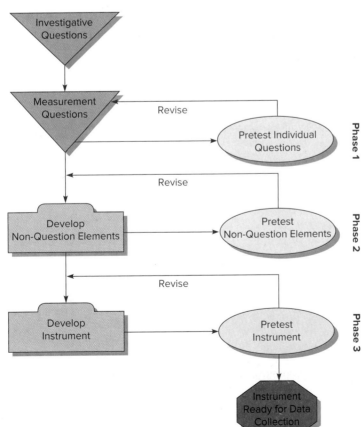

>**Exhibit 11-2** Instrument Design: Phase 1

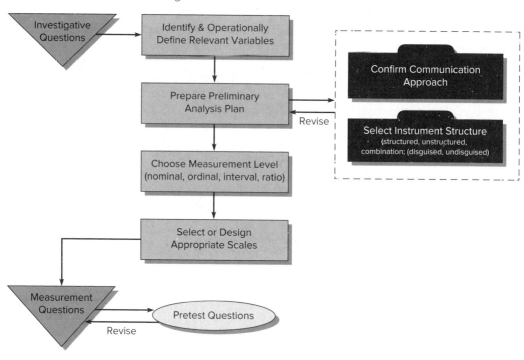

are determined by the scale types used in the instrument. Nominal, ordinal, interval, and ratio scales all have different characteristics that influence data analysis (statistical choices and hypothesis testing). Exhibit 11-3 provides a review of measurement scales by data levels. As Exhibit 11-2 clearly shows, it is important to plan the analysis before choosing a scale on which the measurement question will be based.

A good way to test how well the measurement questions will meet the needs of the analysis plan is to develop **dummy tables** during the preliminary analysis planning. Each table cross-tabulates two or more variables developed from the investigative needs. For example, *Parade Magazine* publishes

>**Exhibit 11-3** Summary of Scales by Data Levels

Scale Type	Characteristics	Empirical Operations
Nominal	Classification (mutually exclusive and collectively exhaustive categories), but no order, distance, or natural origin	• Count (frequency distribution); *mode* as central tendency; No measure of dispersion • Used with other variables to discern patterns, reveal relationships
Ordinal	Classification and order, but no distance or natural origin	• Determination of greater or lesser value • Count (frequency distribution); median as central tendency; nonparametric statistics
Interval	Classification, order, and distance (equal intervals), but no natural origin	• Determination of equality of intervals or differences • Count (frequency distribution); mean or median as measure of central tendency; measure of dispersion is standard deviation or interquartile range; parametric tests
Ratio	Classification, order, distance, and natural origin	• Determination of equality of ratios • Any of the above statistical operations, plus multiplication and division; mean as central tendency; coefficients of variation as measure of dispersion

>**Exhibit 11-4** Dummy Table for American Eating Habits

| Age | Use of Convenience Foods | | | | |
	Always Use	Use Frequently	Use Sometimes	Rarely Use	Never Use
18–24					
25–34					
35–44					
45–54					
55–64					
65+					

stories based on a biennial study of American eating habits.[1] To help make assignments to its writers, it might be interested to know whether age influences the use of convenience foods or whether those leading a healthy lifestyle eat fewer convenience foods. So it will develop a dummy table for each hypothesis (age by frequency of use of convenience foods; healthy lifestyle by frequency of use of convenience foods, etc.). Plotting the dummy table helps the researcher see what level of data is needed for each variable (e.g., ordinal data for age and frequency of use) and thus what types of scales would be appropriate for each question. Exhibit 11-4 shows a sample dummy table for the *Parade* study.

The number of hours spent on data analysis is a major cost of any research project. Too expansive a preliminary analysis plan can reveal unnecessary measurement questions. *The guiding principle of instrument design is always to ask* or *measure only what is needed.*

Confirm Communication Approach

Communication-based research may be conducted by personal interview, telephone, mail, computer (intranet and Internet), or some combination of these (called *hybrid studies*). Decisions regarding which method to use as well as where to interact with the participant (at home, at a neutral site, at the sponsor's place of business, etc.) will affect the design of the measurement instrument. In personal interviewing, as well as computer and mobile phone surveying, it is possible to use graphics and other questioning tools more easily than it is in questioning done by mail or regular phone. The different delivery mechanisms result in different introductions, instructions, instrument layout, and conclusions. For example, researchers may use intercept designs, conducting personal interviews with participants at central locations like shopping malls, stores, sports stadiums, amusement parks, or state fairs. The intercept study poses several instrument challenges.

We need to know the survey methodology before we design the measurement instrument because some measurement questions are difficult to answer without the visual aid of seeing the responses.

Select Instrument Structure

Question Structure

The various scale types offer options that include **unstructured questions** (or *free-response* or *open-ended questions*), which give participants the option of choosing their own words) and **structured questions** (or *closed questions*), where the specific response alternatives are provided. Unstructured questions range from those in which the participants express themselves extensively to those in which participants' latitude is restricted by space, layout, or instructions (e.g., choose one word or phrase, or answer in 40 characters or less).

Structured questions typically are categorized as dichotomous, multiple-choice, checklist, rating, or ranking response strategies. Several situational factors affect the decision of whether to use structured or unstructured questions. The factors include:

- Objectives of the study.
- Participant's level of information about the topic.
- Degree to which participant has thought through the topic.
- Ease with which participant communicates.
- Participant's motivation level to share information.

Participants often offer different alternatives than those provided in structured questions when asked questions in an unstructured way. That's why researchers sometimes pilot test a question in both ways, to be sure they include the appropriate response options within structured questions.[2]

Disguising Objectives and Sponsors

Another consideration in communication instrument design is whether the purpose of the study should be disguised. A **disguised question** is designed to conceal the question's true purpose. Some degree of disguise is often present in survey questions, especially to shield the study's sponsor. We disguise the sponsor and the objective of a study if the researcher believes that participants will respond differently than they would if both or either was known.

The accepted wisdom among researchers is that they must disguise the study's objective or sponsor in order to obtain unbiased data. The decision about when to use disguised questions within surveys may be made easier by identifying four situations where disguising the study objective is or is not an issue:

- Willingly shared, conscious-level information.
- Reluctantly shared, conscious-level information.
- Knowable, limited-conscious-level information.
- Subconscious-level information.

In surveys requesting conscious-level information that should be willingly shared, either disguised or undisguised questions may be used, but the situation rarely requires disguised techniques.

Example: Have you attended the showing of a foreign language film in the last six months?

Sometimes the participant knows the information we seek but is reluctant to share it for a variety of reasons. Exhibit 11-7 in the next section offers additional insights as to why participants might not be entirely honest. When we ask for an opinion on some topic on which participants may hold a socially unacceptable view, we often use projective techniques. In this type of disguised question, the researcher phrases the questions in a hypothetical way or asks how other people in the participant's experience would answer the question. We use projective techniques so that participants will express their true feelings and avoid giving stereotyped answers. The assumption is that responses to these questions will indirectly reveal the participants' opinions.

Example: Have you downloaded copyrighted music from the Internet without paying for it? (nonprojective)

Example: Do you know people who have downloaded copyrighted music from the Internet without paying for it? (projective)

Not all information is at the participant's conscious level. Given some time—and motivation—the participant can express this information. Asking about individual attitudes when participants know they hold the attitude but have not explored why they hold the attitude may encourage the use of disguised questions. A classic example is a study of government bond buying during World War II.[3] A survey sought reasons why, among people with equal ability to buy, some bought more war bonds than others. Frequent buyers had been personally solicited to buy bonds, while most infrequent buyers had not received personal solicitation. No direct *why* question to participants could have provided the answer to this question because participants did not know they were receiving differing solicitation approaches.

Example: What is it about air travel during stormy weather that attracts you?

In assessing buying behavior, we accept that some motivations are subconscious. This is true for attitudinal information as well. Seeking insight into the basic motivations underlying attitudes or consumption practices may or may not require disguised techniques. Projective techniques (such as sentence completion tests, cartoon or balloon tests, and word association tests) thoroughly disguise the study objective, but they are often difficult to interpret.

Example: Would you say, then, that the comment you just made indicates you would or would not be likely to shop at Galaxy Stores? (survey probe during personal interview)

>Select or Craft a Measurement Scale

Technology has affected the instrument development process, not just the method of the survey's delivery. Today's software, hardware, and Internet and intranet infrastructures allow researchers to (1) write instruments more quickly by tapping question banks for appropriate, tested questions and templates of instruments; (2) create visually driven instruments that enhance the process for the participant; (3) use questionnaire software to guide the process and eliminate separate manual data entry; and (4) build questionnaires that save time in data analysis.[4]

Selecting and constructing a measurement question requires choosing an appropriate scale (Exhibit 11-5). The appropriateness of a scale requires the consideration of several factors that influence the reliability,

>**Exhibit 11-5** Measurement Questions: Select the Scales

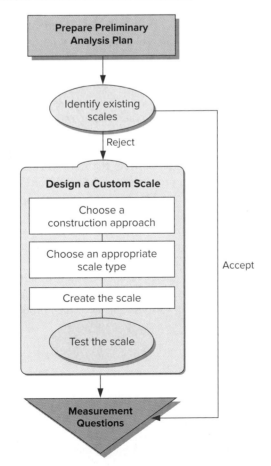

validity, and practicality of the scale. In developing the preliminary analysis plan, we examined the role of the first two:

- Research objectives.
- Response types.
- Number of dimensions.
- Balanced or unbalanced.
- Forced or unforced choices.
- Number of scale points.
- Rater errors.

Research Objectives

Research study objectives are too numerous to list (including, but not limited to studies of attitude, attitude change, persuasion, awareness, purchase intention, cognition and action, and actual and repeat actions). Researchers, however, face two general types of scaling objectives:

- To measure characteristics of the participants who participate in the study.
- To use participants as judges of the indicants of *objects* or *properties* presented to them.

Assume you are conducting a study of employees concerning their attitudes toward a change in corporate identity (a company logo, signage, letterhead, web page, etc.). With the first study objective, your scale would measure the employees' orientation as favorable or unfavorable. You might combine each person's answers to form an indicator of overall favorableness. The emphasis in this first study is on measuring attitudinal differences among people. With the second objective, you might use the same data, but you are now interested in how satisfied people are with different design options. Each participant is asked to choose the object he or she favors or the preferred solution. Participants judge which *object* has more of some characteristic or which design solution is closest to the company's stated objectives.

Response Types

Measurement scales fall into one of four general types: rating, ranking, categorization, and sorting. A **rating scale** is used when participants score an *object*, *property*, or its indicant without making a direct comparison to another object. For example, they may be asked to evaluate the styling of a new automobile on a 7-point rating scale. **Ranking scales** constrain the study participant to making comparisons and determining order among two or more properties (or their indicants) or objects. Participants may be asked to choose which one of a pair of cars has more attractive styling. A *choice* scale requires that participants choose one alternative over another. They could also be asked to rank-order the importance of comfort, ergonomics, performance, and price for a particular vehicle. **Categorization** asks participants to put themselves or property indicants in groups or categories. Asking auto show attendees to identify their gender or ethnic background or to indicate whether a particular prototype design would appeal to a youthful or mature driver would require a category response strategy. **Sorting** requires that participants sort objects or properties on some criterion. For example, participants might be handed cards that contain photos or images or verbal statements of various vehicles or their properties, and asked to sort them based on performance.

Number of Dimensions

Measurement scales are either *unidimensional* or *multidimensional*. With a **unidimensional scale**, one seeks to measure only one attribute of the participant or object. One measure of an actor's "star power" (a hypothetical construct) is his or her ability to "carry" a movie. It is a single dimension. Several items may be used to measure this dimension and by combining them into a single measure, an agent may place clients along a linear continuum of star power. A **multidimensional scale** recognizes that an object might be better described with several dimensions than on a unidimensional continuum. The actor's star power might be better expressed by other distinct dimensions—tickets sold for his or her last three movies, speed of attracting financial resources, number of scripts received, number of lead roles offered, and media buzz (media coverage, Tweets, YouTube videos) on his or her last three movies.

Balanced or Unbalanced

A **balanced rating scale** has an equal number of categories above and below the midpoint. Generally, rating scales should be balanced, with an equal number of favorable and unfavorable response choices. However, scales may be balanced with or without an indifference or midpoint option. A balanced scale might take the form of "very good—good—average—poor—very poor." An **unbalanced rating scale** has an unequal number of favorable and unfavorable response choices. An example of an unbalanced scale that has only one unfavorable descriptive term and four favorable terms is "poor—fair—good—very good—excellent." The scale designer expects that the mean ratings will be near "good" (as it is the center-most position on the scale) and that there will be a symmetrical distribution of answers around that point, but the scale does not allow participants who are unfavorable to express the intensity of their attitude.

The use of an unbalanced rating scale can be justified in studies in which a researcher knows in advance that nearly all participants' scores will lean in one direction or the other. Raters are inclined to score attitude objects higher if the objects are very familiar and if they are ego-involved.[5] Brand-loyal customers are also expected to respond favorably. When researchers know that one side of the scale is not likely to be used, they try to achieve precision on the side that will most often receive the participant's attention. Unbalanced scales are also considered when participants are known to be either "easy raters" or "hard raters." An unbalanced scale can help compensate for the **error of leniency** (participant ratings are consistently overly positive) and an **error of strictness** (participant ratings are consistently overly negative).

Forced or Unforced Choices

A **forced-choice rating scale** requires that participants select one of the offered alternatives. However, not all participants will have an opinion on every *object* or *property*, or their attitude will not be strong. An **unforced-choice rating scale** provides participants with an opportunity to express no opinion when they are unable to make a choice among the alternatives offered. Researchers often exclude the response choice "no opinion," "undecided," "don't know," "uncertain," or "neutral" when they know that most participants have an attitude on the topic. It is reasonable in this circumstance to constrain participants so that they focus on alternatives carefully and do not idly choose the middle position. However, when many participants are clearly undecided and the scale does not allow them to express their uncertainty, the forced-choice scale biases results. Researchers discover such bias when a larger percentage of participants express an attitude than did so in previous studies on the same issue. Some of this bias is attributable to participants providing meaningless responses or reacting to questions about which they have no attitudes. This affects the statistical measures of the mean and median, which shift toward the scale's midpoint, making it difficult to discern attitudinal differences throughout the instrument.[6] Understanding neutral answers is a challenge for researchers. In a customer satisfaction study that focused on the overall satisfaction question with a company in the electronics industry, an unforced scale was used. Study results, however, revealed that 75 percent of those in the "neutral" participant group could be converted to brand loyalists if the company excelled (received highly favorable ratings) on only 2 of the 26 other scaled questions in the study.[7] Thus, the participants in the neutral group weren't truly neutral, and a forced-choice scale would have revealed the desired information.

Number of Scale Points

What is the ideal number of points for a rating scale? A scale should be appropriate for its purpose. For a scale to be useful, it should match the stimulus presented and extract information proportionate to the complexity of the attitude object (concept, or construct). A product that requires little effort

>**Exhibit 11-6** Characteristics of Scale Types

Characteristic	Dichotomous	Multiple Choice	Checklist	Rating	Ranking	Free Response
Data level	Nominal	Nominal, ordinal, or ratio	Nominal	Ordinal or interval*	Ordinal	Nominal or ratio
Usual number of answer alternatives provided	2	3 to 10	10 or fewer	3 to 7	10 or fewer	None
Desired number of participant answers	1	1	10 or fewer	1 per item	7 or fewer	1
Used to provide . . .	Classification	Classification, order, or specific numerical estimate	Classification	Order or distance	Order	Classification, (of idea), order, or specific numerical estimate

* Researchers differ in the ways they treat data from certain scales. If you are unable to establish the linearity of the measured variables or you cannot be confident that you have equal intervals, it is proper to treat data from these scales as ordinal.

or thought to purchase, is habitually bought, or has a benefit that fades quickly (low-involvement products like gum or candy) can be measured generally with a simple scale. A 3-point scale (better than average—average—worse than average) is probably sufficient for a deodorant, a fast-food burger, gift-wrapping, or a snack. There is little support for choosing a scale with 5 or more points in this instance. But when the issue is complex, plays an important role in the consumer's life, and is costly (e.g., financial security, job satisfaction, job safety, job harassment), a scale with 5 to 11 points should be considered.

The characteristics of *reliability* and *validity* are important factors affecting measurement decisions.[8]

- As the number of scale points increases, the *reliability* of the measure increases.[9]
- Scales with more points may produce more valid results. Some studies, using scales with 11 points produced more *valid* results than 3-, 5-, or 7-point scales.[10]
- Some objects require greater measurement sensitivity and the opportunity to extract more variance, which additional scale points provide.
- A larger number of scale points are needed to produce accuracy when using single-dimension versus multiple-dimension scales.[11]
- In cross-cultural measurement, the cultural practices may condition participants to a standard metric—a 10-point scale in Italy, for example.

Exhibit 11-6 previews the scales discussed in this chapter along with the characteristics of scale types.

Participant Errors

The value of rating scales depends on the assumption that a person can and will make good judgments in answering the questions. Before accepting participants' ratings, we should consider their tendencies to make errors of central tendency and halo effect.[12] Some raters are reluctant to give extreme judgments, and this fact accounts for the **error of central tendency**. Participants may also be consistently "easy raters" (*error of leniency*) or consistently "hard raters" (*error of strictness*). These errors most often occur when the rater does not know the object or property being rated. To address these tendencies, researchers can:

- Adjust the strength of descriptive adjectives that anchor a scale.
- Space the intermediate descriptive phrases farther apart.
- Provide smaller differences in meaning between the steps near the ends of the scale than between the steps near the center.
- Use more points in the scale.

>**Exhibit 11-7** Factors That Affect Participant Honesty*

Syndrome	Description	Example
Peacock	Desire to be perceived as smarter, wealthier, happier, or better than others.	Respondents who claim to shop Harrods in London (twice as many as those who do).
Pleaser	Desire to help by providing answers they think the researchers want to hear, to please or avoid offending or being socially stigmatized.	Respondents give a politically correct or assumed correct answer about degree to which they revere their elders, respect their spouse, etc.
Gamer	Adaption of answers to play the system.	Participants who fake membership to a specific demographic to participate in high remuneration study; that they drive an expensive car when they don't or that they have cancer when they don't.
Disengager	Don't want to think deeply about a subject.	Participants who falsify ad recall or purchase behavior (didn't recall or didn't buy) when they actually did.
Self-delusionist	Participants who lie to themselves.	Respondents who falsify behavior, such as the level they recycle.
Unconscious decision maker	Participants who are dominated by irrational decision making.	Respondents who cannot predict with any certainty their future behavior.
Ignoramus	Participant who never knew or doesn't remember an answer.	Respondents who provide false information—such as they can't identify on a map where they live or remember what they ate for supper the previous evening.

The **halo effect** is the systematic bias that the rater introduces by carrying over a generalized impression of the subject from one rating to another. An instructor expects the student who does well on the first question of an examination to do well on the second. You conclude a report is good because you like its form, or you believe someone is intelligent because you agree with him or her. Halo effect is especially difficult to avoid when the property being studied is not clearly defined, is not easily observed, is not frequently discussed, involves reactions with others, or is a trait of high moral importance.[13] Ways of counteracting the halo effect include having the participant rate one trait at a time, revealing one trait per page (as in an Internet or mobile survey, where the participant cannot return to change his or her answer), or periodically reversing the terms that anchor the endpoints of the scale, so positive attributes are not always on the same end of each scale.

Exhibit 11-7 summarizes other factors that affect participant honesty.

>The Nature of Attitudes

In business, research is generally conducted to measure behavior, knowledge, and attitudes. Questions also measure characteristics and status of the participants (e.g., age, income, education level, employment status, type of car one drives, housing type, etc.). Developing questions that measure attitudes are some of the most difficult. So, we will use attitudes to develop your understanding of the process of scale selection and question development.

An **attitude** is a learned, stable predisposition to respond to oneself, other persons, objects, or issues in a consistently favorable or unfavorable way.[14] Important aspects of this definition include the learned nature of attitudes, their relative permanence, and their association with socially significant events and objects. Because an attitude is a *predisposition*, it would seem that the more favorable one's attitude is toward something (e.g., an object, issue, behavior, person), the more likely one would embrace it, and behave accordingly (e.g., acquire the product, vote for the issue, exercise, form a friendship). But, as we will see, that is not always the case.

Let's use an example to illustrate the nature of attitudes:

1. Sally is convinced that Apple has great talent, terrific products, and superior opportunities for growth.

2. Sally loves working at Apple.

3. Sally expects to stay with the firm and work hard to achieve rapid promotions for greater visibility and influence.

The first statement is an example of a *cognitively* based attitude. It represents Sally's memories, evaluations, and beliefs about the properties of the object. A *belief* is an estimate (probability) about the truth of something. In this case, it is the likelihood that the characteristics she attributes to her work environment are true. The statement "I think the cellular market will expand rapidly to incorporate radio and video" is also derived from cognition and belief.

The second statement above is an *affectively* based attitude. It represents Sally's feelings, intuition, values, and emotions toward the object. "I love the Yankees" and "I hate broccoli" are other examples of emotionally-oriented attitudes.

Researchers recognize a third component, *conative* or behaviorally based attitudes. The third statement reflects Sally's expectations and behavioral intentions toward her firm and the instrumental behaviors necessary to achieve her future goals. "I plan to buy a Lexus" or "I intend to see (blank) movie" are examples of a conative attitudinal statement. If we choose one particular type of scale, we can craft multiple attitudinal statements and ask participants the degree to which they agree with them.

The Relationship between Attitudes and Behavior

In crafting a measurement scale designed to measure attitudes, you need to know that while attitudes lead to behavioral intentions they do not always lead to actual behaviors. Moreover, behaviors can influence attitudes. For example, a positive experience with a product or service reinforces a positive attitude or makes a customer question a negative attitude. This is one reason that restaurants where you have a bad dining experience may give you a coupon for a free meal on your next visit or may tell you your meal is free. They know a bad experience contributes mightily to formation of negative attitudes.

Business researchers treat attitudes as a **hypothetical construct**—a construct inferred only from data, not observed directly—because of its complexity. Researchers are cautious about the ways certain aspects of measured attitudes predict behavior. Several factors have an effect on the applicability of attitudinal research:

- Specific attitudes are better predictors of behavior than general ones.

- Strong attitudes are better predictors of behavior than weak attitudes composed of little intensity or topical interest. Strength is affected by *accessibility* (how well the object is remembered and brought to consciousness), how extreme the attitude is, the degree of confidence in it, and its personal relevance—how it relates to a person's self-interest.

- Direct experiences with the attitude object (when the attitude is formed, during repeated exposure, or through reminders) produce behavior more reliably.

- Attitudes have three components: affective (emotion based), behavioral (experience based), and cognitive (knowledge based).

- Cognitive-based attitudes influence behaviors better than affective-based attitudes.

- Affective-based attitudes are often better predictors of consumption behaviors.

- Using multiple measurements of attitude or several behavioral assessments across time and environments improves prediction.

- The influence of reference groups (interpersonal support, urges of compliance, peer pressure) and the individual's inclination to conform to these influences improves the attitude-behavior linkage.[15]

Researchers measure and analyze attitudes because attitudes offer insights about behavior. Many of the attitude measurement scales used have been tested for reliability and validity, but often we craft unique scales that don't share those standards. An example is an instrument that measures attitudes about a particular tourist attraction, employment policy, product, or candidate, as well as the person's intention to attend an event, buy, or vote in a union election. Neither the attitude nor the behavioral intent, alone or together, is effective in predicting the person's actual behavior if the measurement question used to assess it has not been designed carefully. Nevertheless, managers know that the measurement of attitudes is important because attitudes reflect past experience and shape future behavior.

Attitude Scaling

Scaling is the "procedure for the assignment of numbers (or other symbols) to a *property* of *objects* in order to impart some of the characteristics of numbers to the properties in question."[16] **Attitude scaling** then is the process of assessing a person's disposition (from an extremely favorable disposition to an extremely unfavorable one) toward an *object* or its *properties* using a number that represents a person's score on an attitudinal continuum range. Procedurally, we assign numbers to an *indicants* of the property of objects. For example, lots of people complain about the weather. To do so, one assigns a number scale to the various levels of heat and cold and calls it a thermometer. To measure the temperature of the air, you know that a property of temperature is that its variation leads to an expansion or contraction of mercury. A glass tube with mercury provides an *indicant* of temperature change by the rise or fall of the mercury in the tube. Similarly, during your college search, your attitude toward a university could be measured on numerous scales that capture indicants of the different dimensions of your awareness, feelings, or behavioral intentions toward the school.

>Rating Questions

We use rating scales to create **rating questions** to judge properties of objects without reference to other similar objects. These ratings may be in such forms as "like–dislike," "approve–indifferent–disapprove," or other responses using even more categories. For example, a researcher asks questions about participants' attitudes toward the taste of a soft drink. The responses are "thirst quenching," "sour," "strong bubbly," "orange taste," and "syrupy." These answers alone do not provide a means of discerning the degree of favorability and thus would be of limited value to the researcher. However, with a properly constructed scale, the researcher could develop a taste profile for the target brand.

Examples of rating scales we discuss in this section are shown as measurement questions in Exhibit 11-8. Because this exhibit serves as an overview of in this section, we will refer you to the exhibit frequently.[17] When we develop a measurement question, we describe it by its scale name. So, a multiple-choice question is developed using a multiple-choice, single-response scale; a dichotomous-choice question uses a simple category scale; a checklist question, uses a multiple-choice, multiple-response scale, and so forth.

Simple Category Questions

Dichotomous-choice questions are developed using a simple category scale. The **simple category scale** (also called a *dichotomous scale*) offers two mutually exclusive response choices. In Exhibit 11-8 they are "yes" and "no," but they could just as easily be "important" and "unimportant," "agree" and "disagree," or another set of discrete categories if the question were different. This response strategy is particularly useful for demographic questions or where a dichotomous response is adequate for categorization of the variable.

When there are multiple options for the participant but only one answer is sought, the question is built on a **multiple-choice, single-response scale** is appropriate to develop a **multiple-choice question**. Our example in Exhibit 11-8 has five options. The primary alternatives should encompass 90 percent of the range of responses, with the "other" category completing the participant's list. When there is no possibility for an "other" response or exhaustiveness of categories is not critical, the "other" response may be omitted. Both the multiple-choice, single-response scale and the simple category scale produce nominal data.

>**Exhibit 11-8** Sample Rating Scales as Measurement Questions

Simple Category Scale
(dichotomous)
data: nominal

"I plan to purchase tablet in the next 12 months."
☐ Yes
☐ No

**Multiple-Choice,
Single-Response Scale**
data: nominal

"What newspaper do you read most often for financial news?"
☐ *East City Gazette*
☐ *West City Tribune*
☐ Regional newspaper
☐ National newspaper
☐ Other (specify: _____)

**Multiple-Choice,
Multiple-Response
Scale** (checklist)
data: nominal

"Check *any* of the sources you consulted when designing your office."
☐ Online planning services
☐ Magazines
☐ Independent contractor/builder
☐ Developer's models/plans
☐ Designer
☐ Architect
☐ Other (specify: _____)

**Likert Scale
Summated Rating**
data: interval

"The Internet is superior to traditional libraries for comprehensive searches."

STRONGLY AGREE (5)	AGREE (4)	NEITHER AGREE NOR DISAGREE (3)	DISAGREE (2)	STRONGLY DISAGREE (1)

**Semantic Differential
Scale**
data: interval

Lands' End

FAST ___ : ___ : ___ : ___ : ___ : ___ : ___ : SLOW
HIGH QUALITY ___ : ___ : ___ : ___ : ___ : ___ : ___ : LOW QUALITY

Numerical Scale
data: ordinal or
interval*

EXTREMELY FAVORABLE   5   4   3   2   1   EXTREMELY UNFAVORABLE

Employee's cooperation in teams ____
Employee's knowledge of task ____
Employee's planning effectiveness ____

**Multiple Rating
List Scale**
data: ordinal or
interval

"Please indicate the importance of each service characteristic."

	IMPORTANT						UNIMPORTANT
Fast, reliable repair	7	6	5	4	3	2	1
Service at my location	7	6	5	4	3	2	1
Maintenance by manufacturer	7	6	5	4	3	2	1
Knowledgeable technicians	7	6	5	4	3	2	1
Notification of upgrades	7	6	5	4	3	2	1
Service contract after warranty	7	6	5	4	3	2	1

>**Exhibit 11-8** Sample Rating Scales as Measurement Questions (cont'd)

Constant-Sum Scale
data: ratio

> Take all the supplier characteristics we've just discussed together and now consider cost. Divide 100 points between the two, based on the relative importance of each.
>
> Being one of the lowest cost suppliers [   ]
>
> All other aspects of supplier performance [   ]
>
> Sum [100]

Stapel Scale
data: ordinal or*
interval

(Company Name)

+5	+5	+5
+4	+4	+4
+3	+3	+3
+2	+2	+2
+1	+1	+1
Technology Leader	Exciting Products	World-Class Reputation
−1	−1	−1
−2	−2	−2
−3	−3	−3
−4	−4	−4
−5	−5	−5

Graphic Rating Scale
data: ordinal or*
interval or ratio

> How likely are you to recommend (company) to others? (Place an X at the position on the line that best reflects your judgment.)
>
> VERY LIKELY |————————————————| VERY UNLIKELY

Visual Graphic Rating Scale
data: ordinal or*
interval or ratio

> How likely are you to recommend (company) to others? (Place an X at the position on the line that best reflects your judgment.)

* Researchers differ in the ways they treat data from certain scales. If you are unable to establish the linearity of the measured variables or you cannot be confident that you have equal intervals, it is proper to treat data from these scales as ordinal.

A question built on a variation, the **multiple-choice, multiple-response scale** (also called a *checklist*), allows the participant to select one or several alternatives. In the **checklist question** in Exhibit 11-8, we are measuring seven items with one question, and it is possible that all seven sources for office design assistance were consulted. The cumulative feature of this scale can be beneficial when a complete picture of the participant's choice is desired, but it may also present a problem for reporting when research sponsors expect the responses to sum to 100 percent. This scale generates nominal data.

Simple attitude scales are easy to develop, are inexpensive, and can be designed to be highly specific. They provide useful information and are adequate if developed skillfully. There are also weaknesses. The design approach is subjective. The researcher's insight and ability offer the only assurance that the *properties* chosen are a representative sample of the universe of attitudes about the attitude *object*. We have no evidence that each person will view all *properties* with the same frame of reference as will other people. Although custom-designed scales are frequently used, there has been a great effort to develop construction techniques that overcome some of their deficiencies.

Toluna and VOSS Measure Water

According to a Toluna survey, 58 percent of Americans tend to focus more on healthy lifestyle choices leading into the warmer months, and of those people, 61 percent say they try to drink more water. However, 39 percent of Americans have a hard time drinking water because of the lack of flavor. Norway artesian water supplier VOSS wanted to capitalize on this tendency to drink more water as well as their customers' loyalty to the brand and expressed interest—through social media—in more flavors.

VOSS wanted to assess adding two flavors to their sparkling water line-up: Lemon Cucumber and Tangerine Lemongrass. While delicious on their own, these two flavors could pair well with a large variety of foods, as well as be perfect complements to a variety of spirits. They turned to Toluna, a leading provider of on-demand, real-time digital consumer insights, for the assessment. Toluna draws on its 9 million-member social community and a robust mobile-optimized research platform to help companies worldwide survey attitudes and behavior. Its *Real-Time Research* can deliver a representative sample of more than 1,000 in hours rather than weeks, using the client's own questions.

For VOSS, in one six-hour period, Toluna surveyed 1,894 nationally representative respondents drawn from its proprietary panel. As panel members, Toluna already had a rich demographic profile on each participant, so the short survey focused on drawing out behavior and attitude information. "The VOSS survey contained just 11 questions," shared Daniel Enson, research director for Toluna. One single-response multiple choice question asked directly about water's lack of flavor:

When thinking of water, is the lack of flavor a turn-off for you?

> *Yes, I don't like water because of the lack of flavor.*
> *Yes, but I still try to drink water because it is healthy.*
> *I am indifferent about the lack of flavor in water.*
> *No, I like the taste of water.*
> *No, I drink water for reasons other than taste.*

Another single-response multiple-choice question assessed the types of foods participants ate when drinking spirits:

©John Lund/Sam Diephuis/Blend Images LLC

What types of food do you like to eat while you have a cocktail? Please select one.

> *Salty finger foods (peanuts, pretzels, etc.)*
> *Light finger foods (cheeses, bread & butter, chips and salsa, etc.)*
> *Heavy finger foods (chicken fingers, mozzarella sticks, etc.)*
> *Healthier appetizers (salads, veggies and dip, etc.)*
> *Bar food (burgers, nachos, fish & chips, etc.)*
> *Other types of food*

Several questions addressed drinking behaviors and motivation for drinking water (healthier lifestyle, losing weight, watching calories). And one question offered flavor options to consider:

What flavors do you associate with spring/summer time beverages and cocktails? Please select all that apply.

> *Lemon*
> *Cucumber*
> *Orange/Tangerine*
> *Strawberry*
> *Mint*
> *Other*

www.toluna-group.com; www.vosswater.com

>**pic**profile

Can you use social media research to discover a new pet food? Del Monte, the maker of Snausages, certainly thinks so. Using social media as a platform for launching discussions, Del Monte invited more than 300 dog lovers to its site and asked them a series of questions, including, "What does your dog eat for breakfast?" "Would you buy more treats for your dog if they contained vitamins and minerals?" A large number of the participants indicated their dogs preferred eggs and bacon for breakfast. These dog owners also tried to use foods that were rich in Omega 3, antioxidants, and vitamins. Using this research, Del Monte created Snausages Breakfast Bites, shaped like fried eggs and bacon strips and fortified to be nutritious with extra calcium, antioxidants, and Omega 3 and 6. It took just six weeks to bring this new snack food to market. Today you can find Snausages Breakfast Bites in every pet store in the country. **www.snausages.com**

Summated Rating Questions

The **Likert scale**, developed by Rensis Likert (pronounced Lick-ert), is the most frequently used variation of the summated rating question. Questions based on **summated rating scales** consist of statements that express either a favorable or an unfavorable attitude toward the object of interest. The participant is asked to agree or disagree with each statement. Each response is given a numerical score to reflect its degree of attitudinal favorableness, and the scores may be summed to measure the participant's overall attitude. Summation is *not* necessary and in some instances may actually be misleading, as our caution below clearly shows.

In Exhibit 11-8, the participant chooses one of five levels of agreement. This is the traditional Likert scale because it meets Likert's rules for construction and testing. The numbers indicate the value to be assigned to each possible answer, with 1 the least favorable impression of Internet superiority and 5 the most favorable. Likert scales may also use 7 and 9 scale points. Technically, such question is a Likert-type question as its construction is less rigorous than the process Likert created. However, the advantages of the 7- and 9- point scales are a better approximation of a normal response curve and extraction of more variability among respondents.

Conscientious researchers are careful that each item meets an empirical test for discriminating ability between favorable and unfavorable attitudes. Originally, creating a Likert scale involved a procedure known as *item analysis*. Exhibit 11-9 provides the steps for selecting Likert statements (items) for the scale using item analysis. The values for each choice are normally not part of the measurement instrument, but they are shown in Exhibit 11-10 to illustrate the scoring system.

Although item analysis is helpful in weeding out attitudinal statements that do not discriminate well, the summation procedure causes interpretation problems for researchers. The following example on website banner ads shows that the same summated score can mean different things:

1. This banner ad provides the relevant information I expect.

2. I would bookmark this site to use in the future.

>**Exhibit 11-9** How to Perform a Likert Item Analysis

Item analysis assesses each item (statement) in a Likert scale based on how well it discriminates between those people whose total score is high and those whose total score is low.

Step 1	Collect a large number of statements that meet the following criteria • Each statement is relevant to the attitude being studied. • Each statement reflects a favorable or unfavorable position on that attitude.
Step 2	Select people similar to study participants (participant stand-ins) to read each statement.
Step 3	Participant stand-ins indicate their level of their agreement with each statement, using a 5-point scale. A scale value of 1 indicates a strongly unfavorable attitude (strongly disagree). A value of 5 indicates a strongly favorable attitude (strongly agree). The other intensities, 2 (disagree), 3 (neither agree nor disagree), 4 (agree), are mid-range attitudes (see Exhibit 11-3). • To ensure consistent results, the assigned numerical values are reversed if the statement is worded negatively. The number 1 is always strongly unfavorable and 5 is always strongly favorable.
Step 4	Add each participant stand-in's responses to secure a total score.
Step 5	Array these total scores from highest to lowest; then and select some portion—generally defined as the top and bottom 10 to 25 percent of the distribution—to represent the highest and lowest total scores. • The two extreme groups represent people with the most favorable and least favorable attitudes toward the attitude being studied. These extremes are the two criterion groups by which individual Likert statements (items) are evaluated. • Discard the middle group's scores (50 to 80 percent of participant stand-ins), as they are not highly discriminatory on the attitude.
Step 6	Calculate the mean scores for each scale item among the low scorers and high scorers.
Step 7	Test the mean scores for statistical significance by computing a t value for each statement.
Step 8	Rank order the statements by their t values from highest to lowest.
Step 9	Select 20–25 statements (items) with the highest t values (statistically significant difference between mean scores) to include in the final Likert scale.

Researchers have found that a larger number of items for each attitude object improves the reliability of the Likert scale. As an approximate indicator of a statement's discrimination power, one authority suggests using only those statements whose t value is 1.75 or greater, provided there are 25 or more participant stand-ins in each group. See Exhibit 11-5 for an example.

Source: Adapted from Allen L. Edwards, *Techniques of Attitude Scale Construction* (New York: Appleton-Century-Crofts, 1957), pp. 152–54.

3. This banner ad is annoying.

4. I would click for deeper links to discover more details.

If a 5-point scale is used, the maximum favorable score would be 20 (assuming 5 is assigned to the strongly agree response and question 3, a negative, is reverse-scored). Approximately one-half of the statements are worded favorably and the other half unfavorably to safeguard against halo effects. The problem of summation arises because different patterns are concealed by the same total score. One participant could find the website's ad relevant, worth returning to, and somewhat pleasing but not desire deeper information, whereas another could find the ad annoying but have favorable attitudes on the other three questions, thereby producing the same total score.

The Likert scale has many advantages that account for its popularity. It is easy and quick to construct.[18] Likert scales are probably more reliable and provide a greater volume of data than many other scales. The scale produces interval data.

Any question that asks for levels of agreement, might have problems with **acquiescence bias** (a tendency for participants to agree with an item or statement). Less educated and less informed participants show more acquiescence bias.[19] An alternative question format, the paired comparison, diminishes this bias.

>**Exhibit 11-10** Evaluating a Scale Statement by Item Analysis

Response Categories	Low Total Score Group				High Total Score Group			
	X	f	fX	X(fX)	X	f	fX	X(fX)
① {Strongly agree	5	3	15	75	5	22	110	550
Agree	4	4	16	64	4	30	120	480
Undecided	3	29	87	261	3	15	45	135
Disagree	2	22	44	88	2	4	8	16
Strongly disagree}	1	15	15	15	1	2	2	2
Total		73	177	503 ←— ②—→		73	285	1,183
		n_L	ΣX_L	$\Sigma X(fX)_L$		n_H	ΣX_H	$\Sigma X(fX)_H$

$$\bar{X}_L = \frac{177}{73} = 2.42 \quad \longleftarrow \quad ③ \quad \longrightarrow \quad \bar{X}_H = \frac{285}{73} = 3.90$$

$$\Sigma(X_L - \bar{X}_L)^2 = 503 - \frac{(177)^2}{73} \quad \longleftarrow \quad ④ \quad \longrightarrow \quad \Sigma(X_H - \bar{X}_H)^2 = 1{,}183 - \frac{(285)^2}{73}$$

$$= 73.84 \qquad\qquad\qquad\qquad = 70.33$$

$$t = \frac{\bar{X}_H - \bar{X}_L}{\sqrt{\dfrac{\Sigma(X_H - \bar{X}_H)^2 + \Sigma(X_L - \bar{X}_L)^2}{n(n-1)}}} \quad \longleftarrow \quad ⑤$$

$$= \frac{3.90 - 2.42}{\sqrt{\dfrac{70.33 + 73.84}{73(73-1)}}}$$

$$= 8.92 \quad \longleftarrow \quad ⑥$$

Legend:

① For each of the response categories, the scale's value (X) is multiplied by the frequency or number of participants (f) who chose that value. These values produce the product (fX).This number is then multiplied by X. For example, there are 3 participants in the low-score group who scored a 5 (strongly agreed with the statement): (fX) = (3) (5) = 15; (X)(fX) = (5) (15) = 75.

② The frequencies and products are summed.

③ A mean score for each group is computed.

④ Deviation scores are computed, squared, and summed as required by the formula.

⑤ The data are tested in a modified t-test that compares high- and low-scoring groups for the item. Notice the mean scores in the numerator of the formula.

⑥ The calculated value is compared with a criterion, 1.75. If the calculated value (in this case, 8.92) is equal to or exceeds the criterion, the statement is said to be a good discriminator of the measured attitude. (If it is less than the criterion, we would consider it a poor discriminator of the target attitude and delete it from the measuring instrument.) We then select the next measurement item and repeat the process.

For the statement "My digital camera's features are exciting," we select the data from the bottom 25 percent of the distribution (low total score group) and the top 25 percent (high total score group). There are 73 people in each group. The remaining 50 percent of the middle of the distribution is not considered for this analysis.

Semantic Differential Questions

Questions based on the **semantic differential (SD) scale** measure the psychological meanings of an attitude object using bipolar adjectives. The SD scale is based on the proposition that an object can have several dimensions of connotative meaning. The meanings are located in multidimensional property space, called *semantic space*. Connotative meanings are suggested or implied meanings, in addition to the explicit meaning of an object. For example, a roaring fire in a fireplace may connote

Maritz Discovers Better Way to Measure Customer Satisfaction

Customer satisfaction in the service industries has long been measured by asking for a rating on overall satisfaction, followed by ratings of satisfaction with various influential attributes. These ratings are usually provided on a 5- or 7-point scale. Researchers at Maritz Research, long a leader in ground-breaking research methodology, believe they have discovered a better approach. They've named the approach "Make or Break" customer satisfaction.

The new questionnaire moves to a noncompensatory model in asking questions. Participants at a hotel, for example, are asked first to scale their overall satisfaction. Then, rather than asking satisfied customers to evaluate a series of attributes individually using that same scale, they are asked to identify from a series of attributes if ONE made their experience so wonderful as to make them ignore any deficiencies in other attributes. Dissatisfied customers are treated similarly. They are presented the same attributes but asked to identify if ONE made their experience so horrendous that no positives in the other attributes could save the overall experience from being terrible. Only after this initial checklist question is each participant asked to evaluate remaining attributes on the provided scale.

1. Please indicate how satisfied you were with your (blank experience) using the scale below: [1] Completely Satisfied, [2] Somewhat Satisfied, [3] Neither Satisfied Nor Dissatisfied, [4] Somewhat Dissatisfied, [5] Dissatisfied.
2a. If 1 to 3, ask: Was the performance on any of these aspects so **good** as, all by itself, to make your overall (blank experience) satisfactory?
2b. If 4 or 5, ask: Was the performance on any of these aspects so **bad** as, all by itself, to make your overall (blank experience) unsatisfactory?

List of aspects followed.

Only after this initial gridded checklist question are respondents asked to evaluate any attributes not mentioned in 2a or 2b on the provided scale.

Maritz has conducted several split-sample tests, in several industries, that demonstrate the new measurement questions are able to better predict customer return behavior. It also provides managers with evidence of the importance, either negative or positive, of critical customer service attributes.
www.maritzcx.com

romantic as well as its more explicit meaning of *burning flammable material within a brick kiln*. One restaurant trying to attract patrons on slow Tuesday evenings offered a special Tuesday menu and called it "down-home cooking." Yankee pot roast, stew, and chicken pot pie, although not its usual cuisine, carried the connotative meaning of *comfort foods* and brought patrons into the restaurant, making Tuesday one of the busiest nights of the week. Advertisers, salespeople, and product and package designers have long known that they must use words, shapes, associations, and images to activate a person's connotative meanings.

Osgood and his associates developed the semantic differential method to measure the psychological meanings of an object to an individual.[20] They produced a list of 289 bipolar adjective pairs, which were reduced to 76 pairs and formed into rating scales for attitude research. Their analysis allowed them to conclude that semantic space is multidimensional rather than unidimensional. Three factors contributed most to meaningful judgments by participants: (1) evaluation, (2) potency, and (3) activity. This means any semantic differential question must contain adjective pairs that cover all three dimensions. The pairs from the historical thesaurus study (Exhibit 11-11) illustrate the wide applicability of the technique to persons, abstract concepts, events, institutions, and physical objects.[21]

Business researchers often developed their own adjective or phrase pairs and have focused on the evaluative dimension more often than potency or activity. The positive benefit is that the questions created are specific to management questions. One study explored a retail store image using 35 pairs of words or phrases classified into eight groups. These word pairs were especially created for the study. Excerpts from this scale are presented in Exhibit 11-12. Other categories of scale items were "general characteristics of the company," "physical characteristics of the store," "prices charged by the store," "store personnel," "advertising by the store," and "your friends and the store." Because the scale pairs are closely associated with the characteristics of the store and its use, one could develop image profiles of various stores.

>**Exhibit 11-11** Results of the Thesaurus Study

Evaluation (E)	Potency (P)	Activity (A)	
Good–bad	Hard–soft	Active–passive	
Positive–negative	Strong–weak	Fast–slow	
Optimistic–pessimistic	Heavy–light	Hot–cold	
Complete–incomplete	Masculine–feminine	Excitable–calm	
Timely–untimely	Severe–lenient		
	Tenacious–yielding		
Subcategories of Evaluation			
Meek Goodness	**Dynamic Goodness**	**Dependable Goodness**	**Hedonistic Goodness**
Clean–dirty	Successful–unsuccessful	True–false	Pleasurable–painful
Kind–cruel	High–low	Reputable–disreputable	Beautiful–ugly
Sociable–unsociable	Meaningful–meaningless	Believing–skeptical	Sociable–unsociable
Light–dark	Important–unimportant	Wise–foolish	Meaningful–meaningless
Altruistic–egotistical	Progressive–regressive	Healthy–sick	
Grateful–ungrateful	Clean–dirty		
Beautiful–ugly			
Harmonious–dissonant			

Source: Adapted from Charles E. Osgood, G. J. Suci, and P. H. Tannenbaum, *The Measurement of Meaning* (Urbana: University of Illinois Press, 1957), table 5, pp. 52–61.

The semantic differential has several advantages. It is an efficient and easy way to secure attitudes from a large sample. These attitudes may be measured in both direction and intensity. The total set of responses provides a comprehensive picture of the meaning of an object and a measure of the person doing the rating. It is a standardized technique that is easily repeated but escapes many problems of response distortion found with more direct methods. It produces interval data. Basic instructions for constructing an SD scale are found in Exhibit 11-13.

>**Exhibit 11-12** Adapting SD Scales for Retail Store Image Study

Convenience of Reaching the Store from Your Location	
Nearby	____:____:____:____:____:____:____: Distant
Short time required to reach store	____:____:____:____:____:____:____: Long time required to reach store
Difficult drive	____:____:____:____:____:____:____: Easy drive
Difficult to find parking place	____:____:____:____:____:____:____: Easy to find parking place
Convenient to other stores I shop	____:____:____:____:____:____:____: Inconvenient to other stores I shop

Products Offered	
Wide selection of different kinds of products	____:____:____:____:____:____:____: Limited selection of different kinds of products
Fully stocked	____:____:____:____:____:____:____: Understocked
Undependable products	____:____:____:____:____:____:____: Dependable products
High quality	____:____:____:____:____:____:____: Low quality
Numerous brands	____:____:____:____:____:____:____: Few brands
Unknown brands	____:____:____:____:____:____:____: Well-known brands

Source: Robert F. Kelly and Ronald Stephenson, "The Semantic Differential: An Information Source for Designing Retail Patronage Appeals," *Journal of Marketing* 31 (October 1967), p. 45.

>**Exhibit 11-13** How to Construct an SD Scale

Step 1	Select the variable; chosen by judgment and reflects the nature of the investigative question.
Step 2	Identify possible nouns, noun phrases, adjectives, or visual stimuli to represent the variable.
Step 3	Select bipolar word pairs, phrase pairs, or visual pairs appropriate to assess the *object* or *property*. If the traditional Osgood adjectives are used, several criteria guide your selection: • Choose adjectives that allow connotative perceptions to be expressed. • Choose three bipolar pairs for each dimension: evaluation, potency, and activity. (Scores on the individual items can be averaged, by factor, to improve reliability.) • Choose pairs that will be *stable* across participants and variables. (One pair that fails this test is "large–small"; may describe a property when judging a physical object such as automobile but may be used connotatively with abstract concepts such as product quality.) • Choose pairs that are *linear* between polar opposites and passes through the origin. (A pair that fails this test is "rugged–delicate," which is nonlinear as both objectives have favorable meanings.)
Step 4	Create the scoring system and assign a positive value to each point on the scale. (Most SD scales have 7 points with values of 7, 6, 5, 4, 3, 2, and 1. A "0" point is arbitrary.)
Step 5	Randomly select half the pairs and reverse score them to minimize the *halo effect*.
Step 6	Order the bipolar pairs so all representing a single dimension (e.g. evaluation) are not together in the final measurement question.

Source: This instructional table is developed from material included in Charles E. Osgood, G. J. Suci, and P. H. Tannenbaum, *The Measurement of Meaning* (Urbana: University of Illinois Press, 1957).

In Exhibit 11-14, an SD question is being used by a panel of corporate leaders evaluating candidates for a high-level position in their industry's lobbying association. The selection of the concepts is driven by the characteristics they believe the candidate must possess to be successful in advancing their industry's agenda. There are three candidates.

Based on the panel's requirements, researchers choose 10 bipolar pairs to score the three candidates. The letters along the left side, which show the relevant attitude dimension, would be omitted from the actual scale, as would the numerical values shown. Note that the bipolar pairs representing evaluation, potency, and activity scales are mixed, so that the items representing one dimension are not together.

To analyze the results, the set of evaluation (E) values is averaged, as are those for the potency (P) and activity (A) dimensions. The data are plotted in a "snake diagram" in Exhibit 11-15. For data presentation, the adjective pairs are reordered so that the bipolar pairs representing evaluation, potency, and activity are grouped together, with the ideal factor reflected by the left side of the scale.

>**Exhibit 11-14** SD Scale for Analyzing Industry Association Candidates

Analyze (candidate) for current position:

(E)	Sociable	(7): ___ : ___ : ___ : ___ : ___ : ___ : ___ : (1)	Unsociable
(P)	Weak	(1): ___ : ___ : ___ : ___ : ___ : ___ : ___ : (7)	Strong
(A)	Active	(7): ___ : ___ : ___ : ___ : ___ : ___ : ___ : (1)	Passive
(E)	Progressive	(7): ___ : ___ : ___ : ___ : ___ : ___ : ___ : (1)	Regressive
(P)	Yielding	(1): ___ : ___ : ___ : ___ : ___ : ___ : ___ : (7)	Tenacious
(A)	Slow	(1): ___ : ___ : ___ : ___ : ___ : ___ : ___ : (7)	Fast
(E)	True	(7): ___ : ___ : ___ : ___ : ___ : ___ : ___ : (1)	False
(P)	Heavy	(7): ___ : ___ : ___ : ___ : ___ : ___ : ___ : (1)	Light
(A)	Hot	(7): ___ : ___ : ___ : ___ : ___ : ___ : ___ : (1)	Cold
(E)	Unsuccessful	(1): ___ : ___ : ___ : ___ : ___ : ___ : ___ : (7)	Successful

>**Exhibit 11-15** Graphic Representation of SD Analysis

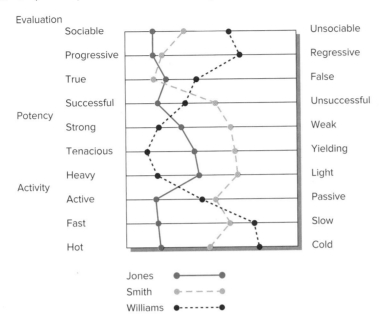

Numerical/Multiple Rating List Questions

Questions built using **numerical scales** have equal intervals that separate each numeric scale point, as shown in Exhibit 11-8. The verbal anchors serve as the labels for the extreme points. Numerical scales are often 5-point scales but may have 7 or 10 points. The participants enter a number from the scale next to each item. If numerous questions about a product's performance were included in the example, the scale would provide both an absolute measure of importance and a relative measure (ranking) of the various items rated. The scale's linearity, simplicity, and production of ordinal or interval data make it popular with managers and researchers. When evaluating a new product concept, purchase intent is frequently measured with a 5- to 7-point numerical scale, with the anchors being "definitely would buy" and "definitely would not buy."

Questions built using a **multiple rating list scale** (Exhibit 11-8) are similar to numerical scale questions but differ in two ways: (1) the question accepts a circled or highlighted response from the participant, and (2) the layout facilitates visualization of the results. The advantage is that a mental map of the participant's evaluations is evident to both the participant and the researcher. This scale produces interval data.

Stapel Scale Questions

Questions built using the **Stapel scale** are used as an alternative to semantic differential questions, especially when it is difficult to find bipolar adjectives that match the investigative question. In the example in Exhibit 11-8, there are three attributes of corporate image. The scale is composed of the word (or phrase) identifying the image dimension and a set of 10 response categories for each of the three attributes. Ratings range from +5 to −5, with participants selecting a number that describes the company very accurately to very inaccurately. The more accurate the description, the larger is the positive number. Similarly, the less accurate the description, the larger is the negative number chosen. Fewer response categories are sometimes used. Like the Likert, SD, and numerical scales, questions designed as Stapel scales usually produce interval data.

Constant-Sum Questions

A question that helps the researcher discover proportions is one based on the **constant-sum scale**. With a constant-sum question, the participant is asked to allocate points to more than one attribute or property indicant, such that they total a constant sum, usually 100 or 10. In the Exhibit 11-8 example, two categories are presented that must sum to 100. In the restaurant example, the participant distributes 100 points among four categories:

> You have 100 points to distribute among the following characteristics of the Dallas Steakhouse. Indicate the relative importance of each attribute in making your decision to eat at the restaurant; the more points you give the attribute, the more important the attribute in your decision.
>
> _____ Food Quality
> _____ Atmosphere
> _____ Service
> _____ Price
> 100 TOTAL

Up to 10 properties of the object may be used in a constant-sum question, but both participant precision and patience suffer when too many stimuli are proportioned and summed. A participant's ability to add is also taxed in paper-and-pencil surveys; this is not a response strategy that can be effectively used with children or the uneducated. Mobile- and computer-based research studies have made the use of this scale far easier, as the software sums the items as numbers are entered. It rejects an entry if the sum exceeds 100 and it alerts the participant if the sum of 100 is not reached.

The advantage of the constant-sum question is its compatibility with 100 percent and the fact that alternatives that are perceived to be equal can be so scored—unlike the case with most ranking scales. The constant-sum question is used effectively to record attitudes, behavior, and behavioral intent; it produces interval data.

Graphic Rating Questions

A question built on the **graphic rating scale** was originally created to enable researchers to discern fine differences. Theoretically, an infinite number of ratings are possible if participants are sophisticated enough to differentiate and record them. In a graphic-rating-scale question, participants mark their response at any point along a line between two response choices. Usually, the data is a measure of length (millimeters) from either endpoint. The results are treated as interval data. The difficulty is in coding and analysis. This scale requires more time than scales with predetermined categories and value codes.

Never_____X_____Always

Questions designed using the **visual graphic rating scale** (see Exhibit 11-8) use pictures, icons, or other visuals to communicate with the participant and represent a variety of data types. These graphic scales are often used with children, whose more limited vocabulary prevents the use of scales anchored with words.

>Ranking Questions

In **ranking questions**, questions built on ranking scales, the participant directly compares two or more objects and makes choices among them. Frequently, in questions based on ranking scales, the participant is asked to select one as the "best" or the "most preferred." When there are only two choices, this approach is satisfactory, but in analyzing results such questions can generate ties when more than two choices are used. For example, assume participants are asked to select the most preferred among three or more payment models. In response, 40 percent choose model A, 30 percent choose model B, and 30 percent choose model C. Which is the preferred model? The analyst would be taking a risk to suggest that A is most preferred. Perhaps that interpretation is correct, but 60 percent of the participants chose some model other than A. Perhaps all participants who chose B and C would place A last, preferring either B or C to A. This ambiguity can be avoided by using some of the techniques described in this section.

In a question built on the **paired-comparison scale**, the participant can express attitudes unambiguously by choosing between two _objects_ or _properties_. Typical of a paired-comparison question would be the sports car preference example in Exhibit 11-16. The number of judgments required in a paired

Assume you are asked by Galaxy Department Stores to study the shopping habits and preferences of teen girls. Galaxy is seeking a way to compete with specialty stores that are far more successful in serving this market segment. Galaxy is considering the construction of an intrastore boutique catering to these teens. What measurement issues would determine your construction of measurement scales?

>**Exhibit 11-16** Sample Ranking Scales as Measurement Questions

Paired-Comparison Scale
data: ordinal

"For each pair of two-seat sports cars listed, place a check beside the one you would most prefer if you had to choose between the two."

____ BMW Z4 M Coupe   ____ Chevrolet Corvette Z06
____ Porsche Cayman S   ____ Porsche Cayman S

____ Chevrolet Corvette Z06   ____ Porsche Cayman S
____ BMW Z4 M Coupe   ____ Dodge Viper SRT10

____ Chevrolet Corvette Z06   ____ Dodge Viper SRT10
____ Dodge Viper SRT10   ____ BMW Z4 M Coupe

Forced Ranking Scale
data: ordinal

"Rank the radar detection features in your order of preference. Place the number 1 next to the most preferred, 2 by the second choice, and so forth."

____ User programming
____ Cordless capability
____ Small size
____ Long-range warning
____ Minimal false alarms

Comparative Scale
data: ordinal

"Compared to your previous hair dryer's performance, the new one is":

SUPERIOR		ABOUT THE SAME		INFERIOR
____	____	____	____	____
1	2	3	4	5

>**Exhibit 11-17** Response Patterns of 200 Heavy Users' Paired Comparisons on Five Alternative Package Designs

Paired-comparison data may be treated in several ways. If there is substantial consistency, we will find that if A is preferred to B, and B to C, then A will be consistently preferred to C. This condition of transitivity need not always be true but should occur most of the time. When it does, take the total number of preferences among the comparisons as the score for that stimulus. Assume a manager is considering five distinct packaging designs. She would like to know how heavy users would rank these designs. One option would be to ask a sample of the heavy-users segment to pair-compare the packaging designs. With a rough comparison of the total preferences for each option, it is apparent that B is the most popular.

	Designs				
	A	**B**	**C**	**D**	**E**
A	—	164*	138	50	70
B	36	—	54	14	30
C	62	146	—	32	50
D	150	186	168	—	118
E	130	170	150	82	—
Total	378	**666**	510	178	268
Rank order	3	**1**	2	5	4

* Interpret this cell as 164 of 200 customers preferred suggested design B (column) to design A (row).

comparison is $[(n)(n-1)/2]$, where n is the number of stimuli or objects to be judged. When four cars are evaluated, the participant evaluates six paired comparisons $[(4)(3)/2 = 6]$.

In another example, we might compare location proposals being considered for a new manufacturing plant (see Exhibit 11-17). Generally, there are more than two stimuli to judge, resulting in a potentially tedious task for participants. If 15 suggestions for design proposals are available, 105 paired comparisons would be made.

Reducing the number of comparisons per participant without reducing the number of objects can lighten this burden. You can present each participant with only a sample of the pairs. In this way, each pair of objects must be compared an equal number of times. Another procedure is to choose a few objects that are believed to cover the range of attractiveness at equal intervals. All other stimuli are then compared to these few standard objects. If 36 automobiles are to be judged, four may be selected as standards and the others divided into four groups of eight each. Within each group, the eight are compared to each other. Then the 32 are individually compared to each of the four standard automobiles. This reduces the number of comparisons from 630 to 240.

Paired comparisons run the risk that participants will tire to the point that they give ill-considered answers or refuse to continue. Opinions differ about the upper limit, but five or six objects or properties are reasonable when the participant has other questions in the measurement instrument to answer. If the data collection consists only of paired comparisons, as many as 10 stimuli are reasonable. Questions built using a paired comparison scale provide ordinal data.

The question built on the **forced ranking scale**, shown in Exhibit 11-16, lists attributes that are ranked relative to each other. This method is faster than paired comparisons and is usually easier and more motivating to the participant. With five items, it takes 10 paired comparisons to complete the task; a question based on a forced-ranking scale of five objects or properties is easier for the participant. Also, questions using forced-choice ranking have no transitivity problem—where A is preferred to B, and B to C, but C is preferred to A—although they do assume a false unidimensionality.

A drawback to forced ranking is the number of stimuli that can be handled by this method. Five objects can be ranked easily, but participants may grow careless in ranking 10 or more items. In addition, rank ordering produces ordinal data because the distance between preferences is unknown.

Often the manager is interested in benchmarking. This calls for a standard by which other programs, processes, events, or people can be compared. Questions built using the **comparative scale** are ideal for such comparisons if the participants are familiar with the standard. In the Exhibit 11-16 example, the standard is the participant's previous hair dryer. The new dryer is being assessed relative to it. The provision to

Paired Comparison Increases Hospitality

Should Northwest Airlines, Marriott, or Alaskan Airlines attempt to attract the business of Americans with disabilities? If so, what would it take to capture the segment? Eric Lipp, executive director of the Open Doors Organization (ODO), an advocacy organization for those with disabilities, sponsored a study to find out. High on his agenda was providing an incentive to the travel industry to make accommodations to attract the 22 million adults with disabilities who have traveled in the last two years on 63 million trips—and who may want to travel more. "We now estimate that Americans with disabilities currently spent $13.2 billion in travel expenditures and that amount would at least double [to $27.2 billion] if travel businesses were more attuned to the needs of those with disabilities."

ODO hired Harris Interactive, a global market research and consulting firm best known for The Harris Poll and for pioneering the Internet method to conduct scientifically accurate market research. Harris Interactive conducted a hybrid study via both online and phone surveys to determine the magnitude of the disability travel segment, its purchasing power, and the accommodations the segment needed to increase travel. "Those with disabilities can't all be reached with one method," explained Laura Light, project director with Harris Interactive. "The nature of their physical limitation might preclude one method or the other." And how did the firm evaluate all the possible accommodations—from Braille safety cards on airplanes to a designated person to handle problems in a hotel? Harris Interactive used its proprietary *COMPASS™* methodology, which uses paired comparisons as a measurement tool. "*COMPASS* saves the participant time and energy," explained Light. "Even with a long list, *COMPASS* can be done quickly." In the ODO study, *COMPASS* was used twice: once to measure 17 possible airline accommodations and once to measure 23 possible hotel accommodations. By having each participant evaluate only a portion of the large number of accommodation pairs rather than the full list (136 for airline accommodations and 253 for hotel accommodations), each question was answered in under four minutes. By using this process with all members of the sample, Harris Interactive is able to rank-order the items and measure the magnitude of difference between items. This makes it easier for Delta, Marriott, or Alaskan Airlines to make the right choices about accommodations for those with disabilities.

To learn more about this research, read the case "Open Doors: Extending Hospitality to Travelers with Disabilities" available from Connect

www.opendoorsnfp.org; www.harrisinteractive.com

compare yet other dryers to the standard is not shown in the example but is nonetheless available to the researcher.

Some researchers treat the data produced by comparative-scales questions as interval data since the scoring reflects an interval between the standard and what is being compared. Some would treat the rank of the item as ordinal data unless the linearity of the variables in question could be supported.

>Sorting Questions

Q-sorts require participants to sort of a deck of cards into piles that represent points along a continuum. Designing a question based on a Q-sort scale involves the selection of a set of verbal statements, phrases, single words, or photos each depicted on a separate card. For statistical stability, the number of cards should not be less than 60 and, for convenience, not be more than 120. After the cards are created, they are shuffled, and the participant is instructed to sort the cards into a set of piles (usually 7 to 11), each pile representing a point on the criterion continuum. The left-most pile represents the concept statements, words or images, which are "most valuable," "favorable," "agreeable," and so forth. The right-most pile contains the least favorable cards. The researcher asks the participant to fill the center, or neutral, pile with the cards about which the participant is indecisive. In the case of a *structured* sort, the distribution of cards allowed in each pile is predetermined. With an *unstructured* sort, only the number of piles will be predetermined. Although the distribution of cards in most structured sorts resembles a normal distribution, there is some controversy about analyzing the data as ordinal data versus interval data. With today's technology, you can use Q-sorts with computer-based surveys.

The purpose of sorting is to get a conceptual representation of the sorter's attitude toward the attitude object and to compare the relationships between people. The relative ranking of concepts allows researchers to derive clusters of individuals possessing similar preferences. By varying the instructions, this type of question can be used to describe products, services, behavioral intentions, and a host of other applications. Special facilities with advanced technology permit card sorts on large computerized screens. In the example below, participants are asked to complete a structured sort of cards containing the names of magazines. The scale values and the number of cards in each pile are predetermined, although the distribution in this case represents a normal statistical distribution.

What magazines do you want Singapore Airlines to carry for its in-flight service?

Most Preferred										Least Preferred	
10	9	8	7	6	5	4	3	2	1	0	(scale value)
3	4	7	10	13	16	13	10	7	4	3	(number of cards per pile)

>Cumulative Questions

Total scores of questions built on **cumulative scales** have the same meaning. Given a person's total score, it is possible to estimate which items were answered positively and negatively. A pioneering scale of this type was the scalogram. **Scalogram analysis** is a procedure for determining whether a set of items forms a unidimensional scale.[22] A scale is unidimensional if the responses fall into a pattern in which endorsement of the item reflecting the extreme position results in endorsing all items that are less extreme.

Assume we are surveying opinions regarding a new style of running shoe. We have developed a preference scale of four items:

1. The Airsole is good-looking.
2. I will insist on Airsole next time because it is great-looking.
3. The appearance of Airsole is acceptable to me.
4. I prefer the Airsole style to other styles.

Participants indicate whether they agree or disagree. If these items form a unidimensional scale, the response patterns will approach the ideal configuration shown in Exhibit 11-18. Item 2 is the most

>**Exhibit 11-18** Ideal Scalogram Response Pattern*

	Item			
2	**4**	**1**	**3**	**Participant Score**
X	X	X	X	4
—	X	X	X	3
—	—	X	X	2
—	—	—	X	1
—	—	—	—	0

* X = agree; — = disagree.

		Item			
Case	**2**	**4**	**1**	**3**	**Participant Score**
1	X	X	X	X	4
2	—	X	X	X	3
3	—	—	X	X	2
4	—	—	—	X	1
5	—	—	—	—	0

extreme position of the four attitude statements. A participant who agrees with item 2 will agree with all four items. The items are ordered in the scalogram left to right, from most to least extreme. If each agreement renders a score of 1, a score of 4 indicates all statements are agreed upon and represents the most favorable attitude. Persons with a score of 3 should disagree with item 2 but agree with all others, and so on. According to scalogram theory, this pattern confirms that the universe of content (attitude toward the appearance of this running shoe) is scalable.

The scalogram and similar procedures for discovering underlying structure are useful for assessing attitudes and behaviors that are highly structured, such as social distance, organizational hierarchies, and evolutionary product stages.[23] The scalogram is used much less often today but retains potential for specific applications.

>Find or Craft Measurement Questions

Once you know the scale you want to use for each variable, you need to actually write or find each question. There are several factors that influence any measurement question.

- Question coverage.
- Question wording.
- Question's frame of reference.
- Question personalization.
- Structure, number, and order of response alternatives.

Question Coverage

Question coverage refers to the number of questions needed to adequately measure the variable as operationally defined. Sometimes you can cover a variable with a single question. For example, we won't need more than one question to ask a participant's age. But if the variable represents a more complex construct, we might need a series of questions. For example, if we want to know a participant's attitude about safety practices, we might write a question about the whether they feel safe on the job, followed by a question about various practices and how safe the participants feels when following each practice.

Question Wording

Every word you use in your question has the potential to bias your participant's response. The difficulties caused by question wording are perceived to exceed most other sources of distortion in survey research.[24]

Shared vocabulary between the researcher and the participant is critical, but not sufficient. It's always best to use words that are common to the participant's language. Unless your sample is very narrowly defined, this means technical terms or jargon specific to company or industry are unlikely to be used. Sometimes even simple, established words have more than one meaning; the question then requires an operational definition applied to one or a series of questions. For example, the word *profit*, even with a knowledgeable business sample, can be measured in dollars at the gross and net level or as a percentage calculated with costs or revenue as its base. *Safe* is another word that might have different meanings for the participant. Does safe mean "free from physical harm," "free from coercion," "free from bullying," "free from sexual harassment," or something else entirely? We look for precision in question wording, but this often means longer and more complex sentences, which aren't ideal for measurement questions.

Target questions need not be constructed solely of words. Computer-assisted surveys, computer-administered surveys, online and mobile surveys, interview guides, and (to a lesser extent) printed surveys often incorporate visual images as part of the questioning process. One of the strengths of computer-based and mobile surveys is their ability to incorporate video stimuli as part of the measurement question.

Question designers need to avoid several specific question-wording problems:[25] leading questions, double-barreled questions, questions with unsupported assumptions. A **leading question** suggests to the participant the desired answer; its biased phrasing makes the question worthless.

What did you think when think when the shampoo lathered so nicely?

A **double-barreled question** asks two or more questions but provides the response option to answer only one. In analysis, you don't know which question the participant was answering. Worse, such a question is likely to be skipped. Too many such questions frustrate a participant and make it increasingly likely that they will stop answering the questionnaire. The solution is simple: separate the questions.

Please rate your satisfaction with the comfort and cleanliness of your room.

A question based on an **unsupported assumption** is one that assumes (rightly or wrongly) an implied affirmative answer to an unasked question in order to answer the current question. If the participant is only given the response scale for the asked question, with no response option to indicate an answer to the unasked question, the question data must factor in missing data from many participants. This type of question also presents participants with evidence that their opinion might not be valuable, encouraging them to question whether they should continue. In the question below, we can solve the missing data issue by adding a response option (did not participate in online training) to the 5-point response scale (likelihood to recommend).

How likely would you be to recommend XYZ's online software training to a colleague?

For mobile surveys, questions are often abbreviated. A rule of thumb is if you can remove a word with-out affecting the meaning of the question, do so. So rather than asking gender: "What is your gender?" (response choices: are male, female) or "Are you male or female?" (response choices: male, female), the question might be abbreviated to "Are you . . . ? (response choices: male, female). This abbreviation is easier to accomplish with classification questions, where the response categories are expected.

Frame of Reference

Each of us understands concepts, constructs words, and expressions in light of our own experiences. A woman participating in an intercept survey at her son's school might use her "mom" frame of reference to answer questions, rather than her "lawyer" frame of reference. Because you don't know what frames of reference are in a participant's day-to-day life, you should provide a frame of reference in any question that requires one. For example, a participant is asked to "evaluate (store)." On what basis should the evaluation be made? Store layout? Customer service? Product selection? Credit policy? Quality of advertising?

Any behavior question needs a **behavior time frame**. An appropriate time frame is determined by the **behavior cycle** (how much time is required for the behavior and between behavior events), as well as the **behavior frequency** (how often a participant executes a particular behavior). The most common errors of time frame are (1) failing to provide a time frame, (2) using a time frame that is too inclusive given the behavior cycle and frequency (e.g., "Have you ever had a cold?"), and (3) using a time frame that is out of sync with the behavior frequency and is therefore impossible to answer (e.g. "In the last 12 months, how often have you checked your email?"). There also is a danger in using too narrow a behavior time frame. We may ask about movie attendance in the last 7 days, although this is too short a behavior time span on which to base audience attendance estimates at some times during the year. It may be better to ask about attendance, for the last 30 or 60 days, especially if you are moving into peak times for movie attendance, around the winter holidays and summer. Many question designers suggest a question about behavior should lead with a behavior time frame.

Precision is also important in behavior time frames. Assume you ask a participant: "In the last week, did you work outside the home for pay?" Is their frame of reference the "prior 7 days," or the "prior week counting Sunday through Saturday," or the "prior work week counting Monday through Friday"? Also, **memory decay**, the inability to accurately recall details after passage of time, is a problem for researchers. Decay most affects short-term memory, but recall of events stored in long-term memory is usually believed possible only if the event was significant in the participant's life and the researcher can connect with those significant memories. So if a question asks for recall of something insignificant, the participant might want a "don't know" or "don't remember" response as an option. Without it, researchers fear that participants will be accommodating and offer some response—any response—to be cooperative.

Response Alternatives

A general rule of thumb for determining the number of response alternatives is that they should cover 90 percent of participant's expected answers. You can always add an "other" category to catch the 10%, but you don't want a large percent of participants to choose this. Pretesting can reveal whether your alternatives have fulfilled this guideline.

Bias can factor into the data when order of responses, and items, is considered. Computer-assisted questionnaires can be coded to randomize the order of alternatives. This helps protect against **recency effect** (choosing the last or most recent option), **primacy effect** (choosing the first option given), and the **error of central tendency** (choosing the middle option). Primacy effect dominates in visual surveys—self-administered via web, mobile, or mail—while recency effect dominates in oral surveys—phone and personal interview surveys.[26] Using the split-ballot technique can counteract this bias: different segments of the sample are presented questions with the same alternatives but arranged in different order.

In most multiple-choice questions, there is also a problem of ensuring that the choices represent a one-dimensional scale—that is, the alternatives to a given question should represent different aspects of the same conceptual dimension. In a college selection checklist question, we could list features associated with a college that might be attractive to a student. This list should only include factors within the concept dimension "college attractiveness factors within the control of the college" (strong academic reputation, high-quality faculty, array of majors). The list should not mention other factors in the same checklist that might affect a school choice decision but represent a different conceptual dimension (parents and peer advice, local alumni efforts, number of friends who attend, and recommendation of high school counselor are factors not within the control of the college).

Researchers are interested in offering a fair balance of choices when a participant's position is unknown. A question formed with a *balanced scale* has an equal number of positive to negative response options. You can also have a neutral center point in a balanced array of options. A question formed with an *unbalanced scale* offers more responses on the positive or negative side. You are likely to design a question with unbalanced alternatives if you have prior knowledge of the participant's stance on the issue, object, etc., and want more discernment on that side of the scale. Numeric alternatives are usually ordered from lowest to highest or highest to lowest. It's also necessary to make sure the numbers are reasonable. If we ask, "Which of the following numbers is closest to the number of students currently enrolled in American colleges and universities?" the responses might be: a. 75,000, b. 750,000, c. 10,000,000, d. 25,000,000, e. 50,000,000. It should be obvious to most participants that the first three of these alternatives choices are not reasonable, given the estimated U.S. population is 323.1 million,[27] the 26th largest institution in the United States (Ohio State) enrolls 64,000 students, and University of Phoenix[28] enrolls 150,000 students.[29]

Response alternatives can also offer **unstructured responses** (open-ended or free-response questions) or **structured responses** (questions that restrict the response to verbal, visual, or numeric alternatives). The factors that influence this choice in response are the participant's level of information about the question's topic, their degree of thought about the topic, the ease with which they communicate, their level of willingness to share information, and the time available for analysis.[30]

We covered scale points in discussing question types. The general rule of thumb here is that you want a sufficient number to allow discernment between options. If the participant's has not given the issue or topic much thought, a 3-point scales might be sufficient. If they have given it extensive consideration, 7- or 10-point scales should be appropriate. Exhibit 11-19 provides a summary of the major issues related to developing measurement questions, discussed in this and previous sections of this chapter.

>**Exhibit 11-19** A Summary of the Major Issues Related to Measurement Questions

Issue Category	Fundamental Issue
Question Content	
1. Purposeful versus interesting	Does the question ask for data that will be merely interesting or truly useful to the manager in making a decision?
2. Incomplete or unfocused	Will the question reveal what the manager needs to know?
3. Double-barreled questions	Does the question ask the participant for too much information? Would the desired single response be accurate for all parts of the question?
4. Precision	Does the question ask precisely what the manager needs to know?
5. Time for thought	Is it reasonable to assume that the participant can frame an answer to the question?
6. Participation at the expense of accuracy	Does the question pressure the participant for a response regardless of knowledge or experience?
7. Presumed knowledge	Does the question assume the participant has knowledge he or she may not have?
8. Recall and memory decay	Does the question ask the participant for information that relates to thoughts or activity too far in the participant's past to be remembered?
9. Balance (general vs. specific)	Does the question ask the participant to generalize or summarize behavior that may have no discernable pattern?
10. Objectivity	Does the question omit or include information that will bias the participant's response?
11. Sensitive information	Does the question ask the participant to reveal embarrassing, shameful, or ego-related information?
Question Wording	
12. Shared vocabulary	Does the question use words that have no meaning or a different meaning for the participant?
13. Unsupported assumption	Does the question assume a prior experience, a precondition, or prior knowledge that the participant does not or may not have?
14. Frame of reference	Is the question worded from the participant's, rather than the researcher's, perspective?
15. Biased wording	Does the question contain wording that implies the researcher's desire for the participant to respond in one way versus another?
16. Personalization vs. projection	Is it necessary for the participant to reveal personal attitudes and behavior, or may the participant project these attitudes and behaviors to someone like him or her?
17. Adequate alternatives	Does the question provide a mutually exhaustive list of alternatives to encompass realistic or likely participant attitudes and behaviors?
Response Strategy Choice	
18. Objective of the study	Is the question designed to classify or label attitudes, conditions, and behaviors or to reveal them?
19. Level of information	Does the participant possess the level of information appropriate for participation in the study?
20. Thoroughness of prior thought	Has the participant developed an attitude on the issue being asked?
21. Communication skill	Does the participant have sufficient command of the language to answer the question?
22. Participant motivation	Is the level of motivation sufficient to encourage the participant to give thoughtful, revealing answers?
23. Method of access	Is the question appropriate for the participant's method of accessing the instrument?

Sources of Existing Questions

The tools of data collection should be adapted to the problem, not the reverse. Thus, the focus of this chapter has been on crafting questions to answer specific investigative questions. But inventing, refining, and pretesting questions demands considerable time and effort. For some topics, a careful review of the related literature and an examination of existing instrument sourcebooks can shorten this process. Increasingly, companies that specialize in survey research and survey software maintain question banks of pretested questions.

Several compilations are recommended in the Sources appendix at the end of the chapter.[31] Borrowing from existing sources is not without risk. It is quite difficult to generalize the reliability and validity of selected questions or portions of a questionnaire that have been taken out of the original context. Researchers whose questions or instruments you borrow may not have reported sampling and testing procedures needed to judge the quality of the question.

>**snap**shot

The SurveyMonkey Question Bank

Each researcher wants to think that his or her management dilemma or situation is unique and that no other researcher has the same insight into the situation as he or she does. That sets the stage for designing situation-specific measurement scales for research. But the problem is that often those custom questions aren't properly vetted—tested in research situations to assure their validity and reliability, absence of bias, etc.

As a result, drawing questions from banks of bias-free questions is a better approach. If you can't find the precise question you feel is critical, you are likely to find one that is sufficiently close that only slight modifications will provide a perfect fit without introducing error. So where do we turn for these tested questions, especially in this day of mobile surveys? The answer might be as close as the software you use to launch a survey.

SurveyMonkey customers create 3+ million surveys and ask almost 33 million questions each year. Some of these are previously vetted questions and others are custom questions. To build its question bank, SurveyMonkey used a subset of these surveys, scanning for the most commonly surveyed topics (like customer feedback, employee satisfaction, health care, demographics, etc.). For each topical area, it randomly chose 10 percent of surveys on that topic, ensuring that each and every SurveyMonkey survey on that topic had an equal and independent chance of being selected. Using this process, it narrowed the 33 million questions to roughly 20,000 questions. Then it asked its methodology experts to rewrite the questions created by SurveyMonkey customers so that these questions asked only the construct of interest and nothing more. Those experts eliminated questions with obvious answer bias—questions that subconsciously pressured the respondent to answer in one direction or another. They eliminated double questions that asked more than one question but offered only one response option.

©monkeybusinessimages/Getty Images

They brought the response options in line with the construct being measured in each question. All together, 1,500 restructured questions made it into the SurveyMonkey Question Bank.

You can also turn to government organizations—such as the Centers for Disease Control and Prevention (CDC) or nonprofits like the Pew Research Center or the Kaiser Family Foundation—that conduct hundreds of surveys each year with tested questions. Another source of current survey methodology expertise is QUEST. The QUEST (QUestionnaire Evaluation STandards) network is a group of those currently involved in survey question and instrument evaluation. The core of the group consists of members from federal statistical agencies and research organizations in the Unites States, Europe, and other countries. This group meets every 18 months and shares their insights on the web. Check out these sources for tested questions.

www.surveymonkey.com; wwwn.cdc.gov/qbank/; kkf.org; www.pewresearch.org

Language, phrasing, and idioms can also pose problems. Questions tend to age or become outdated and may not appear (or sound) as relevant to a participant as freshly worded questions. Integrating previously used and customized questions also is problematic. Often, adjacent questions in one questionnaire are relied on to carry context. If you select one question from a contextual series, the borrowed question is left without its necessary meaning.[32] Whether an instrument is constructed with designed questions or adapted with questions borrowed or licensed from others, pretesting is still recommended.

Pretesting

On measurement questions, we **pretest** questions by fielding individual questions to a sample of participant surrogates and getting an evaluation from research colleagues. This is a critical step in developing valid measurement questions. Feedback can reveal unanswerable questions, difficult-to-answer questions, those with an inappropriate rating scale, double-barreled or leading questions, unsupported assumptions, those that need instructions or operational definitions, and more. Don't skip this valuable step in measurement question development.

>summary

LO11-1 Instrument design is a three-phase process. Central to Phase 1 of instrument design is conversion of the investigative questions to scale selection with the use of a preliminary analysis plan. This plan contains the procedures planned for the data to be collected. The creation of dummy tables, mock-ups for cross-tabulations of two or more variables, is used to identify the search for relationships and patterns at the core of the research question. These tables are used to determine the level of data (nominal, ordinal, interval, ratio) that is needed for each variable so that the right scale can be selected for selection or creation of a measurement question. Planned research design decisions—the communication approach and the level of structure—contribute to the preliminary analysis plan. Too extensive a preliminary analysis plan indicates high data analysis costs and alerts the researcher to a problem: too large a measurement instrument for a single study, requiring the data analysis plan to be corrected.

LO11-2 Selecting and constructing an appropriate scale for a measurement question requires the consideration of several factors that influence the reliability, validity, and practicality of the scale. Two broad research objectives are to measure characteristics of the individuals who participate in studies and to use participants as judges of the objects or indicants presented to them.

Measurement scales fall into one of four general response types: rating, ranking, categorization, and sorting. Measurement scales are either unidimensional or multidimensional. A balanced rating scale has an equal number of categories above and below the midpoint, whereas an unbalanced rating scale has an unequal number of favorable and unfavorable response choices. An unforced-choice rating scale provides participants with an opportunity to express no opinion when they are unable to make a choice among the alternatives offered. A forced-choice scale requires that they select one of the offered alternatives. The ideal number of points for a rating scale should match the stimulus presented and extract information proportionate to the complexity of the attitude object. The value of rating scales depends on the assumption that a rater can and will make good judgments. Errors of central tendency, halo effect, leniency, and strictness adversely affect responses.

LO11-3 Business researchers are interested in measuring knowledge, behaviors, and attitudes, as well as characteristics of participants. The measurement of attitudes is often the best tool available to understand past experience and anticipate future behavior. Attitudes are learned, stable predispositions to respond to oneself, other persons, objects, or issues in a consistently favorable or unfavorable way. Attitudes are generally thought to be composed of three components: affective, cognitive, and behavioral intentions.

Rating scales have several uses, design features, and requirements. The simple category scale offers two mutually exclusive response choices. The multiple-choice, single-response scale offers the rater several options, including "other." The multiple-choice, multiple-response scale (also called a checklist) allows the rater to select one or several alternatives, thereby providing a cumulative feature.

The Likert scale consists of a series of statements, and the participant is asked to agree or disagree with each statement. Summation is possible with this scale although not necessary and in some instances undesirable.

The semantic differential (SD) scale measures the psychological meanings of an attitude object. Researchers use this scale for studies of brand and institutional image. The method consists of a set of bipolar rating scales, usually with 7 points, by which one or more participants rate one or more concepts on each scale item. The Stapel scale is used as an alternative to the semantic differential, especially when it is difficult to find bipolar adjectives that match the investigative question. Participants select a plus number for the characteristic that describes the attitude object. Ratings range from +5 to −5, and participants select a number that describes the object very accurately to very inaccurately.

Numerical scales have equal intervals that separate their numeric scale points. Verbal anchors serve as the labels for the extreme points. Numerical scales are often 5-point scales but may have 7 or 10 points. A multiple rating list scale is similar to the numerical scale but accepts a circled response from the rater, and the layout allows visualization of the results.

A scale that helps the researcher discover proportions is the constant-sum scale. The participant distributes 100 points among up to 10 categories. The graphic rating scale was originally created to enable researchers to discern fine differences. Raters check their response at any point along a continuum. Visual graphic rating scales use pictures, icons, or other visuals to communicate with children or others whose limited vocabulary prevents the use of scales anchored with words.

Ranking scales allow the participant to compare two or more objects and make choices among them. Frequently, the participant is asked to select one as the "best" or the "most preferred." When there are only two choices, as with the paired-comparison scale, the participant can express attitudes unambiguously by choosing between two objects. The forced ranking scale lists attributes that are ranked relative to each other. This method is faster than paired comparisons and more user-friendly. Often the researcher is interested in benchmarking. This calls for a standard by which training programs, processes, brands, point-of-sale purchases, or people can be compared. The comparative scale is ideal for such comparisons if the participants are familiar with the standard.

Q-sorts are a form of scaling that requires sorting of a deck of cards into piles that represent points along a continuum. The purpose of sorting is to get a conceptual representation of the sorter's attitude toward the attitude object and to compare the relationships between people. Given a person's total score, it is possible to estimate which items were answered positively and negatively on cumulative scales. A pioneering cumulative scale was the scalogram, a procedure for determining whether a set of items forms a unidimensional scale.

LO11-4 Several factors influence any measurement question: coverage, wording, participant's frame of reference, personalization, and number and order of response alternatives. A question's coverage refers to the number of questions needed to adequately the measure the variable as operationally defined. Variables often require more than one question or more than one item within a question. Question wording refers to word choices within the question and is influenced by shared vocabulary or shared interpretation of images or symbols. Word problems to avoid include leading questions (inclusion of word that create bias), double-barreled questions (those that ask more than one question with only one response), and unsupported assumptions.

Participants have any number of frames of reference due to the various roles they play in their lives. Specifying the role you want them to assume when asking a question is critical. One important frame of reference relates to time. Behavior questions require time frames that are dependent on the behavior cycle (amount of time for the behavior and between behavior events), as well as behavior frequency (how often a participant executes a particular behavior). When crafting behavior questions, omitting the time frame, or using one that is too broad, or out of sync with behavior cycle or frequency can create biased results.

Response alternatives need to cover a large percentage of possible responses. This involves selecting the right number of scale points, the right words/images/symbols to anchor those points, and making alternative responses reasonable. While numeric alternatives are usually put in order of highest–lowest or lowest–highest, verbal alternatives are usually randomized to avoid biased results.

There are numerous sources for existing questions, not all of which have been tested for validity and reliability. The risks of using preexisting questions involve their lack of customization for a particular management problem, their age, coverage, word choice, etc. Integrating preexisting questions with custom-designed questions involves adjusting the contextual context of the preexisting question, which might alter the accuracy of participant responses. Pretesting is strongly recommended to avoid the numerous potential problems associated with measurement questions discussed in this chapter.

>**key**terms

>**discussion**questions

Terms in Review

1 Discuss the relative merits of and problems with:

   a Rating and ranking scales.

   b Likert and semantic differential scales.

   c Unidimensional and multidimensional scales.

Making Research Decisions

2 Assume you are Menu Foods and you planned a major research study just prior to the largest pet food recall in our history. You plan to proceed with the study and feel you must add one or more questions to measure the consumer's confidence that your firm will be able to recover.

Design a question for each of the following scale types that will measure that confidence.

   a Constant-sum scale.

   b Likert-type summated scale.

   c Semantic differential scale.

   d Stapel scale.

   e Forced ranking scale.

3 An investigative question in your employee satisfaction study seeks to assess employee "job involvement." Create a measurement question that uses the following scales. Which question do your recommend and why?

   a A graphic rating scale.

   b A multiple rating list.

4 You receive the results of a paired-comparison preference test of four soft drinks from a sample of 200 persons. The results are as follows:

	Koak	Zip	Pabze	Mr. Peepers
Koak	—	50*	115	35
Zip	150	—	160	70
Pabze	85	40	—	45
Mr. Peepers	165	130	155	—

*Read as 50 persons preferred Zip to Koak.

   a How do these brands rank in overall preference in this sample?

   b Develop an interval scale for these four brands.

5 One of the problems in developing rating questions is the choice of response categories to use. Below are samples of some widely used scaling responses. Do you see any problems with them?

   a Yes—Depends—No

   b Excellent—Good—Fair—Poor

   c Excellent—Good—Average—Fair—Poor

   d Strongly Approve—Approve—Uncertain—Disapprove—Strongly Disapprove

6 You are working on a consumer perception study of four brands of bicycles. You will need to develop measurement questions to accomplish the tasks listed below. Prepare a preliminary analysis plan, including the dummy tables, and specify which data levels (nominal, ordinal, interval, ratio) are necessary in scale selection.

   a Prepare an overall assessment of all the brands.

   b Provide a comparison of the brands for each of the following dimensions:

   (1) Styling.

   (2) Durability.

   (3) Gear quality.

   (4) Brand image.

7 Below is a Likert-type scale that might be used to evaluate your opinion of the educational degree program in which you are enrolled. There are five response categories: Strongly Agree, Agree, Neither Agree nor Disagree, Disagree, and Strongly Disagree. If Strongly Agree (SA) represents the most positive attitude, how would you value the items below? Record your answers to the items.

   a This program is not very challenging.　　SA A N D SD

   b The general level of teaching is good.　　SA A N D SD

   c I really think I am learning a lot from this program.　　SA A N D SD

   d Students' suggestions are given little attention here.　　SA A N D SD

   e This program does a good job of preparing one for a career.　　SA A N D SD

   f This program is below my expectations.　　SA A N D SD

In what two different ways could such responses be used? What would be the purpose of each?

8 The third-generation iPad disappointed many who had expected not only a higher-resolution screen (delivered) but Siri, Apple's much-ballyhooed speak-and-it-responds app developed for the iPhone 4S (not delivered). Apple indicated it wasn't included because Siri for the iPad wasn't ready. Design the questions that could have revealed expectations of iPad3 devotees.

9 Following are six questions. Evaluate each on its strengths and weaknesses

   a Do you read *National Geographic* magazine regularly?

   b What percentage of your time is spent asking for information from others in your organization?

   c When did you first start chewing gum?

   d How much discretionary buying power do you have each year?

   e Do you think the president is doing a good job now?

From Concept to Practice

10 Using the response strategies within Exhibit 11-8 or 11-16, which would be appropriate to understanding the various indicants of student demand for the academic program in which you are majoring?

From the Headlines

11 Discount department store Kohl's recently announced its customers would "have a new easy, secure and private way to pay in stores with the rollout of Apple Pay, as well as the ability to use Apple Pay within the Kohl's app. Kohl's customers will also be able to add their Kohl's Charge card as a form of payment within Apple Pay." Some analysts were surprised that the announcement came from Kohl's before it came from technology-focused Best Buy or more upscale Macy's. Let's say as a researcher this decision was being considered. While your typical shopper was older, you wanted to attract the Millennials and they were more technologically attuned. What information do you need about your shopper and the targeted Millennials to make this substantial investment worthwhile? What type of scale will you use, and why?

>cases*

*You will find a description of each case in the Case Abstracts section of this textbook. Check the Case Index to determine whether a case provides data, the research instrument, video, or other supplementary material. Cases and case supplements are available in Connect.

Sample Computer-Based Questions and Guidelines for Mobile Q

>**Exhibit SCa-1** Computer-Based Measurement Question Options

Where have you seen advertising for MindWriter laptop computers?

Free Response/Open Question
using textbox

I plan to purchase a MindWriter laptop in the next 3 months.

◉ Yes
◉ No

Dichotomous-Choice Question
using radio buttons
(may also use pull-down box)

My next laptop computer will have . . .

◉ More memory.
◉ More processing speed.

Paired Comparison
using radio buttons
(may also use pull-down box)

What ONE magazine do you read most often for computing news?

◉ PC Magazine
◉ Wired
◉ Computing Magazine
◉ Computing World
◉ PC Computing
◉ Laptop

Multiple Choice, Single Response
using radio buttons
(may also use pull-down box
or checkbox)

>**Exhibit SCa-1** Computer-Based Measurement Question Options (cont'd)

What ONE magazine do you read most often for computing news?

| Please select your answer | V |

| V |
| PC Magazine |
| Wired |
| Computing Magazine |
| Computing World |
| PC Computing |
| Laptop |

Multiple Choice, Single Response
using pull-down box

Checklist
using checkbox
(may also use radio buttons)

Which of the following computing magazines did you look at in the last 30 days?

☐ PC Magazine
☑ Wired
☐ Computing Magazine
☐ Computing World
☐ PC Computing
☐ Laptop

Please indicate the importance of each of the characteristics in choosing your next laptop. [Select one answer in each row. Scroll to see the complete list of options.]

	Very Important		Neither Important nor Unimportant		Not at all Important
Fast reliable repair service	◎	◯	◯	◯	◎
Service at my location	◯	◯	◉	◯	◯
Maintenance by the manufacturer	◉	◯	◯	◯	◯
Knowledgeable technicians	◉	◯	◯	◯	◯
Notification of upgrades	◯	◯	◯	◯	◎

(may also use checkboxes)
Requires a single response per line.
The longer the list, the more likely
the participant must scroll.

Ranking Question
using pull-down box
(may also use textboxes,
in which ranks are entered)
This question asks for
a limited ranking of
only three of the
listed elements.

From the list below, please choose the three most important service options when choosing your next laptop.

Fast reliable repair service	— V
Service at my location	—
	1
Maintenance by the manufacturer	2
Knowledgeable technicians	3
Notification of upgrades	— V

>**snap**shot

The Challenges and Solutions to Mobile Questionnaire Design[33]

"As researchers, we need to be sensitive to the unique challenges respondents face when completing surveys on mobile devices," shared Kristin Luck, CEO of Decipher. "Small screens, inflexible device-specific user input methods, and potentially slow data transfer speeds all combine to make the survey completion process more difficult than on a typical computer. Couple those hindrances with reduced attention spans and a lower frustration threshold and it's clear that, as researchers, we must be proactive in the design of both the questionnaire and user-interface in order to accommodate mobile respondents and provide them with an excellent survey experience."

Decipher researchers follow key guidelines when designing surveys for mobile devices like smartphones and tablets.

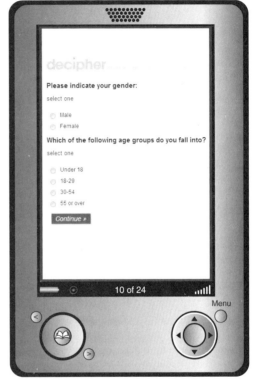

Courtesy of Decipher

- **Ask 10 or fewer questions**
  - Minimize page refreshes—longer wait times reduce participation.
  - Ask few questions per page—many mobile devices have limited memory.
- **Use simple question modes—to minimize scrolling**
  - Keep question and answer text short—due to smaller screens.
  - If unavoidable, limit scrolling to one dimension (vertical is better than horizontal).
  - Use single-response or multiple-response radio button or checkbox questions rather than multidimension grid questions.
  - Limit open-end questions—to minimize typing.
  - Keep answer options to a short list.
  - For necessary longer answer-list options, use dropdown box (but limit these as they require more clicks to answer).
- **Minimize all nonessential content**
  - If used, limit logos to the first or last survey page.
  - Limit privacy policy to first or last survey page.
  - Debate use of progress bar—it may encourage completion but also may require scrolling.

- **Minimize distraction**
  - Use simple, high-contrast color schemes—phones have limited color palettes.
  - Minimize JavaScript due to bandwidth concerns.
  - Eliminate Flash elements on surveys—due to incompatibility with iPhone.

Luck is passionate about making sure that researchers recognize the special requirements of designing for mobile as mobile surveys grow in use and projected use, She shares her expertise at conferences worldwide.

www.decipherinc.com

Sources of Measurement Questions

>Appendix Sa-1 Sources of Questions

Printed Sources		
Author(s)	**Title**	**Source**
William Bearden, R. Netemeyer, and Kelly L. Haws	*Handbook of Marketing Scales: Multi-Item Measures for Marketing and Consumer Behavior Research*	London: Sage Publications Inc., 2010
Alec Gallup and Frank Newport, eds.	*The Gallup Poll Cumulative Index: Public Opinion, 1998–2007*	Lanham, MD: Rowman & Littlefield Publishers Inc., 2008
John P. Robinson, Philip R. Shaver, and Lawrence S. Wrightsman	*Measures of Personality and Social-Psychological Attitudes*	San Diego, CA: Academic Press, 1990, 1999
John Robinson, Phillip R. Shaver, and L. Wrightsman	*Measures of Political Attitudes*	San Diego, CA: Academic Press, 1990, 1999
Alec M. Gallup	*The Gallup Poll: Public Opinion 2010*	Lanham, MD: Rowman & Littlefield Publishers Inc., 2011
Gordon Bruner, Paul Hensel, and Karen E. James	*Marketing Scales Handbook, Volume IV: Consumer Behavior*	Mason, OH: South-Western Educational Pub, 2005
Elizabeth H. Hastings and Philip K. Hastings, eds.	*Index to International Public Opinion, 1996–1997*	Westport, CT: Greenwood Publishing Group, 1998
Elizabeth Martin, Diana McDuffee, and Stanley Presser	*Sourcebook of Harris National Surveys: Repeated Questions 1963–1976*	Chapel Hill, NC: Institute for Research in Social Science, 1981
Philip E. Converse, Jean D. Dotson, Wendy J. Hoag, and William H. McGee III, eds.	*American Social Attitudes Data Sourcebook, 1947–1978*	Cambridge, MA: Harvard University Press, 1980
Philip K. Hastings and Jessie C. Southwick, eds.	*Survey Data for Trend Analysis: An Index to Repeated Questions in the U.S. National Surveys Held by the Roper Public Opinion Research Center*	Williamsburg, MA: Roper Public Opinion Center, 1975
National Opinion Research Center	*General Social Surveys 1972–2000: Cumulative Code Book*	Ann Arbor, MI: ICPSR, 2000
John P. Robinson	*Measures of Occupational Attitudes and Occupational Characteristics*	Ann Arbor, MI: Institute for Social Research, University of Michigan, 1971.
Web Sources		
Interuniversity Consortium for Political and Social Research (general social survey)	www.icpsr.umich.edu	
iPoll (contains more than 500,000 questions in its searchable database)	www.ropercenter.cornell.edu	
Pew Research Center	www.pewresearch.org	
The Odum Institute (houses the Louis Harris Opinion Polls)	http://www.irss.unc.edu/odum/home2.jsp	
Kaiser Family Foundation Health Poll Search	www.kff.org/kaiserpolls/healthpoll.cfm	
Polling the Nations (more than 14,000 surveys)	www.orspub.com	
SurveyMonkey Question Bank	www.SurveyMonkey.com	

Source: This list was compiled from numerous recommendations and the experience of various practicing researchers. It is not intended to be a comprehensive list but should be sufficient to get you started.

More on Effective Measurement Questions

Numerous issues influence whether the questions we ask on questionnaires generate the decision-making data that managers sorely need. Each of the issues summarized in the Measurement Questions chapter is more fully discussed here.

Question Content

Should This Question Be Asked?

Purposeful versus Interesting. Questions that merely produce "interesting information" cannot be justified on either economic or research grounds. Challenge each question's function. Does it contribute significant information toward answering the research question? Will its omission limit or prevent the thorough analysis of other data? Can we infer the answer from another question? A good question designer knows the value of learning more from fewer questions.

Is the Question of Proper Scope and Coverage?

Incomplete or Unfocused. We can test this content issue by asking, "Will this question reveal all we need to know?" We sometimes ask participants to reveal their motivations for particular behaviors or attitudes by asking them, "Why?" This simple question is inadequate to probe the range of most causal relationships. When studying product use behavior, for example, we learn more by directing two or three questions on product use to the heavy-use consumer and only one question to the light user.

Questions are also inadequate if they do not provide the information you need to interpret responses fully.

Double-Barreled Questions. Does the question request so much content that it should be broken into two or more questions? While reducing the overall number of questions in a study is highly desirable, don't try to ask double-barreled questions.

Here's another common example posed to menswear retailers: "Are this year's shoe sales and gross profits higher than last year's?" Couldn't sales be higher with stagnant profits, or profits higher with level or lower sales? This second example is more typical of the problem of double-barreled questions.

A less obvious double-barreled question is the question we ask to identify a family's or a group's TV station preference. Because a single station is unlikely, a better question would ask the station preference of each family member separately or, alternatively, screen for the group member who most often controls channel selection on Monday evenings during prime time. Also, it's highly probable that no one station would serve as an individual's preferred station when we cover a wide range of time (8 to 11 p.m.). This reveals another problem, the imprecise question.

Precision. To test a question for precision, ask, "Does the question ask precisely what we want and need to know?" We sometimes ask for a participant's income when we really want to know the family's total annual income before taxes in the past calendar year. We ask what a participant purchased "last week" when we really want to know what he or she purchased in a "typical 7-day period during the past 90 days." The Albany Clinic's patients were asked for cold and flu history during the time frame "ever." It is hard to imagine an adult who has never experienced a cold or flu and equally hard to assume an adult hasn't been treated for one or both at some time in his or her life.

A second precision issue deals with common vocabulary between researcher and participant. To test your question for this problem, ask, Do I need to offer operational definitions of concepts and constructs used in the question?

Can the Participant Answer Adequately?

Time for Thought. Although the question may address the topic, is it asked in such a way that the participant will be able to frame an answer, or is it reasonable to assume that the participant can determine the answer? This is also a question that drives sample design, but once the ideal sample case is determined, researchers often assume that participants who fit the sample profile have all the answers, preferably on the tips of their tongues. To frame a response to some questions takes time and thought; such questions are best left to self-administered questionnaires.

Participation at the Expense of Accuracy Participants, once committed to an interview, typically want to cooperate in surveys; thus they assume giving any answer is more helpful than denying knowledge of a topic. Their desire to impress the interviewer may encourage them to give answers based on no information. A classic illustration of this problem occurred with the following question:[34] "Which of the following statements most closely coincides with your opinion of the Metallic Metals Act?" The response pattern shows that 70 percent of those interviewed had a fairly clear opinion of the Metallic Metals Act; however, there is no such act. The participants apparently assumed that if a question was asked, they should provide an answer. Given reasonable-sounding choices, they selected one even though they knew nothing about the topic.

To counteract this tendency to respond at any cost, *screen questions* are used to qualify a participant's knowledge. A screen question would likely *branch* or *skip* the participant to other questions.

Assuming that participants have prior knowledge or understanding may be risky. The risk is getting many answers that have little basis in fact. The Metallic Metals Act illustration may be challenged as unusual, but in another case a Gallup report revealed that 45 percent of the persons surveyed did not know what a "lobbyist in Washington" was and 88 percent could not give a correct description of "jurisdictional strike."[35] This points to the need for operational definitions as part of question wording.

Presumed Knowledge.

The question designer should consider the participants' information level when determining the content and appropriateness of a question. In some studies, the degree of participant expertise can be substantial, and simplified explanations are inappropriate and discourage participation. In asking the public about gross margins in menswear stores, we would want to be sure the "general-public" participant understands the nature of "gross margin." If our sample unit were a merchant, explanations might not be needed. A high level of knowledge among our sample cases, however, may not eliminate the need for operational definitions. Among merchants, gross margin per unit in dollars is commonly accepted as the difference between cost and selling price; but when offered as a percentage rather than a dollar figure, it can be calculated as a percentage of unit selling price or as a percentage of unit cost. A participant answering from the "cost" frame of reference would calculate gross margin at 100 percent; another participant, using the same dollars and the "selling price" frame of reference, would calculate gross margin at 50 percent. If a construct is involved and differing interpretations of a concept are feasible, operational definitions may still be needed.

Recall and Memory Decay.

The adequacy problem also occurs when you ask questions that overtax participants' recall ability. People cannot recall much that has happened in their past, unless it was dramatic. Your mother may remember everything about your arrival if you were her first child: the weather, time of day, even what she ate prior to your birth. If you have several siblings, her memory of subsequent births may be less complete. If the events surveyed are of incidental interest to participants, they will probably be unable to recall them correctly even a short time later. An unaided recall question, "What radio programs did you listen to last night?" might identify as few as 10 percent of those individuals who actually listened to a program.[36]

Balance (General versus Specific).

Answering adequacy also depends on the proper balance between generality and specificity. We often ask questions in terms too general and detached from participants' experiences. Asking for average annual consumption of a product may make an unrealistic demand for generalization on people who do not think in such terms. Why not ask how often the product was used last week or last month? Too often participants are asked to recall individual use experiences over an extended time and to average them for us. This is asking participants to do the researcher's work and encourages substantial response errors. It may also contribute to a higher refusal rate and higher discontinuation rate.

There is a danger in being too narrow in the time frame applied to behavior questions. We may ask about movie attendance for the last seven days, although this is too short a time span on which to base attendance estimates. It may be better to ask about attendance, say, for the last 30 days. There are no firm rules about this generality-specificity problem. Developing the right level of generality depends on the subject, industry, setting, and experience of the question designer.

Objectivity.

The ability of participants to answer adequately is also often distorted by questions whose content is biased by what is included or omitted. The question may explicitly mention only the positive or negative aspects of the topic or make unwarranted assumptions about the participant's position. Consider Exhibit Ma-1, an experiment in which two forms of a question were asked. Fifty-seven randomly chosen graduate business students answered version A, and 56 answered version B. Their responses are shown in Exhibit Ma-2. The probable cause of the difference in level of brand preference expressed is that A is an unsupported assumption. It assumes and suggests that everyone has a favorite brand of ice cream and

>**Exhibit Ma-1** A Test of Alternative Response Strategies

A. What is your favorite brand of ice cream? _____

B. Some people have a favorite brand of ice cream, do you? (please check)

    ☐ I do not have a favorite brand of ice cream (Skip to Q #)

    ☐ I do have a favorite brand of ice cream.

    What is your favorite brand ? _____

>**Exhibit Ma-2** Results of Alternative Response
Strategies Test

Response	Version A	Version B
Named a favorite brand	77%*	39%*
Named a favorite flavor rather than a brand	19	18
Had no favorite brand	4	43
	100%	100%
	n = 57	n = 56

Significant difference at the 0.001 level.

will report it. Version B indicates the participant need not have a favorite.

A deficiency in both versions is that about one participant in five misinterpreted the meaning of the term *brand*. This misinterpretation cannot be attributed to low education, low intelligence, lack of exposure to the topic, or quick or lazy reading of the question. The subjects were students who had taken at least one course in marketing in which branding was prominently treated.

Will the Participants Answer Willingly?

Sensitive Information. Even if participants have the information, they may be unwilling to give it. Some topics are considered too sensitive to discuss with strangers. These vary from person to person, but one study suggests the most sensitive topics concern money matters and family life.[37] More than one-fourth of those interviewed mentioned these as the topics about which they would be "least willing to answer questions." Participants of lower socioeconomic status also included political matters in this "least willing" list.

Participants also may be unwilling to give correct answers for ego reasons. Many exaggerate their incomes, the number of cars they own, their social status, and the amount of high-prestige literature they read. They also minimize their age and the amount of low-prestige literature they read. When participants perceive the topic as irrelevant to their own interests or to their perception of the survey's purpose. They participate halfheartedly, often answer with "don't know," give negative replies, give stereotypical responses, or refuse to answer.

You can learn more about crafting questions dealing with sensitive information by reading "Measuring Attitudes on Sensitive Subjects" in Student Resources at www.mhheducation.com/schindler13e.

Question Wording

Shared Vocabulary. Because surveying is an exchange of ideas between researcher and participant, each must understand what the other says, and this is possible only if the vocabulary used is common to both parties.[38] Two problems arise. First, the words must be simple enough to allow adequate communication with persons of limited education. This is dealt with by reducing the level of word difficulty to simple English words and phrases (more is said about this in the section on word clarity).

Technical language is the second issue. Even highly educated participants cannot answer questions stated in unfamiliar technical terms. Technical language also poses difficulties for interviewers. In one study of how corporation executives handled various financial problems, interviewers had to be conversant with technical financial terms. This necessity presented the researcher with two alternatives—hiring people knowledgeable in finance and teaching them interviewing skills or teaching financial concepts to experienced interviewers.[39] This vocabulary problem also exists in situations where similar or identical studies are conducted in different countries and multiple languages.

A great obstacle to effective question wording is the choice of words. Questions to be asked of the public should be restricted to the 2,000 most common words in the English language.[40] Even the use of simple words is not enough. Many words have vague references or meanings that must be gleaned from their context. In a repair study, technicians were asked, "How many radio sets did you repair last month?" This question may seem unambiguous, but participants interpreted it in two ways. Some viewed it as a question of them alone; others interpreted "you" more inclusively, as referring to the total output of the shop. There is also the possibility of misinterpreting "last month," depending on the timing of the questioning. Using "during the last 30 days" would be much more precise and unambiguous. Typical of the many problem words are these: *any, could, would, should, fair, near, often, average,* and *regular.* One author recommends that after stating a question as precisely as possible, we should test each word against this checklist:

- Does the word chosen mean what we intend?
- Does the word have multiple meanings? If so, does the context make the intended meaning clear?
- Does the word chosen have more than one pronunciation? Is there any word with similar pronunciation with which the chosen word might be confused?
- Is a simpler word or phrase suggested or possible?[41]

We cause other problems when we use abstract concepts that have many overtones or emotional qualifications.[42] Without concrete referents, meanings are too vague for the researcher's needs. Examples of such words are *business, government,* and *society.*

Shared vocabulary issues are addressed by using the following:

- Simple rather than complex words.
- Commonly known, unambiguous words.
- Precise words.
- Interviewers with content knowledge.

Unsupported Assumptions   Unwarranted assumptions contribute to many problems of question wording. A metropolitan newspaper, *Midwest Daily*, conducted a study in an attempt to discover what readers would like in its redesigned lifestyle section. One notable question asked readers: "Who selects your clothes? You or the man in your life?" In this age of educated, working, independent women, the question managed to offend a significant portion of the female readership. In addition, *Midwest Daily* discovered that many of its female readers were younger than researchers originally assumed and the only man in their lives was their father, not the spousal or romantic relationship alluded to by the questions that followed. Once men reached this question, they assumed that the paper was interested in serving only the needs of female readers. The unwarranted assumptions built into the questionnaire caused a significantly smaller response rate than expected and caused several of the answers to be uninterpretable.

Frame of Reference   Inherent in word meaning problems is also the matter of a frame of reference. Each of us understands concepts, words, and expressions in light of our own experience. The U.S. Bureau of the Census wanted to know how many people were in the labor market. To learn whether a person was employed, it asked, "Did you do any work for pay or profit last week?" The researchers erroneously assumed there would be a common frame of reference between the interviewer and participants on the meaning of *work*. Unfortunately, many participants viewed themselves primarily or foremost as homemakers or students. They failed to report that they also worked at a job during the week. This difference in frame of reference resulted in a consistent underestimation of the number of people working in the United States.

In a subsequent version of the study, this question was replaced by two questions, the first of which sought a statement on the participant's major activity during the week. If the participant gave a nonwork classification, a second question was asked to determine if he or she had done any work for pay besides this major activity. This revision increased the estimate of total employment by more than 1 million people, half of them working 35 hours or more per week.[43]

The frame of reference can be controlled in two ways. First, the interviewer may seek to learn the frame of reference used by the participant. When asking participants to evaluate their reasons for judging a retail store as unattractive, the interviewer must learn the frames of reference they use. Is the store being evaluated in terms of its particular features and layout, the failure of management to respond to a complaint made by the participant, the preference of the participant for another store, or the participant's recent difficulty in returning an unwanted item?

Second, it is useful to specify the frame of reference for the participant. In asking for an opinion about the new store design, the interviewer might specify that the question should be answered based on the participant's opinion of the layout, the clarity and placement of signage, the ease of finding merchandise, or another frame of reference.

Biased Wording   Bias is the distortion of responses in one direction. It can result from many of the problems already discussed, but word choice is often the major source. Obviously, such words or phrases as *politically correct* or *fundamentalist* must be used with great care. Strong adjectives can be particularly distorting. One alleged opinion survey concerned with the subject of preparation for death included the following question: "Do you think that decent, low-cost funerals are sensible?" Who could be against anything that is *decent* or *sensible*? There is a question about whether this was a legitimate survey or a burial service sales campaign, but it shows how suggestive an adjective can be.

Congressional representatives have been known to use surveys as a means of communicating with their constituencies. Questions are worded, however, to imply the issue stance that the representative favors. Can you tell the representative's stance in the following question?

> *Example:*   Would you have me vote for a balanced budget if it means higher costs for the supplemental Social Security benefits that you have already earned?

We can also strongly bias the participant by using prestigious names in a question. In a historic survey on whether the war and navy departments should be combined into a single defense department, one survey said, "General Eisenhower says the army and navy should be combined," while the other version omitted his name. Given the first version (name included), 49 percent of the participants approved of having one department; given the second version, only 29 percent favored one department.[44] Just imagine using LeBron James's or Stephen Curry's name in a survey question asked of teen boys interested in basketball. The power of aspirational reference groups to sway opinion and attitude is well established in communication; it shouldn't be underestimated in survey design.

We also can bias response through the use of superlatives, slang expressions, and fad words. These are best excluded unless they are critical to the objective of the question. Ethnic and religious references should also be stated with extreme care.

Personalization.   How personalized should a question be? Should we ask, "What would you do about . . . ?" Or should we ask, "What would people with whom you work do about . . . ?" The effect of personalization is shown in a classic example reported by Cantril.[45] A split test—in which a portion of the sample received one question, with another portion receiving a second question—was made of a question concerning attitudes about the expansion of U.S. armed forces in 1940, as noted in Exhibit Ma-3.

Should the United States do any of the following at this time?
   A. Increase our armed forces further, even if it means more taxes.

Should the United States do any of the following at this time?
   B. Increase our armed forces further, even if you have to pay a special tax.

Eighty-eight percent of those answering question A thought the armed forces should be increased, while only 79 percent of those answering question B favored increasing the armed forces.

Source: Hadley Cantril, ed., *Gauging Public Opinion* (Princeton, NJ: Princeton University Press, 1944), p. 48.

These and other examples show that personalizing questions changes responses, but the direction of the influence is not clear. We cannot tell whether personalization or no personalization is superior. Perhaps the best that can be said is that when either form is acceptable, we should choose that which appears to present the issues more realistically. If there are doubts, then split survey versions should be used (one segment of the sample should get one question version, while a second segment should receive the alternative question version).

Adequate Alternatives. Have we adequately expressed the alternatives with respect to the purpose of the question? It is usually wise to express each alternative explicitly to avoid bias. This is illustrated well with a pair of questions that were asked of matched samples of participants.[46] The question forms that were used are noted in Exhibit Ma-4.

Often the above issues are simultaneously present in a single question. **Exhibit Ma-5** reveals several questions drawn from actual mail surveys. We've identified the problem issues and suggest one solution for improvement.

While the suggested improvement might not be the only possible solution, it does correct the issues identified. What other solutions could be applied to correct the problems identified?

>Exhibit Ma-4 Expressing Alternatives

The way a question is asked can influence the results. Consider these two alternative questions judging companies' images in the community in the face of layoffs:

A. Do you think most manufacturing companies that lay off workers during slack periods could arrange things to avoid layoffs and give steady work right through the year?
B. Do you think most manufacturing companies that lay off workers in slack periods could avoid layoffs and provide steady work right through the year, or do you think layoffs are unavoidable?

The Results:

When Asked . . .	A	B
Company could avoid layoffs	63%	35%
Could not avoid layoffs	22	41
No opinion	15	24

Source: Hadley Cantril, ed., Gauging Public Opinion (Princeton, NJ: Princeton University Press, 1944), p. 48.

Response Strategy

The objectives of the study; characteristics of participants, especially their level of information, level of motivation to participate, and ease of communication; the nature of the topic(s) being studied; the type of scale needed; and your analysis plan dictate the response strategy.

Objective of the Study. If the objective of the question is only to classify the participant on some stated point of view, then the closed question will serve well. Assume you are interested only in whether a participant approves or disapproves of a certain corporate policy. A closed question will provide this answer. This response strategy ignores the full scope of the participant's opinion and the events that helped shape the attitude at its foundation. If the objective is to explore this wider territory, then an open-ended question (free-response strategy) is preferable.

Open-ended questions are appropriate when the objective is to discover opinions and degrees of knowledge. They are also appropriate when the interviewer seeks sources of information, dates of events, and suggestions or when probes are used to secure more information. When the topic of a question is outside the participant's experience, the open-ended question may offer the better way to learn his or her level of information. Closed questions are better when there is a clear frame of reference, the participant's level of information is predictable, and the researcher believes the participant understands the topic.

Open-ended questions also help to uncover certainty of feelings and expressions of intensity, although well-designed closed questions can do the same.

Thoroughness of Prior Thought. If a participant has developed a clear opinion on the topic, a closed question does well. If an answer has not been thought out, an open-ended question may give the participant a chance to ponder a reply, and then elaborate on and revise it.

Communication Skill. Open-ended questions require a stronger grasp of vocabulary and a greater ability to frame responses than do closed questions.

Participant Motivation. Experience has shown that closed questions typically require less motivation and answering them is less threatening to participants. But the

>**Exhibit Ma-5** Reconstructing Questions

Problem/Solution	Poor Measurement Question	Improved Measurement Question

Problems: Checklist appears to offer options that are neither exhaustive nor mutually exclusive. Also, it doesn't fully address the content needs of understanding why people choose a hotel when they travel for personal reasons versus business reasons.
 	
Solution: Organize the alternatives. Create subsets within choices; use color or shading to highlight subsets. For coding ease, expand the alternatives so the participant does not frequently choose "Other."
	If your purpose for THIS hotel stay included personal pleasure, for what ONE purpose specifically?
	❑ Visit friend/relative
	❑ Weekend escape
	❑ Sporting event
	❑ Sightseeing
	❑ Family event
	❑ Vacation
	❑ Other: _____
		Which reason BEST explains your purpose for THIS personal pleasure hotel stay?
		❑ Dining
		❑ Shopping
		❑ Entertainment
		   . . . was this for a . . .
		   ❑ Sport-related event?
		   ❑ Theater, musical, or other performance?
		   ❑ Museum or exhibit?
		❑ Visit friend/relative
		   . . . was this for a special event?
		      ❑ YES ❑ NO
		❑ Vacation
		   . . . was this primarily for . . .
		      ❑ Sightseeing?
		      ❑ Weekend escape?
		❑ Other:_____

Problems: Double-barreled question; no time frame for the behavior; "frequently" is an undefined construct for eating behavior; depending on the study's purpose, "order" is not as powerful a concept for measurement as others (e.g., purchase, consume, or eat)
 	
Solution: Split the questions; expand the response alternatives; clearly define the construct you want to measure.
	When you eat out, do you frequently order appetizers and dessert?
	❑ YES ❑ NO
		Considering your personal eating experiences away from home in the last 30 days, did you purchase an appetizer or dessert more than half the time?
		
		      More Than Half Less Than Half
		      the Time the Time
		Purchased
		  an appetizer ❑ ❑
		  a dessert ❑ ❑
		❑ Purchased neither appetizers nor desserts.

Problem: Nonspecific time frame; likely to experience memory decay; nonspecific screen (not asking what you really need to know to qualify a participant). **Solution:** Replace "ever" with a more appropriate time frame; screen for the desired behavior.	Have you ever attended a college basketball game? ❑ YES ❑ NO	In the last six months, have you been a spectator at a basketball game played by college teams on a college campus? ❑ YES ❑ NO
Problem: Question faces serious memory decay as a coat may not be purchased each year; isn't asking if the coat was a personal purchase or for someone else; nor do you know the type of coat purchased; nor do you know whether the coat was purchased for full price or at a discount. **Solution:** Limit the time frame; specify the coat type.	How much did you pay for the last coat you purchased?	Did you purchase a dress coat for your personal use in the last 60 days? ❑ YES ❑ NO Thinking of this dress coat, how much did you pay? (to the nearest dollar) $ _____.00 Was this coat purchase made at a discounted price? ❑ YES ❑ NO

response alternatives sometimes suggest which answer is appropriate; for this reason, closed questions may be biased.

While the open-ended question offers many advantages, closed questions are generally preferable in large surveys. They reduce the variability of response, make fewer demands on interviewer skills, are less costly to administer, and are much easier to code and analyze. After adequate exploration and testing, we can often develop closed questions that will perform as effectively as open-ended questions in many situations. Experimental studies suggest that closed questions are equal or superior to open-ended questions in many more applications than is commonly believed.[47]

A good place to start when crafting questions is a review of tested questions. See the chapter Appendix: Sources of Measurement Questions.

>chapter 12

Stage 3: Measurement Instruments

"As an industry we need to get comfortable with mobile survey formats because there are fundamental differences in survey design and we also need to be focused on building our mobile capabilities as part of our sampling practice."

Kristin Luck,
strategic and research consultant,
and founder, Women in Research

>learningobjectives

After reading this chapter, you should understand . . .

LO12-1   The process of developing the measurement instrument.

LO12-2   The major categories of elements within a measurement instrument and the purpose each plays.

LO12-3   What the researcher is doing in Phase 2 and Phase 3 and the motivations for specific decisions.

LO12-4   The role of pretesting during Phases 2 and 3.

>Instrument Design

A **measurement instrument** is a sequenced list of questions, crafted using various scale options, complete with an introduction, section transitions, instructions, and a conclusion. It is the primary tool used to extract information from a participant in a structured interview or observation. In this chapter, we will focus on the measurement instrument for communication-based research, frequently called a *questionnaire* or *interview guide*, depending on the survey methodology.

Think of the process of instrument design as similar to playing with a jigsaw puzzle: you first organize the pieces before you attempt to put it together to see the picture it represents. Some puzzle enthusiasts approach the pieces strategically. They organize the pieces based on color (blue, red, green), pattern (pattern or solid, part of a face, part of a building), shape (straight edges versus curved), etc. They might start with sections: constructing the corners or a particular image within the puzzle. As they work to "solve" the puzzle, they might be working on several of these smaller puzzle sections at the same time. As they pick up a new piece, they look to see whether it fits in a section they have started or fits with a part of the image they have yet to start. Puzzle building can take hours—or days or weeks—depending on the number of pieces, the image's complexity, and the other demands on the puzzle builder's time. For some, puzzle building is a collaborative process: a group of people works on it together. Collaboration might help find the missing piece in a section, the perfect section for a piece, speed up the process, or just be more fun. So the process that results is: collect the pieces (hopefully, they are all in the box), organize the pieces by some strategy, put individual sections together, get help when you need it, then put the sections together to form the total picture.

Novice researchers often think instrument development is a fairly simple process—put the measurement questions together and you're done. But experienced researchers know their first draft

is never the final instrument. It needs to be tested and refined, often several times, before its ready to launch.

Exhibit 12-1 depicts instrument design within the research process. The procedures followed in developing an instrument vary from study to study, but the flowchart suggests three phases: (1) develop and refine the measurement questions, (2) develop and refine the non-question elements, and (3) develop and refine the measurement instrument.

As we developed measurement questions in the previous chapter (Phase 1), we'll start in this chapter with Phase 2.

>Phase 2: Gather and Sort the Pieces

As you experienced in the previous chapter, the creation of a survey question is not a haphazard or arbitrary process. It is exacting and requires paying significant attention to detail and

>**Exhibit 12-1** Instrument Design within the Research Process

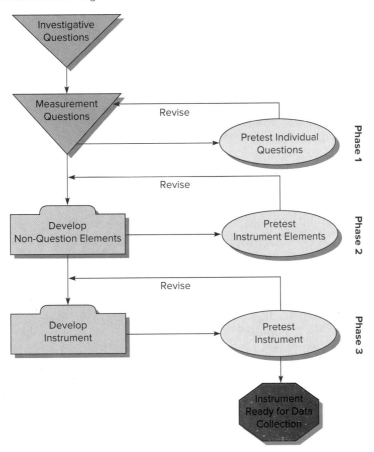

simultaneously addressing numerous issues. Whether you create, borrow, or license a question, you generate specific measurement questions considering subject content, the wording of each question (influenced by the degree of disguise and the need to provide operational definitions for constructs and concepts), and response strategy (each producing a different level of data as needed for your preliminary analysis plan).

In Phase 2, (see Exhibit 12-2) the researcher gathers the measurement questions and non-question elements in preparation to create a measurement instrument with appropriate scope (topics) and coverage (questions within topics). While in the previous chapter the focus was on measurement question design, here we focus on making sure we have a collection of the appropriate questions for fulfilling the research objective. A measurement instrument needs three categories of measurement questions and several non-question elements:

- Administrative questions.
- Classification questions.
- Target questions.
- Non-question elements

The non-question elements include the introduction, transitions, instructions, and a conclusion. We discuss these in the next major section.

>**Exhibit 12-2** Instrument Design Phase 2: Gather and Sort the Pieces

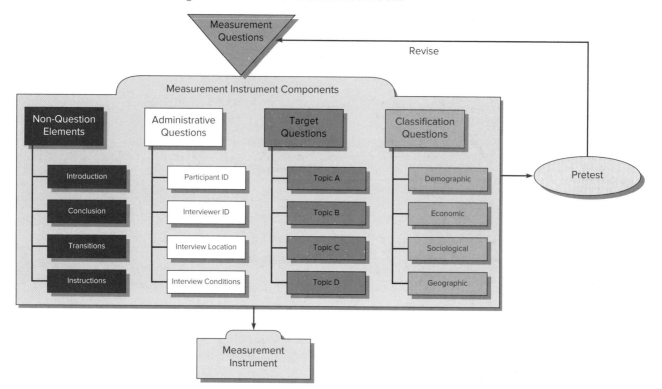

The measurement instrument should accomplish the following:

• Encourage an individual to participate.
• Help establish and maintain rapport with the participant.
• Encourage a participant to provide accurate responses.
• Encourage a participant to provide an adequate amount of information.
• Discourage a participant from refusing to answer specific questions.
• Discourage a participant from early discontinuation of participation.
• Leave the participant with a positive attitude about survey participation.

Question Types

Administrative Questions

Administrative questions identify the (1) participant, (2) interviewer, (3) interview location, and (4) research conditions.

1. Researchers assign each participant a unique identification number; this becomes their case number in a data set. With current technology, this might be in the form of an electronically read code (e.g., barcode) that is scanned during data entry process. It might also be the number that is used by the participant to access a computer-based survey. Other administrative questions about participants may include an assessment of the presence of children or other adults (personal interview), re-contact time (phone surveys), willingness or reluctance, etc. Administrative questions often contain contact information used later for follow-up clarification: an address, email address, or phone number.

>snapshot

Does Cupid Deserve a Place in the Office Cubicle?

As a manager, should you encourage or discourage office romance? Spherion Inc., a leading recruiting and staffing company, recently sponsored its latest Spherion® Workplace Snapshot survey. "The results of this survey confirms what we know intuitively—that many workers find opportunities for romance where they work," shared John Heins, senior vice president and chief human resources officer at Spherion.

The workplace romance findings were collected using the Harris Interactive QuickQuery online omnibus, an online survey fielded two to three times per week. A U.S. sample of 1,588 employed adults, aged 18 or older, were polled in a three-day period in January. Results were weighted to bring them in line with the actual U.S. population.

According to the survey, nearly 40 percent of workers (30 percent of women, 47 percent of men) would consider dating a co-worker or have done so. Approximately 25 percent (27 percent of men, 23 percent of women) of such romances result in marriage. While 41 percent of workers (47 percent of women, 36 percent of men) think an office romance will jeopardize their job security or advancement, 42 percent conduct their romance openly. "The new wrinkle is the explosion of online venues such as blogs, YouTube, and social networking sites, which provide very public means for personal news to be shared," commented Heins. "Becoming a target of gossip on the Internet does have the potential to affect career advancement and security."

© E. Audras/PhotoAlto

Only 16 percent of workers' employers have a policy regarding workplace romance. Although most of us will spend one-third of each day at work, Boswell Group's founding psychoanalyst Kerry Sulkowicz reminds us that "if there's any reporting relationship between the two [people involved], the less powerful person will be the one asked to change jobs or leave."

www.spherion.com; harrisinteractive.com; www.boswellgroup.com

2. Interviewers also are assigned unique identification numbers, information about their gender, age, and ethnicity might be collected when the survey is conducted in person or by phone.

3. Depending on study methodology, interview location might include city, type of environment (e.g., mall, theme park, sports arena) and location within the environment (e.g., outside Macy's at Seminole Mall for intercept studies), whether the study is conducted inside or outside, and the methodology (phone, personal interview, mobile or computer self-administered survey, etc.).

4. Research conditions include such items as day of week, time of day, weather, congestion level, other events or situations occurring at the time of the survey, distractions, etc.

Not all administrative questions are asked but all are recorded; they are necessary to study patterns within the data and identify possible error sources. This information becomes part of each case's data record. Free-response (open-ended) questions may be the most efficient way to structure many of these questions, but dichotomous choice, multiple-choice, or checklist questions may also be used.

Classification Questions

Classification questions allow participants' responses to target questions to be grouped so that patterns are revealed, and can be studied and tested, and insights can be discovered. **Classification questions** cover demographic, economic, geographic, and sociological variables. The topics covered by such questions include age, education, family composition, marital status, income, employment status and type of employment, social class, ethnicity, language, political affiliation, etc. This group may also include questions about behavior and attitudes (charitable giving, environmental sustainability, use of ride-sharing services, etc.) that are not covered but seem related to the target questions. The choice of classification questions differs for each measurement instrument, as each one must serve a purpose in analyzing the data for a specific research objective. Sometimes such questions may seem intrusive or unnecessary to a participant, so researchers are careful to explain how they are used.

Some classification questions may appear early in the measurement instrument; these **screen questions** determine whether a participant has the requisite level of knowledge to participate. Some classifications questions, when used within the instrument, serve as **filter questions**; they determine whether a participant is asked one or more questions within a target question topic or excluded from answering. In order to engage the participant early in the core issues of any survey, many instrument designers place the bulk of classification questions in a separate section at the end of an instrument.

Classification questions may be free-response (e.g., age), dichotomous choice (e.g., gender), multiple-choice (e.g., income, education, employment, race, language, type housing), or rating questions (e.g., degree to which you recycle).

Target Questions

Target questions address the investigative questions of a specific study. Of the three categories of questions, target questions represent the largest number and are the most important. Researchers use these questions, in conjunction with classification questions, to discover patterns that will help the manager make critical decisions.

To facilitate answering a survey, target questions are grouped by topics within an instrument. Based on the research objective, any hypotheses being tested, and the investigative questions, the researcher determines the topics to be covered in the instrument, the number of topics to be covered (**instrument scope**), and the number and breadth of questions needed in each group (**instrument coverage**). Researchers may arbitrarily limit the scope and coverage of any particular instrument. When the investigative questions form a long list, the strategy may be to survey participants using multiple instruments over time or select a separate sample so that the survey time frame is not too long. Agile surveys do just this, keeping the measurement instrument short.

Target questions should minimize shifts in frame of reference without notification. This is especially true of behavior questions that provide a time frame. Participants often interpret one question in light of earlier questions and may miss shifts of perspective or subject unless they are clearly stated. Participants fail to listen carefully and frequently jump to conclusions about the importance of a given question before it is completely stated. Their answers are strongly influenced by their own experiences (their frame of reference). Any change in subject or topic needs to be obvious. Most questionnaires that cover a range of topics are divided into sections using topic labels with clearly defined transitions between sections to alert the participant to the change in frame of reference. Exhibit 12-5 provides a sample of a transition in a study when measurement questions changed to personal and family-related questions.

Target questions may be *structured* (present the participants with a fixed set of choices; *closed questions*) or *unstructured* (provide the participant with a frame of reference for their self-crafted answer; *open-ended questions*). Target questions are designed using the full range of measurement scales. To facilitate answering a survey more quickly, instrument designers tend to use fewer question types within a single measurement instrument; this allows the participant to get familiar with question structure.

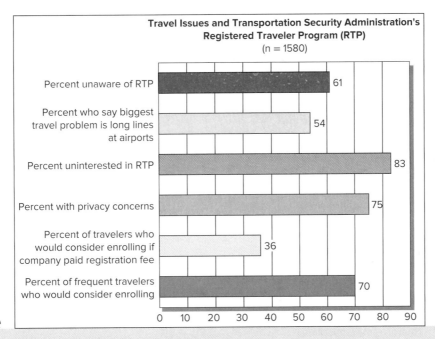

>**pic**profile

Organizations use questionnaires to measure all sorts of activities and attitudes. Deloitte & Touche USA LLP used an online questionnaire to measure understanding of the Registered Traveler Program for the Transportation Security Administration. This program promises that registered travelers will not have to contend with long lines at terminal entrances. Some findings from this survey are noted in the accompanying graph. **www.tsa.gov; www.deloitte.com**

Pretesting: Scope and Coverage

It is during this phase that a researcher might collaborate with research colleagues. From these colleagues, a researcher may seek evaluation of an instrument's topics (scope) and a topic's questions (the coverage). Colleagues also can spot when questions assigned to one topic seem better suited to a different topic, alerting a researcher to potential order problems. Or they may suggest a different order of topics than the plan proposes. Rather than developing an instrument during this phase, the researcher provides a mock-up of the question topics, including each question's focus within a topic, and requests feedback. Obtaining feedback before an instrument is created saves valuable time, as well as prevents bias and error.

A second round of pretesting might order the topics and provide the actual questions for the topic, but not designated in any order. Seeing a question in the context of its topic for the first time might lead to recommendations about question inclusion (drop or add). Of course, the colleague also might suggest that a question should be asked in a different way or that a different scale would be more appropriate given the other questions within the topic.

Responsibility Fulfillment

In this phase, the research has many responsibilities. Exhibit 12-3 summarizes how actions during this phase can fulfill those responsibilities.

>Phase 2: Non-Question Elements

We have our pretested measurement questions grouped by classification, target, and administrative questions, and we've pretested the target topics for appropriate scope and coverage. Now we need the elements that begin and end the instrument, and build rapport and quality.

>**Exhibit 12-3** Actions That Fulfill Phase 2 Responsibilities

Responsibilities	Actions
Encourage an individual to participate.	• Provide appropriate introduction.
Help establish and maintain rapport with the participant.	• Provide information on anonymity and confidentiality. • Order high-interest topics early; order sensitive topics at the end. • Provide clear instructions.
Encourage each participant to provide accurate responses.	• Provide operational definitions as necessary • Use common vocabulary in instructions and transitions
Encourage each participant to provide an adequate amount of information.	• Order questions from general to specific. • Use color/design features to enable participant to see full range of tasks and response options. • Include prompts to complete a skipped or missed question.
Discourage each participant from refusing to answer specific questions.	• Establish rapport early. • Provide a prompt when a question is skipped or missed that stresses its importance.
Discourage each participant from early discontinuation of participation.	• Order topics based on participant interest. • Keep all questions relating to the same topic together. • Show appreciation for the participant's time by restricting topics and questions to what is critical. • Provide a *status bar* on computer/mobile surveys. • Vary response strategy to avoid boredom. • When using the same scale use repetitive response categories, when possible. • Use visual stimuli as part of question, instruction, or transition. • Use visual response options (mobile/computer).
Leave the participant with a positive attitude about survey participation.	• Include topics and questions that make the participant feel knowledgeable, having contributed to something important. • Ask meaningful questions related to the topics. • Thank the participant in the conclusion.

Rapport has been studied in research as a result and as behaviors. For example, **rapport** is described as creating respondent motivation, generating freely given and adequate answers, but also as "a relationship characterized by agreement, mutual understanding, or empathy that makes communication possible or easy" or as "harmonious accord or relation that fosters cooperation, communication, or trust."[1] Rapport is viewed as a positive for encouraging participation (reducing response bias), but it can be viewed as a negative if it causes a participant to try to ingratiate themselves to the researcher or interviewer (**social desirability bias**) and thus provide inaccurate answers in an attempt to be accepted. Most researchers approach the building of rapport as a necessary function of the instrument; without rapport, motivation to participate and to complete an instrument declines.[2]

As depicted in Exhibit 12-4, this part of Phase 2 is focused on elements that can (1) enhance rapport with the participant by making it easier, less stressful, and more enjoyable to complete the

>**Exhibit 12-4** Phase 2: Flowchart for Instrument Design

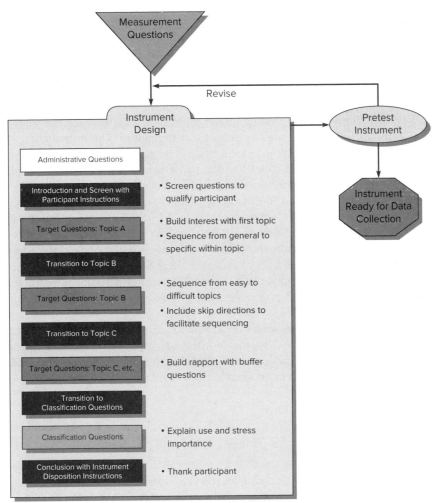

survey process and (2) ensure high-quality results by providing elements that make thorough and accurate responses possible by diminishing motivation to discontinue the survey process. These elements are:

1. The introduction.
2. Transitions.
3. Instructions for the interviewer.
4. Instructions the participant.
5. The conclusion.

The measurement instrument non-question elements should accomplish the following:

- Encourage the participant to participate in the survey.
- Facilitate the participant's understanding of the process, including the time or activity commitment.
- Facilitate the participant's understanding of target groups of questions being asked.
- Make answering the questions easier; provide operational definitions when necessary.
- Encourage the participant to complete the questionnaire.
- Alleviate any concerns participants might have so they view the experience as valuable and worth their time.

Non-Question Elements

Introduction

The introduction must supply the participant with the motivation to participate in the study. When an interviewer is used, the introduction provides the interviewer's first name to help establish critical rapport with the potential participant. It must reveal enough about the forthcoming questions, usually by revealing some or all of the topics to be covered, for participants to judge their interest level and their ability to provide the desired information. In any communication study, the introduction must reveal the amount of time necessary for participation. The introduction also reveals the research organization or sponsor (unless the study is disguised) and, broadly, the objective of the study. It may include a statement about how the participant was selected. It attempts to alleviate concerns about anonymity and confidentiality, and usually contains a confidentiality statement about how the data will be handled. Additionally, more than two-thirds of phone surveys contain a statement that the interviewer is "not selling anything."[3] If Institution Review Board practices are being followed, the introduction will include a statement that indicates participation is voluntary. Answering the first question implies consent. The introduction is the perfect place to encourage participants to answer truthfully, by telling them that there are "no right answers" because this reduces social desirability bias. Broadly, the introduction provides participant instruction for proceeding with the survey. Exhibit 12-5 provides a sample introduction and other components of an instrument.

If participants have not been prescreened, the introduction leads with one or more screen questions to determine if the potential participant has the knowledge or experience necessary to participate in the study. If they have insufficient knowledge or background, the introduction will provide the survey discontinuation statement (e.g., "We are only speaking today with people who have a dog at least 5 years old. Thank you for speaking with me.")

Transitions

Transitions are descriptive statements that are designed to alert the participant to a change in topic or a shift in question group. Transitions may include an introduction and operational definitions necessary to answer subsequent questions. If all questions in the topic use the same response scale, that scale might be included in the transition. Change of time frame is also possible in a transition. Exhibit 12-5 provides a sample of a transition in a study when measurement questions changed to personal and family-related questions.

Interviewer Instructions

Besides skip directions, interviewers are usually provided with instructions for the following to ensure that protocols are followed consistently.

- *Terminating an unqualified participant*—defines for the interviewer how to terminate an interview when the participant does not correctly answer the screen or filter questions.

- *Terminating a discontinued interview*—defines for the interviewer how to conclude an interview when the participant decides to discontinue.

- *Moving between questions on an instrument*—defining for an interviewer or participant how to move between questions or topic sections of an instrument (*skip directions*) when movement is dependent on the specific answer to a question or when branched questions are used.

- *Disposing of a completed questionnaire*—defines for an interviewer how to submit the completed measurement instrument.

These instructions may be embedded in computer-assisted interviews, or may be covered in training for all other interview types. The first two types of instructions are designed to maintain rapport and give the participant a good feeling about the survey and its parties, even if termination is their choice. The last is to assure that the data collected will be included in the final data set.

>**Exhibit 12-5** Sample Components of Communication Instruments

Component	Example
Introduction	
a. Phone/personal interview	Good evening. May I please speak with (name of participant)?
	Mr. (participant's last name), I'm (your name), calling on behalf of XYZ Corporation. You recently had your laptop serviced at our CareCenter. Could you take five minutes to tell us what you thought of the service provided by the Center?
b. Online (often delivered via email)	You've recently had your laptop serviced at our CareCenter. Could you take five minutes to tell us what you thought of the service provided by the Center? Just click the link below.
Transition	The next set of questions asks about your family and how you enjoy spending your nonworking or personal time.
Instructions for . . .	
a. Terminating (following filter or screen question)	*Phone:* I'm sorry, today we are only talking with individuals who eat cereal at least three days per week, but thank you for speaking with me. (Pause for participant reply.) Good-bye.
	Online: You do not qualify for this particular study. Click below to see other studies for which you might qualify.
b. Participant discontinuation	Would there be a time I could call back to complete the interview? (Pause; record time.) We'll call you back then at (repeat day, time). Thank you for talking with me this evening.
	Or:
	I appreciate your spending some time talking with me. Thank you.
c. Skip directions (between questions or groups of questions . . . paper or phone)	3. Did you purchase boxed cereal in the last 7 days? ❏ Yes ❏ No (skip to question 7)
d. Disposition instructions	*Paper survey:* A postage-paid envelope was included with your survey. Please refold your completed survey and mail it to us in the postage-paid envelope.
	Online: Please click DONE to submit your survey and enter the contest.
Conclusion	
a. Phone or personal interview	That's my last question. Your insights and the ideas of other valuable customers will help us to make the CareCenter the best it can be. Thank you for talking with us this evening. (Pause for participant reply.) Good evening.
b. Self-administered (usually precedes the disposition instructions)	Thank you for sharing your ideas about the CareCenter. Your insights will help us serve you better.
c. Post-survey contact	If you have any questions about this survey, please contact Pamela Schindler at 123-456-7890.

Participant Instructions

Besides skip directions, participants are usually provided with instructions for the following:

- *Accessing the measurement instrument*—defines for a participant how to access the measurement instrument and open it. This may be done as part of the introduction or by an email or call that recruited the participant.

- *Using survey software*—defines for the participant how to move from page to page or screen to screen, whether returning to previous questions is permitted (computer based), whether saving responses or submitting responses periodically is required, how to respond to "correction" instructions (embedded instructions about finishing a question, such as answering a skipped item in a multi-item rating question), how to alert the researcher if the participant is having problems, how to upload images or video, etc.

- *Answering a particular question or set of questions*—provides an explanation or instructions for a particular question or group (e.g., providing a scale that is consistent for several questions or describing the details for an activity that is part of a question).

- *Disposing of a completed questionnaire*—defines for a participant completing a self-administered instrument how to submit the completed questionnaire. This may be as simple as "Click FINISHED to send your answers to us." or "Please return the questionnaire to us in the provided postage-paid envelope through the U.S. Postal Service."

These instructions are usually embedded in computer-based surveys. For self-administered surveys delivered by email or mail, they may be printed on the measurement instrument or on a separate instruction sheet that accompanies the instrument.

Conclusion

The role of the conclusion is to leave the participant with the impression that his or her involvement has been valuable. Subsequent researchers may need this individual to participate in new studies. If every instrument expresses appreciation for participation, cooperation in subsequent studies is more likely. A conclusion should always include a sincere thank you for participation. It will usually include a statement about follow-up contact for clarification. It is likely to include a statement about whom a participant might contact if they have questions (name and phone or name and email). It may include an offer to share of the findings. If compensation was offered, it will likely include directions for obtaining compensation. A sample conclusion is shown in Exhibit 12-5.

Overcoming Instrument Problems

The researcher can do several things to help improve survey results, among them:

- Build rapport with the participant.
- Pretest all the survey elements. (See Appendix: Pretesting available from Connect.)

Build Rapport with the Participant

Most information can be secured by direct undisguised questioning if rapport has been developed. Rapport is particularly useful in building participant interest in the project; the more interest participants have, the more cooperation they will give. One can also overcome participant unwillingness by providing compensation for completing the instrument. This approach has been especially successful in mail surveys and is increasingly used in computer-based surveys.

The assurance of confidentiality also can increase participants' motivation. One approach is to give discrete assurances, both by question wording and by interviewer comments and actions, that all types of behavior, attitudes, and positions on controversial or sensitive subjects are acceptable and normal. Where you can say so truthfully, guarantee that participants' answers will be used only in combined statistical totals (aggregate data), not matched to an individual participant. If participants are convinced that their replies contribute to some important purpose, they are more likely to be candid, even about taboo topics. If a researcher's organization uses an Institutional Review Board to review instruments before use, the board may require an instruction indicating that any response—in fact, participation—is voluntary. This is especially important where surveys are conducted with internal participants (e.g., employees).

Pretest Non-Question Elements

Given the importance of the introduction in building rapport, it is wise to pretest these elements. Providing just the introduction to a sample of participant surrogates and asking questions about their willingness to participate will give the researcher an indication of whether the introduction needs to be revised. Based only on the introduction, the sample can also tell the researcher what topics participant surrogates expect the instrument to cover and whether they believe they would have difficulty with those topics.

>**Exhibit 12-6** Actions That Fulfill Phase 2 Responsibilities: Non-Question Elements

Responsibilities	Actions
Encourage the participant to participate in the survey.	• Provide an introduction that boosts the participants self-value. • Provide an appropriate incentive for participation.
Facilitate the participant's understanding of the process, including the time or activity commitment.	• Specify the longest amount of time for completion in introduction. • Provide a status bar (amount of measurement questions completed) with each question (computer/mobile). • Specify types of activities critical to the study.
Facilitate the participant's understanding of target groups of questions being asked. }	• Create transitions between target question groups to shift participant's frame of reference.
Make answering the questions easier.	• Provide operational definitions for key concepts, constructs, variables.
Encourage the participant to complete the questionnaire.	• Send reminders to participate (email, phone). • Supply in-instrument prompts to complete unanswered or skipped questions.
Alleviate any concerns participants might have, so they view the experience as valuable and worth their time.	• Provide contact person and phone for any follow-up issues.

The researcher can share topics and ask whether participant surrogates would need explanations between the planned topics. If complex activities, like uploading videos or pictures, are planned as part of the survey process, the researcher may test whether planned instructions are sufficient.

The conclusion is responsible for ensuring that the instrument is returned to the researcher and for leaving a favorable impression of the survey and its sponsor or researcher. Leaving a favorable impression means that the participant is satisfied with the process and has no concerns. If it doesn't accomplish its purpose, it should be revised. This element is not as frequently tested as the introduction and instructions, but should be.

We devote an appendix to pretesting; it's available from Connect.

Responsibility Fulfillment

Exhibit 12-6 provides a summary of the actions that researchers can take to fulfill the responsibilities of rapport development and quality.

> Phase 3: Organize the Pieces

As depicted in Exhibit 12-1, Phase 3 of instrument design is a multistep process that results in a finished measurement instrument. Its steps are:

1. Place the introduction, including screen questions.
2. Determine the order of topics.
3. Determine question order within topics.
4. Determine classification section placement.
5. Determine classification question order.
6. Place transitions.
7. Place instructions.
8. Place conclusion.
9. Determine physical design.

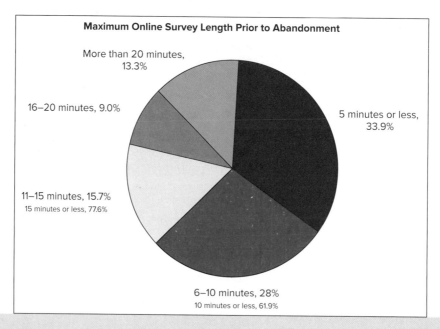

Maximum Online Survey Length Prior to Abandonment

More than 20 minutes, 13.3%

16–20 minutes, 9.0%

5 minutes or less, 33.9%

11–15 minutes, 15.7%
15 minutes or less, 77.6%

6–10 minutes, 28%
10 minutes or less, 61.9%

>**pic**profile

As survey participation declines, measurement instrument length is of increasing concern. InsightExpress studied the web survey process and revealed that people taking web surveys prefer shorter to longer surveys, consistent with what we know about phone, mobile, and intercept survey participants. While 77 percent were likely to complete a survey that took 15 minutes or less, almost one in three participants needed a survey to be 5 minutes or less for full completion. As participating in online surveys in no longer a novelty, prospective participants are likely to become even more reluctant to give significant time to the survey process. Therefore, it is critical that researchers ask only what is necessary. www.insightexpress.com

We will concentrate in this section on placement of topics, questions within topics, facilitating the flow between questions, and placement of classification questions. Tasks 1, 6, and 8 have a given location (beginning of the instrument, as an entry to a specific topic, or end of the instrument, respectively). Task 7 is either at the beginning of a topic or before a specific question, depending on the instruction.

Besides accomplishing the research objective, the measurement instrument should accomplish the following:

- Encourage the participant to participate in the survey.
- Facilitate the participant's understanding of the process, including the time or activity commitment.
- Facilitate the participant's understanding of target groups of questions being asked.
- Provide necessary operations definitions to make answering the questions easier.
- Encourage the participant to complete the questionnaire.
- Alleviate any concerns participants might have, so they view the experience as valuable and worth their time.

Order Topics and Questions

Topics

Researchers have a tendency to want to order the topics based on the research objective and investigative questions. This is logical, from their perspective, because that is the researcher's focus. But this is the wrong strategy. The order of topics should be determined by the need to establish and maintain the participant's interest and motivation to complete. This means topics with high interest or human-interest value should start the instrument. Topics should follow in an order that facilitates ease of answering the questions, based on topics that came before, and limits jumps in subject for the participant. It is this need to build interest that argues against loading classification questions early in the instrument.

>**snap**shot

New Vehicle Survey

Let's assume you recently bought a new car. About three months later you received a survey form in the mail. You had been encouraged several times during the purchase process to complete the survey when it came. Now it has arrived and you are amazed and overwhelmed.

The cover page gives you two options to complete, the pencil-and-paper version in your hand or a computer-based version online. The pencil-and-paper version is printed on over-sized paper and stapled like a booklet. On the cover page is a request for completion. It indicates this is an industry-wide, not a dealer study. The industry will use the "relevant insights" you provide "to help automobile manufacturers take decisive action with regards to future products and services" and "help create the next generation of products the automotive industry produces." As an incentive, participants will be entered into a contest for eight cash prizes, ranging from $1,000 to $10,000. This prize entry is offered because they "appreciate and respect" the participant's time. The survey has a bar code and, for the online version, a password that are person specific. In very small type, below the required contest language about not needing to purchase to win, is a statement that the research company is "committed to protecting" participant privacy "within applicable laws."

The printed survey is 10 pages long and printed in very small 7-point type. It has 64 target questions and 13 classification questions. Nine of the 64 target questions are rating scales. Of these nine, 7 are multi-item rating scales; the fewest items per question is 3, while the most has 77 items. Of these nine, 3 questions have more than 66 items each. Of these nine, 4 are semantic differentials with between 18 and 35 items. Two of the rating scales are 4-point forced-choice scales, without a neutral point; the remaining 5 are 5-point scales, 3 of which are unbalanced with a 3:2 or 4:1 ratio of positive to negative rating points. While there are some dichotomous choice questions, most of the remaining questions are multiple choice or checklists. Five questions are open-ended, asking for accessories purchased, brand and model purchased, finance provider, and useful website URLs.

The question topics are numbered and in the order in which they appear in the survey:

1. New vehicle satisfaction
2. Vehicle equipment
3. Vehicle use and equipment

©Syda Productions/Shutterstock

4. Vehicle perception
5. Feature satisfaction
6. Features sought
7. Vehicle financing
8. Car shopping experience
9. Aftermarket accessories
10. Previous vehicle information
11. Additional vehicles in household
12. Next vehicle purchase
13. Vehicle fuel information
14. Sources of purchase information
15. Rating of new vehicle on
   - Exterior styling
   - Interior styling
   - Driving/riding
   - Overall
16. Problems
17. Internet use
18. Personal lifestyle and vehicle
19. Self-driving vehicles

Without seeing a single question, as a researcher how would you evaluate this measurement instrument?

In the Snapshot: New Vehicle Survey, the topics are listed in order. We can see the first topic, new vehicle satisfaction, is a rapport builder. The questions include one on satisfaction and one on likelihood to recommend. They are quick and easy to answer. Satisfaction level and recommendation likelihood will likely be used when examining other variables to look for patterns in participant responses. This topic and thee questions are important to the researcher for that purpose. And there is no problem with front-loading them in the instrument to ease the participant into the survey. Thus, we've found the first problem: the order doesn't build participant interest or motivation.

The second topic, vehicle equipment and usage, is really two topics: a series of questions about how the vehicle will be used and who will drive it, along with an equipment inventory. Glance down the list and see where we might find topics related to features or equipment. Are they in topic 3? No, but you will find feature questions in topic 6 and topic 9. You've found the second instrument problem, one that could have been spotted by pretesting, and we're still on the first page. The instrument should keep like topics clustered together.

On the first page, the researcher has presented us with two (really three) topics, and 13 questions, without stimulating our interest. The introduction promised that the researcher was interested in participant insights on creating the next generation of vehicles. No question about that on the first page. But note, topic 19 (on page 9 of the 10-page survey) is on self-driving vehicles; it's one rating question, contain two items using a 5-point, balanced, agreement scale. That topic appears just before the classification questions. If you had agreed to the survey on the promise of the introduction, would you continue?

By ordering the topics from the researcher's perspective, we may lose the participants before they get to what we really want to know: why are they satisfied or not with their new vehicle and what their insights tell us about future directions for the automotive industry.

From this example, we've highlighted four guidelines:

- Order topics based on participant interest, not research objective or investigative questions.
- Order topics to establish participant rapport, interest, and maintain engagement.
- Cluster related topics together.
- Order classification questions (not used as screens or filters) at the end of the instrument.

Within topics, target questions usually move from the simple to the complex. Deferring more complex questions until the participant is more comfortable with the survey process can reduce the number of neutral or "don't know" responses, as well as reduce discontinuations.

- Start topics with easier questions, followed by more complex questions.
- Order topics from easier-to-answer to more-difficult-to answer.

Target Questions

Target questions generally are ordered from general to more specific questions within a topic. The objective of using this *funnel approach* is to learn the participant's frame of reference and to extract the full range of desired information, while limiting the distortion effect that earlier questions might have on later ones within a topic. There is always the potential risk of interaction whenever two or more questions are related, as participants may try to "correctly align" their responses. This can be particularly problematic in self-administered surveys where the participant can return to earlier questions by flipping a page or clicking a "previous" button and then change his or her initial answers. We'll never know if the response we receive is their well-thought-out initial answer or an adjusted, politically or socially correct one.

When asking related opinion questions, a prior question could make participants more or less likely to agree with a second, more specific question.[4] Without pretesting the order, you won't know the nature of the effect. Thus, target question order can have two types of order effects: **contrast effect** (where the order results in a greater difference in responses between the first and second question) and **assimilation effect** (where order results in more similarity in responses between the first and the second question).

- Order questions from general to specific to limit the distortion effect, but test for contrast and assimilation effects.
- Limit participant's ability to change earlier answers based on subsequent questions.

If a topic deals with a sensitive subject, researchers may start the topic with **buffer questions**, designed to build rapport and put the participant at ease. These are broad, neutral questions on the topic that don't require a participant to take a stand on the sensitive issue. For example, "In the last 30 days, have you personally used a streaming service to watch a movie?" before asking "Should anyone be able to access movies with graphic sexual content with streaming services?" In tests, sensitive questions that followed buffer questions have been shown to extract markedly different responses compared with when participants are directly asked a sensitive question without buffers.[5]

Facilitate Topic and Measurement Question Sequencing

The design of measurement instruments is influenced by the need to relate each question to the others in the instrument. Often, the content of one question (called a **branched question**) assumes other questions have been asked and answered in a certain way. In computer-based instruments or computer-assisted instruments, such branching is handled by internal coding of the initial question. The PicProfile indicates a typical branch question; it reveals the elimination of alternatives not chosen in one question when asking the second question, thus shortening the participant's time.

Instructions also are a primary tool to facilitate sequencing Three types of sequencing result in **skip directions**. These instructions indicate where the participant or interviewer should go within the instrument—a question, topic or section— given one or a series of responses. These instructions can be embedded in the instrument (paper or computer-based) or provided to the interviewer. Computer-based instruments and computer-assisted interviewing make skipping fairly easy; once a pre-programmed response is entered, the computer automatically skips the participant ahead. The first type is a question-to-question skip: a question screens for experience or knowledge, and the participant is judged unable to answer the next question without it:

Example: In the last two weeks, have you used (product)? ❑ Yes ❑ No (If No, skip to Q3)

2. Which of the following attributes do you like about the automobile you just saw? (Select all that apply.)

- ☑ Overall appeal
- ☑ Headroom
- ❑ Design
- ❑ Color
- ☑ Height from the ground
- ❑ Other _____
- ❑ None of the above

[Next Question]

3. For those items that you selected, how important is each? (Provide one answer for each attribute.)

	Extremely important		Neither important nor unimportant		Not at all important	Don't know
a) Overall appeal	○	○	○	○	○	○
b) Height from the ground	○	○	○	○	○	○
c) Headroom	○	○	○	○	○	○

>**pic**profile

One of the attractions of using a web survey is the ease with which participants follow branching questions immediately customized to their response patterns. In this survey, participants were shown several pictures of a prototype vehicle. Those who responded to question 2 by selecting one or more of the attributes in the checklist question were sequenced to a version of question 3 that related only to their particular responses to question 2. Note also that in question 3 the researcher chose not to force an answer, allowing the participant to indicate he or she had no opinion ("Don't know") on the issue of level of importance.

>**Exhibit 12-7** Skip Logic Diagrams, Two Options

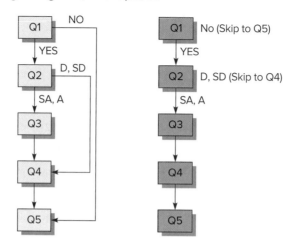

The second type is a question-to-topic skip: a question screens for experience or knowledge, and the participant is judged unable to answer any question within that topic without it:

Example: In the last six months, did you complete sexual harassment training?
❏ Yes ❏ No (If No, skip to Section on Safety)

The third type is the question-to-classification skip. This is determined by the answer to one or several previous questions and results when a participant passes an initial screen but subsequent responses indicate they are not qualified for the survey.

Researchers have developed all sorts of tools and approaches to help with sequencing. One favorite is a **skip logic diagram**, a graphical presentation of measurement questions in a measurement instrument indicating the skip direction. These can be created simply with paper and pencil. Some researchers print individual questions on pieces of paper, arrange them on a surface, attach Post-Its with the skip directions, then take pictures of the final result. Others map the skip directions using flow-chart or design software. Exhibit 12-7 provides two options for the design of a skip logic diagram. Any skip logic diagram, regardless of its origin, is a helpful aid when developing complex computer-based instruments, especially prior to entering questions into computerized survey software.

The basic principle used to guide sequence decisions is this: The nature and needs of the participant must determine the sequence of questions and the organization of the interview schedule.

Classification Questions

By the end of a survey process, participants may be tired, as well as increasingly concerned about the personal information they have shared. Researchers add to this often unvoiced concern by asking more personal questions in the classification section. At the start of this section of an instrument, researchers often reiterate that the data collected in this section of questions are used to permit comparison of the participant's responses with others, that the data are used for finding patterns in the data, and that data are viewed in the aggregate, or in groups, not individually.

Most classification questions are dichotomous, multiple-choice, or free-response questions that are easy to answer. But some ask for very personal information that hit sensitive "hot buttons," making some participants reluctant to answer. Religious affiliation, ethnicity, sexual orientation, and income are all sensitive question topics; make sure your research objective demands that these be collected before you build them into your instrument. Sensitive questions can be the reason a survey is discontinued.

When ordering classification questions, determine which are critical for pattern discovery and ask those first. This particular question or questions might have been used to screen or filter earlier questions, so there will be no need to ask it again within this section. It's always a good idea to have an instruction if classification questions are skipped, sharing with the participants the importance of such questions in the data analysis. Researchers generally order the most sensitive questions at the end, to avoid discontinuation.

- Consider using critical classification questions as screens or filters within the instrument.
- Order more critical classification questions early in the section.
- Order the more sensitive classification questions at the end of the section.

Pretest The Instrument

There is no more important **pretest** than fielding the instrument to participant surrogates and research colleagues. This test by participant surrogates is where you get your **completion estimate**—the time a participant will likely take to complete the measurement instrument. You always compute the longest and the average times; it's best to include the longest time as the estimate in the introduction. "This survey will take you up to 10 minutes to complete." Besides providing a completion estimate, participant surrogates can reveal missing or unclear instructions, difficulties with transitions, question order problems, scale problems, and more. Even when you test individual target or classification questions and non-question elements separately, when the instrument is in its completed form, these perform differently.

The researcher him- or herself should test the whole instrument, in all its various configurations, to see if skip directions and branch questions are working. But there is no substitute for field testing these elements with participant surrogates. What works for the researcher who is intimately familiar with the instrument may not work as smoothly for the participant.

Asking a research colleague to take the survey can also be enlightening. What you thought was a logical transition between topics might be revealed as a problem. Colleagues can also point out problems with order, both topic and question within topic. They might also recommend eliminating a question or group of questions, or adding one, once they see the whole instrument. Reviewing colleague instruments is an expected service in the industry; so if you ask for a review, expect to give one in return. Reviewing other researcher's instruments is a great way to sharpen your own instrument design skills.

Many businesses have government contracts and are subject to federal, state, and local laws, policies, and procedures that regulate research on human subjects. One of these, implemented in 1966 by the Department of Health and Human Services is the Institutional Review Board (IRB) risk assessment. Many institutions require all research to comply with the guidelines of this process.[6] A researcher's strict adherence to the IRB process can identify measurement issues and prevent subsequent problems.

Several of the cases with this text provide measurement instruments. Consult the Case Abstracts at the end of the book for which have instruments. You can access these through Connect.

Physical Design

How the measurement instrument looks and functions, when all the parts are compiled, are important aspects of instrument design. These aspects are getting increasing attention from researchers as options are expanding.

- How will visual elements (color, pictures, video) be used?
- How will questions be presented?

Computer-Based Instruments

Visual Design Most computer-assisted telephone surveys, computer-assisted personal interviews, and computer-based surveys have a wider range of design options. Software requires that designers choose color schemes, logo inclusion identifying the manager-sponsor or the research company (if the survey is disguised), and logo placement (first screen only, first and last screen only, each screen).

Visual elements like color are used for reading clarity, especially in distinguishing rows of multi-item rating scales (see Exhibit 12-8). Color is also used to quickly identify and imply the importance

>**Exhibit 12-8** Facilitate Reading and Accurate Response with Color

Q#: How much do you agree or disagree with each of the following statements?	Strongly Agree	Agree	Neither Agree or Disagree	Disagree	Strongly Disagree
My vehicle is my sanctuary.	❏	❏	❏	❏	❏
My vehicle is a reflection of my achievement.	❏	❏	❏	❏	❏
My favorite hobby is working on my car.	❏	❏	❏	❏	❏
My vehicle gives me a feeling of adventure.	❏	❏	❏	❏	❏
The brand of vehicle I buy makes a statement about who I am.	❏	❏	❏	❏	❏
I choose my vehicle to reward myself of my hard work.	❏	❏	❏	❏	❏

of instructions and operational definitions. Depending on the software, these elements may be designed to appear as pop-up windows rather than as a lead-in or part of the question.

Visual elements are increasingly being used for actual response categories (e.g, using male/female symbols for gender rather than words in mobile surveys). Visual images or video can also be used as part of a question, rather than long verbal descriptions, as visuals increase interest and engagement.

Question Presentation For mobile surveys, most questions are presented individually or in groups of two, due to the nature of their smaller screens and to prevent the need for scrolling. For desktop or

When the participant selects her answer, the symbol's background changes color.

Courtesy of FocusVision. Used with Permission

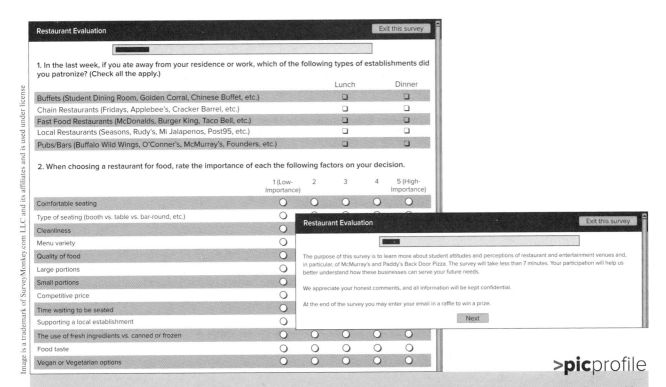

>**pic**profile

Online surveys are increasingly common due, in large part, to their speed in data collection. They also offer versatility for use with various types of measurement scales; flexibility in containing not only verbal, but graphical, photographic, video, and digital stimuli; access to difficult-to-contact or inaccessible participants; and lower cost of large-sample completion. The visual appearance of the measurement question is very important in getting the participant to click through to completion. This invitation from the researcher was the opening screen of the questionnaire and was designed to encourage participation; notice both the mention of time, and the inducement of an incentive. The first screen of the questionnaire indicates two response types: a multiple-choice, multiple-response and a multi-item rating grid. If you look closely, you can also see a scroll bar on the first screen. Some designers will put only one question to a screen in an online questionnaire believing that participants who have to scroll may not fully complete the survey. This is especially true for mobile surveys where you won't see multiple-item grid scales. This survey was designed and fielded through SurveyMonkey. **www.surveymonkey.com**

surveys completed on laptop or tablet computers, questions might be presented within topic groups, or subsets of topic groups, per screen, as with larger screens scrolling is not as problematic. Increasingly, instrument designers are following the mantra, "mobile first," in designing layout, unless the participant is restricted to a particular type of computer equipment to participate.

Another decision in this area is whether the instrument is designed to submit the participant's response after individual questions when the participant clicks for the next question or only at the end of the instrument. The research industry uses both methods, but just like saving your work regularly when you are writing a term paper, having the participant save their work when moving to the next screen is logical and protects the data from power outages or software snafus.

Paper-and-Pencil Instruments

Appearance of an instrument used in a survey employing a face-to-face interview considers issues of practicality and attention more than attractiveness. For interviewers using paper-and-pencil questionnaires, the decisions of physical design are numerous. Introductions and screen questions might be on separate pages. Instructions might be divided with some on separate sheets of paper and others embedded near relevant questions. Conclusions might contain administrative questions on a separate sheet. The designer must consider whether instrument pages should be attached or separate: Which way will it be easier for the interviewer? If participants are offered response cards that detail scale points or verbal or visual descriptions, the material (size, lamination, color) is decided as well as the content. In some intercept interviews, participants are handed electronic tablets rather than paper cards; these screens must be designed and, if multiple screens are needed, these must be ordered for the interviewer.

For the self-administered paper instrument, size of paper (card, letter-sized, or legal-sized paper), color, and thickness all play a role. Some instruments are multipage; the designer must determine whether to organize pages as loose sheets (usually used with one or two sheets), attached sheets (usually used with three or more sheets), or folded booklets (usually used with five or more sheets). The designer also must decide whether to print questions on both sides or a sheet or only one side (usually determined by paper weight, mailing cost, and visual clarity).

Other critical issues of design are how to note topic shifts (paper instruments can use color, but often don't due to cost), and the type font and size of questions (chosen for clarity and ease of reading). Other design concerns include how to make instructions obvious (using a box that contains the text, bold text, oversized text, or shaded or colored backgrounds behind text are some of the options), whether to put the introduction within a cover letter or on the instrument, where to put discontinuation instructions if participants don't "pass" screen questions (these are often boxed below the screen question and include whether the instrument should be returned). When using a paper-and-pencil self-administered survey, a critical design question relates to the disposition of the survey: what size envelope should be provided, should a stamp or postal meter mark be used for postage, should the envelope contain any participant ID symbol (an ID number, a barcode, etc.).

Pretesting: Physical Design

Researchers rely on prior practice, research colleagues, and an understanding of participants gained from participant surrogates during pretesting of the elements to make physical design decisions. It's fairly easy to test different color schemes or use of visual versus verbal elements when using a computer-based instrument, and such decisions are well worth testing. What you are looking for during such pretests are heightened engagement and clarity.

Responsibility Fulfillment

Exhibit 12-9 provides a summary of actions that fulfill Phase 3 responsibilities.

>**Exhibit 12-9** Actions That Fulfill Phase 3 Responsibilities

Responsibilities	Actions
Place the introduction, including screen questions.	• Include description of major topics and critical activities within the introduction.
	• Include completion estimate.
	• Include primary screen question immediately following introduction.
	• Place discontinuation instructions (if participant fails screen question), immediately following screen question.
Determine the order of topics	• Order topics based on participant interest.
	• Order topics to establish rapport, interest and maintain engagement.
	• Order topics of major interest early.
	• Order from easier-to-answer topics to more difficult-to-answer topics.
	• Order sensitive topics later.
	• Cluster related topics together.
	• Determine and apply skip logic diagrams.

>**Exhibit 12-9** Actions That Fulfill Phase 3 Responsibilities (cont'd)

Responsibilities	Actions
Determine question order within each topic	• Order easier-to-answer questions before harder-to-answer/complex questions. • Order general questions before specific questions. • Test for contrast and assimilation effects. • Start sensitive topics with buffer questions to put participants at ease. • Determine branch question(s). • Determine and apply skip logic diagrams.
Determine classification section placement	• Place classification questions section at end of instrument. • Place classification questions used as screen question(s) early.
Determine classification question order.	• Order more critical classification questions early in section. • Order questions requiring sensitive information later.
Place transitions	• Place transitions (including operational definitions, if necessary) between topic sections.
Place instructions	• Place starting instructions at end of introduction. • Place skip instructions within relevant questions or topics. • Place instrument disposition instructions at end of instrument.
Place conclusion	• Provide contact information following submission of instrument (web) or at end of instrument (paper) • Provide incentive collection information following submission of instrument (web) or at end of instrument (paper).
Determine physical design	• Use color to facilitate reading. • Add visually obvious operational definitions for key concepts, constructs, and variables. • Add visually obvious transitions between topics. • Use visual design to facilitate interest and maintain rapport.

>summary

LO12-1 The measurement instrument, the primary tool for collecting data in a communication-based study, is a sequenced list of questions, crafted using various scale options, complete with an introduction, section transitions, instructions, and a conclusion. Instrument design is a multiphase process:
(1) develop and refine the measurement questions,
(2) develop and refine the instrument elements, and
(3) develop and refine the measurement instrument. Instrument design is like building a jigsaw puzzle: You collect the pieces (measurement questions, introduction, conclusion, transitions, instructions), organize them, and then compile them together in order to build the picture.

LO12-2 Instruments obtain three general classes of questions. Target questions address the investigative questions and are the most important and most numerous; these are the focus of any research project. Classification questions concern participant characteristics and allow participants' answers to be grouped for analysis. Administrative questions identify the participant, interviewer, and interview location and conditions; these

are used to label case records and to identify possible sources of differences or error.

LO12-3 During Phase 2, as the researcher designs the measurement instrument their actions must encourage participation, establish and maintain rapport, encourage accurate and thorough responses, discourage answer refusal, discourage early discontinuation, and leave the participant with a positive attitude about participation. They accomplish these responsibilities by chosing topics that stimulate interest, organize topics with participant interest in mind, building each topic with only relevant and critical questions to respect participant time, writing engaging introductions, respectful conclusions, and clear and precise instructions.

In Phase 2, ensuring that an instrument has all three types of questions (administrative, target, and classification) is paramount. Pretesting in the first part of Phase 2 evaluates the instruments scope and coverage. Also in Phase 2, instrument elements that are responsible for building rapport with the participant and ensuring quality are addressed through development of the introduction, conclusion, topic transitions, and instructions.

In Phase 3, organization of all the collected pieces is finalized, and the physical design is addressed. Topic and question sequence or order are addressed. Sequencing can drastically affect participant willingness to cooperate and the quality of responses. Generally, the sequence should begin with efforts to awaken the participant's interest in continuing the survey. Early questions should be simple rather than complex, easy rather than difficult, nonthreatening, and obviously germane to the announced objective of the study. Frame-of-reference changes should be minimal, and questions should be sequenced so that early questions do not distort replies to later ones. Classification question placement should not interfere with participant interest, and so should be placed at the end of the instrument.

Physical design includes visual design, such as color, logo inclusion and placement, use of pictures and video elements for interest and engagement, as well as clarity. It also deals with question delivery in terms of the number of questions delivered per screen. The mantra "mobile first" currently dominates the industry. In paper-and-pencil surveys, interviewer-controlled instruments are dominated by issues of practicality and attention as well as by attractiveness. Care is given to how skip and branch questions are addressed in determining if instruments are divided differently than designed for a self-administered instrument. Issues of paper weight, color, and size are also addressed. Most critical is how topic shifts and instructions are brought to interviewer attention.

LO12-4 Pretesting is the process of evaluating the appropriateness of question scales, the scope and coverage of topics and questions within topics, the organization of those topics and questions, and the rapport and quality elements. Pretesting in Phase 2 is designed to evaluate whether the topics and questions provide a motivating and engaging introduction, thorough instructions to promote thorough and accurate responses, transitions that encourage the participation through to completion, and a conclusion that leaves the participants feeling positive about their participation while ensuring that they correctly submit their instrument for analysis. Phase 2 also assesses the scope (number of topics) and the coverage (questions within each topic) of the instrument to ensure that it meets the needs of investigative questions and the research objective. Pretesting is conducted with both participant surrogates and with research colleagues. Phase 3 pretesting is conducted to ensure that the various parts work together—especially organizational tools like skip directions, filter questions, and branch questions—and to ensure that participants experience no difficulties. Pretesting should also evaluate physical design decisions, layout, color use, questions per screen, paper weight and color, how instructions and definitions are highlighted, etc.

>keyterms

administrative questions 296	filter question 298	skip directions 309
assimilation effect 308	instrument coverage 298	skip logic diagram 310
branched question 309	instrument scope 298	social desirability bias 300
buffer question 309	measurement instrument 294	target question 298
classification question 298	pretest 311	transition 302
completion estimate 311	rapport 300	
contrast effect 308	screen question 298	

>discussionquestions

Terms in Review

1 Distinguish between the following:

   a Administrative and classification questions.

   b Screen and buffer questions.

   c Instruction and a transition.

   d Rapport and social desirability bias.

   e Measurement instrument and measurement question.

2 What is the function of a skip logic diagram?

3 Summarize the instrument design decisions that would result in decreased participant rapport.

4 What would you say are four major faults of measurement instrument design? Justify your choices.

5 One design problem in the development of measurement instruments concerns the sequence of questions.

What suggestions would you give to a novice researcher designing his or her first questionnaire?

6 What invalid assumptions might a researcher make in instrument design? How would each affect the instrument?

Making Research Decisions

7 In a class project, students developed a brief self-administered questionnaire by which they might quickly evaluate a professor. One student submitted the following instrument. Evaluate the organization and the rapport and quality elements of the instrument.

Professor Evaluation Form

1 Overall, how would you rate this professor?

❑ Good

❑ Fair

❑ Poor

2 Does this professor

a Have good class delivery? _____

b Know the subject? _____

c Have a positive attitude toward the subject? _____

d Grade fairly? _____

e Have a sense of humor? _____

f Use audiovisuals, case examples, or other classroom aids? _____

g Return exams promptly? _____

3 What is the professor's strongest point? _____

4 What is the professor's weakest point? _____

5 What kind of class does the professor teach? _____

6 Is this course required? _____

7 Would you take another course from this professor? _____

8 Assume the American Society of Training Directors is studying its membership in order to enhance member benefits and attract new members. Below is a copy of a cover letter and mail questionnaire received by a member of the society.

a Evaluate the cover letter as an introduction.

b Identify question type, develop the topic list, organize questions by topic or type, then evaluate the scope and coverage of the study.

Dear ASTD Member:

The ASTD is evaluating the perception of value of membership among its members. Enclosed is a short questionnaire and a return envelope. I hope you will take a few minutes and fill out the questionnaire as soon as possible, because the sooner the information is returned to me, the better.

Sincerely,

Director of Membership

Directions: Please answer as briefly as possible.

1 With what company did you enter the field of training?

2 How long have you been in the field of training?

3 How long have you been in the training department of the company with which you are presently employed?

4 Is the training department a subset of another department? If so, what department?

5 For what functions (other than training) is your department responsible?

6 How many people, including yourself, are in the training department of your company (local plant or establishment)?

7 What degrees do you hold and from what institutions?

a Undergraduate?

b Graduate?

8 Why were you chosen for training? What special qualifications prompted your entry into training?

9 What experience would you consider necessary for an individual to enter into the field of training with your company? Include both educational requirements and actual experience.

9 Government economic data reveal that young adults, not middle-aged or older adults, are having the most difficult time in today's economy. Although the nation's labor market shows a decline in the unemployment rate, the percentage of young adults, ages 18 to 24, currently employed (54 percent) is at the lowest level since government data collection began in 1948. If you were working for a national survey organization doing a general public survey of young adults and older adults, what topics and questions would you design into your survey to elaborate on this finding?

From Concept to Practice

10 Using Exhibit 12-7, develop a skip logic diagram for the instrument you design in the next question.

From the Headlines

11 A recent study of Ivy League college students showed 20 percent had tried performance-enhancing drugs to improve their academic performance. A Royal Society study found senior employees find the effects even more powerful than do 19-year-olds. A *Financial Times* article claimed these drugs are "becoming popular among city lawyers, bankers, and other professionals keen to gain a competitive advantage over colleagues." A *Nature* readership study showed 20 percent had used or were using such drugs. Scientists predict the use of cognitive enhancers is likely to increase as bioethical and psychological concerns are overcome. While users reported headaches, jitteriness, anxiety, and sleeplessness, such side effects didn't appear to discourage use. Design the measurement instrument that would assess whether the employees in your firm or college were using so-called "smart drugs" to enhance their ability to work harder, longer, or smarter.

>cases*

* You will find a description of each case in the Case Abstracts section of this textbook. Check the Case Index to determine whether a case provides data, the research instrument, video, or other supplementary material. Cases and case supplements are available in Connect.

>**additional**content

You'll find the following appendix available in Connect.

Appendix: Pretesting Options and Discoveries

>part IV

Chapter 13 **Stage 3: Collect, Prepare, and Examine Data**

Collect, Prepare, and Examine the Data

>chapter 13

Stage 3:
Collect, Prepare, and Examine Data

"A well-crafted, thoughtful visualization makes the light bulb go off. You just don't get that with a spreadsheet."

Dana Zuber,
associate director of analytics
Butler, Shine, Stern & Partners Dana Zuber,

>learningobjectives

After reading this chapter, you should understand . . .

LO13-1 The tasks of data collection.

LO13-2 The use of content analysis to postcode textual and verbal data.

LO13-3 The importance of editing raw data to assure it is complete, accurate, and correctly coded.

LO13-4 The exploratory data analysis techniques that provide visual representations of the data.

LO13-5 How cross-tabulation examines relationships between variables.

Dana Zuber, *downloaded* June 22, 2017 (http://get.tableau.com/asset/
how-build-dashboards-persuade-inform-and-engage.html?cid=70132
000001HCNA&ls=Advertisement&lsd=DBM%20-%20Retarget%20
-%20How%20to%20Build%20Dashboards&adgroup=Retarget%20-%20
DBM&creative=building&distribution=DBM&creative=building&dclid=CMHOwqm
nnswCFUYagQodwwwKWQ#preview).

The goal for this phase of the research process is to have a clean data file, suitable for the next phase: data analysis and interpretation. This phase of the research process involves multiple activities (see Exhibit 13-1), including:

- Collect the data
- Enter the data
- Prepare the data
  - Postcoding data
  - Editing data
- Examine the Data

>**Exhibit 13-1** Data Collection, Preparation, and Examination in the Research Process

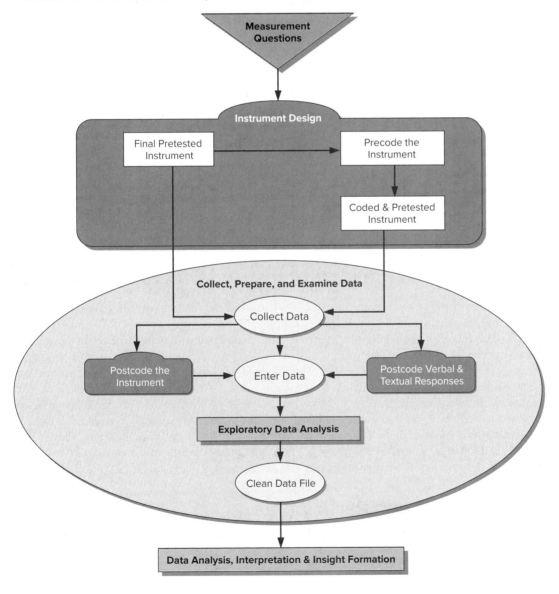

>Collect the Data

Data collection involves the collective actions that field a measurement instrument. The following tasks are included:

1. Train the data collectors.
2. Determine the data collection timeline.
3. Determine and implement an instrument disposition process.
4. Invite the chosen participants.
5. Activate the survey.
6. Remind the participant to complete the survey and return the instrument.
7. Enter the data.

Train the Data Collectors

Training is a critical step if the measurement instrument is complex or the interviewer has some latitude in selecting participants. Knowing how to follow skip directions and other instructions is crucial to data quality. While computer-assisted interviewing feeds the questions to the interviewer, they need to know the whole instrument and where likely pitfalls are located. Interviewers are also trained in approaching prospective participants and minimizing bias, including word emphasis, facial expressions, use of response aids, etc. Making sure the interviewer knows how to submit the completed measurement instrument is usually also part of training.

Determine the Data Collection Timeline

While your research study has a timeline, your actual data collection needs its own timeline. At minimum, it needs to include the survey activation dates and times (start and stop times), when data entry starts and is expected to finish, when data editing starts and finishes, and when the clean data file is ready. It may also include dates and times for training of data collectors when phone and personal interviewers are used.

Determine and Implement Instrument Disposition

Completed measurement instruments are of little value unless they are returned. **Instrument disposition** refers to the procedure(s) by which the completed instrument is returned to the researcher. Some paper-and-pencil instruments are mailed, others are inserted in drop boxes, emailed, or uploaded. Each of these methods needs prior setup—obtaining and placing drop boxes, setting up a special email account or post-office box, and determining a cloud upload location. These methods also need directions, which can be included with the instrument or provided separately. If the sample case is pre-recruited for the survey, the researcher might send directions for instrument completion and collection before the survey starts. Computer-based surveys still need a process for submitting, although if you are using survey software, this process is embedded in the instrument. It might be as simple as adding a line to your instrument's conclusion: "Please click the FINISHED button to send us your answers." If activities other than the measurement instrument are included, such as video or photo elements prepared by the participant, these need to be uploaded.

Invite the Chosen Participants

The invitation is critical to gaining cooperation and it is the first step in building rapport with the participant.

Regardless of the mode by which the survey is conducted, participants may be invited by phone, email, or mail. Participants may also be prescreened as part of this invitation process. Preparing the screen questions and preparing the invitation script, email, or letter are part of the data collection process. Even if a firm is hired to recruit a sample, the researcher will want some say in what the participant is told, what compensation is offered, etc. For intercept studies, the invitation approach is part of interviewer training.

Activate the Survey

The researcher must determine when the instrument is ready to launch. **Survey activation** is the decision that launches the survey; it indicates the researcher has addressed all known measurement instrument problems, and the process is as error-free as he or she can make it.

Remind the Participants

Participants are busy people. They have lives, and participating in research is not a top priority for most of them. Recognizing this, a researcher can dramatically increase the study's response rate by reminding participants if measurement instruments are not submitted or returned. Reminders often use email or phone contact. Multiple reminders are possible, depending on the nature of the probability sample the researcher is using.

Enter the Data

Data entry is a set of processes that including coding (some done prior to data collection when closed questions are used and some done following data collection) and data file creation. Without data entry, the researcher has nothing to analyze. This is the critical last step of data collection and prior to data preparation.

>Enter the Data

Data entry converts data gathered by secondary or primary methods into a medium for data viewing and manipulation. Once data for a particular study is entered, it creates a data file. Various software programs allow users to define data fields and link files so that storage, retrieval, and updating are simplified. The relationship among *data fields*, *data records*, *files*, and *databases* is illustrated in Exhibit 13-2. Many

>**Exhibit 13-2** Data Fields, Records, Files, and Databases

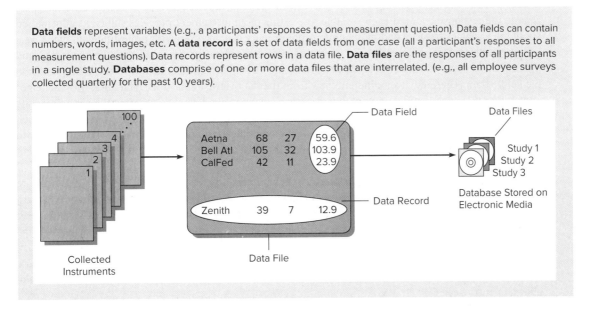

Data fields represent variables (e.g., a participants' responses to one measurement question). Data fields can contain numbers, words, images, etc. A **data record** is a set of data fields from one case (all a participant's responses to all measurement questions). Data records represent rows in a data file. **Data files** are the responses of all participants in a single study. **Databases** comprise of one or more data files that are interrelated. (e.g., all employee surveys collected quarterly for the past 10 years).

>**Exhibit 13-3** Partial Data File

Each row is a *data record*. Each column is a *variable*. In this *data file*, questions 1, 3, 5 are nominal variables that have two response categories. Question 6 uses multiple columns because it is a multi-item rating question, using a 1-to-5 scale; each item is a variable, so each needs its own column. Data can be entered into a spreadsheet, then imported into SPSS or other statistical analysis software—or you can enter data directly into a statistical analysis software program. Each participant is assigned an identification number (CaseID). After a descriptive statistical summary reveals odd value codes or missing data, you can use a CaseID to locate an original measurement instrument to clean the data file.

Microsoft Excel - Sample Survey Spreadsheet

Case ID	Q1	Q2	Q3	Q4	Q5	Q6a	Q6b	Q6c	Q6d	Q6e	Q6f
0001	1	2	1	10	2	1	2	1	1	4	4
0002	2	5	2	7	1	2	2	3	2	4	5
0003	1	2	1	6	2	2	4	3	4	4	4
0004	1	2	1	1	1	3	4	4	4	5	4
0005	2	6	2	8	2	3	5	4	2	5	1
0006	2	1	2	8	2	3	5	2	2	3	1
0007	1	3	1	8	1	2	5	3	5	3	3
0008	2	4	2	5	2	3	3	4	5	1	3
0009	1	2	1	9	1	3	2	4	5	2	5
0010	2	2	2	9	2	4	2	5	5	3	5
0011	2	5	2	9	1	4	1	1	3	1	5
0012	1	2	1	9	1	2	2	2	3	2	2
0013	2	1	2	3	2	5	3	3	4	2	1
0014	1	6	1	2	2	3	4	4	5	5	2
0015	2	4	2	3	1	1	4	3	1	5	3
0016	2	3	2	4	2	5	5	5	2	5	4
0017	1	3	1	6	1	5	5	2	1	1	4
0018	2	3	2	5	2	5	5	2	2	2	3

statistics programs for personal computers and charting and graphics applications have data editors similar to the Excel spreadsheet format shown in Exhibit 13-3. This is a convenient and flexible means for entering and viewing data.

Critical to accurate data entry, as well as data preparation and data analysis, is a coding scheme. A **coding scheme** (*codebook*), contains each variable in the study and specifies the application of *mapping rules* to the response codes of each variable. Pretesting of an instrument provides sufficient information about the variables to test a coding scheme. A preliminary scheme used with pretesting data may reveal coding problems that will need to be corrected before the data for the final study are collected and processed. In many statistical analysis programs, the coding scheme is integral to setting up the data file before data is entered; it's a different view from the data view similar to Exhibit 13-3. Most schemes contain the variable identification number (ID), variable name and label, location of the variable's code in the data record (a column designation), response option codes and labels, and type of variable (which determines its possible statistical procedures). The computerized coding scheme is often too wide to show here, so Exhibit 13-4 provides a paper-based version of a few variables within a larger measurement instrument.

Keyboarding remains a mainstay for researchers who need to create a dataset immediately and store it in a minimal space on a variety of media. It can be a slow, exacting process to enter hundreds of variables for each of thousands of instruments and to do it correctly. However, researchers have profited from more efficient ways for not only speeding up the data-entry process, but also increasing its accuracy: participant entry of data through online or mobile surveys; barcode, optical character and mark recognition for paper surveys; voice recognition for phone surveys; and electronic tablet use by intercept interviewers. Database programs, including spreadsheets and statistical analysis packages, serve as valuable data-entry devices.

>**Exhibit 13-4** Sample Coding Scheme of Some Instrument Questions

Normally, all variables within the instrument would appear in order in the coding scheme. A selection of variables was drawn from the coding scheme of an insurance instrument to show what different variables might look like. Variable IDs starting with A refer to administrative questions; those starting with Q, target questions; those starting with C, classification questions. You might use different letters to start variable IDs, such as S for screen questions, B for branch questions, etc. Or you might choose different designations for target questions, using a different letter to designate a topic of questions rather than a standardized Q. The number following the letter refers to the actual question number on the instrument. As Q6 is a multi-item checklist, each item is a variable, so the variable ID notes this with a small alpha character following the question number. The variable IDs appear in every descriptive statistics, cross-tabulation, or statistical test you request when working within SPSS, SAS, etc. For all elements in your scheme, not just your response codes, make your choices meaningful to you and others reading data analysis files.

Variable ID	Location	Variable Label	Response Codes	Variable Type
A1	1	Interviewer Number	Assigned	Nominal
A2	2	Participant ID	Assigned	Nominal
Q5	10	Evaluation of Current Policy	1=Excellent, 2=Good, 3=Fair, 4=Poor	Ordinal
Q6a	11	Reason for Purchase-Bought Home	1=Yes, 2=No	Nominal
Q6b	12	Reason for Purchase-Birth of Child	1=Yes, 2=No	Nominal
Q6c	13	Reason for Purchase-Death of Relative	1=Yes, 2=No	Nominal
Q6d	14	Reason for Purchase-Promoted	1=Yes, 2=No	Nominal
Q6e	15	Reason for Purchase-Changed Job/Carrier	1=Yes, 2=No	Nominal
Q6f	16	Reason for Purchase-Paid College Expenses	1=Yes, 2=No	Nominal
Q6g	17	Reason for Purchase-Acquired Assets	1=Yes, 2=No	Nominal
Q6h	18	Reason for Purchase-Retired	1=Yes, 2=No	Nominal
Q6i	19	Reason for Purchase-Changed Marital Status	1=Yes, 2=No	Nominal
Q6j	20	Reason for Purchase-Started Business	1=Yes, 2=No	Nominal
Q6k	21	Reason for Purchase-Expanded Business	1=Yes, 2=No	Nominal
Q6l	22	Reason for Purchase-Parent's Death/Illness	1=Yes, 2=No	Nominal
Q6m	23	Reason for Purchase-Agent Contact	1=Yes, 2=No	Nominal
Q6n	24	Reason for Purchase-Other	1=Yes, 2=No	Nominal
C1	30	Gender	1=Male, 2=Female, 3=Other, 9=Missing	Nominal
C2	31	Marital Status	1=Married, 2=Widowed, 3=Divorced, 4=Separated, 5=Never Married	Nominal
C3	32	Housing Ownership	1=Own, 2=Rent, 3=Other, 9=Missing	Nominal
C4	33	Birth Year	2 Digits	Ratio
C5	34	5-Digit Zipcode	5-Digit Code, 99999=Missing	Nominal

>Prepare the Data

Seasoned researchers know that data is not ready for analysis in its raw state. **Data preparation** includes two tasks: post-collection coding of data and editing data. Decisions the researcher makes during each phase can ensure data accuracy and their conversion from raw to processed forms that are more appropriate for analysis. Preparing a descriptive statistical summary of the collected data for each variable is the tool used to assess the coding scheme for coding errors and identify data entry errors. Exhibit 13-1 reflects the steps in this phase of the research process.

Postcollection Coding of Data

Coding Textual and Verbal Responses

If your instrument contains open-ended questions, these need to be coded prior to analysis. Even when categories are anticipated and precoded for open-ended questions, once data are collected, researchers find it useful to reassess the predetermined categories. During instrument development, at least the types of content are anticipated; but the largest part of coding takes place after the data are collected.

Content analysis as a methodology uses a systematic, objective approach to code message characteristics so researchers can treat diverse textual or verbal content quantitatively as they look for patterns and draw inferences. In business intelligence, content analysis is a primary methodology. While it can work with small samples, it works best with larger ones. As a result, content-analyzing transcripts of a focus group—unless these groups have been repeated numerous times, are large (e.g., online *supergroups*), or encompass people who are very influential on the topic—won't add much value.[1] Content analysis can be used to analyze written, audio, or video data from experiments, observations, surveys, and secondary data studies. The textual data to be content-analyzed include transcripts of interviews and open-ended survey responses. But researchers also use content analysis on employee evaluations, annual reports, financial analyst reports, advertisements, promotional brochures, press releases, speeches, web pages, social media posts, historical documents, and conference proceedings, as well as magazine and newspaper articles. For example, 81 percent of the U.S. population has a social media account, and by 2020 more than 3 billion people worldwide are expected to have a social media presence. Imagine the content a business might analyze.[2] Ipsos recently used crowdsourcing (a private online community) to assess product names for a company. They analyzed the recommended names not just for word use, but also for the themes of those names. The participants were able to react to the name recommendations of other members, and this let them spot additional topics and themes that would have been problematic.[3]

In this chapter, we'll look at the coding of semantic content—word use and the meaning of those words to open questions. As do all quantitative techniques, content analysis is not a software-only analytical methodology; it uses both software calculations along with human input and interpretation to provide managers with critical decision-making insights. Analyzing enormous volumes of open-ended

>**snap**shot

How Might You Code Word Data?

There are three ways to code word data: humans, algorithm-based automated, and user-guided automated.

The biggest advantage of human coding is the ability to understand complex meaning in context. A machine, or software, is unlikely to pick up on sarcasm in a text, for example, but a human can. "Humans can also understand statements in a much broader context, not limited to a single sentence or post," shared Malgorzata Kolling, senior consultant/research manager at OdinText. But human coding is at a significant disadvantage compared to

the two other methods on several other criteria. The greatest strengths of automated coding are its speed and low cost, but it fails the complex meaning understanding criterion. User-guided automated coding (like OdinText) beats its competitors on all criteria by being better able to process meaning more like a human while doing it with speed and accuracy. The accompanying chart summarizes the criteria for method selection.

www.odintext.com

Criteria	Human Coding	Algorithm-Based Automated Coding	User-Guided Automated Coding
Speed	Slow	Fast	Fast
Cost	High	Low	Low
Accuracy	Low	High	High
Need for intra-rater reliability assessment	High	None	None
Need for multiple raters	Depends on data set size	None	None
Need for inter-rater reliability assessment	High	None	None
Number of usable codes	Small	Unlimited	Unlimited
User control of codes	High	None	High
Ability to change codes in progress	Yes, but must repeat process	Yes, but must repeat process	Yes
Understanding of meaning in context	High	None	Some, increasing

responses slows the analysis process and increases the opportunity for error. The variety of answers to a single question can be staggering, hampering postcollection categorization.

Coding for content analysis starts by determining which units of data will be analyzed. One researcher suggests that three types of data units may be selected: context, sampling, or recording.[4] **Context units** refer to the objective of the research (if you are studying employee performance, then a unit might be the written description of performance in an official evaluation form). **Sampling units** are what text elements the researcher will code (words, phrases, sentences, paragraphs, etc.). **Recording units** are the ideas embedded in the content. So "Sam Smith is a great performer with significant management potential" would reveal two recording units "performance" and "management potential."

Recording units can be syntactical, referential, propositional, or thematic. Each type is the basis for coding texts into mutually exclusive categories in a researcher's search for meaning.

- *Syntactical* units are the specific, author-defined words, phrases, sentences, or paragraphs. Words are the smallest and most reliable data units to analyze. Although we can certainly count these units, we are more interested in their meaning in context.

- *Referential units* describe *objects* by using words and phrases. Participants may refer to an *object* as a "classic," a "power performer," or "ranked first in safety." Researchers use referential units to make inferences about attitudes, values, or preferences. Thus, we might determine the words that are most commonly used to describe A versus B. We ask, "Are these descriptions for A more likely to lead to favorable opinions and thus to preference and ultimately selection, compared to the descriptions used for B?"

- *Propositional* units are *assertions* about an *object*. For example, a researcher assessing advertising for magazine subscriptions might find the claim, "Subscribers who respond to offer A will save $15 over the single issue rate." The propositional unit is "savings."

- *Thematic* units are topics contained within (and across) texts; they represent higher-level abstractions inferred from the text and its context. The responses to an open-ended question about purchase behavior may reflect a temporal theme: the past ("I never purchased an alternative brand before you changed the package"), the present ("I really like the new packaging"), or the future ("I would buy the product more often if it came in more flavors"). We could also look at the comments as relating to the themes or topics of "packaging" versus a product characteristic, "flavors."

In terms of coding, researchers must establish **intra-rater reliability** (the same rater must assign codes in the same way consistently for each text analyzed). If more than one person is coding the content, **inter-rater reliability** (different raters must assign codes in the same way to the same text) becomes important. As with all other research methodologies, the analytical use of content analysis is influenced by decisions the researcher makes prior to data collection. Computerized content analysis does guard against selective perception of the content, provides for the rigorous application of reliability and validity criteria, and is amenable to computerization.

Let's look at an informal application of content analysis to an open question. In this example, which we are processing without the use of content analysis software, suppose employees in the sales department of a manufacturing firm are asked, "How might company–customer relations be improved?" In precoding, we anticipate that responses will focus on locus of responsibility (company, customer, company and customer, other). A sample from 100 responses included:

- We should treat the customer with more respect.

- We should stop trying to speed up the sales process when the customer has expressed objections or concerns. (buying process)

- We should have software that permits real-time tracking of a customer's order.

- Our laptops are outdated. We can't work with the latest software or access information quickly when we are in the field.

- My [the sales department] manager is rude with customers when he gets calls while I'm in the field. He should be transferred or fired.

- Management should stop pressuring us to meet sales quotas when our customers have restricted their open-to-buy status.

>**Exhibit 13-5** Open Question Coding (after revision)

Question: "How can company–customer relations be improved?"

Locus of Responsibility	Frequency (*n* = 100)
A. Management	
1. Sales manager	10
2. Sales process	20
3. Other	7
5. No action area identified	3
B. Salesperson	
1. Training	15
C. Customer	
1. Buying processes	12
2. Other	8
3. No action area identified	5
D. Environmental conditions	
E. Technology	20
F. Other	

The first pass through the data produces a few general categories within locus of responsibility that expand on our original categories. The second pass produces categories for action planning: human relations (fire or transfer manager), technology (replace laptops, software), training (customer respect, sales supervision), management (buying process, sales process), strategic planning, and others. We even have an indication that no action is desired. Exhibit 13-5 shows how each response might be categorized, which makes it possible to get an accurate frequency count of the new categorization for this question.

Content analysis software applies statistical algorithms to textual and verbal data. This permits stemming, aliasing, and exclusion processes. *Stemming* uses derivations of common root words to create aliases (e.g., using *searching, searches, searched,* for *search*). *Aliasing* searches for synonyms (*wise* or *smart* for *intelligent*). *Exclusion* filters out trivial words (*be, is, the, of*) in the search for meaning.[5]

When you are using menu-driven programs, an auto-categorization option creates manageable categories by clustering terms that occur together throughout the textual or verbal dataset. Then, with a few keystrokes, you can modify categorization parameters and refine your results. Once your categories are consistent with the research and investigative questions, you select what you want to export to a data file or in tab-delimited format. The output, in the form of tables and plots, serves as modules for your final report. Exhibit 13-6 shows a plot produced by a content analysis of restaurant complaint data. The distances between pairs of terms reveal how likely it is that the terms occur together, and the colors represent categories.

Coding Closed Questions

The responses to closed questions include those for which answers can be anticipated. It is possible to **precode** closed questions (assign value codes to response categories during the instrument design stage). With computerized survey design and computer-assisted, computer-administered, or online collection of data, precoding is necessary because the software tallies data as they are collected. Once data are collected and we understand the division of each data field into its various categories by code, we may decide that the original mapping rule is not as valuable as our preliminary analysis plan predicted. For example, assume the coding scheme used a 7-point scale in which the researcher offered the participant three levels of agreement, three levels of disagreement, and one neutral position; collected data showed a 3-point scale, with fewer fine nuances of agreement-disagreement would be better for data

>**Exhibit 13-6** Proximity Plot of Restaurant Complaints

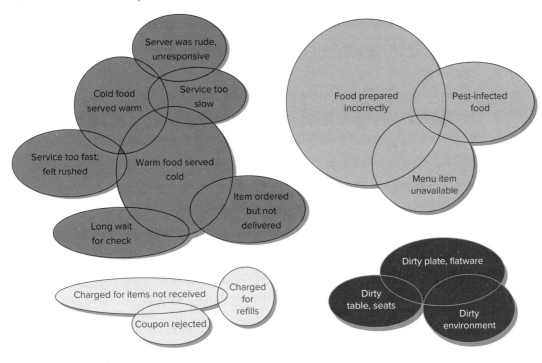

analysis. **Recoding** variables involves developing new mapping rules and assigning new codes based on the merging of initial variable categories. Recoding during data examination is useful when trying to understand the patterns within data.

>Edit the Data

Editing is a process for verifying that variables have used the designated coding scheme and that all data collected is entered correctly. It detects errors and omissions, corrects them when possible, and certifies that maximum data quality standards are achieved. Reviewing a descriptive statistical summary of the collected data for each variable is the task used to identify errors. While online surveys and their subsequent participant data entry for structured questions have eliminated some editing problems, these methodologies do not eliminate the need for a thorough editing.

Editing's purpose is to guarantee that data are:

- Complete
- Accurate
- Appropriately coded

Complete

Data are complete when all data collected are ready for analysis. Sometimes data are in a form that cannot be adequately analyzed. For example, during the stress of data collection in a personal interview and paper-and-pencil recording in an observation or experiment, the researcher may use abbreviations and special symbols. Soon after the interview, experiment, or observation, the data collector should translate those abbreviations or shorthand. When entry gaps are present from interviews, editing may determine that a callback should be made; callbacks are preferable to guessing what the participant probably would have said, thereby injecting bias.

>**Exhibit 13-7** Categories of DK Responses

Categories of DK Responses	Type
1. Participant ignorant of information that is readily available to them.	Legitimate
2. Participant asked for a level of information they don't have.	Legitimate
3. Participant has not yet made a judgment.	Legitimate
4. Participant does not have the information needed at the moment to answer the question.	Legitimate
5. Participant is reluctant to provide the information.	Injects bias
6. Participant feels the question warrants no consideration.	Injects bias

"Don't Know" Responses

When a group of participants chooses the "Don't Know" response option, each may mean something different. The **"don't know" (DK) response** presents special problems for data preparation. When the DK response group is small, it is not troublesome. But when it is large, it is of major concern. Does this mean the measurement question that elicited the DK response is useless? The answer is, "It all depends."

Most DK answers are of two types.[6] First, there is the legitimate DK response when the participant does not know the answer. It is reasonable to expect that some legitimate DK responses might be made to any question appropriately including the DK response option. As a researcher, this response might meet our research objectives; we expected DK responses and consider them to be useful. These should be examined as you would any other response. In the second type, however, a DK reply illustrates the researcher's failure to get the appropriate information with the measurement question(s). Such questions would elicit DK responses of both types and thus will bias the data; editing will likely exclude all DK responses from analysis in this later situation. Within both types, there are several categories of DK responses as summarized in Exhibit 13-7.

For example, consider the following illustrative questions and match them to the categories in Exhibit 13-7:

A. Who developed the Managerial Grid concept?

B. Do you believe the new president's fiscal policy is sound?

C. Do you like your present job?

D. Which of the various brands of chewing gum do you believe has the best quality?

E. How often in the last 12 months did you go to the movies?

In A there seems to be little reason to withhold a correct answer if known; it fits category 1. In B, it is not immediately clear whether the participant is ignorant of the president's fiscal policy or knows the policy but has not made a judgment about it; the DK response fits categories 1 or 3. The researcher should have asked two questions: In the first, the participant's level of knowledge of fiscal policy could be determined. If the participant passed the knowledge test, then a second question could secure judgment on fiscal policy. In C, a DK response is a way of answering, "I do not want to answer that question," or it might be that the participant hasn't been in the job long enough to determine whether it is a good fit (like); it fits category 5 or 3. In D, a DK response might translate to, "This is too unimportant to talk about," or indicate the participant has no experience with chewing gum brands; it fits categories 6 or 2. Finally, in E, the participant is being asked to do some calculation about a topic to which he or she may attach little importance and thus not commit behavior to memory; it fits category 4, but it might also fit 6. As you can see, including the DK responses in analysis when they potentially are of several different interpretations would create problems during data analysis.

Missing Data

Missing data are data from a participant that are not available for one or more variables of interest. In surveys, missing data typically occur when participants intentionally or accidentally skip, refuse to answer, or do not know the answer to measurement question and are reluctant to guess. Missing data also occur due to researcher error, malfunctioning software or equipment, corrupted data files, and changes in the research or instrument design after data were collected from some participants, such as when variables are dropped or added. In longitudinal studies, missing data may result from participants dropping out of the study or being absent for one or more data collection periods.

The strategy for handling missing data consists of a two-step process: (1) the researcher first explores the pattern of missing data to determine the probability that a value is missing rather than observed, then (2) the researcher selects a missing-data correction technique. For example, in a survey on training preferences, assume editing discovered that men were responsible for more missing data on a variable assessing a training event than women. How would editing address this problem? First, the researcher would explore which of three types of missing data are represented:

- **Data missing completely at random (MCAR)**—high probability that missing data for a particular variable are NOT dependent on the variable itself and are NOT dependent on another variable in the data record (e.g., a participant inadvertently skips a question).

- **Data missing at random (MAR)**—high probability that missing data for a particular variable are NOT dependent on the variable itself but ARE dependent on another variable in the data record (e.g., the answer to the first question of a branched-question set might cause missing data to the second question within the branched-question set).

- **Data missing but not missing at random (NMAR)**—high probability that missing data for a particular variable ARE dependent on the variable itself and ARE NOT dependent on other variables in the data record (e.g., participant finds the question unanswerable or too sensitive and skips the question).

In our example, MAR is not applicable because there was no branching, but either MCAR or NMAR are possible. If data are NMAR, then the participant expressed a "no preference" option that wasn't provided by skipping the question. It was a viable response to indicate "no preference" and those data should be factored into the analysis as a separate category of data on that variable. Editing would provide a code for "no preference."

Three techniques are used to salvage data records with missing data:

- **Listwise deletion**—any case with missing data on one variable is deleted from the sample for all analyses of that variable (the default option in most statistical packages like SPSS or SAS); no bias if MAR or MCAR because only complete data records are used for a variable. In our example, men who skipped the question would be excluded. If, however, we exclude men who skipped the question and data are NMAR, not MCAR, deleting men from the sample biases any analysis of training preferences toward women's training preference. Men purposely skipping the question (NMAR) was their expressing "no preference" on training, data that we want to capture.

- **Pairwise deletion**—editing replaces the missing data for a variable with an estimate (e.g., mean or other measure of central tendency); the estimate is determined using all cases that have data for that variable or pair of variables, assumes MCAR, and has a potential for introducing bias. In our example, the missing data from men could be replaced with a measure of central tendency for all men; this will neutralize the strength of opinions expressed at either extreme not just by men, but for the overall sample, depending on the number of men with missing cases.

- **Predictive replacement**—editing replaces the missing data for a variable with an estimate predicted from observed value on another variable; the observed value is used to replace the missing data, assumes MAR, and has a potential for introducing bias. In our example, assume the instrument contained an earlier question requesting a preference for training types; we would use each man's response on that variable as a surrogate for his missing data. However, we potentially inject bias because we don't know that overall preference for a training approach is the same as an assessment of a particular training event.

Accurate

Data validation is a process that attempts to verify that research protocols to avoid data errors were followed and that data are real by identifying fake or inaccurate data. Distinctive response patterns in closed questions will often emerge if data falsification is occurring. To uncover this, editing must analyze—as a set—the instruments used by each interviewer. If interviewer error or bias is suspected, validation may require reinterviewing of some percentage of the participants, at least on some questions. Many research firms will recontact about 10 percent of participants in a data validation process. Phone and personal interviews facilitate this type of data validation. Self-administered computer instruments can be checked for IP address and time of completion; duplicate addresses and tight sequential times make the responses on such instruments suspect. In paper-and-pencil instruments, validation looks for similar handwriting as an indicator, then checks to see if response patterns are similar on suspect instruments.

Data entry can also cause inaccuracy. Sometimes the participant is responsible for the error, and it is obvious that an entry is incorrect—for example, an instrument asks for ratio data in weeks (e.g., expected a number of 4 or fewer), yet the participant responds on some other scale (e.g., 13). Or they might respond with two answers to a question that requested one. In the following question asked of adults 18 or older, one participant checked two categories, indicating that he was retired and currently serving on active duty.

Please indicate your current military status:
❑ Never served in the military
☑ Active duty ❑ Separated ☑ Retired

Editing must determine which of the responses is both consistent with the intent of the question or other information on the instrument and most accurate for this individual participant. If unsure, editing replaces such an answer with an editor code for "no answer" or "unknown."

A researcher might enter data in the wrong location on a data record or enter the wrong response. In these scenarios, editing seeks to detect (revealed by missing cases or out-of-range variable codes) and replace the proper answer by reviewing the original measurement instrument or other information in the data set. This is why coding a case number on a measurement instrument is valuable; it's easier to find the appropriate instrument. The researcher may also recontact the participant for correct information if time and budget allow.

Appropriately Coded

Our preliminary analysis plan called for the study of variables—often in comparison or cross-tabulation with other variables. When we studied measurement, we discussed developing mapping rules to create categories within variables and using these rules to assign numbers to participant's answers [e.g., if the variable is *gender*, the partitions are *male* (1) and *female* (2)]. The categories were assessed as appropriate if they met two criteria: (1) best partitions for data for testing hypotheses and showing relationships and (2) availability of comparison data. These initial codes are assumed to be the ones we will use during analysis. Closed questions, usually precoded as part of instrument design, follow these principles: categories must be mutually exclusive, exhaustive, and focused on a single dimension.

>Examine the Data

Exploratory Data Analysis

Data examination uses **exploratory data analysis (EDA)**, which explores—and reduces—the data using descriptive statistics and some preliminary graphical displays of data. Data analysis and interpretation uses **confirmatory data analysis (CFA)**, an analytical process guided by classical statistical inference in its use of significance testing and confidence to determine whether variables are independent; it is required when attempting to prove causation.[7] One authority has compared exploratory data analysis to the role of police detectives and other investigators and confirmatory analysis to that of judges and the judicial system. The former are involved in the search for clues and evidence; the latter are preoccupied with evaluating the strength of the evidence that is found. Exploratory data analysis is the first step in the search for evidence, without which confirmatory analysis has nothing to evaluate.[8] Exhibit 13-8 shows the relationship of EDA to the preliminary analysis plan. EDA is used in data preparation.

>**Exhibit 13-8** Role of EDA in the Research Process

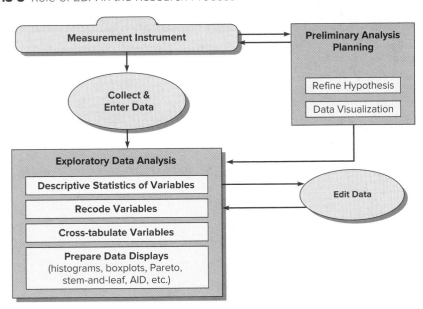

The guide for data examination is the *preliminary analysis plan*, the foundation for the development of the measurement instrument. The convenience of real-time data entry makes it tempting for novice researchers to move directly to statistical analysis, skipping over the first step: the post-data-collection assessment of the preliminary analysis plan. That temptation is even stronger when the data are entered and can be viewed in real time as the research project progresses. One process that survey or statistical analysis software provides is the frequency count for each response option for each variable. The researcher uses this information to assess the value of each procedure within the preliminary analysis plan. For example, let's assume your plan called for a *dummy table* of convenience food use by age groups, but your frequencies show 85 percent of your participants eat convenience foods regularly; it is unlikely that cross-tabulation of "convenience food use" by "age" is going to reveal much of value. By looking at your frequency data, you've just reduced your analysis tasks by one. It may also be true that frequencies might show unexpected patterns—for example, a split pattern on an agreement–disagreement rating question. The researcher must decide whether it would be valuable to the research objective to explore this anomaly, even if it was not anticipated in the preliminary analysis plan.

During EDA, the researcher has the flexibility to respond to the patterns revealed in the preliminary summaries of the data. This flexibility is an important attribute of the process. Because it doesn't follow a rigid structure, EDA is free to take many paths in unraveling the mysteries in the data. While numerical summaries may start the process, visual representations and graphical techniques offer major contributions. Summary statistics, as you will see momentarily, may obscure, conceal, or even misrepresent the underlying structure of the data. When numerical summaries are used exclusively and accepted without visual inspection, the selection of confirmatory models may be based on flawed assumptions.[9] For these reasons, exploratory data analysis should begin with visual inspection. After that, it is not only possible but also desirable to cycle between exploratory and confirmatory approaches.

Frequency Tables, Bar Charts, and Pie Graphs[10]

Several techniques are essential to any data examination. For example, a **frequency table** is a simple device for arraying data. An example is presented in Exhibit 13-9. It arrays data by assigned response code values, from lowest to highest value, with columns for count, percent, valid percent (percent adjusted for missing data), and cumulative percent. This example nominal variable table describes the perceived desirable minimum age to be permitted to own a social networking account. The same data are presented in Exhibit 13-10 using a pie chart and a bar chart. The values and percentages are more

>**Exhibit 13-9** A Frequency Table (Minimum Age for Social Networking)

Value Label	Value	Frequency	Percent	Valid Percent	Cumulative Percent
21 years old	1	60	6	6	6
18 years old min	2	180	18	18	24
16 years old min	3	330	33	33	57
13 years old min	4	280	28	28	85
10 years old min	5	50	5	5	90
Any age	6	60	6	6	96
No opinion	7	40	4	4	100
		1,000	100	100	

Valid Cases 1,000; Missing Cases 0

>**Exhibit 13-10** Nominal Displays of Data (Minimum Age for Social Networking)

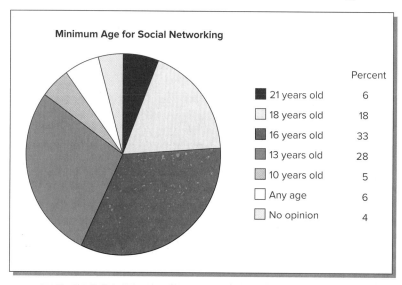

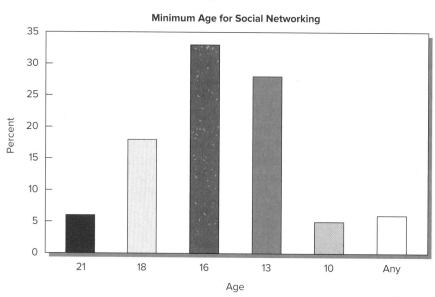

>**Exhibit 13-11** Average Annual Purchases of PrimeSell's Top 50 Customers

Value	Frequency	Percent	Cumulative Percent	Value	Frequency	Percent	Cumulative Percent
54.9	1	2	2	75.6	1	2	54
55.4	1	2	4	76.4	1	2	56
55.6	1	2	6	77.5	1	2	58
56.4	1	2	8	78.9	1	2	60
56.8	1	2	10	80.9	1	2	62
56.9	1	2	12	82.2	1	2	64
57.8	1	2	14	82.5	1	2	66
58.1	1	2	16	86.4	1	2	68
58.2	1	2	18	88.3	1	2	70
58.3	1	2	20	102.5	1	2	72
58.5	1	2	22	104.1	1	2	74
59.9	2	4	26	110.4	1	2	76
61.5	1	2	28	111.9	1	2	78
62.6	1	2	30	118.6	1	2	80
64.8	1	2	32	123.8	1	2	82
66.0	2	4	36	131.2	1	2	84
66.3	1	2	38	140.9	1	2	86
67.6	1	2	40	146.2	1	2	88
69.1	1	2	42	153.2	1	2	90
69.2	1	2	44	163.2	1	2	92
70.5	1	2	46	166.7	1	2	94
72.7	1	2	48	183.2	1	2	96
72.9	1	2	50	206.9	1	2	98
73.5	1	2	52	218.2	1	2	100
				Total	50	100	

readily understood in the graphic format. When the variable of interest is measured at an interval-ratio level and has many potential values, these techniques are not particularly informative. Exhibit 13-11 is a condensed frequency table of the average annual purchases of PrimeSell's top 50 customers. Only two values, 59.9 and 66, have a frequency greater than 1. Thus, the primary contribution of a frequency table for these data is an ordered list of values. If the table were converted to a bar chart, it would have 48 bars of equal length and two bars with two occurrences. Bar charts do not reserve spaces for values where no observations occur within the range. Constructing a pie chart for this variable would also be pointless with the data in its present form, but the frequency table reveals an opportunity to recode the variable so that these techniques might have value.

Histograms

The histogram is a conventional solution for the display of interval-ratio data. **Histograms** are used when it is possible to group the variable's values into intervals. Histograms are constructed with bars (or asterisks) that represent each interval, where the interval quantity determines the height of the bar, and where each interval's bar is the same width and occupies an equal amount of area within graph. You want the number of intervals to represent the expanse of the data. The number of intervals may be arbitrarily chosen. One researcher suggests you calculate the number of intervals based on the square root of the number of observations (after rounding). In the example in Exhibit 13-11, the number of intervals would

The Difference Between Data and Insight

In the face of additional store closures, once-powerful Sears is barely holding on. One category where it still performs strongly is appliances. But as Millennials move into their peak buying years, will Sears capture their business?

In a *Forbes* article, Pam Goodfellow, principal analyst/consumer insights director for Prosper Insights & Analytics™, provides the distinction between *data* and *insight*. "Using Prosper's shopper preference share for appliances (resulting from a quarterly unaided, write-in question posed to consumers), Sears and Lowe's are the dominant players in this category, with

20.9% and 14.3% share respectively, while Best Buy (10.9%) and Home Depot (9.1%) jockey for third and fourth positions. Walmart is a distant fifth (6.7%)." After noting that the distance between Sears and Lowe's as preferred store had shrunk from a high of 16 percent to a low of 4 percent in one year, Goodfellow next looked at the preferences of Millennials (see graph). Her insight: Lowe's is poised to take the position of preferred appliance supplier as Sears continues to stumble, but Home Depot is the competitor Lowe's should watch.

www.prospertechnologiesllc.com

Appliance Store Shopped First Among Millennials
TY Compared to Prior 5-year Average

Store	Value
Home Depot	41.6
Lowe's	19.8
Best Buy	12.2
Walmart	−10.8
Sears	−11.5

Source: Pam Goodfellow, "Lowe's Poised as Successor to the Sears Appliance Empire," *Forbes*, April 26, 2016, downloaded April 26, 2016 (http://www.forbes.com/sites/forbesinsights/2016/04/26/lowes-poised-as-successor-to-the-sears appliance-empire/#109f7f113ha8).

be 8 (square root of 50 = 7.07, rounded up). The interval width should then be approximately equal to the range divided by the number of intervals [(218.2 − 54.9)/8 = 20.4, rounded to 20].[11] Data analysts find histograms useful for (1) displaying all intervals in a distribution, even intervals without observed values, and (2) examining the shape of the distribution for skewness, kurtosis, and the modal pattern. When looking at a histogram, one might ask: Is there a single hump (a mode)? Are subgroups identifiable when multiple modes are present? Are straggling data values detached from the central concentration?[12]

The values for the average annual purchases variable presented in Exhibit 13-11 were measured on a ratio scale and are easily grouped. Other variables possessing an underlying order are similarly appropriate for histograms. A histogram would not be used for a nominal variable that has no order to its categories, such as gender or occupation.

A histogram of the average annual purchases is shown in Exhibit 13-12. Each interval range for the variable of interest, average annual purchases, is shown on the horizontal axis; the frequency or number of observations in each interval is on the vertical axis. The value of the start of each interval is noted at the left of the bar on the horizontal access. The height of the bar corresponds with the frequency of observations in the interval above which it is erected. This histogram was constructed with intervals 20 increments wide. These values are found in PrimeSell's average annual purchases frequency table

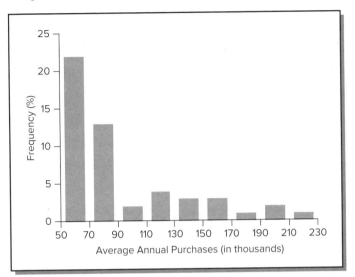

(Exhibit 13-11). Intervals with 0 counts would show gaps in the table and alert the analyst to look for problems with spread. When the upper tail of the distribution is compared with the frequency table, we find three extreme values (183.2, 206.9, and 218.2). Along with the peaked midpoint and reduced number of observations in the upper tail, this histogram warns us of irregularities in the data.

Stem-and-Leaf Displays[13]

The **stem-and-leaf display** is a technique that is closely related to the histogram. It shares some of the histogram's features but offers several unique advantages. It is easy to construct by hand for small samples or may be produced by computer programs. In contrast to histograms, which lose information by grouping data values into intervals, the stem-and-leaf presents actual data values that can be inspected directly, without the use of enclosed bars or asterisks as the representation medium. This feature reveals the distribution of values within the interval and preserves their rank order for finding the median, quartiles, and other summary statistics. It also eases linking a specific observation back to the data file and to the participant that produced it.

Visualization is the second advantage of stem-and-leaf displays. The range of values is apparent at a glance, and both shape and spread impressions are immediate. Patterns in the data—such as gaps where no values exist, areas where values are clustered, or outlying values that differ from the main body of the data—are easily observed.

To develop a stem-and-leaf display for the data in Exhibit 13-11, the first digits of each data item are arranged to the left of a vertical line. Next, we pass through the average annual purchases percentages in the order they were recorded and place the last digit for each item (the unit position, 1.0) to the right of the vertical line. Note that any digit to the right of the decimal point is ignored. The last digit for each item is placed on the horizontal row corresponding to its first digit(s). Now it is a simple matter to rank-order the digits in each row, creating the stem-and-leaf display shown in Exhibit 13-13.

Each line or row is a *stem*, and each piece of information on the stem is a *leaf*. The first stem is:

$$5 \mid 4\ 5\ 5\ 6\ 6\ 6\ 7\ 8\ 8\ 8\ 8\ 9$$

This reflects 12 items in the data set whose first digit is five: 54, 55, 55, 56, 56, 56, 57, 58, 58, 58, 58, and 59. The second stem is:

$$6 \mid 1\ 2\ 4\ 6\ 6\ 7\ 9\ 9$$

It shows that there are eight customers with purchases are in the $60,000 range: 61, 62, 64, 66, 66, 67, 69, and 69.

>**Exhibit 13-13** A Stem-and-Leaf Display of PrimeSell's Average Annual Purchases Data

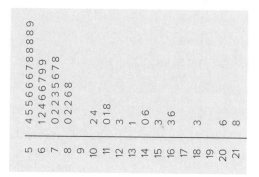

When rotated, a stem-and-leaf display takes on the properties of a histogram.

Pareto Diagrams

The **Pareto diagram** is a bar chart whose percentages sum to 100 percent. The data are derived from a multiple-choice, single-response scale; a multiple-choice, multiple-response scale; or frequency counts of words (or themes) from content analysis. The participants' answers are sorted in decreasing importance, with bar height in descending order from left to right. An analysis of laptop repair complaints is depicted as a Pareto diagram in Exhibit 13-14. The cumulative frequency line in this exhibit shows that the top two problems (the repair did not resolve the customer's problem, and the product was returned multiple times for repair) accounted for 80 percent of the reasons of inadequate repair service. The pictorial array that results reveals that any attempt to improve the service must address the first two problems.

>**Exhibit 13-14** Pareto Diagram of Laptop Repair Complaints

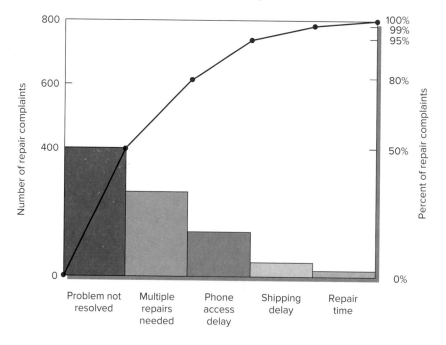

Boxplots[14]

The **boxplot**, or *box-and-whisker plot*, is another technique used frequently in exploratory data analysis.[15] A boxplot reduces the detail of the stem-and-leaf display and provides a different visual image of the distribution's location, spread, shape, tail length, and outliers. Boxplots are extensions of the **five-number summary** of a distribution. This summary consists of the median, the upper and lower quartiles, and the largest and smallest observations. The median and quartiles are used because they are particularly **resistant statistics**. Resistant statistics are unaffected by outliers and change only slightly in response to the replacement of small portions of the data set.[16]

Assume we are examining the following data set

$$[5,6,6,7,7,7,8,8,9], \text{mean}=7, \text{standard deviation}=1.22,$$
$$\text{median}=7, \text{lower quartile}=6, \text{upper quartile}=8$$

if we replace the 9, with 90

$$[5,6,6,7,7,7,8,8,90], \text{mean}=16, \text{standard deviation}=27.78,$$
$$\text{median}=7, \text{lower quartile}=6, \text{upper quartile}=8$$

(The appendix *Describing Data Statistically* at the end of this chapter provides a review of these statistical concepts).

Changing only one of nine values has disturbed the location and spread summaries to the point where they no longer represent the other eight values. Both the mean and the standard deviation are considered **nonresistant statistics**; they are susceptible to the effects of extreme values in the tails of the distribution and do not represent typical values well under conditions of asymmetry. The standard deviation is particularly problematic because it is computed from the squared deviations from the mean.[17] In contrast, the median and quartiles are highly resistant to change. Because of the nature of quartiles, up to 25 percent of the data can be made extreme without perturbing the median, the rectangular composition of the plot, or the quartiles themselves. These characteristics of resistance are incorporated into the construction of boxplots.

Boxplots may be constructed easily by hand or by computer programs. The basic ingredients of the boxplot include:

1. The rectangular plot (encompasses 50 percent of the data values).
2. A center line (marks the median and goes through the width of the box).
3. The edges of the box, called *hinges*.
4. The "whiskers" (extend from the right and left hinges to the largest and smallest values).[18]

These values may be found within 1.5 times the **interquartile range (IQR)** from either edge of the box. These components and their relationships are shown in Exhibit 13-15.

When you are examining data, it is important to separate legitimate outliers from errors in measurement, editing, coding, and data entry. **Outliers**, data points that exceed the interquartile range by 1.5 times, reflect unusual cases and are an important source of information for the study. They are displayed or given special statistical treatment, or other portions of the data set are sometimes shielded from their effects. Extreme outliers, however, can be data entry errors; these variables should be corrected during editing.

Exhibit 13-16 summarizes several comparisons that are of help to the analyst. Boxplots are an excellent diagnostic tool, especially when graphed on the same scale. The upper two plots in the exhibit are both symmetric, but one is larger than the other. Larger box widths are sometimes used when the second variable, from the same measurement scale, comes from a larger sample size. The box widths should be proportional to the square root of the sample size, but not all plotting programs account for this.[19] Right- and left-skewed distributions and those with reduced spread are also presented clearly in the plot comparison. Finally, groups may be compared by means of multiple plots. One variation, in which a notch at the median marks off a confidence interval to test the equality of group medians, takes us a step closer to hypothesis testing.[20] Here the sides of the box return to full width at the upper and lower confidence intervals. When the intervals do not overlap, we can be confident, at a specified confidence level, that the medians of the two populations are different.

>**Exhibit 13-15** Boxplot Components

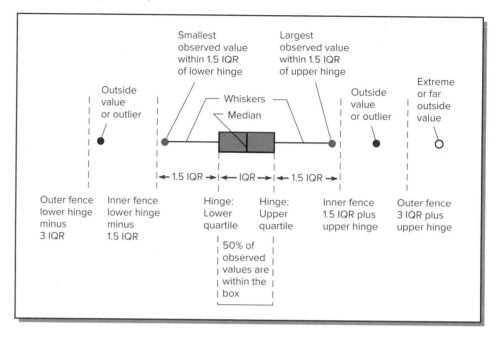

In Exhibit 13-17, multiple boxplots compare five sectors of PrimeSell's customers by their average annual purchases data. The overall impression is one of several potential problems for the analyst: unequal variances, skewness, and extreme outliers. Note the similarities of the profiles of finance and retailing in contrast to the high-tech and insurance sectors. If hypothesis tests are planned, further examination of this plot for each sector would require a stem-and-leaf display and a five-number summary. From this, we could make decisions on the types of tests to select for confirmatory analysis.

>**Exhibit 13-16** Diagnostics with Boxplots

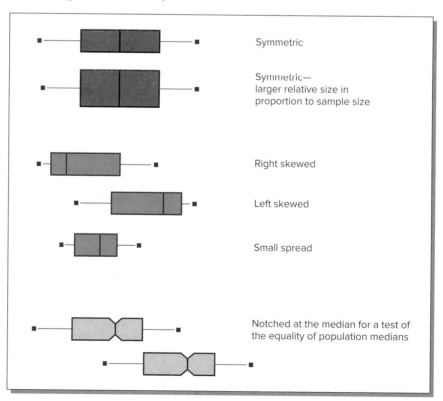

>**Exhibit 13-17** Boxplot Comparison of Customer Sectors

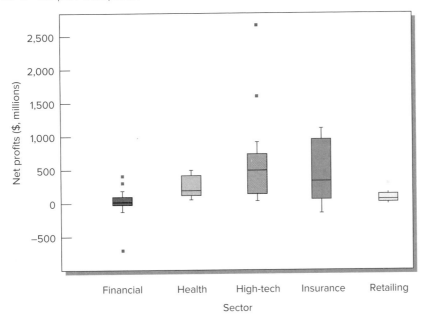

Mapping

Increasingly, when possible, research data are being attached to their geographic dimension. Geographic Information System (GIS) software and coordinate measuring devices have become more affordable and easier to use. Essentially GIS works by linking data sets to each other with at least one common data field (e.g., a household's street address). The GIS allows the researcher to connect target and classification variables from a survey to specific geographic-based databases like U.S. Census data, to develop a richer understanding of the sample's attitudes and behavior. As radio frequency identification (RFID) data become more prevalent, much behavioral data are able to connect with these new geographically rich databases.

The most common way to display such data is with a map. Colors and patterns denoting knowledge, attitude, behavior, or demographic data arrays are superimposed over street maps (finest-level GIS); block-group maps; or county, state, or country maps to help identify the best locations for stores based on demographic, psychographic, and life-stage segmentation data. Florists array promotional response information geographically and use the map to plan targeted promotions. Consumer and business-to-business researchers use mapping of data on ownership, usage level, and price sensitivity in plotting geographic rollouts of new products. Although this is an attractive option for exploratory analysis, it does take specialized software and hardware, as well as the expertise to operate it. Students are encouraged to take specialized courses on GIS to expand their skill set in this growing area.

>Cross-Tabulation

Your preliminary analysis plan contains multiple dummy tables designed to find patterns in your data. In EDA, cross-tabulation is a first step for identifying relationships between variables. **Cross-tabulation** is a technique for comparing data from two or more variables that results in a table. Cross-tabulation is used with classification variables and the study's target variables (operationalized measurement questions). These tables have rows and columns that correspond to the code values of each variable's categories. Exhibit 13-18 is an example of a computer-generated cross-tabulation of gender and selection by one's company for an overseas assignment. This table has two rows for gender and two columns for assignment selection. The combination of the variables with their values produces four cells. Each **cell** contains a count of the cases of the joint classification and also the row, column, and total percentages. The number

>**Exhibit 13-18** SPSS Cross-Tabulation of Gender by Overseas Assignment Opportunity

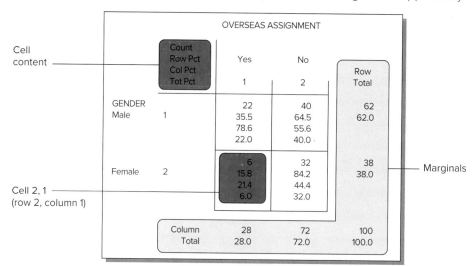

of row cells and column cells is often used to designate the size of the table, as in this 2 × 2 table. The cells are individually identified by their row and column numbers, as illustrated. Row and column totals, called **marginals**, appear at the bottom and right "margins" of the table. They show, separately, the counts and percentages of the rows and columns. In CFA, when cross-tabulation tables are constructed for statistical testing, we call them **contingency tables**, and the test determines if the classification variables are independent of each other.

Throughout this chapter, we have exploited the visual techniques of exploratory data analysis to look beyond numerical summaries and gain insight into the patterns of the data. Few of the approaches have stressed the need for advanced mathematics, and all have an intuitive appeal for the analyst. When the more common ways of summarizing location, spread, and shape have conveyed an inadequate picture of the data, we have used more resistant statistics to protect us from the effects of extreme scores and occasional errors. We have also emphasized the value of transforming the original scale of the data during preliminary analysis rather than at the point of hypothesis testing.

The Importance of Percentages

Percentages serve two purposes in data presentation. First, they simplify the data by reducing all numbers to a range from 0 to 100. Second, they translate the data to a base of 100, important for relative comparisons. In a sampling situation, the number of cases that fall into a category is meaningless unless it is related to some base. A count of 28 overseas assignees has little meaning unless we know it is from a sample of 100. Using the latter as a base, we conclude that 28 percent of this study's sample has an overseas assignment.

Although the preceding is useful, it is even more useful when the research problem calls for a comparison of several distributions of data. Assume the previously reported data were collected five years ago and the present study had a sample of 1,500, of which 360 were selected for overseas assignments. By using percentages, we can see the relative relationships and shifts in the data (see Exhibit 13-19).

With two-dimension tables, the selection of a row or column will accentuate a particular distribution for comparison. Most computer programs offer the option to present percentages in both directions and interchange the placement of each variable on the row or column of the table. This raises the question about which direction the percentages should be predetermined. Researchers find it valuable to be consistent in the construction of cross-tabulated tables, for example always putting the hypothesized independent variable on the row. This makes always choosing row percentages for comparison the default. Of course, if you prefer, you may place your independent variable as the column, and use column percentages. In Exhibit 13-19, gender is the independent variable, placed in rows, and thus we will examine row

>**Exhibit 13-19** Comparison of Percentages in Cross-Tabulation Studies by Overseas Assignment

		Study 1						Study 2		
		OVERSEAS ASSIGNMENT						OVERSEAS ASSIGNMENT		
	Count Row Pct Col Pct Tot Pct	Yes 1	No 2	Row Total			Count Row Pct Col Pct Tot Pct	Yes 1	No 2	Row Total
GENDER Male	1	22 35.5 78.6 22.0	40 64.5 55.6 40.0	62 62.0		GENDER Male	1	225 25.0 62.5 15.0	675 75.0 59.2 45.0	900 60.0
Female	2	6 15.8 21.4 6.0	32 84.2 44.4 32.0	38 38.0		Female	2	135 22.5 37.5 9.0	465 77.5 40.8 31.0	600 40.0
	Column Total	28 28.0	72 72.0	100 100.0			Column Total	360 24.0	1140 76.0	1500 100.0

percentages and ignore column percentages. When percentages are studied by rows, the implication is that gender influences selection for overseas assignments.

Care should be taken in interpreting percentages from tables. Consider again the data in Exhibit 13-19. From the first to the second study, it is apparent that the percentage of females selected for overseas assignments rose from 15.8 to 22.5 percent of their respective samples. This should not be confused with the percentage within each sample who were women with overseas assignments, a number which increased from 6 percent (Study 1) to 9 percent (Study 2). A comparison of the two tables verifies an increase in women with overseas assignments, but we cannot conclude that their gender had anything to do with the increase. Had we evaluated, inappropriately, the column percentages for verification, all we would know is that in the first study 21.4 percent of the sample were women, while in the second study 37.5 percent were women; comparing these numbers tell us nothing about our hypothesis.

Percentages are used by virtually everyone dealing with numbers—but often incorrectly. The following guidelines, if used during analysis, will help to prevent errors in reporting:[21]

- *Averaging percentages.* Percentages should not be averaged unless each is weighted by the size of the group from which it is derived. Thus, a simple average will not suffice; it is necessary to use a weighted average.

- *Use of too large percentages.* This often defeats the purpose of percentages—which is to simplify. A large percentage is difficult to understand and is confusing. If a 1,000 percent increase is experienced, it is better to describe this as a 10-fold increase.

- *Using too small a base.* Percentages hide the base from which they have been computed. A figure of 60 percent when contrasted with 30 percent would appear to suggest a sizable difference. Yet if there are only three cases in the one category and six in the other, the differences would not be as significant as they have been made to appear with percentages.

- *Percentage decreases can never exceed 100 percent.* The higher figure should always be used as the base or denominator. For example, if a price was reduced from $1 to $.25, the decrease (75 cents) would be 75 percent (75/100) of the original dollar price.

Other Table-Based Analysis

It often takes more than a two-way variable analysis to understand a relationship. Even if one finds a statistically significant relationship between two variables, the questions of why and under what conditions remain. The introduction of a **control variable** to interpret the relationship is often necessary. Cross-tabulation tables serve as the framework. Statistical packages like Minitab, SAS, and SPSS have among their modules many options for the construction of *n*-way tables with provision for multiple control

>**Exhibit 13-20** SPSS Cross-Tabulation with Control and Nested Variables

	Control Variable					
	Category 1			Category 2		
	Nested Variable			Nested Variable		
	cat 1	cat 2	cat 3	cat 1	cat 2	cat 3
Stub...	Cells...					

	SEX OF EMPLOYEE			
	MALES		FEMALES	
	MINORITY CLASSIFICATION		MINORITY CLASSIFICATION	
	WHITE	NONWHITE	WHITE	NONWHITE
EMPLOYMENT CATEGORY				
CLERICAL	16%	7%	18%	7%
OFFICE TRAINEE	7%	3%	17%	2%
SECURITY OFFICER	3%	3%		
COLLEGE TRAINEE	7%	0%	1%	
EXEMPT EMPLOYEE	6%	0%	0%	
MBA TRAINEE	1%	0%	0%	
TECHNICAL	1%			

>**Exhibit 13-21** Automatic Interaction Detection Example

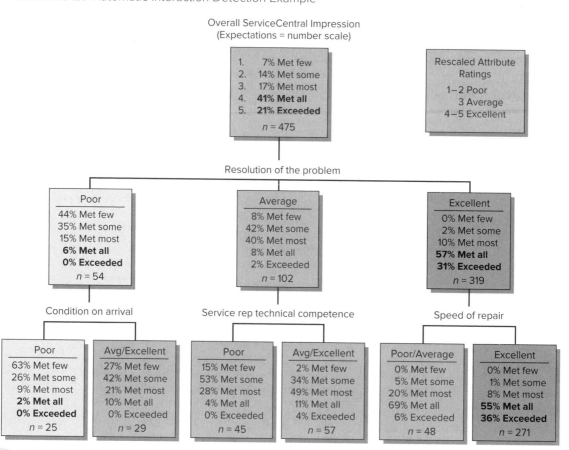

variables. Exhibit 13-20 presents an example in which three variables are handled on the same table. Programs such as these can handle far more complex tables and statistical information.[22]

An advanced variation on *n*-way tables is **automatic interaction detection (AID)**. AID is a computerized statistical process that requires that the researcher identify a dependent variable and a set of predictors or independent variables (up to 300). The computer then searches among the variables for the best single division of the data according to each predictor variable, chooses one, and splits the sample using statistical testing to verify the appropriateness of this choice.

Exhibit 13-21 shows the tree diagram that resulted from an AID study of customer satisfaction with laptop repair service. The initial dependent variable is the overall impression of the repair service. This variable was measured on an interval scale of 1 to 5. The variables that contribute to perceptions of repair effectiveness were also measured on the same scale but were rescaled to ordinal data for this example (1–2 = poor, 3 = average, and 4–5 = excellent). The top box shows that, after recoding, 62 percent of the participants rated the repair service as excellent (41% + 21%). The best predictor of repair effectiveness is "resolution of the problem."

On the left side of the tree, customers who rated "resolution of the problem" as "Poor" have fewer expectations being met or exceeded than the average for the sample (6 percent versus 62 percent). Moving to the far left box on the next row, a "Poor" rating on "condition on arrival" exacerbates this, reducing the total satisfied group to 2 percent. From this example you can see that the researcher separately studied (applied AID to) each subgroup to find the variable that when split again makes the next largest contribution to understanding the consumers' evaluation process—and to the reduction of unexplained variation in each subsample. This analysis alerts decision makers to the best- and worst-case scenarios for laptop repairs, how to recover during a problematic month, and which "key drivers" (independent variables influencing the process) should receive corrective resources.

>summary

LO13-1   Data collection comprises multiple tasks, including training the data collectors, determining the data collection timeline, determining and implementing an instrument disposition process, inviting chosen participants, activating the survey, reminding participants to complete and return the instrument, and entering the data. Each task plays an important role in guaranteeing data quality. Data entry creates a data record for each case and merges data records into a data file suitable for analytical procedures for the research study. Each data record is created using a coding scheme to ensure consistency among data records. This scheme contains each variable name and label, its location in the data file, the mapping rules for assigning codes to each response for each variable, and the code labels.

LO13-2   Data preparation includes any postcollection coding of data and data editing. Postcoding is especially important for textual and verbal responses as open questions are often chosen because participant responses were difficult to anticipate. Content analysis uses a systematic, objective approach to code message characteristics so a researcher can treat diverse textual or verbal content quantitatively as they look for patterns and draw inferences. Researchers can apply content analysis to a variety of cases: interview transcripts, employee evaluations, annual reports, financial analyst reports, advertisements, promotional brochures, press releases, speeches, web pages, social media posts, historical documents, conference proceedings, magazine and newspaper articles, etc.

Coding starts with determining the units to be analyzed: context, sample, or recording. Context units refer to the specific text to be coded that best addresses the research objective. Sample units refer to the type and level of text to be coded (words, phases, sentences, etc.). Recording units refer to the ideas embedded in the content to be coded. There are four types of recording units: syntactical (participant-chosen word choices), referential (to what a participant refers when describing an object), propositional (assertions about an object), and thematic (topics and themes represented in the text). Inter-rater reliability and intra-rater reliability are both critical to data quality when coding textual and verbal data.

LO13-3   Editing is the process for verifying that variables have used the designated coding scheme and that all data collected is entered correctly. Editing attempts to guarantee that data are complete, accurate, and appropriately coded for analysis.

Completeness assessments determine that data is ready for assessment. Don't know (DK) responses are assigned codes as either legitimate or not. There are multiple legitimate reasons for a DK response, and two that are not: intentionally skipping the question to avoid responding to a sensitive issue or as an expression of the unimportance of the topic. Both of these have the potential to inject bias into the data record. Missing data are of three types: data missing completely at random (MCAR), data missing at random (MAR), and data missing but not missing at random (NMAR). There are three techniques used to salvage data records with missing data: listwise deletion (which excludes missing data from analyses of that variable), pairwise deletion (that substitutes an estimate drawn from all data for that variable for the missing data), and predictive replacement (that uses another response from the same record to substitute for the missing data). All modify the affected data record in fundamental ways and each have potential to inject bias into the data.

Accuracy assessments are involved with data validation, a process that attempts to verify that research protocols that avoid data errors were followed and that data are real, by identifying fake or inaccurate data. Data recording and data entry can also cause inaccuracy. Editing attempts to uncover inaccuracies and correct them.

Appropriate coding assessments determine whether codes in the coding scheme, especially those precoded in the measurement instrument, are suitable for analysis given the preliminary frequency summary of collected data. Recoding variables (developing new mapping rules for variables) may be necessary to get the most out of data during analysis.

LO13-4 Exploratory data analysis (EDA) provides a perspective and set of tools to search for clues and patterns in the data. It starts with descriptive statistical processes, including preliminary frequencies and cross-tabulation of the data file. In addition to numerical summaries of location, spread, and shape,

EDA uses visual displays to provide a complete and accurate impression of distributions and variable relationships. Frequency tables are most useful for inspecting the range of responses and their repeated occurrence. Bar charts and pie charts are appropriate for relative comparisons of nominal data. Histograms are optimally used with continuous variables where intervals group the responses. The Pareto diagram is a bar chart whose percentages sum to 100 percent; responses are sorted in decreasing importance, with bar height descending from left to right. Stem-and-leaf displays present actual data values using a histogram-type device that allows inspection of spread and shape. Boxplots use the five-number summary to convey a detailed picture of a distribution's main body, tails, and outliers. Both stem-and-leaf displays and boxplots rely on resistant statistics to overcome the limitations of descriptive measures that are subject to distortion by extreme scores.

LO13-5 The examination of relationships among two or more variables employs cross-tabulation. The tables used for this purpose consist of cells and marginals. Each cell may contain combinations of count, row, column, and total percentages. Various guidelines for displaying tables increase the researcher's ability to understand tabular information: rounding numbers, arranging numbers to see patterns, using percentages and averages, comparing like scales, using design features like whitespace and color to guide the eye to numbers, accurately labeling tables, and summarizing data displays. The tabular structure is the framework for later statistical testing. An advanced variation on n-way tables is automatic interaction detection (AID).

>**key**terms

>discussionquestions

Terms in Review

1 Distinguish between

  a Coding scheme and recoding.

  b Bar chart and histogram.

  c DK response and missing data.

  d Listwise deletion and pairwise deletion.

  e Thematic units and referential units.

2 How should the researcher handle "don't know" responses?

3 How should the researcher handle missing data?

Making Research Decisions

4 Suppose you were preparing two-way tables of percentages for the following pairs of variables. How would you run the percentages?

  a Age and consumption of breakfast cereal.

  b Family income and confidence about the family's future.

  c Marital status and sports participation.

  d Crime rate and unemployment rate.

5 You study the attrition of entering college freshmen (those students who enter college as freshmen but don't stay to graduate). You find the following relationships among attrition, aid, and distance of home from college.

  a What graphical displays would you choose to understand the data?

  b What is your interpretation?

	Aid		Home Near Receiving Aid		Home Far Receiving Aid	
	Yes	No	Yes	No	Yes	No
	%	%	%	%	%	%
Drop Out	25	20	5	15	30	40
Stay	75	80	95	85	70	60

6 A problem facing shoe store managers is that many shoes eventually must be sold at markdown prices. This prompts a manufacturer to conduct a mail survey of shoe store managers in which we ask, "What methods have you found most successful for reducing the problem of high markdowns?" We are interested in extracting as much information as possible from these answers to better understand the full range of strategies that store managers use. Establish what you think are category sets to code 500 responses similar to the 14 given here. Try to develop an integrated set of categories that reflects your theory of markdown management. After developing the set, use it to code the 14 responses.

- Have not found the answer. As long as we buy style shoes, we will have markdowns. We use PMs on slow merchandise, but it does not eliminate markdowns. (*PM* stands for "push-money"—special cash bonuses for selling a particular brand and style of shoe.)

- Using PMs before too old. Also reducing price during season. Holding meetings with salespeople indicating which shoes to push.

- By putting PMs on any slow-selling items and promoting same. More careful check of shoes purchased.

- Keep a close watch on your stock, and mark down when you have to—that is, rather than wait, take a small markdown on a shoe that is not moving at the time.

- Using the PM method.

- Less advance buying—more dependence on in-stock shoes.

- Sales—catch bad guys before it's too late and close out.

- Buy as much good merchandise as you can at special prices to help make up some markdowns.

- Reducing opening buys and depending on fill-in service.

- Buy more frequently, better buying, PMs on slow-moving merchandise.

- Careful buying at lowest prices. Cash on the buying line. Buying closeouts, FDs, overstock, "cancellations." (*FD* stands for "factory-discontinued" style.)

- By buying less "changeable" shoes. Buy only what you need, watch sizes, don't go overboard on new fads.

- Buying more staple merchandise. Buying more from fewer lines. Sticking with better nationally advertised merchandise.

- No successful method with the current style situation. Manufacturers are experimenting, the retailer takes the markdowns—cuts gross profit by about 3 percent—keep your stock at lowest level without losing sales.

7 Select a small sample of class members, work associates, or friends and ask them to answer the following in a paragraph or two: "What are your career aspirations for the next five years?" Use one of the four basic units of content analysis to code their responses. Describe your findings using frequencies for the unit of analysis you selected.

8 A local health agency is experimenting with two appeal letters, A and B, with which to raise funds. It sends out 400 of the A appeal and 400 of the B appeal (each subsample is divided equally among working-class and middle-class neighborhoods). The solicitation secures the results shown in the following table.

a Which appeal is the best?

b Which class responded better to which letter?

c Is appeal or social class a more powerful independent variable?

	Appeal A		Appeal B	
	Middle Class	Working Class	Middle Class	Working Class
	%	%	%	%
Contribution	20	40	15	30
No contribution	80	60	85	70
	100	100	100	100

From Concept to Practice

9 Use the data in Exhibit 13-11 to construct a stem-and-leaf display.

a Where do you find the main body of the distribution?

b How many values reside outside the inner fence(s)?

10 Use the guidelines in appendix: *Better Tables* to develop a table from data in a case with a datafile.

From the Headlines

11 An article posted by *AdAge Media News* revealed that "a study commissioned by the Online Publishers Association found that 54 percent of tablet users prefer free, ad-supported apps over paid ones, up from 40 percent a year ago. At the same time, just 19 percent of users say they prefer to pay more for apps with no ads, down from 30 percent last year."

a Which visual display methods offer an accurate reflection of the data?

b Which visual display provides the most meaning? Why?

>cases*

Agri Comp

Inquiring Minds Want to Know—Now!

Mastering Teacher Leadership

NCRCC: Teeing Up a New Strategic Direction

NetConversions Influences Kelley Blue Book

Proofpoint: Capitalizing on a Reporter's Love of Statistics

* You will find a description of each case in the Case Abstracts section of this textbook. Check the Case Index to determine whether a case provides data, the research instrument, video, or other supplementary material. Cases and case supplements are available in Connect.

Better Tables[1]

Because the researcher's primary job is to discover the message revealed by the data, he or she needs every tool to reveal the message. Authors Sally Bigwood and Melissa Spore, in their book *Presenting Numbers, Tables, and Charts*, suggest that the table is the ultimate tool for extracting knowledge from data.

The presence of any number within a table is for comparison with a similar number—from last year, from another candidate, from another machine, against a goal, and so forth. Using the author's rules for table creation, a researcher exploring data by constructing a table should:

- *Round numbers.*
  - Rounded numbers can be most easily compared, enabling us to more easily determine the ratio or relationship of one number to another.
  - If precision is critical to the number (e.g., you are researching taxes or design specifications or drug interactions), don't round the numbers.

- *Arrange the numbers to reveal patterns.*
  - Order numbers from largest to smallest number.
    - In a vertically arranged table, order the largest number at the top.
    - In a horizontal arrangement, order the largest numbers on the left.
  - When looking for changes over time, order the numbers by year, from most distant (left or top) to most recent.

- *Use averages, totals, or percentages to achieve focus.*
  - An average provides a point for comparison.
    - Don't use an average if the raw data reveal a bimodal distribution.
  - Totals emphasize the big picture.
  - Percentages show proportionate relationships more easily than raw data.

- *Compare like scales in a single table.*
  - Convert numbers to a common scale when the numbers reflect different scales (e.g., grams versus ounces of cereal consumption; monthly salary data versus hourly wage data).

- *Choose simplicity over complexity.*
  - Several smaller tables reveal patterns better rather than one large, complex table.
  - Complex tables are used as a convenient reference source for multiple elements of data.

- *Use whitespace and design to guide the eye to numbers that must be compared and to make patterns and exceptions stand out.*
  - Design a table with a smaller number of columns than rows.
  - Single-space numbers that must be compared.
  - Use gridlines to group numbers within a table; avoid gridlines between numbers that must be compared.
  - Use whitespace to create gutters between numbers in simple tables.
  - Right-align column headers and table numbers.

- *Summarize each data display.*
  - Write a phrase or sentence that summarizes your interpretation of the data presented; don't leave interpretation to chance.
    - Summary statements might be used as the title of a table or chart in the final research report.
    - The summary need not mention any numbers.

- *Label and title tables for clarity of message.*
  - Titles should be comprehensive; include what (subject of the title or message), where (if data have a geographic base), when (date or time period covered), and unit of measure.
  - Include common information in the title; it lengthens a title but shortens the table's column headings.
  - Avoid abbreviations in column headings unless well known by your audience.
  - Avoid footnotes; if used, use symbols—like the asterisk—rather than numbers (numbers used as footnotes can be confused with the content numbers of the table).
  - For reference, provide an undertable source line for later reference.

>**Table 1** Spending by Internet Users in Selected Western European Countries 20XX (Euros in Billions)

	Annual Spending		Annual Purchases
France	Euro	664.5	16
Germany	Euro	658.0	20
Italy	Euro	345.5	14
Spain	Euro	560.1	10
United Kingdom	Euro	2284.9	36

>**Table 2** E5 Per Capita One-Year Online Spending (20XX)

	Annual Spending (Euros)	Average Annual Purchases	Annual Spending (US $)
United Kingdom	2284.9	36	1736.2
Germany	658.0	20	500.0
France	664.5	16	505.0
Italy	345.5	14	262.6
Spain	560.1	10	425.6

Currency exchange rate: 1 US$ = 1.316 euros

An Example

Assume you were determining whether to expand into western Europe with distribution facilities to service online purchases of your specialty goods company.

We start with Table 1, which presents data developed from several studies on online shopping and purchasing behavior in selected countries in western Europe. The data are ordered alphabetically by country. While arranging in alphabetical order may be ideal for randomization or reduction of bias, it isn't a logical choice for clarity of data presentation.

What data might you need to help you make your decision about distribution facilities? Do you need to know the average transaction size? If you don't know the conversion rate of the euro to the dollar, can you interpret the table? Should you put your investment in the United Kingdom or elsewhere?

Table 2 recasts the data using Bigwood and Spore's guidelines. First the table title has changed; now the annual period on which the spending data are based is more obvious, as well as the fact that we are looking at spending per capita for the top five European Union performers, known as the E5. We've also changed the column headers

to reflect currency, and we have right-justified these headers and the numbers. We've rearranged the table by Average Spending (Euro) in descending order and interpreted the (Euro) column by adding a dollar conversion column. We might not need the rightmost column if we were euro spenders ourselves, but if we are more familiar with another currency, the addition of this column helps us interpret the data. With this arrangement, does Germany look attractive? While it might not currently appear to be as strong a contender as the United Kingdom, we know it is fiscally strong and located in a more central location to the other countries being considered.

Table 3 offers a simple addition: the average of the columns. And the table is now ordered by the Average Annual Purchases within the one-year period studied. This presentation allows the interpreter of the data to determine which countries are buying above the average for western Europe and which are buying below the average. Germany is looking pretty good. Right?

Table 4 offers a recasting of the data based on a newly calculated column, Average Transaction (Euros). Germany doesn't look so attractive now. This is especially true if we are a seller of specialty merchandise with higher prices.

>**Table 3** E5 Per Capita One-Year Online Spending (20XX)

	Annual Spending (Euros)	Average Annual Purchases	Annual Spending (US$)	
United Kingdom	2284.9	36	1736.24	Above average frequency buyers
Germany	658.0	20	500.00	Above average frequency buyers
France	664.5	16	504.97	Below average frequency buyers
Italy	345.5	14	262.57	Below average frequency buyers
Spain	560.1	10	425.61	Below average frequency buyers
Average	902.6	19.2	685.88	

Currency exchange rate: 1 US$ = 1.316 euros

>**Table 4** ES Per Capita One-Year Online Spending (20XX)

	Annual Spending (Euros)	Annual Spending (US$)	Average Annual Purchases	Average Transaction (Euros)	Average Transaction (US$)
United Kingdom	2284.9	1736.24	36	63.5	48.23
Spain	560.1	425.61	10	56.0	42.56
France	664.5	504.97	16	41.5	31.56
Germany	658.0	500.00	20	32.9	25.00
Italy	345.5	262.57	14	24.7	18.75
Average	902.6	685.88	19.2	47.0	35.72

Currency exchange rate: 1 US$ = 1.316 euros

Unlike previous tables, Table 5 is ordered from least to most based on the estimated 20X5 Average Transaction and we've used projections for 20X5 purchase data. If you were blurry-eyed from studying numerous tables, you might quickly glance at the table and think Germany as a distribution center should be the obvious choice. While Germany might still be a contender (given its stronger financial position in the European Union), its smaller projected transaction size might make it less so for a specialty goods distributor. So a very important caution on tables: As a researcher, you want to strive for consistency. If you are ordering from most to least, choose this arrangement for every table you do.

After recasting the data in various tables, where would you put your distribution center?

>**Table 5** E5 Per Capita One-Year Online Spending (20XX vs. 20X5)

	Estimated Percent Internet Users 20X5	Estimated Internet Users 20X5 (millions)	Estimated Average Transaction 20X5 (Euros)	Estimated Average Transaction 20X5 (US$)
Germany	89.9	72.2	51.5	37.06
Italy	78.3	45.3	58.6	42.14
France	87.3	56.9	63.8	45.92
United Kingdom	94.9	58.2	95.2	68.48
Spain	77.7	34.5	106.4	76.55
Average	78.3	45.3	58.6	42.14

>**appendix**

Describing Data Statistically[1]

During Stage 3 of the Research Process, data are coded (or recoded), entered, and edited. Creating numerical summaries of this process provides valuable insights to analysts about their effectiveness. In this appendix, we review concepts from your introductory statistics course that offer descriptive tools for cleaning data, discovering problems, and summarizing distributions. A distribution (of data) is an array of value counts from lowest to highest value of a variable, resulting from the tabulation of incidence. Descriptive statistical measures are used to depict the center, spread, and shape of distributions and are helpful as preliminary tools for data description. We will define these measures and describe their use as *descriptive statistics* after introducing a sample data set and an overview of basic concepts.

Reviewing Statistical Concepts

The LCD (liquid crystal display) TV market is an interesting market to watch because of the changes in technology and marketing. Currently the major players in this market are Sharp, LG Electronics/Zenith, Samsung, Sony, Dell, and Panasonic. Only a few other brands earn a noticeable market share. Sharp products currently represent the largest percentage of unit sales. Let's assume we are interested in evaluating annual unit sales increases of several manufacturers. We survey nine manufacturers and we find a *frequency distribution* (an ordered array of all values for a variable) of annual percentage of unit sales increases: 5, 6, 6, 7, 7, 7, 8, 8, 9. From these unit sales scores, we construct a table for arraying the data. It presents value codes from lowest to highest value, with columns for count, percent, percent for missing values, and cumulative percent. An example is presented in Exhibit Da-1.

The table arrays data by assigned numerical value, in this case the actual percentage unit sales increase recorded (far-left column). To discover how many manufacturers were in each unit sales increase category, you

>**Exhibit Da-1** Annual Percentage Unit Sales Increases for LCD TV Manufacturers

A

Unit Sales Increase (%)	Frequency	Percentage	Cumulative Percentage
5	1	11.1	11.1
6	2	22.2	33.3
7	3	33.3	66.7
8	2	22.2	88.9
9	1	11.1	100.0
Total	9	100.0	

B

Company Origin	Unit Sales Increase (%)	Frequency	Percentage	Cumulative Percent
Origin, foreign (1)	6	1	11.1	11.1
	7	2	22.2	33.3
	8	2	22.2	55.5
Origin, domestic (2)	5	1	11.1	66.6
	6	1	11.1	77.7
	7	1	11.1	88.8
	9	1	11.1	100.0
	Total	9	100.0	

would read the frequency column. For example, at the intersection of the frequency column and the second row, there are two companies that posted a 6 percent annual unit sales increase. In the percentage column, you see what percentage of TV manufacturers in the survey gave a response for each level of unit sales increase. The three manufacturers who had unit sales increases of 7 percent represent 33.3 percent of the total number of manufacturers surveyed (3/9 × 100). The cumulative percentage reveals the number of manufacturers that provided a response and *any others that preceded it* in the table. For this example, LCD TV percentage unit sales increases between 5 and 7 percent represent 66.7 percent. The cumulative percentage column is helpful primarily when the data have an underlying order. If, in part B, we create a code for source of origin (foreign = 1, domestic = 2) to each of the nine LCD TV manufacturers, the cumulative percentage column would provide the proportion. The *proportion* is the percentage of elements in the distribution that met a criterion. In this case, the criterion is the origin of manufacture.

In Exhibit Da-2, the bell-shaped curve that is superimposed on the distribution of annual unit sales increases (percent) for LCD TV manufacturers is called the *normal distribution.* The distribution of values for any variable that has a normal distribution is governed by a mathematical equation. This distribution is a symmetrical curve and reflects a frequency distribution of many natural phenomena such as the height of people of a certain gender and age.

Many variables of interest that researchers will measure will have distributions that approximate a *standard normal distribution.* A standard normal distribution is a special case of the normal distribution in which all values are given standard scores. This distribution has a mean of 0 and a standard deviation of 1. For example, a manufacturer that had an annual unit sales increase of 7 percent would be given a standard score of zero since 7 is the mean of the LCD TV distribution. A *standard score* (or *Z score*) tells you how many units a case (a manufacturer in this example) is above or below the mean. The Z score, being standardized, allows us to compare the results of different normal distributions, something we do frequently in research. Assume that Zenith has an annual unit sales increase of 9 percent. To calculate a standard score for this manufacturer, you would find the difference between the value and the mean and divide by the standard deviation of the distribution shown in Exhibit Da-1.

$$\text{Zenith's standard score} = \frac{\text{Value} - \text{Mean}}{\text{Standard deviation}} = \frac{9 - 7}{1.22}$$
$$= 1.64$$

The standard normal distribution, shown in part A of Exhibit Da-3, is a standard of comparison for describing distributions of sample data. It is used with inferential statistics that assume normally distributed variables.

We will come back to this exhibit in a moment. Now let's review some descriptive tools that reveal the important characteristics of distributions. The characteristics of central tendency, variability, and shape are useful tools for summarizing distributions. Their definitions, applications, and formulas fall under the heading of *descriptive statistics.* The definitions will be familiar to most readers.

Measures of Central Tendency

Summarizing information such as that from our collected data of LCD TV manufacturers often requires the description of "typical" values. Suppose we want to know the typical percentage unit sales increase for these companies. We might define *typical* as the average response (mean); the middle value, when the distribution is sorted from lowest to highest (median); or the most frequently occurring value (mode). The common measures of *central tendency* (or center) include the mean, median, and mode.

The *mean* is calculated by the following formula:

$$\overline{X} = \frac{\sum_{i=1}^{n} X_i}{n}$$

For the unit sales increase variable, the distribution of responses is 5, 6, 6, 7, 7, 7, 8, 8, 9. The arithmetic average, or mean (the sum of the nine values divided by 9), is

$$\frac{5 + 6 + 6 + 7 + 7 + 8 + 8 + 9}{9} = 7 \text{ (an average 7\% unit sales increase)}$$

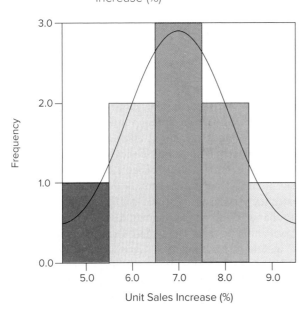

>**Exhibit Da-2** Histogram of Annual Unit Sales Increase (%)

>**Exhibit Da-3** Characteristics of Distributions

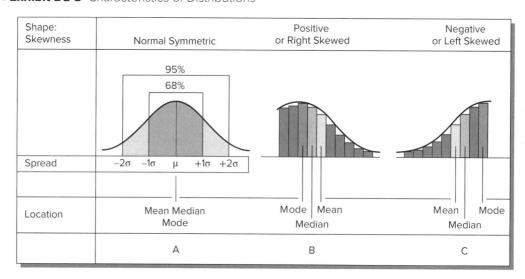

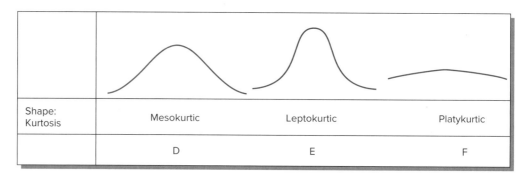

The *median* is the midpoint of the distribution. Half of the observations in the distribution fall above and the other half fall below the median. When the distribution has an even number of observations, the median is the average of the two middle scores. The median is the most appropriate locator of center for ordinal data and has resistance to extreme scores, thereby making it a preferred measure for interval and ratio data when their distributions are not normal. The median is sometimes symbolized by *M* or *mdn*.

From the sample distribution for the percentage unit sales increase variable, the median of the nine values is 7:

5   6   6   7   7   7   8   8   9

If the distribution had 10 values, the median would be the average of the values for the fifth and sixth cases.

The *mode* is the most frequently occurring value. There may be *more than one* mode in a distribution. When there is more than one code that has the highest yet equal frequency, the distribution is bimodal or multimodal. There may be *no* mode in a distribution if every code has an equal number of observations. The mode is the location measure of central tendency for nominal data and a point of reference along with the median and mean for examining spread and shape of distributions. In our LCD TV

percentage unit sales increase example, the most frequently occurring value is 7. As revealed in the frequency distribution in Exhibit Da-2, there are three companies that have unit sales increases of 7 percent.

Notice in Exhibit Da-3, part A, that the mean, median, and mode are the same in a normal distribution. When these measures of central tendency diverge, the distribution is no longer normal.

Measures of Variability

The common measures of *variability,* alternatively referred to as *dispersion* or *spread,* are the variance, standard deviation, range, interquartile range, and quartile deviation. They describe how scores cluster or scatter in a distribution.

The *variance* is a measure of score dispersion about the mean. If all the scores are identical, the variance is 0. The greater the dispersion of scores, the greater the variance. Both the variance and the standard deviation are used with interval and ratio data. The symbol for the sample variance is s^2, and that for the population variance is the Greek letter sigma, squared $(\sigma)^2$. The variance is computed by summing the squared distance from the mean for all cases and dividing the sum by the total number of cases minus 1:

$$\text{Variance} = s^2 = \frac{\text{Sum of the squared distances from mean for all cases}}{(\text{Number of cases} - 1)}$$

$$s^2 = \frac{\sum_{i=1}^{n}(X_i - \overline{X})^2}{n-1}$$

For the percentage unit sales increase variable, we would compute the variance as

$$s^2 = \frac{\begin{array}{c}(5-7)^2 + (6-7)^2 + (6-7)^2 \\ + (7-7)^2 + (7-7)^2 + (7-7)^2 \\ + (8-7)^2 + (8-7)^2 + (9-7)^2\end{array}}{8} = 1.5$$

The *standard deviation* summarizes how far away from the average the data values typically are. It is perhaps the most frequently used measure of spread because it improves interpretability by removing the variance's square and expressing the deviations in their original units (e.g., sales in dollars, not dollars squared). It is also an important concept for descriptive statistics because it reveals the amount of variability within the data file. Like the mean, the standard deviation is affected by extreme scores. The symbol for the sample standard deviation is *s*, and that for a population standard deviation is σ. Alternatively, it is labeled *std. dev.* You can calculate the standard deviation by taking the square root of the variance:

$$s = \sqrt{s^2}$$

The standard deviation for the percentage unit sales increase variable in our example is 1.22:

$$1.22 = \sqrt{1.5}$$

The *range* is the difference between the largest and smallest scores in the distribution. The percentage annual unit sales increase variable has a range of 4 (9 − 5 = 4). Unlike the standard deviation, the range is computed from only the minimum and maximum scores; thus, it is a very rough measure of spread. With the range as a point of comparison, it is possible to get an idea of the homogeneity (small std. dev.) or heterogeneity (large std. dev.) of the distribution. For a homogeneous distribution, the ratio of the range to the standard deviation should be between 2 and 6. A number above 6 would indicate a high degree of heterogeneity. In the percentage unit sales increase example, the ratio is 4/1.22 = 3.28. The range provides useful but limited information for all data. It is mandatory for ordinal data.

The *interquartile range (IQR)* is the difference between the first and third quartiles of the distribution. It is also called the *midspread*. Ordinal or ranked data use this measure in conjunction with the median. It is also used with interval and ratio data when asymmetrical distributions are suspected or for exploratory analysis. Recall the following

relationships: the minimum value of the distribution is the 0 percentile; the maximum, the 100th percentile. The first quartile (Q_1) is the 25th percentile; the median, Q_2, is the 50th percentile. The third quartile (Q_3) is the 75th percentile. For the percentage unit sales increase data, the quartiles are

$$\underline{5 \quad 6 \quad 6 \quad \underset{Q_1}{7} \quad \underset{Q_2}{\mathbf{7}} \quad \underset{Q_3}{7} \quad \underset{Q_4}{8} \quad 8 \quad 9}$$

The quartile deviation, or semi-interquartile range, is expressed as

$$Q = \frac{Q_1 - Q_3}{2}$$

The *quartile deviation* is always used with the median for ordinal data. It is helpful for interval and ratio data when the distribution is stretched (or skewed) by extreme values. In a normal distribution, the median plus one quartile deviation (Q) on either side encompasses 50 percent of the observations. Eight Qs cover approximately the range. Q's relationship with the standard deviation is constant ($Q = .6745s$) when scores are normally distributed. For our annual percentage unit sales increase example, the quartile deviation is 1 [(6 − 8)/2 = 1].

Measures of Shape

The measures of shape, skewness and kurtosis, describe departures from the symmetry of a distribution and its relative flatness (or peakedness), respectively. They use deviation scores ($X - \overline{X}$). *Deviation scores* show us how far any observation is from the mean. The company that posted a percentage unit sales increase of 9 has a deviation score of 2 (9 − 7). The measures of shape are often difficult to interpret when extreme scores are in the distribution. Generally, shape is best communicated through visual displays. (Refer to the graphics in Exhibit Da-3, parts B through F.) From a practical standpoint, the calculation of skewness and kurtosis is easiest with spreadsheet or statistics software.

Skewness is a measure of a distribution's deviation from symmetry. In a symmetrical distribution, the mean, median, and mode are in the same location. A distribution that has cases stretching toward one tail or the other is called *skewed*. As shown in Exhibit Da-3, part B, when the tail stretches to the right, to larger values, it is positively skewed. In part C, scores stretching toward the left, toward smaller values, skew the distribution negatively. Note the relationship between the mean, median, and mode in asymmetrical distributions. The symbol for skewness is *sk*.

$$sk = \frac{n}{(n-1)(n-2)} \sum \left(\frac{x_i - \overline{x}}{s}\right)^3$$

where *s* is the sample standard deviation (the unbiased estimate of sigma).

When a distribution approaches symmetry, *sk* is approximately 0. With a positive skew, *sk* will be a positive number; with negative skew, *sk* will be a negative number. The calculation of skewness for our annual percentage unit sales increase data produces an index of 0 and reveals no skew.

As illustrated in the lower portion of Exhibit Da-3, *kurtosis* is a measure of a distribution's peakedness (or flatness). Distributions that have scores that cluster heavily or pile up in the center (along with more observations than normal in the extreme tails) are peaked or *leptokurtic*. Flat distributions, with scores more evenly distributed and tails fatter than a normal distribution, are called *platykurtic*. Intermediate or *mesokurtic* distributions approach normal—neither too peaked nor too flat. The symbol for kurtosis is *ku*.

$$ku = \left[\frac{n(n + 1)}{(n - 1)(n - 2)(n - 3)} \sum \left(\frac{x_i - \bar{x}}{s} \right)^4 \right] - \frac{3(n - 1)^2}{(n - 2)(n - 3)}$$

where *s* is the sample standard deviation (the unbiased estimate of sigma).

The value of *ku* for a normal or mesokurtic distribution is close to 0. A leptokurtic distribution will have a positive value, and the *platykurtic* distribution will be negative. As with skewness, the larger the absolute value of the index, the more extreme is the characteristic. In the annual percentage unit sales increase example, the kurtosis is calculated as −0.29, which suggested a very slight deviation from a normally shaped curve with some flattening contributed by smaller-than-expected frequencies of the value 7 in the example distribution.

>part V

Analyze and Interpret Data

>**chapter 14**

Stage 4:
Hypothesis Testing

"A fact is a simple statement that everyone believes. It is innocent, unless found guilty. A hypothesis is a novel suggestion that no one wants to believe. It is guilty, until found effective."

Edward Teller, theoretical physicist,
known colloquially as "the father of the hydrogen bomb"
(1908–2003)

>**learning**objectives

After reading this chapter, you should understand. . .

LO14-1 The nature and logic of hypothesis testing.

LO14-2 A statistically significant difference.

LO14-3 The six-step hypothesis testing procedure.

LO14-4 The differences between parametric and nonparametric tests and when to use each.

LO14-5 The factors that influence the selection of an appropriate test of statistical significance.

LO14-6 How to interpret the various test statistics.

>Introduction

Using inductive and deductive reasoning is fundamental to **hypothesis testing**, the process of proving that a hypothesis (unsupported assumption about the relationship between two variables) is valid. (See Exhibit 14-1 for a review of these terms.) Inductive reasoning moves from specific facts to general, but tentative, conclusions. We can never be absolutely sure that inductive conclusions are flawless. With the aid of probability estimates, we can qualify our results and state the degree of confidence we have in these hypotheses. Statistical inference is an application of inductive reasoning. It allows us to reason from evidence found in the sample data to conclusions we wish to make about the target population.

Inferential statistics is the second of two major categories of statistical procedures, the other being descriptive statistics. Researchers use descriptive statistics when exploring data. Under the heading **inferential statistics**, two topics are discussed in this book. The first, estimation of population values, was used in discussing sampling design, but we will return to it here briefly. The second, testing statistical hypotheses, is the primary subject of this chapter. There are more examples of hypothesis tests in this chapter than most students will need for a term project or early assignments in their management careers. A section on nonparametric techniques in Appendix C provides further study for readers with a special interest in nominal and ordinal variables.

After you have detailed your hypotheses in your preliminary analysis plan, the purpose of hypothesis testing is to determine the accuracy of your hypotheses due to the fact that you have collected a sample of data, not a census. Exhibit 14-2 reminds you of the relationships among your design strategy, data collection activities, preliminary analysis, and hypothesis testing.

Researchers evaluate the accuracy of hypotheses by determining the statistical likelihood that the sample data reveal true differences—not random sampling error. We evaluate the importance of a statistically significant difference by weighing the practical significance of any change that we measure.

Although there are two approaches to hypothesis testing, the more established is the classical or sampling-theory approach. **Classical statistics** are found in all of the major statistics books and are widely used in research applications. This approach represents an objective view of probability in which the decision making rests totally on an analysis of available sampling data. A hypothesis is established; it is then rejected or fails to be rejected, based on the sample data collected.

The second approach is known as **Bayesian statistics**, which are an extension of the classical approach. It also uses sampling data, but it goes beyond to consider all other available information. These subjective estimates are based on general experience rather than on specific collected data. Various decision rules are established, cost and other estimates can be introduced, and the expected outcomes of combinations of these elements are used to judge decision alternatives.

Statistical Significance

Following a classical statistics approach, we accept or reject a hypothesis on the basis of data collected from the sample alone. Because any sample will almost surely vary somewhat from its population, we must judge whether the differences are statistically significant or insignificant.

>**Exhibit 14-1** A Review of Key Terms

Hypothesis	• An unsubstantiated assumption about the relationship between concepts and constructs
	• Guides the research
	• Formulated for testing (substantiation)
Induction	• A conclusion based on a specific set of facts
Deduction	• A conclusion based on a set of true and valid premises

>**Exhibit 14-2** Hypothesis Testing and the Research Process

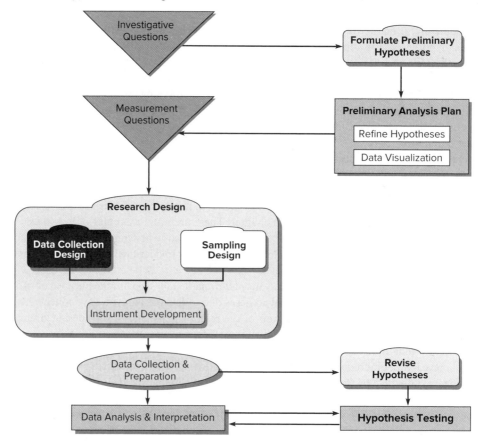

A difference has **statistical significance** if there is good reason to believe the difference does not represent random sampling fluctuations only. For example, Honda, Toyota, Chrysler, Nissan, Ford, and other auto companies produce hybrid vehicles using an advanced technology that combines a small gas engine with an electric motor. The vehicles run on an electric motor at slow speeds but shift to both the gasoline motor and the electric motor at city and higher freeway speeds. Their advertising strategies focus on fuel economy. Let's say that the hybrid Toyota has maintained an average of about 60 miles per gallon (mpg) with a standard deviation of 10 mpg. Suppose researchers discover by analyzing all production vehicles that the mpg is now 61. Is this difference statistically significant from 60? Of course it is, because the difference is based on a *census* of the vehicles and there is no sampling involved. It has been demonstrated conclusively that the population average has moved from 60 to 61 mpg. Although it is of statistical significance, whether it is of **practical significance** is another question. If a manager judges that this variation has no real importance, then it is of little practical significance. One world-wide respected research company says that the most important question a researcher can ask is, "So what?"[1]

Because it would be too expensive to analyze all of a manufacturer's vehicles frequently, we resort to sampling. Assume a sample of 25 cars is randomly selected and the average mpg is calculated to be 64. Is this statistically significant? The answer is not obvious. It is significant if there is good reason to believe the average mpg of the total population has moved up from 60 to 64. Because the evidence consists of only a sample, consider the second possibility: that this is only a random sampling error and thus is not significant. The task is to decide whether such a result from this sample is or is not statistically significant. To answer this question, one needs to consider further the logic of hypothesis testing.

>The Logic of Hypothesis Testing

In classical tests of significance, two kinds of hypotheses are used. The **null hypothesis (H_0)** is used for testing. It is a statement that no difference exists between the *parameter* (a measure taken by a census of the population or a prior measurement of a sample of the population) and the sample statistic being compared to it (a measure from a recently drawn sample of the population). Analysts usually test to determine whether there has been no change in the population of interest or whether a real difference exists. Why not state the hypothesis in a positive form? Why not state that any difference between the sample statistic and the population parameter is due to some reason? Unfortunately, this type of hypothesis cannot be tested definitively. Evidence that is consistent with a hypothesis stated in a positive form can almost never be taken as conclusive grounds for accepting the hypothesis. A finding that is consistent with this type of hypothesis might be consistent with other hypotheses too, and thus it does not demonstrate the truth of the given hypothesis.

For example, suppose a coin is suspected of being biased in favor of heads. The coin is flipped 100 times and the outcome is 52 heads. It would not be correct to jump to the conclusion that the coin is biased simply because more than the expected number of 50 heads resulted. The reason is that 52 heads is consistent with the hypothesis that the coin is fair. On the other hand, flipping 85 or 90 heads in 100 flips would seem to contradict the hypothesis of a fair coin. In this case, there would be a strong case for a biased coin.

In the hybrid-vehicle example, the null hypothesis states that the population parameter of 60 mpg has not changed. A second, **alternative hypothesis (H_A)** holds that there has been a change in average mpg (i.e., the sample statistic of 64 indicates the population value probably is no longer 60). The alternative hypothesis is the logical opposite of the null hypothesis.

The hybrid-car example can be explored further to show how these concepts are used to test for significance:

- The null hypothesis (H_0): There has been no change from the 60 mpg average.

The alternative hypothesis (H_A) may take several forms, depending on the objective of the researchers. The H_A may be of the "not the same" or the "greater than" or "less than" form:

- The average mpg has changed from 60.
- The average mpg has increased (decreased) from 60.

These types of alternative hypotheses correspond with two-tailed and one-tailed tests. A **two-tailed test**, or *nondirectional test*, considers two possibilities: the average could be more than 60 mpg, or it could be less than 60. To test this hypothesis, the regions of rejection are divided into two tails of the distribution. A **one-tailed test**, or *directional test*, places the entire probability of an unlikely outcome into the tail specified by the alternative hypothesis. In Exhibit 14-3, the first diagram represents a nondirectional hypothesis, and the second is a directional hypothesis of the "greater than" variety.

>**Exhibit 14-3** Two- and One-Tailed Tests at the 5 Percent Level of Significance

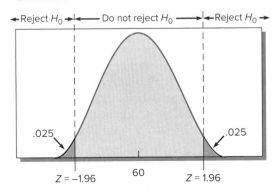

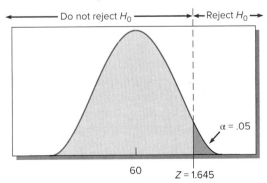

Hypotheses for Exhibit 14-3 may be expressed in the following form:

Null H_0: $\mu = 60$ mpg
Alternative H_A: $\mu \neq 60$ mpg (not the same)

or

Null H_0: $\mu \leq 60$ mpg
Alternative H_A: $\mu > 60$ mpg (greater than)

or

Null H_0: $\mu \geq 60$ mpg
Alternative H_A: $\mu < 60$ mpg (less than)

In testing these hypotheses, researchers adopt this decision rule: Take no corrective action if the analysis shows that one cannot reject the null hypothesis. Note the language "cannot reject" rather than "accept" the null hypothesis. It is argued that a null hypothesis can never be proved and, therefore, cannot be "accepted." Here, again, we see the influence of inductive reasoning. Unlike deduction, where the connections between premises and conclusions provide a legitimate claim of "conclusive proof," inductive conclusions do not possess that advantage. Statistical testing gives only a chance to (1) disprove (reject) or (2) fail to reject the hypothesis. Despite this terminology, it is common to hear "accept the null" rather than the clumsy "fail to reject the null." In this discussion, the less formal *accept* means "fail to reject" the null hypothesis.

If we reject a null hypothesis (find a statistically significant difference), then we are accepting the alternative hypothesis. In either accepting or rejecting a null hypothesis, we can make incorrect decisions. A null hypothesis can be accepted when it should have been rejected or rejected when it should have been accepted.

These problems are illustrated with an analogy to the American legal system.[2] In our system of justice, the innocence of an indicted person is presumed until proof of guilt beyond a reasonable doubt can be established. In hypothesis testing, this is the null hypothesis; there should be no difference between the presumption of innocence and the outcome unless contrary evidence is furnished. Once evidence establishes beyond reasonable doubt that innocence can no longer be maintained, a just conviction is required. This is equivalent to rejecting the null hypothesis and accepting the alternative hypothesis. Incorrect decisions or errors are the other two possible outcomes. We can unjustly convict an innocent person, or we can acquit a guilty person.

Exhibit 14-4 compares the statistical situation to the legal one. One of two conditions exists in nature—either the null hypothesis is true or the alternative hypothesis is true. An indicted person is innocent or guilty. Two decisions can be made about these conditions: one may accept the null hypothesis or reject it (thereby accepting the alternative hypothesis). Two of these situations result in correct decisions; the other two lead to decision errors.

When a **Type I error (α)** is committed, a true null hypothesis is rejected; the innocent person is unjustly convicted. The value is called *the level of significance* and is the probability of rejecting the true null hypothesis. With a **Type II error (β),** one fails to reject a false null hypothesis; the result is an unjust acquittal, with the guilty person going free. In our system of justice, it is more important to reduce the probability of convicting the innocent than that of acquitting the guilty. Similarly, hypothesis testing places a greater emphasis on reducing Type I errors than on Type II errors.

Type I Error

Assume the hybrid manufacturer's problem is complicated by a consumer testing agency's assertion that the average city miles per gallon (mpg) has changed. Assume the population mean is 50 mpg, the standard deviation of the population is 10 mpg, and the size of the sample is 25 vehicles. With this information, we can calculate the standard error of the mean ($\sigma_{\bar{X}}$) (the standard deviation of the distribution of sample means). This hypothetical distribution is pictured in Exhibit 14-5. The standard error of the mean is calculated to be 2 mpg:

$$\sigma_{\bar{X}} = \frac{\sigma}{\sqrt{n}} = \frac{10}{\sqrt{25}} = 2$$

>**Exhibit 14-4** Comparison of Statistical Decisions to Legal Analogy

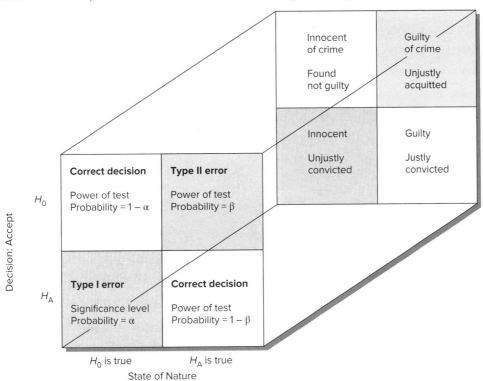

If the decision is to reject H_0 with a 95 percent confidence interval ($\alpha = .05$), a Type I error of .025 in each tail is accepted (this assumes a two-tailed test). In part A of Exhibit 14-5, see the **regions of rejection** indicated by the shaded areas. The area between these two regions is known as the **region of acceptance**. The dividing points between the rejection and acceptance areas are called **critical values**. Because the distribution of sample means is normal, the critical values can be computed in terms of the standardized random variable,[3] where

$Z = 1.96$ (significance level = .05)
$\overline{X}_c$ = the critical value of the sample mean
μ = the population value stated in H_0 = 50
$\sigma_{\overline{X}}$ = the standard error of a distribution of means of samples of 25

Thus, the critical values for the test of the null hypothesis (that the mpg has not changed) are computed as follows:

$$Z = \frac{\overline{X} - \mu}{\sigma_{\overline{X}}}$$

$$-1.96 = \frac{\overline{X}_c - 50}{2}$$

$$\overline{X}_c = 46.08$$

$$1.96 = \frac{\overline{X}_c - 50}{2}$$

$$\overline{X}_c = 53.92$$

If the probability of a Type I error is 5 percent ($\alpha = .05$), the probability of a correct decision if the null hypothesis is true is 95 percent. By changing the probability of a Type I error, you move critical values either closer to or farther away from the assumed parameter of 50. This can be done if a smaller or larger α error is desired and critical values are moved to reflect this. You can also

>snapshot

Testing a Hypothesis for Troy-Bilt®

Marcus Thomas LLC recently conducted an online survey to help Troy-Bilt®, a leading manufacturer of lawn and garden equipment, understand what elements in television advertising help build recall and consideration, specifically within the lawn and garden category.

Marcus Thomas formulated the hypothesis that "consumers who are in the market to purchase a product process television advertising differently than those who are not in the market for lawn and garden equipment," shared Edwige Winans, associate director of research for Marcus Thomas. Carefully selected participants were segmented into groups of equal size, based on whether or not they were planning to purchase lawn or garden equipment (in-market group vs. out-of-market group). To control for category-specific reactions, Marcus Thomas also recruited a control group, those who were in the market for paint and those who were not.

One thousand respondents were asked to watch an eight-minute segment of the DIY Network show *House Crashers* on their computer (to simulate television watching). Four 30-second television ads were embedded following the first four minutes of the show (two for lawn or garden equipment and two for paint), followed by four additional minutes of the show. The study was blind in that respondents did not know its purpose. Ad order was randomized for each respondent to eliminate order bias. In a subsequent online survey, respondents provided both aided and unaided recall measurements of the television spots (to assess which elements in the ads were most memorable), as well as information on how the ads affected perceptions of each brand featured and brand awareness. Several red-herring questions were introduced to ensure participants would not be swayed by their perceived purpose of the study or the merchandise category.

©VStock/Alamy

The test did showcase unique differences in the way consumers process television advertising based on whether they are in-market or not-in-market for lawn and garden products.

The survey Marcus Thomas used is available in Connect.

www.marcusthomasllc.com; www.troybilt.com

change the Type 1 error and the regions of acceptance by changing the size of the sample. For example, if you take a sample of 100, the critical values that provide a Type I error of .05 are 48.04 and 51.96.

The alternative hypothesis concerned a change in either direction from 50, but the manufacturer is interested only in increases in mpg. For this, one uses a one-tailed (greater than) H_A and places the entire region of rejection in the upper tail of the distribution. One can accept a 5 percent α risk and compute a new critical value ($\overline{X}_c$). (See Appendix D, Exhibit D-1, to find the Z value of 1.645 for the area of .05 under the curve.) Substitute this in the Z equation and solve for $\overline{X}_c$:

$$Z = 1.645 = \frac{\overline{X}_c - 50}{2}$$

$$\overline{X}_c = 53.29$$

>**Exhibit 14-5** Probability of Making a Type I Error Given H_0 Is True

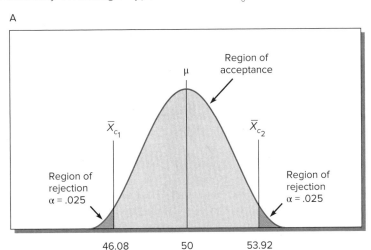

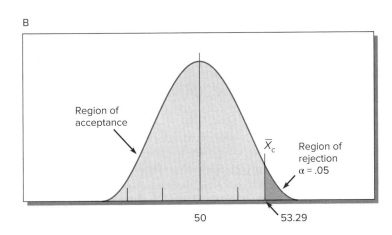

This new critical value, the boundary between the regions of acceptance and rejection, is pictured in part B of Exhibit 14-5.

Type II Error

The manufacturer would commit a Type II error (β) by accepting the null hypothesis ($\mu = 50$) when in truth it had changed. This kind of error is difficult to detect. The probability of committing a β error depends on five factors: (1) the true value of the parameter, (2) the α level we have selected, (3) whether a one- or two-tailed test was chosen to evaluate the hypothesis, (4) the sample standard deviation, and (5) the size of the sample. We secure a different β error if the new β moves from 50 to 54 rather than only to 52. We must compute separate β error estimates for each of a number of assumed new population parameters and $\overline{X}_c$ values.

To illustrate, assume μ has actually moved to 54 from 50. Under these conditions, what is the probability of our making a Type II error if the critical value is set at 53.29? (See Exhibit 14-6.) This may be expressed in the following fashion:

$$P(A_2)S_1 = \alpha = .05 \text{ (assume a one-tailed alternative hypothesis)}$$
$$P(A_1)S_2 = \beta = ?$$
$$\sigma_{\overline{X}} = \frac{\sigma}{\sqrt{n}} = \frac{10}{\sqrt{25}} = 2$$
$$Z = \frac{\overline{X} - \mu}{\sigma_{\overline{X}}} = \frac{53.29 - 54}{2} = -.355$$

>**Exhibit 14-6** Probability of Making a Type II Error

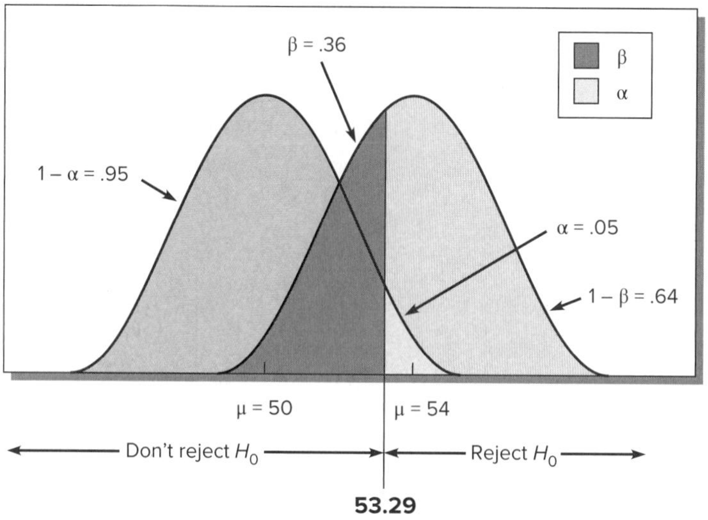

Using Exhibit D-1 in Appendix D, we interpolate between .35 and .36 Z scores to find the .355 Z score. The area between the mean and Z is .1387. β is the tail area, or the area below the Z, and is calculated as

$$\beta = .50 - .1387 = .36$$

This condition is shown in Exhibit 14-6. It is the percent of the area where we would *not* reject the null ($H_0 : \mu = 50$) when, in fact, it was false because the true mean was 54. With an α of .05 and a sample of 25, there is a 36 percent probability of a Type II (β) error if the μ is 54. We also speak of the **power of the test**—that is $(1 - \beta)$. For this example, the power of the test equals 64 percent $(1 - .36)$—that is, we will correctly reject the false null hypothesis with a 64 percent probability. A power of 64 percent is less than the 80 percent minimum percentage recommended by statisticians.

There are several ways to reduce a Type II error. We can shift the critical value closer to the original μ of 50; but to do this, we must accept a bigger α. Whether to take this action depends on the evaluation of the relative α and β risks. It might be desirable to enlarge the acceptable α risk because a worsening of the mileage would probably call for increased efforts to stimulate efficiency. Committing a Type I error would mean only that we engaged in efforts to stimulate efficiency when the situation had not worsened. This act probably would not have many adverse effects even if mpg had not increased.

A second way to reduce Type II error is to increase sample size. For example, if the sample were increased to 100, the power of the test would be much stronger:

$$\sigma_{\bar{X}} = \frac{\sigma}{\sqrt{n}} = \frac{10}{\sqrt{100}} = 1$$

$$Z = \frac{\bar{X} - \mu}{\sigma_{\bar{X}}} = \frac{53.29 - 54}{1} = -.71$$

$$\beta = .50 - .2612 = .24$$

This would reduce the Type II error to 24 percent and increase the power of the test to 76 percent.

A third method seeks to improve both α and β errors simultaneously and is difficult to accomplish. We know that measurement instruments, observations, and recording all produce error. By using a better measurement instrument, tightening the observation and recording processes, or devising a more efficient sample, we can reduce the variability of observations. This diminishes the standard error of estimate and in turn reduces the sampling distributions' spread. The net effect is that there is less tail area in the error regions.

Statistical Testing Procedures

Testing for statistical significance follows a relatively well-defined pattern, although authors differ in the number and sequence of steps. One six-stage sequence is as follows:

1. *State the null hypothesis.* Although the researcher is usually interested in testing a hypothesis of change or differences, the null hypothesis is always used for statistical testing purposes.

2. *Choose the statistical test.* To test a hypothesis, one must choose an appropriate statistical test. There are many tests from which to choose, and there are at least four criteria that can be used in choosing a test. One is the power efficiency of the test. A more powerful test provides the same level of significance with a smaller sample than a less powerful test. In addition, in choosing a test, one can consider how the sample is drawn, the nature of the population, and (importantly) the type of measurement scale used. For instance, some tests are useful only when the sequence of scores is known or when observations are paired; other tests are appropriate only if the population has certain characteristics; still other tests are useful only if the measurement scale is interval or ratio. More attention is given to test selection later in the chapter.

3. *Select the desired level of significance.* The choice of the **level of significance** should be made before we collect the data. The most common level is .05, although .01 is also widely used. Other levels such as .10, .025, or .001 are sometimes chosen. The exact level to choose is largely determined by how much risk one is willing to accept and the effect that this choice has on β risk. The larger the α, the lower is the β.

4. *Compute the calculated difference value.* After the data are collected, use the formula for the appropriate significance test to obtain the calculated value. Although the computation typically results from a software program, we illustrate the procedures in this chapter to help you visualize what is being done.

5. *Obtain the critical test value.* After we compute the calculated t, χ^2, or other measure, we must look up the critical value in the appropriate table for that distribution (or it is provided with the software calculation). The critical value is the criterion that defines the region of rejection from the region of acceptance of the null hypothesis.

6. *Interpret the test.* For most tests if the calculated value is larger than the critical value, we reject the null hypothesis and conclude that the alternative hypothesis is supported (although it is by no means proved). If the critical value is larger, we conclude we have failed to reject the null.[4]

Probability Values (*p* Values)

According to the "interpret the test" step of the statistical test procedure, the conclusion is stated in terms of rejecting or not rejecting the null hypothesis based on a reject region selected before the test is conducted. A second method of presenting the results of a statistical test reports the extent to which the test statistic disagrees with the null hypothesis. This method has become popular because analysts want to know what percentage of the sampling distribution lies beyond the sample statistic on the curve, and most statistical computer programs report the results of statistical tests as probability values (*p* values). The ***p* value** is the probability of observing a sample value as extreme as, or more extreme than, the value actually observed, given that the null hypothesis is true. This area represents the probability of a Type I error that must be assumed if the null hypothesis is rejected. The *p* value is compared to the significance level (α), and on this basis the null hypothesis is either rejected or not rejected.

> If the *p* value is less than the significance level, the null hypothesis is rejected (if *p* value < α, reject the null). If *p* is greater than or equal to the significance level, the null hypothesis is not rejected (if *p* value > α, don't reject the null).

Statistical data analysis programs commonly compute the *p* value during the execution of a hypothesis test. The following example will help illustrate the correct way to interpret a *p* value.

In part B of Exhibit 14-5, the critical value was shown for the situation in which the manufacturer was interested in determining whether the average mpg had increased. The critical value of 53.29 was computed based on a standard deviation of 10, sample size of 25, and the manufacturer's willingness to accept a 5 percent α risk. Suppose that the sample mean equaled 55. Is there enough evidence to reject the null hypothesis? If the *p* value is less than .05, the null hypothesis will be rejected. The *p* value is computed as follows.

The standard deviation of the distribution of sample means is 2. The appropriate *Z* value is

$$Z = \frac{\overline{X} - \mu}{\sigma_{\overline{X}}}$$

$$Z = \frac{55 - 50}{2}$$

$$Z = 2.5$$

The *p* value is determined using the standard normal table. The area between the mean and a *Z* value of 2.5 is .4938. For this one-tailed test, the *p* value is the area above the *Z* value. The probability of observing a *Z* value at least as large as 2.5 is only .0062 (.5000 − .4938 = .0062) if the null hypothesis is true.

This small *p* value represents the risk of rejecting a true null hypothesis. It is the probability of a Type I error if the null hypothesis is rejected. Because the *p* value (*p* = .0062) is smaller than α = .05, the null hypothesis is rejected. The manufacturer can conclude that the average mpg has increased. The probability that this conclusion is wrong is .0062.

>Tests of Significance

Types of Tests

There are two general groups of significance tests: parametric and nonparametric. **Parametric tests** are used when data are derived from interval and ratio measurements. **Nonparametric tests** are used to test hypotheses with nominal and ordinal data. Parametric techniques are the tests of choice if their assumptions are met, as they are more powerful than nonparametric tests. Assumptions for parametric tests include the following:

- The observations must be independent—that is, the selection of any one case should not affect the chances for any other case to be included in the sample.
- The observations should be drawn from normally distributed populations.
- These populations should have equal variances.
- The measurement scales should be at least interval so that arithmetic operations can be used with them.

The researcher is responsible for reviewing the assumptions pertinent to the chosen test. Performing diagnostic checks on the data allows the researcher to select the most appropriate technique. The normality of a distribution may be checked in several ways. We have previously discussed the measures of location, shape, and spread for preliminary analysis and considered graphic techniques for exploring data patterns and examining distributions. Another diagnostic tool is the **normal probability plot**. This plot compares the observed values with those expected from a normal distribution.[5] If the data display the characteristics of normality, the points will fall within a narrow band along a straight line. An example is shown in the upper left panel of Exhibit 14-7.

An alternative way to look at this is to plot the deviations from the straight line. These are shown in a "detrended" plot in the upper right panel of the exhibit. Here we would expect the points to cluster without pattern around a straight line passing horizontally through 0. In the bottom two panels of Exhibit 14-7, there is neither a straight line in the normal probability plot nor a random distribution of points about 0 in the detrended plot. Visually, the bottom two plots tell us the variable is not normally distributed. In addition, two separate tests of the hypothesis that the data come from normal distributions are rejected at a significance level of less than .01.[6]

>**Exhibit 14-7** Probability Plots and Tests of Normality

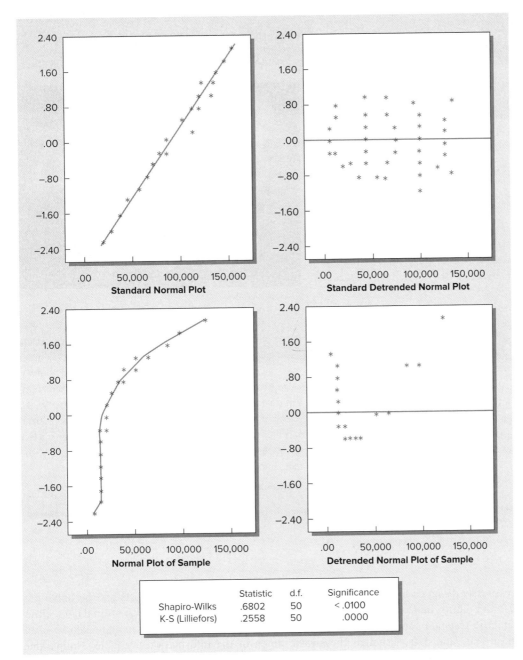

	Statistic	d.f.	Significance
Shapiro-Wilks	.6802	50	< .0100
K-S (Lilliefors)	.2558	50	.0000

If we wished to check another assumption—say, one of equal variance—a spread-and-level plot would be appropriate. Statistical software programs often provide diagnostic tools for checking assumptions. These may be nested within a specific statistical procedure, such as analysis of variance or regression, or provided as a general set of tools for examining assumptions.

Parametric tests place different emphasis on the importance of assumptions. Some tests are quite robust and hold up well despite violations. For others, a departure from linearity or equality of variance may threaten the validity of the results.

Nonparametric tests have fewer and less stringent assumptions. They do not specify normally distributed populations or equality of variance. Some tests require independence of cases; others

>**snap**shot

Testing a Hypothesis of Unrealistic Drug Use in Movies

Are American teens exposed to unrealistic drug usage or to unrealistic consequences from such use? The Office of National Drug Control Policy completed a content analysis of the top 200 rental movies to determine their depiction of substance use. The researchers used the Entertainment Merchants Association's most popular (top 100) home video titles based on rental income during two sequential years. Movies were categorized as follows: action adventure, comedy, or drama. Data were also collected on each title's Motion Picture Association of America (MPAA) rating (G, PG, PG-13, or R). Although technically teens should have been excluded from R-rated titles (which made up 48 percent of the overall sample), the study included all 20 of the most popular teen movies as identified in a prior independent study.

Trained coders watched all 200 movies, paying particular attention to alcohol, tobacco, illicit drugs, over-the-counter medicines, prescription medicines, inhalants, and unidentified pills. Coders ignored substances administered by medical personnel in a hospital or health-related scenario. Substance use included explicit portrayals of consumption. Substance appearance was noted when evidence of materials or paraphernalia was noted without any indication of use. Coders identified dominant messages about substance use and the consequences of use. Coders also noted scenes depicting illicit drug use or those depicting use by characters known to be under 18. Prevalence of use was determined by counting the characters in each

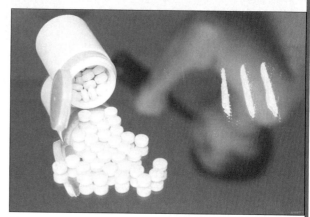

©Janne Tervonen/Alamy

movie and determining not only the percentage of characters using drugs but also whether the character had a major or minor role. Coders profiled characters by age, gender, and ethnicity, as well as other characteristics. Frequency of substance abuse was determined for each five-minute interval of each movie, with the presence or absence of various substances noted, starting with the completion of the title credits and ending when the final credits began. How would the last movie you watched have fared under this scrutiny?

www.whitehouse.gov/ondcp; www.vsda.org

are expressly designed for situations with related cases. Nonparametric tests are the only ones usable with nominal data; they are the only technically correct tests to use with ordinal data, although parametric tests are sometimes employed in this case. Nonparametric tests may also be used for interval and ratio data, although they waste much of the information available. Nonparametric tests are also easy to understand and use. Parametric tests have greater efficiency when their use is appropriate, but even in such cases nonparametric tests often achieve an efficiency as high as 95 percent. This means the nonparametric test with a sample of 100 will provide the same statistical testing power as a parametric test with a sample of 95.

How to Select a Test

In attempting to choose a particular significance test, the researcher should consider at least three questions:

- Does the test involve one sample, two samples, or k (more than two) samples?
- If two samples or k samples are involved, are the individual cases independent or related?
- Is the measurement scale nominal, ordinal, interval, or ratio?

Additional questions may arise once answers to these are known: What is the sample size? If there are several samples, are they of equal size? Have the data been weighted? Have the data been transformed? Often such questions are unique to the selected technique. The answers can complicate the selection, but once a tentative choice is made, standard statistics textbooks will provide further details.

Decision trees provide a more systematic means of selecting techniques. One widely used guide from the Institute for Social Research starts with questions about the number of variables, nature of the variables (continuous, discrete, dichotomous, independent, dependent, and so forth), and level of measurement. It goes through a tree structure asking detailed questions about the nature of the relationships being searched, compared, or tested. More than 130 solutions to data analysis problems are paired with commonly asked questions.[7]

An expert system offers another approach to choosing appropriate statistics. Capitalizing on the power and convenience of computers, expert system programs provide a comprehensive search of the statistical terrain just as a computer search of secondary sources does. Most programs ask about your research objectives, the nature of your data, and the intended audience for your final report. When you are not 100 percent confident of your answers, you can bracket them with an estimate of the degree of your certainty. SPSS and SAS include coaching and help modules with their software for the purpose of selecting the right test.

Selecting Tests Using the Choice Criteria

In this section, we use the three questions discussed in the last section (see bullets) to develop a classification of the major parametric and nonparametric tests and measures. Because parametric tests are preferred for their power when their assumptions are met, we discuss them first in each of the subsections: one-sample tests, two-sample tests, *k*- (more-than-two) sample tests. This is shown in Exhibit 14-8. To illustrate the application of the criteria to test selection, consider that your testing situation involves two samples, the samples are independent, and the data are interval. The figure suggests the *t*-test of differences as the appropriate choice. The most frequently used of the tests listed in Exhibit 14-8 are covered next. For additional examples see Appendix C.

>**Exhibit 14-8** Recommended Statistical Techniques by Measurement Level and Testing Situation

Measurement Scale	One-Sample Case	Two-Samples Tests		*k*-Samples Tests	
		Related Samples	Independent Samples	Related Samples	Independent Samples
Nominal	• Binomial • χ^2 one-sample test	• McNemar	• Fisher exact test • χ^2 two-samples test	• Cochran Q	• χ^2 for *k* samples
Ordinal	• Kolmogorov-Smirnov one-sample test • Runs test	• Sign test • Wilcoxon matched-pairs test	• Median test • Mann-Whitney U • Kolmogorov-Smirnov • Wald-Wolfowitz	• Friedman two-way ANOVA	• Median extension • Kruskal-Wallis one-way ANOVA
Interval and Ratio	• *t*-test • Z test	• *t*-test for paired samples	• *t*-test • Z test	• Repeated-measures ANOVA	• One-way ANOVA • *n*-way ANOVA

Source: This exhibit is partially adapted from Sidney Siegel and N.J. Castellan Jr., *Nonparametric Statistics for the Behavioral Sciences,* 2e. (New York: McGraw-Hill, 1988), flyleaf.

One-Sample Tests

One-sample tests are used when we have a single sample and wish to test the hypothesis that it comes from a specified population. In this case, we encounter questions such as these:

- Is there a difference between observed frequencies and the frequencies we would expect, based on some theory?
- Is there a difference between observed and expected proportions?
- Is it reasonable to conclude that a sample is drawn from a population with some specified distribution (normal, Poisson, and so forth)?
- Is there a significant difference between some measures of central tendency ($\overline{X}$) and its population parameter (μ)?

A number of tests may be appropriate in this situation. The parametric test is discussed first.

Parametric Tests

The **Z test** or **t-test** is used to determine the statistical significance between a sample distribution mean and a parameter.

The **Z distribution** and **t distribution** differ. The *t* has more tail area than that found in the normal distribution. This is a compensation for the lack of information about the population standard deviation. Although the sample standard deviation is used as a proxy figure, the imprecision makes it necessary to go farther away from 0 to include the percentage of values in the *t* distribution necessarily found in the standard normal.

When sample sizes approach 120, the sample standard deviation becomes a very good estimate of the population standard deviation (σ); beyond 120, the *t* and *Z* distributions are virtually identical.

Some typical real-world applications of the one-sample test are:

- Finding the average monthly balance of credit card holders compared to the average monthly balance five years ago.
- Comparing the failure rate of computers in a 20-hour test of quality specifications.
- Discovering the proportion of people who would shop in a new district compared to the assumed population proportion.
- Comparing the average product revenues this year to last year's revenues.

To illustrate the application of the *t*-test in the one-sample case, consider again the hybrid-vehicle problem mentioned earlier. With a sample of 100 vehicles, the researchers find that the mean miles per gallon for the car is 52.5 mpg, with a standard deviation of 14. Do these results indicate the population mean might still be 50?

In this problem, we have only the sample standard deviation (*s*). This must be used in place of the population standard deviation (σ). When we substitute *s* for σ, we use the *t* distribution, especially if the sample size is less than 30. We define *t* as

$$t = \frac{\overline{X} - \mu}{s/\sqrt{n}}$$

This significance test is conducted by following the six-step procedure recommended earlier:

1. *Null hypothesis.*

$$H_0 := 50 \text{ miles per gallon (mpg)}$$
$$H_A :> 50 \text{ mpg (one-tailed test)}$$

2. *Statistical test.* Choose the *t*-test because the data are ratio measurements. Assume the underlying population is normal and we have randomly selected the sample from the population of production vehicles.

3. *Significance level.* Let $\alpha = .05$, with $n = 100$.

4. *Calculated value.*

$$t = \frac{52.5 - 50}{14\sqrt{100}} - \frac{2.5}{1.4} = 1.786 \quad \text{d.f.} = n - 1 = 99$$

5. *Critical test value.* We obtain this by entering the table of critical values of t (see Appendix C, Exhibit D-2, at the back of the book), with 99 degrees of freedom (d.f.) and a level of significance value of .05. We secure a critical value of about 1.66 (interpolated between d.f. = 60 and d.f. = 120 in Exhibit D-2).

6. *Interpretation.* In this case, the calculated value is greater than the critical value (1.786 > 1.66), so we reject the null hypothesis and conclude that the average mpg has increased.

Nonparametric Tests

In a one-sample situation, a variety of nonparametric tests may be used, depending on the measurement scale and other conditions. If the measurement scale is nominal (classificatory only), it is possible to use either the binomial test or the chi-square (χ^2) one-sample test. The binomial test is appropriate when the population is viewed as only two classes, such as male and female, buyer and nonbuyer, and successful and unsuccessful, and all observations fall into one or the other of these categories. The binomial test is particularly useful when the size of the sample is so small that the χ^2 test cannot be used.

Chi-Square Test

Probably the most widely used nonparametric test of significance is the **chi-square (χ^2) test**. It is particularly useful in tests involving nominal data but can be used for higher scales. Typical are cases where persons, events, or objects are grouped in two or more nominal categories such as "yes–no," "favor–undecided–against," or class "A, B, C, or D."

Using this technique, we test for significant differences between the *observed* distribution of data among categories and the *expected* distribution based on the null hypothesis. Chi-square is useful in cases of one-sample analysis, two independent samples, or k independent samples. It must be calculated with actual counts rather than percentages.

In the one-sample case, we establish a null hypothesis based on the expected frequency of objects in each category. Then the deviations of the actual frequencies in each category are compared with the hypothesized frequencies. The greater the difference between them, the less is the probability that these differences can be attributed to chance. The value of χ^2 is the measure that expresses the extent of this difference. The larger the divergence, the larger is the χ^2 value.

The formula by which the χ^2 test is calculated is

$$\chi^2 = \sum_{i=1}^{k} \frac{(O_i - E_i)^2}{E_i}$$

in which

O_i = observed number of cases categorized in the ith category
E_i = expected number of cases in the ith category under H_0
k = the number of categories

There is a different distribution for χ^2 for each number of degrees of freedom (d.f.), defined as $(k - 1)$ or the number of categories in the classification minus 1:

$$\text{d.f.} = k - 1$$

With chi-square contingency tables of the two-samples or k-samples variety, we have both rows and columns in the cross-classification table. In that instance, d.f. is defined as rows minus 1 $(r - 1)$ times columns minus 1 $(c - 1)$:

$$\text{d.f.} = (r - 1)(c - 1)$$

In a 2 × 2 table, there is 1 d.f., and in a 3 × 2 table, there are 2 d.f. Depending on the number of degrees of freedom, we must be certain the numbers in each cell are large enough to make the χ^2 test appropriate. When d.f. = 1, each expected frequency should be at least 5 in size. If d.f. > 1, then the χ^2 test should not be used if more than 20 percent of the expected frequencies are smaller than 5 or when any expected frequency is less than 1. Expected frequencies can often be increased by combining adjacent categories (recoding). Four categories of freshmen, sophomores, juniors, and seniors might be recoded into upper class and lower class. If there are only two categories and still there are too few in a given category it is better to use the binomial test.

Assume Metro University is interested in constructing an on-campus, members-only dining club. A survey of student interest in the club is taken. We interviewed 200 students and learned of their intentions to join the club. We would like to analyze the results by living arrangement (type and location of student housing and eating arrangements). The 200 responses are classified into the four categories shown in the accompanying table.

Living Arrangement	O = Intend to Join	Number Interviewed	Percent (no. interviewed/200)	E = Expected Frequencies (percent × 60)
Dorm/fraternity	16	90	45	27
Apartment/rooming house, nearby	13	40	20	12
Apartment/rooming house, distant	16	40	20	12
Live at home	15	30	15	9
Total	60	200	100	60

Do these variations indicate there is a significant difference among these groups of students, or are they sampling variations only? Proceed as follows:

1. *Null hypothesis.* H_0: $O_i = E_i$. The proportion in the population who intend to join the club is independent of living arrangement. In H_A: $O_i \neq E_i$, the proportion in the population who intend to join the club is dependent on living arrangement.

2. *Statistical test.* Use the one-sample χ^2 to compare the observed distribution to a hypothesized distribution. The χ^2 test is used because the responses are classified into nominal categories and there are sufficient observations.

3. *Significance level.* Let $\alpha = .05$.

4. *Calculated value.*

$$\chi^2 = \sum_{i=1}^{k} \frac{(O_i - E_i)^2}{E_i}$$

Calculate the expected distribution by determining what proportion of the 200 students interviewed were in each group. Then apply these proportions to the number who intend to join the club. Then calculate the following:

$$\chi^2 = \frac{(16-27)^2}{27} + \frac{(13-12)^2}{12} + \frac{(16-12)^2}{12} + \frac{(15-9)^2}{9}$$

$$= 4.48 + 0.08 + 1.33 + 4.0$$

$$= 9.89$$

$$\text{d.f.} = (4-1)(2-1) = 3$$

5. *Critical test value.* Enter the table of critical values of χ^2 (see Exhibit D-3), with 3 d.f., and secure a value of 7.82 for $\alpha = .05$.

6. *Interpretation.* The calculated value (9.89) is greater than the critical value (7.82), so the null hypothesis is rejected and we conclude that intending to join is dependent on living arrangement.

># >snapshot

A/B Testing Comes of Age

Split-run testing of direct mail ads has been a feature of design for more than 100 years. In direct mail ads, the envelope would be changed to see if more people would open the envelope or if the offer (2-for-the-cost-of-one versus 50% off) would be changed for part of the sample to see if more people would buy. Color of the paper, the nature of the salutation, the address on the return mail envelope—any or some combination could be the focus of a test. But never has split-sample testing been a hotter research topic than with the current design of websites.

Google got the whole thing started with its A/B tests. As *Optimizely* profiles the process, when people visit a website, some are diverted to a slightly different version of the landing page. For example, maybe the "buy" button is blue rather than red. Then the visitors to the regular page versus the altered page are tracked. Does the altered page gain more clicks, or longer time spent on the site, or—the holy grail—more purchases? If so, then the new page will displace the former page.

There are countless aspects to a page that can be altered, one at a time or in tandem with other changes: where text is located, its size and color; what headlines might be used; whether still images or video are used; the color scheme of the page; the number of links on the page; or where ads are placed on a site. The list of possible changes to test is endless.

Because research is always being done on a web page, we need to think about what we are seeing when we visit a page. Are we seeing a test page or the standard page that the masses are seeing? The Amazon checkout screen I see may be different than the one you are seeing.

So can anyone with a web page use A/B testing? The answer just a few years ago would be no, but a former Google employee has created *Optimizely*, a software that allows nonprogrammers

©Jukeboxhero/iStock/Getty Images

to drag, resize, retype, replace, insert, and delete at will to create alternate versions of a page to test.

A/B testing can virtually eliminate a deadly error in decision making: having the highest-paid person in a meeting make a design decision based on opinion alone. A/B testing makes it possible to make all decisions based on data. But because small, incremental changes are being tested, a danger lurks. When bold change is needed, the A/B testing mentality may tie the hands of the company webmaster. As Brian Christian, author of *The Most Human Human: What Artificial Intelligence Teaches Us about Being Alive*, writing for *Wired*, put it, "Testing allows you to constantly react to user preferences, but that doesn't necessarily make you agile; 10,000 ongoing tweaks don't add up to a fundamental change of [strategic] direction when one is needed."

www.optimizely.com; www.wired.com; www.google.com; brchristian.com

Two-Independent-Samples Tests

The need to use **two-independent-samples tests** is often encountered in business research. We might compare the purchasing predispositions of a sample of subscribers from two magazines to discover if they are from the same population. Similarly, a test of distribution methods from two channels or the market share movements from two competing products could be compared.

Parametric Tests

The Z and t-tests are frequently used parametric tests for independent samples, although the F test also can be used.

The Z test is used with large sample sizes (exceeding 30 for both independent samples) or with smaller samples when the data are normally distributed and population variances are known. The formula for the Z test is

$$Z = \frac{(\overline{X}_1 - \overline{X}_2) - (\mu_1 - \mu_2)0}{\sqrt{\dfrac{S_1^2}{n_1} + \dfrac{S_2^2}{n_2}}}$$

With small sample sizes, normally distributed populations, and the assumption of equal population variances, the t-test is appropriate:

$$t = \frac{(\overline{X}_1 - \overline{X}_2) - (\mu_1 - \mu_2)0}{\sqrt{S_p^2\left(\dfrac{1}{n_1} + \dfrac{1}{n_2}\right)}}$$

where $(\mu_1 - \mu_2)$ is the difference between the two population means and S_p^2 is associated with the pooled variance estimate:

$$S_p^2 = \frac{(n_1 - 1)S_1^2 + (n_2 - 1)S_2^2}{n_1 + n_2 - 2}$$

To illustrate this application, consider a problem that might face a manager at KDL, a media firm that is evaluating account executive trainees. The manager wishes to test the effectiveness of two methods for training new account executives. The company selects 22 trainees, who are randomly divided into two experimental groups. One receives type A and the other type B training. The trainees are then assigned and managed without regard to the training they have received. At the year's end, the manager reviews the performances of employees in these groups and finds the following results:

	A Group	B Group
Average hourly sales	X-bar$_1$ = \$1,500	X-bar$_2$ = \$1,300
Standard deviation	s_1 = 225	s_2 = 251

Following the standard testing procedure, we will determine whether one training method is superior to the other:

1. *Null hypothesis.*

    H_0: There is no difference in sales results produced by the two training methods.

    H_A: Training method A produces sales results superior to those of method B.

2. *Statistical test.* The t-test is chosen because the data are at least interval and the samples are independent.

3. *Significance level.* $\alpha = .05$ (one-tailed test).

4. *Calculated value.*

$$t = \frac{(1{,}500 - 1{,}300) - 0}{\sqrt{\dfrac{(10)(225)^2 + (10)(251)^2}{20}\left(\dfrac{1}{11} + \dfrac{1}{11}\right)}}$$
$$= \frac{200}{101.63} = 1.97$$

There are $n - 1$ degrees of freedom in each sample, so total d.f. is

$$\text{d.f.} = (11 - 1) + (11 - 1) = 20$$

5. *Critical test value.* Enter Appendix D, Exhibit D-2 with d.f. = 20, one-tailed test, $\alpha = .05$. The critical value is 1.725.

6. *Interpretation.* Since the calculated value is larger than the critical value ($1.97 > 1.725$), reject the null hypothesis and conclude that training method A is superior.

Nonparametric Tests

The chi-square (χ^2) test is appropriate for situations in which a test for differences between samples is required. It is especially valuable for nominal data but can be used with ordinal measurements. When parametric data have been reduced to categories, they are frequently treated with χ^2 although this results in a loss of information. Preparing to solve this problem is the same as presented earlier although the formula differs slightly:

$$\chi^2 = \sum_i \sum_j \frac{(O_{ij} - E_{ij})^2}{E_{ij}}$$

in which

O_{ij} = observed number of cases categorized in the ijth cell

E_{ij} = expected number of cases under H_0 to be categorized in the ijth cell

Suppose TopFlight is implementing a smoke-free workplace policy and is interested in whether smoking affects worker accidents. Because the company has complete reports on on-the-job accidents, a sample of names of workers is drawn from those who were involved in accidents during the last year. A similar sample from among workers who had no reported accidents in the last year is drawn. Members of both groups are interviewed to determine if each is a nonsmoker or smoker and, if a smoker, whether the person classifies himself or herself as a heavy or moderate smoker. The results appear in the following table, with expected values calculated as shown.

On-the-Job Accident

Cell Designation Count Expected Values		Yes	No	Total
Smoker		1,1	1,2	
	Heavy smoker	127	4	16
		8.24	7.75	
		2,1	2,2	
	Moderate	9	6	15
		7.73	7.27	
		3,1	3,2	
	Nonsmoker	13	22	35
		18.03	16.97	
	Column Total	34	32	66

The testing procedure is:

1. *Null hypothesis.*

   H_0: There is no relationship in on-the-job accident occurrences between smokers and nonsmokers.

   H_A: There is a relationship in on-the-job accident occurrences between smokers and nonsmokers.

2. *Statistical test.* χ^2 is appropriate, but it may waste some of the data because the measurement appears to be ordinal.

3. *Significance level.* $\alpha = .05$, with d.f. = $(3 - 1)(2 - 1) = 2$

4. *Calculated value.* The expected distribution is provided by the marginal totals of the table. If there is no relationship between accidents and smoking, there will be the same proportion of smokers in both accident and nonaccident groups. The numbers of expected observations in

each cell are calculated by multiplying the two marginal totals common to a particular cell and dividing this product by n. For example,

$$\frac{34 \times 16}{66} = 8.24, \text{the expected value in cell } (1,1)$$

$$\chi^2 = \frac{(12 - 8.24)^2}{8.24} + \frac{(4 - 7.75)^2}{7.75} + \frac{(9 - 7.73)^2}{7.73} + \frac{(6 - 7.72)^2}{7.72}$$

$$+ \frac{(13 - 18.03)^2}{18.03} + \frac{(22 - 16.97)^2}{16.97}$$

$$= 7.01$$

5. *Critical test value.* Turn to Appendix D, Exhibit D-3, and find the critical value 7.01 with $\alpha = .05$ and d.f. = 2.

6. *Interpretation.* Because the calculated value is greater than the critical value, the null hypothesis is rejected.

For chi-square to operate properly, data must come from random samples of multinomial distributions, and the expected frequencies should not be too small. We previously noted the traditional cautions that expected frequencies (E_i) below 5 should not compose more than 20 percent of the cells, and that no cell should have an E_i of less than 1. Some research has argued that these restrictions are too severe.[8]

In another type of χ^2, the 2×2 table, a correction known as *Yates' correction for continuity* is applied when sample sizes are greater than 40 or when the sample is between 20 and 40 and the values of E_i are 5 or more. (We use this correction because a continuous distribution is approximating a discrete distribution in this table. When the E_i's are small, the approximation is not necessarily a good one.) The formula for this correction is

$$\chi^2 = \frac{n\left(\left|AD - BC\right| - \frac{n}{2}\right)^2}{(A+B)(C+D)(A+C)(B+D)}$$

where the letters represent the cells designated as

A	B
C	D

When the continuity correction is applied to the data shown in Exhibit 14-9, a χ^2 value of 5.25 is obtained. The observed level of significance for this value is .02192. If the level of significance had been set at .01, we would accept the null hypothesis. However, had we calculated χ^2 without correction, the value would have been 6.25, which has an observed level of significance of .01242. Some researchers may be tempted to reject the null at this level. (But note that the critical value of χ^2 at .01 with 1 d.f. is 6.64. See Appendix D, Exhibit D-3.) The literature is in conflict regarding the merits of Yates' correction, but if nothing else, this example suggests one should take care when interpreting 2×2 tables.[9] To err on the conservative side would be in keeping with our prior discussion of Type I errors.

The Mantel-Haenszel test and the likelihood ratio also appear in Exhibit 14-9. The former is used with ordinal data; the latter, based on maximum likelihood theory, produces results similar to Pearson's chi-square.

Two-Related-Samples Tests

The **two-related-samples tests** are used when cases (persons, objects, or events) are closely matched or the phenomena are measured twice. One might compare the consumption of husbands and wives, the performance of employees before and after vacations, or the effects of a marketing test stimulus when persons were randomly assigned to groups and given pretests and posttests. Both parametric and nonparametric tests are applicable under these conditions.

>**Exhibit 14-9** Comparison of Corrected and Noncorrected Chi-Square Results Using SPSS Procedure Cross-Tab

INCOME BY POSSESSION OF MBA

Count		MBA		
		Yes 1	No 2	Row Total
INCOME				
	High 1	30	30	60 60.0
	Low 2	10	30	40 40.0
	Column Total	40 40.0	60 60.0	100 100.0

Chi-Square	Value	D.F.	Significance
Pearson	6.25000	1	.01242
Continuity Correction	5.25174	1	.02192
Likelihood Ratio	6.43786	1	.01117
Mantel-Haenszel	6.18750	1	.01287
Minimum Expected Frequency: 16.000			

Parametric Tests

The t-test for independent samples would be inappropriate for this situation because one of its assumptions is that observations are independent. This problem is solved by a formula in which the difference is found between each matched pair of observations, thereby reducing the two samples to the equivalent of a one-sample case—that is, there are now several differences, each independent of the other, for which one can compute various statistics.

In the following formula, the average difference $\bar{D}$ corresponds to the normal distribution when the α difference is known and the sample size is sufficient. The statistic t with $(n - 1)$ degrees of freedom is defined as

$$t = \frac{\bar{D}}{S_D / \sqrt{n}}$$

where

$$\bar{D} = \frac{\sum D}{n}$$

$$S_D = \sqrt{\frac{\sum D^2 - \frac{(\sum D)^2}{n}}{n - 1}}$$

To illustrate, we use two years of *Forbes* sales data (in millions of dollars) from 10 companies, as listed in Exhibit 14-10.

1. *Null hypothesis.*

   H_0: $\mu = 0$; there is no difference between year 1 and year 2 sales.

   H_A: $\mu \neq 0$; there is a difference between year 1 and year 2 sales.

2. *Statistical test.* The matched- or paired-samples t-test is chosen because there are repeated measures on each company, the data are not independent, and the measurement is ratio.

3. *Significance level.* Let $\alpha = .01$, with $n = 10$ and d.f. $= n - 1$.

>**Exhibit 14-10** Sales Data for Paired-Samples *t*-Test (dollars in millions)

Company	Sales Year 2	Sales Year 1	Difference *D*	*D²*
GM	126932	123505	3427	11744329
GE	54574	49662	4912	24127744
Exxon	86656	78944	7712	59474944
IBM	62710	59512	3198	10227204
Ford	96146	92300	3846	14791716
AT&T	36112	35173	939	881721
Mobil	50220	48111	2109	4447881
DuPont	35099	32427	2672	7139584
Sears	53794	49975	3819	14584761
Amoco	23966	20779	3187	10156969
			$\Sigma D = 35821$	$\Sigma D^2 = 157576853$

4. *Calculated value.*

$$t = \frac{\overline{D}}{S_D / \sqrt{n}} = \frac{3582.10}{570.98} = 6.27$$

5. *Critical test value.* Enter Appendix D, Exhibit D-2, with d.f. = 9, two-tailed test, $\alpha = .01$. The critical value is 3.25.

6. *Interpretation.* Because the calculated value is greater than the critical value (6.27 > 3.25), reject the null hypothesis and conclude there is a statistically significant difference between the two years of sales.

A computer solution to the problem is illustrated in Exhibit 14-11. Notice that an **observed significance level** is printed for the calculated *t* value (highlighted). With SPSS, this is often rounded and would be interpreted as significant at the .0005 level. The correlation coefficient, to the left of the *t* value, is a measure of the relationship between the two pairs of scores. In situations where matching has occurred (such as husbands' and wives' scores), it reveals the degree to which the matching has been effective in reducing the variability of the mean difference.

>**Exhibit 14-11** SPSS Output for Paired-Samples *t*-Test (dollars in millions)

--- *t*-tests for paired samples ---

Variable	Number of Cases	Mean	Standard Deviation	Standard Error
Year 2 Sales	10	62620.9	31777.649	10048.975
Year 1 Sales	10	59038.8	31072.871	9836.104

(Difference Mean)	Standard Deviation	Standard Error	Corr.	2-tail Prob.	*t* Value	Degrees of Freedom	2-tail Prob.
3582.1000	1803.159	570.209	.999	.000	6.28	9	.000

Nonparametric Tests

The *McNemar test* may be used with either nominal or ordinal data and is especially useful with before-after measurement of the same subjects. Test the significance of any observed change by setting up a fourfold table of frequencies to represent the first and second set of responses:

	After	
Before	**Do Not Favor**	**Favor**
Favor	A	B
Do Not Favor	C	D

Because $A + D$ represents the total number of people who changed (B and C are no-change responses), the expectation under a null hypothesis is that $1/2 (A + D)$ cases change in one direction and the same proportion in the other direction. The McNemar test uses a transformation of the χ^2 test:

$$\chi^2 = \frac{(|A - D| - 1)^2}{A + D} \text{ with d.f.} = 1$$

The "minus 1" in the equation is a correction for continuity since the χ^2 is a continuous distribution and the observed frequencies represent a discrete distribution.

To illustrate this test's application, we use survey data from SteelShelf Corporation, whose researchers decided to test a new concept in office seating with employees at the company's headquarters facility. Managers took a random sample of their employees before the test, asking them to complete a questionnaire on their attitudes toward the design concept. On the basis of their responses, the employees were divided into equal groups reflecting their favorable or unfavorable views of the design. After the campaign, the same 200 employees were asked again to complete the questionnaire. They were again classified as to favorable or unfavorable attitudes. The testing process is:

1. *Null hypothesis.*

$$H_0: P(A) = P(D)$$
$$H_A: P(A) \neq P(D)$$

2. *Statistical test.* The McNemar test is chosen because nominal data are used and the study involves before-after measurements of two related samples.

3. *Significance level.* Let $\alpha = .05$, with $n = 200$.

4. *Calculated value.*

$$\chi^2 = \frac{(|10 - 40| - 1)^2}{10 + 40} = \frac{29^2}{50} = 16.82 \quad \text{d.f.} = 1$$

	After	
Before	**Do Not Favor**	**Favor**
Favor	A = 10	B = 90
Do Not Favor	C = 60	D = 40

5. *Critical test value.* Enter Appendix D, Exhibit D-3, and find the critical value to be 3.84 with $\alpha = .05$ and d.f. = 1.

6. *Interpretation.* The calculated value is greater than the critical value (16.82 > 3.84), indicating one should reject the null hypothesis, and conclude that the new concept had a significant positive effect on employees' attitudes. In fact, χ^2 is so large that it would have surpassed an α of .001.

k-Independent-Samples Tests

We often use ***k*-independent-samples tests** in research when three or more samples are involved. Under this condition, we are interested in learning whether the samples might have come from the same or identical populations. When the data are measured on an interval-ratio scale and we can meet the necessary assumptions, analysis of variance and the *F* test are used. If preliminary analysis shows the assumptions cannot be met or if the data were measured on an ordinal or nominal scale, a nonparametric test should be selected.

As with the two-samples case, the samples are assumed to be independent. This is the condition of a completely randomized experiment when participants are randomly assigned to various treatment groups. It is also common for an ex post facto study to require comparison of more than two independent sample means.

Parametric Tests

The statistical method for testing the null hypothesis that the means of several populations are equal is **analysis of variance (ANOVA)**. *One-way analysis of variance* is described in this section. It uses a single-factor, fixed-effects model to compare the effects of one *treatment* or *factor* (brands of coffee, varieties of residential housing, types of retail stores) on a continuous dependent variable (coffee consumption, hours of TV viewing, shopping expenditures). In a fixed-effects model, the levels of the factor are established in advance, and the results cannot be generalized to other levels of treatment. For example, if coffee were Jamaican-grown, Colombian-grown, and Honduran-grown, we could not extend our inferences to coffee grown in Guatemala or Mexico.

To use ANOVA, certain conditions must be met. The samples must be randomly selected from normal populations, and the populations should have equal variances. In addition, the distance from one value to its group's mean should be independent of the distances of other values to that mean (independence of error). ANOVA is reasonably robust, and minor variations from normality and equal variance are tolerable. Nevertheless, the analyst should check the assumptions with the diagnostic techniques previously described.

Analysis of variance, as the name implies, breaks down or partitions total variability into component parts. Unlike the *t*-test, which uses sample standard deviations, ANOVA uses squared deviations of the variance so that computation of distances of the individual data points from their own mean or from the grand mean can be summed (recall that standard deviations sum to zero).

In an ANOVA model, each group has its own mean and values that deviate from that mean. Similarly, all the data points from all of the groups produce an overall *grand mean*. The total deviation is the sum of the squared differences between each data point and the overall grand mean.

The total deviation of any particular data point may be partitioned into *between-groups variance* and *within-groups variance*. The between-groups variance represents the effect of the treatment, or factor. The differences of between-groups means imply that each group was treated differently, and the treatment will appear as deviations of the sample means from the grand mean. Even if this were not so, there would still be some natural variability among subjects and some variability attributable to sampling. The within-groups variance describes the deviations of the data points within each group from the sample mean. This results from variability among subjects and from random variation. It is often called *error*.

Intuitively, we might conclude that when the variability attributable to the treatment exceeds the variability arising from error and random fluctuations, the viability of the null hypothesis begins to diminish. And this is exactly the way the test statistic for analysis of variance works.

The test statistic for ANOVA is the ***F* ratio**. It compares the variance from the last two sources:

$$F = \frac{\text{between-groups variance}}{\text{within-groups variance}} = \frac{\text{mean square}_{\text{between}}}{\text{mean square}_{\text{within}}}$$

where

$$\text{Mean square}_{\text{between}} = \frac{\text{sum of squares}_{\text{between}}}{\text{degrees of freedom}_{\text{between}}}$$

$$\text{Mean square}_{\text{within}} = \frac{\text{sum of squares}_{\text{within}}}{\text{degrees of freedom}_{\text{within}}}$$

To compute the F ratio, the sum of the squared deviations for the numerator and denominator are divided by their respective degrees of freedom. By dividing, we are computing the variance as an average or mean; thus the term **mean square**. The degrees of freedom for the numerator, the mean square between groups, are one less than the number of groups ($k - 1$). The degrees of freedom for the denominator, the mean square within groups, are the total number of observations minus the number of groups ($n - k$).

If the null hypothesis is true, there should be no difference between the population means, and the ratio should be close to 1. If the population means are not equal, the numerator should manifest this difference, and the F ratio should be greater than 1. The F distribution determines the size of ratio necessary to reject the null hypothesis for a particular sample size and level of significance.

To illustrate one-way ANOVA, consider *Travel Industry Magazine*'s reports from international travelers about the quality of in-flight service on various carriers from the United States to Asia. Before writing a feature story coinciding with a peak travel period, the magazine decided to retain a researcher to secure a more balanced perspective on the reactions of travelers. The researcher selected passengers who had current impressions of the meal service, comfort, and friendliness of a major carrier. Three airlines were chosen and 20 passengers were randomly selected for each airline. The data, found in Exhibit 14-12,[10] are used for this and the next two examples. For the one-way analysis of variance problem, we are concerned only with the columns labeled "Flight Service Rating 1" and "Airline." The factor, airline, is the grouping variable for three carriers.

Again, we follow the procedure:

1. *Null hypothesis.*

   H_0: $\mu_{A1} = \mu_{A2} = \mu_{A3}$

   H_A: $\mu_{A1} \neq \mu_{A2} \neq \mu_{A3}$ (The means are not equal.)

2. *Statistical test.* The F ratio is chosen because we have k independent samples, accept the assumptions of analysis of variance, and have interval data.

3. *Significance level.* Let $\alpha = .05$, and d.f. = [numerator ($k - 1$) = ($3 - 1$) = 2], [denominator ($n - k$) = ($60 - 3$) = 57] = (2, 57).

4. *Calculated value.*

$$F = \frac{\text{MS}_b}{\text{MS}_w} = \frac{5822.017}{205.695} = 28.304 \quad \text{d.f.} (2, 57)$$

   See summary in Exhibit 14-13.

5. *Critical test value.* Enter Appendix D, Exhibit D-8, with d.f. (2, 57), $\alpha = .05$. The critical value is 3.16.

6. *Interpretation.* Because the calculated value is greater than the critical value ($28.3 > 3.16$), we reject the null hypothesis and conclude there are statistically significant differences between two or more pairs of means. Note in Exhibit 14-13 that the p value equals .0001. Because the p value (.0001) is less than the significance level (.05), we have a second method for rejecting the null hypothesis.

The ANOVA model summary in Exhibit 14-13 is a standard way of presenting the results of analysis of variance. This table contains the sources of variation, degrees of freedom, sum of squares, mean squares, and calculated F value. The probability of rejecting the null hypothesis is computed up to 100 percent α—that is, the probability value column reports the exact significance for the F ratio being tested.

>**Exhibit 14-12** Data Table: Analysis of Variance Examples*

	Flight Service					Flight Service			
	Rating 1	Rating 2	Airline†	Seat Selection‡		Rating 1	Rating 2	Airline†	Seat Selection‡
1	40	36	1	1	31	52	65	2	2
2	28	28	1	1	32	70	80	2	2
3	36	30	1	1	33	73	79	2	2
4	32	28	1	1	34	72	88	2	2
5	60	40	1	1	35	73	89	2	2
6	12	14	1	1	36	71	72	2	2
7	32	26	1	1	37	55	58	2	2
8	36	30	1	1	38	68	67	2	2
9	44	38	1	1	39	81	85	2	2
10	36	35	1	1	40	78	80	2	2
11	40	42	1	2	41	92	95	3	1
12	68	49	1	2	42	56	60	3	1
13	20	24	1	2	43	64	70	3	1
14	33	35	1	2	44	72	78	3	1
15	65	40	1	2	45	48	65	3	1
16	40	36	1	2	46	52	70	3	1
17	51	29	1	2	47	64	79	3	1
18	25	24	1	2	48	68	81	3	1
19	37	23	1	2	49	76	69	3	1
20	44	41	1	2	50	56	78	3	1
21	56	67	2	1	51	88	92	3	2
22	48	58	2	1	52	79	85	3	2
23	64	78	2	1	53	92	94	3	2
24	56	68	2	1	54	88	93	3	2
25	28	69	2	1	55	73	90	3	2
26	32	74	2	1	56	68	67	3	2
27	42	55	2	1	57	81	85	3	2
28	40	55	2	1	58	95	95	3	2
29	61	80	2	1	59	68	67	3	2
30	58	78	2	1	60	78	83	3	2

*All data are hypothetical.

†Airline: 1 = Lufthansa; 2 = Malaysia Airlines; 3 = Cathay Pacific

‡Seat selection: 1 = economy; 2 = business.

A Priori Contrasts

When we compute a t-test, it is not difficult to discover the reasons why the null is rejected. But with one-way ANOVA, how do we determine which pairs are not equal? We could calculate a series of t-tests, but they would not be independent of each other and the resulting Type I error would increase substantially.

>**Exhibit 14-13** Summary Tables for One-Way ANOVA Example*

Model Summary[†]					
Source	d.f.	Sum of Squares	Mean Square	F Value	p Value
Model (airline)	2	11644.033	5822.017	28.304	0.0001
Residual (error)	57	11724.550	205.694		
Total	59	23368.583			

Means Table				
	Count	Mean	Std. Dev.	Std. Error
Lufthansa	20	38.950	14.006	3.132
Malaysia Airlines	20	58.900	15.089	3.374
Cathay Pacific	20	72.900	13.902	3.108

Scheffè's S Multiple Comparison Procedure[‡]					
	Vs.	Diff.	Crit. Diff.	p Value	
Lufthansa	Malaysia	19.950	11.400	0.0002	S
	Cathay	33.950	11.400	0.0001	S
Malaysia	Cathay	14.000	11.400	0.0122	S

*All data are hypothetical.

[†]Factor: airline; dependent: flight service rating 1.

[‡]S = significantly different at the .05 level; significance level: .05.

This is not recommended. If we decided in advance that a comparison of specific populations was important, a special class of tests known as *a priori* **contrasts** could be used after the null was rejected with the *F* ratio (it is *a priori* because the decision was made before the test).[11]

A modification of the *F* ratio provides one approach for computing contrasts:

$$F = \frac{MS_{CON}}{MS_W}$$

The denominator, the within-groups mean square, is the same as the error term of the one-way's *F* ratio (recorded in the summary table, Exhibit 14-13). We have previously referred to the denominator of the *F* ratio as the error variance estimator. The numerator of the contrast test is defined as

$$MS_{CON} = SS_{CON} = \frac{\left(\sum_j C_j \bar{X}_j\right)^2}{\sum_j \frac{C_j^2}{n}}$$

where

C_j = the contrast coefficient for the group j

n_j = the number of observations recorded for group j

A contrast is useful for experimental and quasi-experimental designs when the researcher is interested in answering specific questions about a subset of the factor. For example, in a comparison of coffee products, we have a factor with six levels. The levels, blends of coffee, are meaningfully ordered. Assume we are particularly interested in two Central American–grown blends and one Colombian blend. Rather than looking at all possible combinations, we can channel the power more effectively by stating the comparisons of interest. This increases our likelihood of detecting differences if they really exist.

Multiple Comparison Tests

For the probabilities associated with the contrast test to be properly used in the report of our findings, it is important that the contrast strategy be devised ahead of the testing. In the airline study, we had no theoretical reason for an *a priori* contrast. However, when we examine the table of mean ratings (Exhibit 14-13), it is apparent that the airline means were quite different. Comparisons after the results are compared require *post hoc* tests or pairwise **multiple comparison tests** (or *range tests*) to determine which means differ. These tests find homogeneous subsets of means that are not different from each other. Multiple comparisons test the difference between each pair of means and indicate significantly different group means at an α level of .05, or another level that you specify. Multiple comparison tests use group means and incorporate the MS_{error} term of the *F* ratio. Together they produce confidence intervals for the population means and a criterion score. Differences between the mean values may be compared.

There are more than a dozen such tests with different optimization goals: maximum number of comparisons, unequal cell size compensation, cell homogeneity, reduction of Type I or Type II errors, and so forth. The merits of various tests have produced considerable debate among statisticians, leaving the researcher without much guidance for the selection of a test. In Exhibit 14-14, we provide a general guide. For the example in Exhibit 14-13, we chose Scheffé's *S*. It is a conservative test that is robust to violations of assumptions.[12] The computer calculated the critical difference criterion as 11.4; all the differences between the pairs of means exceed this. The null hypothesis for the Scheffé S was tested at the .05 level. Therefore, we can conclude that all combinations of flight service mean scores differ from each other.

While the table in Exhibit 14-13 provides information for understanding the rejection of the one-way null hypothesis and the Scheffé null, in Exhibit 14-15 we use plots for the comparisons. The means plot shows relative differences among the three levels of the factor. The means by standard deviations plot

>**Exhibit 14-14** Selection of Multiple Comparison Procedures

Test	Pairwise Comparisons	Complex Comparisons	Equal *n*'s Only	Unequal *n*'s	Equal Variances Assumed	Unequal Variances Not Assumed
Fisher LSD	X			X	X	
Bonferroni	X		X	X		
Tukey HSD	X		X		X	
Tukey-Kramer	X			X	X	
Games-Howell	X			X		X
Tamhane T2	X			X		X
Scheffé *S*		X		X	X	
Brown-Forsythe		X		X		X
Newman-Keuls	X		X		X	
Duncan	X		X		X	
Dunnett's T3						X
Dunnett's C						X

>**Exhibit 14-15** One-Way Analysis of Variance Plots

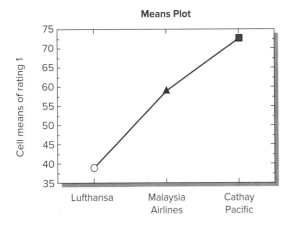
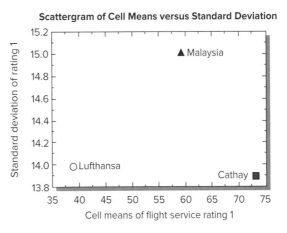

reveals lower variability in the opinions recorded by the hypothetical Lufthansa and Cathay Pacific passengers. Nevertheless, these two groups are sharply divided on the quality of in-flight service, and that is apparent in the plot.

Exploring the Findings with Two-Way ANOVA

Is the airline on which the passengers traveled the only factor influencing perceptions of in-flight service? By extending the one-way ANOVA, we can learn more about the service ratings. There are many possible explanations. We have chosen to look at the seat selection of the travelers in the interest of brevity.

Recall that in Exhibit 14-12, data were provided for the variable seat selection: economy and business-class travelers. Adding this factor to the model, we have a *two-way* analysis of variance. Now three questions may be considered with one model:

- Are differences in flight service ratings attributable to airlines?
- Are differences in flight service ratings attributable to seat selection?
- Do the airline and the seat selection interact with respect to flight service ratings?

The third question reveals a distinct advantage of the two-way model. A separate one-way model on airlines averages out the effects of seat selection. Similarly, a single-factor test of seat selection averages out the effects of the airline choice. But an interaction test of airline by seat selection considers them *jointly*.

Exhibit 14-16 reports a test of the hypotheses for these three questions. The significance level was chosen at the .01 level. We first inspect the interaction effect, airline by seat selection, since the individual *main effects* cannot be considered separately if the factors interact. The interaction was not significant at the .01 level, and the null is accepted. Now the separate main effects, airline and seat selection, can be verified. As with the one-way ANOVA, the null hypothesis for the airline factor was rejected, and seat selection was also rejected (statistically significant at .0001).

Means and standard deviations listed in the table are plotted in Exhibit 14-17. We note a band of similar deviations for economy-class travelers and a band of lower variability for business class—with the exception of one carrier. The plot of cell means confirms visually what we already know from the summary table: there is no interaction between airline and seat selection ($p = .185$). If an interaction had occurred, the lines connecting the cell means would have crossed rather than displaying a parallel pattern.

Analysis of variance is an extremely versatile and powerful method that may be adapted to a wide range of testing applications.

Nonparametric Tests

When there are k independent samples for which nominal data have been collected, the chi-square test is appropriate. It can also be used to classify data at higher measurement levels, but metric information

>**Exhibit 14-16** Summary Table for Two-Way ANOVA Example*

Model Summary†					
Source	d.f.	Sum of Squares	Mean Square	F Value	p Value
Airline	2	11644.033	5822.017	39.178	0.0001
Seat selection	1	3182.817	3182.817	21.418	0.0001
Airline by seat selection	2	517.033	258.517	1.740	0.1853
Residual	54	8024.700	148.606		

Means Table Effect: Airline by Seat Selection				
	Count	Mean	Std. Dev.	Std. Error
Lufthansa economy	10	35.600	12.140	3.839
Lufthansa business	10	42.300	15.550	4.917
Malaysia economy	10	48.500	12.501	3.953
Malaysia business	10	69.300	9.166	2.898
Cathay economy	10	64.800	13.037	4.123
Cathay business	10	81.000	9.603	3.037

*All data are hypothetical.
†Dependent: Flight service rating 1.

is lost when reduced. The k-samples χ^2 test is an extension of the two-independent-samples cases treated earlier. It is calculated and interpreted in the same way.

The Kruskal-Wallis test is appropriate for data that are collected on an ordinal scale or for interval data that do not meet F-test assumptions, that cannot be transformed, or that for another reason prove to be unsuitable for a parametric test. Kruskal-Wallis is a one-way analysis of variance by ranks. It assumes random selection and independence of samples and an underlying continuous distribution.

>**Exhibit 14-17** Two-Way Analysis of Variance Plots

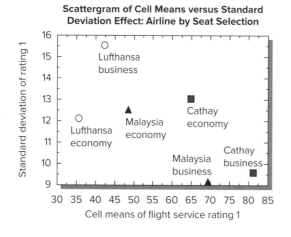

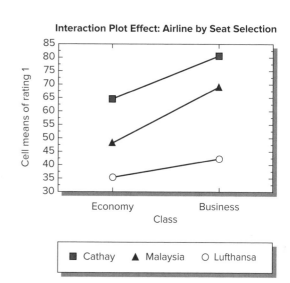

Data are prepared by converting ratings or scores to ranks for each observation being evaluated. The ranks range from the highest to the lowest of all data points in the aggregated samples. The ranks are then tested to decide if they are samples from the same population. An application of this technique is provided in Appendix C.

k-Related-Samples Tests

Parametric Tests

A **k-related-samples test** is required for situations where (1) the grouping factor has more than two levels, (2) observations or subjects are matched or the same participant is measured more than once, and (3) the data are at least interval. In test marketing experiments or ex post facto designs with *k* samples, it is often necessary to measure subjects several times. These repeated measurements are called **trials**. For example, multiple measurements are taken in studies of stock prices, products evaluated by reliability, inventory, sales, and measures of product performance. Hypotheses for these situations may be tested with a univariate or multivariate general linear model. The latter is beyond the scope of this discussion.

The repeated-measures ANOVA is a special type of *n*-way analysis of variance. In this design, the repeated measures of each subject are related just as they are in the related *t*-test when only two measures are present. In this sense, each subject serves as its own control requiring a within-subjects variance effect to be assessed differently than the between-groups variance in a factor like airline or seat selection. The effects of the correlated measures are removed before calculation of the *F* ratio.

This model is an appropriate solution for the data presented in Exhibit 14-12. You will remember that the one-way and two-way examples considered only the first rating of in-flight service. Assume a second rating was obtained after one week by reinterviewing the same respondents. We now have two trials for the dependent variable, and we are interested in the same general question as with the one-way ANOVA, with the addition of how the passage of time affects perceptions of in-flight service.

Following the testing procedure, we state:

1. *Null hypotheses.*

    (1) Airline: H_0: $\mu_{A1} = \mu_{A2} = \mu_{A3}$
    (2) Ratings: H_0: $\mu_{R1} = \mu_{R2}$
    (3) Ratings × airline: H_0: $(\mu_{R2A1} - \mu_{R2A2} - \mu_{R2A3}) = (\mu R_{1A1} - \mu_{R1A2} - \mu_{R1A3})$

    For the alternative hypotheses, we will generalize to the statement that not all the groups have equal means for each of the three hypotheses.

2. *Statistical test.* The *F* test for repeated measures is chosen because we have related trials on the dependent variable for *k* samples, accept the assumptions of analysis of variance, and have interval data.

3. *Significance level.* Let α = .05 and d.f. = [airline (2, 57), ratings (1, 57), ratings by airline (2, 57)].

4. *Calculated values.* See summary in Exhibit 14-18.

5. *Critical test value.* Enter Appendix D, Exhibit D-8, with d.f. (2, 57), α = .05 and (1, 57), α = .05. The critical values are 3.16 (2, 57) and 4.01 (1, 57).

6. *Interpretation.* The statistical results are grounds for rejecting all three null hypotheses and concluding there are statistically significant differences between means in all three instances. We conclude the perceptions of in-flight service were significantly affected by the different airlines, the interval between the two measures had a significant effect on the ratings, and the measures' time interval and the airlines interacted to a significant degree.

The ANOVA summary table in Exhibit 14-18 records the results of the tests. A means table provides the means and standard deviations for all combinations of ratings by airline. A second table of means reports the differences between flight service ratings 1 and 2. In Exhibit 14-19, there is an interaction plot for these data. Note that the second in-flight service rating was improved in two of the three groups after

>**Exhibit 14-18** Summary Tables for Repeated-Measures ANOVA*

Model Summary†					
Source	d.f.	Sum of Squares	Mean Square	F Value	p Value
Airline	2	35527.550	17763.775	67.199	0.0001
Subject (group)	57	15067.650	264.345		
Ratings	1	625.633	625.633	14.318	0.0004
Ratings by air	2	2061.717	1030.858	23.592	0.0001
Ratings by subj	57	2490.650	43.696		

Means Table Ratings by Airline				
	Count	Mean	Std. Dev.	Std. Error
Rating 1, Lufthansa	20	38.950	14.006	3.132
Rating 1, Malaysia	20	58.900	15.089	3.374
Rating 1, Cathay	20	72.900	13.902	3.108
Rating 2, Lufthansa	20	32.400	8.268	1.849
Rating 2, Malaysia	20	72.250	10.572	2.364
Rating 2, Cathay	20	79.800	11.265	2.519

Means Table Effect: Ratings				
	Count	Mean	Std. Dev.	Std. Error
Rating 1	60	56.917	19.902	2.569
Rating 2	60	61.483	23.208	2.996

*All data are hypothetical.
†Dependent: flight service ratings 1 and 2.

one week, but for the third carrier there was a decrease in favorable response. The intersecting lines in the interaction plot reflect this finding.

Nonparametric Tests

When the k related samples have been measured on a nominal scale, the Cochran Q test is a good choice.[13] This test extends the McNemar test, discussed earlier, for studies having more than two samples. It tests the hypothesis that the proportion of cases in a category is equal for several related categories.

When the data are at least ordinal, the Friedman two-way analysis of variance is appropriate. It tests matched samples, ranking each case and calculating the mean rank for each variable across all cases. It uses these ranks to compute a test statistic. The product is a two-way table where the rows represent subjects and the columns represent the treatment conditions.[14] See Appendix C for additional nonparametric tests.

>Exhibit 14-19 Repeated-Measures ANOVA Plot

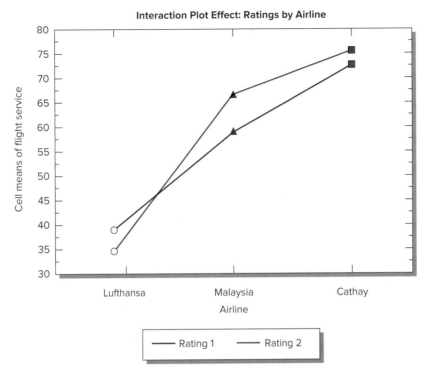

Interaction Plot Effect: Ratings by Airline

>summary

LO14-1 In classical statistics, we make inferences about a population based on evidence gathered from a sample. Although we cannot state unequivocally what is true about the entire population, representative samples allow us to make statements about what is probably true and how much error is likely to be encountered in arriving at a decision. The Bayesian approach also employs sampling statistics but has an additional element of prior information to improve the decision maker's judgment.

LO14-2 A difference between two or more sets of data is statistically significant if it actually occurs in a population. To have a statistically significant finding based on sampling evidence, we must be able to calculate the probability that some observed difference is large enough that there is little chance it could result from random sampling. Probability is the foundation for deciding on the acceptability of the null hypothesis, and sampling statistics facilitate acquiring the estimates.

LO14-3 Hypothesis testing can be viewed as a six-step procedure:

   a Establish a null hypothesis as well as the alternative hypothesis. It is a one-tailed test of significance if the alternative hypothesis states the direction of difference. If no direction of difference is given, it is a two-tailed test.

   b Choose the statistical test on the basis of the assumption about the population distribution and measurement level. The form of the data can also be a factor. In light of these considerations, one typically chooses the test that has the greatest power efficiency or ability to reduce decision errors.

   c Select the desired level of confidence. While $\alpha = .05$ is the most frequently used level, many others are also used. The α is the significance level that we desire and is typically set in advance of the study. Alpha or Type I error is the risk of rejecting a true null hypothesis and represents a decision error. The β or Type II error is the decision error that results from accepting a false null hypothesis. Usually, one determines a level of acceptable α error and then seeks to reduce the β error by increasing the sample size, shifting from a two-tailed to a one-tailed significance test, or both.

   d Compute the actual test value of the data.

   e Obtain the critical test value, usually by referring to a table for the appropriate type of distribution.

   f Interpret the result by comparing the actual test value with the critical test value.

LO14-4 Parametric and nonparametric tests are applicable under the various conditions described in the chapter.

They are also summarized in Exhibit 14-8. Parametric tests operate with interval and ratio data and are preferred when their assumptions can be met. Diagnostic tools examine the data for violations of those assumptions. Nonparametric tests do not require stringent assumptions about population distributions and are useful with less powerful nominal and ordinal measures.

LO14-5 In selecting a significance test, one needs to know, at a minimum, the number of samples, their independence or relatedness, and the measurement level of the data. Statistical tests emphasized in the chapter were the Z and t-tests, analysis of variance, and chi-square. The Z and t-tests may be used to test for the difference between two means. The t-test is chosen when the sample size is small. Variations on the t-test are used for both independent and related samples.

One-way analysis of variance compares the means of several groups. It has a single grouping variable, called a factor, and a continuous dependent variable. Analysis of variance (ANOVA) partitions the total variation among scores into between-groups (treatment) and within-groups (error) variance. The F ratio, the test statistic, determines if the differences are large enough to reject the null hypothesis. ANOVA may be extended to two-way, n-way, repeated-measures, and multivariate applications.

Chi-square is a nonparametric statistic that is used frequently for cross-tabulation or contingency tables. Its applications include testing for differences between proportions in populations and testing for independence. Corrections for chi-square were discussed.

LO14-6 Each of the numerous hypothesis tests generates a statistic, a critical value, which is compared to the value on its appropriate value table at the specified level of significance chosen by the researcher. In business this is usually .05 or .01. If the test's calculated critical value is larger than the value on its appropriate table, the null hypothesis is rejected and we conclude there is a significant relationship between the variables tested. Whether the test reveals that a significant relationship exists (reject the null hypothesis) or that a significant relationship does not exist (accept the null hypothesis), each finding is equally important to interpreting the data, as it supports or refutes a hypothesis that drove the original research. Every time an original hypothesis (alternative hypothesis) is supported or refuted, it influences the development of an insight and possibly a resulting recommendation.

Given that most hypothesis testing statistics are calculated by computer, assuming the researcher selects the appropriate test for the type of data studied, interpreting the statistic is the most important task. For example, for a cross-tabulation of two variables that contains 4 rows and 2 columns and that uses the chi-square hypothesis test, the calculated critical test value is 9.98. Referencing the chi-square values table (D-3) with 3 degrees of freedom [(4 rows-1)(2 columns-1)=3], we see that the test's calculated critical value of 9.98 is larger than the table value of 7.82 at the chosen .05 significance level; we reject the null hypothesis that there is no significant relationship between the variables tested.

>**key**terms

>discussionquestions

Terms in Review

1   Distinguish between the following:

   a   Parametric tests and nonparametric tests.

   b   Type I error and Type II error.

   c   Null hypothesis and alternative hypothesis.

   d   Acceptance region and rejection region.

   e   One-tailed tests and two-tailed tests.

   f   Type II error and the power of the test.

2   Summarize the steps of hypothesis testing. What is the virtue of this procedure?

3   In analysis of variance, what is the purpose of the mean square between and the mean square within? If the null hypothesis is accepted, what do these quantities look like?

4   Describe the assumptions for ANOVA, and explain how they may be diagnosed.

Making Research Decisions

5   Suggest situations where the researcher should be more concerned with Type II error than with Type I error.

   a   How can the probability of a Type I error be reduced? A Type II error?

   b   How does practical significance differ from statistical significance?

   c   Suppose you interview all the members of the freshman and senior classes and find that 65 percent of the freshmen and 62 percent of the seniors favor a proposal to send Help Centers offshore. Is this difference significant?

6   What hypothesis testing procedure would you use in the following situations?

   a   A test classifies applicants as accepted or rejected. On the basis of data on 200 applicants, we test the hypothesis that acceptance is not related to gender.

   b   A company manufactures and markets automobiles in two different countries. We want to know if the gas mileage is the same for vehicles from both facilities. There are samples of 45 units from each facility.

   c   A company has three categories of financial analysts: (1) with professional qualifications but without work experience, (2) with professional qualifications and with work experience, and (3) without professional qualifications but with work experience. A study exists that measures each analyst's motivation level (classified as high, normal, and low). A hypothesis of no relation between analyst category and motivation is to be tested.

   d   A company has 24 salespersons. The test must evaluate whether their sales performance is unchanged or has improved after a training program.

   e   A company has to evaluate whether it should attribute increased sales to product quality, advertising, or an interaction of product quality and advertising.

7   You conduct a survey of a sample of 25 members of this year's graduating business students and find that the average GPA is 3.2. The standard deviation of the sample is 0.4. Over the last 10 years, the average GPA has been 3.0. Is the GPA of this year's students significantly different from the long-run average? At what alpha level would it be significant?

8   You are curious about whether the professors and students at your school are of different political persuasions, so you take a sample of 20 professors and 20 students drawn randomly from each population. You find that 10 professors say they are conservative and 6 students say they are conservative. Is this a statistically significant difference?

9   You contact a random sample of 36 graduates of Western University and learn that their starting salaries averaged $28,000 last year. You then contact a random sample of 40 graduates from Eastern University and find that their average starting salary was $28,800. In each case, the standard deviation of the sample was $1,000.

   a   Test the null hypothesis that there is no difference between average salaries received by the graduates of the two schools.

   b   What assumptions are necessary for this test?

10   A random sample of students is interviewed to determine if there is an association between class and attitude toward corporations. With the following results, test the hypothesis that there is no difference among students on this attitude.

	Favorable	Neutral	Unfavorable
Freshmen	100	50	70
Sophomores	80	60	70
Juniors	50	50	80
Seniors	40	60	90

11   You do a survey of business students and liberal arts school students to find out how many times a week they read a daily newspaper. In each group, you interview 100 students. You find the following:

$\overline{X}_b$ = 4.5 times per week

S_b = 1.5

$\overline{X}_{la}$ = 5.6 times per week

S_{la} = 2.0

Test the hypothesis that there is no significant difference between these two samples.

12 One-Koat Paint Company has developed a new type of porch paint that it hopes will be the most durable on the market. The R&D group tests the new product against the two leading competing products by using a machine that scrubs until it wears through the coating. One-Koat runs five trials with each product and secures the following results (in thousands of scrubs):

Trial	One-Koat	Competitor A	Competitor B
1	37	34	24
2	30	19	25
3	34	22	23
4	28	31	20
5	29	27	20

Test the hypothesis that there are no differences between the means of these products ($\alpha = .05$).

13 A computer manufacturer is introducing a new product specifically targeted at the home market and wishes to compare the effectiveness of three distribution strategies: computer stores, home electronics stores, and department stores. Numbers of sales by 15 salespeople are recorded here:

Electronics store: 5, 4, 3, 3, 3

Department store: 9, 7, 8, 6, 5

Computer store: 7, 4, 8, 4, 3

a Test the hypothesis that there is no difference between the means of the retailers ($\alpha = .05$).

b Select a multiple comparison test, if necessary, to determine which groups differ in mean sales ($\alpha = .05$).

From the Headlines

14 Employers, the military, and colleges use aptitude tests to predict how well someone might perform. Recently, critics have said there isn't much difference in performance above a certain level—that everyone is more or less the same. Now, in a current issue of *Psychological Science,* the authors of a new study find that this isn't true. Instead, the higher your score, the better you perform later. The investigation considered four large studies of people who have taken aptitude tests: the College Board's SAT scores for 150,000 students entering 110 colleges and their freshman GPA. The Army collected 5,000 scores for the Armed Services Vocational Aptitude Battery and later appraised candidates on how well they did their jobs. Two additional data sets contained students' performance on tests in high school and their grades in college. The higher the test scores, the better the subsequent performance. Suggest alternative hypotheses that could equally explain this finding.

>cases*

* You will find a description of each case in the Case Abstracts section of this textbook. Check the Case Index to determine whether a case provides data, the research instrument, video, or other supplementary material. Cases and case supplements are available in Connect.

>chapter 15

Stage 4:
Measures of Association

> "The human brain is an incredible pattern-matching machine."
>
> *Jeff Bezos,*
> *CEO,*
> *Amazon*

>learningobjectives

After reading this chapter, you should understand . . .

LO15-1 How correlation analysis may be applied to study relationships between two or more variables.

LO15-2 The uses, requirements, and interpretation of the product moment correlation coefficient.

LO15-3 How predictions are made with regression analysis using the method of least squares to minimize errors in drawing a line of best fit.

LO15-4 How to test regression models for linearity and whether the equation is effective in fitting the data.

LO15-5 The nonparametric measures of association and the alternatives they offer when key assumptions and requirements for parametric techniques cannot be met.

>Introduction

In the previous chapter, we emphasized testing hypotheses of difference. However, management questions frequently address the study of relationships between two or more variables. Then, a *relational hypothesis* is necessary. In the research question, "Are U.S. kitchen appliances perceived by American consumers to be of better quality than foreign kitchen appliances?" the nature of the relationship between the two variables ("country of origin" and "perceived quality") is not specified. The implication, nonetheless, is that one variable is responsible for the other. A correct relational hypothesis for this question would state that the variables occur together in some specified manner without implying that one causes the other.

Various objectives are served with correlation analysis. The strength, direction, shape, and other features of the relationship may be discovered. Or tactical and strategic questions may be answered by predicting the values of one variable from those of another. Let's look at some typical management questions:

- In e-commerce, excessive catalog costs quickly squeeze margins. Many mailings fail to reach receptive or active buyers. What is the relationship between mailings that delete inactive customers and the improvement in profit margins?

- Medium-size companies often have difficulty attracting the cream of the MBA crop, and when they are successful, they have trouble retaining them. What is the relationship between the candidate's rank based on an executive interview and the rank obtained from testing or managerial assessment?

- Cigarette company marketing allocations shifted a few years ago as a result of multi-state settlements eliminating outdoor and transit advertising. More recently, advertising in magazines with large youth readerships came under scrutiny. During a given period, what is the relationship between point-of-sale expenditures and net profits?

- Aggressive U.S. high-tech companies have advertised heavily in the European chip market, and their sales have grown 20 percent over sales of the three largest European firms. Can we predict next year's sales based on present advertising?

All these questions may be evaluated by means of measures of association. And all call for different techniques based on the level at which the variables were measured or the intent of the question. The first three use nominal, ordinal, and interval data, respectively. The last one is answered through simple linear regression.

With correlation, one calculates an index to measure the nature of the relationship between variables. With regression, an equation is developed to predict the values of a dependent variable. Both are affected by the assumptions of measurement level and the distributions that underlie the data.

Exhibit 15-1 lists some common measures and their uses. The chapter follows the progression of the exhibit, first covering bivariate linear correlation, then examining simple regression, and concluding with nonparametric measures of association. Exploration of data through visual inspection and diagnostic evaluation of assumptions continues to be emphasized.

>Bivariate Correlation Analysis

Bivariate correlation analysis (a correlation of two continuous variables measured on an interval or ratio scale) differs from nonparametric measures of association and regression analysis in two important ways. First, parametric correlation requires two continuous variables measured on an interval or ratio scale. Second, the coefficient does not distinguish between independent and dependent variables. It treats the variables symmetrically since the coefficient r_{xy} has the same interpretation as r_{yx}.

Pearson's Product Moment Coefficient *r*

The **Pearson** (product moment) **correlation coefficient** varies over a range of +1 through 0 to −1. The designation *r* symbolizes the coefficient's estimate of linear association based on sampling data. The coefficient ρ represents the population correlation.

>**Exhibit 15-1** Commonly Used Measures of Association

Measurement	Coefficient	Comments and Uses
Interval and Ratio	**Pearson (product moment) correlation coefficient**	For continuous linearly related variables.
	Correlation ratio (eta)	For nonlinear data or relating a main effect to a continuous dependent variable.
	Biserial	One continuous and one dichotomous variable with an underlying normal distribution.
	Partial correlation	Three variables; relating two with the third's effect taken out.
	Multiple correlation	Three variables; relating one variable with two others.
	Bivariate linear regression	Predicting one variable from another's scores.
Ordinal	**Gamma**	Based on concordant-discordant pairs: $(P - Q)$; proportional reduction in error (PRE) interpretation.
	Kendall's tau b	$P - Q$ based; adjustment for tied ranks.
	Kendall's tau c	$P - Q$ based; adjustment for table dimensions.
	Somers's d	$P - Q$ based; asymmetrical extension of gamma.
	Spearman's rho	Product moment correlation for ranked data.
Nominal	**Phi**	Chi-square (CS) based for 2×2 tables.
	Cramer's V	CS based; adjustment when one table dimension > 2.
	Contingency coefficient C	CS based; flexible data and distribution assumptions.
	Lambda	PRE based interpretation.
	Goodman & Kruskal's tau	PRE based with table marginals emphasis.
	Uncertainty coefficient	Useful for multidimensional tables.
	Kappa	Agreement measure.

Correlation coefficients reveal the magnitude and direction of relationships. The *magnitude* is the degree to which variables move in unison or opposition. The size of a correlation of +.40 is the same as one of −.40. The sign says nothing about size. The degree of correlation is modest. The coefficient's sign signifies the *direction* of the relationship. Direction tells us whether large values on one variable are associated with large values on the other (and small values with small values). When the values correspond in this way, the two variables have a positive relationship: as one increases, the other also increases. Family income, for example, is positively related to household food expenditures. As income increases, food expenditures increase. Other variables are inversely related. Large values on the first variable are associated with small values on the second (and vice versa). The prices of products and services are inversely related to their scarcity. In general, as products decrease in available quantity, their prices rise. The absence of a relationship is expressed by a coefficient of approximately zero.

Discovering Best Practices

Discovering best practices in every field is a mandate for many firms. Such discoveries can significantly improve profitability by reducing resource expenditures, increasing performance, or both. The purpose of such association-based research—regardless of the arena—is to identify those practices. Global management consultancy McKinsey & Company set out to discover best practices for its clients trying to manage distribution in Latin American countries experiencing slowdowns in growth, rising inflation rates, and devaluations in currency.

Unlike in developed countries where large retailers and box stores have overwhelmingly captured distribution, small independent stores (called *fragmented trade*) still sell 40 percent of consumer packaged goods in Latin America. Consumer product goods companies (CPGs) are zeroing in on the emerging middle-class segment by selling through these neighborhood markets and supermarkets throughout the region. To identify best practices, McKinsey surveyed 35 CPGs doing business in Latin America as part of its larger global Customer and Channel Management Survey. To discover best practices, it needed to find companies employing similar practices that were performing markedly better than companies not employing those practices. "This difference in performance between winners and others is bigger than in any other market we studied except China, where the gap is 17 percentage points," shared study author Bruno Furtado.

McKinsey found best-practice CPGs are far more likely to use more evaluative criteria and more forward-looking criteria in choosing fragmented-trade partners. For example, the study discovered best-practice companies were far more likely to use evaluating quality of store-CPG company relationship (50 percent to 6 percent), the CPG company's share within the store (67 percent to 29 percent), store profitability growth potential (33 percent to 6 percent), and a store's potential share of category sales (50 percent to 29 percent) and that monitoring these multiple criteria could lead to significantly better performance.

All best-practice CPGs invested in collaborative store relationships to form power partnerships with stores of all types and sizes—not just larger, low-cost retailers—with 100 percent using multifunctional service teams with key accounts and

©Blend Images/Dave and Les Jacobs/Getty Images

nearly 50 percent of those focused on sales generation; far fewer lower-performing companies used such teams, and among those that did, only 29 percent focused on sales generation activities. All best-practice CPGs invested more in store execution of planograms and inventory control, new product introductions, etc. These companies paid their sales staff 28 percent more, resulting in lower turnover. Best-practice companies centrally managed pricing and promotional activities and tracked competitor prices more frequently, resulting in selling a higher percentage of items at undiscounted prices (78 percent to 63 percent). Their trade-level pricing varied more frequently and was more responsive to local conditions than lower-performing companies. Best-practice companies are using technology and data far more than nonperforming companies, especially in inventory management; these CPGs used point-of-sale photos to track planogram use (75 percent to 17 percent) and tracked inventory (75 percent to 35 percent) at the stock-keeping-unit level.

The study's authors believe that CPGs distributing in Latin America have much to learn from the industry's best-practice users.

www.mckinsey.com

Scatterplots for Exploring Relationships

Scatterplots are essential for understanding the relationships between variables. They provide a means for visual inspection of data that a list of values for two variables cannot. Both the direction and the shape of a relationship are conveyed in a plot. With a little practice, the magnitude of the relationship can be seen.

>**Exhibit 15-2** Scatterplots of Correlations between Two Variables

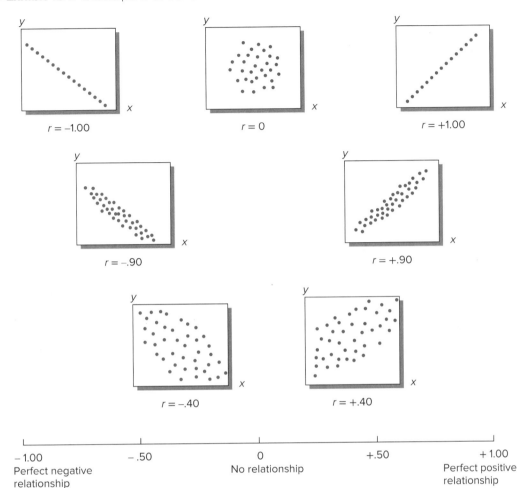

Exhibit 15-2 contains a series of scatterplots that depict some relationships across the range *r*. The three plots on the left side of the figure have their points sloping from the upper left to the lower right of each *x-y* plot.[1] They represent different magnitudes of negative relationships. On the right side of the figure, the three plots have opposite patterns and show positive relationships.

When stronger relationships are apparent (e.g., the ±.90 correlations), the points cluster close to an imaginary straight line passing through the data. The weaker relationships (±.40) depict a more diffuse data cloud with points spread farther from the line.

The shape of linear relationships is characterized by a straight line, whereas nonlinear relationships have curvilinear, parabolic, and compound curves representing their shapes. Pearson's *r* measures relationships in variables that are linearly related. It cannot distinguish linear from nonlinear data. Summary statistics alone do not reveal the appropriateness of the data for the model, which is why inspecting the data is important.

The need for data visualization is illustrated with four small data sets possessing identical summary statistics but displaying strikingly different patterns.[2] Exhibit 15-3 contains these data, and Exhibit 15-4 plots them. In Plot 1 of the figure, the variables are positively related. Their points follow a superimposed straight line through the data. This example is well suited to correlation analysis. In Plot 2, the data are curvilinear in relation to the line, and *r* is an inappropriate measure of their relationship. Plot 3 shows the presence of an influential point that changed a coefficient that would have otherwise been a perfect +1.0. The last plot displays constant values of *x* (similar to what you might find in an animal or quality control experiment). One leverage point establishes the fitted line for these data.

>**Exhibit 15-3** Four Data Sets with the Same Summary Statistics

S_s	X_1	Y_1	X_2	Y_2	X_3	Y_3	X_4	Y_4
1	10	8.04	10	9.14	10	7.46	8	6.58
2	8	6.95	8	8.14	8	6.77	8	5.76
3	13	7.58	13	8.74	13	12.74	8	7.71
4	9	8.81	9	8.77	9	7.11	8	8.84
5	11	8.33	11	9.26	11	7.81	8	8.47
6	14	9.96	14	8.10	14	8.84	8	7.04
7	6	7.24	6	6.13	6	6.08	8	5.25
8	4	4.26	4	3.10	4	5.39	19	12.50
9	12	10.84	12	9.13	12	8.15	8	5.56
10	7	4.82	7	7.26	7	6.42	8	7.91
11	5	5.68	5	4.74	5	5.73	8	6.89
Pearson's r	0.81642		0.81624		0.81629		0.81652	
r^2	0.66654		0.66624		0.66632		0.66671	
Adjusted r^2	0.62949		0.62916		0.62925		0.62967	
Standard error	1.2366		1.23721		1.23631		1.2357	

>**Exhibit 15-4** Different Scatterplots for the Same Summary Statistics

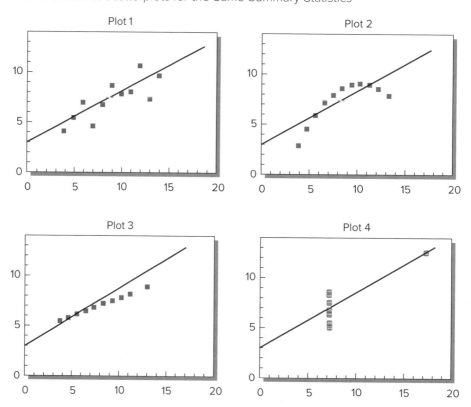

400

We will return to these concepts and the process of drawing the line when we discuss regression. For now, comparing Plots 2 through 4 with Plot 1 suggests the importance of visually inspecting correlation data for underlying patterns to ensure linearity. Careful analysts make scatterplots an integral part of the inspection and exploration of their data. Although small samples may be plotted by hand, statistical software packages save time and offer a variety of plotting procedures.

The Assumptions of *r*

Like other parametric techniques, correlation analysis makes certain assumptions about the data. Many of these assumptions are necessary to test hypotheses about the coefficient.

The first requirement for *r* is **linearity**. All of the examples in Exhibit 15-2, with the exception of $r = 0$, illustrate a relationship between variables that can be described by a straight line passing through the data cloud. When $r = 0$, no pattern is evident that could be described with a single line. Parenthetically, it is also possible to find coefficients of 0 where the variables are highly related but in a nonlinear form. As we have seen, plots make such findings evident.

The second assumption for correlation is a **bivariate normal distribution**—that is, the data are from a random sample of a population where the two variables are normally distributed in a joint manner.

Often these assumptions or the required measurement level cannot be met. Then the analyst should select a nonlinear or nonparametric measure of association, many of which are described later in this chapter.

Computation and Testing of *r*

The population correlation coefficient is

$$\rho = \frac{\text{Cov}(X, Y)}{\sigma_X \sigma_Y} \tag{1}$$

Because population parameters are usually not known to us, we estimate from the random sample of (X, Y) observation pairs.

With the sample estimator of $\text{Cov}(X, Y)$ being $SS_{XY}/(n - 1)$, an estimator of σ_x is

$$\sqrt{SS_X/(n - 1)}$$

and an estimator of σ_y is

$$\sqrt{SS_Y/(n - 1)}$$

We can substitute these estimators for their population counterparts in equation (2), giving us the sample correlation coefficient designated by *r*.

$$r = \frac{SS_{XY}}{\sqrt{SS_X SS_Y}} \tag{2}$$

Another common formula for calculating Pearson's *r* is

$$r = \frac{\sum (X - \bar{X})(Y - \bar{Y})}{(n - 1) S_x S_y} \tag{3}$$

where

n = the number of pairs of cases

S_x, S_y = the standard deviations for X and Y

A variation known as the reflective correlation, used when the data are not centered on their mean values, is:

$$r = \frac{\sum xy}{\sqrt{(\sum x^2)(\sum y^2)}}$$ (4)

because

$$S_x = \sqrt{\frac{\sum x^2}{N}} \quad S_y = \sqrt{\frac{\sum y^2}{N}}$$

If the numerator of equation (4) is divided by n, we have the *covariance*, the amount of deviation that the X and Y distributions have in common. With a positive covariance, the variables move in unison; with a negative one, they move in opposition. When the covariance is 0, there is no relationship. The denominator for equation (4) represents the maximum potential variation that the two distributions share. Thus, correlation may be thought of as a ratio.

Exhibit 15-5 contains a random subsample of 10 firms of the *Forbes* 500 sample. The variables chosen to illustrate the computation of r are cash flow and net profits. Beneath each variable is its mean and standard deviation. In columns 4 and 5, we obtain the deviations of the X and Y values from their means, and in column 6, we find the product. Columns 7 and 8 are the squared deviation scores.

Substituting into the formula, we get

$$r = \frac{224777.23}{\sqrt{138419.71} * \sqrt{422139.76}} = .9298$$

>**Exhibit 15-5** Computation of Pearson's Product Moment Correlation

(1)	(2)	(3)	(4)	(5)	(6)	(7)	(8)
	Net Profits ($, millions)	Cash Flow ($, millions)	Deviations from Means				
Corporation	X	Y	$(X - \bar{X})x$	$(Y - \bar{Y})y$	xy	x^2	y^2
1	82.6	126.5	−93.84	−178.64	16763.58	8805.95	31912.25
2	89.0	191.2	−87.44	−113.94	9962.91	7645.75	12982.32
3	176.0	267.0	−0.44	−38.14	16.78	0.19	1454.66
4	82.3	137.1	−94.14	−168.04	15819.29	8862.34	28237.44
5	413.5	806.8	−37.06	501.66	118923.52	56197.44	251602.56
6	18.1	35.2	158.34	−269.94	42742.30	25071.56	72867.60
7	337.3	425.5	160.86	120.36	19361.11	25875.94	14486.53
8	145.8	380.0	−30.64	74.86	−2293.71	938.81	5604.02
9	172.6	326.6	−3.84	21.36	82.02	14.75	456.25
10	247.2	355.5	70.76	50.36	3563.47	5006.98	2536.13
	$\bar{X} = 176.44$ $s_x = 216.59$	$\bar{Y} = 305.14$ $s_y = 124.01$			$\Sigma xy = 224777.23$		

$\Sigma x^2 = 138419.71$

$\Sigma y^2 = 422139.76$

>**Exhibit 15-6** Plot of *Forbes* 500 Net Profits with Cash Flow

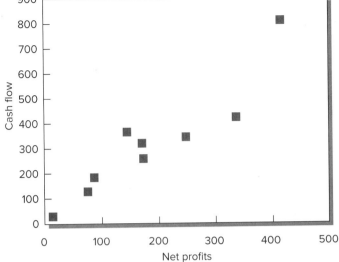

In this subsample, net profits and cash flow are positively related and have a very high coefficient. As net profits increase, cash flow increases; the opposite is also true. Linearity of the variables may be examined with a scatterplot such as the one shown in Exhibit 15-6. The data points fall along a straight line.

Common Variance as an Explanation

The amount of common variance in X (net profits) and Y (cash flow) may be summarized by the **coefficient of determination (r^2)**. As Exhibit 15-7 shows, the overlap between the two variables is the proportion of their common or shared variance.

>**Exhibit 15-7** Diagram of Common Variance

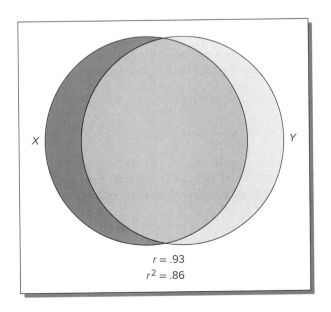

$r = .93$
$r^2 = .86$

The area of overlap represents the percentage of the total relationship accounted for by one variable or the other. So 86 percent of the variance in X is explained by Y, and vice versa.

Testing the Significance of r

Is the coefficient representing the relationship between net profits and cash flow real, or does it occur by chance? This question tries to discover whether our r is a chance deviation from a population p of zero. In other situations, the researcher may wish to know if significant differences exist between two or more r's. In either case, r's significance should be checked before r is used in other calculations or comparisons. For this test, we must have independent random samples from a bivariate normal distribution. Then the Z or t-test may be used for the null hypothesis, $p = 0$.

The formula for small samples is

$$t = \frac{r}{\sqrt{\dfrac{1 - r^2}{n - 2}}}$$

where

$$r = .93$$
$$n = 10$$

Substituting into the equation, we calculate t:

$$t = \frac{.93}{\sqrt{\dfrac{1 - .86}{8}}} = 7.03$$

With $n - 2$ degrees of freedom, the statistical program calculates the value of t (7.03) at a probability less than .005 for the one-tailed alternative, $H_A: p > 0$. We reject the hypothesis that there is no linear relationship between net profits and cash flow in the population. The preceding statistic is appropriate when the null hypothesis states a correlation of 0. It should be used only for a one-tailed test.[3] However, it is often difficult to know in advance whether the variables are positively or negatively related, particularly when a computer removes our contact with the raw data. Software programs produce two-tailed tests for this eventuality. The observed significance level for a one-tailed test is half of the printed two-tailed version in most programs.

Interpretation of Correlations

A correlation coefficient of any magnitude or sign, whatever its statistical significance, does not imply causation. Increased net profits may cause an increase in market value, or improved satisfaction may cause improved performance in certain situations, but correlation provides no evidence of cause and effect. Several alternate explanations may be provided for correlation results:

- X causes Y.
- Y causes X.
- X and Y are activated by one or more other variables.
- X and Y influence each other reciprocally.

Ex post facto studies seldom possess sufficiently powerful designs to demonstrate which of these conditions could be true. By controlling variables under an experimental design, we may obtain more rigorous evidence of causality.

Take care to avoid so-called **artifact correlations**, in which distinct groups combine to give the impression of one. The upper panel of Exhibit 15-8 shows data from two business sectors. If all the data points for the X and Y variables are aggregated and a correlation is computed for a single group, a positive correlation results. Separate calculations for each sector (note that points for sector A

>**Exhibit 15-8** Artifact Correlations

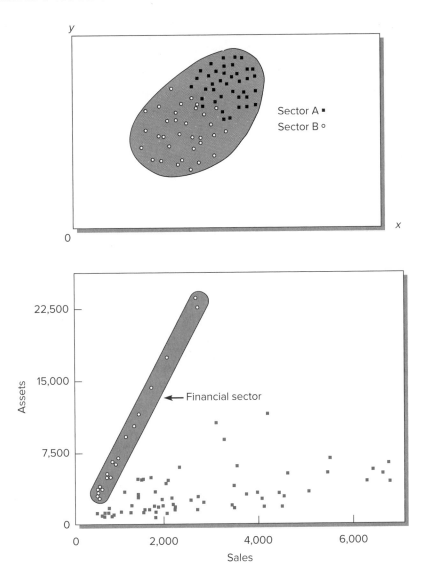

form a circle, as do points for sector B) reveal *no* relationship between the *X* and *Y* variables. A second example, shown in the lower panel, contains a plot of data on assets and sales. We have enclosed and highlighted the data for the financial sector. This is shown as a narrow band enclosed by an ellipse. The companies in this sector score high on assets and low in sales—all are banks. When the data for banks are removed and treated separately, the correlation is nearly perfect (.99). When banks are returned to the sample and the correlation is recalculated, the overall relationship drops to the middle .80s. In short, data hidden or nested within an aggregated set may present a radically different picture.

Another issue affecting interpretation of coefficients concerns practical significance. Even when a coefficient is statistically significant, it must be practically meaningful. In many relationships, other factors combine to make the coefficient's meaning misleading. For example, in nature we expect rainfall and the height of reservoirs to be positively correlated. But in states where water management and flood control mechanisms are complex, an apparently simple relationship may not hold. Techniques like partial and multiple correlation or multiple regression are helpful in sorting out confounding effects.

>snapshot

Is Oscar Showing Some Tarnish?

Each year the movie industry puts its best pictures and its brightest actors, writers, and directors into a competition known as the Oscars. Voted on by members of the Academy of Motion Picture Arts and Sciences, the Oscars is not only designed to recognize excellence, but also, in a blatant way, to increase viewing of movies.

Polaris Marketing Research Inc. and AMC Theatres set out to determine whether the Oscar event had any measurable effect on movie viewership. Launching a brief online survey via Research Now's OmniPulse® omnibus offering, and matching attitudinal and behavior questions to extensive demographic data, Polaris Marketing Research indicates that for a movie, studio, or actor, all the pre-event hype and the Oscar event itself influence a relatively small percentage to view an Oscar-nominated or Oscar-winning movie. Do the accompanying data indicate that women and men respond differently to Oscar, at a level that is statistically significant? How would you determine this?

www.polarismr.com, www.amctheatres.com, www.researchnow.com

©CREATISTA/Shutterstock

The Question: How much do you agree or disagree with the following statements?

	Strongly Agree	Somewhat Agree	Somewhat Disagree	Strongly Disagree	Don't Know
I enjoy following the Oscar nomination process and pre-Oscar buzz.	4	3	2	1	5
I make it a point to see the movies that get Oscar nominations.	4	3	2	1	5
I make it a point to see the movies that win an Oscar.	4	3	2	1	5

The Data:

		Males		Females		
		Strongly Agree/ Agree	Strongly Disagree/ Disagree	Strongly Agree/ Agree	Strongly Disagree/ Disagree	Total
I enjoy following the Oscar nomination process and pre-Oscar buzz.	Count	198	367	316	322	565 males 638 females
	Percent	35.0	65.0	49.5	50.5	
	Mean					1.93 males 2.24 females
I make it a point to see the movies that get Oscar nominations.	Count	199	366	266	372	
	Percent	35.2	64.8	41.7	58.3	
	Mean					1.98 males 2.13 females
I make it a point to see the movies that win an Oscar.	Count	234	331	313	325	
	Percent	41.4	58.6	49.1	50.9	
	Mean					2.10 males 2.31 females

With large samples, even exceedingly low coefficients can be statistically significant. This "significance" only reflects the likelihood of a linear relationship in the population. Should magnitudes less than .30 be reported when they are significant? It depends. We might consider the correlations between variables such as cash flow, sales, market value, or net profits to be interesting revelations of a particular phenomenon whether they were high, moderate, or low. The nature of the study, the characteristics of the sample, or other reasons will be determining factors. *A coefficient is not remarkable simply because it is statistically significant.*

By probing the evidence of direction, magnitude, statistical significance, and common variance together with the study's objectives and limitations, we reduce the chances of reporting trivial findings. Simultaneously, the communication of practical implications to the reader will be improved.

>Simple Linear Regression[4]

In the previous section, we focused on relationships between variables. The product moment correlation was found to represent an index of the magnitude of the relationship, the sign governed the direction, and r^2 explained the common variance. Relationships also serve as a basis for estimation and prediction.

When we take the observed values of X to estimate or predict corresponding Y values, the process is called **simple prediction**.[5] When more than one X variable is used, the outcome is a function of multiple predictors. Simple and multiple predictions are made with a technique called **regression analysis**.

The similarities and differences of correlation and regression are summarized in Exhibit 15-9. Their relatedness would suggest that beneath many correlation problems is a regression analysis that could provide further insight about the relationship of Y with X.

>**Exhibit 15-9** Comparison of Bivariate Linear Correlation and Regression

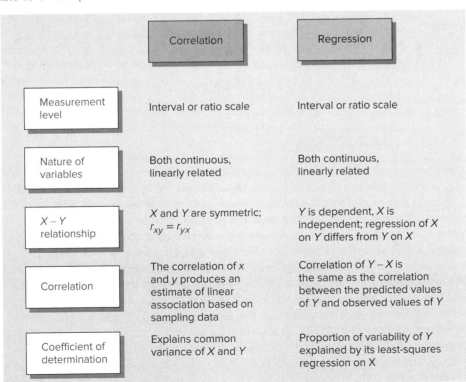

	Correlation	Regression
Measurement level	Interval or ratio scale	Interval or ratio scale
Nature of variables	Both continuous, linearly related	Both continuous, linearly related
X–Y relationship	X and Y are symmetric; $r_{xy} = r_{yx}$	Y is dependent, X is independent; regression of X on Y differs from Y on X
Correlation	The correlation of x and y produces an estimate of linear association based on sampling data	Correlation of Y–X is the same as the correlation between the predicted values of Y and observed values of Y
Coefficient of determination	Explains common variance of X and Y	Proportion of variability of Y explained by its least-squares regression on X

>**Exhibit 15-10** Examples of Different Slopes

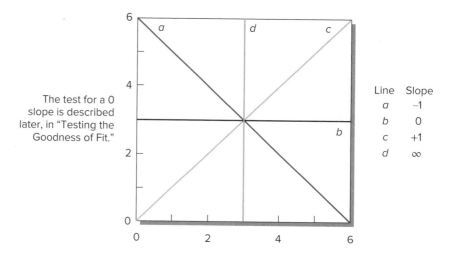

The test for a 0 slope is described later, in "Testing the Goodness of Fit."

Line	Slope
a	−1
b	0
c	+1
d	∞

The Basic Model

A straight line is fundamentally the best way to model the relationship between two continuous variables. The bivariate linear regression may be expressed as

$$Y = \beta_0 + \beta_1 X_i$$

where the value of the dependent variable Y is a linear function of the corresponding value of the independent variable X_i in the ith observation. The slope and the Y intercept are known as **regression coefficients**. The **slope, β_1**, is the change in Y for a 1-unit change in X. It is sometimes called the "rise over run." This is defined by the formula

$$\beta_1 = \frac{\Delta Y}{\Delta X}$$

This is the ratio of change (Δ) in the rise of the line relative to the run or travel along the X axis. Exhibit 15-10 shows a few of the many possible slopes you may encounter.

The **intercept, β_0**, is the value for the linear function when it crosses the Y axis; it is the estimate of Y when $X = 0$. A formula for the intercept based on the mean scores of the X and Y variables is

$$\beta_0 = \overline{Y} - \beta_1 \overline{X}$$

Concept Application

What makes Generation X-ers all over the world select a glass of wine rather than a beer, Jack Daniels and Coke, or Bacardi Breezer? A research report from Australia highlights Generation X attitudes toward wine. The results suggest the top influencers are friends and family, wine reviews, and visits to wineries.[6] From the winery's perspective, tasting from the barrel is not only a widespread sales tool, but also a major determinant of market *en primeur* or futures contracts, which represent about 60 percent of the harvest.

Weather is widely regarded as responsible for pronouncements about a wine's taste and potential quality. A Princeton economist has elaborated on that notion. He suggested that just a few facts about local weather conditions may be better predictors of vintage French red wines than the most refined palates and noses.[7] The regression model developed predicts an auction price index for about 80 wines from winter and harvest rainfall amounts and average growing-season temperatures. Interestingly, the calculations suggested that the 1989 Bordeaux would be one of the best since 1893. French traditionalists reacted hysterically to these methods yet agreed with the conclusion.

Our first example will use one predictor with highly simplified data. Let X represent the average growing-season temperature in degrees Celsius and Y the price of a 12-bottle case in euros. Take, for example, a famous French burgundy such as Romanée Conti St. Vivant, which sells for $340 per bottle (times 12 bottles per case or $4,080). This would be approximately 3,060 euros. The data appear here:

X Average Temperature (Celsius)	Y Price per Case (EUR)
12	2,000
16	3,000
20	4,000
24	5,000
$\overline{X} = 18$	$\overline{Y} = 3,500$

The plotted data in Exhibit 15-11 show a linear relationship between the pairs of points and a perfect positive correlation, $r_{yx} = 1.0$. The slope of the line is calculated:

$$\beta_1 = \frac{Y_i - Y_j}{X_i - X_j} = \frac{4,000 - 3,000}{20 - 16} = \frac{1,000}{4} = 250$$

where the $X_i Y_i$ values are the data points (20, 4,000) and $X_j Y_j$ are points (16, 3,000). The intercept β_0 is $-1,000$, the point at which $X = 0$ in this plot. This area is off the graph and appears in an insert on the figure.

$$\beta_0 = \overline{Y} - \beta_1 \overline{X} = 3,500 - 250(18) = -1,000$$

>**Exhibit 15-11** Plot of Wine Price by Average Growing Temperature

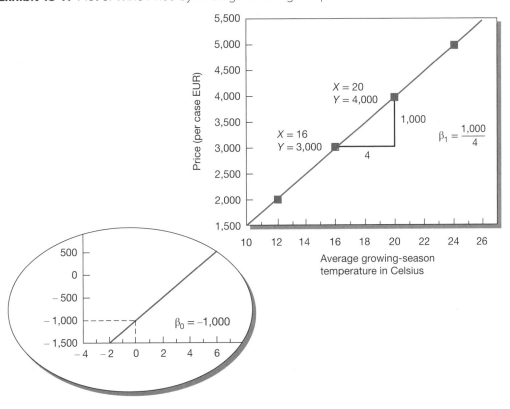

Substituting into the formula, we have the simple regression equation

$$Y = -1,000 + 250\, X_i$$

We could now predict that a warm growing season with 25.5°C temperature would bring a case price of 5,375 euros. $\hat{Y}$ (called *Y-hat*) is the predicted value of *Y*:

$$\hat{Y} = -1,000 + 250(25.5) = 5,375$$

Unfortunately, one rarely comes across a data set composed of four paired values, a perfect correlation, and an easily drawn line. A model based on such data is *deterministic* in that for any value of *X*, there is only one possible corresponding value of *Y*. It is more likely that we will collect data where the values of *Y* vary for each *X* value. Considering Exhibit 15-12, we should expect a distribution of price values for the temperature $X = 16$, another for $X = 20$, and another for each value of *X*. The means of these *Y* distributions will also vary in some systematic way with *X*. These variabilities lead us to construct a *probabilistic* model that also uses a linear function.[8] This function is written

$$Y_i = \beta_0 + \beta_1 X_i + \varepsilon_1$$

where ε symbolizes the deviation of the *i*th observation from the mean, $\beta_0 + \beta_1 X_i$.

As shown in Exhibit 15-12, the actual values of *Y* may be found above or below the regression line represented by the mean value of $Y\,(\beta_0 + \beta_1 X_i)$ for a particular value of *X*. These deviations are the error in fitting the line and are often called the **error term**.

>**Exhibit 15-12** Distribution of *Y* for Observations of *X*

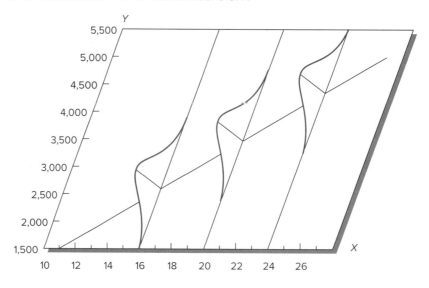

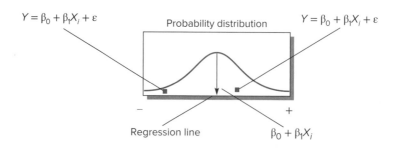

>**Exhibit 15-13** Data for Wine Price Study

	Price (EUR) Y	Temperature (C) X	XY	Y²	X²
1	1,813	11.80	21,393.40	3,286,969.00	139.24
2	2,558	15.70	40,160.60	6,543,364.00	246.49
3	2,628	14.00	36,792.00	6,906,384.00	196.00
4	3,217	22.90	73,669.30	10,349,089.00	524.41
5	3,228	20.00	64,560.00	10,419,984.00	400.00
6	3,629	20.10	72,942.90	13,169,641.00	404.01
7	3,886	17.90	69,559.40	15,100,996.00	320.41
8	4,897	23.40	114,589.80	23,980,609.00	547.56
9	4,933	24.60	121,351.80	24,334,489.00	605.16
10	5,199	25.70	133,614.30	27,029,601.00	660.49
Σ	35,988	196.10	748,633.50	141,121,126.00	4,043.77
Mean	3,598.80	19.61			
s	1,135.66	4.69			
Sum of squares (SS)	11,607,511.59	198.25	42,908.82		

Method of Least Squares

Exhibit 15-13 contains a new data set for the wine price example. Our prediction of Y from X must now account for the fact that the X and Y pairs do not fall neatly along the line. Actually, the relationship could be summarized by several lines. Exhibit 15-14 suggests two alternatives based on visual inspection—both of which produce errors, or vertical distances from the observed values to the line. The **method of least squares** allows us to find a regression line, or line of best fit, that will keep these errors to a minimum. It uses the criterion of minimizing the total squared errors of estimate. When we predict values of Y for each X_i, the difference between the actual Y_i and the predicted $\hat{Y}$ is the error. This error is squared and then summed. The line of best fit is the one that minimizes the total squared errors of prediction.[9]

$$\sum_{i=1}^{n} e_i^2 \text{ minimized}$$

Regression coefficients β_0 and β_1 are used to find the least-squares solution. They are computed as follows:

$$\beta_1 = \frac{\sum XY - \frac{(\sum X)(\sum Y)}{n}}{\sum X^2 - \frac{(\sum X)^2}{n}}$$

$$\hat{\beta}_0 = \overline{Y} - \hat{\beta}_1 \overline{X}$$

>**Exhibit 15-14** Scatterplot and Possible Regression Lines Based on Visual Inspection: Wine Price Study

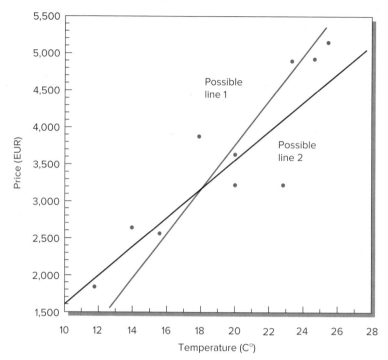

Substituting data from Exhibit 15-13 into both formulas, we get

$$\beta_1 = \frac{748{,}633.5 - \dfrac{(196.1)(35{,}988)}{10}}{4{,}043.77 - \dfrac{(196.1)^2}{10}} = 216.439$$

$$\widehat{\beta}_0 = 3{,}598.8 - (216.439)(19.61) = -645.569$$

The predictive equation is now $\widehat{Y} = -645.57 + 216.44\,X_i$.

Drawing the Regression Line

Before drawing the regression line, we select two values of X to compute. Using values 13 and 24 for X_i, the points are

$$\widehat{Y} = -645.57 + 216.44(13) = 2{,}168.15$$
$$\widehat{Y} = -645.57 + 216.44(24) = 4{,}548.99$$

Comparing the line drawn in Exhibit 15-15 to the trial lines in Exhibit 15-14, one can readily see the success of the least-squares method in minimizing the error of prediction.

Residuals

We now turn our attention to the plot of standardized residuals in Exhibit 15-16. A **residual** is what remains after the line is fit or $(Y_i - \widehat{Y}_i)$. When standardized, residuals are comparable to Z scores with a mean of 0 and a standard deviation of 1. In this plot, the standardized residuals should fall between 2 and −2, be randomly distributed about zero, and show no discernible pattern. All these conditions say the model is applied appropriately.

>**Exhibit 15-15** Drawing the Least-Squares Line: Wine Price Study

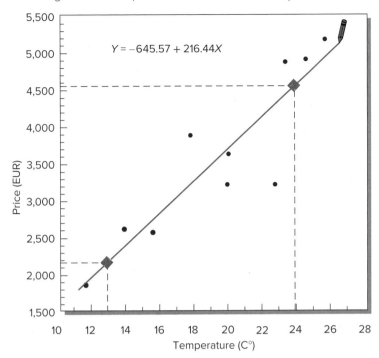

$$Y = -645.57 + 216.44X$$

In our example, we have one residual at −2.2, a random distribution about zero, and few indications of a sequential pattern. It is important to apply other diagnostics to verify that the regression assumptions (normality, linearity, equality of variance, and independence of error) are met. Various software programs provide plots and other checks of regression assumptions.[10]

Predictions

If we wanted to predict the price of a case of investment-grade red wine for a growing season that averages 21°C, our prediction would be

$$\widehat{Y} = -645.57 + 216.44(21) = 3,899.67$$

>**Exhibit 15-16** Plot of Standardized Residuals: Wine Price Study

Case	−3.0	0.0	3.0	Y Price	Predicted Price	Residual
1		* .		1,813	1,908.4112	−95.4112
2		* .		2,558	2,752.5234	−194.5234
3		. *		2,628	2,384.5771	243.4229
4	*	.		3,217	4,310.8844	−1,093.8844
5		* .		3,228	3,683.2112	−455.2112
6		*		3,629	3,704.8551	−75.8551
7		. *		3,886	3,228.6893	657.3107
8		. *		4,897	4,419.1039	477.8961
9		. *		4,933	4,678.8307	254.1693
10		. *		5,199	4,916.9137	282.0863

−3.0	0.0	3.0

©Pressmaster/Shutterstock

This is a *point prediction* of Y and should be corrected for greater precision. As with other confidence estimates, we establish the degree of confidence desired and substitute into the formula

$$\widehat{Y} \pm t_{\alpha/2} s \sqrt{1 + \frac{1}{10} + \frac{(X - \overline{X})^2}{SS_x}}$$

where

$t_{\alpha/2}$ = the two-tailed critical value for t at the desired level (95 percent in this example)

s = the standard error of estimate (also the square root of the mean square error from the analysis of variance of the regression model) (see Exhibit 15-19).

SS_x = the sum of squares for X (see Exhibit 15-13).

$$3,899.67 \pm (2.306)(538.559) \sqrt{1 + \frac{1}{10} + \frac{(21 - 19.61)^2}{198.25}}$$

$$3,899.67 \pm 1,308.29$$

Envirosell: Studies Reveal Left-Hand Retail

World retailers collect and subscribe to numerous data sources, but they need knowledge from the data to craft their merchandising, staffing, and promotion strategies, as well as their store designs. Retail giants (e.g., The Gap, Limited, Starbucks, McDonald's) turn to consultant Paco Underhill when they want to know how consumers buy what they do and what barriers prevent or discourage buying. Underhill describes himself as a "commercial researcher, which means I am part scientist, part artist, and part entrepreneur." His company, Envirosell, has offices in the United States, Milan, Sidney, and São Paulo. Envirosell concentrates on the third segment of retail information, drawn from observation (segment 1 is register data, and segment 2 is communication studies). In an *ABC News* live e-chat, Underhill said, "The principal differences in 1st world shopping patterns are governed more by education and income than by ethnicity . . . but the Brits and Aussies [do] tend to walk as they drive. This sets up some very peculiar retail [shopping] patterns, because their walking patterns set up a left-hand dominance, whereas in the U.S. and much of the rest of the world, our walking patterns set up a right-hand dominance."

www.envirosell.com

©Laura Porter

If you were Gap and about to design a store to open in London, how would you design a study to verify Paco Underhill's conclusion about left-hand dominance?

We are 95 percent confident of our prediction that a case of investment-quality red wine grown in a particular year at 21°C average temperatures will be initially priced at 3,899.67 ± 1,308.29 euros, or from approximately 2,591 to 5,208 EUR. The comparatively large bandwidth results from the amount of error in the model (reflected by r^2), some peculiarities in the Y values, and the use of a single predictor.

It is more likely that we would want to predict the average price of *all* cases grown at 21°C. This prediction would use the same basic formula but omitting the first digit (the 1) under the radical. A narrower *confidence* band is the result since the average of all Y values is being predicted from a given X. In our example, the confidence interval for 95 percent is 3,899.67 ±411.42, or from 3,488 to 4,311 EUR.

The predictor we selected, 21°C, was close to the mean of X (19.61). Because the **prediction and confidence bands** are shaped like a bow tie, predictors farther from the mean have larger bandwidths. For example, X values of 15, 20, and 25 produce confidence bands of ±565, ±397, and ±617, respectively. This is illustrated in Exhibit 15-17. The farther one's selected predictor is from X, the wider is the prediction interval.

Testing the Goodness of Fit

With the regression line plotted and a few illustrative predictions, we should now gather some evidence of **goodness of fit**—how well the model fits the data. The most important test in bivariate linear regression is whether the slope, β_1, is equal to zero.[11] We have already observed a slope of zero in Exhibit 15-10, line *b*. Zero slopes result from various conditions:

- Y is completely unrelated to X, and no systematic pattern is evident.
- There are constant values of Y for every value of X.
- The data are related but represented by a nonlinear function.

>**Exhibit 15-17** Prediction and Confidence Bands on Proximity to X

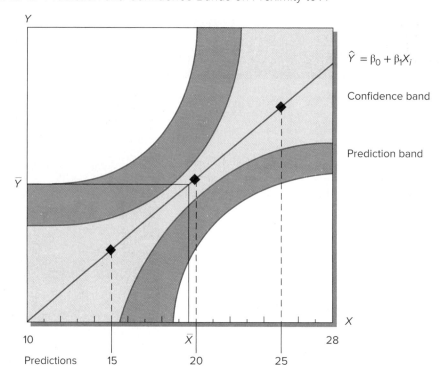

The t-Test

To test whether $\beta_1 = 0$, we use a two-tailed test (since the actual relationship is positive, negative, or zero). The test follows the t distribution for $n - 2$ degrees of freedom:

$$t = \frac{b_1}{s(b_1)} = \frac{216.439}{34.249} = 5.659$$

where b_1 was previously defined as the slope β_1 and $s(b_1)$ is the standard error of β_1.[12]

We reject the null hypothesis, $\beta_1 = 0$, because the calculated t is greater than any t value for 8 degrees of freedom and $\alpha = .01$. Therefore, we conclude that the slope is not equal to zero.

The F Test

Computer printouts generally contain an analysis of variance (ANOVA) table with an F test of the regression model. In bivariate regression, t and F tests produce the same results since t^2 is equal to F. In multiple regression, the F test has an overall role for the model, and each of the independent variables is evaluated with a separate t-test. From the last chapter, recall that ANOVA partitions variance into component parts. For regression, it comprises explained deviations, $\hat{Y} - \bar{Y}$ and unexplained deviations, $Y - \hat{Y}$. Together they constitute the total deviation, $Y - \bar{Y}$. This is shown graphically in Exhibit 15-18. These sources of deviation are squared for all observations and summed across the data points.

In Exhibit 15-19, we develop this concept sequentially, concluding with the F test of the regression model for the wine data. Based on the results presented in that table, we find statistical evidence of a linear relationship between variables. The null hypothesis, $r^2 = 0$, is rejected with $F = 32.02$, d.f. (1, 8), $p < .005$. The alternative hypothesis is accepted. The null hypothesis for the F test had the same effect as $\beta_1 = 0$ because we could select either test. Thus, we conclude that X and Y are linearly related.

>**Exhibit 15-18** Components of Variation

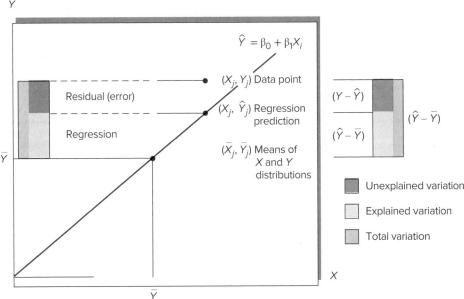

Coefficient of Determination

In predicting the values of Y without any knowledge of X, our best estimate would be $\overline{Y}$, its mean. Each predicted value that does not fall on Y contributes to an error of estimate, $Y - \overline{Y}$. The total squared error for several predictions would be $\sum(Y_i - Y)^2$. By introducing known values of X into a regression equation, we attempt to reduce this error even further. Naturally, this is an improvement over using $\overline{Y}$, and the result is $(\widehat{Y} - \overline{Y})$. The total improvement based on several estimates is $\sum(\widehat{Y}_i - \overline{Y})^2$, the amount of variation explained by the relationship between X and Y in the regression. Based on the formula, the *coefficient of determination* is the ratio of the line of best fit's error over that incurred by using Y. One purpose of testing, then, is to discover whether the regression equation is a more effective predictive device than the mean of the dependent variable.

As in correlation, the coefficient of determination is symbolized by r^2.[13] It has several purposes. As an index of fit, it is interpreted as the total proportion of variance in Y explained by X. As a measure of linear relationship, it tells us how well the regression line fits the data. It is also an important indicator of the predictive accuracy of the equation. Typically, we would like to have an r^2 that explains 80 percent or more of the variation. Lower than that, predictive accuracy begins to fall off. The coefficient of determination, r^2, is calculated like this:

$$r^2 = \frac{\sum_{i=1}^{n}(\widehat{Y} - Y)^2}{\sum_{i=1}^{n}(Y = \overline{Y})^2} = \frac{SS_r}{SS_e} = 1 - \frac{SS_e}{SS_t}$$

For the wine price study, r^2 was found by using the data from the bottom of Exhibit 15-19:

$$r^2 = 1 - \frac{2,320,368.49}{11,607,511.60} = .80$$

Eighty percent of the variance in price may be explained by growing-season temperatures. With actual data and multiple predictors, our results would improve substantially.

>**Exhibit 15-19** Progressive Application of Partitioned Variance Concept

General Concept				
$(\hat{Y} - \bar{Y})$	$+$	$(Y - \hat{Y})$	$=$	$(Y - \bar{Y})$
Explained Variation (the regression relationship between X and Y)		Unexplained Variation (cannot be explained by the regression relationship)		Total Variation

ANOVA Application		
$\sum_{i=1}^{n} (\hat{Y} - \bar{Y})^2$	$\sum_{i=1}^{n} (Y - \hat{Y})^2$	$\sum_{i=1}^{n} (Y - \bar{Y})^2$
SS_r Sum of Squares Regression	SS_e Sum of Squares Error	SS_t Sum of Squares Total

Contents of Summary Table				
Source	Degrees of Freedom	Sum of Squares	Mean Square	F Ratio
Regression	1	SS_r	$MS_r = \dfrac{SS_r}{1}$	$\dfrac{MS_r}{MS_e}$
Error	$n - 2$	SS_e	$MS_e = \dfrac{SS_e}{n-2}$	
Total		SS_t		

ANOVA Summary Table: Test of Regression Model				
Source	Degrees of Freedom	Sum of Squares	Mean Square	F Ratio
Regression	1	9,287,143.11	9,287,143.11	32.02
Residual (error)	8	2,320,368.49	290,046.06	
Total		11,607,511.60		

Significance of $F = .0005$

>Nonparametric Measures of Association[14]

Measures for Nominal Data

Nominal measures are used to assess the strength of relationships in cross-classification tables. They are often used with chi-square or may be used separately. In this section, we provide examples of three statistics based on chi-square and two that follow the proportional reduction in error approach.

There is no fully satisfactory all-purpose measure for categorical data. Some are adversely affected by table shape and number of cells; others are sensitive to sample size or marginals. It is perturbing to find similar statistics reporting different coefficients for the same data. This occurs because of a statistic's particular sensitivity or the way it was devised.

Technically, we would like to find two characteristics with nominal measures:

- When there is no relationship at all, the coefficient should be 0.
- When there is a complete dependency, the coefficient should display unity, or 1.

This does not always happen. In addition to being aware of the sensitivity problem, analysts should be alert to the need for careful selection of tests.

Chi-Square-Based Measures

Exhibit 15-20 reports a 2 × 2 table showing the test of an advertising campaign involving 66 people. The variables are success of the campaign and whether direct mail was used. In this example, the observed significance level is less than the testing level ($\alpha = .05$), and the null hypothesis is rejected. A correction to chi-square is provided. We now turn to measures of association to detect the strength of the relationship. Notice that the exhibit also provides an approximate significance of the coefficient based on the chi-square distribution. This is a test of the null hypothesis that no relationship exists between the variables of direct mail and campaign success.

The first **chi-square-based measure** is applied to direct mail and campaign success. It is called **phi (Φ)**. Phi ranges from 0 to +1.0 and attempts to correct χ^2 proportionately to N. Phi is best employed with 2 × 2 tables like Exhibit 15-20 because its coefficient can exceed +1.0 when applied to larger tables. Phi is calculated

$$\emptyset = \sqrt{\frac{\chi^2}{N}} = \sqrt{\frac{6.16257}{66}} = .30557$$

>**Exhibit 15-20** Chi-Square-Based Measures of Association

		Marketing Campaign Success		
	Count	Yes	No	Row Total
Direct Mail	Yes	21	10	31
	No	13	22	35
	Column Total	34	32	66

Chi-Square	Value	d.f.	Significance
Pearson	6.16257	1	.01305
Continuity correction	4.99836	1	.02537

Minimal expected frequency 15.030

Statistic	Value	Approximate Significance
Phi	.30557	.01305[*]
Cramer's V	.30557	.01305[*]
Contingency coefficient C	.29223	.01305[*]

[*]Pearson chi-square probability.

Phi's coefficient shows a moderate relationship between marketing campaign success and direct mail. There is no suggestion in this interpretation that one variable causes the other, nor is there an indication of the direction of the relationship.

Cramer's V is a modification of phi for larger tables and has a range up to 1.0 for tables of any shape. It is calculated like this:

$$V = \sqrt{\frac{\chi^2}{N(k-1)}} = \sqrt{\frac{6.16257}{66(1)}} = .30557$$

where k = the lesser number of rows or columns. In Exhibit 15-20, the coefficient is the same as phi.

The **contingency coefficient C** is reported last. It is not comparable to other measures and has a different upper limit for various table sizes. The upper limits are determined as

$$\sqrt{\frac{k-1}{k}}$$

where k = the number of columns. For a 2 × 2 table, the upper limit is .71; for a 3 × 3, .82; and for a 4 × 4, .87. Although this statistic operates well with tables having the same number of rows as columns, its upper-limit restriction is not consistent with a criterion of good association measurement. C is calculated as

$$C = \sqrt{\frac{\chi^2}{\chi^2 + N}} = \sqrt{\frac{6.16257}{6.16257 + 66}} = .29223$$

The chief advantage of C is its ability to accommodate data in almost every form: skewed or normal, discrete or continuous, and nominal or ordinal.

Proportional Reduction in Error

Proportional reduction in error (PRE) statistics are the second type used with contingency tables. Lambda and tau are the examples discussed here. The coefficient **lambda (λ)** is based on how well the frequencies of one nominal variable offer predictive evidence about the frequencies of another. Lambda is asymmetrical—allowing calculation for the direction of prediction—and symmetrical, predicting row and column variables equally.

The computation of lambda is straightforward. In Exhibit 15-21, we have results from an opinion survey with a sample of 400 shareholders in publicly traded firms. Of the 400 shareholders, 180 (45 percent) favor capping executives' salaries; 220 (55 percent) do not favor doing so. With this information alone, if asked to predict the opinions of an individual in the sample, we would achieve the best prediction record by always choosing the modal category. Here it is "do not favor." By doing so, however, we would be wrong 180 out of 400 times. The probability estimate for an incorrect classification is .45, $P(1) = (1 - .55)$.

Now suppose we have prior information about the respondents' occupational status and are asked to predict opinion. Would it improve predictive ability? Yes, we would make the predictions by summing the probabilities of all cells that are not the modal value for their rows [e.g., cell (1, 2) is 20/400, or .05]:

$$P(2) = \text{cell }(1, 2)\,.05 + \text{cell }(2, 1)\,.15 + \text{cell }(3, 1)\,.075 = .275$$

Lambda is then calculated:

$$\lambda = \frac{P(1) - P(2)}{P(1)} = \frac{.45 - .275}{.45} = .3889$$

Note that the asymmetric lambda in Exhibit 15-21, where opinion is the dependent variable, reflects this computation. As a result of knowing the respondents' occupational classification, we improve our

>**Exhibit 15-21** Proportional Reduction of Error Measures

What is your opinion about capping executives' salaries?

	Cell designation Count Row Pct.	Favor	Do Not Favor	Row Total
	Managerial	1,1 90 82.0	1,2 20 18.0	110
Occupational Class	White collar	2,1 60 43.0	2,2 80 57.0	140
	Blue collar	3,1 30 20.0	3,2 120 80.0	150
	Column Total	180 45.0%	220 55.0%	400 100.0%

Chi-Square	Value	d.f.	Significance
Pearson	98.38646	2	.00000
Likelihood ratio	104.96542	2	.00000

Minimum expected frequency 49.500

Statistic	Value	ASEI	T Value	Approximate Significance
Lambda:				
Symmetric	.30233	.03955	6.77902	
With occupation dependent	.24000	.03820	5.69495	
With opinion dependent	.38889	.04555	7.08010	
Goodman & Kruskal tau:				
With occupation dependent	.11669	.02076		.00000[*]
With opinion dependent	.24597	.03979		.00000[*]

[*]Based on chi-square approximation.

prediction by 39 percent. If we wish to predict occupational classification from opinion instead of the opposite, a λ of .24 would be secured. This means that 24 percent of the error in predicting occupational class is eliminated by knowledge of opinion on the executives' salary question. Lambda varies between 0 and 1, corresponding with no ability to eliminate errors to elimination of all errors of prediction.

Goodman and Kruskal's **tau (τ)** uses table marginals to reduce prediction errors. In predicting opinion on executives' salaries without any knowledge of occupational class, we would expect a 50.5 percent correct classification and a 49.5 percent probability of error. These are based on the column marginal percentages in Exhibit 15-21.

Column Marginal		Column Percent		Correct Cases
180	*	45	=	81
220	*	55	=	121
Total correct classification				202

Correct classification of the opinion variable = .505 = $\frac{202}{400}$

Probability of error, $P(1) = (1 - .505) = .495$

When additional knowledge of occupational class is used, information for correct classification of the opinion variable is improved to 62.7 percent with a 37.3 percent probability of error. This is obtained by using the cell counts and marginals for occupational class (refer to Exhibit 15-21), as shown below:

Row 1	$\left(\frac{90}{110}\right) 90 + \left(\frac{20}{110}\right) 20$	$=$	$73.6364 + 3.6364$	$=$ 77.2727
Row 2	$\left(\frac{60}{140}\right) 60 + \left(\frac{80}{140}\right) 80$	$=$	$25.7143 + 45.7142$	$=$ 71.4286
Row 3	$\left(\frac{30}{150}\right) 30 + \left(\frac{120}{150}\right) 120$	$=$	$6.0 + 96.0$	102.0000

Total correct classification (with additional information on occupational class) 250.7013

Correct classification of the opinion variable $= .627 = \dfrac{250.7}{400}$

Probability of error, $P(2) = (1 - .627) = .373$

Tau is then computed like this:

$$\tau = \frac{P(1) - P(2)}{P(1)} = \frac{.495 - .373}{.495} = .24597$$

Exhibit 15-21 shows that the information about occupational class has reduced error in predicting opinion to approximately 25 percent. The table also contains information on the test of the null hypothesis that tau = 0 with an approximate observed significance level and asymptotic error (for developing confidence intervals). Based on the small observed significance level, we would conclude that tau is significantly different from a coefficient of 0 and that there is an association between opinion on executives' salaries and occupational class in the population from which the sample was selected. We can also establish the confidence level for the coefficient at the 95 percent level as approximately .25 ± .04.

Measures for Ordinal Data

When data require **ordinal measures**, there are several statistical alternatives. In this section we will illustrate:

• Gamma.

• Kendall's tau *b* and tau *c*.

• Somers's *d*.

• Spearman's rho.

All but Spearman's rank-order correlation are based on the concept of concordant and discordant pairs. None of these statistics require the assumption of a bivariate normal distribution, yet by incorporating order, most produce a range from −1.0 (a perfect negative relationship) to +1.0 (a perfect positive one). Within this range, a coefficient with a larger magnitude (absolute value of the measure) is interpreted as having a stronger relationship. These characteristics allow the analyst to interpret both the direction and the strength of the relationship.

Exhibit 15-22 presents data for 70 managerial employees of KeyDesign, a large industrial design firm. All 70 employees have been evaluated for coronary risk by the firm's health insurer. The management levels are ranked, as are the fitness assessments by the physicians. If we were to use a nominal measure of association with these data (such as Cramer's *V*), the computed value of the statistic would be positive since order is not present in nominal data. But using ordinal measures of association reveals the actual nature of the relationship. In this example, all coefficients have negative signs; therefore, lower levels of fitness are associated with higher management levels.

The information in the exhibit has been arranged so that the number of concordant and discordant pairs of individual observations may be calculated. When a subject that ranks higher on one variable also

>**Exhibit 15-22** Tabled Ranks for Management and Fitness Levels at KeyDesign

		Management Level			
	Count	Lower	Middle	Upper	
	High	14	4	2	20
Fitness	Moderate	18	6	2	26
	Low	2	6	16	24
		34	16	20	70

Statistic	Value*
Gamma	−.70
Kendall's tau *b*	−.51
Kendall's tau *c*	−.50
Somers's *d*	
Symmetric	−.51
With fitness dependent	−.53
With management-level dependent	−.50

*The *t* value for each coefficient is −5.86451.

ranks higher on the other variable, the pairs of observations are said to be **concordant**. If a higher ranking on one variable is accompanied by a lower ranking on the other variable, the pairs of observations are **discordant**. Let *P* stand for concordant pairs and *Q* stand for discordant. When concordant pairs exceed discordant pairs in a $P - Q$ relationship, the statistic reports a positive association between the variables under study. As discordant pairs increase over concordant pairs, the association becomes negative. A balance indicates no relationship between the variables. Exhibit 15-23 summarizes the procedure for calculating the summary terms needed in all the statistics in this discussion.[15]

Goodman and Kruskal's **gamma (γ)** is a statistic that compares concordant and discordant pairs and then standardizes the outcome by maximizing the value of the denominator. It has a proportional reduction in error (PRE) interpretation that connects nicely with what we already know about PRE nominal measures. Gamma is defined as

$$\gamma = \frac{P - Q}{P + Q} = \frac{172 - 992}{172 + 992} = \frac{-820}{1164} = -.70$$

For the fitness data, we conclude that as management level increases, fitness decreases. This is immediately apparent from the larger number of discordant pairs. A more precise explanation for gamma takes its absolute value (ignoring the sign) and relates it to PRE. Hypothetically, if one was trying to predict whether the pairs were concordant or discordant, one might flip a coin and classify the outcome. A better way is to make the prediction based on the preponderance of concordance or discordance; the absolute value of gamma is the proportional reduction in error when prediction is done the second way. For example, you would get a 50 percent hit ratio using the coin. A PRE of .70 improves your hit ratio to 85 percent ($.50 \times .70$) + (.50) = .85.

With a γ of −.70, 85 percent of the pairs are discordant and 15 percent are concordant.[16] There are almost six times as many discordant pairs as concordant pairs. In situations where the data call for a 2 × 2 table, the appropriate modification of gamma is Yule's Q.[17]

Kendall's **tau *b* (τ_b)** is a refinement of gamma that considers tied pairs. A tied pair occurs when participants have the same value on the *X* variable, on the *Y* variable, or on both. For a given sample size, there are $n(n - 1)/2$ pairs of observations.[18] After concordant pairs and discordant pairs are removed, the remainder

>**Exhibit 15-23** Calculation of Concordant (*P*), Discordant (*Q*), Tied (T_x, T_y), and Total Paired Observations: KeyDesign Example

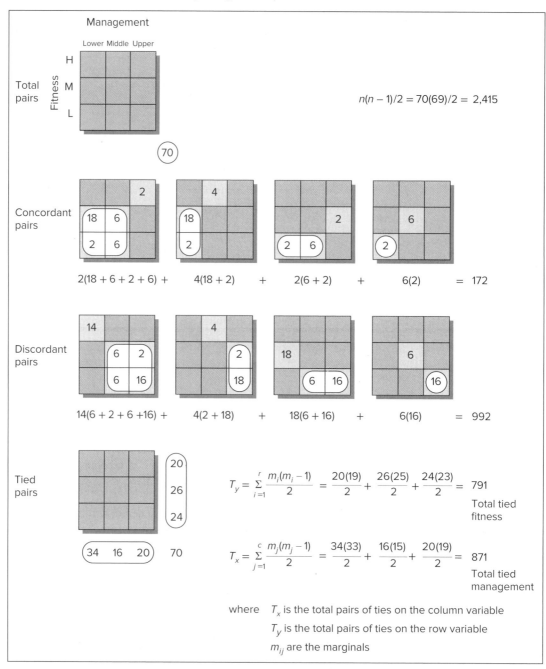

are tied. Tau *b* does not have a PRE interpretation but does provide a range of +1.0 to −1.0 for square tables. Its compensation for ties uses the information found in Exhibit 15-23. It may be calculated as

$$\tau_b = \frac{P - Q}{\sqrt{\left(\frac{n(n-1)}{2} - T_x\right)\left(\frac{n(n-1)}{2} - T_y\right)}}$$

$$= \frac{172 - 992}{\sqrt{(2,415 - 87 -)(2,415 - 791)}} = \boxed{-.51}$$

Kendall's **tau** *c* (τ_c) is another adjustment to the basic *P* − *Q* relationship of gamma. This approach to ordinal association is suitable for tables of any size. Although we illustrate tau *c*, we would select

>snapshot

Advanced Statistics Increase Satisfaction and Release More Funds through ATMs

The Navy Federal Credit Union (NFCU) is the world's largest credit union, with more than $48 billion in assets, 3.9 million members, 220 branch offices, 461 proprietary ATMs, and more than 8,900 employees worldwide. Its clientele represent all Department of Defense military and civilians and their families. According to Alan Payne, Navy's manager of member research and development, it regularly surveys members' satisfaction with lending, savings and checking, and investments and insurance programs using various products from SPSS PASW statistical, modeling, and text analysis modules. Through a combination of statistical techniques, NFCU discovered that members phoning the call center for account information also wanted to know about enhanced services and were receptive to cross-servicing promotions. Payne added that by discovering voice-of-customer insights on satisfaction levels, NFCU realized 15.3 times return on technological investment over a two-month period, creating almost $1.5 million benefit annually.

Boeing Employees' Credit Union (BECU) is another proactive organization using sophisticated analytics. As a top financial cooperative in the United States with more than 744,000 members, two full-service centers, and more than 40 locations, Boeing recently launched an ambitious company-wide research project to improve customer satisfaction. The project focused on whether to allow larger ATM withdrawals and more provisional credit for checks deposited. BECU hypothesized that allowing members to access cash more conveniently would improve retention and generate revenue. Additional objectives were to optimize response rates in direct marketing campaigns, lower per-unit acquisition costs, and identify new branch locations.

Calvin Bierley, market research analyst, in talking about its use of SPSS said, "A risk score model was embedded in the daily transactions processing system to automatically determine how much cash each member can withdraw from an ATM or receive when making deposits." Then through other modeling statistical techniques, BECU identified receptive customers for marketing

©Onoky/SuperStock

campaigns (achieving a 20 to 30 percent response rate on direct mail), saved $1 million annually in staffing by automating provisional credit decisions, increased revenue by $600,000 from new member acquisition and retention, and successfully identified new branch locations.

www.becu.org; www.navyfcu.org; www.spss.com

---

tau b since the cross-classification table for the fitness data is square. The adjustment for table shape is seen in the formula

$$\tau_c = \frac{2m(P-Q)}{N^2(m-1)} = \frac{2(3)(172-992)}{(70)^2(3-1)} = -.50$$

where m is the smaller number of rows or columns.

Somers's d rounds out our coverage of statistics employing the concept of concordant-discordant pairs. This statistic's utility comes from its ability to compensate for tied ranks and adjust for the direction of the dependent variable. Again, we refer to the preliminary calculations provided in Exhibit 15-23 to compute the symmetric and asymmetric d's. As before, the symmetric coefficient (equation 1) takes the row and column variables into account equally. The second and third calculations show fitness as the dependent and management level as the dependent, respectively.

$$d_{sym} = \frac{(P-Q)}{n(n-1)-T_xT_y/2} = \frac{-820}{1,584} = -.51 \tag{1}$$

$$d_{y-x} = \frac{(P-Q)}{\dfrac{n(n-1)}{2}-T_x} = \frac{-820}{2,415-871} = -.53 \tag{2}$$

$$d_{x-y} = \frac{(P-Q)}{\dfrac{n(n-1)}{2}-T_y} = \frac{-820}{2,415-791} = -.50 \tag{3}$$

The **Spearman's rho (ρ)** correlation is another ordinal measure. Along with Kendall's tau, it is used frequently with ordinal data. Rho correlates ranks between two ordered variables. Occasionally, researchers find continuous variables with too many abnormalities to correct. Then scores may be reduced to ranks and calculated with Spearman's rho.

As a special form of Pearson's product moment correlation, rho's strengths outweigh its weaknesses. First, when data are transformed by logs or squaring, rho remains unaffected. Second, outliers or extreme scores that were troublesome before ranking no longer pose a threat since the largest number in the distribution is equal to the sample size. Third, it is an easy statistic to compute. The major deficiency is its sensitivity to tied ranks. Ties distort the coefficient's size. However, there are rarely too many ties to justify the correction formulas available.

To illustrate the use of rho, consider a situation where KDL, a media firm, is recruiting account executive trainees. Assume the field has been narrowed to 10 applicants for final evaluation. They arrive at the company headquarters, go through a battery of tests, and are interviewed by a panel of three executives. The test results are evaluated by an industrial psychologist who then ranks the 10 candidates. The executives produce a composite ranking based on the interviews. Your task is to decide how well these two sets of ranking agree. Exhibit 15-24 contains the data and preliminary calculations. Substituting into the equation, we get

$$r_s = 1 - \frac{6\sum d^2}{n^3-n} = \frac{6(57)}{(10)^3-10} = .654$$

where n is the number of subjects being ranked.

>**Exhibit 15-24** KDL Data for Spearman's Rho

Applicant	Rank by		d	d²
	Panel x	Psychologist y		
1	3.5	6.0	−2.5	6.25
2	10.0	5.0	5.0	25.00
3	6.5	8.0	−1.5	2.25
4	2.0	1.5	0.5	0.25
5	1.0	3.0	−2.0	4.00
6	9.0	7.0	2.0	4.00
7	3.5	1.5	2.0	4.00
8	6.5	9.0	−2.5	6.25
9	8.0	10.0	−2.0	4.00
10	5.0	4.0	1.0	1.00
				57.00

Note: Tied ranks were assigned the average (of ranks) as if no ties had occurred.

The relationship between the panel's and the psychologist's rankings is moderately high, suggesting agreement between the two measures. The test of the null hypothesis that there is no relationship between the measures ($r_s = 0$) is rejected at the .05 level with $n - 2$ degrees of freedom.

$$t = r_s \sqrt{\frac{n-2}{1-r_s^2}} = \sqrt{\frac{8}{1-.4277}} = 2.45$$

>summary

LO15-1 Management questions frequently involve relationships between two or more variables. Correlation analysis may be applied to study such relationships. A correct correlational hypothesis states that the variables occur together in some specified manner without implying that one causes the other.

LO15-2 Parametric correlation requires two continuous variables measured on an interval or ratio scale. The product moment correlation coefficient represents an index of the magnitude of the relationship: Its sign governs the direction, and its square explains the common variance. Bivariate correlation treats X and Y variables symmetrically and is intended for use with variables that are linearly related.

Scatterplots allow the researcher to visually inspect relationship data for appropriateness of the selected statistic. The direction, magnitude, and shape of a relationship are conveyed in a plot. The shape of linear relationships is characterized by a straight line, whereas nonlinear relationships are curvilinear or parabolic or have other curvature. The assumptions of linearity and bivariate normal distribution may be checked through plots and diagnostic tests.

A correlation coefficient of any magnitude or sign, regardless of statistical significance, does not imply causation. Similarly, a coefficient is not remarkable simply because it is statistically significant. Practical significance should be considered in interpreting and reporting findings.

LO15-3 Regression analysis is used to further our insight into the relationship of Y with X. When we take the observed values of X to estimate or predict corresponding Y values, the process is called simple prediction. When more than one X variable is used, the outcome is a function of multiple predictors. Simple and multiple predictions are made with regression analysis.

A straight line is fundamentally the best way to model the relationship between two continuous variables. The method of least squares allows us to find a regression line, or line of best fit that minimizes errors in drawing the line. It uses the criterion of minimizing the total squared errors of estimate. Point predictions made from well-fitted data are subject to error. Prediction and confidence bands may be used to find a range of probable values for Y based on the chosen predictor. The bands are shaped in such a way that predictors farther from the mean have larger bandwidths.

LO15-4 We test regression models for linearity and to discover whether the equation is effective in fitting the data. An important test in bivariate linear regression is whether the slope is equal to zero (i.e., whether the predictor variable X is a significant influence on the criterion variable Y). In bivariate regression, t-tests and F tests of the regression produce the same result since t^2 is equal to F.

LO15-5 Often the assumptions or the required measurement level for parametric techniques cannot be met. Nonparametric measures of association offer alternatives. Nominal measures of association are used to assess the strength of relationships in cross-classification tables. They are often used in conjunction with chi-square or may be based on the proportional reduction in error (PRE) approach.

Phi ranges from 0 to +1.0 and attempts to correct chi-square proportionately to N. Phi is best employed with 2 × 2 tables. Cramer's V is a modification of phi for larger tables and has a range up to 1.0 for tables of any configuration. Lambda, a PRE statistic, is based on how well the frequencies of one nominal variable offer predictive evidence about the frequencies of another. Goodman and Kruskal's tau uses table marginals to reduce prediction errors.

Measures for ordinal data include gamma, Kendall's tau b and tau c, Somers's d, and Spearman's rho. All but Spearman's rank-order correlation are based on the concept of concordant and discordant pairs. None of these statistics require the assumption of a bivariate normal distribution, yet by incorporating order, most produce a range from −1 to +1.

>**key**terms

>**discussion**questions

Terms in Review

1 Distinguish between the following:

   a Regression coefficient and correlation coefficient.

   b $r = 0$ and $\rho = 0$.

   c The test of the true slope, the test of the intercept, and $r^2 = 0$.

   d r^2 and r.

   e A slope of 0.

   f F and t^2.

2 Describe the relationship between the two variables in the four plots.

(a)

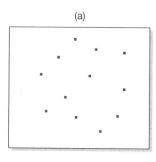

(b)

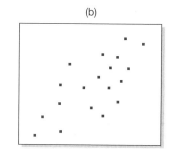

(c)

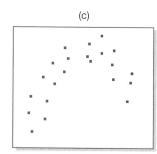

(d)

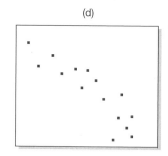

Making Research Decisions

3 A polling organization collected data on a sample of 60 registered voters regarding a tax on the market value of equity transactions as one remedy for the budget deficit.

Opinion about Market Tax	Education		
	High School	College Grad.	MBA
Favorable	15	5	0
Undecided	10	8	2
Unfavorable	0	2	18

a Compute gamma for the table data.

b Compute tau *b* or tau *c* for the same data.

c What accounts for the differences?

d Decide which is more suitable for these data.

4 Using the table data in question 3, compute Somers's *d* symmetric and then use opinion as the dependent variable. Decide which approach is best for reporting the decision.

5 A research team conducted a study of soft-drink preferences among residents in a test market prior to an advertising campaign for a new cola product. Of the participants, 130 are teenagers and 130 are adults. The researchers secured the following results:

	Cola	Noncola
Teenagers	50	80
Adults	90	40

a Calculate an appropriate measure of association, and decide how to present the results. How might this information affect the advertising strategy?

From Concept to Practice

6 Using the following data,

X	Y
3	6
6	10
9	15
12	24
15	21
18	20

a Create a scatterplot.

b Find the least-squares line.

c Plot the line on the diagram.

d Predict: *Y* if *X* is 10.
  Y if *X* is 17.

7 A home pregnancy test claims to be 97 percent accurate when consumers obtain a positive result. To what extent are the variables of "actual clinical condition" and "test readings" related?

a Compute phi, Cramer's *V*, and the contingency coefficient for the following table. What can you say about the strength of the relationship between the two variables?

b Compute lambda for these data. What does this statistic tell you?

Actual Clinical Condition Test Readings of In-Vitro Diagnostic Cross-Tabulation

Count Actual Clinical Condition	Test Readings of In-Vitro Diagnostic		Total
	Positive	Negative	
Pregnant	451 accurate	36 inaccurate	487
Not pregnant	15 inaccurate	183 accurate	198
Total	466	219	685

8 Fill in the missing blocks for the ANOVA summary table on net profits and market value used with regression analysis.

ANOVA Summary Table

	d.f.	Sum of Squares	Mean Square	F
Regression	1	11,116,995.47		
Error			116,104.63	
Total	9	12,045,832.50		

a What does the *F* tell you? (alpha = .05)

b What is the *t* value? Explain its meaning.

Forbes 500 Random Subsample ($, millions)

Assets	Sales	Market Value	Net Profit	Cash Flow	Number of Employees (thousands)
1,034.00	1,510.00	697.00	82.60	126.50	16.60
956.00	785.00	1,271.00	89.00	191.20	5.00
1,890.00	2,533.00	1,783.00	176.00	267.00	44.00
1,133.00	532.00	752.00	82.30	137.10	2.10
11,682.00	3,790.00	4,149.00	413.50	806.80	11.90
6,080.00	635.00	291.00	18.10	35.20	3.70
31,044.00	3,296.00	2,705.00	337.30	425.50	20.10
5,878.00	3,204.00	2,100.00	145.80	380.00	10.80
1,721.00	981.00	1,573.00	172.60	326.60	1.90
2,135.00	2,268.00	2,634.00	247.20	355.50	21.20

9 Secure Spearman rank-order correlations for the largest Pearson coefficient in the matrix from question 8. Explain the differences between the two findings.

10 Using the preceding matrix data (*Forbes* 500), select a pair of variables and run a simple regression. Then investigate the appropriateness of the model for the data using diagnostic tools for evaluating assumptions.

11 For the following data,

X	Y
25	5
19	7
17	12
14	23
12	20
9	25
8	26
7	28
3	20

a Calculate the correlation between *X* and *Y*.

b Interpret the sign of the correlation.

c Interpret the square of the correlation.

d Plot the least-squares line.

e Test for a linear relationship:

(1) $\beta_1 = 0$.

(2) $r = 0$.

(3) An *F* test.

From the Headlines

12 "There is an 'unhealthy correlation' between the building of skyscrapers and subsequent financial crashes," according to Barclays Capital. Examples include the world's first skyscraper, the Equitable Life building in New York (completed in 1873 and coincided with a five-year recession), the Empire State building (the Great Depression was under way), Chicago's Willis Tower—formerly known as the Sears Tower—in 1974 (during an oil shock and when the U.S. dollar's reliance on gold was abandoned), and Malaysia's Petronas Towers in 1997 (corresponding to the Asian financial crisis). Currently, the world's tallest skyscraper is the Burj Khalifa (built just before Dubai's financial troubles). China is the biggest builder of skyscrapers, with 53 percent of all the tall buildings in the world. JPMorgan Chase said that the Chinese property market could drop by as much as 20 percent in value in the country's major cities within the next 12 to 18 months. "Often the world's tallest buildings are . . . [a reflection of] a widespread misallocation of capital and an impending economic correction," Barclays Capital analysts said.

Examine the correlational finding and provide plausible alternatives for their findings.

>cases*

Mastering Teacher Leadership	NCRCC: Teeing Up and New Strategic Direction

*You will find a description of each case in the Case Abstracts section of this textbook. Check the Case Index to determine whether a case provides data, the research instrument, video, or other supplementary material. Cases and case supplements are available in Connect.

>part VI

Chapter 16 **Stage 5: Research Reports: Supported Insights and Recommendations**

Stage 5: Report the Research

>**chapter 16**

Stage 5: Research Reports: Supported Insights and Recommendations

"If you're navigating a dense information jungle, coming across a beautiful graphic or lovely data visualization is a relief. It's like coming across a clearing in the jungle."

David McCandless,
British data journalist,
information designer, and author

>**learning**objectives

After reading this chapter, you should understand . . .

LO16-1 How changes in business and technology are changing research reporting.

LO16-2 How to plan an audience-centric report using audience analysis.

LO16-3 Different report structures and why each is used.

LO16-4 The types and specifications of various types of reports.

LO16-5 The organizational frameworks for reports.

LO16-6 Visualization and how to effectively use different support materials.

LO16-7 The role of compilation, practice, and delivery in achieving audience effect.

LO16-8 The ethical considerations in reporting research results.

>Introduction

In this chapter, the research report refers to both oral and written components; when we want to single out one component or the other, we will do so. Exhibit 16-1 introduces the reporting process and indicates its fit within the research process model.

We've seen three major changes or shifts in emphasis in research reporting in the last few years. The first change is the emphasis on reporting insights rather than only data or information. The second change is the structure of the reporting. The third is the increasing dominance of audience-centric planning rather than the traditional data-centric planning.[1]

>**Exhibit 16-1** Reports and the Research Process

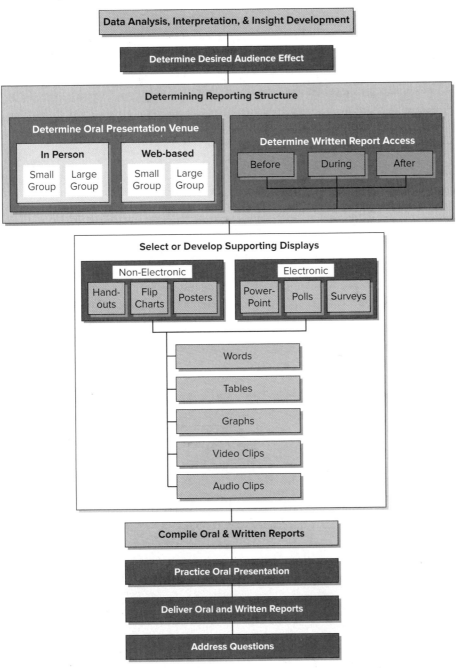

Emphasis on Insights

Business research starts with a management dilemma that the researcher hopes to help solve. To achieve this goal, researchers make choices: to report data, information, insights, recommendations or some combination. To understand this shift in reporting, from data and information to insights, you need to understand the distinctions. Researchers collect **data**—raw, unprocessed facts in the form of numbers, text, pictures, or video collected by either quantitative or qualitative means. Researchers process data into **information** by aggregating and organizing data; applying rules of measurement, statistical summary and testing; and developing data visualizations. Delivering information might once have been enough, but in an ocean of data and information, managers need to find islands of value—they need insights.

Researchers generate **insights** by *analyzing* information. As a conclusion, an insight may be a deduction or in induction. An insight uses the researcher's understanding of the initial management dilemma and all the data developed during the project—both secondary and primary—to interpret the primary data collected during the project. While an insight might come from the results of a single data variable, it is far more likely to be the result of understanding the interaction of several variables. Exhibit 16-2 shows the relationship of data to insights. **Actionable insights**—those that lead to recommendations for specific decisions—have the most value and share the following:[2]

- Aligned with key business goals and strategic initiatives.
- Novel, unusual, or unexpected rather than familiar.
- Clearly communicated, including why the insight is important and how it helps the decision maker.
- Routed to the right decision makers.

To report insights, researchers must combine their knowledge of business with their intimate knowledge of the research sponsor's organization gained while conducting the research. This background knowledge allows the researcher to correctly interpret the data in light of the research question(s) and the foundational management problem or opportunity. When we refer to intimate knowledge of the research sponsor, we allude to such things as the knowledge of the sponsor's level of employee engagement, employees' skills and the company's training capabilities, as well as its organizational culture; a company's products, services, positioning and brand identity, as well as its communication processes; an understanding of its physical plant and technology; and its financial structure and the capabilities of its management.

>**Exhibit 16-2** Relationship of Data to Insights

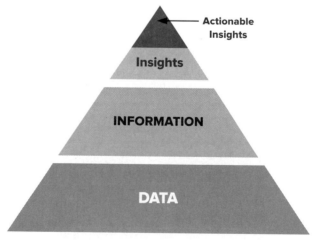

By Brent Dykes, Director of Data Strategy at Domo

In reporting, it is the job of the researcher to (1) make sure the audience understands how any insight was reached and (2) be sure to provide the correct and sufficient support so that the audience can understand its value and embrace the insight. If the report audience cannot embrace the researcher's insights, they will not be able to embrace any recommendations that flow from those insights.

Shift in Reporting Structure

When a research report shifts to insights, the tone of the research report becomes persuasive rather than merely descriptive. In past decades, how the research findings were to be reported might be determined during the proposal stage. It was assumed that the emphasis would be on a detailed, written report of findings and that an oral presentation was secondary, often included only when the budget allowed. These assumptions are no longer valid. The development of sophisticated, technology-based communication tools now allows researchers and managers to meet often while being hundreds, if not thousands, of miles apart. Analysis tools also allow easier querying of the data file to address spontaneous questions and what-if scenarios in real time. As a result, oral presentations, which were once perceived as a luxury in research projects due to extensive travel costs, now are often the first consideration when designing the research report. This has shifted the role of the written component of the report to that of support and substantiation of the oral component.

>**snap**shot

Hitting the Wall Is a Good Thing

What if you could get your audience to not only embrace your findings, but also have a higher retention of the detail that supports your recommendations? What if you could get your audience to embrace your recommendations and arrive at the same conclusions you did while they process your data internally? You can do all that and more with The Wall, a technology that enhances audience engagement, synthesizes data and findings, and allows for storytelling—all within the reporting process.

The Wall is a touch-screen technology that is far more fluid and flexible than PowerPoint for research reporting. While it offers as much structure as you might need, it doesn't tie you to a predetermined linear progression of ideas. Think of a 75-square-foot screen (5 by 15 ft) that is dynamic, multiwindow, and interactive. It allows for free-form or structured display of study stimuli and serves as a central repository for all study information, insights, and recommendations. All your data visualizations can be projected on that screen, along with access to data sets and captured video—for example, from focus groups—at one time. And as you tell your research story, you touch and expand whatever visualization you need to make your point. As Rob Ramirez, executive vice president of strategic development for Schlesinger Associates, reveals, "It's made synthesis and storytelling more powerful."

Ramirez, whose background is in pharma marketing research, shared that Eli Lilly was one early proponent of creating The Wall. Prysm, an Indianapolis-based company that creates visual workspaces, actually manufactures The Wall, which can be found in Schlesinger research facilities in New York, Chicago, and Los Angeles. Some companies have their own

video walls, and Schlesinger can stream directly to that company's wall, reducing the need for travel. "What's done on The Wall is saved instantaneously," explained Ramirez, which makes widely sharing a research reporting session much easier. "While we aren't yet at video topline reports," explained Ramirez, "that's the direction we're moving. We just need better video editing tools."

The Wall can also be used on the front end of research planning. For example, in an attempt to get your product into Walmart, you would likely present research to show how well the product would do at the mega-retailer. The Wall could be used during a "learning book" session by an insight provider on behalf of Walmart to synthesize the data. The Wall's capabilities are critical in assisting the retailer to see its knowledge gaps and help plan research that would provide additional insights but avoid duplication. And it's especially valuable for highly engaging focus groups and triads.

The strength of The Wall for research reporting is "its use to drive ideation and those 'Ah Ha' moments," shared Ramirez.

www.schlesingerassociates.com

Sources: "Announcing The Wall," Schlesinger Associates, April 25, 2016, downloaded May 18, 2016 (http://www.schlesingerassociates.com/whats_new/announcing_the _wall.aspx). "Prysm Visual Workplace," Prysm, downloaded May 18, 2016 (http://www .prysym.com). Rob Ramirez, Executive Vice President, Strategic Development for Schlesinger Associates, phone interview, May 18, 2016, and email interview June 3, 2016. "Wall Locations and Specs," Schlesinger Associates, downloaded May 18, 2016 (http://www.schlesingerassociates.com/qualitative_solutions/interactive_wall/wall _locations_spec.aspx).

>**Exhibit 16-3** Audience-Centric Report Planning

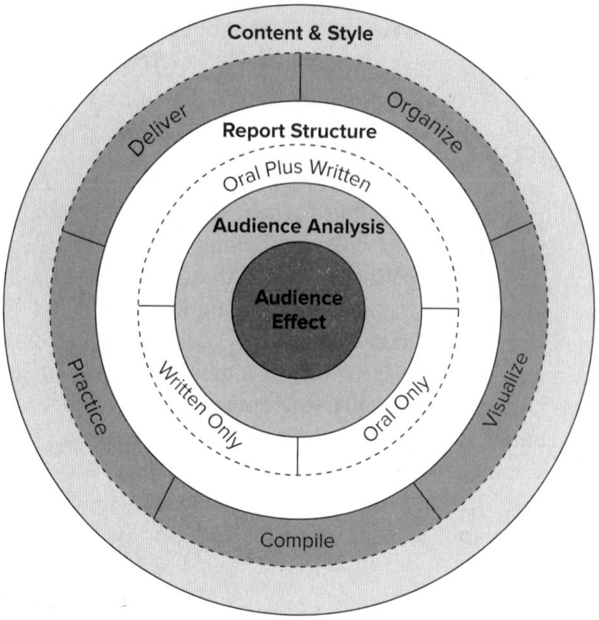

Audience-Centric Planning

Research reports can serve multiple purposes. It is expected that such reports will provide findings, insights, and, increasingly, recommendations for the decision(s) the research sponsor faces. But such presentations might also, for example, be used to raise concerns about previously unknown problems, showcase emerging opportunities, or increase the knowledge of audience members in any number of ways. At its core, the research report should convince the audience to take action related to the research objective. This requires a shift from **data-centric planning**—a focus on the data or information and sharing as much data/information as was discovered—to **audience-centric planning**—a focus on gaining the audience's embrace of data insights and recommendations. The reports resulting from the two different orientations are very different. With data-centric planning, the report is more factual and statistical; with audience-centric planning, the report is more persuasive and tells a story where statistics are a tool, not the focus.

Several factors comprise the research report's plan: (1) desired audience effect, (2) report structure, and (3) content and style. The research question and its foundational management dilemma, and the findings and insights, influence the **desired audience effect** (what we want them to think, feel, and do as a result of the research report). Usually the research sponsor indicates the report structure (the combination of oral and written elements that comprise the research report). This structure is influenced by the audience composition, its size and location, and the time allocated for any oral component of the report. Report content is most often determined by the level and types of support needed to clarify the researcher's insights and recommendations. As we focus on reporting insights, we also need to adjust the report's level of persuasion, which affects both its content and style. If the time is severely limited, then the researcher may recommend topical priorities for the oral report, adjusting the content in both the oral and written components, accordingly. Exhibit 16-3 summarizes audience-centric report planning and the structure of this chapter.

>Audience Analysis

Good researchers understand that the primary purpose of their report is to gain a *desired audience effect*. Overall, the desired audience effect is that they embrace the findings, insights, and recommendations in the report; without this, the researcher's report is likely to languish without action. The ultimate success of the report depends on the researcher's ability to connect with his or her audience and correctly

>**Exhibit 16-4** Sample Audience Profile

The audience is branch bank managers with between 5 and 15 years of experience; half are women. Most have at least some experience with at least two banks. Most have backgrounds in finance or customer service; none have experience in conducting or analyzing research. They perceive themselves as "number people" but are not schooled in statistical analysis.

They know a research project is in progress, but they have not been consulted or kept informed. There is strong concern among the audience that branches are going to be closed. They don't know the closure decision process but fear that the research is the only factor that will be considered in the decision process. They fear they might lose their jobs.

The desired audience effect is to bring the branch managers into the information loop and put the research findings into a positive perspective. We want to alleviate concerns that closure decisions are imminent, and to encourage them to see the insights and recommendations as a means to strengthen their branch effectiveness among their customers.

anticipate audience response. The remote audience for an oral report (using web services to present and connect) requires more, not less, analysis because the presenter has to work doubly hard to establish and maintain the audience connection. Any good report plan should account for the possibility of an unreceptive or unsupportive audience reaction and adjust accordingly.

An analysis of the expected audience for a research report, an **audience analysis**, can be formal or informal. An informal analysis would rely on conversations with opinion leaders within the audience group or with the project liaison or manager-sponsor. A formal analysis might include interviews; a survey of audience members; and compiling written documentation on each member from LinkedIn sites, company websites, résumés, etc. You should summarize your audience analysis into a profile statement, as shown in Exhibit 16-4. This is used for planning purposes only and is not included in the research sponsor's report.

A researcher conducting an audience analysis collects and evaluates the following:[3]

1. *Audience composition:* Who will receive the report?
2. *Research question knowledge:* What background do they have relating to the research question(s)?
3. *Research predispositions:* What are their predispositions relating to the research topics?
4. *Recommendation effects:* How might audience members be affected by the recommendations resulting from the research?
5. *Audience effect:* What is the desired audience effect?
6. *Supplemental purposes:* What other purposes must the report accomplish?

Audience Composition

Research audiences can be large or small, technically savvy or not, skilled in data analysis or not, managers with a knowledge of the research question or not, or some composite of all of these. So we need to know who will receive the report. Is the audience comprised of managers only or a broad range of employees, outside vendors, board members, etc.? Are the managers at a senior level, at lower levels, or at all levels? Are those affected by the research in the audience or only those making the decisions? Years and types of experience, age, authority level, gender, ethnicity, education, economic status, group membership, and organizational culture all affect the audience's perception of information and receptivity. As the audience members for a research report are usually invited, we know who they are ahead of time.

Research Question Knowledge

The research project manager or liaison is likely your best source of knowledge to answer the second audience question: What background do they have relating to the research question(s)? Only the liaison knows what information from the exploratory stages of the research project was widely shared. If the researcher is internal to the organization, then it is a matter of recalling which audience members have been provided what information. If used, interim or progress reports and their distribution can provide this information.

Research Predispositions

Predispositions are the audience's attitudes and beliefs—formed by their experiences, knowledge, and values—about a report's research topics.

- Audience members engage with the research report with a range of past knowledge of the research topics. They will judge the report based on their *selective perception* (what they know and believe).
- As audience members examine report content they capture those threads of information consistent with accumulated knowledge; their processed meanings will fluctuate between agreement/disagreement and clarity/confusion.
- Each audience member organizes his or her unique understanding of the content of the research report, which is dependent on their experience and openness to change.

To be persuasive a researcher's report must address key audience biases.[4] Most of us search for information that confirms what we already believe, our **confirmation bias**. A report must present irrefutable evidence to make the audience question what they believe. With our **anchoring bias**, we rely on our first impressions. This is where a researcher's credibility has importance; if the audience believes the first insight the researcher shares, the audience is likely to believe all insights she shares. An audience is made up of people who are members of groups. These groups influence audience beliefs due to our **conformity bias**; the desire for harmony makes us suppress or withhold opinions that are outside of *groupthink*. Research seeks change, so its report needs to give the audience permission—even encouragement—to think outside the already accepted. We tend to believe stories that resulted in success rather than failure due to our **survivorship bias**. This should influence our choice of stories, quotes, testimonials, etc. Finally, audiences have a **loss-aversion bias**; when faced with an insight or recommendation expressed positively versus negatively, they are more likely to gravitate toward the positive expression. Research reports can use or counter these biases.

As the researcher develops and delivers the report, he or she must attempt to imaginatively construct how the audience will interpret the message. Knowing the audience's predispositions allows the researcher to predict audience resistance, skepticism, or receptivity. Then the researcher can adjust both content and delivery to achieve the desired audience effect. To assess predispositions, audience members can be sent a pre-report survey if the audience is large, or the researcher can confer with opinion leaders within the audience.

Recommendation Effects

While some information might be revealed as data emerge—especially in the current environment of in-progress data tallying—insights and recommendations are less likely to be revealed prior to crafting a research report. Prior to developing a research recommendation, a researcher must assess the effects of any recommendation. Does the research lead to a recommendation to shift production to a different plant, to expand the market presence of a product, or to change a training or compensation program? Then knowing how such a recommendation might be executed is critical. Any employee, from the CEO down, will have some stake in any recommendation. But knowing who has the largest stake, and whether this audience segment would support or fight implementing the recommendation, is invaluable. Historical response of various audience segments to past change recommendations is the researcher's best answer to the audience question: How might they be affected by the recommendations resulting from the research?

Audience Effect

While earlier we described the audience effect as broadly embracing the research's insights and recommendations, the audience effect might be more narrowly defined for any actual report. If, for example, a report is designed for a segment of a broader audience (e.g., a specific department rather than the whole company), then the audience effect might be narrowed to "acceptance of recommendation A" that is related to that segment. The audience effect is always specific to one or more recommendations or insights.

Supplemental Purposes

Research often reveals information that is unexpected but tangential to the research question(s). Depending on the sponsor, this information may be shared in the report or transmitted separately. So determining early if the research report is to focus solely on those findings, insights, and recommendations related to the research question is critical. Only the research sponsor can make this decision.

>Report Structure

How the audience effect is defined leads to the next decision: **report structure**, the way in which research results are reported. There are three possible report structures: (1) oral only, (2) written only, or (3) oral plus written.

The *oral-only* structure implies that there is no official written report. The advantage of the oral-only report is its ability to disseminate the report quickly. It offers some capability for asking questions of the researcher, which is often critical for clarification. In one sense, this structure is misnamed. Most oral-only reports provide some written material as a handout—delivered in person or via email or download. This is often in the form of a slide deck used during the oral presentation. Some researchers may provide a *topline* report handout—a short, two- to three-page summary of the oral's highlights—or an infographic—a visually designed composite of the key graphical displays and data elements presented in the oral, usually summarized on one page or as a visual image file.

As indicated at the beginning of this chapter, the *written-only* structure for research reports is waning as communication tools have advanced. But the written-only format still has appeal as it allows the audience members to digest a large volume of information at his or her own pace. What it doesn't offer is immediate feedback capability. It also has the danger that once delivered, it may find a resting place on a shelf. With no researcher to advocate for the insights and resulting recommendations, written-only reports can be weak on execution of change.

The *oral-plus-written* structure provides the greatest flexibility given the nature of the research results and the audience. An oral report can accompany a brief management report (written for the nonresearcher, with limited information on methodology); the oral report can precede the delivery of a detailed, long, written report; or the oral report can accompany the delivery of a technical report (written for an audience of researchers). Some research may require both technical and management written reports. This combination report structure offers advocacy of research insights and recommendations, as well as immediate clarification of information and analyses, plus the ability to delve into more detail as it is needed during execution of decisions. People perceive any information delivered in an oral and written report to convey more importance than those items related only in the written report.[5]

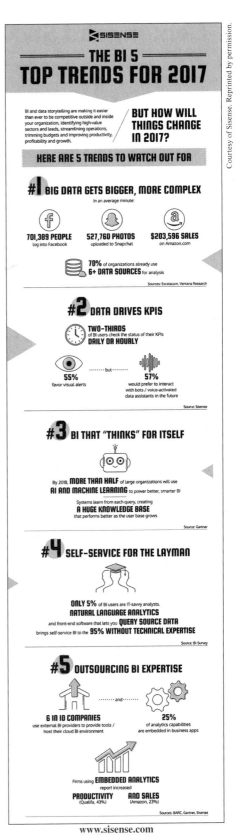

>Content and Style: Organize

Content and style are determined by three planning choices: (1) what information findings, insights, and recommendations should be presented to achieve the audience effect and in what order; (2) how should these be presented; and (3) how, when, and where the report will be delivered. The audience effect, the research conclusions, the report structure, and the level of persuasion needed to achieve the audience effect are all influential. At minimum, this phase of planning must cover organization, visualization, preparation, practice, and delivery.

Oral and written research reports are characterized by their audiences. A **management report**, whether brief (topline) or long, addresses an audience of managers. A **technical report**, whether short or long, addresses an audience of researchers, those knowledgeable in methodology and analysis. An infographic, always a written report and the most visual of the three types, addresses a non-technical audience but may extend beyond managers, to employees, suppliers, customers, etc.

Oral and written research reports contain four critical components (introduction, background, methodology, and findings-insights-recommendations), as well as the possibility for a fifth component, appendices, in some written reports. The presence or absence of each component, and its detail, are determined by the type of report being prepared. Exhibit 16-5 shows the relationship of components to

>**Exhibit 16-5** Research Report Sections by Type of Report

		Written				
			MGT		Technical	
Report Components	Oral	Infographic	Topline	Long	Short	Long
Introduction	1	1	1	1	1	1
Title	✓	✓	✓	✓	✓	✓
Researcher Profile	✓			✓	✓	✓
Executive Summary				✓	✓	✓
Table of Contents				✓		✓
Background	2		2	2	2	2
Problem Statement	✓		✓	✓	✓	✓
Research Objectives	✓		✓	✓	✓	✓
Methodology	3		3, Brief	3	3, Brief	3
Sampling design	✓			✓		✓
Research design	✓			✓		✓
Data collection	✓			✓		✓
Data analysis	✓			✓		✓
Limitations	✓		✓	✓	✓	✓
Findings, Insights & Recommendations	4	2	4	4	4	4
Findings	✓	✓	✓	✓	✓	✓
Insights	✓	✓	✓	✓	✓	✓
Recommendations (optional)	✓		✓	✓	✓	✓
Appendices				5	5	5
Measurement Instruments				✓	✓	✓
Frequencies				✓	✓	✓
Secondary Data Studies						✓
Bibliography						✓

type of report. Within each section, inclusions are based on importance and relevance to resolving the management question and achieving audience effect.

Report Components

Introduction

The introduction prepares the audience for the report, establishes the researcher's credibility, and makes it easy for the audience to navigate the information.[6] It contains the title, the researcher's profile (name, title, company, educational and experiential background) and, in a written report, the executive summary and a table of contents. The title page or slide should include the title of the report, by whom and for whom it was prepared, and the date. A descriptive title is best, and should establish the project's research **scope**—the variables and population studied—by including (1) the variables included in the study, (2) the type of relationship among the variables, and (3) the population to which the results may be applied.[7] Here are three examples of report titles:

Descriptive Study:	Training and Worker Productivity in Branch X
Correlation Study:	The Relationship between Relative National Inflation Rates and Household Purchases of Brand X in International Markets
Causal Study:	The Effect of Various Motivation Methods on Retail Sales Associates' Attitudes and Performance

An **executive summary** can serve two purposes. It may be a report in miniature (sometimes called a *topline report*), covering all the aspects of the project but in abbreviated form. Or it may be a concise summary of only the major information findings, insights, and recommendations, without explanation or persuasion. Two pages are generally sufficient for the second type of executive summary. As a rough guide, any report of several sections that totals more than 10 pages also should have a table of contents. In long written reports, where there are many tables and graphs, each should be listed as a separate entry in the table of contents.

Background

All research reports must contain some background and methodology information, as your audience's knowledge with respect to the project will vary. The purpose of this information is to provide the audience with (1) knowledge critical to interpreting the research findings, (2) establish credibility for the researcher, and (3) establish validity of the findings. The detail of this section in an oral report is determined by the degree to which audience members were involved in research project decisions; the more involved, the less detail. In the written report, this section summarizes the background at various levels of detail depending on the project. Critical background knowledge will likely include the management question, the research objectives, and any information discovered during exploration that was used to develop the measurement instrument or interpret the data.[8]

Methodology

The researcher should summarize the sample design, including a sample profile, as well as the margin of error and level of confidence with which the data were interpreted. The report should also describe the research design, specifically including how data were collected and the rationale for using multiple methods to collect the data; the more complex the design, the more information in this section. The researcher also describes the data analysis; the more technical the audience and the longer the written report, the more detailed the information. The oral report rarely provides much detail on data analysis, except as necessary to understand the findings. Every report should discuss the project's **limitations**—a thoughtful presentation of any significant methodology problems. The researcher increases his credibility when he discusses problems and how these were handled, as well as increasing the audience's ability to judge the study's validity.

Findings, Insights, and Recommendations

This is the largest section of any research report, and the purpose for which your audience gives you their attention. Findings need not include everything you collected and must never include every table or graph you developed and analyzed during examination and data analysis. The primary criterion for inclusions is, "Is the information critical to the audience's understanding of any hypothesis, the insights, and recommendation(s)?" The more selective the researcher is, the more the audience perceives as important each piece of information presented.

In your report, to determine the order of findings and insights, you should start with a plot of all the recommendations you want to make and the insights and data needed to support each. You might create a storyboard of the information with sticky notes, much like a TV commercial is crafted. A decision tree is another tool to map out your plan, as shown in Exhibit 16-6. For the oral report, you have to keep in mind the time allotted and your audience's limited ability to process large amounts of information at one time; some recommendations (as well as their supporting data and insights) will find a place only in the written report.

Once you have all the recommendations—and their support—plotted, you need to arrange their order. There is considerable research to support that an argument's sequence influences short-term and long-term recall, as well as recall accuracy.[9] Whether or not an oral report is included in the report structure, consider each of the following to determine the order of what should be reported:

- *Primacy:* People assign superior importance to what the researcher delivers *first* in a report (primacy effect); it's more influential in building understanding, motivating action.

- *Early:* People remember the first few items a researcher delivers better than those embedded midway in a report.

>**Exhibit 16-6** Research Report Decision Tree

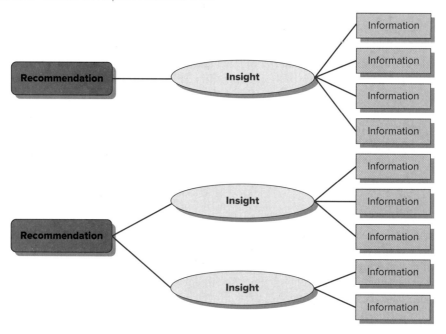

- *Recency:* People remember best what they hear/see *last* in a report (recency effect); information presented last is influential in building understanding and motivating action.

- *Perceptible difference:* People need large differences to discriminate between items and they perceive items with large differences as more important.

Besides perceived importance, two types of relevance influence order: (1) relevance to resolving the management question and (2) relevance to understanding an insight or recommendation. Your audience naturally groups information as you report in order to process the large amount of information, so it's wise to provide them a structure that supports accepting your insights and recommendations.

Increasingly, researchers are expected to offer recommendations. In applied research, these recommendations will usually be for managerial action, with the researcher suggesting one or more alternatives that are supported by the information and insights. Also, researchers may recommend further research initiatives. Recommendations may also be recapped as an additional page concluding the executive summary in a written report or as a separate slide in an oral report. Some researchers use this recommendation slide during a question-and-answer session.

Appendices

Appendices are used in written, not oral, reports and provide a place for complex tables; statistical tests; supporting documents [e.g., research request for proposal (RFP) and research contract]; copies of interview forms, observation checklists, and measurement instruments; instructions to data collectors; and other evidence important for later reference. A technical audience, who wishes to learn about the statistical aspects of the study, will want a complete appendix of statistical tests. If a report used secondary data, one important document in the appendix is the bibliography. A bibliography documents any sources used as background in the study and for preparing the report.

Traditional Frameworks for Organization

A **report framework** is an organizational mechanism that influences not only content order, but also type of support materials. There are several standard organization frameworks that work for research reports. We've summarized several below. Some research companies use a framework template that can be modified for specific reports. But if multiple presentations are made to the same audience of managers using such a template, the report may fail to hold attention and communicate persuasively. Successful researchers pick the framework that best fits a specific project. If a specific framework isn't right for the findings, insights, and recommendations of a particular project, they don't choose it. Thus, an attitude of openness in choosing the framework produces a fresh approach to planning your report.[10]

- *Research brief:* One of the most commonly used structures; starts with an explanation of the genesis of the project, the purpose of the project, and its methodology. This is followed by a discussion of the insights gained, as well as the findings that support these insights. Increasingly, recommendations conclude the report.

- *Topical:* There are several findings and insights to report, but one topic naturally seems to precede the others in order. In a research report of survey research, for example, the presenter could organize according to target question topics of the measurement instrument.

- *Narrative:* Involves the use of stories as the primary vehicle for communicating the research insights and recommendations; these stories are ordered based on impact on the audience. Wrapping research insights with audio and/or video clips and survey verbatim comments enable insights to come alive. This structure can result in more favorable attitudes toward the report and the researcher and contribute to long-term recall,[11] all elements that could result in more action.

- *Classification:* Puts recommendations, and their insights and findings, into categories. In a report about what potential customers revealed in testing prototype iPads, the order of the report could be arranged by iPad features.

- *Motivated sequence:* Follows the way people habitually arrive at a decision despite individual differences. It consists of multiple steps: establish the need for change, provide data to support change, picture the benefits of change, and detail recommendations. In research reports designed to be persuasive rather than merely informative, this organizational framework is powerful because it has as its goal stimulating overt action.

- *Problem/solution:* The first part of the report describes a problem, the middle presents research findings and insights, and the last section presents a recommendation. In research presentations, you start with the management problem, proceed to the research problem and methodology, and conclude with the findings, insights, and recommendations.

- *Climax order:* Material is organized from the least important information to the most important. In a research report, elements are ordered to lead from the foundation findings to the key insights to the recommended action(s).

- *Chronological:* Uses time sequence of the research for a framework. In a research presentation on plant safety issues, the order would be determined by when each research activity (focus group, survey, experiment) occurred.

- *Past/present/future:* The first section discusses the past, the second the covers the present, and the third predicts the future. In a research presentation using predictive modeling of inventory patterns, the organization starts with the data patterns of the past, then the present, then models the future.

- *Cause/effect/solution:* The first part describes the cause of a problem, the second describes its effect, and the third presents a solution. In a research presentation about the effectiveness of Toyota's solution for accelerator pedal malfunction, the presentation starts with the discovery of the engineering defect; describes the effect on sales, brand image, and customer loyalty; then presents information on what the research discovered about solutions which might resonate with the auto-buying public.

- *Pros/cons/recommendations:* Organized around benefits, disadvantages, and how benefits are superior. In a research presentation, what the researcher discovered about benefits of e-books, their perceived disadvantages, and what Amazon might do to enhance the advantage of the Kindle DX would be presented.

- *Spatial:* Material is organized by physical space. In a research report about skiing accidents in Colorado resorts, the presentation might be arranged by each specific ski area within Colorado.

>Content and Style: Visualize

A researcher developing a quality research report must tell a story grounded in the data. This requires the ability to **visualize**—the process of developing a report's textual, tabular, graphical, and video/audio support materials that help the audience share in the researcher's understanding of the data. Given that many research reports now emphasize or include an oral report, thinking about visualization from the orientation of the oral presentation is a good place to start. For many, thinking about what will fit on a presentation screen influences the design of support materials. But PowerPoint experts encourage developing your support materials away from the computer first.[12]

Supporting materials are the leaves on the branches of your organizational framework. They help showcase and validate the insights and recommendations for the audience. In a research report, this not only means the actual data and its interpretation but also the stories or demonstrations that corroborate the data. Supporting materials create interest, clarify the researcher's point, provide emphasis to a point, and offer proof that influences audience belief. Without appropriate supporting materials, a researcher's insights are nothing more than a series of unsupported claims. See the checklist in Exhibit 16-7 for criteria a researcher might use to evaluate his or her support materials.

>**Exhibit 16-7** A Checklist for Better Support Materials

☐ **Relevant**—Each piece of support should be relevant to the point it is supporting and consistent with the topical theme.

☐ **Audience Appropriate**—Each item of support should fit the needs, style, and demands of that particular audience, and fit the chosen report structure.

☐ **Simple**—The report's statistics should be conveyed in quickly understandable terms or through comparisons.

☐ **Detailed**—Each support material needs to be developed to the point that audience members can understand the insight and how it fits the management problem.

☐ **Believable**—The material must be accurate, ethically sourced, and fairly presented.

☐ **Balanced**—The report should include adequate amount of support but show a balance between quantity and variety, while not overburdening the audience.

☐ **Variety**—The report should not rely excessively on one type of support, but should instead use different forms of support.

☐ **Style**—The report should benefit from the power of analogies and metaphors.

☐ **Spatial**—The material must be workable within time and space limits.

☐ **Speaker Specific**—The support should be selected to enhance the researcher's style of delivery as well as the message.

Source: Adapted from Thomas Leech, *How to Prepare, Stage, and Deliver Winning Presentations* (New York: AMACOM, 2004), pp. 98 -102; and the Speech Department at Maui Community College, http://www.hawaii.edu/mauispeech/html/supporting_materials.html, downloaded January 27, 2010.

People learn information in different ways.[13] It helps to know what type of learners comprise your audience in building your support. **Visual learners** prefer to get their information from images, graphs, and models. Too much textual or verbal information is lost on this group. Preparing great graphs and infographics appeal to this group. **Auditory learners** benefit from textual/verbal approaches; stories and examples, both video and audio, help this audience segment understand and believe. **Kinesthetic learners** prefer to learn through personal, tactile experiences. They get bored with long oral presentations and lengthy reports, disengaging or skimming through material quickly. Topline reports or well-written executive summaries and incorporating demonstrations and real examples within the oral report work well to keep this audience segment engaged. If participants did an exercise as part of the research, having the audience try this exercise is an example of what would appeal to a kinesthetic learner. Any research report is delivered to audiences comprising all three types, so your content and style must accommodate them all.

A strong research report relies on a researcher's ability to convince his or her audience of the following:

1. That he or she, as the researcher, is credible.

2. That the findings from the research are credible.

3. That the audience should act upon the insights and recommendations drawn from these findings.

The level of persuasiveness of any report is determined by what Greek philosopher Aristotle described as the three types of proof: ethos, logos, and pathos.[14] A researcher needs all three to convince the audience that the insights and recommendations should be embraced. **Ethos** relies on how well the audience believes that the researcher is qualified to conduct the research. People whose education, experience, and previous performance qualify them to report on a certain issue earn authority.[15] This is why a research report often begins by introducing the researcher with his or her title, experience, and educational background (researcher profile slide and sponsor liaison's introduction in an oral; researcher profile in a written report). However, without prior experience, researchers must borrow ethos by linking their methodology and procedures to credible sources with experience. If a researcher isn't deemed credible, then achieving credibility for the results and the recommendations would be near impossible.

People perceive messages based on their state of mind. If their emotional disposition is positive, they are more likely to be receptive to the message; if it is negative, they will be less receptive to the message.[16] The researcher must arouse emotions exactly because they have the power to modify the audience's

Forrester Research: Finding the Dramatic Story Line

Forrester Research is a firm that does issue-driven research in numerous industries and sells many of its reports by subscription. Forrester takes a modular approach to report writing, whether it's a "brief" drafted in a few hours or a report that might take as many as 30 hours. Each report has three main sections. The "Market Overview" section describes the data collected from interviews, surveys, and secondary searches. It starts by revealing simpler problems and moves on to more complex ones. It doesn't rehash information the audience knows but provides only those data that are new. The "Analysis" section interprets the findings. And the "What It Means" section speculates on the implications of the findings and the analysis.

In one such study, the Market Overview would relate the finding that "40 percent of the time auto dealers have the wrong cars." In the Analysis section, the report would relate that with all the data car manufacturers have about what cars—and features within cars—are selling, a dealer with access to this information should be able to improve his or her inventory mix. Senior analyst Mark Bunger relates that the What It Means section is

speculative. "We develop the W-I-M chain—if 'a' was found, then isn't 'b' likely? Or if 'b,' then 'c'; and if 'c,' then 'd.' A lot of deduction and conjecture based on solid knowledge and experience within the industry ends up in the last section of the report. So if 40 percent of the time dealers have the wrong cars, and the manufacturers have the information dealers need, then dealers could improve the inventory to reduce that rate to, say, 20 percent. And for those prospects who still can't find the car they want? They might be likely to custom build to order to achieve satisfaction." This speculative section is the smallest section of the report.

And when it comes to writing reports, Forrester researchers take the time to find the right words to relay their information. The title takes on special significance, as subscribers often choose the reports they access based on the title. "We'll get more people reading a report if we title it something intriguing like 'Will ad skipping kill television?' than if we call it something drier like 'The implications of technology on viewer control activities in television ad exposure.'"

www.forrester.com

Sources: Mark Bunger, senior analyst, Forrester Research, interviewed January 22, 2004. "Making Auto Retail Lean," TechStrategy report, Forrester Research, downloaded January 5, 2004 (http://www.forrester.com/ER/Research/Report/Summary/0,1338,32782,00.html).

predispositions and, thus, its judgments. **Pathos** relies on the researcher developing an emotional connection with his or her audience. It involves an appeal to an audience's sense of identity, self-interest, and emotions. Pathos-based appeals take advantage of common biases: We naturally move in the direction of what is advantageous, what serves our interests or the interests of any group of which we are a part. Establishing pathos is why understanding an audience's predispositions and the effects of your recommendations on various audience members are so critical.

Logos, the logical argument, is the core of most research presentations; it is normally used to describe facts and findings that support the researcher's insights about research results. It should not, however, be the only content of the report. Logos may sway cynical listeners, but many in an audience distrust statistics. They perceive statistics as misleading, confusing, inaccurate, or, potentially, unethically applied. Researchers prone to build their reports solely on logos reduce the likelihood that they will achieve their desired audience effect—implementation of recommended actions inherent in the research insights.

The following list presents examples of frequently used materials for supporting your insights and recommendations. Exhibit 16-8 relates Aristotle's proofs to these frequently used materials:

- **Facts** are verifiable data about situations that exist or events that are known to have occurred. Facts often involve statistical data that can be demonstrated to be true. Facts are not in dispute and thus provide powerful support. Facts are the foundation of many research reports as they build *logos*. Examples of facts in research would be product sales, participant complaints about restaurant service, or employee turnover.

- **Statistics** are numerical data used in the collection, analysis, and interpretation of data, but also found in data collection planning, measurement, and design. Statistics are useful and expected for

>**Exhibit 16-8** Aristotle's Proofs and Desired Audience Effect

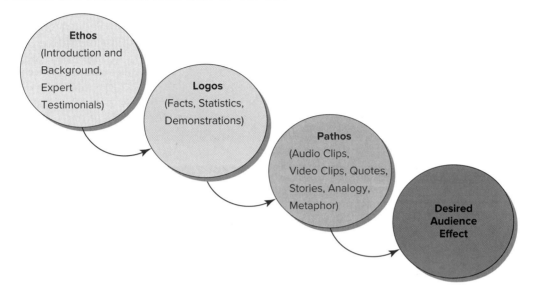

research reports. To be a credible source of support, the audience needs to know that a statistic is valid and reliable, used correctly, properly interpreted, and relevant to the point. Such statistics contribute to *logos*. Statistics used sparingly reduce audience fatigue. Researchers use visuals to facilitate understanding of statistics.

- **Story** relates the particulars of a single act or occurrence or course of events to clarify a concept or construct or bring an insight to life; it might relate the responses of an individual participant via a quote, audio clip, or video clip. Another example might relate the impact of a recommended action based on the responses of a single participant or group of participants. Brief stories make research come alive and provide credibility to insights; they contribute to *pathos*.

- **Demonstration** teaches something new through activity by involving the audience in an experience to clarify a finding. It appeals to visual and kinesthetic learners, especially if there is an opportunity to handle objects or reenact a participant activity during an oral presentation. As the audience's guide, the researcher takes them through a *show-and-tell* process, revealing each step of an activity from start to finish.[17] Demonstration contributes to *pathos* and *ethos*.

- **Testimony/expert opinion** uses the opinions of recognized experts to enhance a researcher's credibility for the audience on a specific topic. When used as testimonials, opinions of credible third-party endorsers allow the audience to absorb success stories. This is often in the form of a video clip, a quote, or participation of a recognized expert. These opinions represent an excellent source of support because they enhance *ethos*.

- **Analogy** is a comparison between two different things to highlight a point of similarity. An analogy is not offered as conclusive proof for an insight, but a good analogy may be useful to clarify the insight. Research might ask participants to compare a car brand to a particular type of house, to clarify their perceptions of style. "Brand X is like a Victorian house, with all its busy features and fussy details." Or "Brand Y is like a log cabin, sturdy and functional but not modern." Sharing these analogies makes insights about participants' perception of the construct of style come alive. Analogies contribute to *pathos*.

- **Metaphor** is an implicit comparison between two unlike things that actually have something important in common, used to provide clarity on a construct or complex insight. A metaphor expresses the unfamiliar in terms of the familiar, achieving its effect via association, comparison, and resemblance. Metaphors "carry" meaning from one word, image, or idea to another. When a participant says, "A Mercedes is an eagle, but my Ford is a plow horse," he's speaking metaphorically. Using metaphors contributes to *pathos*.

Storytelling Lessons from Pixar Applied to Research

Pixar Animation Studios has created acclaimed animated feature and short films for over 25 years. It is a worldwide success at telling stories. You've watched their stories since you were a child—*Toy Story; Monsters, Inc.; Ratatouille; Finding Nemo*—and each made you laugh, shiver in fear, cheer, even cry. What Pixar does so well is tell a story that engages our attention while imparting a lesson. Emma Coats, a blogger and former Pixar storyteller has summarized several storytelling lessons. As researchers, we can learn from Pixar.

Pixar Lessons	Research Report Application
	Research Report Preparation
• Pull apart prior stories you liked. You have to recognize what works before you can use it.	Use other research stories (review cases, topline reports) to help craft yours.
• Keep in mind what's interesting for the audience, not what's fun for the writer.	Conduct a comprehensive audience analysis.
• Identify with your characters; what would make you act?	Identify with your audience's problem, and understand what will be involved to correct it.
	Craft the Research Story
• You won't see what the story is about until you're at the end of it. The ending is hard. Write it first.	Start with the end—the action you want them to take or the research insight you want them to embrace.
• Put your story on paper. If it's in your head, it's a perfect idea that can't be fixed.	Map your story—the order of your data insights—and discuss your research story idea with your colleagues/ team.
• Take the building blocks of a story you dislike and rearrange them until you do. What did you learn?	If your research story isn't persuasive, engaging, or memorable, try rearranging the order of your data exhibits and insights, make different visualization choices, or both.
• Simplify, focus, combine characters, hop over detours. You're not losing valuable stuff; you're setting the story free.	Simplify your story. The audience doesn't need to know every phase of your analysis, just the key data so they may embrace your insights, recommendations. Delete what isn't critical.
• A coincidence that gets your character into trouble is acceptable; a coincidence that gets them out of trouble is cheating.	In your story, spend less time/space on what led to the situation than on what will correct the problem or take advantage of the opportunity.
	Present/Write the Research Story
• Challenge your "character." Take what your character is good at and throw the polar opposite at them.	Establish rapport by recognizing your audience's strengths and successes and how they will use these to address the problem or opportunity. But challenge them to take the different path that your recommendation suggests and embrace different skills.
• Honesty in feelings lends credibility to your characters. If you were your character, what would you feel?	Infuse empathy into your research report.
• The heart of your story is the belief that's burning within you.	Be passionate in your delivery of the key insights and recommendation(s).
• Give your characters opinions. Passive or malleable is death to your audience.	Take a firm stand on recommendation(s), as the core of your research story.
• What are the stakes? Give us reasons to root for the character.	Make the stakes of inaction clear, and the rewards of action even clearer.
	Debrief
• Finish your story and move on. Do better next time.	Always learn from each research report, and apply those lessons on the next research project.

Source: The lessons were developed using the insights provided by Emma Coats in her, "Pixar's 22 Rules to Phenomenal Storytelling," Slideshare, downloaded May 28, 2016 (http://www.slideshare.net/powerfulpoint/pixar-22rulestophenomenalstorytellingpowerfulpointsslideshare/24). The applications are the contribution of the author. "About," Pixar, downloaded May 28, 2016 (http://www.pixar.com/about).

Presenting Findings

The purpose of presenting findings is to support insights and recommendations. While a variety of support materials should be used in a research report to connect with different members of the audience, facts and statistics remain the core of many reports and deserve special attention. The presentation of statistics in research reports is a special challenge for researchers. There are three basic ways to present findings: (1) words/text, (2) tables, or (3) graphs.[18]

Words/Text

When there are a small number of statistics to present, words work well. Words can be phrases, sentences or paragraphs, lists, bullet points, or some combination.

> *Walmart regained its number-1 rank in the* Forbes *500 due to its strong sales performance (11% increase; $351.1 billion). Although Walmart surpassed number-2-ranked ExxonMobil in sales, Walmart's profitability ($11.2 billion) was far below the oil giant ($39.5 billion).*

OR

> • *Walmart is the second largest business in the* Fortune *500 with revenues up by 6 percent but with profits down by 4.2 percent.*

The drawback to using words is that the statistics are somewhat buried in prose. Thus, the researcher must highlight the relevant statistic in some way. During an oral presentation, the researcher might literally pull out the statistic on a single slide or enlarge it, change its color, or bold it and talk around it. In a written report, the researcher might stylistically bold the statistic or use a pull-out, repeating the statistic in a box alongside the prose much as a newspaper article does to highlight a quote. Words also are most often used to report insights and recommendations (as seen later in Exhibits 16-16 and 16-17).

Words are often used exclusively in qualitative research reports, even though statistics are not presented, as verbatim quotes are the core findings. Usually a brief title, followed by quotes, is the format. For example, you might see something like the following on a findings page or an oral report slide:[19]

> *Small companies lack information about green energy.*
>
> *"I have not heard much about green energy alternatives."* Energy buyer, small company.
>
> *"None of the energy companies told me how to buy green energy."* Business owner, small company.
>
> *"I asked about green, but never received a quote."* Plant engineer, small company.

Tables

Tables are presentations of data or statistics in rows and columns built from cross-tabulated data; these data are related to each other and need to be presented together to facilitate comparison. *Summary tables* contain only a few key pieces of data closely related to a specific finding or insight. To make them inviting to the audience, the researcher omits unimportant details and collapses multiple classifications into recoded classifications. In an oral presentation, a table is accompanied by an explanation so that the audience easily captures the point. Visual aids can highlight the table elements as the presenter talks. In a written report, tables may be presented alone or can be accompanied by explanatory text. The more complex the table, the more an explanation is necessary.

General tables tend to be large, complex, and detailed. A researcher might generate many of these in a search for patterns. They can serve as the repository for multiple statistical findings of a study. While appropriate for a written report, these complex tables are not appropriate for an oral report. Exhibit 16-9 shows an abbreviated example. Unless such a table contains information central to supporting an insight or conclusion, it is relegated to an appendix in a detailed written report.

>**Exhibit 16-9** Sample Abbreviated General Table

Percent Internet Use among U.S. Adults*	Internet Use at Least Occasionally	Receive Email	Home Internet or Email Use	High-Speed Connection at Home	Use Internet for Info about Hobby	Make a Phone Call Online
Percent Distribution						
Gender						
Men	48	70	90	90	49	22
Women	52	72	89	89	51	21
Education						
Less Than High School	40	27	73	72	35	11
High School Graduate	68	63	85	86	62	15
Some College	86	84	91	92	48	22
College Graduate	93	92	96	94	42	29
Ethnicity						
White	79	75	91	90	49	20
Black	68	62	83	83	56	15
Hispanic	66	58	85	88	52	23

*Refers to adults 18 or older, with access within the 30 days prior to their participation in the tracking study.

Source: Pew Research Center's Internet & American Life Project, Tracking Study, July 25–August 26, 2011 (Tables: AACTIV31, AACTIV12, I_User, Home3NW, Modem3b, Emlocc, IntUse.)

Exhibit 16-9 also illustrates the various parts of a table. Any table should contain enough information for the audience to understand its contents. The title should explain the subject of the table, how the data are classified, the time period, or other related matters. A subtitle is sometimes included under the title to explain something of additional importance. For example, this may be the measurement question, the measurement units, etc. The table stub clearly identifies the rows, while column heads do the same for columns. The body of the table contains the data, while the footnotes contain any needed explanations. Footnotes should be identified by letters or symbols such as asterisks, rather than by numbers, to avoid confusion with data values. Finally, there should be a source note if the data do not come from the project's primary data.

Graphs

A **graph** is a diagram showing the relationship of various values from a single variable or between two or more variables. While graphs reveal less information than a table, their use

- Implies that the information is of greater importance.
- Conveys comparisons more easily.
- Increases audience retention of the information.

In order for the audience to understand how the researcher reached his or her conclusions and recommendations, it is important that graphs (1) give accurate visual impressions of information (**data clarity**) and (2) be easily interpreted.

There are many different types of graphs. Graph selection should always be made based on (1) how it clarifies the information and (2) familiarity to the audience. Some graph types that a researcher developed during data exploration or analysis, and that speak clearly to the researcher, might not be appropriate for the research report. Still others, due to their complexity, might be appropriate for a written report but would not be appropriate for the oral report. Graphs that achieve dimensionality with shadowing, while they might look good to a designer, often reduce clarity of the data you are trying to present; most seasoned researchers avoid these. Simplicity, while not offering great style, is often the best rule in graph design. Researchers often choose a limited number of types of graphs when visualizing a report to increase the speed with which an audience member can interpret each new graph. However, variety has its purpose; when information is presented differently than previous information, it is perceived as more important.[20] Exhibit 16-10 shows the most common graphs and how they should be used.

Line Graphs   A **line graph** uses lines of different colors or patterns to connect data points; these are used primarily to display time series drawn from cross-tabulated data.

There are several guidelines for designing a line graph:

- Put the time units of the independent variable on the horizontal axis.
- Use different line types (solid, dashed, dotted, dash-dot) and colors to distinguish multiple lines.
- Use a solid line for the most important data.
- Put the dependent variable on the vertical axis.
- Use a zero baseline on the vertical access to avoid introducing visual bias.
- Avoid more than four lines on one graph.

Regardless of graph type, choosing the appropriate horizontal and vertical scales for clarity and to avoid perceptual confusion is a first consideration. Exhibit 16-11 uses different baselines. Part A uses a zero baseline, which places the curve well up on the chart and gives a better perception of the relation between the absolute size of cable systems and the changes on a five-year interval. Part B, with a baseline at 35 million, gives the impression that growth was more rapid. When space or other reasons dictate condensing a scale, use the zero base point with a prominent break (part C) to warn the audience that the scale has been reduced.

The balance of size between vertical and horizontal scales also affects the reader's impression of the data. In part C, the space between horizontal guidelines is half that in part B. This changes the slope of the curve, creating a different perception of growth rate.

Another distortion with line graphs occurs when we present relative and absolute changes among two or more sets of data. Arithmetic scales, where each space unit has identical value, is the default. Exhibit 16-12, part A correctly shows absolute differences between variables using an arithmetic scale. If we are interested in rates of growth, using a semi-logarithmic scale (part B) is more accurate. A semi-logarithmic scale uses a logarithm along one axis (usually the vertical or Y axis) and an arithmetic scale along the other axis (usually the horizontal or X axis). Semi-logarithmic graphs preserve percentage relationships across the scale. In part A, notice that sales of both light and heavy trucks have grown since Year01 but heavy-truck sales are only a small segment of U.S. sales of trucks and have a much flatter growth curve. Part B shows that while light trucks had a major growth spurt between Year10–Year20, a spurt not shared by heavy trucks, since then both growth patterns have been more consistent with each other. From the calculated growth rate provided in the table, in two of the last four five-year periods examined, the growth in heavy-truck sales actually exceeded the growth in light-truck sales, even while light-truck sales far exceeded heavy-truck sales.

Area Graphs   An **area graph** displays total frequency, group frequency, and time series data; a.k.a. *stratus graph* or *surface graph*. It consists of the area under a line that has been divided into component parts, it is best used to show changes in patterns over time (see Exhibit 16-13).

Pie Graphs   A **pie graph** represents data categories within a single variable as slices of a circle to represent 100 percent of a frequency distribution of a single variable; stacked pie graphs can be used for time series data but are more difficult for the audience to interpret. Pie graphs can easily mislead the reader

>**Exhibit 16-10** Graph Options for Oral and Written Reports

For components of a whole or frequency

   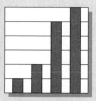 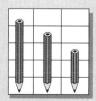 

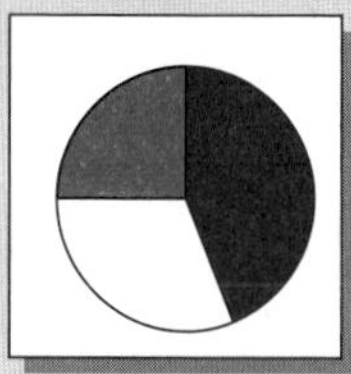

Pie:
Shows relationship of parts to the whole. Wedges are row values of data.

Exploded Pie:
Draws attention to critical component within the whole.

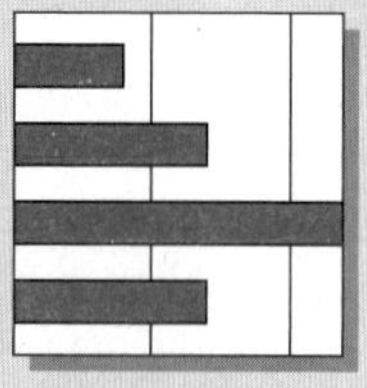

Simple Bar:
Places categories on the Y axis and amounts or percentages on the X axis.

Simple Column:
Places categories on the X axis and amounts or percentages on the Y axis.

Pictograph:
Represents values as pictures; either bar or column.

Stacked Bar:
Shows amounts of component variables; either bars or columns.

For relationship or comparisons

  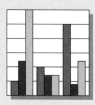 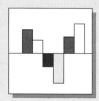  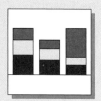

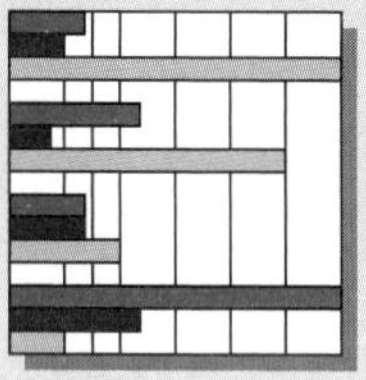

Bar:
Compares different entities on the same variable or component of a variable.

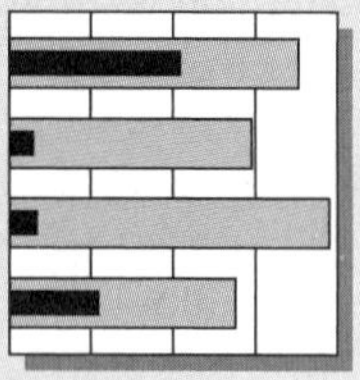

Bullet Bar:
Compares different entities on the same variable or component of a variable.

Column:
Compares different entities on the same variable or component of a variable.

Deviations (Bar or Column):
Positions categories on X axis and values on Y axis. Deviations distinguish positive from negative values.

Mirror Image Bar:
Positions categories on Y axis and values on X axis as mirror images for different entities.

Side-by-Side Stacked Bar:
Compares components of two or more items of interest for two or more segments.

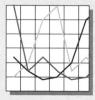 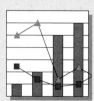  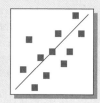

Line:
Compares values over time to show changes in trends.

Column with Line:
Item of most interest is presented in bars and compared to items represented by lines; categories on X axis and values on Y axis.

Area (surface):
Like line chart, compares changing values but emphasizes relative value of each series.

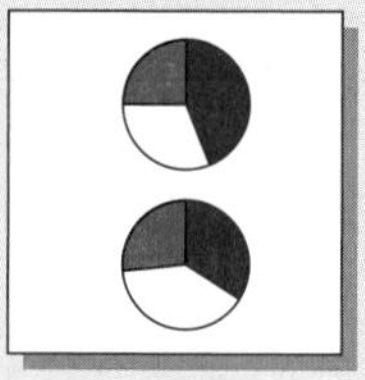

Multiple Pie:
Uses same data as stacked pie but plots separate pies for each column of data without stacking.

Scatterplot with Trend Line:
Shows if pattern exists for a variable; X axis and values on Y axis.

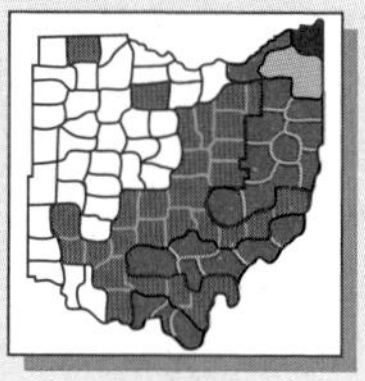

Geograph:
Shows data patterns by some geographic base.

For relationship or comparisons, Written Report Only

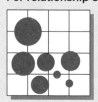 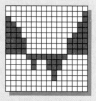   

Bubble:
Used to introduce third variable (dots of different sizes). Axes could be sales, profits; bubbles are assets.

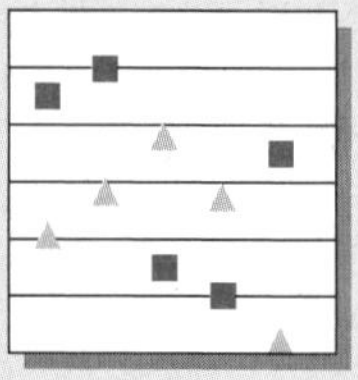

Multiple Item Scatterplot:
Multiple items are represented by different lines, with distinct markers for variables; categories on X axis and values on Y axis.

Filled Line:
Similar to line chart, but uses fill to highlight series.

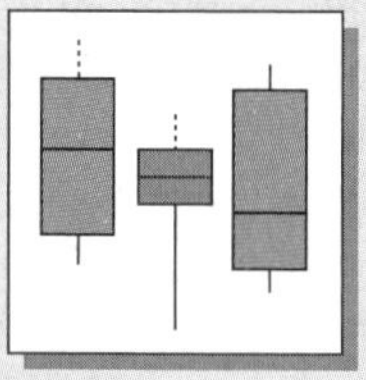

Boxplots:
Displays distribution(s) and compares characteristics of shape.

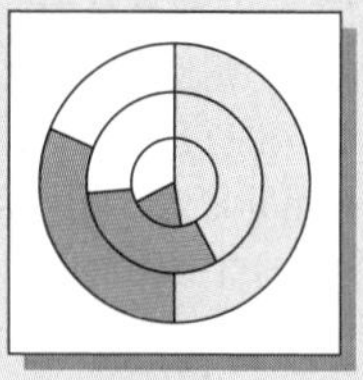

Stacked Pie:
Same as pie but displays two or more data series.

Spider (and Radar):
Radiating lines are categories; values are distances from center (shows multiple variables—e.g., performance, ratings, progress).

>**Exhibit 16-11** Cable Subscribers, Year01–Year30

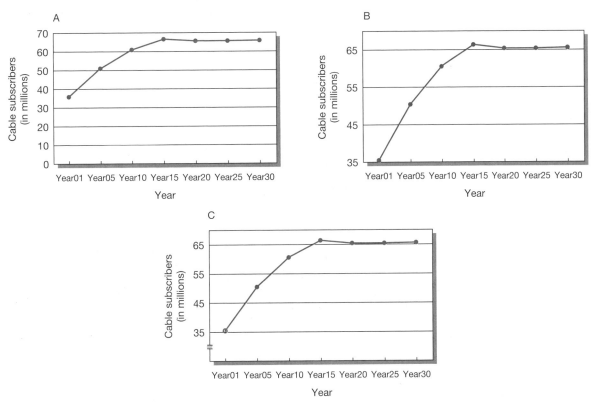

>**Exhibit 16-12** U.S. Truck Sales, Year01–Year30 (in thousands)

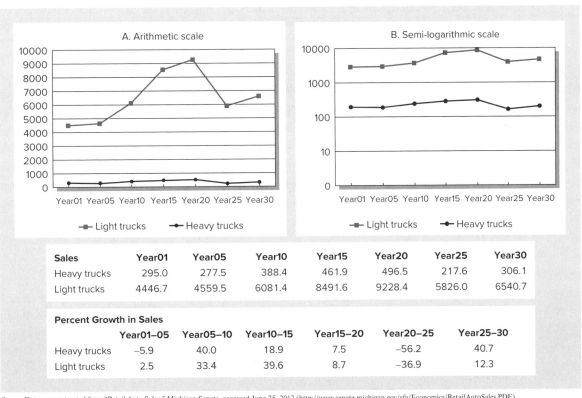

Sales	Year01	Year05	Year10	Year15	Year20	Year25	Year30
Heavy trucks	295.0	277.5	388.4	461.9	496.5	217.6	306.1
Light trucks	4446.7	4559.5	6081.4	8491.6	9228.4	5826.0	6540.7

Percent Growth in Sales	Year01–05	Year05–10	Year10–15	Year15–20	Year20–25	Year25–30
Heavy trucks	−5.9	40.0	18.9	7.5	−56.2	40.7
Light trucks	2.5	33.4	39.6	8.7	−36.9	12.3

Source: Data were extracted from "Retail Auto Sales," Michigan Senate, accessed June 25, 2012 (http://www.senate.michigan.gov/sfa/Economics/RetailAutoSales.PDF).

>**Exhibit 16-13** Area Graphs: A Stratum and Two Pies

Notice that the two pie charts seem to indicate a decrease in the "under 25" category relative to the stratum chart. The "under 25" category did in fact decrease (from 40 to 33 percent) but not as dramatically as the stratum to pie comparison would suggest. Also note that the sample size changed from 100 to 180 units between Year01 and Year25. It is important not to use a pie chart alone in a time series, to avoid giving erroneous impressions.

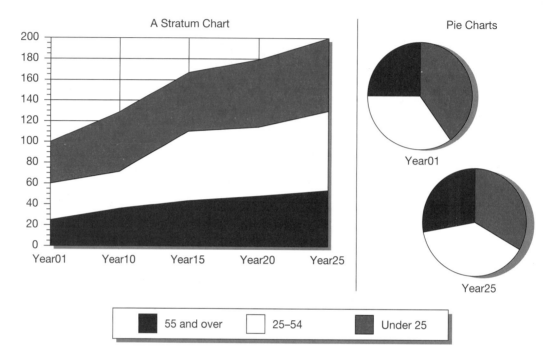

or be improperly prepared. Research shows that readers' perceptions of the percentages represented by the pie slices are consistently inaccurate.[21] Consider the following suggestions when designing pie charts:

- Label each slice with its label and the percentage or amount that is represented; eliminate legend.
- Put the largest slice at 12 o'clock and move clockwise in descending order.
- Use light colors for large slices, darker colors for smaller slices.
- Use color to communicate your most important message.[22] [Use a dominant color (e.g., red) with black and white slices to command the attention and be memorable].
- Do not use a single pie to show change over time; use a series of pie charts and complement these with an area chart.

As shown in Exhibit 16-13, pie charts portray frequency data in interesting ways. In addition, they can be stacked to show relationships between two sets of data, but without labels they are difficult to interpret.

Bar Graphs   One of the most commonly understood of all graphs a **bar graph**, representing cross-tabulated data as either horizontal or vertical bars (*column bar graph*). Quantities are represented on one axis, usually done as percentages to promote easy comparison. The alternative axis is usually a nominal, ordinal, or interval variable. Variations of bar graphs are numerous, as previously shown in Exhibit 16-10. Column bar graphs are generally used for time series and for quantitative classifications. Bar charts using horizontal bars work better with longer category labels and can be used for all manner of nominal, ordinal, and interval data. *Stacked bar graphs* are especially useful if the researcher wants the audience to consider collapsing the scale without sacrificing the detail of the scale. *Deviations bar graphs* and *mirror image bar graphs* are great at showcasing differences (see Exhibit 16-14). The simple bar graphs are always the best for oral presentations; more complex bar graphs showing more than two variables in a single chart, can be used for written reports, but audience familiarity with the bar graph should be considered in the researcher's choice.

>**Exhibit 16-14** Simplifying Visuals

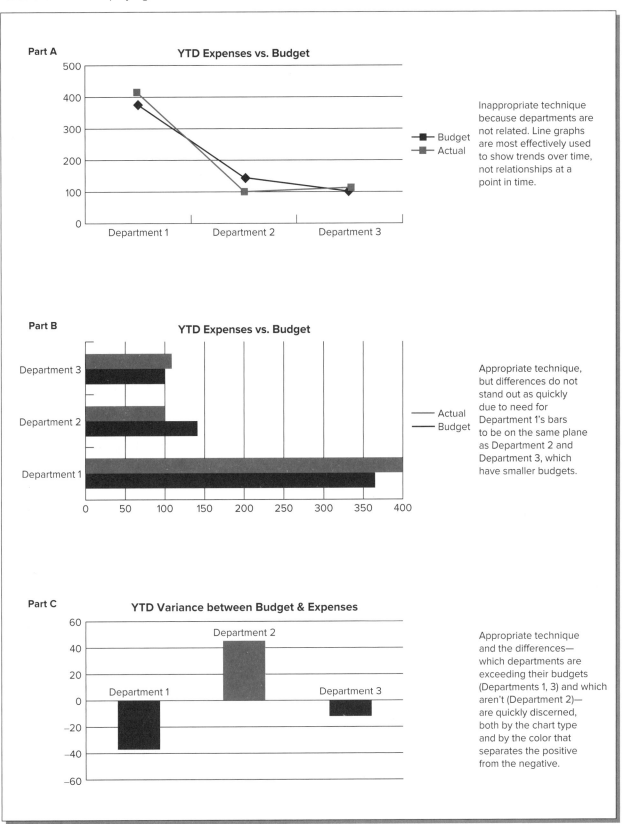

Part A

YTD Expenses vs. Budget

Legend: Budget, Actual

Inappropriate technique because departments are not related. Line graphs are most effectively used to show trends over time, not relationships at a point in time.

Part B

YTD Expenses vs. Budget

Legend: Actual, Budget

Appropriate technique, but differences do not stand out as quickly due to need for Department 1's bars to be on the same plane as Department 2 and Department 3, which have smaller budgets.

Part C

YTD Variance between Budget & Expenses

Appropriate technique and the differences—which departments are exceeding their budgets (Departments 1, 3) and which aren't (Department 2)—are quickly discerned, both by the chart type and by the color that separates the positive from the negative.

>**Exhibit 16-15** 3-D Graphs

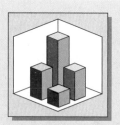   

3-D Column:
A variation on column charts, they compare variables to each other or over time. Axes: *X* = categories, *Y* = series, *Z* = values. Other variations include 3-D area charts and connect-the-dots scatter charts.

3-D Ribbon:
This example is a one-wall plot showing columns of data (series) as ribbons. One or more columns are used. Axes: *X* = categories, *Y* = series, *Z* = values.

3-D Wireframe:
A variation of a contour or response surface; suitable for changes in time and multivariate data. Axes: *X* = categories, *Y* = series, *Z* = values.

3-D Surface Line:
Handles three columns of data and plots *XYZ* coordinates to show a response surface. Helpful for multivariate applications.

A **pictograph**, which uses pictorial symbols (an oil drum for barrels of oil, a stick figure for people, or a pine tree for wood) rather than bars to represent frequency data, can be incomprehensible to an audience. It is proper to stack or align same-size images to express more quantity and to show fractions of an image to show less. Because each picture represents a set quantity of an actual object, changing the scale of a picture rather than stacking pictures is problematic. This misleads the audience into believing the increase is larger than it really is. The exception is a graphic that is easily substituted for a bar, such as the pencils in Exhibit 16-10. Pictographs might be used in an oral report, but they are more likely to be used when research is reported in magazines and newspapers. They are far more difficult to interpret quickly than a simple bar chart.

Geographs   A **geograph** uses a map to show variations in regional data (Exhibit 16-10). They can be used for product sales, distribution status, media consumption, promotional response rates, per-capita rates of consumption, worker productivity, demographics, or any of a number of other geographically-specific variables. The resulting graph allows the user to "drill" through the layers and visualize the relationships. With better software and government agencies providing geocodes and reference points, geographic spatial displays are becoming a more common form of graph in business research. One study of response times to distress calls used a geograph as valuable support for a recommendation to change the location of a planned fire house.[23]

3-D Graphs   With current charting techniques, virtually all graphs can now be made to have dimension. These are not 3-D graphs. A **3-D graph** allows you to compare three or more variables from the sample in one graph. If you want to display several quarters of sales results for Hertz, Avis, Budget, and National, you have 3-D data. Surface charts and 3-D scatter charts are helpful for displaying complex data patterns if the underlying distributions are multivariate. Finally, be careful about converting line graphs to ribbon graphs and area graphs to 3-D area graphs; these can be hard for an audience to understand, and your primary objective in graphical presentation is always data clarity. Exhibit 16-15 shows some sample 3-D graphs that might be appropriate for a written technical report. 3-D graphs are rarely used in oral reports with nontechnical audiences due to complexity in interpretation.

Visualization Specifically for the Oral Report

Oral visualization has some special properties because the audience has a limited period of time to take in visual information and no, or limited, ability to play back auditory information for clarity.[24]

- Pictures enhance memorability of research information. The picture must have a very close relationship with the slide topic; if not, a picture adds clutter and reduces data clarity.
- Audio and video clips enhance understanding and improve persuasiveness. Electronically delivered written reports can contain links to clips stored on a cloud-based server.
- Motion enhances data clarity. Enlarging numbers, exploding graphs to highlight a section, and changing color of a data item while the audience watches can add emphasis in an oral report.
- **Whitespace**, leaving empty space around key visuals and text on the slide, enhances data clarity; the greater the white space, the more your audience is focused on the element within that space.
- Large type size enhances data clarity; the bigger the physical venue, the larger the text on a slide. If you prepare a slide with 30-point text, you'll be unlikely to overload it.
- Reducing clutter enhances data clarity; only one graph per slide is the rule and limit text (e.g., substitute key word prompts for sentences).
- Presentation-flow markers pace a presentation. Each presentation slide serves as the prompt to discuss the insight and its corollary recommendation, but the flow marker lets you know where you are in the total oral report.

>Content and Style: Compile

Eventually you actually have to prepare your oral report script and presentation aids and your written report. Exhibit 16-16 provides a sample written report findings page for a written report, and Exhibit 16-17 provides a sample oral findings slide of the same data. There is one primary rule in preparing these: Limit the number of insights on any given slide or page because this speeds audience understanding.

>**Exhibit 16-16** A Sample Findings Page for the Written Report

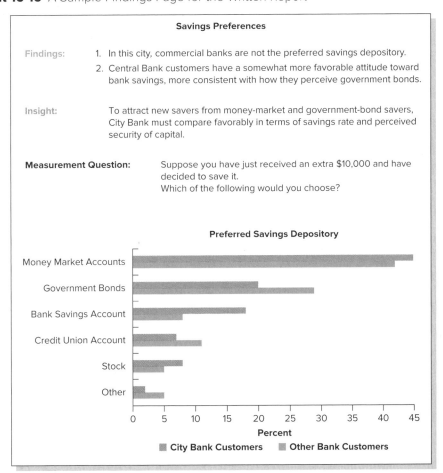

Savings Preferences

Findings:
1. In this city, commercial banks are not the preferred savings depository.
2. Central Bank customers have a somewhat more favorable attitude toward bank savings, more consistent with how they perceive government bonds.

Insight:
To attract new savers from money-market and government-bond savers, City Bank must compare favorably in terms of savings rate and perceived security of capital.

Measurement Question:
Suppose you have just received an extra $10,000 and have decided to save it.
Which of the following would you choose?

Preferred Savings Depository

(Bar chart with categories: Money Market Accounts, Government Bonds, Bank Savings Account, Credit Union Account, Stock, Other; x-axis "Percent" from 0 to 45. Legend: City Bank Customers, Other Bank Customers)

>**Exhibit 16-17** A Sample Oral Report Slide

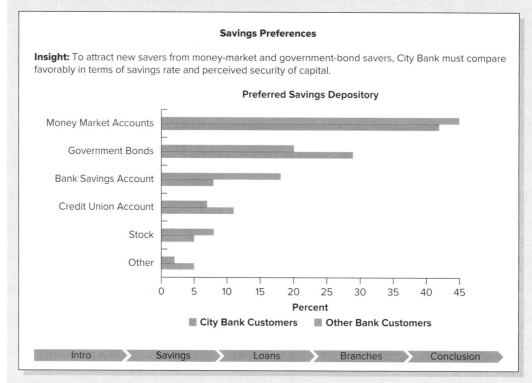

Assuming a written report is provided, any oral report slide should use the same presentation style as in a written report of the same information (words/table/graph). Oral slides contain less information, though, as the researcher supplements the slide with comments. Note also that oral report slides often contain a flow diagram to remind the speaker and the audience where the researcher is in the report. Here the flow diagram indicates the presentation is focused on the Savings section of the report.

Both written and oral reports share three important decisions: use of jargon, language level, and tone. **Jargon** is specialized language that is shared by a group, profession, or discipline. As you have learned, research has its own language. Unless your audience is full of research professionals, however, it's unlikely you'll want to immerse your audience in research jargon; it will obscure the meaning necessary to achieve audience effect. When concepts and constructs are used, define them clearly; analogy, metaphor, and stories help.

Language level refers to vocabulary and sentence structure. In terms of language level, the more complex the subject, the more simplistic the report's language level needs to be. A written report or oral script can be analyzed by software to assess its readability level; you want to shoot for something a high school senior might understand. Even magazines like *The New Yorker*, with highly educated audiences, rarely write above a 12 on the Gunning scale (appropriate for a high school senior). Opt for short, known words rather than the long, unfamiliar words. Opt for short sentences rather than complex or run-on sentences. It only takes one word the audience doesn't know or understand to lose them.

A report's **tone** is its style or manner of expression. Research is serious business, so your tone should be professional and business-like, not casual. And to win over an audience, phrase insights and recommendations positively, not negatively;[25] for example, say, "End users want autonomy over software choices" as opposed to "End users don't want the Information Systems Department (ISD) telling them what software to use." The latter would put the ISD on the defensive and diminish your chances of getting them to consider change.

We haven't mentioned size of a written report because it has to be as long as is necessary to answer the research objectives. It also should be not one word longer. No matter how wonderful your research findings, there will always be those managers who just don't have the time to read a lengthy written report.

If you reduce the information you need to present to the most important answers—those that that address the research objectives—you can present these in a graphic dashboard (a visual display of the most important information needed to achieve one or more objectives and consolidated and arranged on a single [computer] screen; each display is linked to its data)[26] or an **infographic** (a visual display of the most important information needed to achieve one or more objectives, consolidated in a single digital image file; not linked to its data).[27] Even if these consolidated visuals don't replace the written report as the manager-sponsor might expect, such visualization tools keep you focused on the objective.

Infographics

Infographics, a relatively new written report form for researchers, are effective because of their visual element and deserve some attention here:

> An infographic (short for information graphic) is a type of picture that blends data with design, helping individuals and organizations concisely communicate messages to their audience.[28]

Humans receive far more information from vision than their others senses.[29] Additionally, the brain processes pictures all at once, while it processes text in a linear fashion; thus it takes much longer to extract information from text.[30] The researcher may use an infographic to link to a more complete report because the infographic can be used to prime the audience and stimulate their interest.[31] The shorter attention span of internet users (sometimes referred to as *slivers* of attention) has also contributed to the increasing popularity and effectiveness of infographics.[32] With advanced technology, "attention to information has become a form of currency."[33] When an infographic is shared, you're not asking receivers to spend much of that currency.

Three basic provisions of communication are assessed when designing an infographic—appeal, comprehension, and retention.[34] Appeal choices engage the audience. Comprehension choices make the information easy to understand. Retention choices help the audience remember the data presented. When infographics are being used for business research, comprehension choices dominate the design. The Web offers a wealth of infographic templates and software for creating custom-designed ones. Each visual element (position, size, shape, and color) can be utilized in its own way to represent relationships between different types of data. Studies have shown that spatial position—where you put each element and how you connect each element—influences the effectiveness of visual displays of data and leads to the fastest and easiest understanding by the audience.[35] Therefore, researchers often use position and size to represent the most important relationships being depicted in an infographic.

Refer to the end-of-chapter appendix, *Better Reports*, for some helpful tools to improve research reports. Chapter 17, *An Integrated Example*, provides sample pages from a topline management report.

>Content and Style: Practice

The oral report has one defining factor that the written report does not—the need for practice. During practice, you can determine the time it takes to explain various insights, mark your script or note cards to indicate pauses, experiment with various audience-engagement exercises, cue audio and video clips, prepare responses to anticipated questions, stage the presentation environment (seating arrangement, lighting, sound, screen placement, etc.) and rehearse contingency plans for things that might go wrong. Practice pays dividends by reducing **performance anxiety** (fear produced by the need to make a presentation in front of an audience or before a camera), which negatively affects presentation quality. Malcolm Gladwell, in his bestselling book, *Outliers*, presents the case for the "The 10,000-Hour Rule," claiming that the key to success—from the Beatles to Bill Gates—is repeated practice of a specific task for 10,000 hours.[36] Whether you practice 20 hours or 6 hours, the time you spend rehearsing is the difference between achieving your desired audience effect and disappointment.

Even with practice, you might need a few tips because presenting statistics is difficult orally. Voice elements convey emphasis; learn to adjust volume, inflection, tone, pitch, and rhythm. Pauses in an oral report convey importance. Scripts enhance presentation planning but diminish credibility and audience connection if read in an oral research report. If you must use notes, use keyword prompts. Nonverbal communication can support or weaken a research report. Clothing, body movements, body position, eye contact, and gestures all add to or detract from the message. Dress professionally, stand erect, maintain eye contact to establish and maintain rapport, and limit hand gestures to using your laser pointer to highlight something on a slide. Of course, if you are delivering your oral report via the Web or an intranet, and if your technology shows the slides but not you, then these nonverbal cues are not a concern. See the chapter appendix, *Better Reports*, for some helpful tips.

>Content and Style: Deliver

Usually, the research sponsor and the researcher determine the delivery of the research report.

Oral reports can be delivered several ways: (1) in a physical venue where both the researcher and audience members are in attendance, (2) via a Web-based delivery platform or intranet, or (3) in combination. The first offers the best possible opportunity to influence the audience to embrace insights and recommendations, but with a higher price; the second offers the ability to reach a geographically dispersed audience at a lower cost, but with reduced opportunity to build emotional connection, a key to achieving desired audience effect. The combination offers the benefits of both, but also their drawbacks.

Written reports also can be delivered in several ways: (1) in person, (2) via mail or other delivery courier, (3) via an attachment to email, (4) as a download from a cloud-based server or intranet. The first two require printing the report, which increases the project's cost, but ensures that each member of the audience receives a copy in the desired format. This is especially important if the report uses color. The last two provide documentable delivery at a lower cost while providing the audience with a color-correct, electronic version of the report in a widely used format (e.g., Adobe Acrobat PDF). Electronic reports are both searchable and extractable, allowing audience members to share the report with a wider audience, in whole or in part.

Written reports can also precede the oral, be delivered at the time of the oral, or follow the oral. If delivered before the oral, the oral's purpose shifts to clarification and persuasion. The oral should not duplicate the report in such an instance, but it should contain enough information to communicate with those who haven't read the report. If the written report is delivered at the same time as the oral, the written report serves as a handout where the audience can take notes or jot down questions. The researcher can often refer the audience to a particular page in the report as the oral progresses. If delivery follows an oral report, the report serves as detail for recall or a reminder of highlights.

>Ethical Considerations in Reporting

Whether the researcher is an employee of the research sponsor or an external supplier, to achieve and maintain an effective researcher-sponsor relationship, the report must fulfill several ethical responsibilities: (1) the sponsor's right to quality research, (2) absence of coercion, and (3) the sponsor's right to findings nondisclosure.

An important ethical consideration for the researcher and the sponsor is contained within the sponsor's **right to quality** research. As this right relates to reporting, it includes (1) providing visualization and data-reporting techniques and tools appropriate for the data collected and (2) maximizing the sponsor's value for the resources expended. The ethical researcher reports findings in ways that minimize the drawing of false conclusions. This means using words, tables, and graphs that show the data objectively. Maximizing value includes not expending resources on unnecessary reports (or unnecessarily expensive reports), support materials, handouts, etc.

Occasionally, the researcher may be asked by sponsors to participate in unethical reporting behavior. Some examples to avoid are:

- Falsifying data presentations or interpretations to meet a predetermined objective or biased perspective.
- Omitting sections of data analysis and insights that conflict with a desired objective or perspective.
- Making recommendations beyond the scope of the data collected.
- Violating participant confidentiality.

To follow an ethical course, the researcher should take the following actions while reporting:

- Educate the audience to the purpose and scope of the research to deflect questions that ask the researcher to go beyond the research's scope.
- Explain the researcher's role in fact finding and interpreting those facts versus the sponsor's role in decision making.
- Explain how distorting data truth leads to future problems for the sponsor.
- To maintain participant confidentiality, when video clips of participants are used in reports, obtain prior consent. Keep video clips and written quotes anonymous by using only demographic or psychographic descriptors (e.g., female, age 45, 15-year employee).

Even if a sponsor feels no need to hide its identity or the study's purpose during data collection, most sponsors want the research data, findings, and insights to be confidential, often even after any management decision is made. Thus, sponsors usually demand and receive **findings nondisclosure** between themselves or their researchers and any interested, but unapproved, parties. In today's digital world, this means controlling the safety and distribution of any data reports, support materials, and presentation materials maintained on the researcher's or other cloud servers.

>summary

LO16-1 Three major changes in business and technology are altering the process of reporting. The first is the emphasis on insights rather than data, which demands the researcher to be better educated in business rather than just in research methodology. The second is report structure; the increasing sophistication of communication tools has shifted the emphasis on reporting to feature the oral report or the oral report in combination with a written report. The third is in the central focus of the planning process, shifting from data-centric planning to audience-centric planning.

LO16-2 The audience-centric planning process starts at its core with an audience analysis that influences the determination of the desired audience effect. Fanning out from this central core is the selection of the report structure, followed by a five-phase content and style process: organize, visualize, compile, practice, and deliver. Audience analysis involves collecting information about audience composition, research question knowledge, research predispositions, recommendation effects, audience effects, and any supplemental purposes. Within predispositions, we must address several audience biases, including confirmation, anchoring bias, conformity, survivorship, and loss aversion. An audience analysis can be formal or informal. An audience profile statement is the summary of what was discovered about the audience during the audience analysis.

LO16-3 In determining report structure, researchers have three basic options: an oral-only report, a written-only report, or a combination of oral and written reports. Due to changes in communication technology, the

oral report is getting primary attention because it allows the researcher to more strongly influence the audience effect and reaches a wider audience. The written-only structure is waning due, in part, to the increasing sophistication of data analysis and the need for the researcher to serve as interpreter and sometimes teacher in this process.

LO16-4 The report components include its introduction; background; methodology; finding, insights, and recommendations; and in the written report, appendices and bibliography. The presentation time allotted and the needs of the research sponsor determine the types of reports within the chosen report structure. The written report, in its many variations—management (infographic, topline, long) and technical (short or long)—offer the ability to share all the research findings and insights, or some subset of these, given the audience.

LO16-5 In the third phase of audience-centric planning, the researcher selects the organizational report framework. The options include: research brief, motivated sequence, narrative, topical, spatial, classification, climax order, problem/solution, chronological, past/present/future, cause/effect/solution, and pros/cons/recommendation. The most commonly used of these is the research brief. Researchers, however, should consider each project as a unique opportunity to choose the best framework to tell the research story and achieve the desired audience effect.

LO16-6 The second component activity within the last planning phase (content and style) is to visualize. Visualization is influenced by the audience's learning style (visual, auditory or kinesthetic) and the level of pathos, logos, and ethos needed to persuade the audience. Visualization includes selection and preparation of the best possible support materials to encourage the audience to embrace the research insights and recommendations. There are several types of support a researcher might use: facts, statistics, stories, demonstration, testimony/expert opinion, analogy, and metaphor. Facts and statistics are the core of most research reports, but these should not be the only support provided. Presenting statistics presents special challenges for researchers, given the possibility that the audience might misunderstand or misconstrue findings if incorrectly presented.

LO16-7 The last three activities within the content and style phase are compilation, practice, and delivery. Compilation includes not only the preparation of the written report to include all the support materials, but also the development of the oral presentation and its aids. It is the selection of the oral report within the report structure that determines the need for practice. During practice, the researcher determines the time it takes to explain various insights, marks a script or notecards to indicate pauses, experiments with various audience-engagement exercises, cues audio and video clips, prepares responses to anticipated questions, stages the presentation environment (seating arrangement, lighting, sound, screen placement, etc.), and rehearses contingency plans for things that might go wrong. Practice is the difference between a stellar result in achieving audience effect and disappointment.

LO16-8 Whether the researcher is an employee of the research sponsor or an external supplier, to achieve and maintain an effective researcher–sponsor relationship, the report must fulfill several ethical responsibilities, including (1) the sponsor's right to quality research, (2) the absence of researcher coercion, and (3) the sponsor's right to findings nondisclosure. The first requires choosing visualization and data-reporting techniques and tools appropriate for the data collected and maximizing the sponsor's value. The second requires explaining and maintaining the researcher's role, living within the scope of the data collected, and not violating participant confidentiality. The third requires controlling the safety and distribution of any data reports, support materials, and presentation materials printed or maintained on the researcher's or other cloud servers.

>**key**terms

>discussionquestions

Terms in Review

1 Distinguish between the following:

   a Technical report and management report.

   b The motivated sequence and the cause/effect/solution pattern of organization.

   c Jargon and language level.

   d Audience analysis and audience profile statement.

   e Conformity bias and confirmation bias.

2 Describe *logos, ethos,* and *pathos* and how each should influence the research report.

3 What are the three types of learners, and how does each type influence the research report.

Making Research Decisions

4 The day before your research oral report, you are suffering from pounding heart, a slight tremor in your hands, and stomach problems. What specific measures might you take to build your confidence and reduce your performance anxiety?

5 What report structure and type of report would you suggest be written in each of the following cases?

   a The president of the company has asked for a study of the company's pension plan and its comparison to the plans of other firms in the industry.

   b Your division manager has asked you to prepare a forecast of promotional budget needs for the division for the next 12 months.

   c The National Institutes of Health has given you a grant to study the relationship between advertising of prescription drugs and subsequent sales and consumption of those drugs.

6 Which type of graph would you recommend to show each of the following? Why?

   a A comparison of changes in average annual per capita income for the United States and Japan from 2000 to 2018.

   b The percentage composition of average family expenditure patterns, by the major types of expenditures, for families whose heads are under age 35 compared with families whose heads are 55 or older.

   c A comparison of the changes in charitable giving between December 31, 2007 and December 31, 2017.

7 Describe how you would conduct an audience analysis of your business research class.

8 Prepare mock-ups of visual aids that you might use in an oral presentation on these topics:

   a How to write a research report.

   b The outlook for the economy over the next year.

   c A major analytical article in a *Bloomberg Businessweek* article.

9 Your class team in research methods has completed a project for a financial institution on branch location effectiveness to determine which, if any, branches might be closed. What information would you collect for your audience analysis as you plan your report?

From Concept to Practice

10 Using Exhibit 16-10 choose an appropriate graphing technique and defend its use to show the difference between men's and women's attitudes on the top five Super Bowl ads. (According to Nielsen, women are hardwired for big-picture thinking, multi-tasking, "gut" reasoning, social and verbal skills, and worry/empathy. Men are preconditioned for concrete thinking, goal-oriented tasks, logical solutions, competition/defense.)

11 Use Exhibit 16-5 and the sample infographic to plan an infographic of your course project or of a research study you have read about in one of the cases in this text.

12 Choose any case containing data from the text website and prepare a findings page and slide, similar to the ones in Exhibit 16-16 and Exhibit 16-17.

From the Headlines

13 According to a National Federation of Independent Business (NFIB) report, "The Index of Small Business Optimism," the level of optimism declined in February 2016 to 92. The report's Optimism Index contains questions on employment, capital outlays, inventories, the economy in general, sales, credit, expansion, and earnings, among others. None of the 10 index components posted a gain, six posted small declines from January, and four were unchanged. How would you report this information to members? Justify your choices.

14 You are preparing to give a research presentation about the effectiveness of Toyota's advertising to restore public confidence in the wake of its product recalls involving accelerator pedal malfunction and antilock braking problems for high-tech hybrid vehicles. Which of the organizational frameworks would be appropriate for your purpose? Why?

>cases*

Inquiring Minds Want to Know—NOW!

Mastering Teacher Leadership

NCRCC: Teeing Up and New Strategic Direction

Ohio Lottery: Innovative Research Design Drives Winning

Proofpoint: Capitalizing on a Reporter's Love of Statistics

* You will find a description of each case in the Case Abstracts section of this textbook. Check the Case Index to determine whether a case provides data, the research instrument, video, or other supplementary material. Cases and case supplements are available in Connect.

Better Reports

Tips for Better Oral Reports

Psychological Foundations[1]

In his book *Clear and to the Point*, author Stephen Kosslyn argues that audience members of any presentation "should not have to search through a visual or conceptual haystack to find the needle you are talking about." Thus the process of *visualization* involves developing and organizing support materials that help the audience share in your understanding of the research findings. The composition and knowledge of the audience, the venue, and amount of time all influence choices in visualization.

Several psychological principles influence your audience's understanding of your findings. The *principle of relevance* infers that only information critical to understanding should be presented. Information that is presented verbally along with visual support will be perceived as more relevant than that mentioned only verbally without visual support. But the principle also indicates that we do not want to overwhelm the audience with too much information.

In the process of exploring your data, prior to developing a research presentation, you developed numerous tables, graphs, and textual summaries. Not all of these support materials, whether you use handouts, flip charts, or slides, can or should be used in most presentations due to time constraints. Any limitations in your audience's knowledge level (*principle of appropriate knowledge*) or their inability to process large amounts of information at one time (*principle of capacity limitations*) should reduce the complexity of your support materials. A familiar visualization technique—a bar or column chart or table—will always convey information more quickly than an unfamiliar one. However, you can design even appropriate and familiar techniques in too complex a fashion by including unnecessary information. Your audience, after all, has only moments to digest visually what you may have been studying for days or weeks.

Prescriptions for Better Slides

Researchers can learn from designers when preparing support materials. Exhibit Ba-1 provides some of their best tips for preparing oral report support materials.

Tips for Better Delivery

The *extemporaneous presentation* (audience-centered and made from minimal notes) is the proven choice for research presentations. This mode permits the researcher to be natural, conversational, and flexible. Preparation for this mode consists of developing outlines and developing key word prompt notecards. In this way, you can try lines of argument, experiment with various supporting materials, and develop memorable phraseology (the sound bites that will later be shared). During preparation, the main points are fixed sequentially in your mind, and supporting connections are made.

We rule out several alternative modes for the reasons noted:

- *Impromptu delivery* (no formal preparation; a "talk" without support documents or slides): Your reputation and the research effort should not be jeopardized by "winging it."
- *Memorization* (exact wording of a presentation script is memorized): Precludes establishing rapport with the audience members by adapting to their reactions while you speak as it produces a self- or speaker-centered presentation; a slip in memory can be a catastrophe.
- *Manuscript reading* (verbatim delivery of a presentation script): This heads-down preoccupation with text precludes establishing rapport. Most researchers are not trained to read aloud nor have the equipment (e.g., teleprompter) to do so professionally.

Scripts and Notes. Ditch the script! Manuscripts are often required for ceremonial speeches but are inappropriate for the majority of business presentations. They have no place in research presentations where audience members want to engage in information exchange, not be read a document.

Scripts are important in the planning phase but should be shelved by the time you get to practice. Here are one author's suggestions for evolving from ideation and organizing to becoming scriptless:

- Write the script in full sentences in the notes section of PowerPoint—no more than four to five sentences per slide.
- Do not script every word; just rework your material removing filler words from sentences, leaving only keywords.
- Highlight keywords and use them without regard to details to get key points into memory.
- Memorize the one key idea for each slide: ask, "What is my audience's take-home message from this slide?"
- Practice the presentation without notes using the slide's keywords, graph, or visual as the prompt.[2]

>**Exhibit Ba-1** Design Principles Checklist for Oral Support Materials

Successful visual design is achieved by what Reynolds describes as "careful reduction of the nonessential"; give the audience only what they need to understand your findings, insights, and recommendations. Ideas reduced to their most simplistic "stick" in the mind of the audience. Besides simplicity, clarity, relationship and visibility are important. Using the collective ideas of Reynolds, Duarte, Kosslyn, and Altman, the ideas below should improve the design of your oral report's support materials.

Images & Diagrams	
❑	Use simplistic flow diagram, like arrows, on slides to denote content location within the whole
❑	When image or diagram is used...
	❑ it is not used solely for appearance; it evokes emotion, introduces an abstract idea, represents a finding or insight
	❑ a specific image has close association with message you are trying to deliver
	❑ only one visual is used per slide
	❑ additional text is reduced or eliminated
	❑ any image with "direction" (arms, fingers) points to content, not off slide
	❑ headers, titles, and colors are used to group information
	❑ only audience-familiar graph types, images, and language are used
	❑ only the part of a graph that makes the point is used
	❑ corresponding categories, from graph to graph, are denoted the same way (e.g., same color for 18-14 year olds across slides)
❑	Element size is used to convey importance; larger is more important
❑	Color is used to convey importance
❑	Combination graphs (e.g., bar graph overlaid with line graph) are minimized or eliminated
Visibility	
❑	Graphic or pictorial backgrounds are eliminated
❑	Text uses high contrast color with background
❑	Text uses size for emphasis; larger, more emphasis
❑	Text size is large enough to be easily read (rule: oldest age divided by 2)
❑	Text in table is highlighted when discussing that element
❑	Statistic in sentence or paragraph is highlighted when discussing that element
❑	Visual aid is large enough for room and audience size
❑	In-chart animations are used to draw attention to a discussed element
❑	Colors in graphs are used to highlight or contrast an element
❑	Any support material uses whitespace to focus interest on key visual, text, or statistic
❑	Copies of support materials are available when supersizing visual aids is not available
Simplicity	
❑	Numbered lists are used when order is conveyed
❑	Bullet lists are used when order is not implied; number of points is limited per slide
❑	Unnecessary borders (around legends, titles, axis titles) are eliminated

Audiences accept speaker notecards, and their presence does wonders in allaying speaker fear. Even if you never use them, they are there for psychological support. Many prefer to use cards for their briefing notes. Card contents vary widely, but here are some general guidelines for their design:

- Place preliminary remarks on the first card.
- Use the remaining cards to carry a major section of the presentation. The amount of detail depends on the need for precision and the speaker's memory but should not become a mini-manuscript containing, for example, the details of supporting information.

- If using PowerPoint, match cards to slides.
- Content might include keywords and phrases, illustrations, statistics, dates, and a pronunciation guide for difficult words. Include quotes and ideas that bear repeating.
- Along the margin, place instructions or cues, such as SLOW, FAST, EMPHASIZE, SLIDE, TURN CHART, and BACK TO CHART 3.
- Sequentially number your cards or notes; you can return them quickly to order if they are accidentally shuffled.

>**Exhibit Ba-2** Using Key Word Prompts as a Substitute for Notes

Key Word Prompt	Presentation Script
1st HDTV	The 2012 London Olympics were the first to use HDTV freeze-frame technology.
3 times	London has hosted the Olympics three times, more than any other city.
22 medals	Michael Phelps increased his total Olympic medals to 22, 19 of them gold, swimming in three Olympics—Sidney, Beijing, and London.
204 countries	204 countries were represented in the 2012 London Olympics.
10,960 athletes	10,960 athletes competed in the 2012 London Olympics.
80,000 seats	London Olympic Stadium was configured to hold 80,000 for the opening ceremony.
160,000 tons	Londoners moved tons of soil to create the London Aquatic Center.

When cards are not suited to the occasion, you might consider the example in Exhibit Ba-2, which uses the previous advice on how a slide's keyword can serve as the prompter. In this example, the speaker is presenting, among other things, numerical information on the Olympics in London.[3]

Success Is in the Details

Reduce Clutter. *Clutter* in a speech includes repetition of fillers such as "ah," "um," "you know," "like," "basically," or "exactly." Clutter in a research presentation gives the impression of hesitancy and lack of competence.

Reduce or Eliminate Jargon. *Jargon,* language specific to a profession or academic discipline, is considered meaningless and generally unintelligible to people outside of that group. Using jargon is a particular danger in delivery of a research presentation where your audience may not be schooled in the techniques of research or of statistical analysis. Jargon also reduces the simplicity of the message. A thorough audience analysis should help you know how much, if any, research and statistical jargon you may safely include. There are many types of business jargon or buzzwords (see BuzzWhack.com) to avoid. Exhibit Ba-3 offers a few examples.[4]

Use Nonverbal Communication. *Nonverbal communication* is meaning conveyed through other than verbal means; it encompasses clothing and bodily characteristics, physical environment (physical space and time), movement and body position (including kinesics, posture, gesture, touch), eye gaze, and paralanguage (nonverbal cues of the voice). Studies on the topic cite that nonverbal communication can account for between 50 and 93 percent of the actual message received.[5] While a researcher making a presentation can use nonverbal communication to his or her advantage, it is equally important that he or she minimizes distracting or contradictory nonverbal messages that interfere with achieving the purpose of the presentation. The complexity of this topic is such that we can only focus on four admonitions for the presenter.

- *Eye contact:* A research presenter needs to know what is on his or her visual aids so that the aid does not demand his or her full attention; the audience should have that attention. The frequency of eye contact with the audience helps to establish rapport and comfort and makes the speaker approachable. When a researcher is perceived as approachable, the audience feels free to ask questions. Presenters who make eye contact show concern, warmth, and authenticity. Lack of eye contact, common with inexperienced presenters, is particularly bothersome to an audience. If you find eye contact difficult, practice using one drama coaches' advice: Scan the room slowly, tracing an X or Z with your eyes, but varying

>**Exhibit Ba-3** Business Jargon Translations

Jargon	Clearer Meaning	Jargon	Clearer Meaning
Swim lane	Specific responsibility	Move the needle	Generate a reaction
SWAT team	Group of "experts" assembled to solve a problem or tackle an opportunity	Burning platform	Impending crisis
Leverage knowledge capital	Steal someone's idea	Drill down	Examined more closely
Peel the onion	Delve into a problem, one aspect at a time	Reinvent the flat tire	Repeatedly make a mistake
Ocular inspection	Look at carefully	Relanguage	Reword or rewrite
Hard stop	Definitive ending time	Low-hanging fruit	Easily accomplished task

the pattern size to avoid looking predictable. Stop and look at individuals long enough to communicate with them personally before moving on to another.

- *Gestures:* Gestures convey animation. A speaking style that is animated and lively gains audience attention, facilitates learning, and makes content more interesting. In addition to hand gestures, facial expression (particularly smiling) is a powerful cue that transmits happiness, friendliness, warmth, liking, and affiliation. When you smile often, you will be perceived as more approachable. Luckily for the research presenter, gesturing to visual aids is almost mandatory and gets you started in the right direction. But a caution, you can over-gesture in a presentation, distracting the audience with your body language.

- *Posture and body orientation:* You communicate numerous messages by the way you walk and stand. Standing erect, but not rigid, and leaning slightly forward communicates that you are approachable, receptive, engaged, and friendly. Interpersonal closeness results when you and your audience face each other and nothing blocks the audience's view, such as a lectern. Speaking with your back turned or looking too long at a slide communicates disinterest. In some rooms, there is too much distance between you and your audience. To offset this, moving about the room increases interaction with your audience. Proximity enables you to make better eye contact and reveals your confidence.

- *Paralanguage:* This facet of nonverbal communication includes such vocal elements as tone, pitch, rhythm, pause, timbre, loudness, and inflection. Modulate your voice to accentuate key words for impact.[6] Vary volume, tone quality, and rate of speaking. Any of these can be used successfully to add interest and emphasis to the message and engage audience attention. Practice varying these seven elements of your voice to avoid a major criticism of presenters: speaking in a monotone. When an audience tunes out in a research presentation, they may miss an insight critical to a major recommendation.

Arrangements for Facilities and Equipment. Arrangements for the oral report occasion and venue, referred to as *staging*, involve detailed management of facilities, operational problems, and equipment (lecterns, lights, projectors, cords, controls, sound systems, video, internet conferencing, electronic boards, racks for charts, displays/models/props). Staging requires attention to the meeting room, seating arrangement, screens and lighting, testing of virtually everything, along with preparation/backup for disasters. Refer to Exhibit Ba-4 for a detailed checklist of the activities involved in perfecting the arrangements.

>**Exhibit Ba-4** Facilities and Equipment Checklist

Source	Item	Considerations
☐ Facilities	Meeting room	• On-site vs. off-site
		• Adjacent facilities and noise
		• Plain walls: distraction avoidance
		• Clock placement
		• Ingres-egress opposite speaker
		• Barriers between presenter and audience
	Lighting	• Rheostats
		• Screen proximity and wash-out
		• Access to bulbs and fixtures
	Electrical power	• Outlets: location
		• Power extensions
	Lectern	• Moveable vs. fixed vs. podium
		• Location and visibility
		• Size adequate for presenter's equipment
	Temperature	• Adjustable vs. central
		• Effect on audience
	Seating	• Theater vs. conference style
		• Conference table for small group: about 10 to 15
		• Individual tables for larger group: 5 to 6 per table
		• U-shape for visibility and interaction

>Exhibit Ba-4 Facilities and Equipment Checklist (cont'd)

Source	Item	Considerations
☐ Projection Screens	Size	• 1/6 distance from screen to last viewer
	Visibility	• Side angle and elevation
	Projection	• 4 feet above floor level; keystoning
	Interfering barrier	• Columns, hanging fixtures, lighting
	Brightness	• Reflectivity: black and white vs. color
		• Dim vs. dark room
☐ Sound System	Microphone	• Need for professional sound specialist
		• System control access
		• Handheld: 6 to 10 inches vertical from chin
		• Fixed-handheld vs. wireless
		• Feedback proximity
		• Desirability of portable systems
☐ AV Equipment	LCD projector	• Portable vs. installed in room
		• Projector-PC compatibility
		• Computer power
		• Operating location in room
		• Wireless controller/mouse
		• Wireless keyboard (meeting-related)
	Video	• DVD/camcorder/VCR
		• Web streaming
		• Teleprompter
		• Playback monitor size
		• System tests
	Video conferencing/Webinars	• PC vs. Mac requirements
		• VoIP
		• Speaker systems
		• One broadcast vs. two-way interaction
		• Supported browsers
	Flipcharts/posters	• Size and visibility
		• Support systems—racks
	Electronic whiteboards	• Simulation of PC desktop
		• Create video files
		• Digital storytelling
		• Brainstorming
		• Port over to PowerPoint
		• Use for review/repetition

Source: This checklist was adapted in part from Thomas Leech, *How to Prepare, Stage, and Deliver Winning Presentations* (New York: AMACOM, 2004), pp. 167–187.

Rehearsal Is Essential
What do super-achievers and star performers have in common? Practice.

Practice identifies the following:

• Content and stylistic ideas, like placement of pauses or rephrasing of awkward wording.

• Appropriate gestures or use of support materials.

• Appropriate staging of the environment.

• Duration of your oral report.

• Contingency plans to counter things that might go wrong.

• Possible audience reactions.

To get honest feedback from practice session observers, stick with open-ended questions such as the following: (1) Which supporting evidence was most effective? Why? Which supporting evidence was ineffective? Why? (2) Did the order of findings or arguments help support the conclusion? Why/Why not? (3) What was the most powerful element in the presentation? Why? (4) What would improve the presentation?[7]

Consider video recording your oral report to capture your habits—both good and bad. As you watch the video, look for:

- *Eye contact:* You should have a minimum of 75 percent eye contact in practice to obtain a higher goal in the presentation.

- *Body language:* Watch for unconscious gestures (e.g., touching hair, touching your face, standing awkwardly, pulling at your clothes) and gestures unsynchronized with your words.

- *Vocal characteristics:* Watch for irregular breathing with long sentences, pauses in the wrong places, dropping or raising your voice at the end of sentences, repeated phrases as transitions (e.g., "and then I," "now," or "next"), rapid pace of delivery, repeated fillers words, and negligible variation in tone or pace.

- *Energy level:* Do not underestimate the energy level necessary to generate enthusiasm for your insights and recommendations. Is your presentation inspiring or boring?

Control Performance Anxiety. *Performance anxiety* arises in anticipation of a performance event and causes negative effects on presentation quality. Performance anxiety has numerous physical symptoms: fluttering or pounding heart, tremor in the hands and legs, stomach cramping or nausea, facial nerve tics, flushing, hives, and dry mouth. Performance anxiety at various levels occurs to people of all experience levels and backgrounds, from students to seasoned professionals.[8]

Research found five common denominators among individuals who experience performance anxiety—all based in negative self-perception:[9]

1. I perceive or imagine the presence of significant others who are able to judge me.

2. I consider the possibility of my visible failure at a task.

3. I feel a need to do well to avoid failure.

4. I feel uncertain as to whether I will do well.

5. I focus on my own behavior and appearance.

The study's authors suggest several ways to reduce anxiety; these are summarized in Exhibit Ba-5. In short, they suggest you focus on "process rather than results, the moment of experience rather than the future, positive approach goals rather than negative avoidance goals, and self-acceptance rather than self doubt."[10] Beyond being overwhelmingly prepared, researchers suggest meditation and relaxation techniques, including exercise; talking with a few audience members before you speak to build your confidence and audience rapport; and while being introduced, sit calmly and breathe slow, deep breaths.

The Web-Delivered Oral Report

Noted presenter Nancy Duarte reminds us of the need to treat your audience as your first priority: "They didn't come to your presentation to see you. They came to find out what you can do for them. Success means giving them a reason for taking their time, providing content that resonates, and ensuring that it's clear what they are to do."[11]

A Web-delivered presentation involves

- A Web presentation platform (e.g., Live Meeting, WebEx, etc.).

- A presenter who remotely controls the delivery of the presentation visual aids to the audience's computer while he or she speaks to the audience via computer or a controlled-access phone line.

- An invited audience who participate via the Web from their offices or a web-equipped room.

- Various participation opportunities—most notably the ability of the audience to type in questions throughout the presentation and the ability of the presenter to respond to questions. Most offer the ability to poll the audience on their understanding of material or their consensus on a conclusion or recommendation.

- An archived copy for later viewing but without the opportunity to participate.

The biggest problems in planning for a Web-delivered presentation are the lower level of audience rapport affecting the pathos of the presentation and the longer time frame needed for planning, as is noted in Exhibit Ba-6. Such a presentation format does, however, permit the audience to be large and offers built-in processes for pre-contact (all attendees must register, which is useful for audience analysis) and follow-up (useful for determining the effectiveness of the presentation). Web-delivered research presentations often use post-presentation surveys to query the audience's understanding, solicit additional questions, and deliver copies of the written report. These are actions the face-to-face presentation does not often duplicate.

Keep Your Audience Focused

Once thought of as a "20-minute fatigue factor," audiences are now believed to become bored in 10 minutes—not 11 but 10.[12] Research presenters should observe this *10-minute rule* by varying their content by interspersing straight talk with graphs, videos, demonstrations, questions, and other means that allow the brain to seek new stimuli. Exhibit Ba-7 provides a checklist for an in-person oral report.

>**Exhibit Ba-5** Address Performance Anxiety

Suggested Strategy	Anxiety Reducing Actions
Reduce the imagined power of others.	• Remind yourself that you know the methodology and the findings far better than anyone in the audience. • Remind yourself that you have new information and new insights that could help resolve the manager's problem. • See yourself as the audience's partner in solving their problem. • Wear clothing that increases your power (suits win out over casual apparel).

Eliminate imagining negative possibilities.	• Remind yourself of the positive outcomes of the sponsor adopting your recommendations (e.g., their company grows, avoids layoffs, etc.)
	• Plan for contingencies
	  • Create a disaster kit with extra power cords, projection bulbs, and laptop.
	  • Burn your presentation to CD, as well as to a USB thumb drive.
	  • Make multiple copies of your script note cards or slide note pages, put them in different places (luggage, backpack, car).
	  • Have multiple copies of handouts of your slides as a backup to a PowerPoint malfunction.

Hold the performance in perspective.	• Think of the presentation as an opportunity for career-enhancing experience. • Remind yourself of what you'll be doing later today or tomorrow that will provide you great joy. • Plan a dinner with friends the evening following the presentation. • Plan a celebration with your teammates for after the presentation.
Control your own performance.	• Get some exercise to burn off your nervous energy. • Eat a couple of hours before you go onstage to avoid low blood sugar (can make you feel light-headed) or too much undigested food (can make you nauseous). • Craft your support materials with great care. • Develop strong examples, exercises, slides, and handouts. • Practice, Practice. Practice. • Apply the visualization techniques that the professionals use. • Rest shaking hands on the podium to hide trembling.
Increase your awareness of others without considering them judges.	• Meet your audience (all or at least some) before your presentation. • Learn something personal about a few audience members that makes them appear more human (e.g., they have kids who eat bark, they like cherry Kool-Aid, they hate sunshine (or snow), they have a chihuahua named Brutus, etc.)

Tips for Better Written Reports

Judging a report as competently written is often the key first step to a manager's decision to use the findings in decision making and also to consider implementation of the researcher's recommendations.

Don't Skimp on Prewriting

While some research reports are actually written in PowerPoint or other slide preparation software, most are written in document writing software like Word or Publisher. Many researchers step away from their computer when planning their report and find the outline is a useful tool. If you'd prefer to outline via computer, Microsoft Word provides templates.

Two styles of outlining are widely used—the topic outline and the sentence outline. In the *topic outline*, a keyword or two are used. The assumption is that the writer knows its significance and will later remember the nature of the argument represented by that word or phrase, or alternatively, the writer knows a point should be made but is not yet sure how to make it.

The *sentence outline* expresses the essential thoughts associated with the specific topic. This approach leaves less development work for later writing, other than elaboration and explanation to improve readability. It has the obvious advantages of pushing the writer to make decisions on what to include and how to say it. It is probably the best outlining style for the inexperienced researcher because it divides the writing job into its two major components—what to say and how to say it.

Exhibit Ba-8 offers an example of the type of detail found with each of these outlining formats:

>**Exhibit Ba-6** Checklist for Oral Web-Delivered Reports

When	Who	What
6 weeks before	Researcher & Sponsor	☐ Plan report priorities
		☐ Finalize audience list, with emails
		☐ Finalize audience analysis
		☐ Determine time length
		☐ Determine how questions will be handled, during or at end
		☐ Determine technical specifications
3 weeks before	Researcher	☐ Prepare invitation for attendees
	Researcher through Sponsor	☐ Email invitation to attendees
2 weeks before	Researcher	☐ Finalize presentation materials, in-presentation polls, post-presentation survey
1 week before	Researcher	☐ Prepare email reminder for attendees with audio and web link information
	Researcher through Sponsor	☐ Email reminder to attendees with audio and web link information
	Researcher	☐ Practice run-through with equipment, all presenters
5 days before	Researcher	☐ Prepare system compatibility check email
	Researcher through Sponsor	☐ Email attendees requesting system compatibility check
2 days before	Researcher	☐ Practice with equipment
1 day before	Researcher	☐ Prepare email reminder with audio and Web link information
	Researcher	☐ Prepare "Thank You for Attending" email with process, contact information for asking questions; may include link to written report, if available
1 hour before	Researcher through Sponsor	☐ Email reminder to attendees with audio and web link information
1 hour after	Researcher through Sponsor	☐ Email "Thank You for Attending" email
1–2 days after	Researcher through Sponsor	☐ Email link to archived recorded report
	Researcher to Attendee	☐ Respond to emailed questions
	Researcher through Sponsor	☐ Email post-presentation survey
Within one week after	Researcher	☐ Evaluate post-presentation survey and make notes for future changes, respond to sponsor to address concerns

Readability

As a researcher, you assume that your manager-sponsor and anyone with whom he or she shares the report have a high interest level. But reports often end up on shelves (or buried in hard drives), unread. You can obtain higher readership if you determine that your report is written at a level appropriate for the audience. To test writing for difficulty level, use a standard *readability index*. The Flesch Reading Ease Score gives a score between 0 and 100, with the desired range between 50 and 60. The lower the score, the harder the material is to read. This appendix meets that goal. The Flesch-Kincaid Grade Level and Gunning's Fog Index both provide a score that corresponds with the grade level needed to easily read and understand the document. This appendix calculates at 10.5 (anyone who has completed the 10 grade should find the report understandable). Microsoft Word calculates these indexes.

Use Templates When Appropriate

Many research firms follow templates for developing various types of written reports. For a topline report of a few pages, S&P Global follows a template that includes (1) one or more findings pages, each with up to eight small color graphs; (2) a "key assumptions" page with multiple numbered paragraphs; (3) a "key forecasts" page each containing up to six graphs; (4) a "key risks and opportunities" page; and (5) a "financial summary" page with text description and graphs.[13] If you are writing a report within a slide program like PowerPoint, check out slide templates at such sites as slidegeeks.com. For infographic reports, you can find numerous templates online (many for free) along with the software to create them; check out venngage.com, easel.ly, piktochart.com, and infogram.com. Some companies go the extra step beyond infographic to creating better graphics in all types of reports; check out visme.co.

>**Exhibit Ba-7** Checklist for In-Person Delivered Oral Report

When	Who	What
6 weeks before	Researcher & Sponsor	☐ Plan report priorities
		☐ Finalize audience list, with emails
		☐ Determine time length
		☐ Determine how questions will be handled, during or at end
		☐ Determine technical specifications
	Researcher	☐ Finalize audience analysis
3 weeks before	Researcher	☐ Prepare invitation for attendees
	Researcher through Sponsor	☐ Email invitation to attendees
2 weeks before	Researcher	☐ Finalize presentation materials, in-presentation polls, post-presentation survey
1 week before	Researcher	☐ Prepare email reminder for attendees
	Researcher through Sponsor	☐ Email reminder to attendees
	Researcher	☐ Design room layout, screen placement, seat arrangement
2 days before	Researcher	☐ Practice, Practice, Practice with equipment
1 day before	Researcher	☐ Prepare email reminder
	Researcher	☐ Prepare "Thank You for Attending" email with process, contact information for asking questions; may include link to written report, if available.
	Researcher	☐ Practice run-through with equipment, all presenters, if possible
1 hour before	Researcher through Sponsor	☐ Email reminder to attendees
1 hour after	Researcher through Sponsor	☐ Email "Thank You for Attending" email
1–2 days after	Researcher to Attendee	☐ Respond to emailed questions
	Researcher through Sponsor to Attendee	☐ Email post-presentation survey
Within 1 week after	Researcher	☐ Evaluate post-presentation survey and respond to sponsor to address concerns; make notes on implications for future oral reports

>**Exhibit Ba-8** Outline Formats

Topic Outline	Sentence Outline
I. Demand	I. Demand for refrigerators
A. How measured	A. Measured in terms of factory shipments as reported to the U.S. Department of Commerce.
1. Voluntary error	1. Error is introduced into year-to-year comparisons because reporting is voluntary.
2. Shipping error	2. A second factor is variations from month to month because of shipping and invoicing patterns.
a. Monthly variance	a. Variations up to 30 percent this year depending on whether shipments were measured by actual shipment data or invoice date.

We provided one template for a findings page in the chapter. Exhibit Ba-9 offers another that uses a one-column format, with lots of whitespace to showcase graphs or statistics; we've seen this template used many times in research reports. Researchers caution against multiple-column text formats because the reader has to do lots of scrolling if the report is delivered in an electronic format like an Adobe Acrobat PDF file. This is the format in which many electronic reports are delivered because color is maintained for graphs, and it's a standard format that most computers—from desktop to laptop to tablet—can handle.

Exhibit Ba-10 provides a checklist for writing the written report.

>**Exhibit Ba-9** Alternative Findings Page Template for Written Report

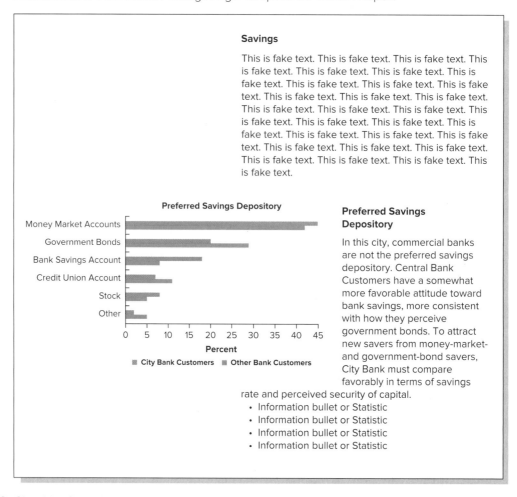

Savings

This is fake text. This is fake text.

Preferred Savings Depository

In this city, commercial banks are not the preferred savings depository. Central Bank Customers have a somewhat more favorable attitude toward bank savings, more consistent with how they perceive government bonds. To attract new savers from money-market- and government-bond savers, City Bank must compare favorably in terms of savings rate and perceived security of capital.

- Information bullet or Statistic
- Information bullet or Statistic
- Information bullet or Statistic
- Information bullet or Statistic

>**Exhibit Ba-10** Checklist for Writing the Written Report

Timing	Who	What
6 weeks before due	Researcher & Sponsor	☐ Clarify the reports purpose
		☐ Determine how report will be used
		☐ Determine audience and type of report
		☐ Determine method and time of delivery
		☐ Determine how questions will be addressed
5 weeks before due	Researcher	☐ Finalize introduction, background, and methodology sections
		☐ Develop Findings/Insights/Recommendations section
		☐ Develop appendices (if needed)
2 weeks before due	Researcher	☐ Polish final report
7 days before due	Researcher	☐ Finalize report
5 days before due	Researcher	☐ Print report (paper, PDF, etc)
		☐ Prepare letter or email per delivery method
1–2 days before oral, at time of oral, following oral or on date due	Researcher	☐ Delivery report based on determined method and scheduled
1 day before oral	Researcher	☐ Prepare email reminder for audience with day, time of oral report
	Researcher forwarded by Sponsor	☐ Email reminder to audience with day, time of oral report
		☐ Prepare email (re: answering questions)
1 hour after oral	Researcher forwarded by Sponsor	☐ Email report to audience about process and contact information for asking questions; may include link to PDF written report, if provided.
1–2 days after oral	Researcher forwarded by Sponsor	☐ Email link to archived recorded report, if available
	Researcher to Audience	☐ Respond to emailed questions

>part VII

Research Project Overview

>chapter 17

An Integrated Example

"I approach each project with a new insecurity, almost like the first project I ever did. And I get the sweats. I go in and start working; I'm not sure where I'm going. If I knew where I was going I wouldn't do it."

Frank Gehry
Award-winning architect

>learningobjectives

After reading this chapter, you should understand . . .

LO17-1 How the various stages of and steps within the research process work together to complete a research project.

LO17-2 What decisions are made behind the scenes of a research project.

Visionary Insights (VI) is a full-service research firm, providing both quantitative and qualitative research for a variety of clients. In this example, you'll meet several principals of the firm as they take on a project for *BrainSavvy*, a manufacturer of high-technology products for both home and industry.[1]

The Visionary Insights players:

- Bedford Chance, partner and business development officer.
- Dayton Wager, partner and senior project manager.
  - Chardon Kirk, research associate, specializes in data analysis, reports to Wager.

- Celina Gamble, partner and senior project manager.
  - Ethan Hilliard, research associate, reports to Gamble.
  - Zoe Gahanna, research associate, reports to Gamble.

BrainSavvy principals and people influential in the project:

- Parma Mason, new chief operating officer (COO) for BrainSavvy personal computers and the client liaison for the ServiceCentral research project; reports to CEO.
  - Zane Bet, ServiceCentral's manager; supervises both call center and physical repair center for BrainSavvy products; reports to Mason.
    - Julie Breck, manages ServiceCentral's call center; reports to Bet.
- Logan Park, Director of Research for BrainSavvy, reports to CEO.
- Zach Powell, account liaison for FastDelivery, contracted delivery agent for ServiceCentral's repair division; contract issued by Bet.

>The Need for Research

Parma Mason, COO for BrainSavvy personal computers, has sent several research companies a request for proposal (RFP). This RFP (Exhibit 17-1) outlines a problem Brain-Savvy is having with its after-purchase service program, ServiceCentral. While most of the companies have done previous research for BrainSavvy, she also sends the RFP to two companies recommended by colleagues in another industry. One of these is Visionary Insights, a highly recommended company but not one BrainSavvy has worked with before.

>Receipt of an RFP at Visionary Insights

In his position as business development officer, Bedford Chance solicits research business for VI. He is the person who receives RFPs from companies and determines whether Visionary Insights can make a proposal, based on current contracts and workload and its capabilities. It is his responsibility to avoid conflicts of interest or overloading the firm's talent and facilities. He is also the one who identifies research opportunities in the marketplace and prepares unsolicited proposals.

Chance has received an RFP from Parma Mason at BrainSavvy, requesting a research proposal to address a problem BrainSavvy is having with its after-purchase

>Exhibit 17-1 BrainSavvy RFP for ServiceCentral Project

BrainSavvy RFP for ServiceCentral© Project

BrainSavvy is a world-wide technology leader serving the consumer, industrial and government markets with a wide array of technology products. BrainSavvy is traded on the New York Stock Exchange and currently holds a AAA Standard & Poor's rating.

Background
ServiceCentral is the in-bound technical assistance call center and physical repair center for all BrainSavvy-branded laptops and tablets. The call center operates 24-7, fielding more than 1,000 calls per day. The repair facility handles between 500–1,000 repairs a month. In the last several months, complaints in the call center (transcripts available) and letters to the manager of the ServiceCentral repair facility have increased.

Contractual Needs
Requirements for research and evaluation support are described in the two tasks below.

Task 1. RESEARCH. Design, conduct, analyze, and provide conclusions and recommendations relevant to identifying and correcting ServiceCentral's key problems.
This research will help direct corrections to ServiceCentral processes or determine whether any process should be outsourced.

> **Task 1a.** Qualitative research among those experiencing problems to better understand the situation and circumstance of the complaint.
> Level of effort: multiple focus groups with approximately 20 participants or in-depth interviews. [Alternative suggestions invited.]
> **Task 1b.** Benchmark survey using a probability sample drawn from ServiceCentral users to judge satisfaction, effect of their negative experience on ServiceCentral or BrainSavvy's image. Recommendations for evaluating survey validity and reliability should be included. [Method to be part of your recommendation]
> Level of effort: approximately 500 surveys [Alternative suggestions invited.]

We anticipate repeating this research in the future to help gauge change and progress. However, at this time we are interested only in the first benchmark survey.

Anticipated Time Schedule

August 10, 20XX	Proposal submitted
August 20, 20XX	Contract awarded; begin development of all tasks
September 6, 20XX	Approval of revised proposal
September 16, 20XX	Qualitative research completed
October 1, 20XX	Conduct survey
November 1, 20XX	Present findings survey and recommendations

Proposal Instructions
We invite you to submit a proposal addressing one or both of the tasks described above. Your proposal should include:

Summary Statement of the Problem: Problem as you see it after examining addition information provided on the secure website: www.brainsavvy.com.research-SC; password access code: VisionaryInsights-SC.

Technical Section: Methodology proposed, with details.

Management Section: Who will comprise the research team, including education, experience, and certifications or other credentials; name and contact information of the project liaison; how project tasks will be allocated among team members; any services that must be outsourced, and to what firms, including their liaison with contact information; detailed timeline for the project.

Pricing Section: Detailed breakdown of project costs.

Submit Pre-Proposal Questions to:

Parma Mason, COO, BrainSavvy personal computers
  Email: Parma.Mason@brainsavvy.com
  Phone: (800) 272-4672 or (800) 277-2880
  Mobile: (272) 467-2889

servicing operation, ServiceCentral. BrainSavvy is a key player in the technology field and capturing its business would open up many opportunities in the technology market. Chance determines that VI has no current conflicts of interest and that, given current contracts, VI could deliver within BrainSavvy's time frame. Based on prior projects, Chance concludes VI has the capabilities to address this project as outlined. He forwards the RFP to partners Celina Gamble and Dayton Wager to develop the proposal.

They decide it is in the company's best interests for them to work as a team, given their teams' different methodology strengths and the possibility of more business from BrainSavvy in the future.

The VI Proposal for BrainSavvy Research

"The RFP doesn't indicate what information will be available from BrainSavvy's business intelligence system. Knowing that would be a big plus," claims Celina. "Like so many other RFPs, it mentions the need for a survey. However, given that a growing number of complaints about post-purchase service started the process, that seems logical. It would have been helpful if we knew what critical event convinced them that research was necessary."

"We'll need to delve into tech industry background," says Dayton. "We've only had one tech industry client, so we'll need more information to convince BrainSavvy that we are the right firm for the job. The secure website it created describes the ServiceCentral operation in some detail but doesn't detail its processes. It's still a good resource. We should also find out more about the team that will award the contract; I'll assign one of the staff to use LinkedIn to scope out Parma Mason and the others."

"I'll assign one of my team to collect articles on BrainSavvy and about the technology arena," decides Celina. "Let's meet on Thursday to discuss these and develop the proposal."

"Okay. And I'll develop several plausible research designs to consider," relates Dayton. "I think our standard proposal template should work well, given what they are asking for. If your profile is up-to-date, I'll get it started. (See Exhibit 17-2.) Is it my turn or yours to be primary liaison with the client?"

"My current profile is on the server. And it's your turn as liaison," confirms Celina. "I'll be done with the Deerfield project before the BrainSavvy project is awarded."

The Proposal Review at BrainSavvy

Mason and her team develop 10 criteria for firm selection before they receive any proposals, including knowledge of tech industry, experience in tech industry research, firm's reputation in public media, credentials of principals, and capabilities in both quantitative and qualitative research. As proposals come in, each team member independently reviews the proposal and assigns each factor a score from 1 to 10 and adds those for a total score. It is determined that the firms with the three highest total scores will be invited to interview.

Following the proposal due date, the team meets to set dates for onsite interviews and the order for the three presentations. Mason contacts the top three firms and invites each to present at BrainSavvy headquarters in Chicago. Visionary Insights is among the finalists and will present last. Before that date, Mason and her team meet to develop criteria for firm selection based on the oral presentation.

The BrainSavvy Finalist Interview

Mason's pre-RFP research revealed that VI has a reputation for merging traditional methodologies with creative, emerging approaches; she and her team are looking forward to learning more. Visionary Insights has brought its lead team (Chance, Wager, and Gamble) to the BrainSavvy selection interview. Mason approaches the VI team and, after initial greetings, brings them to a conference room where the BrainSavvy team is gathered.

>**Exhibit 17-2** Proposal to BrainSavvy

Proposal for BrainSavvy's ServiceCentral Project

Visionary Insights
Research Solutions to Complicated Problems

Statement of the Problem

BrainSavvy promises to provide a rapid response to customers' service problems. But ServiceCentral, the dedicated servicing facility for BrainSavvy-branded personal computers, is experiencing a shortage of trained technical operators in its telephone center. The package courier, *FastDelivery,* contracted to pick up and deliver customers' machines to ServiceCentral, has provided irregular execution. ServiceCentral is also experiencing parts availability problems for some machines. Recent ServiceCentral call center logs show complaints about ServiceCentral; it is unknown how representative these complaints are or what implications these complaints may have for satisfaction with BrainSavvy products.

The purpose of this research is to discover the level of satisfaction with ServiceCentral. Specifically, we intend to identify the component and overall levels of customer satisfaction with ServiceCentral, in order to discover the importance of various types of product failure on satisfaction levels. Component satisfaction is critical to the assessment as they reveal:
- How customer tolerance levels for repair performance affect overall satisfaction.
- Which process components should be immediately improved to elevate the overall satisfaction of those BrainSavvy customers experiencing product failures.

High levels of user satisfaction translate into positive word-of-mouth product endorsements. These endorsements influence the purchase outcomes for friends and relatives, as well as business associates. Critical incidents, such as product failures, have the potential to either undermine existing satisfaction levels. Appropriate responses to critical incidents preserve and even increase the resulting levels of customer satisfaction.

Technical Section

Research Design:
Phase 1,   Exploration: We recommend exploratory interviews with the service manager, the call center manager, and the independent package company's account executive, followed by content analysis of call center logs and complaint letters and an inventory of ServiceCentral's internal and external processes.

Phase 2,   Qualitative: We recommend focus groups with a small group of dissatisfied customers to assist in identifying component satisfaction elements.

Phase 3,   Sampling Design: The ServiceCentral log will serve as the sampling frame to draw a probability sample.

Phase 4,   Quantitative: We propose an online customer satisfaction survey, customized to identified ServiceCentral problems and desired performance rubrics, and pilot-tested before activation.

Phase 5,   Data Analysis: We propose using overall satisfaction in a regression with component satisfaction scores, and developing a performance grid to identify corrective measures based on priority.

Phase 6,   Non-Response Assessment, Qualitative: Using phone interviews, we propose contacting a small sample from those invited but not participating in the online survey; the data will be used to compare participants and non-participants responses.

Management Section

Visionary Insight Team:
Dayton Wager, lead researcher, quantitative. Wager, is a partner and 20-year veteran in quantitative research; a graduate of MIT and University of Florida, Wager holds a PhD in mathematics. Wager will serve as project liaison and oversee all quantitative methods and analysis.

Celina Gamble, lead researcher, qualitative. Gamble is a partner and 15-year veteran with experience in both quantitative and qualitative research methods. She holds an MBA and a Master of data analytics, and is a certified focus group moderator. Gamble will oversee all exploratory and qualitative research and assist in questionnaire design.

Additional team members will be drawn from both Wager and Gamble's teams, as needed.

Outsourced Services:
Graphic design of online survey, GraphicWorks; this Atlanta firm has done our graphics work for more than 20 online survey projects.

Online survey platform, SurveyMonkey; this platform is the number 1 survey platform for business.

Online focus group platform, iTracks; this platform is the leader in the industry.

Secure online file-sharing platform, Dropbox; this platform was recently named as number 2 in the Forbes Cloud 100.

(continued)

>**Exhibit 17-2** Proposal to BrainSavvy (cont'd)

Proposal for BrainSavvy's ServiceCentral Project

Visionary Insights
Research Solutions to Complicated Problems

TimeFrame
    Phase 1: August 20-September 6, 20XX
    Phase 2: September 6–12, 20XX
    Phase 3: September 6–22, 20XX
    Phase 4: Development of custom questionnaire: September 22–29, 20XX
    Phase 4: Survey in progress: September 30–October 6, 20XX
    Phase 4: Data preparation, exploration, and analysis: October 6–20, 20XX
    Phase 5: Non-response assessment: October 6–20, 20XX
    Final Report: November 1, 20XX

Pricing Section:

Item	Cost
Focus groups	$ 1,550.00
Travel costs	2,500.00
Questionnaire development	1,850.00
Equipment/supplies	1,325.00
Graphics design services	800.00
Secure survey fielding account	400.00
Secure file-sharing site	300.00
Secure online-focus group platform	600.00
Monthly data files (each)	50.00
Monthly reports (each)	1,850.00
Total one-time project costs	**$11,175.00**
Subsequent monthly run costs (each)	$2,150.00
Subsequent survey software for 11 months	800.00

Contact Information
    Bedford Chance, partner
            Email: Bedford.Chance@visionaryinsights.com
            Phone: 800-467-4448
            Mobile: 407-847-4660

    Dayton Wager, partner
            Email: Dayton.Wager@visionaryinsights.com
            Phone: 800-467-4448
            Mobile: 407-847-4661

    Celina Gamble, partner
            Email: Celina.Gamble@visionaryinsights.com
            Phone: 800-467-4448
            Mobile: 407-847-4662

The VI interview starts with Bedford Chance's five-minute presentation on VI and its capabilities. Chance shares some impressive results accomplished for former clients in noncompetitive industries. The last slide in his presentation features a top industry award VI recently won for its customer satisfaction methodology. Celina Gamble and Dayton Wager present their ideas for the possible research design, based on what they know so far about the problem, but stress this might be adjusted if their exploratory phase reveals anything unknown. During the question-and-answer session that follows, Celina Gamble demonstrates significant current knowledge of the technology industry, confidence, and expertise. Dayton Wager, obviously the methodology guru at VI, demonstrates a strong grasp of current and emerging methodologies and how these would be applied in BrainSavvy's situation. Chance concludes VI's presentation by thanking Mason and her team for the opportunity. Mason concludes the session, thanking the VI team and letting them know BrainSavvy will award the contract within 72 hours.

Visionary Insights Captures the Research Contract

Based on the proposal and interview, Visionary Insights is the unanimous choice. Mason contacts Chance the next day by phone. "We've chosen Visionary Insights for the BrainSavvy contract. Congratulations."

"Thank you," accepts Chance. "You've made the right choice."

"I've got three seats on a flight to Dallas next Wednesday," shares Mason. "Can Wager and Gamble join me for an 8:00 a.m. flight? They need to see ServiceCentral in operation. We'll be back by 5:30 p.m. I'd like to lay the groundwork for the project and better understand the number crunching that's already been done. I'll introduce them to other people they will be working with and share more details about the concerns we have about ServiceCentral."

"I'll contact them and have Dayton Wager contact you directly. He will be your primary contact during the project."

>Stage 1: Clarify the Research Question

The Dallas Trip

"The trip was very informative," declares Wager. "Although Zane Bet wants the sun, the sky, and the moon. She wants to know the demographic characteristics of her users . . . their job descriptions . . . their salaries . . . their ethnicities . . . their education. Wants to know the perception of BrainSavvy; wants to know their satisfaction with the purchase channel and with ServiceCentral, too."

"What Dayton is trying to say is that you need to keep your eye on the bottom line, Parma, or your return-on-research-investment will fall," shares Gamble. "You can bet someone will want to know how you and Zane can justify asking all these questions. They will ask, 'What is going to be the payoff in knowing the ethnicity of customers who use ServiceCentral?' And if you or Zane can't justify needing the information, if one of you can't establish that the dollar benefit of knowing is at least as great as the dollar cost of finding out, the question will get struck from the survey. And, there is a negative correlation between survey length and number of completes."

"So you feel we need to propose an exploratory study to whittle down the information to critical items, followed by a larger study?" asked Parma.

"A pilot study could help. Zane wants to know the customers' perceptions of BrainSavvy's overall quality. But we have to ask ourselves, 'Are these customers really qualified to form independent opinions, or will they simply be parroting what they have read in magazines or online?' A pilot study of a few hundred might help determine if it is really useful to ask them their overall impression of the product. But we are getting way ahead of ourselves. You need to let Celina and me put our heads together and come up with the plausible research questions. Right now, all we have are information needs. These are not the same."

"Today's tour of ServiceCentral really helped me understand the context of management's concern," comments Parma. "Did you or Celina have a chance to look over any of the customer letters Zane gave you?"

"I did," shares Celina, "and I asked Zane to provide the call center transcripts for any service problems. He said he'd get those to me no later than tomorrow. Some letters did catch my eye; one customer wrote: 'My BrainSavvy was badly damaged on arrival. I could not believe its condition when I unpacked it.' And another said, 'The service technicians seemed to be unable to understand my complaint. But once they understood it, they performed immediate repairs.' We will collaborate to boil these down, and possibly dozens more like them, to critical themes. This will help us better understand the scope of the problem. You don't want BrainSavvy to pay for everything Zane says she wants, just what she wants that has a payoff and is researchable. We first need to agree on a research question, and we have work before we get there. We'll likely want to confer with managers in both the call center and the repair facility."

"Once we've completed our own exploratory assessment," explains Dayton, "we'll come back to you with who we want to contact. And once we've completed those interviews, we'll discuss some plausible research questions. We'll then help you put them in order of priority. For the moment, you need to let us do what we do best and why you hired us."

VI Project Structure and Exploration

Dayton and Celina brainstorm the next morning; set up a team; and determine the exploration strategy (Exhibit 17-3), tasks, and assignments. After reviewing current project assignments, they determine which research associates they wanted on their team for the BrainSavvy project and how and who will brief the team. They set up a Dropbox for the project and share it with team members. They upload one folder to include the scanned customer letters and another to contain the call transcripts. Other folders

>**Exhibit 17-3** Exploration Strategy for BrainSavvy

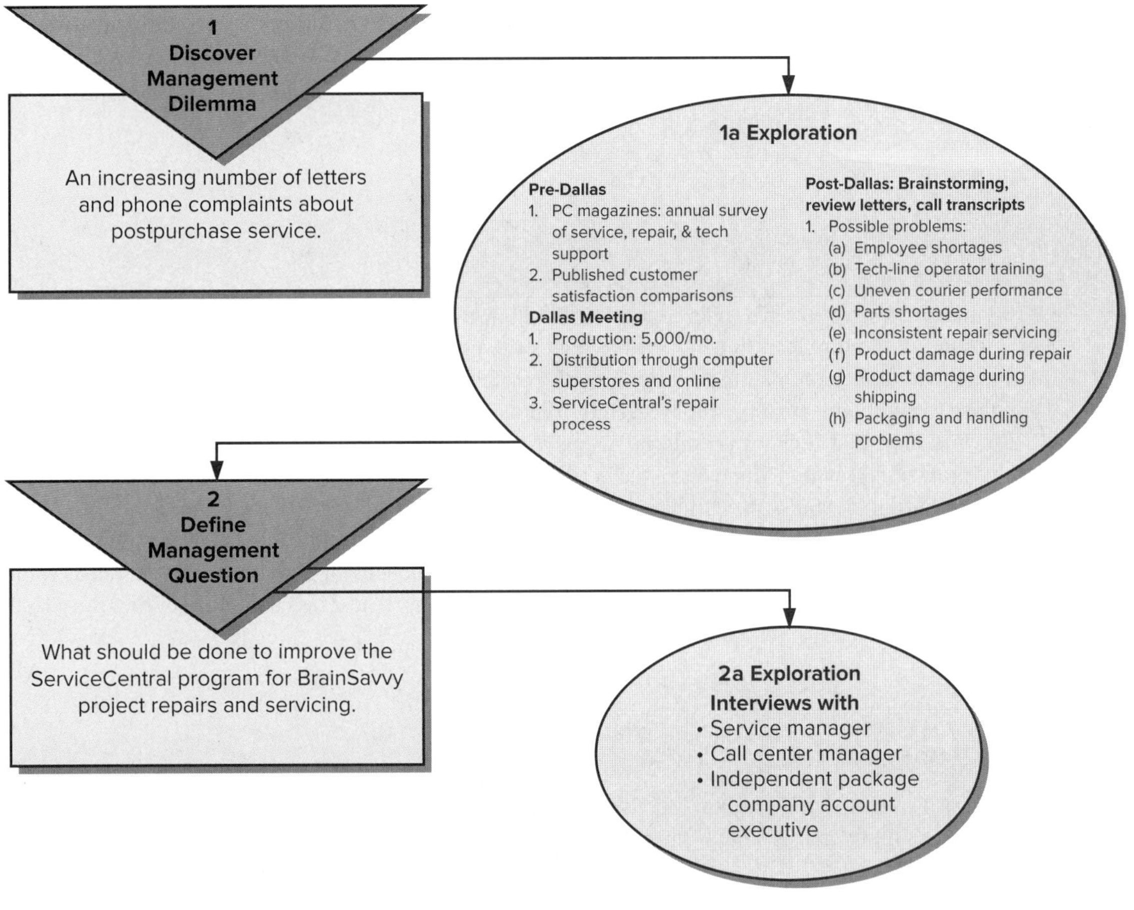

1 Discover Management Dilemma

An increasing number of letters and phone complaints about postpurchase service.

1a Exploration

Pre-Dallas
1. PC magazines: annual survey of service, repair, & tech support
2. Published customer satisfaction comparisons

Dallas Meeting
1. Production: 5,000/mo.
2. Distribution through computer superstores and online
3. ServiceCentral's repair process

Post-Dallas: Brainstorming, review letters, call transcripts
1. Possible problems:
   (a) Employee shortages
   (b) Tech-line operator training
   (c) Uneven courier performance
   (d) Parts shortages
   (e) Inconsistent repair servicing
   (f) Product damage during repair
   (g) Product damage during shipping
   (h) Packaging and handling problems

2 Define Management Question

What should be done to improve the ServiceCentral program for BrainSavvy project repairs and servicing.

2a Exploration
Interviews with
- Service manager
- Call center manager
- Independent package company account executive

will contain summaries of all secondary data searches and copies of any important articles, as well as all summaries of expert interviews. They agree on a file-naming protocol. Together they create a summary of each of their Dallas meetings and upload these files to a client-meeting-notes folder on Dropbox. Having met at least two of the individuals they want to interview, they define the objectives for these expert interviews that they will try to set up for the next day.

Later that day, Dayton and Celina reconvene. "I've assigned Zoe to review the transcripts and summarize the major themes. We'll have that later this afternoon or early tomorrow," discloses Celina. "And Ethan will research whether technical products have differing measurement issues for satisfaction than other industries we've studied. He's also searching for an industrywide study on laptop satisfaction, something we might use as a benchmark. I think we might want to determine if laptops have any special problems associated with construction, operation, use patterns, or repairs."

"I'm on that," claimed Dayton. "I've set up our call with Zane Bet, ServiceCentral's manager, tomorrow morning at 8:00. It's just one of the questions I've slated for the interview. The interview guide is uploaded to Dropbox."

"I need to ask Zane about a particularly troubling call transcript I found before handing the task over to Zoe," reveals Celina. She's sure to remember it. Tomorrow, I'll follow up with Parma; she's searching BrainSavvy archives for prior satisfaction studies."

"I uploaded my summary from my visit to Best Buy last night to Dropbox. When we get the team together, I'll share what the salesman said while they attempted to sell me one. That experience convinced me I don't have enough knowledge about BrainSavvy's laptops," shares Dayton. "When you check in with Parma, see if she can arrange for us to have loaners—one of each model—for at least a few weeks. We could have the team put them through some tests."

"Will do. I asked Parma to set up some fake registry info so that our team could make disguised calls to ServiceCentral. I've set up our interview tomorrow at 2:00 with Julie Breck, who manages the call center," revealed Celina. "And the interview with Zach Powell, FastDelivery's account executive for BrainSavvy, is at 4:30. It's important that the whole team listen to all the interviews. I'll arrange to have them recorded and archived for those who can't sit in."

Interviews

"It was a coup to discover what all is contained within ServiceCentral customer database: types of problem, location of the problem, remedy used to correct the problem, technician who did the service, production information about plant, date, production employees, part sources, and more," exclaims Celina. "And their warranty information database sounds like a treasure trove."

"But troubling that they have done little analysis of that data to arrive at their decision to do research," proclaims Dayton. "Zane just emailed a link to a Dropbox she set up to share that data with us. I'll assign Chardon to start a preliminary analysis."

"Ethan did a great job distilling the secondary data search," approved Celina. "He got tens of thousands of hits on his broad internet search. But he found us that benchmark laptop survey, as well as some key articles that will be helpful on each of the research questions. And Zoe's summary of the transcripts is equally valuable."

Data File Analysis

"Parma wasn't surprised by the analysis that Chardon did on the ServiceCentral database," confirms Dayton. "She's more comfortable having data insights to confirm the anecdotal evidence from the transcripts and letters."

>**Exhibit 17-4** Pareto Diagram of ServiceCentral Complaints from BrainSavvy's Data File Analysis

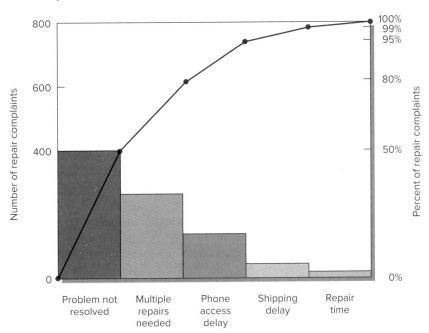

"The cumulative frequency line in the Chardon's Pareto diagram (Exhibit 17-4) shows that the top two problems (the repair did not resolve the customer's problem and the product was returned multiple times for repair) accounted for 80 percent of the perceptions of inadequate repair service. And his proximity plot (Exhibit 17-5) shows all the problems.

>**Exhibit 17-5** Proximity Plot of Problems from ServiceCentral's Data File Analysis

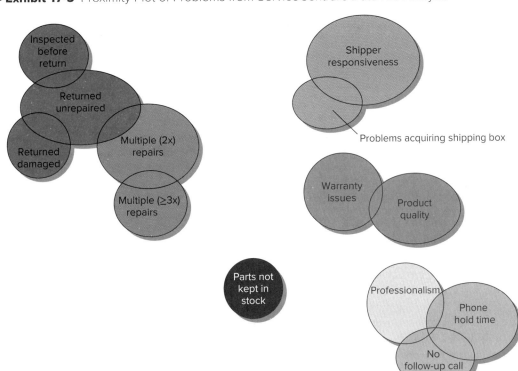

Process Modeling

"I've used your notes and mine from the Bet, Breck, and Powell interviews to develop the process models for both the phone-technical-assistance-only and the phone-technical-assistance-plus-physical-repair processes," shared Dayton. "Both are fairly straightforward. When a customer calls, a technician is assigned randomly based on who is available. They take the customer's phone, email, home address, and model number, and enter it into a database by incident number. They listen to the customer's description of the problem and enter this as a summary in real time. Based on the category of the problem, they ask a predetermined series of questions and enter the answers. Customer answers guide the technician in the steps and activities they use to resolve the issue over the phone. If the machine is operational, they connect with the customer through online screen-to-screen sharing software while the customer is on the phone.

"If the technician is unable to resolve the issue with the phone call, they provide the customer with a service code and dispatch FastDelivery to pick up the laptop before 6 p.m. that day (if the call comes through before 3 p.m.) or the following day by 10 a.m. (if it comes through between 3 p.m. and midnight). ServiceCentral's software generates a template report that contains all the data from the call and screen-share. It is accessible electronically by the repair facility; the file name is the assigned service code number. The damaged laptop is delivered to Dallas by 8 a.m. or 2 p.m. and slated for service the day it is received. A repair technician is assigned once the service code is assigned. If the service record is incomplete, ServiceCentral's repair technician calls the customer—it's never the same technician who diagnosed the problem. The call is usually after receipt of the laptop, but not always. The laptop is repaired the same day it is received, with courier pickup that evening and redelivery to the customer by 10 a.m. the following day at an address of their choosing—all within 48 hours of the call. That's the ideal. If parts aren't available, or the machine is more seriously compromised, it takes longer. There's no standard procedure for customer contact if a delay occurs.

"Not as much information was available on the FastDelivery process. It provides the packaging material, but it sources this locally. Courier drivers package the laptop at the customer's location. When the repair is complete, the repair technician brings the repaired laptop to the FastDelivery operation inside ServiceCentral. FastDelivery's representative repacks the laptop for shipment using the same type of packaging material, again locally sourced. FastDelivery can track the package's location at any point along the pickup-to-Dallas or Dallas-to-customer routes, so it has information on timing at each point along both routes; and we know the distance each laptop traveled and how far each traveled by truck and plane. As far as I can tell, no one photographs the laptop at the point of customer pickup, ServiceCentral arrival, or departure."

Focus Groups

"Using Chardon's analysis of the ServiceCentral data file, I recruited the focus group participants," relates Celina, "into three groups based on their BrainSavvy laptop model; I also have one mixed-model group with such severe damage that their laptops were replaced. The first two groups are this evening, with the others tomorrow. Zoe is assisting. We should have insights to share by late the following afternoon."

Investigative and Research Questions

"So, we know there are technician shortages in both the call center and the repair facility and problems getting new technicians trained quickly and adequately, all of which affect repair diagnostics; the courier is inconsistent in meeting promised pickup and delivery; an increasing number of laptops are returned unrepaired or damaged, sometimes severely, so we might question the adequacy of the packaging material or its use; and BrainSavvy has parts delivery problems affecting both manufacturer and repair—all of which reduce the speed of problem resolution," summarizes Celina.

"The possible investigative questions (Exhibit 17-6) and research questions (Exhibit 17-7) lists are growing," says Dayton. "Chardon's analysis should help us prioritize these for Parma."

>**Exhibit 17-6** VI's Investigative Questions for BrainSavvy's Service Central Project

Define Investigative Questions

1. How well is the call center helping the customers? Is it helping the customers with instructions? What percentage of customers' technical problems is the center solving without callbacks? How long do customers wait on the phone? How competent are technicians?

2. How good is the transportation company? Does it package laptops appropriately? Does it pick up and deliver laptops responsively? How long do customers wait for pickup? Delivery? Are the laptops damaged due to package handling? What available packaging alternatives are cost-effective?

3. How good is the repair group? What is the sequencing of the repair program, diagnostics through completion? Is the repair complete? Are customers' problems resolved? Are new repair problems emerging? Are customers' repair-time expectations being met?

4. What is the timing of repair from call-center contact to resolution? From call-center contact to pickup? From pickup to return delivery?

5. How is condition assessed and recorded at time of pickup/packaging, arrival at ServiceCentral, repackaging for delivery, and customer location?

6. What is the overall satisfaction with ServiceCentral and with the BrainSavvy product?

>**Exhibit 17-7** BrainSavvy's Possible Research Questions Following Interviews

Define Research Question(s)

Should the tech-support operator be given more intensive training?

Should FastDelivery be replaced?

Should the repair diagnostic and repair sequencing operations be modified?

Should the return packaging be modified to premolded, rigid form inserts, or conforming-expanding foam protection?

Should metropolitan repair centers be established to complement or replace ServiceCentral's repair facilities?

>Stage 2: Research Design

Sampling Design

"BrainSavvy keeps excellent records in ServiceCentral. It has phone, address, and email address for every customer who has had a laptop repaired at ServiceCentral in the last five years. Admittedly, some information may no longer be valid, and, due to memory decay, we should focus on those who had repairs in the last three months. This is a big step toward developing a sample frame," concludes Dayton.

"Based on our exploration," asserts Celina, "the target population should be all BrainSavvy laptop customers over 18 years of age who have had a ServiceCentral repair experience on their personal Brain-Savvy laptop in the prior three months. I'd define a case as any individual within that target population, regardless of location, ethnicity, age, or gender."

"Because he is familiar with the database, let's assign Chardon the task of building the sample frame," agreed Dayton. "But let's adjust it by removing people who have purchased or acquired a new BrainSavvy laptop and submitted their new warranty information since the repair experience, unless they have had a repair experience with the new laptop. It's unlikely these individuals will be using their originally repaired BrainSavvy and would have less information about its current operation."

"Remind him after the adjustment to randomize the cases alphabetically," reminds Celina. "We don't want all the participants to own only one model or to have been serviced by the same technician."

"Given the investment BrainSavvy has already made in ServiceCentral, we'll want to be confident that any recommendation is thoroughly supported by the data. With a clean sample frame," asserts Celina, "we could use a simple random probability sample or a systematic probability sample. What's your choice? I'm leaning toward the lower cost, easier to implement systematic sampling."

"Let's use systematic. I'd like to use perceived quality of service and likelihood to repurchase as our parameters of interest," explains Dayton. "According to the benchmark technology study Ethan discovered, the last is measured on a 5-point scale. And given the number of customers in the ServiceCentral database, we might want to draw at least 100 from each month."

Data Collection Design

Online Survey

Following exploration, the whole team has gathered together to brainstorm question topics for the online survey component of the design.

"It's not enough to know a customer is dissatisfied; ServiceCentral's management needs to know what processes, employees, part, and time sequences within the ServiceCentral program lead to dissatisfaction," reveals Celina. "So our instrument needs to include measurement of these topics."

"By using data from the benchmark technology satisfaction study," said Chardon, "we can establish convergent reliability."

"But I'm convinced we need a custom-designed scale for the evaluation of satisfaction," asserts Dayton. "We'll need to convince BrainSavvy."

Are Custom-Designed Measurement Questions Necessary?   Dayton and Celina video conference with Parma Mason and Logan Park, Director of Research for BrainSavvy. "Why is developing and testing customized questions necessary? It seems unnecessarily time consuming. Why reinvent the wheel when we have a satisfaction scale?" asked Park.

"When we held focus groups with your customers," shared Celina, "they continually referred to the need for your product service to 'meet expectations' or 'exceed expectations.' None of the current scales developed for customer satisfaction deal with expectations. We need a scale that does. Your company credo—'Underpromise and exceed expectations'—stresses the importance of a unique scale that ranges in five steps from 'Met no expectations' to 'Exceeded expectations,' but we need to name the in-between intervals so that the psychological spacing is equal between increments."

"Because of the way you are running your service operation," adds Dayton, "you'll want great precision and reliability. Besides setting up your own repair force, we understand you have contracted with an outside organization to provide repairs in certain geographic areas, with the intention after six months of comparing the performance of the inside and outside repair organizations and giving the future work to whichever performs better. We feel that such an important decision, which involves the job security of ServiceCentral employees, must have full credibility."

Park nods. "Okay, I'm willing to try a new scale. We'll want to assess the quality of the questions as we might want to use them with other satisfaction measures, too. Nice job, so far, Parma; you seem to have gotten a quick start with BrainSavvy. I look forward to seeing the research results, Dayton. Celina, now that we've met, I'm sure you served as moderator on some focus groups done for my prior employer; it's great to have someone of your caliber on our team."

Crafting the Custom-Designed Questions

"The Likert scale is a possibility for comparison to a custom BrainSavvy scale," hypothesizes Dayton, "now that we have Logan Park's endorsement for the customized scale."

Dayton is considering testing three scales (Exhibit 17-8): a Likert scale, a hybrid numerical rating scale with verbal anchors, and a hybrid expectation scale with each scale point having a verbal and numeric anchor. All are 5-point scales that are presumed to measure at the interval level.

For preliminary evaluation, Dayton needs a statement or question that can accompany each scale. Returning to VI's list of investigative questions, he finds a question that seems to capture the essence of the repair process: Are customers' problems resolved? Translated into an assertion for the scale, the statement becomes "Resolution of problem that prompted service/repair." Dayton has read an article that indicates Likert scales and scales similar to BrainSavvy's hybrid numerical scale frequently produce a heavy concentration of 4s and 5s—as an *error of leniency* is a common problem in customer satisfaction research. The authors suggest a 7-point scale to remedy this, but Dayton thinks the term "exceeded" on the expectation scale could compensate for scores that cluster on the positive end. He chooses the 5-point scale and refines the wording of the verbal anchors. Then he develops appropriate measurement questions for each of the investigative questions.

> **Exhibit 17-8** Scale Test for BrainSavvy ServiceCentral Project

Likert Scale				
The problem that prompted service/repair was resolved.				
Strongly Disagree	Disagree	Neither Agree nor Disagree	Agree	Strongly Agree
1	2	3	4	5

Numerical Scale (BrainSavvy Favorite)				
To what extent are you satisfied that the problem that prompted service/repair was resolved?				
Very Dissatisfied				Very Satisfied
1	2	3	4	5

Hybrid Expectation Scale				
Resolution of the problem that prompted service/repair.				
Met No Expectations	Met Some Expectations	Met Most Expectations	Met All Expectations	Exceeded Expectations
1	2	3	4	5

>**Exhibit 17-9** Plot of ServiceCentral Scale Evaluation

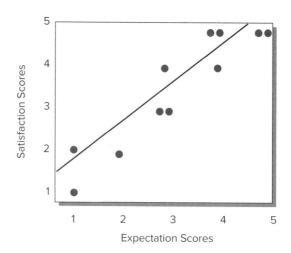

Parma wants to see the questions before the test so she can get feedback from the BrainSavvy research experts. They suggest it is unlikely that ServiceCentral would meet *none* of the customers' expectations. And, given *errors of strictness*, "no" should be replaced by the term "few" so that the low end of the scale would be more relevant. Dayton concedes their point and adjusts the response category to "Met few Expectations."

Now ready for a pilot test, Dayton, Celina, and Parma decide to compare only the expectation scale with BrainSavvy's numerical rating scale because the typical Likert scale would require that they create more potential assertion statements than they plan to use in the actual survey. Dayton chooses the *delayed equivalent forms* method for reliability testing. Using the ServiceCentral database, 30 participants are selected arbitrarily from those who have had recent repair service. They are recruited by phone and put into two groups (A and B). They are immediately provided a link via email to the first online survey; one week later they will be sent an email with a link to a second survey with the alternative scale. To group A, VI will administer the expectation scale followed by the numerical scale; to group B, the numerical scale is followed by the expectation scale.

Subsequently, Ethan correlates the numerical satisfaction scores with the expectation scores and plots the results (Exhibit 17-9). On the problem resolution question, the participants' scores from the

>**close**up

BrainSavvy Measurement Instrument

BrainSavvy

The BrainSavvy measurement instrument simplifies answering by using only two different attitudinal response strategies. The first is based on the custom-designed expectations scale, and the second based on a common likelihood scale. Each uses five response points—the first employing numerical codes along with verbal codes, while the second uses verbal anchors only. It asks for detailed identification information to permit follow-up, but it uses no gender, ethnicity, age, or other demographic descriptors to group the data because the most important variable, satisfaction level, is covered.

The instrument basically answers the question "How did ServiceCentral's program work for you?" It accomplishes this by setting up the 10 factors of interest: "Please answer the first set of questions using the following scale." The second scale basically addresses likely behaviors by asking, "Given your experience with ServiceCentral, how likely would you be to use it again or repurchase BrainSavvy?" Because the sample includes only ServiceCentral users, the underlying assumption that participants have used the service is acceptable. The language is appropriate for the participant's likely level of education. And the open-ended question used for comments adds the flexibility to capture any unusual circumstances not covered by the structured list of factors. (See Exhibit 17-10.)

>**Exhibit 17-10** Paper Mockup of BrainSavvy's ServiceCentral Questionnaire

BrainSavvy personal computers offer you ease of use and maintenance. When you need service, we want you to rely on **ServiceCentral**, wherever you may be. That's why we're asking you to take a moment to tell us how well we served you.

BrainSavvy

Please answer the first set of questions using the following scale:

Met **Few** Expectations 1	Met **Some** Expectations 2	Met **Most** Expectations 3	Met **All** Expectations 4	**Exceeded** Expectations 5

	1	2	3	4	5
1. Telephone assistance with your problem:					
a. Responsiveness	○	○	○	○	○
b. Technical competence	○	○	○	○	○
2. The courier service's effectiveness:	○	○	○	○	○
a. Arrangements	○	○	○	○	○
b. Pickup speed	○	○	○	○	○
c. Delivery speed	○	○	○	○	○
3. Speed of the overall repair process	○	○	○	○	○
4. Resolution of the problem that prompted service/repair	○	○	○	○	○
5. Condition of your BrainSavvy upon arrival	○	○	○	○	○
6. Overall impression of ServiceCentral's effectiveness	○	○	○	○	○

How likely would you be to . . .

	Very Unlikely	Somewhat Unlikely	Neither Unlikely nor Likely	Somewhat Likely	Very Likely
7. Use ServiceCentral on another occasion	○	○	○	○	○
8. Repurchase another BrainSavvy based on:					
a. Service/repair experience	○	○	○	○	○
b. Product performance	○	○	○	○	○

Please share any additional comments or suggestions

How may we contact you to follow up on any problems you have experienced?

Last Name _____   First Name _____   Email _____

City _____   State _____   Zipcode _____   Phone _____

Service Code

Thank you for your participation.

SUBMIT

When taken by laptop, participants will see the introduction first, followed by a single screen with the expectations scale and questions 1–6, followed by a screen with the likely scale and questions 7–8. The comment box will appear on the fourth screen, and the identifying information will appear on the last screen, along with the Thank You conclusion. Each screen will have a submit button: all screens will use <NEXT> except the last, which will use <SUBMIT>. If participants skip a factor, when they click <NEXT>, they will get a prompt to answer the factor they skipped. The status bar will appear at the top of each screen.

Each survey includes a disguised Service Code number unique to each participant. This links their responses and comments to the details of the call center and repair service logs for their repair experience. This will let BrainSavvy do a deeper analysis than it has contracted for, if the managers later change their minds.

numerical satisfaction scale and those from the expectation scale are positively correlated. The correlation index is .90 (1.00 is a perfect positive correlation). This reveals the equivalence of both scales. On another reliability issue, stability, a check of the test-retest reliability over a one-week interval produces a correlation index of .93 for the expectation scale, but the BrainSavvy numerical satisfaction scale has a lower index ($r = .75$). This implies that the expectation scale is more likely to produce stable and consistent results. Finally, as shown in the plot, the data for the resolution question measured on both scales are linear (they cluster around a straight line). Additionally, no "order-of-presentation" effects are found.

The team concludes that the preferred expectation scale has tested well and is a good replacement for BrainSavvy's existing numerical satisfaction scale. VI will use the new expectation scale for the BrainSavvy's research on the ServiceCentral project.

Measurement Instrument   "One of the selling points of the Best Buy pitch was the enhanced graphics capability online," affirms Dayton. "So we can assume purchasers will be using the online features. The online survey will be fairly simple. And with email addresses, we can do email invites and email reminders to participate in the survey."

"We should anticipate that some will take the survey on their phones, so we should ask them to take it on their laptop or design it for phone," said Celina. "As the study is both direct and undisguised, we should use the BrainSavvy logo on each online survey page to reinforce that participants are contributing to improvements."

"Agreed. We should have Parma send the invitation we create and use both her picture and her title to personalize and emphasize the survey's importance to BrainSavvy. I'm thinking it should be fairly straightforward," shares Dayton. "Something like: 'You've recently had your BrainSavvy laptop serviced at ServiceCentral. Please take five minutes to tell us what you thought of the service provided. Just click the link below.'"

"I'd modify that slightly," suggested Celina. "'You've recently had your BrainSavvy laptop serviced at ServiceCentral. We are constantly looking for ways to serve you better. Please take five minutes to tell us what you thought of the service provided. Just click the link below.' This might encourage participants to give us ideas in the open question box, not just reinforce complaints."

>Stage 3: Data Collection, Preparation, and Examination

Activate the Survey

"We'll be ready to launch the survey on August X, as planned," claimed Dayton. "It will likely take some follow-up emails to get a large number of targeted participants to respond. We should have the data ready to analyze about a week after the survey launches, after we've prepped and cleaned it. So that means we should be finalizing our data analysis plan now."

The Analysis Plan

It was decided that question 6, overall impression of ServiceCentral's effectiveness, is the variable that will be used to assess patterns in all other variables. Thus, each dummy table would look similar to the one below:

	Call Center Technical Competence				
Overall Impression	**Met Few**	**Met Some**	**Met Most**	**Met All**	**Exceeded All**
Met Few Expectations					
Met Some Expectations					
Met Most Expectations					
Met All Expectations					
Exceeded All Expectations					

All variables could also be cross-tabulated using likelihood to use ServiceCentral again or likelihood to repurchase BrainSavvy again based on the ServiceCentral experience, as shown below:

	Call Center Technical Competence				
Likely to again use ServiceCentral	**Met Few**	**Met Some**	**Met Most**	**Met All**	**Exceeded All**
Very Unlikely					
Somewhat Unlikely					
Neither Unlikely nor Likely					
Somewhat Likely					
Very Likely					

	Call Center Technical Competence				
Likely to purchase another BrainSavvy laptop	**Met Few**	**Met Some**	**Met Most**	**Met All**	**Exceeded All**
Very Unlikely					
Somewhat Unlikely					
Neither Unlikely nor Likely					
Somewhat Likely					
Very Likely					

Data Preparation and Examination

"I see Chardon is done with data prep," shares Celina. "Ethan and Chardon are ready to tackle the preliminary analysis on the quantitative data as soon as we give them the go ahead. Zoe has been building her coding scheme of the comment data as the comments have come in, so she's ready to run her preliminary content analysis."

"Tell them to start, but keep us posted to any unusual findings," said Dayton. "I want the exploratory data analysis done by Friday. So we can start the more rigorous analysis on Monday morning."

>Stage 4: Analyze the Data

"I really found the AID [automatic interaction detection] diagram of value," compliments Celina (Exhibit 17-11). "Using the overall impression of the repair service was the right choice as the initial dependent variable."

"On this analysis, we recoded several of the variables. As you can see on the left side," points out Chardon, "customers who rated 'resolution of the problem' as poor have fewer expectations being met or exceeded than the average for the sample (6 percent versus 62 percent). A poor rating on 'condition on arrival' exacerbates this, reducing the total satisfied group to 2 percent. We applied AID to each subgroup to find the variable that, when split, again helps understand the customer's evaluation process. On the right side, it was 'speed of service' that was most influential. This analysis alerts decision makers at BrainSavvy to the best- and worst-case scenarios for ServiceCentral. It's also a good indicator for how to recover during a problematic month, as well as which key drivers influence the process and should receive corrective resources."

Conference Call with Parma the Following Tuesday

"Is that chart I glimpse on the table one of mine?" asks Parma as she connects with Dayton and Celina via video conference call.

>**Exhibit 17-11** Automatic Interaction Detection of ServiceCentral's Repair Satisfaction

Overall ServiceCentral Impression
(Expectations = number scale)

1.	7% Met few
2.	14% Met some
3.	17% Met most
4.	**41% Met all**
5.	**21% Exceeded**

n = 475

Rescaled Attribute
Ratings

1–2 Poor
3 Average
4–5 Excellent

Resolution of the problem

Poor

44% Met few
35% Met some
15% Met most
6% Met all
0% Exceeded
n = 54

Average

8% Met few
42% Met some
40% Met most
8% Met all
2% Exceeded
n = 102

Excellent

0% Met few
2% Met some
10% Met most
57% Met all
31% Exceeded
n = 319

Condition on arrival

Poor

63% Met few
26% Met some
9% Met most
2% Met all
0% Exceeded
n = 25

Avg/Excellent

27% Met few
42% Met some
21% Met most
10% Met all
0% Exceeded
n = 29

Service rep technical competence

Poor

15% Met few
53% Met some
28% Met most
4% Met all
0% Exceeded
n = 45

Avg/Excellent

2% Met few
34% Met some
49% Met most
11% Met all
4% Exceeded
n = 57

Speed of repair

Poor/Average

0% Met few
5% Met some
20% Met most
69% Met all
6% Exceeded
n = 48

Excellent

0% Met few
1% Met some
8% Met most
55% Met all
36% Exceeded
n = 271

"It's one of nearly 50 tables and charts we will analyze before distilling our findings into your report," shared Celina, as she moved the chart out of range of the camera. "But it's just as likely you won't see this one because it's a boxplot and not likely to make it into the management topline report you requested. We do a variety of analytical exercises to reveal findings, insights, and, ultimately, our recommendations."

"I'm not pressuring to see the results, not much at least. I'm really calling to see if it would be possible to move up the oral presentation by one day. Logan Park wants to be at the presentation, but he has to be out of the country on the date we set," explained Parma.

Dayton and Celina shared a glance. They had expected this request as a big technology summit in London was all over the news. "We can do that, assuming we can get our flights changed," stated Dayton.

"Cancel your reservations," announced Parma. "I've arranged for you to use the company jet. What time would be convenient for it to pick you up between 8 and 11? The presentation is still scheduled for 2:00 p.m."

>Stage 5: Report the Research

"It's been a grueling few days to meet the shorter deadline, but I'm pleased with what we discovered and what we have to share with Parma and BrainSavvy," divulges Dayton. "Tell Ethan, nice job on the report graphics; we couldn't have put it together so fast if not for his charting skills. All the copies are made and packaged. Thanks for taking the lead on the oral. It was a great idea to divide the two reports. Are we ready for tomorrow?"

"Absolutely," affirms Celina. "Parma said to prepare for an extensive Q&A, so I've drafted a series of questions and prepared answers. If you want to see the oral support materials, you can review them in Dropbox. I'm leaving now to get ready for our 9 a.m. flight. I'm taking both portable projectors. Don't forget to bring your laptop as a backup. See you tomorrow."

"I'll have the topline report copies and the technical report with me, in case they have more detailed questions than you prepared for. See you tomorrow."

Oral Report

"While there will be several in the room," Parma noted, "the presentation will be web-delivered to a larger group."

Celina introduces herself and Dayton, then starts the presentation. Dayton joins her during the Q&A, especially to handle the more statistically oriented questions asked by Logan Park.

"Based on the poll results that are on your screen, you have reached a strong consensus on your first priority. The research strongly supports that you should be negotiating a stronger contract with your courier to address the in-transit damage issues. Congratulations," concluded Celina.

"That wraps up our briefing today. After reading the summary report, Celina and I are happy to respond via email to any follow-up questions any of you might have," invites Dayton. "For those of you off-site, Parma will deliver this report to your email shortly. Our email address is on screen, and it is also on the cover of the report. Parma, I'm handing control of the Web-meeting back to you."

As Parma starts to conclude the meeting, Celina is holding up a sign facing Dayton that reads, "Turn off your microphone." Dayton smiles and clicks off his mic.

"Thank you, Celina and Dayton. The research has clarified some critical issues for us and you have helped us focus on some probable solutions," approves Parma. Turning to the audience, Parma continues, "I'll be following up soon with an email that contains a link to the recorded archive of this presentation, allowing you to share this presentation with your staff. You will also be asked to participate in a brief survey when you close the Web-presentation window. I'd really appreciate your taking the three minutes it will take to complete the survey. This concludes the meeting. Thank you all for attending."

As soon as the audience audio is disconnected, Logan approaches. "That went well, Dayton. The use of the Q&A tool to obtain their pre-report ideas for action was a stroke of genius. When you posted the results as a poll and had them indicate their first priority, they were all over the board. It helped them understand that one purpose of the research and today's meeting was to bring them all together."

"Celina gets the credit for that stroke of genius," claims Dayton after removing his microphone and clicking off his speakerphone. "She is a strong proponent of interaction in our briefings. And she continually invents new ways to get people involved and keep them engaged."

"Kudos, Celina," congratulates Parma. "Who gets the credit for using the perceptual map?"

"Those honors actually go to our research associate, Zoe Gahanna," shares Celina. "I told her we needed a visual way to showcase the most important issues. She did a great job. I'll pass on your praise."

"Well," asked Parma, "where do we go from here?"

"Dayton and I will field any questions for the next week from you or your staff," explains Celina. "Then we will consider this project complete—until you contact us again."

>Post-Project Team Debriefing

Dayton, Celina, and Bedford sit with the team in the conference room. It's an active session with each discussing what could have gone better and what they might do differently in a similar project next time.

"BrainSavvy sent us two additional RFPs this morning, one competitive and one just for us," shared Bedford. "That's a strong indication of their pleasure with our work. And Parma recommended us to the CenterCity Symphony; we got its RFP this morning."

"Parma also indicated we should expect to receive a contract for a continuation of the ServiceCentral project; it will involve a monthly survey plus log assessment for the next 12 months; she said she discussed this with you at the presentation."

"She did. The cost overview and the invoices for the completed BrainSavvy project are in the financial documents folder on Dropbox," shares Dayton.

"I'll arrange for accounting to send out the BrainSavvy invoice," concludes Bedford.

"What are the new BrainSavvy projects?" asks Celina.

"The non-competitive RFP requests a study to provide data to justify making an advertising claim for BrainSavvy's new 9000 model. It's got a really short turnaround, so they want us to considering online qualitative with agile quant. Celina, it's more your type of project than Dayton's. We don't have any conflicts. After you review the RFP, let me know if you can do it in their time frame."

"I'll review it and get back to you," decides Celina.

"I need to check some possible conflicts before we consider the second project," explains Bedford. "If we're clear, I'll get back with you, Dayton, on the details."

"We're going to get a load of new business from this one project! Great job everyone!"

>The Continuation Contract

Three and a Half Months Later

"I see you're still tweaking the report," observes Celina. "I thought we had agreed it was finished at yesterday's meeting, and that the template we designed for the initial report worked well."

"I'm concerned that BrainSavvy hasn't made as much progress in the last few months as it had planned," explains Dayton. "I want to make sure that we're providing enough direction."

"Understood. But we agreed that the direction was clear," argues Celina. "Remember, we'll have the opportunity to be persuasive during our conference call with Parma, which is in 30 minutes. You promised her she'd have the topline before the call."

BrainSavvy's December TopLine Report

Visionary Insights
Research Solutions to Complicated Problems

ServiceCentral
Monthly Customer Survey Results

December 20XX

Prepared for Parma Mason
BrainSavvy Corporation
January 20XX

Prepared by
Dayton Wager and Celina Gamble

BrainSavvy CONFIDENTIAL

200 Magic Tower, Orlando, Florida 32827
407.555.4321 info@visiaionaryinsights.com www.visionaryinsights.com

BrainSavvy ServiceCentral December Results

Introduction

This report is based on the December data collected from the BrainSavvy ServiceCentral Survey. The survey asks customers about their satisfaction with the ServiceCentral repair and service system. Its secondary purpose is to identify monthly improvement targets for management.

The findings are organized into the following sections: (1) an executive summary, (2) methodology, (3) service improvement grid, (4) findings, and (5) open-ended question responses.

Executive Summary

The highest degrees of satisfaction with ServiceCentral were found in the categories of "delivery speed" and "pickup speed." Average scores on these items were between 4.2 and 4.4 on a 5-point scale. "Speed of repair," "condition on arrival," and "overall impression of ServiceCentral's effectiveness" also scored relatively well. They were above the *met all expectations* level (see appropriate charts).

Several questions were below the *met all expectations* level. From the lowest, "Call Center's responsiveness," to "Call Center's technical competence," and "courier service's arrangements," the average scores ranged from 2.0 to 3.9. In general, ratings have improved since November, with the exception of "condition on arrival."

The three items generating the most negative comments are (1) problems with the courier's arrangements, (2) long telephone waits, and (3) transfer among many people at the Call Center. These same comments carry over for the last two months. ServiceCentral's criteria for Dissatisfied Customers consist of negative comments in the Comments/Suggestions section or ratings of less than 3.0 on questions one through eight. Forty-three percent of the sample met these criteria, down from 56 percent last month. By counting only customers' comments (positive/negative or +/−), the percentage of Dissatisfied Customers would be 32 percent.

The ratio of negative to positive comments was 1.7 to 1, an improvement over November's ratio (2.3 to 1).

When the expectation-based satisfaction scores are adjusted for perceived importance, "ServiceCentral responsiveness," "technician competence," and "courier arrangements" are identified as action arenas. "Repair speed" and "problem resolution" maintained high importance scores and are also rated above average.

Methodology

The data collection instrument is an online survey. Participation is solicited via email among users of the ServiceCentral program.

The survey consists of 12 satisfaction questions measured on 5-point scales. The questions record the degree to which the components of the ServiceCentral process (arrangements for receiving the customer's computer through return of the repaired product) meet customers' *expectations*. A final categorical question asks whether customers will use ServiceCentral again. Space for suggestions is provided.

Sample

The sample consisted of 175 customers who provided impressions of ServiceCentral's effectiveness. For the four-week period, the response rate was 35 percent with no incentive given. Nothing is yet known about the differences between participants and nonparticipants.

Visionary Insights
Research Solutions to Complicated Problems

200 Magic Tower, Orlando, Florida 32827
407.555.4321 info@visiaionaryinsights.com
www.visionaryinsights.com

>closeupcont'd

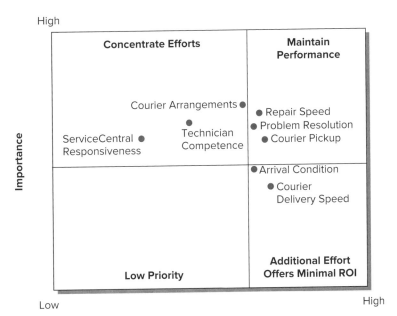

ServiceCentral Performance

Service Improvement Grid

Based on importance and mean rating, the quadrants are labeled to identify actionable items and to highlight those that bear watching for improvement or deterioration.

The **Concentrate Efforts** quadrant is the area where customers are marginally satisfied with service but consider service issues important. Question 1a, "ServiceCentral responsiveness," Question 1b, "technician competence," and Question 2a, "courier arrangements," are found here. "Technical competence" was similarly rated last month. Its perceived importance was rated higher in previous months. "Courier arrangements" has increased in perceived importance over previous reports.

In the **Maintain Performance** quadrant, ServiceCentral has, on average, *met all expectations* with the "repair speed" and "courier pickup" questions. Their mean scores are greater than 4.0 and considered important by respondents. "Problem resolution" has improved but remains a borderline concern.

Additional Effort Offers Minimal ROI contains two questions. Question 5, "arrival condition," has improved its ratings over last month but has dropped slightly on the importance scale because the average of importance scores (horizontal line) moved upward. Question 2c, "courier delivery speed," has a high satisfaction rating, but respondents considered this item to have lower importance than most issues in ServiceCentral.

There are no items in the **Low Priority** quadrant.

Visionary Insights
Research Solutions to Complicated Problems

200 Magic Tower, Orlando, Florida 32827
407.555.4321 info@visiaionaryinsights.com
www.visionaryinsights.com

Findings

The figures that follow provide (1) a comparison of the mean scores for each of the questions for the last three months and (2) individual question results. The latter contains frequencies for the scale values, percentages for each category, mean scores, standard deviations, and valid cases for each question. (See Appendix for question wording and placement.)

The three-month comparison (October, November, December) shows results for all scaled questions. December data bars reveal improvements on all average scores (vertical axis) except Question 5, "arrival condition." Most aspects of the service/repair process have shown improvement over the three-month period.

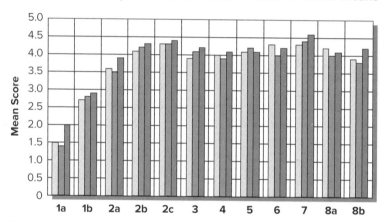

3-Month Comparison of All Factors Based on Factor Means

Dec. Mean: 1.98 2.89 3.89 4.19 4.44 4.17 4.10 4.14 4.24 4.54 4.02 4.09

October   November   December

Visionary Insights
Research Solutions to Complicated Problems

200 Magic Tower, Orlando, Florida 32827
407.555.4321 info@visiaionaryinsights.com
www.visionaryinsights.com

>closeupcont'd

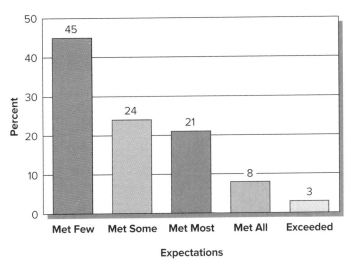

ServiceCentral's Call Center Responsiveness

Mean Score: 1.98   Standard Deviation: 1.09   Valid Cases: 159

Question 1a. ServiceCentral's Responsiveness

This question has the lowest mean score of the survey. Using a top-box method of reporting (combining the top two categories), 11 percent of the respondents felt that the Call Center met or exceeded their expectations for service responsiveness, still far below your goal. This has improved only marginally since November and has significant implications for program targets. Based on our visit and recent results, we recommend that you begin immediately the contingency programs we discussed: additional training for call center technicians and implementation of the proposed staffing plan.

Visionary Insights

Research Solutions to Complicated Problems

200 Magic Tower, Orlando, Florida 32827
407.555.4321 info@visiaionaryinsights.com
www.visionaryinsights.com

>**close**up**cont'd**

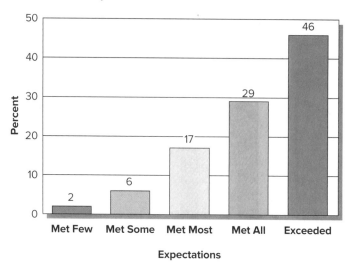

Overall Impression of ServiceCentral's Effectiveness

Mean Score: 4.14   Standard Deviation: 0.98   Valid Cases: 169

Question 6. Overall Impression of ServiceCentral's Effectiveness

ServiceCentral has increased the number of truly satisfied respondents with 46 percent (versus 43 percent in November) in the exceeded expectations category. The top-box score has increased to 75 percent of respondents (against 70 percent in November).

Visionary Insights
Research Solutions to Complicated Problems

200 Magic Tower, Orlando, Florida 32827
407.555.4321 info@visiaionaryinsights.com
www.visionaryinsights.com

>closeupcont'd

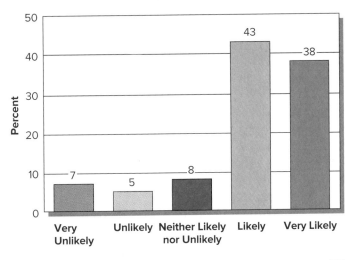

**Likelihood of Repurchasing BrainSavvy
Based on ServiceCentral Experience**

Mean Score: 4.02   Standard Deviation: 1.10   Valid Cases: 165

Question 8a. Likelihood of Repurchasing BrainSavvy Based on Service/Repair Experience

Respondents' average scores (4.02) for this likelihood scale are the highest this month since measurement began. Improvement of the courier service's arrangements with customers and the resolution of the problem that prompted service appear to be the best predictors of repurchase at this time.

Visionary Insights

Research Solutions to Complicated Problems

200 Magic Tower, Orlando, Florida 32827
407.555.4321 info@visiaionaryinsights.com
www.visionaryinsights.com

>**close**up**cont'd**

Patterns in the Open-Ended Questions

The following categories were found when the comments and suggestions were analyzed. The ratio of negative to positive comments was 1.7 to 1. Pickup problems continue to be "courier only" problems and coordination between ServiceCentral's telephone call center and the courier. Customers complain of holding on the phone for long periods and being transferred among support people. Problems with service are split between large problems that have not been fixed and small, nuisance problems that customers are prepared to live with. Positive comments commend turnaround and service and also praise specific technical operators.

Positive Comments   **(38)/(38.3%)**

About ServiceCentral process (13)/34.2%

Quick response (12)/31.6%

Great service (7)/18.4%

Helpful phone personnel (6)/15.8%

Negative Comments   **(61)/(61.6%)**

Shipping   (19)/31.1%
Pickup problems (15)

Delivery problems (2)

Box damage (1)

The courier charged customer (1)

Call Center   (20)/32.8%
Too long on hold (9)

Transferred call too frequently/confusion (8)

Untrained/hard to understand (2)

Won't use BrainSavvy call center again (1)

Service   (16)/26.2%
Problem continues (5)

Small things not fixed/damaged (6)

Took too long (2–7 weeks) (2)

Provide more information on what was done (2)

Offer extended warranty (1)

Product   (6)/9.8%
Multiple repairs needed (3)

Paint wears off (2)

General dislike of product (1)

BrainSavvy shouldn't need to be repaired (4)

Visionary Insights
Research Solutions to Complicated Problems

200 Magic Tower, Orlando, Florida 32827
407.555.4321 info@visiaionaryinsights.com
www.visionaryinsights.com

>closeupcont'd

Appendix

BrainSavvy personal computers offer you ease of use and maintenance. When you need service, we want you to rely on **ServiceCentral**, wherever you may be. That's why we're asking you to take a moment to tell us how well we served you.

BrainSavvy

Please answer the first set of questions using the following scale:

Met **Few** Expectations 1	Met **Some** Expectations 2	Met **Most** Expectations 3	Met **All** Expectations 4	**Exceeded** Expectations 5

	1	2	3	4	5
1. Telephone assistance with your problem:					
a. Responsiveness	○	○	○	○	○
b. Technical competence	○	○	○	○	○
2. The courier service's effectiveness:	○	○	○	○	○
a. Arrangements	○	○	○	○	○
b. Pickup speed	○	○	○	○	○
c. Delivery speed	○	○	○	○	○
3. Speed of the overall repair process	○	○	○	○	○
4. Resolution of the problem that prompted service/repair	○	○	○	○	○
5. Condition of your BrainSavvy upon arrival	○	○	○	○	○
6. Overall impression of ServiceCentral's effectiveness	○	○	○	○	○

How likely would you be to . . .

	Very Unlikely	Somewhat Unlikely	Neither Unlikely nor Likely	Somewhat Likely	Very Likely
7. Use ServiceCentral on another occasion	○	○	○	○	○
8. Repurchase another BrainSavvy based on:					
a. Service/repair experience	○	○	○	○	○
b. Product performance	○	○	○	○	○

Please share any additional comments or suggestions

How may we contact you to follow up on any problems you have experienced?

Last Name _____ First Name _____ Email _____

City _____ State _____ Zipcode _____ Phone _____

Service Code

Thank you for your participation.

SUBMIT

Visionary Insights

Research Solutions to Complicated Problems

200 Magic Tower, Orlando, Florida 32827
407.555.4321 info@visiaionaryinsights.com
www.visionaryinsights.com

>summary

LO17-1   Visionary Insights (VI) wins a contract with BrainSavvy to help it determine how to improve its ServiceCentral repair program. It is plagued with customer complaints about issues not being resolved and laptops being returned damaged. Exploration leads to the development of investigative and research questions and a determination to do a Web-based self-administered survey of prior ServiceCentral users via a probability sampling procedure.

Along this journey, VI partners perform exploratory research (including expert interviews, process analysis, focus groups, literature searchers, data file analysis, and more), pilot test measurement scales, and develop custom-designed questions for the survey. In an in-person and Web-delivered oral presentation, the VI team reveals their discoveries and guides the BrainSavvy team to arenas where changes will have the greatest likelihood to improve ServiceCentral.

LO17-2   Behind the scenes, RFPs are issued by BrainSavvy, accepted and responded to by VI, and reviewed and chosen by BrainSavvy. The VI team is formed, the file structure is developed, and responsibilities are allocated among team members. Conversations and meetings during the project are revealed.

>discussionquestions

Terms in Review

1   What **hypotheses** are driving the BrainSavvy research?

2   Build the **management-research question hierarchy** for the BrainSavvy project.

3   What types of **management questions** are involved in this project?

4   How did VI use **expert interviews** during exploration? What were some of the likely questions on VI's interview discussion guides?

5   During the **focus groups,** what issues will VI need to manage?

6   What are the possible sources of **error** in this project?

7   What supports the use of a **multiple rating list** scale for the development of the survey **measurement instrument?**

8   VI chose a **systematic probability sample** for this project. What are some of the disadvantages associated with this type of **sampling design** and were these a major problem for this project?

Making Research Decisions

9   Develop the **recruitment screener** for the focus groups used during exploration.

10   What factors might influence individuals to agree to participate in the survey?

11   Why might VI have chosen a web-based **self-administered survey** rather than a **telephone survey?**

12   Why did VI insist on a **custom-designed measurement question** for the survey questionnaire?

13   Evaluate the **sampling design** decisions, excluding the decision to use a systematic probability sample.

From Concept to Practice

14   Evaluate the **measurement questions** in Exhibit 17-10.

15   Evaluate the **measurement instrument** in Exhibit 17-10.

16   Evaluate the topline **management report** in the CloseUp.

>case index

Check the Case Index to determine whether a case provides data, the measurement instrument, video, or other supplementary material. Cases and case supplements are available in Connect.

Case	Type	Ch 01	Ch 02	Ch 03	Ch 04	Ch 05	Ch 06	Ch 07	Ch 08	Ch 09	Ch 10	Ch 11	Ch 12	Ch 13	Ch 14	Ch 15	Ch 16
A GEM of a Study	W, T				X												
AgriComp	W, D													X			
Akron Children's Hospital	W, V		X	X		X	X			X		X		X	X		X
Calling Up Attendance	W, I		X	X	X	X						X	X				X
Campbell-Ewald Pumps Awareness into the American Heart Association	W, V				X	X				X							
Campbell-Ewald: R-E-S-P-E-C-T Spells Loyalty	W	X				X					X	X	X		X	X	X
Can Research Rescue the Red Cross?	W					X				X			X				
Covering Kids with HealthCare	VC		X		X		X			X							
Cummins Engines	VC				X							X					
Data Development, Inc	VC									X	X						
Donatos: Finding the New Pizza	W, V		X	X						X	X	X					
Envirosell	VC							X									
Goodyear's Aquatred	VC		X	X		X											
HeroBuilders.com	W	X	X	X													
Inquiring Minds Want to Know—Now!	W, I		X	X	X	X				X	X	X		X	X		X
Lexus SC430	VC		X				X			X							
Mastering Teacher Leadership	W, I, D		X	X						X	X	X		X	X	X	X
Marcus Thomas Tests Hypothesis for Troy-Bilt® Creative Development	W, I		X			X				X		X		X	X		
McDonald's Tests Catfish Sandwich	W	X							X								
NCRCC: Teeing Up a New Strategic Direction	W, I, T, D		X	X			X			X	X	X	X	X	X	X	X
NetConversions Influences Kelley Blue Book	W, T				X			X	X					X			
Ohio Lottery: Innovative Research Design Drives Winning	W, Q, T, V		X	X			X			X	X	X					X
Open Doors: Extending Hospitality to Travelers with Disabilities	W	X			X	X	X										
Pebble Beach Co.	VC										X	X	X				
Proofpoint: Capitalizing on a Reporter's Love of Statistics	W, T				X							X	X	X	X		X
Ramada Demonstrates Its *Personal Best*™	W		X	X	X	X	X			X		X	X				
Starbucks, Bank One, and Visa Launch Starbucks Card Duetto™ Visa	VC				X	X											
State Farm: Dangerous Intersections	W		X		X	X		X			X						
The Catalyst for Women in Financial Services	W, T				X	X											
USTA: Come Out Swinging	W, I, VC		X	X	X	X					X	X	X			X	
Volkswagen's Beetle	VC											X	X		X		
Yahoo!: *Consumer Direct Marries Purchase Metrics to Banner Ads*	W		X	X	X	X					X	X					

LEGEND:

W = Written Case
D = Data File
VC = Video Case
V = Some Video Material
I = Instrument
Q = Some Measurement Quuestions
T = Some Table/Graphed Data

508

>A GEM of a Study

The Global Entrepreneurship Monitor Entrepreneurial Assessment, a joint project of the Kauffman Center for Entrepreneurship Leadership at Babson College and the London Business School, has undertaken a long-term, large-scale project to prove the causal links between a government's economic policies and initiatives, the resulting entrepreneurial activity, and subsequent economic growth. This case describes multiple-stage research, including thousands of interviews in several countries by established research firms. **www.babson.edu**; **www.lsbf.org.uk**; **www.gemconsortium.org**

>AgriComp

AgriComp, a supplier of computer systems for farmers, has surveyed its dealers on whether to change its procedure for settling warranty claim disputes. Currently, local dealers handle warranty services for customers via local repair followed by a reimbursement claim to AgriComp. Denied claims follow an internal company appeal process. Dealers have been complaining about the fairness of the appeal process and in a recent survey were asked to respond to an alternative process, an impartial mediator. The student is asked to review survey results and determine whether the costly external mediator process would be worth implementing to keep the dealers happy.

>Akron Children's Hospital

Northeastern Ohio is a highly competitive health care market, especially for the care of seriously ill children. With powerhouse health care institutions like the Cleveland Clinic venturing into the children's care segment, Akron Children's Hospital needed a way to differentiate itself. The research profiled in this case helped develop the positioning of Akron Children's Hospital and its promotional approach and resulted in an increase in its bed-occupancy rate, a key metric in the health care industry. **www.akronchildrens.org**; **www.marcusthomasllc.com**

>Calling Up Attendance

This case examines a study by Prince Marketing for TCS Management Group. TCS Management Group, Inc., part of Aspect Communications, is the leading provider of workforce management software, especially related to call center management. The study discusses measures of customer satisfaction and aims to predict attendance at a two-day educational event, Users Forum. **www.aspect.com**

>Campbell-Ewald Pumps Awareness into the American Heart Association

You wouldn't think that an organization that does as much good as the American Heart Association would have low awareness, but at the start of the described research program its unaided awareness level was just 16 percent. For a company reliant on contributions, low awareness is a major problem. This case profiles the research behind the American Heart Association's first-ever paid advertising campaign. **www.c-e.com**; **www.americanheart.org**

>Campbell-Ewald: R-E-S-P-E-C-T Spells Loyalty

Campbell-Ewald, the Detroit-based marketing communications company, part of the global Interpublic Group of Companies, is an award-winning consultancy. This case describes the research behind its effort to measure and improve customer loyalty and the development of its five respect principles that lead to enhanced customer commitment. **www.c-e.com**

>Can Research Rescue the Red Cross?

The American Red Cross seemed in its true element following September 11, 2001. It was flooded with donations to do its highly needed and regarded work. Most of those donations went to its Liberty Fund. But shortly after it started to disburse the funds, the media began asking questions. And the American Red Cross soon wore a patina of tarnish. Learn about the research that evaluated Americans' perception of the Red Cross and how research by Wirthlin Worldwide (now part of Harris Interactive) helped craft a new and highly effective donation solicitation process. **harris-interactive.com**; **www.redcross.org**

>Covering Kids with Health Care

This video case describes the research done to increase enrollment in the federal government's SCHIP program. Managed at the state level, the State Children's Health Insurance Program provides basic health coverage for the children of the nation's working poor. Research by Wirthlin Worldwide (now Harris Interactive) revealed why families weren't enrolling, and findings were used by GMMB, Inc., to develop a major advertising and public relations initiative to increase enrollment. The research and campaign were sponsored by the Robert Wood Johnson Foundation. (Video duration: 16 minutes) **www.rwjf.org**; **harris-interactive.com**; **www.gmmb.com**

>Cummins Engines

Cummins Engines makes advanced, fuel-efficient diesel power systems and engine-related components and specializes in customized diesel engine production. Shipping more than 1,000 engines per day to customers and dealers on every continent, Cummins has a long history of innovation, from winning performances at the Indianapolis 500 to the first natural gas–fueled engine to pass California's tough emissions regulations. This case focuses on the Signature 600 engine, the newest and most advanced diesel engine on the market. (Video duration: 14 minutes) **www.cummins.com**

>Data Development Corporation

This video case profiles Data Development Corporation (DDC), a leader in in-home and office personal interviewing. DDC has fielded more than 20,000 studies since 1960; it currently has four offices in the United States, with global capabilities in 80 countries worldwide. DDC WATS centers have 170 CATI (computer-assisted telephone interviewing) stations. The company offers a network of CAPI (computer-assisted personal interviewing) in more than 180 mall locations, as well as interactive software (STORE) simulations of store shelving, buildings, and so on, to develop and evaluate logos, signage, packaging, and the like. DDC's Internet Survey Group offers Web-based studies. (Video duration: 11 minutes)

>Donatos: Finding the New Pizza

The pizza segment of the fast-food industry is very aggressive. As people's tastes change and new diets become the rage, restaurant chains must decide if and how to respond. This case focuses on the research behind the introduction of Donato's low-carbohydrate pizza and how the company collapsed its normal product-development research process to take advantage of a current trend. **www.donatos.com**

>Envirosell

Envirosell specializes in behavioral research, specifically in the retail environment. It has done this for *Fortune* 500 companies including banks, stores, and restaurant chains, as well as consumer product companies. In this video case, the managing director, research director, and senior analyst share information from several observational studies done in banks, as well as music, general-merchandise, and other retail environments. Envirosell, which has offices in the United States, Europe, Brazil, Japan, Mexico, and Turkey, strives to understand what people buy and how to get them to buy more. (Video duration: 10 minutes) **www.envirosell.com**

>Goodyear's Aquatred

This video case profiles the genesis of the Goodyear Aquatred tire. In 1993, the Aquatred tire, winner of more than a dozen awards, including Japan's prestigious Good Product Design Award, reached more than 2 million units in sales in the United States. This revolutionary tire pumps away more gallons of water per second as you drive at highway speeds. And a new tread rubber compound provides road-hugging traction and extends the tread life. The Aquatred tire segmented the market in a way that had not been done before. (Video duration: 14 minutes) **www.goodyear.com**

>HeroBuilders.com

Emil Vicale, president of BBC Design Group, used rapid prototyping technology (RPT) to build wax or plastic three-dimensional prototypes of his clients' designs. But this same technology can be used to custom-manufacture dolls. Shortly after September 11, 2001, Vicale Corporation, BBC's parent company, purchased an e-commerce toy company. Vicale's first action figure was made to honor the heroes who emerged from that event. Using RPT, he crafted a doll with the head of George W. Bush and the body of Arnold Schwarzenegger. Other figures followed. This case is about a design firm that used exploratory research to define a niche in the action-figure business. **www.herobuilders.com**

>Inquiring Minds Want to Know—NOW!

This case describes a multistage communication study undertaken by the research department of Penton Media, a publisher of business trade magazines, to determine the long-term viability of a reader and advertiser service, the *reader service card*, a postcard-size device used by readers to request additional information from a particular advertiser. **www.penton.com**

>Lexus SC 430

This video case follows the research used to develop the newest Lexus, the SC 430, the line's hard-top convertible. From auto show interviews to qual-quant clinics and positioning analysis, learn about how Team One Advertising, Lexus's U.S. agency of record used research to position this latest entry into the crowded sport coupe category. (Video duration: 8 minutes) **www.teamone-usa.com**; **www.lexus.com**

>Marcus Thomas Tests Hypothesis for Troy-Bilt® Creative Development

Troy-Bilt® works with Marcus Thomas LLC to develop marketing communications, including television advertising campaigns. As part of its creative development, Marcus Thomas needed to understand what motivated the yardwork enthusiast and what makes television advertising most effective within the lawn and garden industry. Marcus Thomas developed a hypothesis that "consumers who are in the market to purchase a product process television advertising differently than those who are not in the market for lawn and garden equipment." It used an online survey employing a control group, with embedded video, to test this hypothesis and develop the subsequent ad campaign. **www.marcusthomasllc.com**; **www.troybilt.com**

>Mastering Teacher Leadership

This case is about a multistage communication study of teachers by Wittenberg University's Department of Education to determine the viability of starting a Master of Education program for Ohio-certified teachers working within school districts serving a five-county area. **www.wittenberg.edu**

>McDonald's Tests Catfish Sandwich

This case describes the test marketing for McDonald's catfish sandwich in the southeastern United States. It asks students to assume they are the new product development team and to assess the research design described. **www.mcdonalds.com**

>NCRCC: Teeing Up a New Strategic Direction

The NCR Country Club started out as a benefit for thousands of National Cash Register employees. By the late 1990s, those employees were aging rapidly and the core membership needed to be increased. NCRCC offers two golf courses. One is an award-winning, championship-hosting course on the PGA tour. But the club wasn't attracting new members, especially younger families. This case is about a membership study done as part of a larger management initiative to evaluate several strategic directions the club might take to expand its membership. **www.ncrcountryclub.com**

>NetConversions Influences Kelley Blue Book

Kelley Blue Book (KBB) is one of the most visited automotive sites on the Web. Visitors flock there to estimate the price of a car they might buy or sell. KBB needed to enhance its site's performance for advertisers, who had become a major source of revenue as sales of the printed *Kelley Blue Book* had declined. NetConversions, a Web analytic service that evaluates website performance, conducted the research; it is now part of Microsoft. This case reveals how websites are evaluated so that new design elements can be developed and tested. **www.microsoft.com/en-us/**; **www.kelleybluebook.com**

>Ohio Lottery: Innovative Research Design Drives Winning

The Ohio Lottery was originally developed as an additional source of public school funding. Today proceeds from lottery games annually provide approximately 7 percent of the public educational budget. This research was originally undertaken because the lottery director wanted a deeper understanding of lottery players and insight into nonplayers. The research design described in this case is multistage and incorporates the use of both qualitative and quantitative research. This case reveals the research that guides the current Ohio Lottery promotional program that encourages play of its various games. **www.marcusthomasllc.com**; **orcinternational.com**; **www.ohiolottery.com**

>Open Doors: Extending Hospitality to Travelers with Disabilities

Eric Lipp started the Open Doors Organization (ODO) to help travelers with disabilities. In order to get the attention of the travel and hospitality industries, and to effect changes desired by people with disabilities, ODO undertook a major research project to estimate the expenditures of persons with disabilities and the accommodations that would be necessary to get them to travel more. Harris Interactive was chosen to field the multimethod survey. This case describes the methodology and the effects of the first round of a multiphase study. **www.opendoorsnfp.org**; **harris-interactive.com**

>Pebble Beach Co.

This case profiles the Pebble Beach Company, a 5,300-acre complex in Monterey, California, that offers three lodging options (Casa Palmero opened in September 1999, The Inn at Spanish Bay opened in 1989, and the Lodge at Pebble Beach opened in 1919), four golf courses, plus a new five-hole "golf links," eight restaurants, and an oceanside Beach and Tennis Club. Pebble Beach has repeatedly won awards as America's best travel resort and was host to the 2004 AT&T Pro-Amateur championship, the U.S. Open in 2000, the Callaway Golf Pebble Beach Invitational in 2004, and the newest tournament on the 2005 PGA Champions tour (First Tee Open). In January 1999, The Inn at Spanish Bay was granted the coveted Mobil Five-Star Award from the 1999 *Mobil Travel Guide*. Pebble Beach achieves its quality status by focusing on seven core values. The company is land-locked, so it must develop ever-creative ways to make the facilities it has more intensively profit-generating. (Video duration: 11 minutes) **www.pebblebeach.com**

>Proofpoint: Capitalizing on a Reporter's Love of Statistics

Proofpoint provides antispam software and email security software solutions for large enterprises. Their software products stop spam, protect against email viruses, ensure that outbound email messages comply with both corporate policies and external regulations, and prevent leaks of confidential information via email and other network protocols like blogs and text-messaging. Proofpoint knew from its customer inquiries that the IT professional was increasingly concerned with outbound information privacy compliance issues. Believing that painting this broader picture would earn them valuable space and airtime in the business, IT, and mainstream media, Proofpoint sponsored a series of surveys among IT professionals. This case is about those surveys. **www.proofpoint.com**

>Ramada Demonstrates Its *Personal Best*™

This case describes syndicated research in the hospitality industry that revealed trends in customer satisfaction and Ramada's proprietary research leading to the development of the *Personal Best*™ employee hiring, training, and motivation program. **www.ramada.com**

>Starbucks, Bank One, and Visa Launch Starbucks Card Duetto™ Visa

In the very mature financial services industry, it is rare for a new financial product to garner much attention, let alone be named one of *BusinessWeek*'s outstanding products of the year. But what started as a way for Starbucks to add value to its existing Starbucks Card program developed into a financial product that many other institutions are interested in exploring. This case reveals the research that was done to develop this new payment option for Starbucks customers. (Video duration: 11 minutes) **www.starbucks.com**; **www.chase.com**; **www.visa.com**

>State Farm: Dangerous Intersections

State Farm, the nation's largest auto insurer, distributed a list of the 10 most dangerous intersections in the United States based on crashes resulting in claims by its policyholders. What started as a study to reduce risk turned into an ongoing study that directs a major public relations effort: State Farm provides funds for communities to further research their dangerous intersections and initiate improvements based on the research. This case tells how the State Farm Dangerous Intersections initiative got started and how it is done. **www.statefarm.com**

>The Catalyst for Women in Financial Services

Smith Barney (now Morgan Stanley Smith Barney) was ordered by the court, in settling the landmark sexual harassment case, to evaluate the climate for personal development and advancement through promotion not only in Smith Barney but, as a comparative, in other financial services firms. The case describes the methodology used to sample both men's and women's beliefs and attitudes, as well as reveals some of the basic findings. **www.catalyst.org**; **morganstanley.com**

>USTA: Come Out Swinging

The United States Tennis Association funded one of the most aggressive surveys ever undertaken about a single sport in order to revitalize tennis in the minds of consumers. The survey results were supplemented with qualitative research by Vigilante (owned by Publicis Groupe), a specialist in urban communication campaigns. What resulted was a full-scale marketing initiative involving the establishment of Tennis Welcome Centers and the Come Out Swinging advertising, merchandising, and public relations campaigns. This case reveals the research and how the marketing initiative developed. (Video duration: 11 minutes) **www.usta.com**; **www.publicisgroupe.com/en**; **www.thetaylorgroup.com**

>Volkswagen's Beetle

This video case profiles the history of the original Beetle in the U.S. market from its introduction in 1949 to its demise in 1979 and then follows the initial two years of the New Beetle's rebirth, 1998 and 1999. The Beetle became a symbol of the 1960s rebelliousness, but it lost the love of a generation when it stressed engineering over style and low-cost operation, two factors that baby boomers considered crucial in the 1970s. By 1974, the Beetle had lost ground to its aggressive Japanese rivals for the value segment of the U.S. automobile market. In 1998, when the Beetle was reintroduced in the United States, it surpassed all sales estimates. The second year it doubled its sales. Historically, the Beetle is the world's best-selling car, having sold in more countries than any other automobile, with 21 million cars sold in its lifetime. (Video duration: 16 minutes) **www.vw.com**

>Yahoo!: *Consumer Direct* Marries Purchase Metrics to Banner Ads

As little as two years ago, many advertising pundits were bemoaning the inevitable demise of the banner ad on the Internet. But maybe they were too quick to judge. This case reveals how Yahoo!, in combination with ACNielsen's *Homescan®*, has developed a methodology *(Consumer Direct)* to evaluate the true effectiveness of banner ads, from ad exposure to shopping cart. It also reveals the role Dynamic Logic (now part of Kantar Millward Brown) played in conducting post-exposure ad evaluation. **www.yahoo.com**; **www.ncppanel.com**; **www.millwardbrowndigital.com**

>appendices

Business Research Proposals and RFPs (with Sample RFP)

>Proposing Research

There are four primary reasons for a manager to develop a research proposal: (1) clarify his or her thoughts for self-conducted research, (2) clarify his or her thoughts in order to delegate the research to a subordinate, (3) provide background and direction to an in-house research department, and (4) seek outside assistance from a research professional. While some may view the proposal process as unnecessary work, the more inexperienced the manager, the more important it is to have an adequately documented proposal. In the proposal process, Exhibit a-1, the left side addresses the process when research expertise is sought (reason 4); this type of proposal is called the *request for proposal (RFP)*. The right side of the exhibit addresses reasons 1, 2, and 3: the internal proposal. With advanced technology and software, many managers are tackling their own research or delegating it to a subordinate. So, we will explore the internal proposal first.

The Research Proposal

The purpose of the research proposal is to discuss what has led to the decision that research will have value, to present the research question, and to suggest a plausible, affordable research design. The *research proposal* is essentially a road map; it describes what, why, how, where, and by whom the research will be done and includes the following:

1. The management question to be researched.
2. The research efforts of others who have worked on related management questions.
3. The investigative questions for solving the management question,
4. The research design.
5. The benefit of doing this particular research project.[1]
6. Potential problems that may be encountered and methods for avoiding or dealing with them.

The process of writing a proposal encourages the manager to plan and review the project's logical steps. During stage one of the research process, the manager used exploratory research of several types to help define the management question, develop investigative questions, refine the research question(s), and value and budget for research. Developing the proposal offers the opportunity to spot flaws in logic, and errors in assumptions or even management questions.

Another benefit of the proposal is the discipline it brings to the manager. Many managers, when requesting research from an in-house research departmental, may not adequately define the problem they are addressing. The research proposal acts as a catalyst for discussion between the person conducting the research and the manager. The researcher translates the management question, as described by the manager, into the research question and outlines the objectives of the study. Upon review, the manager may discover that the interpretation of the problem does not encompass all the original symptoms. The proposal, then, serves as the basis for additional discussion between the manager and the researcher until all aspects of the management question are understood. Parts of the management question may not be researchable (not subject to empirical study). An alternate design, such as a qualitative study, may need to be proposed. Upon completion of the discussions, the manager and researcher should agree on

> **Exhibit a-1** The Research Proposal Process

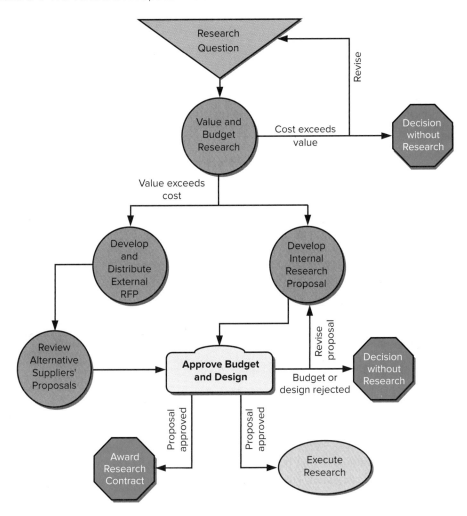

a carefully worded research question. As Exhibit a-2 reveals, proposal development can work in an iterative fashion until the sponsor authorizes the research to proceed.

Any in-house researcher uses the approved research proposal as a guide throughout the research project. Progress can be monitored and milestones noted. Comparison of the research project results with the proposal is also one step in the process of evaluating the overall research. At completion, the proposal provides an outline for the final research report.[2] Comparing the final report with the stated proposal objectives makes it is easy for the manager to decide if the research goal—a better decision on the management question—has been achieved.

A thorough proposal process is likely to reveal all possible cost-related activities, thus making cost estimation more accurate. Because many of these cost-associated activities are related to time, a proposal benefits a manager by revealing a time frame for the project. These time and cost estimates encourage managers and those assigned to do the research to plan the project so that work progresses steadily toward the deadline.

There are two general levels of complexity in proposals: small-scale studies and large-scale studies. The small-scale study, common in business, is often within the manager's budget discretion. It can be either an internal study or contracted to an outside research supplier using an RFP. The large-scale study often exceeds the manager's budget approval and must receive approval at a higher level. Such studies usually require professional research expertise and usually require an RFP, and its more complex, detailed proposal, if an in-house research department is not available.

> **Exhibit a-2** Proposal Development

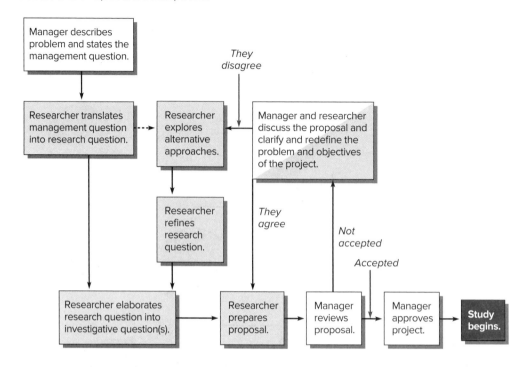

>Proposal Structure

Exhibit a-3 displays a set of modules for building the various proposals. Their order suggests an outline for a proposal. This exhibit is a general guide; sometimes more or less appropriate for a specific purpose.

Executive Summary

The *executive summary* is essentially an informative abstract, giving executives the chance to grasp the essentials of the proposal without having to read the details.[3] It allows a busy manager, internal research department head, or subordinate to understand quickly the elements of the proposal. Externally, it allows a research company to determine if its expertise fits the needs of the requesting organization and if it has a conflict of interest with other research projects in progress. The goal of the summary is to secure a positive evaluation by the executive who will pass the proposal on to the staff for a full evaluation. As such, the executive summary should include brief statements of the management dilemma and management question, the research objectives/research question(s), and the benefits of the proposed research design.

Problem Statement

Internally, the *problem statement* section needs to convince the approving manager to continue reading the proposal. You should capture the reader's attention by stating the management dilemma, its background and consequences, and the resulting management question. The importance of answering the management question should be emphasized here if a separate module on the importance/benefits of the study is not included later in the proposal. In addition, this section should include any restrictions or areas of the management question that will not be addressed.

Problem statements too broadly defined cannot be addressed adequately in one study. It is important that the management question distinguish the primary problem from related problems clearly. After

> **Exhibit a-3** Proposals Modules for Internal Proposals and RFPs

Proposal Types / Proposal Modules	Management Proposals			
	Internal		RFP	
	Small-Scale	Large-Scale	Small-Scale	Large-Scale
Executive summary	✔	✔	✔	✔
Problem statement	✔	✔	✔	✔
Research objectives	✔	✔	✔	✔
Literature review		✔		✔
Importance/ benefits of study		✔	✔	✔
Research design	✔	✔	✔	✔
Data analysis				✔
Nature and form of results	✔	✔	✔	✔
Qualification of researchers			✔	✔
Budget	✔	✔	✔	✔
Schedule	✔	✔	✔	✔
Facilities and special resources		✔	✔	✔
Project management		✔		✔
Bibliography		✔		✔
Appendices/ glossary of terms		✔		✔
Measurement instrument		✔		✔

reading this section, the approving manager should know the management dilemma and the question, its significance, and why something should be done to change the status quo.[4]

In an external RFP proposal, internal experts, usually managers, define the problem. Alternatively, an expert or a group of experts may be retained to assist in defining the research question and then writing the remainder of the RFP. Once the problem is defined, the technical section of the RFP can be written.

When a firm receives an RFP, the problem statement might be in the letter soliciting a research proposal. This same letter would introduce the organization soliciting the proposal. Here is an example:

Our call center currently operates without an automated recording and monitoring process. We have 10 dedicated reviewers sustaining this function. In addition, our call center supervisors spend six hours per month monitoring the quality of our reviewers. The reviewers rely on a manually generated schedule to select representatives and times for monitoring. When representatives are on active calls during the monitoring schedule, it is problematic to trace them. However, reviewers have access to the online scheduling software. Thus, they can view the account screens selected by the representative using our own software tool.

The quality of our customer service and the resulting customer satisfaction are of vital importance. We need to significantly increase the efficiency of our customer call monitoring through automation and a recorded database for agent review. We also need to discover the extent to which these technical changes to our process will improve customer perceptions of service.

Research Objectives

The *research objectives* module addresses the purpose of the investigation. It is here that you lay out exactly what is being planned by the proposed research. In a descriptive study, the objectives can be stated as the research question. If the proposal is for a causal study, then the objectives can be restated as a hypothesis.

For the manager, the objectives module reveals specific, concrete, and achievable goals—the same that will be used to judge the effectiveness of the research and its report. It is best to list the objectives either in order of importance or in general terms first and then move to specific terms (i.e., research question followed by underlying investigative questions). The research question(s) or hypotheses should be highlighted for quick identification.

For an RFP, the research objectives section provides the guidelines for judging the submitting research companies' proposals by verifying that each objective is discussed in the research design. It is also used for judging the effectiveness of the research and the final report by verifying that each objective is addressed in the data analysis, results, and recommendation.

Literature Review

The *literature review* section examines recent or historically significant research studies, company data, or industry reports that act as a basis for the proposed study and presents a brief review of the information, not a comprehensive report. Information is always sourced, and particularly interesting material might be quoted. This section emphasizes important results and conclusions of other studies, the relevant data and trends from exploratory research, and particular methods or designs that could be duplicated or should be avoided due to research design weaknesses. If the problem has a historical background, the literature review begins with the earliest references.

The literature review may also explain the need for the proposed research as it reveals shortcomings and/or informational gaps in secondary data sources. This analysis may go beyond scrutinizing the availability or conclusions of past studies and their data to assessing the accuracy of secondary sources, the credibility of these sources, and the appropriateness of earlier studies in dealing with the current management dilemma. This section ends with a summary of the important aspects of the literature and interprets them in terms of the manager's problem.

Regardless of the intended audience, in the small-scale project proposal, the literature review is not included; the findings are reviewed briefly with the research design section.

Importance/Benefits of the Study

In the *importance/benefits* section, you describe explicit benefits that will accrue from doing the research now. Usually, this section is not more than a few paragraphs. This section is where the manager must be the advocate for the research.

Research Design

The *research design* module describes what the researcher will do in technical terms. This section should include as many subsections as needed to show the phases of the project. It includes information on sampling design (including sample selection and size), data collection design (including method), measurement instruments, procedures, and ethical requirements. When more than one way exists to approach the design, the section reveals the methods rejected and why the selected design is superior. In an RFP these are stated as hypotheticals For small-scale projects, this section would include data analysis design.

Data Analysis

It is in the *data analysis* section that the manager describes proposed handling of the data and the theoretical basis for using selected techniques. It specifies the types of data to be obtained and the interpretations that will be made in the analysis.

In an RFP, it specifies whether data are to be turned over to the sponsor for proprietary reasons. This section guides the manager when determining whether the researcher supplier follows correct assumptions and uses theoretically-sound data analysis procedures.

This module is often an arduous section to write. You can make it easier to write, read, and understand your proposed data analysis by using sample charts and tables featuring "dummy" data. When there is no statistical or analytical expertise in the company, managers may hire professional help to develop this section.

Nature and Form of Results

In the *nature and form of results* section, the manager specifies the form (oral only, written only, oral plus written; management report, topline report, infographic, technical report, etc.) and nature of the results. Statistical conclusions, applied findings, recommendations, action plans, models, strategic plans, graphs, and so forth are examples of the types of results a manager might expect. For an RFP, this section guides the research company in developing the research report(s). The audience of the report should be noted in this section.

Qualifications of Researchers

The *qualifications* section is primarily used when a researcher is responding to an RFP. It should begin with the principal investigator and then provide similar information on all individuals involved with the project. Two elements are critical:[5]

1. Professional research competence (relevant research experience, the highest academic degree held, and memberships in business and technical societies).
2. Relevant management experience.

With so many individuals, research specialty firms, and general consultancies providing research services, the manager needs assurance that the researcher is professionally competent. Past research experience is the best barometer of competence, followed by their academic qualifications. To document relevant research experience, the researcher provides concise descriptions of similar projects. Highest degree usually follows the person's name (e.g., S. Researcher, PhD in Statistics). Society memberships provide some evidence that the researcher is cognizant of the latest methodologies and techniques. These follow the relevant research experience as a string or bulleted list, with organization name followed by term of membership and any relevant leadership positions.

Researchers are increasingly in the business of providing consulting advice, not just research services. And businesses are looking for quality advice. Comparatively, the researcher who demonstrates relevant management or industry experience will be more likely to receive a favorable nod to his or her proposal. The format of this information should follow that used for relevant research experience. The entire curriculum vitae of each researcher need not be included unless required by the RFP. However, researchers often place complete vitae information in an appendix for review by interested sponsors.

Research companies often subcontract specific research activities to firms or individuals that offer specific services, resources, or facilities. This is especially true for studies involving qualitative research methods such as in-depth personal interviews and focus groups. Usually, brief profiles of these companies are provided in this section only if their inclusion enhances the credibility of the researcher. Otherwise, profiles of such subcontractors are included in an appendix of the final report, rather than in the proposal.

Budget

Typically, the *budget* should be no more than one to two pages. The budget statement in an internal research proposal is based on employee and overhead costs.

Exhibit a-4 shows one format that can be used for small-scale research projects. For a large-scale study, any additional information, backup details, quotes from vendors, and hourly time and payment calculations should be put into an appendix if required or kept in the a file for future reference.

In a response to an RFP, the detail the researcher presents may vary depending on both the manager's requirements and the research company's policy. Here, rather than separating the "other costs," Exhibit a-4 shows these costs embedded in a combined rate. One reason external research agencies avoid giving detailed budgets is the possibility that disclosures of their costing practices will make their calculations public knowledge, reducing their negotiating flexibility. Because budget statements embody a work strategy depicted in financial terms that could be used by the recipient of the proposal to develop a replicate research plan, vendors are often doubly careful.

The budget section of any company's response to an RFP states the total fee payable for the assignment. When it is accompanied by a proposed schedule of payment, this is frequently detailed in a purchase order. Like other large-ticket-price services delivered over time in stages (e.g., building a home), payments can be paid at stages of completion. Sometimes a retainer is paid at the beginning of the contract, then a percentage at an intermediate stage, and the balance on completion of the project.

It is extremely important that you retain all information you use to generate your budget. If you use quotes from external contractors, get the quotation in writing for your records. If you estimate time for interviews, keep explicit notes on how you made the estimate. When the time comes to do the work, you should know exactly how much money is budgeted for each particular task.[6]

> **Exhibit a-4** Sample Proposal Budget for a Research Project

Items	Rate	Total Days	Charge
A. Salaries			
1. Research director	$200/hr	20 hours	$ 4,000
2. Research associate	100/hr	10 hours	1,000
3. Research assistants (2)	20/hr	300 hours	6,000
4. Secretarial (1)	12/hr	100 hours	1,200
Subtotal			$12,200
B. Other costs			
5. Employee services and benefits			
6. Travel			$ 2,500
7. Office supplies			100
8. Telephone			800
9. Rent			
10. Other equipment			
11. Publication and storage costs			100
Subtotal			$ 3,500
C. Total of direct costs			$15,700
D. Overhead support			$ 5,480
E. Total funding requested			$21,180

Some costs are more elusive than others. Do not forget to build the cost of proposal writing into your fee. Publication and delivery of final reports can be a last-minute expense that may be easily overlooked in preliminary budgets.

Schedule

Your *schedule* should include the major phases of the project, their timetables, and the milestones that signify completion of a phase. For example, major phases may be (1) exploratory interviews, (2) final research proposal, (3) final measurement instrument, (4) field interviews, (5) editing and coding, (6) data analysis, and (7) report generation. Each of these phases should have an estimated time schedule and people assigned to the work.

It may be helpful to you and your sponsor if you chart your schedule. You can use a Gantt chart or the critical path method (CPM) of scheduling. In a CPM chart, the nodes represent major milestones, and the arrows suggest the work needed to get to the milestone. More than one arrow pointing to a node indicates all those tasks must be completed before the milestone has been met. Usually a number is placed along the arrow showing the number of days or weeks required for that task to be completed. The pathway from start to end that takes the longest time to complete is called the critical path, because any delay in an activity along that path will delay the end of the entire project. An example of a CPM chart is shown in Exhibit a-5, with a Gantt chart in Exhibit a-6. Software programs designed for project management simplify scheduling and charting the schedule. Most are available for personal computers.[7]

Facilities and Special Resources

Often, projects will require special *facilities or resources*. For example, a project may need specialized facilities for focus group sessions or computer-assisted telephone or other interviewing facilities. Additionally, a project might require sophisticated data analysis, and time on an appropriate system might be required. These requirements vary from study to study. The manager should carefully list the relevant facilities and resources that will be used and include any costs in the proposal's budget.

> **Exhibit a-5** CPM Schedule of Research Project

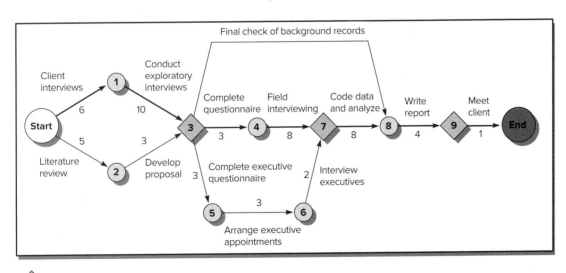

Milestones:
3 Proposal approval
7 Interviews completed
9 Final report completed

Critical Path:
S–1–3–4–7–8–9–E

Time to Completion:
40 working days

> **Exhibit a-6** Gantt Chart of a Research Project

Day	Task Duration
Client Interviews	Days 1–6
Literature Review	Days 1–6
Exploratory Interviews	Days 7–13
Justify Research Design	Days 14–16
Submit Proposal for Design	Day 16
Receive Approval for Design	Day 18
Develop Executive Interview Guide	Days 18–19
Arrange Executive Interviews	Days 20–21
Conduct Executive Interviews	Days 22–23
Executive Interviews Completed	Day 24
Complete Questionnaire	Days 21–23
Survey in Progress	Days 24–29
Survey Completed	
Prepare Data	Days 29–31
Analyze Data	Days 32–34
Prepare Report(s)	Days 35–38
Report Completed	Days 38–39
Deliver Oral Report	Day 40

Project Management

The purpose of the *project management* section is to help the manager organize and control the project; the schedule is the most important tool for this task. It includes:

- The research team's organization.
- Management procedures and controls for executing the research plan.
- Examples of management and technical reports.
- The research team's relationship to the manager-sponsor.
- Financial and legal responsibilities.

Bibliography

For all projects that require a literature review, a *bibliography* is necessary. Use the bibliographic format required by the manager. If none is specified, a standard style manual will provide the details necessary to prepare the bibliography.[8] Many of these sources also offer suggestions for successful proposal writing. In most small scale studies, where a literature review is not performed, a bibliography is not supplied.

Appendices

Glossary   The manager should include a glossary of terms whenever there are many words unique to the research topic and not understood by researcher. This is a simple section consisting of terms and definitions, similar in format to the glossary in this textbook.

Measurement Instrument   For large projects, it is appropriate to include samples of the measurement instruments if they are available when you assemble the proposal. This allows the sponsor to discuss particular changes in one or more of the instruments. If the proposal includes the development of a custom-designed measurement instrument, omit this appendix section.

Other   Any detail that reinforces the body of the proposal can be included in an appendix. This includes researcher vitae, profiles of firms or individuals to which work will be subcontracted, budget details, and lengthy descriptions of special facilities or resources.

>Create a Request for Proposal

When the manager has insufficient expertise or insufficient time, he or she may request the assistance of a professional research company to execute a project. The *request for proposal (RFP)* is a formal document issued by a corporate research department or manager-sponsor to solicit services from research suppliers. Developing a well-written RFP takes time and planning. However, the benefit to the sponsoring organization is an opportunity to formalize the process of documenting, justifying, and authorizing the procurement of research. RFPs also provide a chance to evaluate different proposed research designs and offer the means of establishing, monitoring, and controlling the performance of the winning research supplier. A sample of an RFP proposal concludes this appendix.

The manager must complete several tasks in the RFP process: (1) qualify potential research suppliers, (2) write and distribute the RFP (usually 8 to 10 weeks before the requested proposal due date), (3) be available to answer research supplier questions or hold pre-bid conferences, (4) evaluate submissions on known criteria, (5) award contracts and start the project on published dates, and (6) provide a critique to any research supplier who submitted a proposal. This last task helps unsuccessful bidders become competitive in the future and maintains goodwill for future projects.

A well-written RFP allows an organization to request high-quality proposals for dealing with complex problems. When not done properly, the RFP process will take longer, cost more, and not provide a complete long-term solution. Therefore, when a manager decides to put a research project to bid using an RFP, it is essential that time and effort be invested at the beginning.

First, the manager invites a qualified research supplier to submit a proposal, by a particular deadline, in accordance with a specific, detailed format. Each sponsoring firm may have its own requirements, and these are reflected not only in the format of the RFP but in how it is distributed. Managers must determine which vendors have the capability to complete the project on time. When the process is not open to all bidders, criteria such as industry experience, reputation, geographic location, quality of previous work, size of staff, and strategic alliances with other vendors determine which bidders will be eligible to receive the RFP. Firms may limit supplier invitations to bidders that they have solicited before, or to research companies or independent researchers that have provided prior services.

Although RFPs differ somewhat from firm to firm, the general components follow:

- Proposal administration information.
- Summary statement of the problem.
- Technical section.
- Management section.
- Contracts and licensing section.
- Pricing section.

Proposal Administration

This section is an overview of important information on the administration of the project itself. It establishes the dates of the RFP process—when the RFP is released, when the RFP team is available for questions, the date the proposal is due, and the dates of the evaluation and supplier selections. It includes all requirements for preparing the proposal and describes how proposals will be evaluated. Contact names, addresses, and relevant telephone and fax numbers are listed.

Summary Problem Statement

The summary statement often takes the form of a letter introducing the sponsoring organization issuing the RFP and explaining its needs.

Technical Section

Technical information needed by the research supplier to create the proposal is presented in this section. It begins by describing the problem(s) to be addressed and the technical details of each requirement. It loosely describes the services to be performed and the equipment, software, and documentation required, if these are known. This section should be neither too specific nor too general to allow the research suppliers reasonable flexibility and creativity in research design—after all, you are hiring them for their expertise—but it should also constrain them to meet the needs of the sponsor. Typically, the following would be included:

- Problem statement.
- Description of functional requirements (what actual phases will be included in the research).
- Identification of constraints (what might limit research design creativity).

The RFP functional requirements assist research suppliers in testing the comprehensiveness of their proposed research. Managers may ask the proposed researcher to answer questions. Using the service-call-center problem discussed earlier, these questions might include:

Recording

- What proportion of calls does your proposed solution record?
- To what degree is your proposed system scalable?
- Can the representatives detect that they are being recorded?

System Integration and Retrieval

- Can you integrate multiple sources of information into the recording platform?
- Does your proposed solution offer redundancy in the event of a failure?
- Does your proposed solution store conversations along with their corresponding call-tag data in a single database?
- Can the recorded calls be replayed immediately?
- How does your proposed solution search calls for replay?
- What volume of long-term archived storage is available?

Evaluation and Analysis

- Can call data be displayed visually for analysis?
- How are calls selected for evaluation/scoring?
- Can values be assigned to each question and "rep performance" or "rep skill" category?
- Does your solution offer data mining capabilities?
- In what ways does your solution support managerial analysis of operations and business performance?
- How does your solution support the customer satisfaction philosophy?

One strategy for dealing with constraints includes specifying what is anticipated. If the manager requires that the research supplier offer creative solutions, the RFP describes the constraints within which any research design must work. A manager might be interested in using the benchmarks from previous studies and thus needs consistency in its current project; here is an example of constraints.

- The sample sizes and breakdowns for various markets are:
  - Europe: 500 completed surveys.
  - Asia: 500 completed surveys.
  - United States: 300 completed surveys.
    - Regional differences.
    - Differentiation by segment and brand.

- Proposed sample proportion for distributors/resellers:
  - Retailers = 90–95% of respondents.
  - Wholesale Distributors = 5–10%.

Building technical quality control into the RFP subsequently strengthens the project. When the technical section contains thorough specifications and clear criteria for evaluating proposals, both low and high bidders can provide the requisite quality for consideration. In addition, if an RFP requires that the research supplier provide technical reports during the project, project management is less costly for the sponsoring firm. When a thorough understanding of the constraints is unknown, managers may schedule a planning meeting with possible research companies to clarify and examine options prior to their RFP response.

Management Section

Each project requires some level of project management. The manager's timing on schedules, plans, and reports is included in this section. This section also lists the requirements for implementation schedules, training and reporting schedules, quality control, and other documentation. If specific supplier qualifications are needed, they should be requested here. The nature and frequency of progress reports is also indicated, as is any clerical, printing, or data processing services that the manager will provide. References from the supplier's customers may also be requested. Increasingly, the manager builds detailed documentation websites to provide information to those invited to submit proposals. These website URLs are documented in this section of the RFP.

Contracts and Licensing Section

The research supplier is often privy to a firm's strategies and tactics long before such competitive moves are undertaken. The research supplier is also aware of challenges facing the firm and actions being considered to address those challenges. Nondisclosure of such information is therefore critical. It is in this context that the sponsor should discuss the safeguarding of intellectual property and the use of copyrights. This section may contain several critical elements: (1) sample contracts, (2) sample nondisclosure agreements, (3) agreements on use of trademarks and copyrights, (4) disposition of the data file, and (4) disposition of the results/report. The manager should provide anything that the research supplier is expected to sign. Terms of payment and required benchmarks are also set forth here. Because the RFP is usually a part of the final contract, it should be worded precisely to avoid problems of interpretation. If a task is not described in the RFP or during contract negotiations, the firm may not be able to require that the supplier complete it.

Pricing Section

To cost the proposal, research suppliers must receive all needed information. A format that lists all anticipated activities helps the manager compare the cost of proposals with different research designs. The following list shows examples of items that could be included in costing of the proposal:

Services		Deliverables
• Data collection.	• Internet design and activation.	• Brochures/literature.
• Data analysis.	• Facilities and equipment.	• Videotapes.
• Meetings with client.	• Extensions to work agreements.	• Reports.
• Travel.	• Report preparation.	• Infographics.
• Instrument design.	• Report reproduction.	• Transcriptions.
• Mail and telephone.	• Computer models.	
• Respondent incentives.	• Project management.	
• Pilot tests.	• Manpower and training.	

Ethical standards are integral to designing the pricing section. For example, a manager would *not* send a research supplier an RFP to (1) help the manager plan its project budget, (2) estimate costs and ideas for a project the sponsor intends to execute in-house, or (3) create the impression of a competitive bid when the sponsor has already determined the supplier for the project.

Format

The format requirements for RFPs differ widely. The preceding sections reflect informational requirements rather than an RFP outline. A typical RFP might use the following order:

- Instructions to bidders.
- Background.
  - Overview or profile of the buyer's company.
  - Project overview.
  - Project requirements.
- Research supplier information.
  - Company profile.
  - History and description.
  - Legal summary (active lawsuits or pending litigation).
  - Partnerships and alliances.
  - References.
- Proposed solution.
- Services and support.
- Cost proposal.
  - Services pricing.
  - Maintenance pricing.
  - Contractual terms and conditions.

>Qualify a Researcher to Receive the RFP

Because each research project is often unique, industry practice suggests that careful consideration should be used when qualifying potential research suppliers to receive an RFP. Exhibit a-7 offers a checklist developed from recommendations of industry practitioners and associations.

>Evaluate a Research Company's Proposal

Proposals are subject to either formal or informal reviews. *Formal reviews* are regularly done for solicited proposals as part of the RFP process. The formal review process varies but typically includes:

- Development of review criteria, using RFP guidelines.
- Assignment of points to each criterion, using a universal scale.
- Assignment of a weight for each criterion, based on importance of each criterion.
- Generation of a score for each proposal, representing the sum of all weighted criterion scores.

The manager-sponsor should assign the criteria, the weights, and the scale to be used for scoring each criterion before the RFP proposal deadline. If a manager has an in-house research department and if using its services is competitive, then a formal review might be used. The RFP solicited proposal should be evaluated with this checklist of criteria in hand. Points are recorded for each criterion, reflecting the manager's assessment of how well the proposal meets the company's needs

> **Exhibit a-7** Checklist for Qualifying RFP Research Suppliers

Research Supplier

❏ Research experience and industry status including appropriate accreditation.

   ❏ Scope/type of research performed (quantitative vs. qualitative vs. both; advertising creative development, product testing, site location, etc.).

      ❏ Knowledge of specific research methodologies (e.g. research with children, visual ethnography, conjoint analysis).

  ❏ Types of clients.

   ❏ Knowledge of specific markets.

     ❏ International links or associations, if needed.

   ❏ No conflicts of interest.

  ❏ Code of ethical performance.

Research Supplier's Staff

❏ Skill and experience to manage the project.

❏ Skill and experience to conduct desired research.

   ❏ Specialist skills, when needed (psychologists, anthropologists, Internet technologists, etc.).

❏ Understanding of the various business functions.

Research Supplier's Facilities, Procedures, and Quality Management

❏ Compatible project management system.

❏ Compatible contractual arrangements, including billing.

❏ Compatible client complaint and satisfaction handling procedures.

❏ Desired quality assurance procedures.

❏ Desired organization, procedures, and appropriate facilities.

   ❏ Data collection (interviewers, interviewer training, CATI, CAPI, proprietary methodologies, etc.).

     ❏ Field operations.

     ❏ Lab settings (taste testing, product testing, etc.).

   ❏ Data handling (internal or subcontracted, software used, etc.).

   ❏ Developing/drawing samples.

❏ Compatible standard reporting procedures and guidelines.

❏ Desired results presentation practices.

Source: This checklist was developed from recommendations of industry practitioners and material on the ESOMAR, website: http://www.esomar.nl/guidelines /CommissioningResearch.htm, downloaded April 2003.

relative to that criterion (e.g., 1 through 10, with 10 being the largest number of points assigned to the best proposal for a particular criterion). After the review, the weighted criterion scores are added to provide a cumulative total. The proposal with the highest number of points wins the contract.

During RFP proposal review, a research proposal allows the manager to assess the sincerity of the researcher's purpose, the clarity of his or her design, the extent of his or her relevant background material, and the researcher's expertise for undertaking the project. Depending on the type of research and the manager, various aspects of a standard proposal design are emphasized. The proposal displays the researcher's discipline, organization, and logic. It thus allows the manager to assess both the researcher and the proposed design; to compare them against competing proposals on current organizational, scholastic, or scientific needs; and to make the best selection for the project. A poorly planned, poorly written, or poorly organized proposal damages the researcher's reputation more than the decision not to submit a proposal.

Small-scale projects, especially internal ones, are more prone to informal evaluation. In an *informal review*, the project needs, and thus the criteria, are well understood but are not usually well documented. In contrast to the formal review, a system of points is not used and the criteria are not ranked. The evaluation process uses the manager's judgment and impressions. Exhibit a-8 shows Sara Arens's informal review of a proposal presented to her as a member of her county's Economic Development Council.

In practice, many factors contribute to an RFP's acceptance and funding. Primarily, the content discussed earlier must be included to the level of detail required by the manager-sponsor. Beyond the required modules, other factors can quickly eliminate a proposal from consideration or improve the sponsor's reception of the proposal, among them:

- Neatness.
- Organization in terms of being both logical and easily understood.
- Completeness in fulfilling the RFP's specifications, including budget and schedule.
- Appropriateness of writing style.
- Submission within the RFP's timeline.

A poorly presented, unclear, or disorganized proposal will not get serious attention from the reviewing manager. For a solicited proposal in the RFP process, multiple reviewers may be evaluating only a given section, the reviewer should be able to page through the proposal to any section of interest. Solicited proposals often use a technical writing style, yet a manager must be able to understand the problem statement, the research design, and the methodology.

The proposal also must meet specific RFP guidelines set by the sponsoring manager, including budgetary restrictions and schedule deadlines. A schedule that does not meet the expected deadlines will disqualify the proposal. A budget that is too high for the allocated funds will be rejected. Conversely, a low budget compared to competing proposals suggests that something is missing or there is something wrong with the researchers.

Finally, a late proposal will not be reviewed. Although current project disqualification due to lateness may appear to be the worst result here, there is a possible longer-term effect created. Lateness communicates a level of disrespect for the sponsor—that the researcher's schedule is more important than the sponsor's. A late proposal also communicates a weakness in project management, which raises an issue of professional competence. This concern about competence may continue to plague the researcher during future project proposal reviews.

Evaluating an Unsolicited Research Proposal

Previously, we focused on the solicited proposal, the result of a research supplier's interest in delivering a company's research project. An *unsolicited proposal* represents a suggestion by a researcher for research that might be done. For an example, a consulting firm might propose a research project to a client that has retained the consultancy for other purposes. As another example, a research firm might propose an omnibus study to members of a trade association to address problems arising from a change in the cultural or political-legal environments. The unsolicited proposal has the advantage of not competing against others but the disadvantage of having to speculate on the ramifications of a management dilemma facing the firm's management. In addition to being an outsider assessing an internal problem, the researcher writing an unsolicited proposal must decide to whom the document should be sent. Such proposals are often time sensitive, so the window of opportunity might close before a redirected proposal finds its appropriate recipient.

> **Exhibit a-8** Informal Proposal Evaluation

Sara Arens

200 ShellPoint Tower
Palm Beach, Florida 33480

Mr. Harry Shipley, President
Economic Development Council
1800 ShellPoint Tower
Palm Beach, Florida 33480

Dear Harry,

I have reviewed Robert Buffet's proposal for an investigation of the job creation practices of local companies and, in short, I am very much concerned with several aspects of the "proposal." It is not really a proposal at all, because it lacks sufficient detail.

First, let me mention that I shared Buffet's proposal with Mr. Jason Henry, my partner. Mr. Buffet and his organization may one day represent competition for us, and you must therefore be aware of a potential conflict of interest and perhaps discount the opinions stated here. Since I am delivering this letter to you in two days rather than the two weeks you requested, you may wish to discuss my comments with others.

What you and Mr. Buffet gave me is an abbreviated research plan for our county, but since it lacks many features found in a comprehensive proposal, I immediately saw it was not the full proposal that had been funded by the state commerce secretary. I called Tallahassee and reached a young woman who hemmed and hawed and refused to say if she was authorized to mail me the full proposal. Finally, I gave up arguing and gave her your address and told her she could mail it to you.

I then made several calls to people in Tallahassee whom I know. Did you know that this research idea is being floated by our senior U.S. senator, who is eager to throw a monkey wrench into the president's tax incentives plan? The senator whispered it to the governor and the governor whispered it to her commerce secretary, and here we are.

The problem statement is rather long and convoluted, but, in short, it poses the questions: Are new high-tech companies creating jobs for residents of our county? Or are they bringing technical and manufacturing workers from outside the state and bypassing the local work force? Or are they doing research in these companies with a low level of manufacturing job creation? Or are they investing in "smart" capital equipment that does not create jobs? If you cut through the verbiage, I think you can see the project is dead on the mark with its questions.

The research objectives section is fairly straightforward. Buffet's people are going to identify all the companies in this county in the NAICS code groups associated with "high tech" and collect information on the number of locally hired employees in various job categories, chiefly in production, and also collect data on capital investments, debt, and other financial data, which Jason says makes good sense to collect and ought to be easy to do.

There is a section called Importance of the Study, which is full of platitudes and does not get around to mentioning the pending tax legislation. But at least the platitudes are brief.

I become nervous in the Design section. It calls for Mr. Buffet's group to go on site with a "team" and conduct in-depth interviews with the chief operating officer (COO), treasurer, and comptroller of each company and enter the data into a spreadsheet. I have double-checked this with Jason and also with a banker friend, and both of them assure me that a simple questionnaire might be mailed to the COO. There is no need whatsoever to send in a team to conduct open-ended interviews. Although there might be a noncompliance problem associated with filling out a form, this might appropriately be attended to by pointing out the auspices—the state commerce secretary and your Economic Development Council—with an interview request as a last resort.

The proposal contains no budget and no specific list of researchers who will comprise the team. The firm would have carte blanche to go in with anyone on their payroll and try to induce the subjects to stray beyond the stated research objectives to talk about anything at all. Obviously such license would be a marketing tool and might allow the researchers to collect a list of researchable problems not related to the secretary's needs, as stated in the problem section.

I strongly advise you to tell Mr. Buffet to collect the information through a simple mail survey. Offer to send it out under your council's letterhead, or see if you can get the commerce office or even the governor's office to send it out. But do not subject your local business community to unstructured, free-ranging visits, which are clearly not justified by the research objectives.

Sincerely,

Sara

Sample RFP: Covering Kids[9]

Wirthlin Worldwide earned the Ogilvy Research Award for creative and effective research instrumental in the development of the Covering Kids advertising campaign. This RFP from sponsor Robert Wood Johnson Foundation started the process that resulted in enrolling more than one million additional children for a health insurance initiative.

March 13, 20xx

Name
Firm
Address
City, State Zip code

Dear XXXX:

As you know, we are working with GMMB&A to support the national Covering Kids Initiative (CKI). We appreciate your recent response to a proposal to support this effort's marketing research requirements. Since that time, we have further refined our requirements. We hope that you will be willing to review this request, and revise your previous proposal in any ways needed to meet these altered needs.

The Covering Kids Initiative is a $47 million national program of the Foundation that works to enroll eligible children in Medicaid and the Federal-State Children's Health Insurance Programs (SCHIP). Three-year grants for the Covering Kids Initiative support coalitions in 49 states and the District of Columbia. These coalitions conduct outreach initiatives and work to simplify and coordinate the enrollment processes for health coverage programs for low-income children. In its first two years of activity, the CKI has focused largely on simplifying the enrollment process. During the second year, in addition to continuing a focus on simplification and coordination, there will be target marketing campaigns to encourage adults to enroll eligible children in both the SCHIP and Medicaid programs.

The Foundation will work with its Covering Kids communications contractor to support these CKI coalitions in marketing, advertising, public relations, coalition building, and cause-related partnerships at the national and state levels. The tasks described here will help provide direction for the strategic development of communications and provide support for testing and measuring communications campaigns in six markets prior to introduction nationwide.

Background

There are approximately five million uninsured children in the US eligible for either SCHIP or Medicaid. While income eligibility requirements in the federally funded SCHIP programs vary from state-to-state, they all generally cover children in households of four with incomes up to $33,400 (higher in some states). About half of the eligible-uninsured Americans are non-Hispanic white, about 30% are African-American, another 20% are Hispanic/Latino. Although the numbers are much smaller, a large proportion of Native-Americans are also eligible but not covered.

There are many reasons why so many eligible children are not enrolled. Some primary barriers to enrollment are: lack of awareness of the availability of health programs, especially SCHIP; lack of knowledge of eligibility criteria for these programs; complicated/onerous application processes; a stigma attached to government-funded health care programs (especially for working parents); the lack of outreach experience and expertise (most states have never conducted outreach for programs like Medicaid).

The primary challenge for this project is to create a nationwide campaign to enroll children—yet the "fulfillment mechanisms" (the state SCHIP and Medicaid programs) vary from state to state. Many states have developed their own distinct marketing and branding campaigns so that the SCHIP programs in Connecticut (HUSKY B) and in Georgia (PeachCare) and in Illinois (KidsCare) resemble traditional private health plans more than they do government programs based on income eligibility. A national 1-877-KIDS-NOW phone number is in use that seamlessly routes calls through to the appropriate state program office. We will likely use that toll-free number as a marketing and fulfillment mechanism for this effort.

The communications campaign will target specific groups of parents and other adults who could play a key role in enrolling eligible children in existing programs. Specific messages will be tested for use with subsets of low-income Americans, including African-Americans, Hispanic/Latino, Native Americans and others. The campaigns will first be tested and measured in six regional markets before national advertising begins. Ad buys and other communications activities will be coupled with local enrollment events. Communications activities and enrollment events will likely intensify twice annually, during the back-to-school and winter cold and flu seasons.

Contractual Needs

Requirements for market research and evaluation support are described in the two tasks below.

Task 1. MARKET RESEARCH. Design, conduct, analyze, and provide conclusions relevant to communications planning.

Task 1a. Develop an in-depth comprehensive profile (through a series of in-depth interviews) of the families of eligible-but-uninsured children—who are they, where are they, why are they not enrolled, the most effective messages/concepts to move individuals in specific groups to enroll in SCHIP/Medicaid, what messages/words/concepts are definite turn-offs among specific groups, etc.

Of particular interest:

- Hispanic/Latino rural/urban
- African-American rural/urban
- Native American rural/urban
- White rural/urban
- Parents of children enrolled in SCHIP
- Parents of children enrolled in Medicaid
- Parents of uninsured children eligible for SCHIP and/or Medicaid who haven't applied
- Parents of uninsured children eligible for SCHIP and/or Medicaid who have applied but are not enrolled

Level of effort: approximately 120 in-depth interviews. [Alternative suggestions invited.]

Task 1b. Qualitative research among opinion leaders: their perceptions of SCHIP; their definition of success/failure, etc. These might include federal and state legislative staff, regulatory staff, child health advocates, constituency group leaders, and media gatekeepers.

Level of effort: approximately 25 in-depth interviews. [Alternative suggestions invited.]

Evaluation Task

Task 1. A comprehensive national survey. This survey will: help direct communications development; provide content for news placement; provide a pre-campaign benchmark (baseline data). We anticipate repeating this survey in the future to help gauge change and progress. However, at this time we are interested only in one benchmark survey.

We are considering two options for survey sampling: (a) a national sample including oversamples of lower-income families as described above, or (b) a sample consisting of lower-income families with sufficient subsets (described above) to be statistically reliable. We are interested in receiving recommendations regarding which option to pursue as well as a description of how this work would be done.

Task 2. An evaluation of the media campaign in six test markets. Because the national advertising and public relations components of the communication campaign will be large in scope and level of effort, this test market phase will be used to test and refine media messages, techniques, and decisions. The test market evaluation is critical to decision making for this effort.

Six mid-sized media markets will be selected to obtain a mix of the targeted demographic groups and geographic diversity. The Foundation will provide the list of selected sites to the contractor. The advertising and public relations test phase will span 4–6 weeks, planned for late August–early September 2000. The market test will be planned and executed through close collaboration with the communications contractor, the Covering Kids National Program Office and coalitions in the target markets, and the Foundation. It will be designed to gauge heightened awareness, perceptions of target audiences, willingness to apply, and impact of campaign on overcoming any attitudinal barriers to applying.

This market test will include

Task 2a. Benchmark survey—a random sample telephone survey with oversamples of target audiences. To include both benchmarking questions (such as awareness, attitude, intention measures) and message development questions (such as questions about message concepts, language).

Task 2b. Post-campaign survey—a brief telephone follow-up survey using same sampling; to include questions to assess recall/awareness, attitudes, intentions.

Task 2c. Tracking of callers to the promoted toll-free number—the Foundation/National Program Office will provide a liaison to the toll-free manager(s). At this time it is not clear whether this will include only the national toll-free number or/and some state operated numbers. This task will include both compiling and analyzing call data and identifying ways to re-contact callers to assess further actions.

Task 2d. Follow-up with callers—brief telephone survey to identify any questions taken. Phone numbers will be provided through the liaison described above. [Alternative method of assessment may be needed.]

Alternative suggestions for test market evaluation, with approximately the same level of effort required, are acceptable.

Anticipated Time Schedule

April 20xx	contract awarded begin development of all tasks
May 20xx	conduct national survey
June 20xx	conduct research with potential beneficiaries, opinion leaders conduct benchmark survey in 6 test markets
August 20xx	begin ads in test markets begin telephone tracking
September 20xx	conduct testing market post-test surveys begin follow-up with telephone callers
October 20xx	present findings of national survey present findings from caller callbacks

Proposal Instructions

We invite you to submit a proposal addressing one or both of the tasks described above. Your proposal should address:

- Your approach to conducting the work.
- Any alternative methods or procedures you would like to suggest for accomplishing the work described (optional).
- A discussion of any anticipated challenges to completing these tasks, and how you would propose handling the challenges.
- Comments on methodology and other recommendations for producing the needed information.
- Specific work to be performed, description of the deliverables to be provided, and all costs (included out-of-pocket costs), by task.

- Relevant experience and expertise
- References.

The Foundation is not seeking lengthy or elaborate proposals. Rather, proposals should succinctly provide information that will permit a review using the criteria listed below.

Review Criteria

In reviewing proposals, we will consider:

- Your approach to the needs and tasks described here, including recommended methodology.
- Anticipated problems and how these would be handled.
- Company and staff experience in conducting similar market research and evaluation.
- Company and staff experience in conducting qualitative and quantitative research with a similar population.
- Company and staff experience with a health insurance or similar health care issue.
- Personnel, task and time line, project management.
- Proposed budget.
- Ability to respond to time schedule.

In addition, we will expect that your company has no conflicts of interest with the Foundation.
Proposals will be due no later than COB Monday, March 27, delivered to

Stuart Schear (Four Copies)
Senior Communications Officer
The Robert Wood Johnson Foundation
Address
City, State Zip code
Phone

Kristine Hartvigsen (Three Copies)
Covering Kids National Program Office
Address
City, State Zip code
Phone

David Smith (Four Copies)
GMMB&A
Address
City, State Zip code
Phone

Elaine Bratic Arkin (One Copy)
Address
City, State Zip code
Phone

We anticipate notifying those who submit proposals of our decision no later than April 1, 2000. I am available by e-mail @ smr@rwjf.org to answer any questions you might have. The following websites offer a wealth of information as well:

< http://www.coveringkids.org>—the website for "Covering Kids," the RWJF-funded initiative that these tasks will support
< http://www.insurekidsnow.gov>—the HHS/HCFA website for the CHIP programs
< http://www.cbpp.org>—the Center on Budget and Policy Priorities

Thank you for your thoughtful consideration of this request.
If you wish to speak with someone about this project, please call me at 609-951-5799. Either Elaine Arkin, a consultant to the Foundation, or I would be happy to speak with you.

Sincerely,

Stuart Schear
Senior Communications Officer

National U.S. healthcare reform, many parts slated for implementation in 2013, will likely affect SCHIP (the subject of this RFP), but at this time it is unknown exactly in what ways or with what effects.

Focus Group Discussion Guide*

Background

What if your firm manufactures cleansing products in multiple forms—deodorant bar, beauty bar, cream body wash, gel body wash—and your customers are not using the best form for their skin types and activity levels? You might use exploratory focus groups to determine what drivers motivate customers to select the *form* they choose. Given the dramatic growth in this market, you want to hear from women aged 16 to 50 and also from men aged 16 to 25. Also, you need to understand their trade-offs when choosing a specific form.

You turn to a research specialist to conduct focus groups in three cities representative of the category market. Prior to meeting the six groups (two groups in each city; two consisting only of teens), researchers ask each participant to prepare two visual collages using pictures cut from magazines. One collage is to reflect the participant's perceptions and experiences with each form (regardless of personal use experience). A second collage is to depict a month in the participant's life. The Intro and Forms segments of the discussion guide below reference these creative exercises.

Personal Cleansing Form Drivers   Atlanta, Seattle, Phoenix

INTRO (15 min)

 A. ALL ABOUT ME—name, family info, work, play, activities, interests. SHOW LIFE IN THE MONTH COLLAGE

 B. AT SOME POINT ASK: How often shower / bathe?

             Use fragrances / perfume? How often?

             Use scented or unscented deodorant, lotions, etc?

FORMS (60 min)

 A. LISTED ON EASEL "DEODORANT BAR, BEAUTY BAR, CREAM BODY WASH, GEL BODY WASH"

   Here are the different forms of soaps available that we want to learn about.

   How many have ever used _____? Still using or moved on / rejected?

 B. EASEL RESPONSES (BE SURE PICTURES ARE LABELED) Show and describe your picture collage (from homework), as you tell what you like / not, what **associate** w/_____ form.

    What else **like?** / **why use?**

    What **not like** about _____? Why not using (more often)?

    How compare to other forms—advantages / disadvantages?

    What **wish for** this form . . . what would make it **better / perfect** for you?

    How / why **begin** to use? Specifically, what **remember** about _____ form then?

    How find out about it? (ads, TV commercial, friends) What details remember about the ad—what show, who in it?

   REPEAT FOR ALL FORMS

 C. LINE UP THE FORMS—When you think about these different forms, are they **basically the same**—just a different form or do you think of these as different products with **different results**? Describe.

D. EXPLAIN CHART—Line these attributes up in the order you think is **best to worst for each of the attributes** listed on the paper.

CLEANLINESS / SKIN CARE / GERM KILL / DEODORANCY / LATHER / SCENT / VALUE

Why put in this order? What experience / notice with this form for (*attribute above*)?

What about the form makes that difference?

How much do you care about (*attributes above*)? Why / not? Affect whether you'd buy it?

E. SHOW EXAMPLES OF BRANDS WITH BOTH BAR AND BODY WASH—

Oil of Olay / Dove / Lever 2000 / Dial

So to summarize with some specific brands, whether you have tried or not, what would you **expect to be the difference,** if any, when using the bar of _____ brand vs. the body wash?

What difference, if any, in how they make you feel emotionally after bathing with the bar vs. body wash?

BRANDS (30 min)

A. Now let's focus on different brands. Write your favorite on your name card.

LINE UP EXAMPLES OF THOSE COMMONLY USED.

B. How many of you have used _____ ? How often / long ago?

Why **use / choose** (at store)? What like (better) about _____ .

Why **NOT** use (more often)?

C. How many have **tried Oil of Olay / Dove / Lever 2000 / Dial?** Why / not (more recently)?

What associate with (brand above)? What stand for? What makes it different / unique vs. other brands?

SUMMARY (15 min)

A. There are 3 basic considerations when choosing a soap—**brand, form, price.** Put them in order of what matters most, 2nd, 3rd. For example, you go to the store to buy, and your usual form isn't available in your usual brand, etc. What would you buy?

MAKE A CHART OF RESPONSES

B. Now think about 3 benefits we've discussed—**skin care, scent, cleanliness.** Put these in order of importance. Describe order.

Why is _____ more important than _____ ?

(MISC—TIME PERMITTING)

C. What do you see / notice in the store when shopping this aisle? New things? Switch around?

ADULTS—How many of you buy soap for other family members? Who? How do you decide which form / brand to choose for your husband / teen?

D. TEENS ONLY—Let's talk a bit more about how you learn about new types brands or versions of soaps. Where have you seen ads?

(Mall / locker room / Channel 1/ dressing rooms / etc.)

What do you remember about it? What show / say / what was the main idea?

What do you think of celebrity endorsements?

CONCLUSION

* This discussion guide was developed by Pam Hay, an independent qualitative consultant for more than 24 years with a career focused on consumable goods (personal care products, health and beauty aids, and OTC drugs). Her experiences include conducting focus groups, individual depth interviews, ethnographic home visits, and multifunctional consumer direct processes for the purposes of concept development, advertising evaluation, insight exploration, consumer segmentation, and product development.

Nonparametric Significance Tests

This appendix contains additional nonparametric tests of hypotheses to augment those described in the chapter on Hypothesis Testing.

One-Sample Test

Kolmogorov-Smirnov Test

This test is appropriate when the data are at least ordinal and the research situation calls for a comparison of an observed sample distribution with a theoretical distribution. Under these conditions, the Kolmogorov-Smirnov (KS) one-sample test is more powerful than the χ^2 test and can be used for small samples when the χ^2 test cannot. The KS is a test of goodness of fit in which we specify the *cumulative* frequency distribution that would occur under the theoretical distribution and compare that with the observed cumulative frequency distribution. The theoretical distribution represents our expectations under H_0. We determine the point of greatest divergence between the observed and theoretical distributions and identify this value as D (maximum deviation). From a table of critical values for D, we determine whether such a large divergence is likely on the basis of random sampling variations from the theoretical distribution. The value for D is calculated as follows:

$$D = \text{maxium} \left| F_0(X) - F_T(X) \right|$$

in which

$F_0(X)$ = the observed cumulative frequency distribution of a random sample of n observations. Where X is any possible score, $F_0(X) = k/n$, where k = the number of observations equal to or less than X.

$F_T(X)$ = the theoretical frequency distribution under H_0.

We illustrate the KS test, with an analysis of the results of the dining club study, in terms of various class levels. Take an equal number of interviews from each class, but secure unequal numbers of people interested in joining. Assume class levels are ordinal measurements. The testing process is as follows (see accompanying table):

	Freshman	Sophomore	Junior	Senior	Graduate
Number in each class	5	9	11	16	19
$F_0(X)$	5/60	14/60	25/60	41/60	60/60
$F_T(X)$	12/60	24/60	36/60	48/60	60/60
$\|F_0(X) - F_T(X)\|$	7/60	10/60	11/60	7/60	0

$D = 11/60 = .183; n = 60$

1. *Null hypothesis.*

   H_0: There is no difference among student classes as to their intention of joining the dining club.

   H_A: There is a difference among students in various classes as to their intention of joining the dining club.

2. *Statistical test.* Choose the KS one-sample test because the data are ordinal measures and we are interested in comparing an observed distribution with a theoretical one.

3. *Significance level.* $\alpha = .05$, $n = 60$.

4. *Calculated value.* $D = $ maximum $|F_0(X) - F_T(X)|$.

5. *Critical test value.* We enter the table of critical values of D in the KS one-sample test (see Appendix d, Exhibit d-5) and learn that with $\alpha = .05$, the critical value for D is

$$D = \frac{1.36}{\sqrt{60}} = .175$$

6. *Interpretation.* The calculated value is greater than the critical value, indicating we should reject the null hypothesis.

Two-Samples Tests

Sign Test

The sign test is used with matched pairs when the only information is the identification of the pair member that is larger or smaller or has more or less of some characteristic. Under H_0, one would expect the number of cases in which $X_A > X_B$ to equal the number of pairs in which $X_B > X_A$. All ties are dropped from the analysis, and n is adjusted to allow for these eliminated pairs. This test is based on the binomial expansion and has a good power efficiency for small samples.

Wilcoxon Matched-Pairs Test

When you can determine both *direction* and *magnitude* of difference between carefully matched pairs, use the Wilcoxon matched-pairs test. This test has excellent efficiency and can be more powerful than the *t*-test in cases where the latter is not particularly appropriate. The mechanics of calculation are also quite simple. Find the difference score (d_i) between each pair of values, and rank-order the differences from smallest to largest without regard to sign. The actual signs of each difference are then added to the rank values, and the test statistic T is calculated. T is the sum of the ranks with the less frequent sign. Typical of such research situations might be a study where husband and wife are matched, where twins are used, where a given subject is used in a before/after study, or where the outputs of two similar machines are compared.

Two types of ties may occur with this test. When two observations are equal, the d score becomes zero, and we drop this pair of observations from the calculation. When two or more pairs have the same d value, we average their rank positions. For example, if two pairs have a rank score of 1, we assign the rank of 1.5 to each and rank the next largest difference as third. When $n < 25$, use the table of critical values (see Appendix d, Exhibit d-4). When $n > 25$, the sampling distribution of T is approximately normal with

$$\text{Mean} = \mu_T = \frac{n(n + 1)}{4}$$

$$\text{Standard deviation} = \sigma_T \sqrt{\frac{n(n + 1)(2n + 1)}{24}}$$

The formula for the test is

$$z = \frac{T - \mu_T}{\sigma_T}$$

Suppose you conduct an experiment on the effect of brand name on quality perception. Ten subjects are recruited and asked to taste and compare two samples of a product, one identified as a well-known drink and the other as a new product being tested. In truth, however, the samples are identical. The subjects are then asked to rate the two samples on a set of scale items judged to be ordinal. Test these results for significance by the usual procedure.

1. *Null hypothesis.*
   H_0: There is no difference between the perceived qualities of the two samples.
   H_A: There is a difference in the perceived quality of the two samples.

2. *Statistical test.* The Wilcoxon matched-pairs test is used because the study is of related samples in which the differences can be ranked in magnitude.

3. *Significance level.* $\alpha = .05$, with $n = 10$ pairs of comparisons minus any pairs with a d of zero.

4. *Calculated value.* T equals the sum of the ranks with the less frequent sign. Assume we secure the following results:

Pair	Branded	Unbranded	d_i	Rank of d_i	Rank with Less Frequent Sign
1	52	48	4	4	
2	37	32	5	5.5*	
3	50	52	−2	−2	2
4	45	32	13	9	
5	56	59	−3	−3	3
6	51	50	1	1	
7	40	29	11	8	
8	59	54	5	5.5*	
9	38	38	0	*	
10	40	32	8	7	$T = 5$

* There are two types of tie situations. We drop out the pair with the type of tie shown by pair 9. Pairs 2 and 8 have a tie in rank of difference. In this case, we average the ranks and assign the average value to each.

5. *Critical test value.* Enter the table of critical values of T with $n = 9$ (see Appendix d, Exhibit d-4) and find that the critical value with $\alpha = .05$ is 6. Note that with this test, the calculated value must be smaller than the critical value to reject the null hypothesis.

6. *Interpretation.* Since the calculated value is less than the critical value, reject the null hypothesis.

Kolmogorov-Smirnov Two-Samples Test

When a researcher has two independent samples of ordinal data, the Kolmogorov-Smirnov (KS) two-samples test is useful. Like the one-sample test, this two-samples test is concerned with the agreement between two cumulative distributions, but both represent sample values. If the two samples have been drawn from the same population, the cumulative distributions of the samples should be fairly close to each other, showing only random deviations from the population distribution. If the cumulative distributions show a large enough maximum deviation D, it is evidence for rejecting the H_0. To secure the maximum deviation, one should use as many intervals as are available so as not to obscure the maximum cumulative difference.

The two-samples KS formula is

$$D = \text{maximum} \mid F_{N1}(X) - F_{N2}(X) \mid \text{ (two-tailed test)}$$
$$D = \text{maximum} \mid F_{N1}(X) - F_{N2}(X) \mid \text{ (one-tailed test)}$$

D is calculated in the same manner as before, but the table for critical values for the numerator of D, K_D (two-samples test) is presented in Appendix d, Exhibit d-6, when $n_1 = n_2$ and is less than 40 observations. When n_1 and/or n_2 is larger than 40, D from Appendix d, Exhibit d-7, should be used. With this larger sample, it is not necessary that $n_1 = n_2$.

Here we use a different sample from a tobacco industry advertising study. Suppose the smoking classifications represent an ordinal scale (heavy smoker, moderate smoker, non-smoker), and you test these data with KS two-samples test for young and old age groups. Proceed as follows:

1. *Null hypothesis.*

   H_0: There is no difference in ages of smokers and nonsmokers.

   H_A: The older the person, the more likely he or she is to be a heavy smoker.

2. *Statistical test.* The KS two-samples test is used because it is assumed the data are ordinal.

3. *Significance level.* $\alpha = .05$. $n_1 = n_2 = 34$.

4. *Calculated value.* See the one-sample calculation (KS test) and compare with the table below.

5. *Critical test value.* We enter Appendix d, Exhibit d-6, with $n = 34$ to find that $K_D = 11$ when $p \leq .05$ for a one-tailed distribution.

	Heavy Smoker	Moderate Smoker	Nonsmoker
$F_{n1}(X)$	12/34	21/34	34/34
$F_{n2}(X)$	4/34	10/34	34/34
$d_i = K_{D/n}$	8/34	11/34	0

6. *Interpretation.* Because the critical value equals the largest calculated value, we reject the null hypothesis.

Mann-Whitney *U* Test

This test is also used with two independent samples if the data are at least ordinal; it is an alternative to the *t*-test without the latter's limiting assumptions. When the larger of the two samples is 20 or less, there are special tables for interpreting U; when the larger sample exceeds 20, a normal curve approximation is used.

In calculating the U test, treat all observations in a combined fashion and rank them, algebraically, from smallest to largest. The largest negative score receives the lowest rank. In case of ties, assign the average rank as in other tests. With this test, you can also test samples that are unequal. After the ranking, the rank values for each sample are totaled. Compute the U statistic as follows:

$$U = n_1 n_2 + \frac{n_1(n_1 + 1)}{2} - R_1$$

or

$$U = n_1 n_2 + \frac{n_2(n_2 - 1)}{2} - R_2$$

in which

n_1 = number in sample 1
n_2 = number in sample 2
R_1 = sum of ranks in sample 1

With this equation, you can secure two U values, one using R_1 and the second using R_2. For testing purposes, use the smaller U.

An example may help to clarify the U statistic calculation procedure. Let's consider the sales training example with the t distribution discussion. Recall that salespeople with training method A averaged higher sales than salespeople with training method B. Although these data are ratio measures, one still might not want to accept the other assumptions that underlie the t-test. What kind of a result could be secured with the U test? While the U test is designed for ordinal data, it can be used with interval and ratio measurements.

1. *Null hypothesis.*

   H_0: There is no difference in sales results produced by the two training methods.

   H_A: Training method A produces sales results superior to the results of method B.

2. *Statistical test.* The Mann-Whitney U test is chosen because the measurement is at least ordinal, and the assumptions under the parametric t-test are rejected.

3. *Significance level.* $\alpha = .05$ (one-tailed test).

4. *Calculated value.*

Sales per Week per Salesperson			
Training Method A	**Rank**	**Training Method B**	**Rank**
1,500	15	1,340	10
1,540	16	1,300	8.5
1,860	22	1,620	18
1,230	6	1,070	3
1,370	12	1,210	5
1,550	17	1,170	4
1,840	21	1,770	20
1,250	7	950	1
1,300	8.5	1,380	13
1,350	11	1,460	14
1,710	19	1,030	2
	$R_1 = 154.5$		$R_2 = 98.5$

$$U = (11)(11) + \frac{11(11 + 1)}{2} - 154.5 = 32.5 \qquad U = (11)(11) + \frac{11(11 + 1)}{2} - 98.5 = 88.5$$

5. *Critical test value.* Enter Appendix d, Exhibit d-9, with $n_1 = n_2 = 11$, and find a critical value of 34 for $\alpha = 0.5$, one-tailed test. Note that with this test, the calculated value must be smaller than the critical value to reject the null hypothesis.

6. *Interpretation.* Because the calculated value is smaller than the critical value ($34 > 32.5$), reject the null hypothesis and conclude that training method A is probably superior.

Thus, one would reject the null hypothesis at $\alpha = .05$ in a one-tailed test using either the t *test* or the U test. In this example, the U test has approximately the same power as the parametric test.

When $n > 20$ in one of the samples, the sampling distribution of U approaches the normal distribution with

$$\text{Mean} \quad = \quad \mu_U = \frac{n_1 n_2}{2}$$

$$\text{Standard deviation} \quad \sigma_U = \sqrt{\frac{(n_1)(n_2)(n_1 + n_2 + 1)}{12}}$$

and

$$z = \frac{U - \mu_U}{\sigma_U}$$

Other Nonparametric Tests

Other tests are appropriate under certain conditions when testing two independent samples. When the measurement is only nominal, the Fisher exact probability test may be used. When the data are at least ordinal, use the median and Wald-Wolfowitz runs tests.

k-**Samples Tests** You can use tests more powerful than χ^2 with data that are at least ordinal in nature. One such test is an extension of the median test mentioned earlier. We illustrate here the application of a second ordinal measurement test known as the Kruskal-Wallis one-way analysis of variance.

Kruskal-Wallis Test

This is a generalized version of the Mann-Whitney test. With it we rank all scores in the entire pool of observations from smallest to largest. The rank sum of each sample is then calculated, with ties being distributed as in other examples. We then compute the value of *H* as follows:

$$H = \frac{12}{N(N + 1)}\sum_{j=1}^{k}\frac{T_j^2}{n_j} - 3(N + 1)$$

where

T_j = sum of ranks in column j
n_j = number of cases in jth sample
$N = \Sigma w_j$ total number of cases
k = number of samples

When there are a number of ties, it is recommended that a correction factor (*C*) be calculated and used to correct the *H* value as follows:

$$C = 1 - \left\{ \frac{\sum_i^G (t_i^3 - t_i)}{N^3 - N} \right\}$$

where

G = number of sets of tied observations
t_i = number tied in any set i

$$H' = H / C$$

To secure the critical value for *H'*, use the table for the distribution of χ^2 (see Appendix d, Exhibit d-3), and enter it with the value of *H'* and d.f. = $k - 1$.

To illustrate the application of this test, use the price discount experiment problem. The data and calculations are shown in Exhibit c-1 and indicate that, by the Kruskal-Wallis test, one again barely fails to reject the null hypothesis with $\alpha = .05$.

>**Exhibit c-1** Kruskal-Wallis One-Way Analysis of Variance (price differentials).

One Cent		Three Cents		Five Cents	
X_A	Rank	X_B	Rank	X_C	Rank
6	1	8	5	9	8.5
7	2.5	9	8.5	9	8.5
8	5	8	5	11	14
7	2.5	10	11.5	10	11.5
9	8.5	11	14	14	18
11	14	13	16.5	13	16.5
	$T_j = 33.5$		60.5		77.0

$T_i = 33.5$

$T = 33.5 + 60.5 + 77.0$

$\quad = 171$

$H = \dfrac{12}{18(18+1)}\left[\dfrac{33.5^2 + 60.5^2 + 77^2}{6}\right] - 3(18+1)$

$\quad = \dfrac{12}{342}\left[\dfrac{1{,}122.25 + 3{,}660.25 + 5{,}929}{6}\right] - 57$

$\quad = 0.0351\left[\dfrac{10{,}711.5}{6}\right] - 57$

$H = 5.66$

$C = 1 - \left(\dfrac{3\left[(2)^3 - 2\right] + 2\left[(3)^3 - 3\right] + 4\left[(4)^3 - 4\right]}{18^3 - 18}\right)$

$\quad = 1 - \dfrac{18 + 48 + 60}{5814}$

$\quad = .978$

$H' = \dfrac{H}{C} = \dfrac{5.66}{.978} = 5.79$

$d.f. = k - 1 = 2$

$p > .05$

>appendixd

Selected Statistical Tables

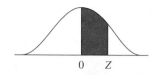

>**Exhibit d-1** Areas of the Standard Normal Distribution

| | | | | | Second Decimal Place in z | | | | | |
z	0.00	0.01	0.02	0.03	0.04	0.05	0.06	0.07	0.08	0.09
0.0	0.0000	0.0040	0.0080	0.0120	0.0160	0.0199	0.0239	0.0279	0.0319	0.0359
0.1	0.0398	0.0438	0.0478	0.0517	0.0557	0.0596	0.0636	0.0675	0.0714	0.0753
0.2	0.0793	0.0832	0.0871	0.0910	0.0948	0.0987	0.1026	0.1064	0.1103	0.1141
0.3	0.1179	0.1217	0.1255	0.1293	0.1331	0.1368	0.1406	0.1443	0.1480	0.1517
0.4	0.1554	0.1591	0.1628	0.1664	0.1700	0.1736	0.1772	0.1808	0.1844	0.1879
0.5	0.1915	0.1950	0.1985	0.2019	0.2054	0.2088	0.2123	0.2157	0.2190	0.2224
0.6	0.2257	0.2291	0.2324	0.2357	0.2389	0.2422	0.2454	0.2486	0.2517	0.2549
0.7	0.2580	0.2611	0.2642	0.2673	0.2704	0.2734	0.2764	0.2794	0.2823	0.2852
0.8	0.2881	0.2910	0.2939	0.2967	0.2995	0.3023	0.3051	0.3078	0.3106	0.3133
0.9	0.3159	0.3186	0.3212	0.3238	0.3264	0.3289	0.3315	0.3340	0.3365	0.3389
1.0	0.3413	0.3438	0.3461	0.3485	0.3508	0.3531	0.3554	0.3577	0.3599	0.3621
1.1	0.3643	0.3665	0.3686	0.3708	0.3729	0.3749	0.3770	0.3790	0.3810	0.3830
1.2	0.3849	0.3869	0.3888	0.3907	0.3925	0.3944	0.3962	0.3980	0.3997	0.4015
1.3	0.4032	0.4049	0.4066	0.4082	0.4099	0.4115	0.4131	0.4147	0.4162	0.4177
1.4	0.4192	0.4207	0.4222	0.4236	0.4251	0.4265	0.4279	0.4292	0.4306	0.4319
1.5	0.4332	0.4345	0.4357	0.4370	0.4382	0.4394	0.4406	0.4418	0.4429	0.4441
1.6	0.4452	0.4463	0.4474	0.4484	0.4495	0.4505	0.4515	0.4525	0.4535	0.4545
1.7	0.4554	0.4564	0.4573	0.4582	0.4591	0.4599	0.4608	0.4616	0.4625	0.4633
1.8	0.4641	0.4649	0.4656	0.4664	0.4671	0.4678	0.4686	0.4693	0.4699	0.4706
1.9	0.4713	0.4719	0.4726	0.4732	0.4738	0.4744	0.4750	0.4756	0.4761	0.4767
2.0	0.4772	0.4778	0.4783	0.4788	0.4793	0.4798	0.4803	0.4808	0.4812	0.4817
2.1	0.4821	0.4826	0.4830	0.4834	0.4838	0.4842	0.4846	0.4850	0.4854	0.4857
2.2	0.4861	0.4864	0.4868	0.4871	0.4875	0.4878	0.4881	0.4884	0.4887	0.4890
2.3	0.4893	0.4896	0.4898	0.4901	0.4904	0.4906	0.4909	0.4911	0.4913	0.4916
2.4	0.4918	0.4920	0.4922	0.4925	0.4927	0.4929	0.4931	0.4932	0.4934	0.4936
2.5	0.4938	0.4940	0.4941	0.4943	0.4945	0.4946	0.4948	0.4949	0.4951	0.4952
2.6	0.4953	0.4955	0.4956	0.4957	0.4959	0.4960	0.4961	0.4962	0.4963	0.4964
2.7	0.4965	0.4966	0.4967	0.4968	0.4969	0.4970	0.4971	0.4972	0.4973	0.4974
2.8	0.4974	0.4975	0.4976	0.4977	0.4977	0.4978	0.4979	0.4979	0.4980	0.4981
2.9	0.4981	0.4982	0.4982	0.4983	0.4984	0.4984	0.4985	0.4985	0.4986	0.4986
3.0	0.4987	0.4987	0.4987	0.4988	0.4988	0.4989	0.4989	0.4989	0.4990	0.4990
3.1	0.4990	0.4991	0.4991	0.4991	0.4992	0.4992	0.4992	0.4992	0.4993	0.4993
3.2	0.4993	0.4993	0.4994	0.4994	0.4994	0.4994	0.4994	0.4995	0.4995	0.4995
3.3	0.4995	0.4995	0.4995	0.4996	0.4996	0.4996	0.4996	0.4996	0.4996	0.4997
3.4	0.4997	0.4997	0.4997	0.4997	0.4997	0.4997	0.4997	0.4997	0.4997	0.4998
3.5	0.4998									
4.0	0.49997									
4.5	0.499997									
5.0	0.4999997									
6.0	0.499999999									

>**Exhibit d-2**   Critical Values of *t* for Given Probability Levels

	Level of Significance for One-Tailed Test					
	.10	.05	.025	.01	.005	.0005
	Level of Significance for Two-Tailed Test					
d.f.	.20	.10	.05	.02	.01	.001
1	3.078	6.314	12.706	31.821	63.657	636.619
2	1.886	2.920	4.303	6.965	9.925	31.598
3	1.638	2.353	3.182	4.541	5.841	12.941
4	1.533	2.132	2.776	3.747	4.604	8.610
5	1.476	2.015	2.571	3.365	4.032	6.859
6	1.440	1.943	2.447	3.143	3.707	5.959
7	1.415	1.895	2.365	2.998	3.499	5.405
8	1.397	1.860	2.306	2.896	3.355	5.041
9	1.383	1.833	2.262	2.821	3.250	4.781
10	1.372	1.812	2.228	2.764	3.169	4.587
11	1.363	1.796	2.201	2.718	3.106	4.437
12	1.356	1.782	2.179	2.681	3.055	4.318
13	1.350	1.771	2.160	2.650	3.012	4.221
14	1.345	1.761	2.145	2.624	2.977	4.140
15	1.341	1.753	2.131	2.602	2.947	4.073
16	1.337	1.746	2.120	2.583	2.921	4.015
17	1.333	1.740	2.110	2.567	2.898	3.965
18	1.330	1.734	2.101	2.552	2.878	3.922
19	1.328	1.729	2.093	2.539	2.861	3.883
20	1.325	1.725	2.086	2.528	2.845	3.850
21	1.323	1.721	2.080	2.518	2.831	3.819
22	1.321	1.717	2.074	2.508	2.819	3.792
23	1.319	1.714	2.069	2.500	2.807	3.767
24	1.318	1.711	2.064	2.492	2.797	3.745
25	1.316	1.708	2.060	2.485	2.787	3.725
26	1.315	1.706	2.056	2.479	2.779	3.707
27	1.314	1.703	2.052	2.473	2.771	3.690
28	1.313	1.701	2.048	2.467	2.763	3.674
29	1.311	1.699	2.045	2.462	2.756	3.659
30	1.310	1.697	2.042	2.457	2.750	3.646
40	1.303	1.684	2.021	2.423	2.704	3.551
60	1.296	1.671	2.000	2.390	2.660	3.460
120	1.289	1.658	1.980	2.358	2.617	3.373
∞	1.282	1.645	1.960	2.326	2.576	3.291

Source: Abridged from Table III of R. A. Fisher and F. Yates, *Statistical Tables for Biological, Agricultural, and Medical Research,* 6th ed., published by Oliver and Boyd Ltd., Edinburgh, 1963. By permission of the publishers.

>**Exhibit d-3** Critical Values of the Chi-Square Distribution

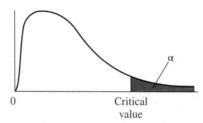

0   Critical
value

			Probability		
d.f.	.10	.05	.02	.01	.001
1	2.71	3.84	5.41	6.64	10.83
2	4.60	5.99	7.82	9.21	13.82
3	6.25	7.82	9.84	11.34	16.27
4	7.78	9.49	11.67	13.28	18.46
5	9.24	11.07	13.39	15.09	20.52
6	10.64	12.59	15.03	16.81	22.46
7	12.02	14.07	16.62	18.48	24.32
8	13.36	15.51	18.17	20.09	26.12
9	14.68	16.92	19.68	21.67	27.88
10	15.99	18.31	21.16	23.21	29.59
11	17.28	19.68	22.62	24.72	31.26
12	18.55	21.03	24.05	26.22	32.91
13	19.81	22.36	25.47	27.69	34.53
14	21.06	23.68	26.87	29.14	36.12
15	22.31	25.00	28.26	30.58	37.70
16	23.54	26.30	29.63	32.00	39.29
17	24.77	27.59	31.00	33.41	40.75
18	25.99	28.87	32.35	34.80	42.31
19	27.20	30.14	33.69	36.19	43.82
20	28.41	31.41	35.02	37.57	45.32
21	29.62	32.67	36.34	38.93	46.80
22	30.81	33.92	37.66	40.29	48.27
23	32.01	35.17	38.97	41.64	49.73
24	33.20	36.42	40.27	42.98	51.18
25	34.38	37.65	41.57	44.31	52.62
26	35.56	38.88	42.86	45.64	54.05
27	36.74	40.11	44.14	46.96	55.48
28	37.92	41.34	45.42	48.28	56.89
29	39.09	42.56	46.69	49.59	58.30
30	40.26	43.77	47.96	50.89	59.70

Source: Abridged from Table IV of Fisher and Yates, *Statistical Tables for Biological, Agricultural, and Medical Research,* 6th ed., published by Oliver and Boyd Ltd., Edinburgh, 1963. By permission of the publishers.

>**Exhibit d-4** Critical Values of T in the Wilcoxon Matched-Pairs Test

	Level of Significance for One-Tailed Test		
	.025	.01	.005
	Level of Significance for Two-Tailed Test		
n	.05	.02	.01
6	0	–	–
7	2	0	–
8	4	2	0
9	6	3	2
10	8	5	3
11	11	7	5
12	14	10	7
13	17	13	10
14	21	16	13
15	25	20	16
16	30	24	20
17	35	28	23
18	40	33	28
19	46	38	32
20	52	43	38
21	59	49	43
22	66	56	49
23	73	62	55
24	81	69	61
25	89	77	68

Source: Adapted from Table 1 of F. Wilcoxon, *Some Rapid Approximate Statistical Procedures* (New York: American Cyanamid Company, 1949), p. 13, with the kind permission of the publisher.

>**Exhibit d-5** Critical Values of D in the Kolmogorov-Smirnov One-Sample Test

| | Level of Significance for $D = $ Maximum $|F_o(X) - S_N(X)|$ | | | | |
Sample Size n	.20	.15	.10	.05	.01
1	.900	.925	.950	.975	.995
2	.684	.726	.776	.842	.929
3	.565	.597	.642	.708	.828
4	.494	.525	.564	.624	.733
5	.446	.474	.510	.565	.669
6	.410	.436	.470	.521	.618
7	.381	.405	.438	.486	.577
8	.358	.381	.411	.457	.543
9	.339	.360	.388	.432	.514
10	.322	.342	.368	.410	.490
11	.307	.326	.352	.391	.468
12	.295	.313	.338	.375	.450
13	.284	.302	.325	.361	.433
14	.274	.292	.314	.349	.418
15	.266	.283	.304	.338	.404
16	.258	.274	.295	.328	.392
17	.250	.266	.286	.318	.381
18	.244	.259	.278	.309	.371
19	.237	.252	.272	.301	.363
20	.231	.246	.264	.294	.356
25	.21	.22	.24	.27	.32
30	.19	.20	.22	.24	.29
35	.18	.19	.21	.23	.27
Over 35	$\dfrac{1.07}{\sqrt{N}}$	$\dfrac{1.14}{\sqrt{N}}$	$\dfrac{1.22}{\sqrt{N}}$	$\dfrac{1.36}{\sqrt{N}}$	$\dfrac{1.63}{\sqrt{N}}$

Source: F. J. Massey Jr., "The Kolmogorov-Smirnov Test for Goodness of Fit," *Journal of the American Statistical Association* 46, p. 70. Adapted with the kind permission of the publisher.

>**Exhibit d-6** Critical Values of K_D in the Kolmogorov-Smirnov
Two-Samples Test (small samples)

	One-Tailed Test		Two-Tailed Test	
n	$\alpha = .05$	$\alpha = .01$	$\alpha = .05$	$\alpha = .01$
3	3	–	–	–
4	4	–	4	–
5	4	5	5	5
6	5	6	5	6
7	5	6	6	6
8	5	6	6	7
9	6	7	6	7
10	6	7	7	8
11	6	8	7	8
12	6	8	7	8
13	7	8	7	9
14	7	8	8	9
15	7	9	8	9
16	7	9	8	10
17	8	9	8	10
18	8	10	9	10
19	8	10	9	10
20	8	10	9	11
21	8	10	9	11
22	9	11	9	11
23	9	11	10	11
24	9	11	10	12
25	9	11	10	12
26	9	11	10	12
27	9	12	10	12
28	10	12	11	13
29	10	12	11	13
30	10	12	11	13
35	11	13	12	
40	11	14	13	

Source: One-tailed test—abridged from I. A. Goodman, "Kolmogorov-Smirnov Tests for Psychological Research," *Psychological Bulletin* 51 (1951), p. 167, copyright (1951) by the American Psychological Association. Reprinted by permission. Two-tailed test—derived from Table 1 of F. J. Massey Jr., "The Distribution of the Maximum Deviation between Two Sample Cumulative Step Functions," *Annals of Mathematical Statistics* 23 (1951), pp. 126–27, with the kind permission of the publisher.

>**Exhibit d-7** Critical Values of D in the Kolmogorov-Smirnov Two-Samples Test for Large Samples (two-tailed)

Level of Significance	Value of D So Large as to Call for Rejection of H_0 at the Indicated Level of Significance, Where D = Maximum $|S_{n_1}(X) = S_2(X)|$
.10	$1.22\sqrt{\dfrac{n_1 + n_2}{n_1 n_2}}$
.05	$1.36\sqrt{\dfrac{n_1 + n_2}{n_1 n_2}}$
.025	$1.48\sqrt{\dfrac{n_1 + n_2}{n_1 n_2}}$
.01	$1.63\sqrt{\dfrac{n_1 + n_2}{n_1 n_2}}$
.005	$1.73\sqrt{\dfrac{n_1 + n_2}{n_1 n_2}}$
.001	$1.95\sqrt{\dfrac{n_1 + n_2}{n_1 n_2}}$

Source: Adapted from N. Smirnov, "Table for Estimating the Goodness of Fit of Empirical Distribution," *Annals of Mathematical Statistics* 18 (1948), pp. 280–81, with the kind permission of the publisher.

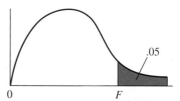

>**Exhibit d-8** Critical Values of the *F* Distribution for α = .05

n_2	Degrees of Freedom for Numerator								
	1	**2**	**3**	**4**	**5**	**6**	**7**	**8**	**9**
1	161.40	199.50	215.70	224.60	230.20	234.00	236.80	238.90	240.50
2	18.51	19.00	19.16	19.25	19.30	19.33	19.35	19.37	19.38
3	10.13	9.55	9.28	9.12	9.01	8.94	8.89	8.85	8.81
4	7.71	6.94	6.59	6.39	6.26	6.16	6.09	6.04	6.00
5	6.61	5.79	5.41	5.19	5.05	4.95	4.88	4.82	4.77
6	5.99	5.14	4.76	4.53	4.39	4.28	4.21	4.15	4.10
7	5.59	4.74	4.35	4.12	3.97	3.87	3.79	3.73	3.68
8	5.32	4.46	4.07	3.84	3.69	3.58	3.50	3.44	3.39
9	5.12	4.26	3.86	3.63	3.48	3.37	3.29	3.23	3.18
10	4.96	4.10	3.71	3.48	3.33	3.22	3.14	3.07	3.02
11	4.84	3.98	3.59	3.36	3.20	3.09	3.01	2.95	2.90
12	4.75	3.89	3.49	3.26	3.11	3.00	2.91	2.85	2.80
13	4.67	3.81	3.41	3.18	3.03	2.92	2.83	2.77	2.71
14	4.60	3.74	3.34	3.11	2.96	2.85	2.76	2.70	2.65
15	4.54	3.68	3.29	3.06	2.90	2.79	2.71	2.64	2.59
16	4.49	3.63	3.24	3.01	2.85	2.74	2.66	2.59	2.54
17	4.45	3.59	3.20	2.96	2.81	2.70	2.61	2.55	2.49
18	4.41	3.55	3.16	2.93	2.77	2.66	2.58	2.51	2.46
19	4.38	3.52	3.13	2.90	2.74	2.63	2.54	2.48	2.42
20	4.35	3.49	3.10	2.87	2.71	2.60	2.51	2.45	2.39
21	4.32	3.47	3.07	2.84	2.68	2.57	2.49	2.42	2.37
22	4.30	3.44	3.05	2.82	2.66	2.55	2.46	2.40	2.34
23	4.28	3.42	3.03	2.80	2.64	2.53	2.44	2.37	2.32
24	4.26	3.40	3.01	2.78	2.62	2.51	2.42	2.36	2.30
25	4.24	3.39	2.99	2.76	2.60	2.49	2.40	2.34	2.28
26	4.23	3.37	2.98	2.74	2.59	2.47	2.39	2.32	2.27
27	4.21	3.35	2.96	2.73	2.57	2.46	2.37	2.31	2.25
28	4.20	3.34	2.95	2.71	2.56	2.45	2.36	2.29	2.24
29	4.18	3.33	2.93	2.70	2.55	2.43	2.35	2.28	2.22
30	4.17	3.32	2.92	2.69	2.53	2.42	2.33	2.27	2.21
40	4.08	3.23	2.84	2.61	2.45	2.34	2.25	2.18	2.12
60	4.00	3.15	2.76	2.53	2.37	2.25	2.17	2.10	2.04
120	3.92	3.07	2.68	2.45	2.29	2.17	2.09	2.02	1.96
∞	3.84	3.00	2.60	2.37	2.21	2.10	2.01	1.94	1.88

Degrees of Freedom for Denominator

			Degrees of Freedom for Numerator (cont'd)							
n_2	10	12	15	20	24	30	40	80	120	∞
1	241.90	243.90	245.90	248.00	249.10	250.10	251.10	252.20	253.30	243.30
2	19.40	19.41	19.43	19.45	19.45	19.46	19.47	19.48	19.49	19.50
3	8.79	8.74	8.70	8.66	8.64	8.62	8.59	8.57	8.55	8.53
4	5.96	5.91	5.86	5.80	5.77	5.75	5.72	5.69	5.66	5.63
5	4.74	4.68	4.62	4.56	4.53	4.50	4.46	4.43	4.40	4.36
6	4.06	4.00	3.94	3.87	3.84	3.81	3.77	3.74	3.70	3.67
7	3.64	3.57	3.51	3.44	3.41	3.38	3.34	3.30	3.27	3.23
8	3.35	3.28	3.22	3.15	3.12	3.08	3.04	3.01	2.97	2.93
9	3.14	3.07	3.01	2.94	2.90	2.86	2.83	2.79	2.75	2.71
10	2.98	2.91	2.85	2.77	2.74	2.70	2.66	2.62	2.58	2.54
11	2.85	2.79	2.72	2.65	2.61	2.57	2.53	2.49	2.45	2.40
12	2.75	2.69	2.62	2.54	2.51	2.47	2.43	2.38	2.34	2.30
13	2.67	2.60	2.53	2.46	2.42	2.38	2.34	2.30	2.25	2.21
14	2.60	2.53	2.46	2.39	2.35	2.31	2.27	2.22	2.18	2.13
15	2.54	2.48	2.40	2.33	2.29	2.25	2.20	2.16	2.11	2.07
16	2.49	2.42	2.35	2.28	2.24	2.19	2.15	2.11	2.06	2.01
17	2.45	2.38	2.31	2.23	2.19	2.15	2.10	2.06	2.01	1.96
18	2.41	2.34	2.27	2.19	2.15	2.11	2.06	2.02	1.97	1.92
19	2.38	2.31	2.23	2.16	2.11	2.07	2.03	1.98	1.93	1.88
20	2.35	2.28	2.20	2.12	2.08	2.04	1.99	1.95	1.90	1.84
21	2.32	2.25	2.18	2.10	2.05	2.01	1.96	1.92	1.87	1.81
22	2.30	2.23	2.15	2.07	2.03	1.98	1.94	1.89	1.84	1.78
23	2.27	2.20	2.13	2.05	2.01	1.96	1.91	1.86	1.81	1.76
24	2.25	2.18	2.11	2.03	1.98	1.94	1.89	1.84	1.79	1.73
25	2.24	2.16	2.09	2.01	1.96	1.92	1.87	1.82	1.77	1.71
26	2.22	2.15	2.07	1.99	1.95	1.90	1.85	1.80	1.75	1.69
27	2.20	2.13	2.06	1.97	1.93	1.88	1.84	1.79	1.73	1.67
28	2.19	2.12	2.04	1.96	1.91	1.87	1.82	1.77	1.71	1.65
29	2.18	2.10	2.03	1.94	1.90	1.85	1.81	1.75	1.70	1.64
30	2.16	2.09	2.01	1.93	1.89	1.84	1.79	1.74	1.68	1.62
40	2.08	2.00	1.92	1.84	1.79	1.74	1.69	1.64	1.58	1.51
60	1.99	1.92	1.84	1.75	1.70	1.65	1.59	1.53	1.47	1.39
120	1.91	1.83	1.75	1.66	1.61	1.55	1.50	1.43	1.35	1.25
∞	1.83	1.75	1.67	1.57	1.52	1.46	1.39	1.32	1.22	1.00

Source: Reprinted by permission from *Statistical Methods* by George W. Snedecor and William G. Cochran, 6th edition, © 1967 by Iowa State University Press, Ames, Iowa.

>**Exhibit d-9** Partial Table of Critical Values of *U* in the Mann-Whitney Test

	Critical Values for One-Tailed Test at α = .025 or Two-Tailed Test at α = .05											
n_1/n_2	9	10	11	12	13	14	15	16	17	18	19	20
1												
2	0	0	0	1	1	1	1	1	2	2	2	2
3	2	3	3	4	4	5	5	6	6	7	7	8
4	4	5	6	7	8	9	10	11	11	12	13	13
5	7	8	9	11	12	13	14	15	17	18	19	20
6	10	11	13	14	16	17	19	21	22	24	25	27
7	12	14	16	18	20	22	24	26	28	30	32	34
8	15	17	19	22	24	26	29	31	34	36	38	41
9	17	20	23	26	28	31	34	37	39	42	45	48
10	20	23	26	29	33	36	39	42	45	48	52	55
11	23	26	30	33	37	40	44	47	51	55	58	62
12	26	29	33	37	41	45	49	53	57	61	66	69
13	28	33	37	41	45	50	54	59	63	67	72	76
14	31	36	40	45	50	55	59	64	67	74	78	83
15	34	39	44	49	54	59	64	70	75	80	85	90
16	37	42	47	53	59	64	70	75	81	86	92	98
17	39	45	51	57	63	67	75	81	87	93	99	105
18	42	48	55	61	67	74	80	86	93	99	106	112
19	45	52	58	65	72	78	85	92	99	106	113	119
20	48	55	62	69	76	83	90	98	105	112	119	127

	Critical Values for One-Tailed Test at α = .05 or Two-Tailed Test at α = .10											
n_1/n_2	9	10	11	12	13	14	15	16	17	18	19	20
1											0	0
2	1	1	1	2	2	2	3	3	3	4	4	4
3	3	4	5	5	6	7	7	8	9	9	10	11
4	6	7	8	9	10	11	12	14	15	16	17	18
5	9	11	12	13	15	16	18	19	20	22	23	25
6	12	14	16	17	19	21	23	25	26	28	30	32
7	15	17	19	21	24	26	28	30	33	35	37	39
8	18	20	23	26	28	31	33	36	39	41	44	47
9	21	24	27	30	33	36	39	42	45	48	51	54
10	24	27	31	34	37	41	44	48	51	55	58	62
11	27	31	34	38	42	46	50	54	57	61	65	69
12	30	34	38	42	47	51	55	60	64	68	72	77
13	33	37	42	47	51	56	61	65	70	75	80	84
14	36	41	46	51	56	61	66	71	77	82	87	92
15	39	44	50	55	61	66	72	77	83	88	94	100
16	42	48	54	60	65	71	77	83	89	95	101	107
17	45	51	57	64	70	77	83	89	96	102	109	115
18	48	55	61	68	75	82	88	95	102	109	116	123
19	51	58	65	72	80	87	94	101	109	116	123	130
20	54	62	69	77	84	92	100	107	115	123	130	138

Source: Abridged from D. Auble, "Extended Tables from the Mann-Whitney Statistic," *Bulletin of the Institute of Educational Research at Indiana University* 1, no. 2, reprinted with permission. For tables for other-size samples, consult this source.

>**Exhibit d-10** Random Numbers

97446	30328	05262	77371	13523	62057	44349	85884	94555	23288
15453	75591	60540	77137	09485	27632	05477	99154	78720	10323
69995	77086	55217	53721	85713	27854	41981	88981	90041	20878
69726	58696	27272	38148	52521	73807	29685	49152	20309	58734
23604	31948	16926	26360	76957	99925	86045	11617	32777	38670
13640	17233	58650	47819	24935	28670	33415	77202	92492	40290
90779	09199	51169	94892	34271	22068	13923	53535	56358	50258
71068	19459	32339	10124	13012	79706	07611	52600	83088	26829
55019	79001	34442	16335	06428	52873	65316	01480	72204	39494
20879	50235	17389	25260	34039	99967	48044	05067	69284	53867
00380	11595	49372	95214	98529	46593	77046	27176	39668	20566
68142	40800	20527	79212	14166	84948	11748	69540	84288	37211
42667	89566	20440	57230	35356	01884	79921	94772	29882	24695
07756	78430	45576	86596	56720	65529	44211	18447	53921	92722
45221	31130	44312	63534	47741	02465	50629	94983	05984	88375
20140	77481	61686	82836	41058	41331	04290	61212	60294	95954
54922	25436	33804	51907	73223	66423	68706	36589	45267	35327
48340	30832	72209	07644	52747	40751	06808	85349	18005	52323
23603	84387	20416	88084	33103	41511	59391	71600	35091	52722
12548	01033	22974	59596	92087	02116	63524	00627	41778	24392
15251	87584	12942	03771	91413	75652	19468	83889	98531	91529
65548	59670	57355	18874	63601	55111	07278	32560	40028	36079
48488	76170	46282	76427	41693	04506	80979	26654	62159	83017
02862	15665	62159	15159	69576	20328	68873	28152	66087	39405
67929	06754	45842	66365	80848	15262	55144	37816	08421	30071
73237	07607	31615	04892	50989	87347	14393	21165	68169	70788
13788	20327	07960	95917	75112	01398	26381	41377	33549	19754
43877	66485	40825	45923	74410	69693	76959	70973	26343	63781
14047	08369	56414	78533	76378	44204	71493	68861	31042	81873
88383	46755	51342	13505	55324	52950	22244	28028	73486	98797
29567	16379	41994	65947	58926	50953	09388	00405	29874	44954
20508	60995	41539	26396	99825	25652	28089	57224	35222	58922
64178	76768	75747	32854	32893	61152	58565	33128	33354	16056
26373	51147	90362	93309	13175	66385	57822	31138	12893	68607
10083	47656	59241	73630	99200	94672	59785	95449	99279	25488
11683	14347	04369	98719	75005	43633	24125	30532	54830	95387
56548	76293	50904	88579	24621	94291	56881	35062	48765	22078
35292	47291	82610	27777	43965	31802	98444	88929	54383	93141
51329	87645	51623	08971	50704	82395	33916	95859	99788	97885
51860	19180	39324	68483	78650	74750	64893	58042	82878	20619
23886	01257	07945	71175	31243	87167	42829	44601	08769	26417
80028	82310	43989	09242	15056	48250	04529	96941	48190	69644
83946	46858	09164	18858	12672	55190	02820	45861	29104	75386
00000	41586	25972	25356	54260	95691	99431	89903	22306	43863
90615	12848	23376	29458	48239	37628	59265	50152	30340	40713
42003	10738	55835	48218	23204	19188	13556	06610	77667	88068
86135	26174	07834	17007	97938	96728	15689	77544	89186	41252
54436	10828	41212	19836	89476	53685	28085	22878	71868	35048
14545	72034	32131	38783	58588	47499	50945	97045	42357	53536
43925	49879	13339	78773	95626	67119	93023	96832	09757	98545

Source: The Rand Corporation, *A Million Random Digits with 100,000 Normal Deviates* (Glencoe, IL: Free Press, 1955), p. 225.

>references

Chapter 1

1. This example is based on an on-air interview with David Green, Hobby Lobby's CEO, on *CBS This Morning*, April 25, 2017 (http://www.cbsnews.com/news/hobby-lobby-ceo-david-green-new-book/), and on his book, *Giving It All Away . . . and Getting It All Back Again: The Way of Living Generously*. (Grand Rapids, MI: Zondervan, 2017).

2. Sam Ransbotham, David Kiron, and Pamela Kirk Prentice, "Beyond the Hype: The Hard Work Behind Analytics Success, research white paper from *MIT/Sloan Management Review* and SAS, Spring 2016, downloaded April 27, 2016 (http://marketing.mitsmr.com/PDF/57381-MITSMR-SAS-Analytics2016.pdf?utm_source=WhatCounts%2c+Publicaster+Edition&utm_medium=email&utm_campaign=darpt16&utm_content=Download+the+Report+%28PDF%29&cid=1).

3. Material for this paragraph was drawn from the research industry's annual retrospective by Leonard F. Murphy, "GRIT Report," *GreenBook*, June 2016, downloaded June 30, 2016 (https://www.greenbook.org/images/GRIT/2016_grit/GRIT_Report_2016_Edition.pdf); and "10 Trends to Watch For in 2017," Seifert Technologies Inc., downloaded April 18, 2017 (http://techbit.guide/show.php?a=1571&source=linkedin&cid=19735&ref=026A1CJ01K).

4. "Our Business," Siemens AG, downloaded April 26, 2016 (http://www.siemens.com/businesses/us/en/); and "About," Siemens AG, downloaded April 26, 2016 (http://www.usa.siemens.com/en/about_us.htm?stc=usccc025276&s_kwcid=AL!462!3!47804445220!e!!s!!siemens&ef_id=VfRMpgAABbGt39PL:20160426154333:s).

5. Gerhard Kress, director of mobility data services at Siemens AG, "The Internet of Things in Motion: Analytics and Transportation," Web seminar sponsored by Teredata and *MIT/Sloan Management Review*, April 26, 2016.

6. "The Definitive Guide to Data Blending," Alteryx, downloaded April 25, 2016 (http://pages.alteryx.com/rs/alteryx/images/ALT_WPDefGuideDataBlending-WithGraphics38.pdf).

7. Merriam-Webster, downloaded February 10, 2016 (http://www.merriam-webster.com/dictionary/gestalt).

8. "Customer," *Merriam-Webster's Dictionary,* downloaded July 7, 2016 (http://www.merriam-webster.com/thesaurus/customer).

9. Fred N. Kerlinger, *Foundations of Behavioral Research,* 3rd ed. (New York: Holt, Rinehart & Winston, 1986), pp. 436–37.

10. Kenneth R. Hoover, *The Elements of Social Scientific Thinking,* 5th ed. (New York: St. Martin's Press, 1991), p. 71.

11. Bruce Tuckman, *Conducting Educational Research* (New York: Harcourt Brace Jovanovich, 1972), p. 45.

12. "Employee Theft Statistics," *StatisticsBrain*, April 1, 2017, downloaded April 15, 2017 (http://www.statisticbrain.com/employee-theft-statistics/). Statistics were drawn from Association of Certified Fraud Examiners, Easy Small Business HR, Institute for Corporate Productivity, and Jack L. Hayes International Inc. Also, "The 2015 Hiscox Embezzlement Watchlist: A Snapshot of Employee Theft in the US," Hiscox, downloaded April 15, 2017 (http://www.hiscoxbroker.com/shared-documents/2015%20Hiscox%20Embezzlement%20Watchlist.pdf).

13. Howard Kahane, *Logic and Philosophy,* 2nd ed. (Belmont, CA: Wadsworth, 1973), p. 3.

14. Originally published by John Dewey, "Systematic Inference: Induction and Deduction," *How We Think* (Lexington, MA: D.C. Heath, 1910), Chap. 7, pp. 79-100, downloaded April 27, 2016 (https://brocku.ca/MeadProject/Dewey/Dewey_1910a/Dewey_1910_g.html).

15. Based on John Dewey, *How We Think* (Boston: Heath, 1910); and John R. Platt, "Strong Inference," *Science,* October 16, 1964, pp. 347–53.

16. The original theory was developed by economist Raymond Vernon, "International Investment and International Trade in the Product Cycle," *Quarterly Journal of Economics* 80, no. 2 (1966), pp. 190-207. It has been interpreted and enriched by numerous authors, including Roger A Kerin, Eric N. Berkowitz, Steven W. Hartley, and William Rudelius, *Marketing,* 7th ed. (Burr Ridge, IL: Irwin/McGraw-Hill, 2003), pp. 294–302.

References for Snapshots, PicProfiles, Captions, and Pull Quotes
Big vs Small Data

1. Martin Lindstrom, *Small Data: The Tiny Clues That Uncover Huge Trends,* St. Martin's Press (February 23, 2016), pp. 1–2.

2. "Why Small Data Is the New Big Data," Knowledge@Wharton, March 24, 2016. Downloaded March 25, 2016 http://adage.com/article/special-report-4as-conference/tipping-point-j/303268/?utm_source=daily_email&utm_medium=newsletter&utm_campaign=adage&ttl=1459463433).

Cyber Security

1. Richard Cassidy, Cyber Security Evangelist, AlertLogic, "Behind The Scenes: Cybercrime Threat Landscape," Brightalk webcast, April 27, 2016, downloaded May 26, 2016 (https://www.brighttalk.com/webcast/11587/201299?autoclick=true&utm_medium=web&utm_source=brighttalk-promoted&utm_campaign=player-page-feed&utm_content=promoted).

Identifying and Defining Constructs

1. George Slefo, "Digital Conference: Marketers Chime in on Elephants in the Room, Known and Unknown," AdAge, April 05, 2016, downloaded April 6, 2016 (http://adage.com/article/special-report-digital-conference/marketers-chime-elephants-digital/303413/?utm_source=daily_email&utm_medium=newsletter&utm_campaign=adage&ttl=1460499287).

MIT/Sloan

1. Sam Ransbotham, David Kiron, and Pamela Kirk Prentice, "Beyond the Hype: The Hard Work Behind Analytics Success," MIT Sloan, April 2016, downloaded April 29, 2016 (http://marketing.mitsmr.com/PDF/57381-MITSMR-SAS-Analytics2016.pdf?utm_source=WhatCounts%2c+Publicaster+Edition&utm_medium=email&utm_campaign=darpt16&utm_content=Download+the+Report+%28PDF%29&cid=1).

PullQuote

1. William C. Pink, "How Big Data Liberates Research," Millward Brown, downloaded May 4, 2016 (http://www.millwardbrown.com/docs/default-source/insight-documents/points-of-view/Millward_Brown_POV_How_Big_Data_Liberates_Research.pdf).

Chapter 2

1. "GRIT Report: Greenbook Research Industry Trends Report, 2016 Q3-Q4," Greenbook, p. 5, downloaded April 21, 2017, https://www.greenbook.org/images/GRIT/2017/GRIT2016-Q3-4.pdf.

2. Paul D. Leedy, *How to Read Research and Understand It* (New York: Macmillan, 1981), pp. 67–70.

3. Some examples are the ESOMAR Research Effectiveness Award, the Advertising Research Foundation (ARF) David Ogilvy Award, and the Michael R. Losey Excellence in Human Resource Research Award.

4. "The Hottest Trends in Workplace Collaboration," Polycom, May 2016, downloaded May 2, 2016, http://polycom.lookbookhq.com /defy-distance-collaboration/asset.

5. "GRIT Report: Greenbook Research Industry Trends Report, 2016 Q3-Q4," Greenbook, downloaded April 21, 2017, https://www .greenbook.org/images/GRIT/2017/GRIT2016-Q3-4.pdf.

6. Roger Cohen, "For U.S. Publishers, Awash in Red Ink, the Moment of Truth Looms," *International Herald Tribune*, March 6, 1990, p. 6.

7. Carl M. Moore, *Group Techniques for Idea Building,* 2nd ed. (Thousand Oaks, CA: Sage Publications, 1994).

8. Fred N. Kerlinger, *Foundations of Behavioral Research,* 3rd ed. (New York: Holt, Rinehart & Winston, 1986), pp. 436–37.

9. Walter B. Reitman, "Heuristic Decision Procedures, Open Constraints, and the Structure of Ill-Defined Problems," in *Human Judgments and Optimality,* ed. Maynard W. Shelly II and Glenn L. Bryan (New York: Wiley, 1964), p. 285.

References for Snapshots, PicProfiles, CloseUps and PullQuotes
2016 GRIT Report

1. "GRIT Report: Greenbook Research Industry Trends Report, 2016 Q3-Q4," GreenBook® | New York AMA Communication Services Inc., February 2016, p. 5 and 70, downloaded April 21, 2017, (https:// www.greenbook.org/images/GRIT/2017/GRIT2016-Q3-4.pdf).

Marcus Thomas, LLC & QualVu

1. "Case Study: Leveraging Technology in Marketing Research: Du- rable Baby Goods Consumer Insights" Marcus Thomas, LLC, provided via email, 2012.

2. Jennifer Hirt-Marchand, associate partner, strategic insights executive, and Edwige Winans, associate research director, Marcus Thomas, LLC, phone interview January 31, 2012.

3. "QualVu, Durable Baby Goods Project" Discussion Guide, provided by email, 2012.

4. QualVu demonstration, February 13, 2012 (https://qualvu.webex. com/ qualvu/j.php?J=854496039).

5. Guadalupe Pagalday, marketing manager, QualVu, phone interview February 13, 2012.

Programmatic Algorithms

1. Jack Neff, "Programmatic Pays Off Big for P&G, but Obstacles Loom," *AdAge,* April 01, 2016, downloaded April 01, 2016 (http://adage.com/article/digital/programmatic-pays-big-p -g-obstacles-loom/303350/?utm_source=daily_email&utm _medium=newsletter&utm_campaign=adage&ttl=1460071426).

2. Michael Benisch, "What's Under the Hood of Programmatic?" Rocket Fuel Inc., downloaded April 1, 2016 (http://info.rocketfuel.com/rs /rocketfuel/images/WhatsUndertheHoodofProgrammatic.pdf).

Project Leaving the Country

1. "Help End the Market Research Professions' Secret," November 19, 2009, accessed January 24, 2010 (http://www.tomhcanderson .com/ 2009/11/19/help-end-the-market-research-professions -final-dirty- little-secret/).

2. "Recent Survey Data about Offshoring." Study conducted by Foundation for Transparency in Offshoring, November 2009, accessed January 24, 2010 (http://www.offshoringtransparency .org/images/charts/ngmr4.jpg).

PullQuote

1. James Covert, "Microsoft sues US government over secret data requests," *New York Post,* April 14, 2016, downloaded May 2, 2016, (Http://mypost.com/2106/04/14/microsoft -sues-us-government-over-data-requests/).

Chapter 3

1. You can explore the latest census form and learn about the process at Census.gov. The form, and why each question is asked, can be found here: https://www.census.gov/2010census/about/interactive-form .php. According to "Census 2010: Final Report to Congress, Final Report No. OIG-11-020-I," Census Bureau, June 27, 2011, downloaded May 11, 2017, https://www.oig.doc.gov/OIGPublications /OIG-11-030-I.pdf, the decennial census cost $12 billion, $4 billion more than the previous one in 2000.

2. "Our Surveys & Programs," U.S. Census Bureau, downloaded May 11, 2017, https://www.census.gov/programs-surveys/censuses.html.

3. "About This Encyclopedia," *TDM Encyclopedia,* Victoria Transport Policy Institute, accessed February 2, 2007, http://www.vtpi.org /tdm/tdm12.htm.

4. "Encyclopedia of Private Equity and Venture Capital," VC Experts Inc., accessed February 2, 2007, http://vcexperts.com/vce/library /encyclopedia/.

5. *Occupational Outlook Handbook*, U.S. Bureau of Labor Statistics, accessed February 2, 2007, http://www.bls.gov/oco/ocoiab.htm.

6. Joseph B. Sieczka and Robert E. Thornton, eds., "Potato Association of American Handbook," Potato Association of America, accessed February 2, 2007, http://cropandsoil.oregonstate.edu /classes/CSS322/Cppina.htm.

7. *North American Industry Classification System (NAICS), United States 2017,* Executive Office of the President, Office of Management and Budget, accessed October 18, 2017 (https://www.census .gov/eos/www/naics/index.html).

8. *Associations Unlimited,* Gale Inc., accessed February 2007, http:// www.gale.com/servlet/ItemDetailServlet?region59&imprint5 000&titleCode5GAL7&type54&id5110996.

9. *Green Book: A Guide for Buyers of Marketing Research Services,* AMA Communication Services Inc., accessed April 28, 2017, http://www.greenbook.org/; and *Blue Book Marketing Research Services and Focus Group Facility Directory*, Insights Association, accessed April 28, 2017, https://bluebook.insightsassociation.org/. Organizations are included in the directory by joining the trade group that sponsors the directory.

10. B. DePompe, "There's Gold in Databases," *CMP Publications,* January 8, 1996, http://techweb.cmp.com/iwk.

11. "Data Mining: Plumbing the Depths of Corporate Databases," *Computer World Customer Publication,* insert to *ComputerWorld,* April 21, 1997, pp. 6, 18.

12. "Data Mining: Plumbing the Depths," p. 12.

13. Robert D. Buzzell, Donald F. Cox, and Rex V. Brown, *Marketing Research and Information Systems* (New York: McGraw-Hill, 1969), p. 595.

References for Snapshots, PicProfiles, CloseUps
Art of Asking Questions

1. Madeline Johnson, "Investing in Resting: Is Airbnb a Top 2016 IPO Candidate?" Zacks.com, December 11, 2015, downloaded April 8, 2016 (http://www.zacks.com/stock/news/200846 /investing-in-resting-is-airbnb-a-top-2016-ipo-candidate).

2. Stephan Leman, Brand Trust, and Warren Berger, A More Beautiful Question, "A More Beautiful Question," IIeX Insight Innovation Exchange NA, Atlanta, June ?, 2015, "downloaded April 8, 2016 (http://insightinnovation.org/wp-content/uploads/2015/06 /PDF/question.pdf).

3. Warren Berger, *A More Beautiful Question: The Power of Inquiry to Spark Breakthrough Ideas,* Bloomsbury Publishing, Inc.: New York, New York, USA: March 4, 2014, pp 88-91.

4. Warren Berger, "Why should you be stuck without a bed if I've got an extra air mattress?" amorebeaurtifulquestion.com, downloaded April 8, 2016 (http://amorebeautifulquestion.com /airbnbs-10-billion-valuation-started-beautiful-question/).

Housing and Millennials

1. Carl Bialik, Andrew Flowers, Reuben Fischer-Baum and Dhrumil Mehia, "Uber Is Serving New York's Outer Boroughs More Than Taxis Are," *FiveThirtyEight Newsletter,* August 10, 2015, downloaded March 31, 2016 (http://fivethirtyeight.com/features /uber-is-serving-new-yorks-outer-boroughs-more-than-taxis-are/).

2. "How a Walk Score Works," Redfin.com, downloaded March 31, 2016 (https://www.redfin.com/how-walk-score-works).

3. Glenn Kelman, "The American City Was Built for Cars. What Will Happen When They All Leave," March 30, 2016, downloaded March 31, 2016 (https://www.linkedin.com/pulse/american-cities -were-built-cars-what-happen-when-all-leave-kelman?trk=eml-b2 _content_ecosystem_digest-hero-14-null&midToken=AQFnVvJjNg dZAg&fromEmail=fromEmail&ut=1ovAj36Bgo9Tc1).

4. Kirsten Korosec, "Elon Musk Says Tesla Vehicles Will Drive Themselves in Two Years," *Fortune,* December 21, 2015, downloaded March 31, 2016 (http://fortune.com/2015/12/21 /elon-musk-interview/).

Interviews Refine Management Question

1. Jason Atkins, "The War on Incentive Entitlement," Tire Business, April 5, 2016, downloaded April 13, 2016 (http://www.tire business.com/article/20160405/SPONSORED/160409979 /the-war-on-incentive-entitlement).

PullQuote

1. Warren Berger, "What is a Beautiful Question?," Amorebeauti fulquestion.com, downloaded April 8, 2016 (http://amorebeauti fulquestion.com/what-is-a-beautiful-question/).

Secondary Data

1. "About Netvibes," Netvibes, downloaded April 14, 2016 (http:// about.netvibes.com/).

2. Michael Chui, James Manyika, and Mehdi Miremadi, "Four Fundamentals of Workplace Automation," *McKinsey Quarterly,* November 2015, downloaded April 14, 2016 (http://www .mckinsey.com/business-functions/business-technology /our-insights/four-fundamentals-of-workplace-automation).

3. "Netvibes Business Case: Global CPG leader, Elle & Vire, saves hours each week on digital monitoring with Netvibes Dashboards," Netvibes, downloaded April 14, 2016 (http://www.netvibes.com /en/case/elle-vire-analyses-data-and-optimizes-marketing-strategy -with-netvibes-dashboards-6e46e957271a).

4. "Netvibes Business Case: Luxury Automotive Manufacturer analyzes car models and competitors with Netvibes Dashboards," Netvibes, downloaded April 14, 2016 (http://www.netvibes.com /en/case/luxury-automotive-manufacturer-analyzes-car-models -and-competitors-with-netvibes-dashboards-291a65552d11).

5. "Integrating Web and Social Data into your Marketing Research Strategy: Real-World Case Study with a Luxury Automotive Manufacturer," webseminar sponsored by Greenbook and Netvibes, April 13, 2016, downloaded April 14, 2016 (http://www .greenbookblog.org/other/51-Netvibes/2.25.16-572948-Greenbook -Integrating%20Web%20and%20Social%20Data%20into%20 your%20Market%20Research%20Strategy.mp4).

Chapter 4

1. This material was developed using information provided by research collaborators, as well as material from Bernard S. Phillips, *Social Research Strategy and Tactics,* 2nd ed. (London: Macmillan Publishing, 1971), p. 93 (with permission); and Fred N. Kerlinger, *Foundations of Behavioral Research,* 3rd ed. (New York: Holt, Rinehart & Winston, 1986), p. 279.

2. The complexity of data collection design tends to confuse students. That confusion is addressed by encasing the vast array of design decisions into a classification scheme. Some of these design decisions defy such forced order. So this scheme, like others, may either include or exclude too much.

3. Scientists often want universals (applicable everywhere or in all cases), and universals can be falsified by a single-counter instance. [W. Charles Redding, "Research Setting: Field Studies," in *Methods of Research in Communication,* ed. Philip Emmert and William D. Brooks (Boston: Houghton Mifflin, 1970), pp. 140–42.] Thus case studies have been unfairly maligned because they extract information from a small sample. [See Abraham Kaplan, *Conduct of Inquiry* (San Francisco: Chandler, 1964), p. 37.] Case studies have a rich history in business research.

4. Virtual reality (VR) investigates how the brain integrates multi-sensory information. Researchers can use VR to manipulate the spatial and temporal properties of sensory information, then translate this information to the design of more immersive and engaging experiences in games, in packages on store shelves, in store or workplace design, etc. For an example, see the video on 20/20 Research's website, http://www.2020research.com/virtual-reality/.

5. The Hawthorne studies, comparing two groups of workers in the Western Electric plant and their responses to changes in the physical conditions of their work environment, established that the performance of employees is influenced by their surroundings and by the people that they are working with as much as by their own innate abilities. To learn more, read E. Mayo, *The Human Problems of an Industrial Civilisation* (New York: Macmillan, 1933; 2nd ed., Cambridge, MA: Harvard University, 1946).

6. W. Charles Redding, "Research Setting: Field Studies," in *Methods of Research in Communication,* ed. Philip Emmert and William D. Brooks (Boston: Houghton Mifflin, 1970), pp. 140–42.

References for Snapshots, PicProfiles, CloseUps & Captions
Agile Research

1. Bella Tumini, brand manager Suja, and Matt Marta, CEO Gut-Check, "How Suja Used Agile Market Research to Assess the Risk

of Updating Their Product Branding," Quirk's Marketing Research Review webinar, June 22, 2016.

2. Lisa Whetstone, Director of Marketing, and Cassandra McNeill, Marketing Content Manager, GutCheck, email interview, July 27, 2016.

AIG

1. Julia Smith, Global Head of People Excellence, AIG, "Reframing Performance Management Conversations: AIGs Transformation Story," Webinar sponsored by Talent Management, March 16, 2016.

2. Steven Pinker, "Daniel Kahneman changed the way we think about thinking. But what do other thinkers think of him?" *The Guardian,* February 16, 2014, downloaded March 25, 2016 (https://www.theguardian.com/science/2014/feb/16 /daniel-kahneman-thinking-fast-and-slow-tributes).

Marcus Thomas: Emotional Face

1. Edwige Winans, associate research director, Marcus Thomas, LLC, email interview, April 12, 2016.

2. Edwige Winans, "Connecting through the Heart: The Importance of Measuring Emotions in Creative Testing," February 9, 2016.

3. Jennifer Hirt-Marchand, partner, Marcus Thomas LLC, email interview, April 11, 2016.

4. Orlando Wood, "How Emotional Tugs Trump Rational Pushes," *Journal of Advertising Research,* Vol. 52, No. 1, March 2012.

Project Leaving Country

1. "Help End the Market Research Professions' Secret," November 19, 2009, accessed January 24, 2010 (http://www.tomhcanderson .com/2009/11/19/help-end-the-market-research-professions -final-dirty-little-secret/).

2. "Recent Survey Data about Offshoring." Study conducted by Foundation for Transparency in Offshoring, November 2009, accessed January 24, 2010 (http://www.offshoringtransparency.org/images /charts/ngmr4.jpg).

PullQuote

1. Nick Drew, VP Insights and Strategy, Fresh Intelligence, and Zoe Dowling, Lead Research Strategist, FocusVision, "Snack Attack: Using Mobile Digital Qual to Hack the Snack Aisle," August 5, 2016, downloaded august 7, 2016 (https://www.focusvision.com /cpg/snack-attack-using-mobile-digital-qual-hack-snack-aisle/).

TIAA

1. John Cendroski, Senior Talent Management Advisor, and Michelle Shail, Manager of Talent Management, TIAA, "It's Not About Ratings, It's About Enabling Employee Performance: TIAA's Journey," Talent Management and SilkRoad webcast, May 26, 2016 (http://event.lvl3 .on24.com/event/11/82/49/3/rt/1/documents/resourceList1398 875993694/526_tm_silkroad_final.pdf?dummy=dummyBody).

Chapter 5

1. Amir D. Aczel, *Complete Business Statistics* (Burr Ridge, IL: Irwin, 1996), p. 180.

2. N. L. Rynolds, A. C. Simintiras, and A. Diamantopoulus, "Theoretical Justification of Sampling Choices in International Marketing Research: Key Issues and Guidelines for Researchers," downloaded May 28, 2004 (http://www.questia.com /PM.qst?a[H11005]o&d[H11005]5001902692).

3. Family Health International, "Sampling Approaches," and "Weighting in Multi-Stage Sampling," in *Guidelines for Repeated Behavioral Surveys in Populations at Risk of HIV* (Durham, NC: FHI, 2000), Chaps. 4 and 5, pp. 29–65.

4. Standard international sampling systems are based on standards such as ISO 2859 and ISO 3951.

5. A. Parasuraman, *Marketing Research,* 2nd ed. (Reading, MA: Addison-Wesley, 1991), p. 477.

6. "Census 2010: Final Report to Congress," U.S. Department of Commerce, Office of Inspector General, Final Report No. OIG -11-03-I, July 27, 2011, downloaded May 8, 2017 (https://www.oig .doc.gov/OIGPublications/OIG-11-030-I.pdf).

7. W. E. Deming, *Sample Design in Business Research* (New York: Wiley, 1960), p. 26.

8. Henry Assael and John Keon, "Nonsampling versus Sampling Errors in Survey Research," *Journal of Marketing Research* (Spring 1982), pp. 114–23. In this study, nonsampling error was 90 percent of all error.

9. Proportions are hypothetical.

10. Fred N. Kerlinger, *Foundations of Behavioral Research,* 3rd ed. (New York: Holt, Rinehart & Winston, 1986), p. 72.

11. All estimates of costs are hypothetical.

12. "Internet/Broadband Fact Sheet," Pew Research Center, January 12, 2017, downloaded May 9, 2017 (http://www.pewinternet.org /fact-sheet/internet-broadband/).

13. Monica Anderson, "Digital Divide Persists Even as Lower-Income Americans Make Gains in Tech Adoption," Pew Research Center, March 22, 2017, downloaded May 9, 2017 (http://www.pewresearch .org/fact-tank/2017/03/22/digital-divide-persists-even-as-lower -income-americans-make-gains-in-tech-adoption/).

14. Nielsen Portable People Meter research uses responses from 65,000 panelists on an average day with its more than 80,000 installed meters. "Nielsen to Increase Portable People Meter Sample Size by 10% across 48 Radio Metro Meters," Nielsen press release, December 21, 2016 (http://www.nielsen.com/us/en/press-room /2016/nielsen-to-increase-portable-people-meter-sample-size-by -10-percent-across-48-radio-metro-areas.html).

15. Leslie Kish, *Survey Sampling* (New York: Wiley, 1965), p. 188.

16. Ibid., pp. 76–77.

17. Typically, stratification is carried out before the actual sampling, but when this is not possible, it is still possible to stratify after the fact. Ibid., p. 90.

18. W. G. Cochran, *Sampling Techniques,* 2nd ed. (New York: Wiley, 1963), p. 134.

19. Ibid., p. 96.

20. Kish, *Survey Sampling*, p. 94.

21. For detailed treatment of these and other cluster sampling methods and problems, see ibid., pp. 148–247.

22. J. H. Lorie and H. V. Roberts, *Basic Methods of Marketing Research* (New York: McGraw-Hill, 1951), p. 120.

23. Kish, *Survey Sampling*, p. 156.

24. For specifics on these problems and how to solve them, the reader is referred to the many good sampling texts. Two that have been mentioned already are Kish, *Survey Sampling*, Chap. 5, 6, and 7; and Cochran, *Sampling Techniques*, Chaps. 9, 10, and 11.

References for Snapshots, PicProfiles, CloseUps, Captions, and Pull Quotes
Ford

1. David Kiley, "The Fight for Ford's Future," BusinessWeek, August 11, 2008, pp. 40–43.

Keynote

1. "About Us," Keynote Systems, accessed August 11, 2006 (http://www.keynote.com/about_us/about_us_tpl.html).

2. Danny Sullivan, "Hitwise Search Engine Ratings," SearchEngine-Watch.com, August 23, 2006, accessed April 20, 2007 (http://searchenginewatch.com/showPage.html?page53099931).

3. Keynote_SES_Deck.ppt, PowerPoint presentation presented by Lance Jones, senior research analyst, Keynote Systems to Search Engine Strategies 2006 Conference and Expo, New York, February 27, 2006.

4. Lance Jones, "How Online Consumers Use and View Search Engines," webseminar presented by American Marketing Association, July 26, 2006.

5. Lance Jones, senior research analyst, Keynote Systems, interviewed August 11, 2006.

Pullquote

1. "G-Eazy." BrainyQuote.com. Xplore Inc, 2017, downloaded May 25, 2017 (https://www.brainyquote.com/quotes/quotes/g/geazy696145.html).

Research for Good

1. Sean Case, co-founder, Research for Good, interviewed via e-mail, May 5, 2012.

2. Sean Case, "Research for Good: Sampling with Purpose," Research for Good Web seminar, May 2, 2012.

SSI, Mixed Access Sampling

1. Alina Selyukh, "The Daredevils Without Landlines — And Why Health Experts Are Tracking Them," NPR, May 4, 2017, downloaded May 9, 2017 (http://www.npr.org/sections/alltechconsidered/2015/12/03/458225197/the-daredevils-without-landlines-and-why-health-experts-are-tracking-them).

2. "Internet/Broadband Fact Sheet," Pew Research Center, January 12, 2017, downloaded May 9, 2017 (http://www.pewinternet.org/fact-sheet/internet-broadband/).

3. Monica Anderson, "Digital divide persists even as lower-income Americans make gains in tech adoption," Pew Research Center, March 22, 2017, downloaded May 9, 2017 (http://www.pewresearch.org/fact-tank/2017/03/22/digital-divide-persists-even-as-lower-income-americans-make-gains-in-tech-adoption/).

4. Pete Cape and Keith Phillips, "Solving the Mode Mystery: The Cost, Coverage and Quality Tradeoffs of Picking (and Mixing) Online and Offline," American Marketing Association webinar, June 13, 2012, accessed June 14, 2012 (https://cc.readytalk.com/cc/playback/Playbackdo; https://cc.readytalk.com/cc/playback/Playback.do?id=dn79fd).

5. Pete Cape, global knowledge director, SSI, interviewed via e-mail, June 19, 2012.

Sources of Error graphic

1. Exhibit 5-5 was modified from one created by Dr. Nicola Petty, of Statistics Learning Centre and used with permission. Dr. Petty has developed a series of videos and blog posts to make statistical concepts more understandable. See: Nicola Ward Petty, "Sampling Error and Nonsampling Error," September 4, 2014, downloaded May 15, 2017 (https://learnandteachstatistics.wordpress.com/2014/09/04/sampling-and-non-sampling-error/).

Who's Taking Your Surveys

1. Jessica Broome, principal, Jessica Broome Research, phone interview, June 17, 2016 and August 7, 2016.

2. Kerry Hecht, Director of Research Services, Recollective, a division of Ramius Corporation, phone interview, June 17, 2016; August 3, 2016; and August 7, 2016.

3. Tom H. C. Anderson, "Look who's Talking, Part 1: Who are the most Frequently Mentioned Research Panels?" OdinText Blog, May 13, 2016, downloaded May 13, 2016 (http://odintext.com/blog/look-whos-talking-part-1full-research-panels/)

4. "Thoughtful answer, consistent result: Putting our survey panel to the test," SurveyMonkey, June 2016, downloaded June 30< 2016 (https://www.surveymonkey.com/wp-content/uploads/2016/06/Audience_panel_quality_report.pdf?&utm_source=email&utm_medium=SM_CRM_MKTG_PA&utm_content=sm4biz-june-newsletter&utm_campaign=email_NL&family=SME&date=2016-06-06&program=7013A000000mL14QAE&source=email&recent=email&cvosrc=email-mkto.sme.7013A000000mL14QAE&mkt_tok=eyJpIjoiWWpVNE1Ea3hZVFl5TURRaaiIsInQiOiJSMnJneDlkNEMwXC9jZnZhWkpDQ2J6ZjEzSW9WRGwxMERoU3Y2VmhDaVV3czREVktIOWlvWmVTb0FjUStONEh6ckEwZ1VZUHNkRE43dG1pUDBaaeE1yVUlyUG41YTludmUyY0o1VGJJV2o1OGs9In0%3D).

Chapter 6

1. Leonard F. Murphy, "GRIT Report," Greenbook, June 2016, downloaded June 30, 2016 (https://www.greenbook.org/images/GRIT/2016_grit/GRIT_Report_2016_Edition.pdf).

2. Leonard Murphy, "Research Innovation during Disruptive Change: 10 Key Takeaways from Market Research in the Mobile World," GreenBook, July 24, 2012, accessed July 16, 2012 (http://www.greenbookblog.org/2012/07/24/research-innovation-during-disruptive-change-10-key-takeaways-from-market-research-in-the-mobile-world); and Ray Fischer, "Online Ual Methods and Toots for Testing Concepts and Ideas," Aha! Webinar, April 11, 2017.

3. Murphy, "Research Innovation during Disruptive Change."

4. This list was developed from numerous sources, including David Carson, Audrey Gilmore, Chad Perry, and Kjell Gronhaug, *Qualitative Marketing Research* (Thousand Oaks, CA: Sage Publications, 2001), pp. 67–68, which references Norman Denzin and Y. Lincoln, *Handbook of Qualitative Research* (London: Sage Publications, 1994); Y. Lincoln and E. Guba, *Naturalistic Inquiry* (Newbury, CA: Sage Publications, 1985); M. Q. Patton, *Qualitative Evaluation and Research Methods,* 2nd ed. (Newbury Park, CA: Sage Publications, 1990); A. M. Pettigrew, "On Studying Organizational Cultures," *Administrative Science Quarterly* 24 (1979), pp. 570–81; Mellanie Wallendorf, Russel Belk, and John Sherry, "The Sacred and the Profane in Consumer Behavior: Theodicy on the Odyssey," *Journal of Consumer Research* 16 (June 1989), pp. 1–38.

5. John Van Maanen, "Reclaiming Qualitative Methods for Organizational Research: A Preface," *Administrative Science Quarterly* 24 (December 1979), pp. 520–24.

6. Judith Langer, *The Mirrored Window: Focus Groups from a Moderator's Point of View* (Ithaca, NY: Paramount Market Publishing, 2001), p. 26.

7. Carson, Gilmore, Perry, and Gronhaug, *Qualitative Marketing Research*, p. 65.

8. Adrian Holliday, *Doing and Writing Qualitative Research* (London: Sage Publications, 2002), pp. 71–72, 99, 105.

9. Patricia I. Fusch and Lawrence R. Ness, "Are We There Yet? Data Saturation in Qualitative Research," *The Qualitative Report* 20, no. 9 (2015), pp. 1408–16, downloaded May 13, 2017 (http://tqr .nova.edu/wp-content/uploads/2015/09/fusch1.pdf).

10. *Making Connections,* AT&T (video).

11. Jennifer Mason, *Qualitative Researching,* 2nd ed. (London: Sage Publications, 2002).

12. Hy Mariampolski, *Qualitative Market Research: A Comprehensive Guide* (Thousand Oaks, CA: Sage Publications, 2001), p. 79.

13. Rick Kendall, "Thoughts on The Economist's Big Rethink," Green-Book, March 20, 2014, downloaded May 17, 2017 (http://www .greenbookblog.org/2014/03/20/thoughts-on-the-economists -big-rethink/).

14. Ibid.

15. Mariampolski, *Qualitative Market Research,* pp. 31, 85.

16. Laura Jett, "How to Keep Online Respondents Engaged and Focused: Projective Techniques," GutCheck, July 21, 2015, downloaded April 21, 2016 (http://blog.gutcheckit.com /how-to-keep-online-respondents-engaged-and-focused-projective -techniques).

17. These techniques were culled from various qualitative research company sources, as well as Jett,"How to Keep Online Respondents Engaged and Focused: Projective Techniques"; Christine Daymon and Immy Holloway, *Qualitative Research Methods in Public Relations and Marketing Communications* (London: Sage Publications, 2002), pp. 223–25; and Hy Mariampolski, *Qualitative Market Research: A Comprehensive Guide* (Thousand Oaks, CA: Sage Publications, 2001), pp. 206–19.

18. Langer, *The Mirrored Window,* p. 41.

19. "Services: Research: Case Studies: Cracking the Low-Involvement Ceiling," Primary Insights, downloaded January 1, 2003 (http:// www.primaryinsights.com/services.cfm?cid=15&cscont=Cracking Ceiling.cfm).

20. P. Hawe, D. Degeling, and J. Hall, *Evaluating Health Promotion: A Health Worker's Guide* (Artarmon, N.S.W.: MacLennan & Petty, 1990).

21. Dennis W. Rook, "Out-of-Focus Groups," *Marketing Research* 15, no. 2 (Summer 2003), pp. 10–15.

22. "Shoppers Speak Out in Focus Groups," *Discount Store News* 36, no. 5 (March 3, 1997), pp. 23–26.

23. Martin Bauer and George Gaskell, eds., *Qualitative Researching with Text, Image, and Sound: A Practical Handbook* (London: Sage Publications, 2000), pp. 48–51.

24. "How Nonprofits Are Using Focus Groups," *Nonprofit World* 14, no. 5 (September–October 1996), p. 37.

25. Carson et al., *Qualitative Marketing Research,* pp. 114–15.

26. Rook, "Out-of-Focus Groups," p. 13.

27. Carson et al., *Qualitative Marketing Research,* pp. 91–94, 100–6.

28. Tom Peters and Robert Waterman, *In Search of Excellence: Lessons from America's Best Run Companies* (New York: HarperCollins, 1982). *In Search of Excellence* was reprinted in 2012 in celebration of the 30th anniversary of its publication.

29. Carson et al., *Qualitative Marketing Research,* pp. 159–63.

30. Uwe Flick, *An Introduction to Qualitative Research*, 2nd ed. (London: Sage Publications, 2002), pp. 262–63.

References for Snapshots, PicProfiles, Captions, and Pull Quotes
Anderson Analytics

1. Tom Anderson, founder and president, Anderson Analytics, interviewed March 8, 2006.

Digital Transformation

1. "Digital Transformation: A Roadmap for Billion-Dollar Organizations; Findings from Phase 1 of the Digital Transformation Study Conducted by the MIT Center for Digital Business and Capgemini Consulting," Capgemini Consulting, downloaded March 31, 2016 (https://www.capgemini.com/resource-file -access/resource/pdf/Digital_Transformation__A_Road-Map _for_Billion-Dollar_Organizations.pdf).

2. George Westerman, Didier Bonnet and Andrew McAfee, "The Nine Elements of Digital Transformation," MIT Sloan Management Review, January 07, 2014, downloaded March 31, 2016 (http://sloanreview.mit.edu/article/the-nine-elements-of -digital-transformation/).

Focus Group Problems

1. Robert W. Kahle, Dominator, Cynics, and Wallflowers (Ithaca, NY: Parmount Market Publishing, Inc., 2006), pp. 22–33.

Maritz Travel

1. Edwige Winans, associate research director, Marcus Thomas LLC, email interview April 15, 2016.

2. "Let Us Put Our Expertise to Work," Maritz Travel, downloaded April 16, 2016 (http://www.maritztravel.com/About /Our-Approach).

3. "Maritz Travel: Creating Equity-Driven Brand Portfolio Strategy Using 'Voice of the Customer,'" Marcus Thomas, February 4, 2016.

Pull Quote

1. "How One Beauty Expert Uses Agile Market Research To Arrive at Winning Concepts," Gutcheck and Quirk marketing Research, webinar, February 17, 2016, downloaded April 15, 2016 (http:// info.gutcheckit.com/thank-you-here-is-your-quirks-beauty -webinar-recording-021716?submissionGuid=0f5bc367-66d8-4f86 -8b38-6f1859567f70).

Qual & Smart Phones

1. Dan Weber, CEO iTracks, phone interview and product demonstration, May 3, 2017.

2. "Mobile Fact Sheet: Internet/Broadband," Pew Research Center, January 12, 2017, downloaded May 3, 2017 (http://www .pewinternet.org/fact-sheet/mobile/).

3. Dan Coates, "Case Study: Using Insights to Energize Your Retail Channel," YPulse at 2016 EVOLVE Qualitative Research Week, November 22, 2016, downloaded May 4, 2017 (https://www .youtube.com/watch?v=XcPuDjLu3CM&feature=youtu.be).

4. "iTracksGo 2.0 Release", iTracks, published Mar 19, 2017, downloaded May 4, 2017 (https://www.youtube.com /watch?v=zkZTc5nuz9c).

5. iMarkIt," iTracks, published July 8, 2016, downloaded May 4, 2017 (https://www.youtube.com/watch?v=2yPpkOQabww).

6. iTracks IDI Software," iTracks, published October 26, 2015, downloaded May 4, 2017 (https://www.youtube.com /watch?v=xWgyd4KN9ZE).

7. iTracks Mobile Focus Group Software, iTracks, published September 17, 2012, downloaded May 4, 2017 (https://www .youtube.com/watch?v=hwH3YTKGM9o)

Chapter 7

1. "Why the Technology to Track Missing Planes Hasn't Taken Off," *CBS This Morning*, May 20, 2016, downloaded May 20, 2016 (http://www.cbsnews.com/news/why-airplanes-slow-to-adopt-technology-to-stream-flight-data/).

2. Louise H. Kidder and Charles M. Judd, *Research Methods in Social Relations*, 5th ed. (New York: Holt, Rinehart & Winston, 1986), p. 291.

3. K. E. Weick, "Systematic Observational Methods," in *The Handbook of Social Psychology,* vol. 2, ed. G. Lindzey and E. Aronson (Reading, MA: Addison-Wesley, 1968), p. 360.

4. R. Bales, *Interaction Process Analysis* (Reading, MA: Addison-Wesley, 1950).

5. Weick, "Systematic Observational Methods," p. 381.

6. Louise H. Kidder and Charles M. Judd, *Research Methods in Social Relations*, 5th ed. (New York: Holt, Rinehart & Winston, 1986), p. 292.

7. Kenneth D. Bailey, *Methods of Social Science,* 2nd ed. (New York: Free Press, 1982), pp. 252-54.

8. Donald F. Roy, "'Banana Time,' Job Satisfaction, and Informal Interaction," *Human Organization* 18, no. 4 (Winter 1959-60), pp. 151-68.

9. Robert F. Bales, *Personality and Interpersonal Behavior* (New York: Holt, Rinehart & Winston, 1970).

10. E. J. Webb, D. T. Campbell, R. D. Schwartz, L. Sechrest, and J.B. Grove, *Nonreactive Measures in the Social Sciences,* 2nd ed. (Boston: Houghton Mifflin, 1981).

11. W. L. Rathje and W. W. Hughes, "The Garbage Project as a Nonreactive Approach: Garbage In . . . Garbage Out?" in *Perspectives on Attitude Assessment: Surveys and Their Alternatives,* ed. H. W. Sinaiko and L. A. Broedling (Washington, DC: Smithsonian Institution, 1975).

12. William Grimes, "If It's Scientific, It's 'Garbology,'" *International Herald Tribune,* August 15-16, 1992, p. 17.

13. Dorothy Leonard and Jeffrey F. Rayport, "Spark Innovation through Empathic Design," *Harvard Business Review*, November-December, 1997, downloaded May 18, 2017 (https://hbr.org/1997/11/spark-innovation-through-empathic-design).

14. Erin Long-Crowell, "The Halo Effect: Definition, Advantages & Disadvantages," *Psychology 104: Social Psychology*, study.com, downloaded May 17, 2017 (http://study.com/academy/lesson/the-halo-effect-definition-advantages-disadvantages.html).

15. "What Is Observer Drift?" *Psychology Dictionary*, downloaded May 19, 2017 (http://psychologydictionary.org/observer-drift/?utm_source=TrendMD&utm_medium=cpc&utm_campaign=Psychology_Dictionary_TrendMD_0).

16. Kidder and Judd, *Research Methods in Social Relations,* pp. 298-99.

17. Marc G. Berman, John Jonides, and Richard Lewis, "In Search of Decay in Verbal Short Term Memory," *Journal of Experimental Psychology: Learning, Memory, and Cognition* 35, no. 2 (March 2009), pp. 317-33, downloaded May 23, 2017 (https://www.ncbi.nlm.nih.gov/pmc/articles/PMC3980403/).

18. Jordon Gaines Lewis, "This is How the Brain Filters Out Unimportant Details," *Psychology Today*, February 11, 2015, downloaded May 24, 2017 (https://www.psychologytoday.com/blog/brain-babble/201502/is-how-the-brain-filters-out-unimportant-details).

References for Snapshots, Picprofiles, Captions, CloseUps and Pull Quotes

CloseUp: Job Enrichment

1. Frederick J. Herzberg, "One More Time: How Do You Motivate Employees?" Harvard Business Review (January–February 1968), pp. 53-62.

Sticky

1. Justin Ohanessian, Sticky, phone interview, June 3, 2016; email interviews, June 20, 27, 30 and July 7 and 10, 2016.

2. https://sticky.ad/

3. https://sticky.ad/about/

4. Emotion, Sticky, June 3, 2016 (https://sticky.ad/how-it-works/).

5. "Micro Survey," Sticky, June 3, 2016 (https://sticky.ad/how-it-works/).

6. "Web-based Eye Tracking," Sticky, June 3, 2016 (https://sticky.ad/how-it-works/).

7. Jennifer Breese, 5 Insightful Instagram Statistics That You Should Know," SproutSocial, January 22, 2015, downloaded June 4, 2016 (http://sproutsocial.com/insights/5-instagram-stats/).

8. Nate Elliott, "Instagram Is The King Of Social Engagement," Forester, April 29, 2014, downloaded June 4, 2016 (http://blogs.forrester.com/nate_elliott/14-04-29-instagram_is_the_king_of_social_engagement).

Police Cameras

1. Seth Stoughton, email interview, April 03, 2016.

2. Seth Stoughton, Geoffrey Alpert, and Jeff Noble, "Why Police Need Constructive Criticism," The Atlantic, December 23, 2015, downloaded April 2, 2016 (http://www.theatlantic.com/politics/archive/2015/12/officer-porter-mistrial-police-culture/421656/).

3. Timothy Williams, James Thomas, Samuel Jacoby, and Damien Cave, "Police Body Cameras: What Do You See?" The New York Times, April 1, 2016, downloaded April 2, 2016 (http://www.nytimes.com/interactive/2016/04/01/us/police-bodycam-video.html?emc=edit_th_20160402&nl=todaysheadlines&nlid=20495303&_r=0).

PullQuote

1. Katie Hafner, BrainyQuote.com, 2017, downloaded May 24, 2017 (https://www.brainyquote.com/quotes/quotes/k/katiehafne739479.html)

Chapter 8

1. The work of John Stuart Mill in the 19th century is the standard for determining causation.

2. From *Methods in Social Research* by William J. Goode and Paul K. Hatt. Copyright (c) 1952, McGraw-Hill Book Company. Used with permission of McGraw-Hill Book Company.

3. This section on variable relationships was developed using Morris Rosenberg, *The Logic of Survey Analysis* (New York: Basic Books, 1968), p. 3; and Rhona E Johnsen and David Ford, "Developing the Concept of Asymmetrical and Symmetrical Relationships: Linking Relationship Characteristics and Firms' Capabilities," 2002, downloaded May 6, 2017 (http://impgroup.org/uploads/papers/452.pdf).

4. Morris R. Cohen and Ernest Nagel, *An Introduction to Logic and Scientific Method* (New York: Harcourt, Brace, 1934), Chap. 13; and Blalock, *Causal Inferences,* p. 14.

5. Bibb Latane and J. M. Darley, *The Unresponsive Bystander: Why Doesn't He Help?* (New York: Appleton-Century-Crofts, 1970),

pp. 69–77. Research into the responses of bystanders who witness crimes was stimulated by an incident in New York City, where Kitty Genovese was attacked and killed in the presence of 38 witnesses who refused to come to her aid or to summon authorities.

6. This section is largely adapted from Julian L. Simon and Paul Burstein, *Basic Research Methods in Social Science,* 3rd ed. (New York: Random House, 1985), pp. 128–33.

7. For a thorough explanation of this topic, see Helena C. Kraemer and Sue Thiemann, *How Many Subjects? Statistical Power Analysis in Research* (Beverly Hills, CA: Sage Publications, 1987).

8. Kenneth D. Bailey, *Methods of Social Research,* 2nd ed. (New York: Free Press, 1982), pp. 230–33.

9. The concept of a quota matrix and the tabular form for Exhibit 8–6 was adapted from Earl R. Babbie, *The Practice of Social Research,* 5th ed. (Belmont, CA: Wadsworth, 1989), pp. 218–19.

10. Donald T. Campbell and Julian C. Stanley, *Experimental and Quasi-Experimental Designs for Research* (Chicago: Rand McNally, 1963), p. 5.

11. Thomas D. Cook and Donald T. Campbell, "The Design and Conduct of Quasi-Experiments and True Experiments in Field Settings," in *Handbook of Industrial and Organizational Psychology,* ed. Marvin D. Dunnette (Chicago: Rand McNally, 1976), p. 223.

12. William J. Paul Jr., Keith B. Robertson, and Frederick Herzberg, "Job Enrichment Pays Off," *Harvard Business Review* (March–April 1969), pp. 61–78.

13. For an in-depth discussion of many quasi-experimental designs and their internal validity, see ibid., pp. 246–98.

a. Frederick J. Herzberg, "One More Time: How Do You Motivate Employees?" *Harvard Business Review* (January–February 1968), pp. 53–62.

References for Snapshots, PicProfiles, Captions, and Pull Quotes
Employee Health

1. "Why Some Workplace Health Incentive Programs Don't Work - and Some Do," Knowledge@Wharton, April 4, 2016, downloaded April 6, 2016 (http://knowledge.wharton.upenn.edu/article /workplace-health-incentive-programs-dont-work/?utm_source=kw _newsletter&utm_medium=email&utm_campaign=2016-04-06).

MIT SENSEable City Lab

1. Carlo Ratti, director SENSEable City Lab, MIT, "How Future Workspaces Will Improve Productivity and Creativity," webinar sponsored by Xively, June 16, 2016.

PullQuote

1. Jeff Bezos, CEO Amazon, BrainyQuote.com, 2017, downloaded April 26, 2017 (https://www.brainyquote.com/quotes/j /jeffbezos450000.html).

Robotic Experiments

1. "A night in Japan's robot hotel," CBS News, July 22, 2015, downloaded May 23, 2016 (http://www.cbsnews.com/news /inside-japan-robot-hotel-hennna-where-staff-are-robots/).

2. Craig Trudell, Yuki Hagiwara and Ma Jie, "Herald Toyota's Vision of Future," Bloomberg, April 7, 2014, downloaded May 23, 2016 (http://www.bloomberg.com/news/articles/2014-04-06 /humans-replacing-robots-herald-toyota-s-vision-of-future).

3. Judith Aquino, "Automate or Humanize? The Great Customer Service Debate," 1to1 Media, May 23, 2016, downloaded May 23, 2016 (http://www.1to1media.com

/view.aspx?docid=35796&utm_content=title&utm_source =1to1weekly&utm_medium=email&utm_campaign=05232016).

4. Larry Downes, Happy birthday to Moore's Law," The Washington Post, April 16, 2015, downloaded May 29, 2016 (https://www .washingtonpost.com/news/innovations/wp/2015/04/16 /happy-birthday-to-moores-law/).

5. Matt McFarland, "Ex-McDonald's CEO says raising the minimum wage will help robots take jobs," Washington Post, May 25, 2016, downloaded May 29, 2016 (https://www.washingtonpost.com /news/innovations/wp/2016/05/25/ex-mcdonalds-ceo-says-raising -the-minimum-wage-will-help-robots-take-jobs/).

6. Julie Vogtman and Agata Pelka, "Minimum Wage Update: State and Local Highlights," National Women's Law Center Blog, June 5, 2015, downloaded May 23, 2017 (https://nwlc.org/blog /minimum-wage-update-state-local-highlights/).

7. Julie Vogtman, "The Fight for $15 is Winning for Women and Families," National Women's Law Center, April 2017, downloaded May 23, 2017 (https://nwlc.org/wp-content /uploads/2017/04/The-Fight-for-15-is-Winning.pdf).

ZeoTap

1. Kate Kaye, "Mercedes-Benz Uses Tough-to-Get Telco Data to Target Ads for the E-Class," Advertising Age, May 24, 2016, downloaded May 24, 2016 (http://adage.com/article /datadriven-marketing/startup-zeotap-helps-turn-telco-data -mobile-ad-dollars/304127/?utm_source=daily_email&utm _medium=newsletter&utm_campaign=adage&ttl=1464647285).

Chapter 9

1. "Harness the Conversation: Business in Today's Social World," Cvent, accessed March 8, 2012 (http://www.cvent.com/en/sem /business-in-todays-social-world-survey-ebook.shtml).

2. "Internet/Broadband Fact Sheet," Pew Research Center, January 12, 2017 (http://www.pewinternet.org/fact-sheet/internet -broadband/).

3. Ibid.

4. Stephen J. Blumberg and Julian V. Luke, "Wireless Substitution: Early Release of Estimates From the National Health Interview Survey, July–December 2016," National Center for Health Statistics, May 2017, downloaded May 29, 2017 (https://www.cdc.gov /nchs/data/nhis/earlyrelease/wireless201705.pdf).

5. This conclusion has been reached by several researchers. "A Future without Key Social and Economic Statistics for the Country," U.S. Census Bureau, posted May 11, 2012, accessed July 20, 2012 (http://directorsblog.blogs.census.gov/2012 /05/11/a-future-without-key-social-and-economic-statistics-for-the -country/); "Assessing the Representativeness of Public Opinion Surveys," Pew Research Center, May 15, 2012, accessed July 20, 2012 (http://www.people-press.org/2012/05/15/assessing -the-representativeness-of-public-opinion-surveys/); "House GOP Votes to Kill Census' American Community Survey," *Daily KOS,* posted May 15, 2012, accessed July 20, 2012 (http://www.dailykos .com/story/2012/05/15/1091881/-House-GOP-Votes-to-Kill-Census -American-Community-Survey); Scott Keeter, "Survey Research, Its New Frontiers and Democracy," address to the 67th Annual Conference of the American Association for Public Opinion Research, May 18, 2012, accessed July 20, 2012 (http://pewresearch .org/pubs/2270/polling-survey-research-cellphone-only-households -random-samples).

6. Edith de Leeuw and William Nicholls II, "Technology Innovations in Data Collection: Acceptance, Data Quality, and Costs," *Sociological Research Online* 1, no. 4 (1996) (http://www.socresonline.org.uk/1/4/leeuw.html).

7. Personal experience of the author.

8. de Leeuw and Nicholls II, "Technology Innovations in Data Collection."

9. Don A. Dillman, *Mail and Telephone Surveys* (New York: Wiley, 1978), p. 6.

10. de Leeuw and Nicholls II, "Technology Innovations in Data Collection."

11. Dillman, *Mail and Telephone Surveys,* pp. 160–61.

12. Ibid., pp. 12, 22–24.

13. "Total Design Method," February 4, 2000 (http://survey.sesrc.wsu.edu/tdm.htm). Don Dillman is professor of sociology and rural sociology and deputy director of research and development of the Social and Economic Sciences Research Center at Washington State University.

14. Leslie Kanuk and Conrad Berenson, "Mail Surveys and Response Rates: A Literature Review," *Journal of Marketing Research,* November 1975, pp. 440–53; Arnold S. Linsky, "Stimulating Responses to Mailed Questionnaires: A Review," *Public Opinion Quarterly* 39 (1975), pp. 82–101.

15. Kanuk and Berenson, "Mail Surveys," p. 450. Reprinted from the *Journal of Marketing Research,* published by the American Marketing Association.

16. Robert M. Groves and Robert L. Kahn, *Surveys by Telephone* (New York: Academic Press, 1979), p. 223.

17. "Data Collection and Processing Services," Survey Research Center at the University of Michigan, accessed April 27, 2012 (http://www.src.isr.umich.edu/content.aspx?id=research_services_sro_data_collection).

18. Michael J. Havice, "Measuring Nonresponse and Refusals to an Electronic Telephone Survey," *Journalism Quarterly*, Fall 1990, pp. 521–30.

19. See, for example, J. H. Frey Jr., *Survey Research by Telephone* (Beverly Hills, CA: Sage Publications, 1989).

20. "2003 CMOR Respondent Cooperation and Industry Image Study Topline Report," CMOR, downloaded November 23, 2003 (http://www.cmor.org/resp_coop_news1003_2.htm). CMOR, founded in 1992 as the Council for Marketing and Opinion Research, tries to improve access to consumers for its more than 150 member trade associations and research companies, to increase respondent awareness of the value of research, and to increase respondent cooperation rates.

21. Scott Keeter, Nick Hatley, Courtney Kennedy, and Arnold Lau, "What Low Response Rates Mean for Telephone Surveys," Pew Research Center, May 15, 2017, downloaded June 1, 2017 (http://www.pewresearch.org/2017/05/15/what-low-response-rates-mean-for-telephone-surveys/).

22. Chart 3-8: Percent of U.S. Households with a Telephone by Income by Rural, Urban, Central City Areas, and Total U.S., downloaded December 15, 2003 (http://www.ntia.doc.gov/ntiahome/net2/presentations/slide5.html through slide8.html). See also U.S. Census Bureau, Census 2000 Summary File 3, Matrices H6 and H43.

23. "Wireless Local Number Portability," Federal Communications Commission, downloaded May 22, 2004 (http://www.fcc.gov/cgb/consumerfacts/wirelessportability.html).

24. A block is defined as an exchange group composed of the first four or more digits of a seven-digit number.

25. G. J. Glasser and G. D. Metzger, "Random Digit Dialing as a Method of Telephone Sampling," *Journal of Marketing Research,* February 1972, pp. 59–64; Seymour Sudman, "The Uses of Telephone Directories for Survey Sampling," *Journal of Marketing Research,* May 1973, pp. 204–07.

26. Personal experience of the author, October 2002.

27. Seymour Sudman, *Reducing the Costs of Surveys* (Chicago: Aldine, 1967), p. 65.

28. J. J. Wheatley, "Self-Administered Written Questionnaires or Telephone Interviews," *Journal of Marketing Research,* February 1973, pp. 94–95.

29. Robert M. Groves and Robert L. Kahn, *Surveys by Telephone* (New York: Academic Press, 1979), p. 223.

30. Marilyn Geewax, "FTC Scrubs Do-Not-Call Start Date," Cox News Service, posted September 27, 2003 (http://www.dfw.com/mld/dfw/news/nation/6875595.htm).

31. Floyd J. Fowler Jr., *Survey Research Methods* (Beverly Hills, CA: Sage Publications, 1988), p. 111.

32. B. W. Schyberger, "A Study of Interviewer Behavior," *Journal of Marketing Research*, February 1967, p. 35

33. B. S. Dohrenwend, J. A. Williams Jr., and C. H. Weiss, "Interviewer Biasing Effects: Toward a Reconciliation of Findings," *Public Opinion Quarterly,* Spring 1969, pp. 121–29.

34. One of the top research organizations in the world is the Survey Research Center of the University of Michigan. The material in this section draws heavily on the *Interviewer's Manual,* rev. ed. (Ann Arbor: Survey Research Center, University of Michigan, 1976); and Fowler, *Survey Research Methods,* Chap. 7.

35. Robert L. Kahn and Charles F. Cannell, *The Dynamics of Interviewing* (New York: Wiley, 1957), pp. 45–51.

36. D. Wallace, "A Case for and against Mail Questionnaires," *Public Opinion Quarterly,* Spring 1954, pp. 40–52.

37. Jon Krosnick, "The Art of Asking a Question: The Top 5 Things Researchers Need to Know about Designing Questionnaires," a seminar sponsored by SPSS and American Marketing Association, March 30, 2004.

38. Ibid.

39. There are a number of sources for research services, some of which are annotated. For current listings, consult the latest edition of the *Marketing Services Guide* and the *American Marketing Association Membership Directory* (Chicago: American Marketing Association); *Consultants and Consulting Organizations Directory* (Detroit: Gale Research Corporation); or the research section of *Marketing News.*

40. "Business Opinion Omnibus," BDRC-Continental, downloaded June 1, 2017 (http://bdrc-continental.com/products/business-opinion-omnibus/).

41. "About Gartner," Gartner Inc., downloaded June 1, 2017 (http://www.gartner.com/technology/about.jsp).

42. There are literally dozens of laws influencing survey research relating to privacy and confidentiality. The *Privacy Act of 1974* is the foundation of much of the more specific legislation restricting health information, financial and credit information, and information about or from children. A summary of pre-2010 legislation is available from Jonathan Ishee, "Summary of Selected Laws and Regulations addressing Confidentiality, Privacy,

and Security," Department of Health and Human Services, February 18, 2010, downloaded May 31, 2017 (https://www .healthit.gov/sites/default/files/federal_privacy_laws _table_2_26_10_final_0.pdf).

*Exhibit 9-5 examples are drawn from the personal experience of the author, as well as from Noah Shachtman, "Why the Web Works as a Market Research Tool," *AdAge.com*, Summer 2001 (http://adage .com/tools2001).

*Exhibit 9-7 is influenced by Robert L. Kahn and Charles F. Cannell, "Interviewing," in David L. Sills, ed., *International Encyclopedia of the Social Sciences*, vol. 8, p. 153. Copyright © 1968 by Crowell Collier and Macmillan, Inc.

*Exhibit 9-9 is Based on Nova Southeastern University's review information: http://www.nova.edu/lib/process.html#int_review and Wittenberg University's IRB process.

References for Snapshots, PicProfiles, PullQuotes and Captions
Anderson Analytics-BigEars

1. "New Survey Technology allows you to 'listen' to the voice of the customer: A third of college students say their mobile phone is an extension/reflection of themselves," Anderson Analytics press release, November 9, 2006.
2. Topline Report, Anderson Analytics, November 2006 (http://www .andersonanalytics.com/reports/AndersonAnalyticsBigEars.ppt).

Gamification

1. Betty Adamou, "Betty Adamou Telling Secrets at Esomar 3d #Eso3d," ESOMAR presentation. YouTube, accessed March 12, 2012 (http:// www.youtube.com/watch?v=OcbmpYfzcAQ&context=C48092ffA DvjVQa1PpcFMHbEY2akjr-z8p1GjwN7B2oOsgV6WO2Ak=).
2. Betty Adamou, CEO and founder of Research Through Gaming Ltd (RTG) and editor-in-chief of Game Access, a gamification blog, e-mail interview, March 20, 2012.
3. Gabe Zichermann, "Kids, Games, and Gamification," TEDxKids Brus- sels presentation on June 1, 2011. YouTube, accessed March 12, 2012 (http://www.youtube.com/watch?v=O2N-5maKZ9Q).
4. Gabe Zichermann, "Kids, Games, and Gamification," slidedeck, June 1, 2011, accessed March 12, 2012 (http://www.slideshare.net/ gzicherm/tedxkids-zichermann -the-effect-of-games-on-children).
5. "Gartner Says by 2015, More than 50 Percent of Organizations That Manage Innovation Processes Will Gamify Those Processes," Gartner Group, April 12, 2011, accessed March 12, 2012 (http:// www.gartner.com/it/page.jsp?id=1629214).
6. "Gamification for Research—Voted in the GRIT Top 50 MR Firms of the Future!," Research through Gaming, accessed March 12, 2012 (http://www.researchthroughgaming.com/ thenittygritty .html).
7. "Gamified Engagement," M2 Research, accessed May 18, 2012 (http://www.m2research.com/gamification.htm).
8. Steven Johnson, "This Is Your Brain on Video Games: Gaming Sharpens Thinking, Social Skills, and Perception," *Discover Magazine*, July 9, 2007, accessed March 12, 2012 (http://discovermaga zine.com/2007/brain/video-games/article_view?b_start:int=2&-C).
9. Wanda Meloni and Wolfgang Gruener, "Gamification in 2012: Market Update Consumer and Enterprise Market Trends," M2 Research, accessed May 18, 2012 (http://gamingbusinessreview.com /wp-content/uploads/2012/05/Gamification-in-2012-M2R3.pdf).

GRIT Survey Trends

1. "GRIT Report: Greenbook Research Industry Trends Report, 2016 Q3-Q4," GreenBook® | New York AMA Communication Services Inc., February 2016, p. 5 and 70, downloaded April 21, 2017, (https:// www.greenbook.org/images/GRIT/2017/GRIT2016-Q3-4.pdf).

Marcus Thomas – Prediction Markets

1. Jennifer Hirt-Marchand, "Prediction Market Research Case: Leveraging The Wisdom of Crowds for Audience Refinement," Marcus Thomas, September 25, 2014.
2. Jennifer Hirt-Marchand, associate partner and strategic insights executive, Marcus Thomas LLC, email interview, April 11, 2016.
3. Malcolm Gladwell, *Blink: The Power of Thinking Without Thinking,* Little,Brown-Back Bay Books: New York, NY, April 3, 2007.
4. Paul Taylor, Cary Funk, and Peyton Craighill, "Americans See Weight Problems Everywhere But In the Mirror," PEW Research Center, April 11, 2006, p. 5, downloaded April 11, 2016 (http:// www.pewsocialtrends.org/files/2010/10/Obesity.pdf).
5. Robert S. Duboff, "Forethought Decision Making: The Wisdom of (Expert) Crowds," *Harvard Business Review,* September 2007, p. 1 downloaded April 11, 2016 (http://hawkpartners.com/files /hbr_wisdom_of_expert_crowds_duboff.pdf).

PEW Research Center – Response Rates

1. Scott Keeter, Nick Hatley, Courtney Kennedy and Arnold Lau, "What Low Response Rates Mean for Telephone Surveys," Pew Research Center, May 15, 2017, downloaded June 1, 2017 (http://www.pewresearch.org/2017/05/15/what-low-response -rates-mean-for-telephone-surveys/).

Pullquote

1. Dave Goldberg. BrainyQuote.com, Xplore Inc, 2017, downloaded May 28, 2017 (https://www.brainyquote.com/quotes/quotes/d /davegoldbe718496.html).

RTI - Smart Phones

1. Andy Peytchev, survey methodologist, Research Triangle Institute, interviewed June 8, 2009.
2. David Chartier, "More Americans snipping landlines in favor of cell phones," ARS Technica, May 14, 2008, accessed June 8, 2009 (http://arstechnica.com/business/news/2008/05/more-americans -snipping-landlines-in-favor-of-cell-phones.ars).
3. Stephen J. Blumberg, and Julian V. Luke, "Wireless Substitution: Early Release of Estimates From the National Health Interview Survey, July–December 2007," National Center for Health Statistics, May 13, 2008, accessed June 9, 2009 (http://www.cdc.gov /nchs/data/nhis/earlyrelease/wireless200805.htm).
4. Stephen J. Blumberg, and Julian V. Luke, "Wireless Substitution: Early Release of Estimates From the National Health Interview Survey, July–December 2007-Tables," National Center for Health Statistics, May 13, 2008, accessed June 9, 2009 (http:// www.cdc .gov/nchs/data/nhis/earlyrelease/wireless200805_tables.htm#T2).
5. Stephen J. Blumberg and Julian V. Luke, "Wireless Substitution: Early Release Estimates from the National Health Interview survey, July-December 2016," national Center for Health Statistics, May 4, 2017, downloaded May 31, 2017 (https://www.cdc.gov /nchs/data/nhis/earlyrelease/wireless201705.pdf).

SSI, Mixed Mode Research

1. Pete Cape and Keith Phillips, "Solving the Mode Mystery: The Cost, Coverage and Quality Tradeoffs of Picking (and Mixing)

Online and Offline," American Marketing Association webinar, June 13, 2012, accessed June 14, 2012 (https://cc.readytalk.com /cc/playback/Playback. do; https://cc.readytalk.com/cc/playback /Playback.do?id=dn79fd).

2. Pete Cape, global knowledge director, SSI, via e-mail, June 19, 2012.

Chapter 10

1. Fred N. Kerlinger, *Foundations of Behavioral Research,* 3rd ed. (New York: Holt, Rinehart & Winston, 1986), p. 396; S. Stevens, "Measurement, Statistics, and the Schemapiric View," *Science,* August 1968, p. 384.

2. W. S. Torgerson, *Theory and Method of Scaling* (New York: Wiley, 1958), p. 19.

3. S. S. Stevens, "On the Theory of Scales of Measurement," *Science* 103 (1946), pp. 677–80.

4. I assume the reader has had an introductory statistics course in which measures of central tendency such as arithmetic mean, median, and mode have been treated. Similarly, I assume familiarity with measures of dispersion such as the standard deviation, range, and interquartile range. For a brief review of these concepts, refer to the appendix *Describing Data Statistically* or see an introductory statistics text.

5. Although this might intuitively seem to be the case, consider that one might prefer *a* over *b, b* over *c,* yet *c* over *a.* These results cannot be scaled as ordinal data because there is apparently more than one dimension involved.

6. Parametric tests are appropriate when the measurement is interval or ratio and when one can accept certain assumptions about the underlying distributions of the data with which they are working (normality, independence, constant variance). Nonparametric tests usually involve much weaker assumptions about measurement scales (nominal and ordinal), and the assumptions about the underlying distribution of the population are fewer and less restrictive. More on these tests is found in Chapters 14 and 15 and Appendix C.

7. *Statistical power* is the probability of detecting a meaningful difference if one were to occur. Studies should have power levels of 0.80 or higher (i.e., an 80 percent chance or greater of discerning an effect if one was really there).

8. See Chapters 14 and 15 for a discussion of these procedures.

9. To learn more about Swatch's BeatTime, visit http://www.swatch .com/internettime/internettime.php3.

10. To learn more about Swatch's BeatTime, visit https://www.swatch .com/en/internet-time/.

11. Claire Selltiz, Lawrence S. Wrightsman, and Stuart W. Cook, *Research Methods in Social Relations,* 3d ed. (New York: Holt, Rinehart & Winston, 1976), pp. 164–69.

12. Claire Selltiz, Lawrence S. Wrightsman, and Stuart W. Cook, *Research Methods in Social Relations,* 3rd ed. (New York: Holt, Rinehart & Winston, 1976), pp. 164–69.

13. Robert L. Thorndike and Elizabeth Hagen, *Measurement and Evaluation in Psychology and Education,* 3rd ed. (New York: Wiley, 1969), p. 5.

14. The focus of this chapter is internal validity; external validity was discussed in sampling design and experiments. For more information consult Thomas D. Cook and Donald T. Campbell, "The Design and Conduct of Quasi Experiments and True Experiments in Field Settings," in *Handbook of Industrial and Organizational Psychology,* ed. Marvin D. Dunnette (Chicago: Rand McNally, 1976), p. 223.

15. Examples of other conceptualizations of validity are factorial validity, job-analytic validity, synthetic validity, rational validity, and statistical conclusion validity.

16. *Standards for Educational and Psychological Tests and Manuals* (Washington, DC: American Psychological Association, 1974), p. 26.

17. Wayne F. Cascio, *Applied Psychology in Personnel Management* (Reston, VA: Reston Publishing, 1982), p. 149.

18. Thorndike and Hagen, *Measurement and Evaluation,* p. 168.

19. Cascio, *Applied Psychology,* pp. 135–36.

20. Emanuel J. Mason and William Bramble, *Understanding and Conducting Research* (New York: McGraw-Hill, 1989), p. 268.

21. A problem with this approach is that the way the test is split may influence the internal consistency coefficient. To remedy this, other indexes are used to secure reliability estimates without splitting the test's items. The Kuder-Richardson Formula 20 (KR20) and Cronbach's coefficient alpha are two frequently used examples. Cronbach's alpha has the most utility for multi-item scales at the interval level of measurement. The KR20 is the method from which alpha was generalized and is used to estimate reliability for dichotomous items (see Exhibit 10-8).

22. Thorndike and Hagen, *Measurement and Evaluation,* p. 199.

References for Snapshots, PicProfiles, CloseUps, & Pullquotes
PullQuote

1. David McCandless, "The Beauty of Data Visualization," TedEd Talks, November 23, 2012, downloaded April 26, 2016 (https:// www.youtube.com/watch?v=5Zg-C8AAIGg).

SHL Talent Analytics

1. "2012 *Business Outcomes* Study Report," SHL, accessed June 7, 2012 (http://www.shl.com/assets/SHL-BOS-2012-Web.pdf).

2. Ken Lahti (SHL) and Madeline Laurano (Aberdeen Group), "The Tal- ent Audit: Bridging the Gap between HR and the Business," SHL, webseminar, June 19, 2012.

3. "People Intelligence, A Business Imperative for High-Performing Organizations," Berkin & Associates, accessed June 7, 2012 (http://www.shl.com/assets/091611_Bersin_People_Intelligence _Report.pdf).

4. *"SHL Talent Analytics™*: Data-driven Insights that Boost Organizational Performance," SHL, accessed June 7, 2012 (http://www.shl .com/us/solutions/talent-analytics/).

5. "Transforming the Way Organizations Assess, Hire and Manage Talent," SHL, accessed June 7, 2012 (http://www.shl.com/us /company/who-we-are/).

TiVo Households

a. Alex Midlin, "Drilling Down; Hit TV Shows Have Most-Skipped Ads," *The New York Times,* September 29, 2009, accessed December 24, 2009 (http://query.nytimes.com/gst/fullpage.html?res=9C0 6E3D9143FF93BA1575AC0A96F9C8B63&scp=1&sq=research +measurement&st=nyt).

b. Ibid.

c. Stephanie Olsen, "Watching the Watchers: TiVo Tracks Ad Viewing," *Cnet News: Digital,* July 30, 2008, accessed December 24, 2009 (http://news.cnet.com/8301-1023_3-10002634-93.html).

d. Stuart Elliot, "Advertising; Late-Game Scores for Spots, Too," *The New York Times,* February 3, 2009, accessed December 24, 2009 (http://query.nytimes.com/gst/fullpage.html?res=9D01E4DD 1F38F930A35751C0A96F9C8B63&sec=&spon=&pagewanted=).

e. Ibid.

Marcus Thomas – Faces

1. Edwige Winans, associate research director, Marcus Thomas, LLC, email interview, April 12, 2016.

2. Edwige Winans, "Connecting through the Heart: The Importance of Measuring Emotions in Creative Testing," February 9, 2016.

3. Jennifer Hirt-Marchand, partner, Marcus Thomas LLC, email interview, April 11, 2016.

4. Orlando Wood, "How Emotional Tugs Trump Rational Pushes," *Journal of Advertising Research,* Vol. 52, No. 1, March 2012.

Chapter 11

1. "What America Eats 2003," *Parade,* November 16, 2003. This is the ninth biennial survey of the food habits of the United States; 2,080 men and women, aged 18 to 65, were interviewed in March 2003 by Mark Clements Research.

2. "Questionnaire Design," Pew Research Center, downloaded June 27, 2016 (http://www.pewresearch.org/methodology/u-s-survey-research /questionnaire-design/).

3. Dorwin Cartwright, "Some Principles of Mass Persuasion, " *Human Relations* 2 (1948), p. 266.

4. "Technical Report: The How's and Why's of Survey Research," SPSS Inc., October 16, 2002.

5. J. P. Guilford, *Psychometric Methods* (New York: McGraw-Hill, 1954), pp. 278–79.

6. H. H. Friedman and Taiwo Amoo, "Rating the Rating Scales," *Journal of Marketing Management* 9, no. 3 (Winter 1999), pp. 114–23.

7. Donald R. Cooper, "Converting Neutrals to Loyalists," unpublished paper prepared for the IBM Corporation, New York, 1996.

8. You might want to review these concepts in the previous chapter.

9. G. A. Churchill and J. P. Peter, "Research Design Effects on the Reliability of Rating Scales: A Meta-Analysis," *Journal of Marketing Research* 21 (November 1984), pp. 360–75.

10. See, for example, H. H Friedman and Linda W. Friedman, "On the Danger of Using Too Few Points in a Rating Scale: A Test of Validity," *Journal of Data Collection* 26, no. 2 (1986), pp. 60–63; and Eli P. Cox, "The Optimal Number of Response Alternatives for a Scale: A Review," *Journal of Marketing Research* 17, no. 4 (1980), pp. 407–22.

11. A study of the historic research literature found that more than three-fourths of the attitude scales used were of the 5-point type. An examination of more recent literature suggests that the 5-point scale is still common but there is a growing use of longer scales. For the historic study, see Daniel D. Day, "Methods in Attitude Research," *American Sociological Review* 5 (1940), pp. 395–410. Single- versus multiple-item scaling requirements are discussed in Jum C. Nunnally, *Psychometric Theory* (New York: McGraw-Hill, 1967), Chap. 14 .

12. Guilford, *Psychometric Methods.*

13. P. M. Synonds, "Notes on Rating," *Journal of Applied Psychology* 9 (1925), pp. 188–95.

14. E. Aronson, D. Wilson, and R. Akert, *Social Psychology* (Upper Saddle River, NJ: Prentice Hall, 2002); Robert J. Sternberg, *Cognitive Psychology,* 3rd ed. (Reading, MA: Wadsworth Publishing, 2002); Richard E. Petty and John T. Cacioppo, *Attitudes and Persuasion: Classic and Contemporary Approaches* (Boulder, CO: Westview Press, 1996); and Gordon W. Allport, "Attitudes," in *A Handbook of Social Psychology,* vol. 2, ed. C. A. Murchison (New York: Russell, 1935), 2 vols.

15. See, for example, Robert A. Baron and Donn Byrne, *Social Psychology,* 10th ed. (Boston: Pearson Allyn & Bacon, 2002); and David G. Myers, *Social Psychology,* 7th ed. (New York: McGraw-Hill, 2002).

16. Bernard S. Phillips, *Social Research Strategy and Tactics,* 2nd ed. (New York: Macmillan, 1971), p. 205.

17. This is adapted from Pamela L. Alreck and Robert B. Settle, *The Survey Research Handbook* (Burr Ridge, IL: Irwin, 1995), Chap. 5.

18. One study reported that the construction of a Likert scale took only half the time required to construct a Thurstone scale. See L. L. Thurstone and K. K. Kenney, "A Comparison of the Thurstone and Likert Techniques of Attitude Scale Construction," *Journal of Applied Psychology* 30 (1946), pp. 72–83.

19. "Questionnaire Design," Pew Research Center, downloaded June 27, 2016 (http://www.pewresearch.org/methodology/u-s-survey -research/questionnaire-design/).

20. Charles E. Osgood, G. J. Suci, and P. H. Tannenbaum, *The Measurement of Meaning* (Urbana: University of Illinois Press, 1957).

21. Ibid., p. 49. See also James G. Snider and Charles E. Osgood, eds., *Semantic Differential Technique* (Chicago: Aldine, 1969).

22. Louis Guttman, "A Basis for Scaling Qualitative Data," *American Sociological Review* 9 (1944), pp. 139–50.

23. John P. Robinson, "Toward a More Appropriate Use of Guttman Scaling," *Public Opinion Quarterly* 37 (Summer 1973), pp. 260–67.

24. S. A. Stouffer et al., *Measurement and Prediction: Studies in Social Psychology in World War II,* vol. 4 (Princeton, NJ: Princeton University Press, 1950), p. 709.

25. An excellent example of the question revision process is presented in Stanley Payne, *The Art of Asking Questions* (Princeton, NJ: Princeton University Press, 1951), pp. 214–25. This example illustrates that a relatively simple question can go through as many as 41 different versions before being judged satisfactory.

26. Jon A. Krosnick and Duane F. Alwin, "An Evaluation of a Cognitive Theory of Response-Order Effects in Survey Measurement," *Public Opinion Quarterly* 51, no. 2 (Summer 1987), pp. 201–19.

27. "2016 Population Estimate," U.S. Census, downloaded June 16, 2017 (https://www.census.gov/search-results.html?q=u.s. +population&search.x=11&search.y=13&search=submit&page =1&stateGeo=none&searchtype=web&cssp=Typeahead&%3 Acq_csrf_token=undefined).

28. Goldie Blumenstyk, "U. of Phoenix Looks to Shrink Itself With New Admissions Requirements and Deep Cuts," *The Chronicle of Higher Education,* June 30, 2015 (http://www.chronicle.com /article/U-of-Phoenix-Looks-to-Shrink/231247/).

29. Actual enrollment in 2016 was approximately 40 million according to the NCES. See "Table 302.60: Percentage of 18-24 year olds enrolled in degree-granting postsecondary institutions, by level of institution and sex and race/ethnicity of student 1970-2015," National Center of Education Statistics, downloaded June 14, 2017 (https://www.sec.gov/Archives/edgar/data/929887 /000092988716000225/apol-aug31201610k.htm).

30. Robert L. Kahn and Charles F. Cannell, *The Dynamics of Interviewing* (New York: Wiley, 1957), p. 132.

31. Jean M. Converse and Stanley Presser, *Survey Questions: Handcrafting the Standardized Questionnaire* (Beverly Hills, CA: Sage Publications, 1986), pp. 50–51.

32. Ibid., p. 51.

Appendix: Sample Computer-Based Questions and Guidelines for Mobile Q

1. The snapshot in this appendix was developed with the collaboration of Kristin Luck, CEO Decipher, interview via e-mail, March 20, 2012. Kristin Luck, "Mobile Survey Best Practices," Decipher, March 12,2012, received via e-mail.

Appendix: More on Effective Measurement Questions

1. Sam Gill, "How Do You Stand on Sin?" *Tide,* March 14, 1947, p. 72.
2. Stanley L. Payne, *The Art of Asking Questions* (Princeton, NJ: Princeton University Press, 1951), p. 18.
3. Unaided recall gives respondents no clues as to possible answers. Aided recall gives them a list of radio programs that played last night and then asks them which ones they heard. See Harper W. Boyd Jr. and Ralph Westfall, *Marketing Research*, 3rd ed. (Homewood, IL: Irwin, 1972), p. 293.
4. Gideon Sjoberg, "A Questionnaire on Questionnaires," *Public Opinion Quarterly* 18 (Winter 1954), p. 425.
5. Robert L. Kahn and Charles F. Cannell, *The Dynamics of Interviewing* (New York: Wiley, 1957), p. 108.
6. Ibid., p. 110.
7. Payne, *The Art of Asking Questions,* p. 140.
8. Ibid., p. 141.
9. Ibid., p. 149.
10. Gertrude Bancroft and Emmett H. Welch, "Recent Experiences with Problems of Labor Force Measurement," *Journal of the American Statistical Association* 41 (1946), pp. 303–12.
11. National Opinion Research Center, *Proceedings of the Central City Conference on Public Opinion Research* (Denver, CO: University of Denver, 1946), p. 73.
12. Hadley Cantril, ed., *Gauging Public Opinion* (Princeton, NJ: Princeton University Press, 1944), p. 48.
13. Payne, *The Art of Asking Questions,* pp. 7–8.
14. Barbara Snell Dobrenwend, "Some Effects of Open and Closed Questions on Respondents' Answers," *Human Organization* 24 (Summer 1965), pp. 175–84.

*Exhibit 11-7 was developed from an article by Jon Puleston, "Honesty of Responses: The 7 Factors at Play," GreenBook, March 4, 2012, accessed March 5, 2012 (http://www.greenbookblog.org/2012/03/04/honesty-of-responses-the-7-factors-at-play/).

Appendix: Sources of Measurement Questions

1. Existing questions can serve as a rich source of inspiration for custom-designed questions, as well as specific questions you might use for your measurement instrument. This list was compiled from numerous recommendations and the experience of various practicing researchers. It is not intended to be a comprehensive list but should be sufficient to get you started.

References for Snapshots, PicProfiles, Captions, and Pull Quotes
Maritz Research, Inc.

1. Keith Chrzan and Michael Kemery, "Make or break: a simple non-compensatory customer satisfaction model," *International Journal of Market Research,* Vol. 54, No. 2, 2012.
2. Keith Chrzan, "Make or Break Customer Satisfaction: Improving Customer Satisfaction Measurement with New Methods," 2012. PowerPoint slide set, accessed May 2, 2012 (http://www.slideshare.net/oanaman/make-or-break-customer-satisfaction).

Open Doors

1. "About Harris Interactive," Harris Interactive, downloaded March 20, 2004 (http://www.harrisinteractive.com/about/).
2. Laura Light, research director for public policy and public relations, Harris Interactive, interviewed March 10, 2004.
3. "Research among Adults with Disabilities: Travel and Hospitality," final report prepared by Harris Interactive for Open Doors Organization, delivered January 2002.
4. Eric Lipp, executive director, Open Doors Organization, interviewed March 4, 2004.
5. Steve Struhl, Harris Interactive, interviewed March 10, 2004. Headquartered in Rochester, New York, Harris Interactive combines proprietary methodologies and technology with expertise in predictive, custom, and strategic research. The company conducts international research through wholly owned subsidiaries—London-based HI Europe (www.hieurope.com) and Tokyo-based Harris Interactive Japan—as well as through the Harris Interactive Global Network of local market- and opinion-research firms.

PullQuote

1. David F. Harris, President, Insight and Measurement and Author, email, April 23, 2017.

Snausages

1. Hoag Levins (producer), "How Del Monte Social-Media Strategy Created a New Pet Food: Case Study from the IAB Conference," *Advertising Age,* May 25, 2009, accessed May 28, 2009 (http://adage.com/brightcove/single.php?title=24149973001); http://www.snausages.com/snack-shack/breakfast-bites.htm; http://www.snausages.com/snack-shack/breakfast-bites-ingredients.htm.

Toluna

1. "Case Study: VOSS, Artesian Water from Norway," Toluna, provided via email June 17, 2016.
2. Dan Enson, research director, Toluna, email, June 21, 2016.
3. Dan Enson, research director, Toluna, phone interview, June 14, 2016.
4. "Toluna Sets the New Standard for 'Real-Time Research'," Toluna press release, March 30, 2016, downloaded June 26, 2016 (http://www.toluna-group.com/about-toluna/thought-leadership/news/press-release/toluna-sets-the-new-standard-for-real-time-research).
5. "VOSS Survey," provided via email, June 21, 2016.

Urban Dictionary

1. Tom H. C. Anderson, "Why Text Analytics Needs to Move at the Speed of Slang," OdinText blog, April 18, 2016, downloaded April 20, 2016 (http://odintext.com/blog/why-text-analytics-needs-to-move-at-the-speed-of-slang/).
2. Home page, Urban Dictionary, downloaded April 20, 2016 (http://www.urbandictionary.com/).

Chapter 12

1. "Rapport," *Miriam Webster Dictionary,* downloaded June 13, 2017 (https://www.merriam-webster.com/dictionary/rapport).
2. Brooke Foucault, Joanquin Aguilar, Peter Miller, and Justine Cassel, "Behavioral Correlates of Rapport in Survey Interview," downloaded June 13, 2017 (http://home.isr.umich.edu/files/2013/01/FoucaultAAPOR2009.pdf).
3. Jane Sheppard, "Telephone Survey Practices Study 2000," ResearchInfo.com, June 1, 2000, accessed March 19, 2004 (http://

www.researchinfo.com/docs/library/telephone_survey_ practices _study_2000.cfm).

4. "Questionnaire Design," Pew Research Center, downloaded June 27, 2016 (http://www.pewresearch.org/methodology/u-s -survey-research/questionnaire-design/).

5. Frederick J. Thumin, "Watch for These Unseen Variables," *Journal of Marketing* 26 (July 1962), pp. 58–60.

6. You might want to visit the chapter on survey research for a review of the IRB process.

References for Snapshots, PicProfiles, Captions, and Pull Quotes
Cupid

1. Kerry Sulkowicz, "In Cupid's Cubicle," *BusinessWeek,* February 26, 2007, p. 18.

2. "Be My Valentine? Nearly 40 Percent of Workers Have Had a Workplace Romance, According to Latest Spherion Survey," Spherion Corporation press release: January 29, 2007, accessed February 24, 2007 (http:www.spherion.com/press/releases/2007 /workplace-romance.jsp).

3. "QuickQuery Frequently Asked Questions," Harris Interactive, accessed February 24, 2007 (http://www.harrisinteractive.com /services/pubs/HI_QuickQuery_FAQ_Sheet.pdf).

4. "Consulting on the Psychology of Business," Boswell Group Inc., accessed February 24, 2007 (http://www.boswellgroup.com).

Factors Affecting Respondent Honesty

1. Developed from an article by Jon Puleston, "Honesty of Responses: The 7 Factors at Play," GreenBook, March 4, 2012, accessed March 5, 2012 (http://www.greenbookblog.org /2012/03/04/ honesty-of-responses-the-7-factors-at-play/).

InsightExpress/Time to Abandonment

1. Doug Adams and Bob Ferro, "Not as Easy as It Looks: Best Practices for Online Research," InsightExpress, March 11, 2004. This presentation was part of the American Marketing Association Online Seminar Series.

PullQuote

1. David F. Harris, President, Insight and Measurement and Author, email, April 23, 2017.

TSA/Deloitte

1. "Deloitte Survey: Travelers Are Essentially Uninterested in Registered Traveler Program, Despite Frustration with Long Airport Security Lines; Privacy Concerns Cited; Cost Only a Minor Issue," Hotels, April 4, 2007. Accessed April 16, 2007 (http://www6.lexis nexis.com/publisher/EndUser?Action5UserDisplayFullDocument &orgId5 616&topicId512552&docId51:593960847&start510).

Vehicle Survey

1. This snapshot was developed from a survey experience of the author, following the purchase of a new automobile in February 2017 and receipt of the survey in May 2017.

Chapter 13

1. Tom H.C. Anderson, "Seven Text Analytics Myths Exposed at IIEX," OdinText Blog, June 15, 2017 downloaded June 21, 2017 (http:// odintext.com/blog/7-iiex-text-analytics-myths-exposed/?utm_source =MRX+Leaders&utm_campaign=b75c415402-EMAIL_CAMPAIGN _2017_06_19&utm_medium=email&utm_term=0_28d17bd83e -b75c415402-133618157).

2. Menaka Gopinath, Ipsos Social Media Exchange, "Understanding the Social Dynamic," NewMR Webinar, June 21, 2017.

3. Ibid.

4. Steve Stemler, "An Overview of Content Analysis," *Practical Assessment, Research, & Evaluation* 7, no. 17 (June 2001; updated March 7, 2012), downloaded June 21, 2017 (http://pareonline.net /getvn.asp?v=7&n=17).

5. Based on the operation of the SPSS Inc., product TextSmart.

6. Hans Zeisel, *Say It with Figures,* 6th ed. (New York: Harper & Row, 1985), pp. 48–49.

7. David C. Hoaglin, Frederick Mosteller, and John W. Tukey, eds., *Understanding Robust and Exploratory Data Analysis* (New York: Wiley, 1983), p. 2.

8. John W. Tukey, *Exploratory Data Analysis* (Reading, MA: Addison-Wesley, 1977), pp. 2–3.

9. Frederick Hartwig with Brian E. Dearing, *Exploratory Data Analysis* (Beverly Hills, CA: Sage Publications, 1979), pp. 9–12.

10. The exhibits in this section were created with statistical and graphic programs particularly suited to exploratory data analysis. The author acknowledges the following vendors for evaluation and use of their products: SPSS Inc., 233 S. Wacker Dr., Chicago, IL 60606; and Data Description, P.O. Box 4555, Ithaca, NY 14852.

11. "Constructing a Histogram," downloaded June 20, 2017 (https:// www.oswego.edu/˜srp/stats/hist_con.htm).

12. Paul F. Velleman and David C. Hoaglin, *Applications, Basics, and Computing of Exploratory Data Analysis* (Boston: Duxbury Press, 1981), p. 13.

13. John Hanke, Eastern Washington University, contributed this section. For further references to stem-and-leaf displays, see John D. Emerson and David C. Hoaglin, "Stem-and-Leaf Displays," in *Understanding Robust and Exploratory Data Analysis*, pp. 7–31; and Velleman and Hoaglin, *Applications*, pp. 1–13.

14. This section is adapted from the following excellent discussions of boxplots: Velleman and Hoaglin, *Applications,* pp. 65–76; Hartwig, *Exploratory Data Analysis,* pp. 19–25; John D. Emerson and Judith Strenio, "Boxplots and Batch Comparison," in *Understanding Robust and Exploratory Data Analysis,* pp. 59–93; and Amir D. Aczel, *Complete Business Statistics* (Homewood, IL: Irwin, 1989), pp. 723–28.

15. Tukey, *Exploratory Data Analysis,* pp. 27–55.

16. Hoaglin et al., *Understanding Robust and Exploratory Data Analysis,* p. 2.

17. Several robust estimators that are suitable replacements for the mean and standard deviation—for example, the trimmed mean, trimean, the M-estimators (such as Huber's, Tukey's, Hampel's, and Andrew's estimators), and the median absolute deviation (MAD). See Hoaglin et al., *Understanding Robust and Exploratory Data Analysis,* Chap. 10; and SPSS Inc., *SPSS Base 9.0 User's Guide* (Chicago: SPSS, 1999), Chap. 13.

18. The difference between the definitions of a hinge and a quartile is based on variations in their calculation. *Q1, 25th percentile,* and *lower hinge* are used synonymously, and *Q3, 75th percentile*, and *upper hinge,* similarly. There are technical differences, although they are not significant in this context.

19. R. McGill, J. W. Tukey, and W. A. Larsen, "Variations of Box Plots," *The American Statistician* 14 (1978), pp. 12–16.

20. See J. Chambers, W. Cleveland, B. Kleiner, and John W. Tukey, *Graphical Methods for Data Analysis* (Boston: Duxbury Press, 1983).

21. Harper W. Boyd Jr. and Ralph Westfall, *Marketing Research,* 3rd ed. (Homewood, IL: Irwin, 1972), p. 5.

22. SPSS Inc., *SPSS Tables 8.0* (Chicago: SPSS, 1998), with its system file: Bank Data.

Appendix: Better Tables

1. This appendix was developed from concepts presented in Sally Bigwood and Melissa Spore. *Presenting Numbers, Tables, and Charts* (Oxford: Oxford University Press, 2003). The numbers used throughout this appendix were drawn from numerous sources, including "Europe," *NewMedia TrendWatch*, accessed August 1, 2012 (http://www.newmediatrendwatch.com/regional-overview/103 -europe?showall=1); "EURO to Dollar Exchange Rates," *X-Rates*, accessed July 28, 2012 (http://www.x-rates.com/table/?from=EUR); "Historical Exchange Rates: EURO to Dollar," *Oanda*, accessed July 28, 2012 (http://www.oanda.com/currency/historical-rates/); and Matt Creamer and Rupal Parekh, "Why the Euro Crisis Is Your Business Problem, Too," *Advertising Age*, July 23, 2012, accessed July 28, 2012 (http://adage.com/article/news/euro -crisis-businessproblem/236235/?utm_source=daily_email&utm _medium=newsletter&utm_campaign=adage).

Appendix: Describing Data Statistically

1. This appendix was built from two examples developed for *Business Research Methods*, 8th ed. (New York: McGraw-Hill, 2003), by Donald Cooper and Pamela Schindler. A proportion is the mean of a dichotomous variable when members of a class receive the value of 1, and nonmembers receive a value of 0.

Chapter 14

1. An ad from Lieberman Research Worldwide, originally published in *Advertising Age* magazine and provided by the company to the author, claimed, "We look at the results and ask 'so what'—playing out every possible scenario."

2. A more detailed example is found in Amir D. Aczel and Jayauel Sounderpandian, *Complete Business Statistics,* 5th ed. (New York: Irwin/McGraw-Hill, 2001).

3. The standardized random variable, denoted by Z, is a deviation from expectancy and is expressed in terms of standard deviation units. The mean of the distribution of a standardized random variable is 0, and the standard deviation is 1. With this distribution, the deviation from the mean by any value of X can be expressed in standard deviation units.

4. Procedures for hypothesis testing are reasonably similar across authors. This outline was influenced by Sidney Siegel, *Nonparametric Statistics for the Behavioral Sciences* (New York: McGraw-Hill, 1956), Chap. 2.

5. Marija J. Norusis/SPSS Inc., *SPSS for Windows Base System User's Guide*, Release 6.0 (Chicago: SPSS, 1993), pp. 601–06.

6. For further information on these tests, see ibid., pp. 187–88.

7. F. M. Andrews, L. Klem, T. N. Davidson, P. M. O'Malley, and W. L. Rodgers, *A Guide for Selecting Statistical Techniques for Analyzing Social Science Data* (Ann Arbor: Institute for Social Research, University of Michigan, 1976).

8. See B. S. Everitt, *The Analysis of Contingency Tables* (London: Chapman and Hall, 1977).

9. The critiques are represented by W. J. Conover, "Some Reasons for Not Using the Yates' Continuity Correction on 2 × 2 Contingency Tables," *Journal of the American Statistical Association* 69

(1974), pp. 374–76; and N. Mantel, "Comment and a Suggestion on the Yates' Continuity Correction," *Journal of the American Statistical Association* 69 (1974), pp. 378–80.

10. This data table and the analysis of variance tables and plots in this section were prepared with SuperANOVA™.

11. See, for example, Roger E. Kirk, *Experimental Design: Procedures for the Behavioral Sciences* (Belmont, CA: Brooks/Cole, 1982), pp. 115–33. An exceptionally clear presentation for step-by-step hand computation is found in James L. Bruning and B. L. Kintz, *Computational Handbook of Statistics,* 2nd ed. (Glenview, IL: Scott, Foresman, 1977), pp. 143–68. Also, when you use a computer program, the reference manual typically provides helpful advice in addition to the setup instructions.

12. Kirk, *Experimental Design,* pp. 90–115. Alternatively, see Bruning and Kintz, *Computational Handbook of Statistics,* pp. 113–32.

13. For a discussion and example of the Cochran Q test, see Sidney Siegel and N. J. Castellan Jr., *Nonparametric Statistics for the Behavioral Sciences,* 2nd ed. (New York: McGraw-Hill, 1988).

14. For further details, see ibid.

References for Snapshots, PicProfiles, Captions, and Pull Quotes
A/B Testing

1. "What Is A/B Testing," Optimizely, accessed July 27, 2012 (https://www.optimizely.com/whatisabtesting).

2. Brian Christian, "The A/B Test: Inside the Technology That's Changing the Rules of Business," Wired, April 25, 2012, accessed July 27, 2012 (http://www.wired.com/business/2012/04 /ff_abtesting/all/).

Drug Use in Movies

1. "New Study Looks at Drugs in Movies and Songs," America Cares Inc., April 1999 (http://www.americacares.org/drugs_in_movies .htm).

2. "Substance Use in Popular Movies and Music," Office of National Drug Control Policy, April 1999 (http://www.mediacampaign.org /publications/movies/movie_partIV.html).

Marcus Thomas/Troy-Bilt

1. "Case Study: Uncovering the Inner Workings of Television Advertising," Marcus Thomas, provided via e-mail.

2. Jennifer Hirt-Marchand, associate partner, strategic insights executive, and Edwige Winans, associate research director, Marcus Thomas interviewed January 31, 2012.

3. Edwige Winans, associate research director, Marcus Thomas e-mail June 7, 2012.

4. Troy-Bilt questionnaire provided by Marcus Thomas via e-mail.

PullQuote

1. Edward Teller, accessed May 29, 2012 (http://en.wikiquote.org /wiki/Edward_Teller).

Chapter 15

1. Typically, the X (independent) variable is plotted on the horizontal axis and the Y (dependent) variable on the vertical axis. Although correlation does not distinguish between independent and dependent variables, the convention is useful for consistency in plotting and will be used later with regression.

2. F. J. Anscombe, "Graphs in Statistical Analysis," *American Statistician* 27 (1973), pp. 17–21. Cited in Samprit Chatterjee and Bertram Price, *Regression Analysis by Example* (New York: Wiley, 1977), pp. 7–9.

3. Amir D. Aczel, *Complete Business Statistics*, 2nd ed. (Homewood, IL: Irwin, 1993), p. 433.

4. This section is partially based on the concepts developed by Emanuel J. Mason and William J. Bramble, *Understanding and Conducting Research* (New York: McGraw-Hill, 1989), pp. 172–82; and elaborated in greater detail by Aczel, *Complete Business Statistics*, pp. 414–29.

5. Technically, estimation uses a concurrent criterion variable whereas prediction uses a future criterion. The statistical procedure is the same in either case.

6. Roz Howard and Jenny Stonier, "Marketing Wine to Generation X," for the 2000–2001 NSW Wine Press Club Fellowship. Reported in Murray Almond's "From the Left Island," May 25, 2002 (http://www.wineoftheweek.com/murray/0205genx.html).

7. Peter Passell, "Can Math Predict a Wine? An Economist Takes a Swipe at Some Noses," *International Herald Tribune*, March 5, 1990, p. 1; and Jacques Neher, "Top Quality Bordeaux Cellar Is an Excellent Buy," *International Herald Tribune,* July 9, 1990, p. 8.

8. See Alan Agresti and Barbara Finlay, *Statistical Methods for the Social Sciences* (San Francisco: Dellen Publishing, 1986), pp. 248–49. Also see the discussion of basic regression models in John Neter, William Wasserman, and Michael H. Kutner, *Applied Linear Statistical Models* (Homewood, IL: Irwin, 1990), pp. 23–49.

9. The error term $\varepsilon_1 = Y_i - E\hat{Y}_i$ and the residual $e_1 = (Y_i - \hat{Y}_i)$ are differentiated. The first is based on the vertical deviation of Y_i from the true regression line. It is unknown and estimated. The second is the vertical deviation of Y_i from the fitted Y on the estimated line. See Neter et al., *Applied Linear Statistical Models,* p. 47.

10. For further information on software-generated regression diagnostics, see the most current release of software manuals for SPSS, MINITAB, BMDP, and SAS.

11. Aczel, *Complete Business Statistics*, p. 434.

12. This calculation is normally listed as the standard error of the slope (SE B) on computer printouts. For these data it is further defined as

$$s(b_i) + \frac{8}{\sqrt{SS_x}} = \frac{538.559}{\sqrt{198.249}} = 38.249$$

where

    s = the standard error of estimate (and the square root of the mean square error of the regression)

    SS_x = the sum of squares for the X variable

13. Computer printouts use uppercase (R^2) because most procedures are written to accept multiple and bivariate regression.

14. The table output for this section has been modified from SPSS and is described in Marija J. Norusis/SPSS Inc., *SPSS Base System User's Guide* (Chicago: SPSS, 1990). For further discussion and examples of nonparametric measures of association, see S. Siegel and N. J. Castellan Jr., *Nonparametric Statistics for the Behavioral Sciences,* 2nd ed. (New York: McGraw-Hill, 1988).

15. Calculation of concordant and discordant pairs is adapted from Agresti and Finlay, *Statistical Methods for the Social Sciences,* pp. 221–23.

16. The percentage of concordant plus the percentage of discordant pairs sums to 1.0. Their difference is −.70. The only numbers satisfying these two conditions are .85 and .15 (.85 + .15 = 1.0, .15 − .85 = −.70).

17. G. U. Yule and M. G. Kendall, *An Introduction to the Theory of Statistics* (New York: Hafner, 1950).

18. M. G. Kendall, *Rank Correlation Methods,* 4th ed. (London: Charles W. Griffin, 1970).

Snapshots, CloseUps, PicProfiles, and Exhibits
Advanced Statistics

1. Bob Reczek, "Navy Federal Credit Union Capitalizes on Predictive Analytics Software from SPSS Inc., Wins 2009 Technology ROI Award," News Blaze, September 1, 2009, accessed September 1, 2009 (http://newsblaze.com/story/2009090106065100001.bw/topstory.html).

2. Calvin Bierley, "Boeing Employees' Credit Union," SPSS, accessed November 20, 2009 (http://www.spss.com/success/pdf/Boeing%20Employees%20Credit%20Union%20Customer%20Story.pdf).

3. "Navy Federal Credit Union Capitalizes on Predictive Analytics Software from SPSS Inc., Wins 2009 Technology ROI Award," SPSS press release, September 1, 2009, accessed November 4, 2009 (http://www.spss.com/press/template_view.cfm?PR_ID51114).

4. "Navy Federal Credit Union Fact Sheet," Navy Federal Credit Union, accessed June 25, 2012 (https://www.navyfederal.org/pdf/publications/fact-sheet.pdf).

Best Practices

1. Bruno Furtado, Felipe Ize, Antonio Rocha, and Miguel Suadi, "Lessons from Latin America's leading consumer-goods companies," McKinsey & Company, June 2016, downloaded June 21, 2016 (http://www.mckinsey.com/industries/consumer-packaged-goods/our-insights/lessons-from-latin-americas-leading-consumer-goods-companies?cid=other-eml-alt-mip-mck-oth-1606).

Constellation Wines

1. Natasha Hayes, Group Marketing Director, Ravenswood, Blackstone & Toasted Head, Constellation Wines US. Interviewed August 12, 2009; August 17, 2009; and September 19, 2009.

2. Stuart Elliot, "In Wine We Trust,' Ads Suggest," *New York Times,* August 10, 2009, accessed August 10, 2009 (http://www.nytimes.com/2009/08/10/business/media/10adnewsletter1.html?_r51&adxnnl51&8ad5&emc5seiaa1&adxnnlx51266177729-WbcjIygTDT1As/PYF44/mw).

Envirosell

1. Live e-chat with Paco Underhill, July 8, 1999 (http://www.abcnews.go.com/sections/politics/DailyNews/chat_990511underhill.html).

Oscar

1. Data tables provided by Polaris Marketing Research, April 5, 2012.

2. "Survey Research Shows Low Involvement with Oscars for Most Americans," *PRWeb,* March 8, 2012, accessed April 3, 2012 (http://www.prweb.com/releases/2012/3/prweb9263454.htm).

Quote

1. Jeff Bezos, CEO Amazon, BrainyQuotes, downloaded April 26, 2017 (https://www.brainyquote.com/quotes/quotes/j/jeffbezos450018.html).

Chapter 16

1. This section draws upon content presented during conference sessions and recorded interviews from *Insight Innovation Exchange NA,* Atlanta, Georgia, June 16–18, 2014; *Insight Innovation Exchange NA,* Atlanta, Georgia, June 15–17, 2015; and *Insight Innovation Exchange NA,* Atlanta, Georgia, June 13–15, 2016.

2. Brent Dykes, "Actionable Insights: The Missing Link Between Data and Business Value," *Forbes,* April 26, 2016, downloaded

May 4, 2016 (http://www.forbes.com/sites/brentdykes/2016/04/26/actionable-insights-the-missing-link-between-data-and-business-value/#6c7a15ec65bb).

3. Portions of this section are adapted from: http://www.smsu.edu/Academics/ChallengeProgram/Speech%20110/Audience%20Analysis%20(4).doc, downloaded January 7, 2010; Mary Munter and Dave Paradi, *Guide to PowerPoint* (Upper Saddle River, NJ: Pearson/Prentice Hall, 2009), p. 6; and Doug Losee, "An Adaptation of Constructive Alternativism as Theory for Audience Analysis," presented at the Annual Meeting of the Western Speech Communication Association (Albuquerque, NM, February 19–22, 1983), downloaded January 7, 2010 (http://www.eric.ed.gov/ERICWebPortal/custom/portlets/recordDetails/detailmini.jsp?_nfpb5true&_&ERICExtSearch_SearchValue_05ED229800).

4. These biases, well grounded in psychological theory, were summarized in Jory MacKay, "5 Cognitive Biases That Are Killing Your Decisions," *Life Hacks*, September 26, 2015, downloaded May 18, 2016 (http://thenextweb.com/lifehacks/2015/09/26/5-cognitive-biases-that-are-killing-your-decisions/?utm_content=5%20cognitive%20biases%20that%20are%20killing%20your%20decisions&awesm=tnw.to_b4juC&utm_source=t.co&utm_campaign=share%20button&utm_medium=referral#gref).

5. This comment refers to a principle called informative change, discussed in Stephen Kosslyn, *Clear and to the Point: 8 Principles for Compelling PowerPoint Presentations* (New York: Oxford Press, 2007), pp. 3–12.

6. John M. Penrose Jr., Robert W. Rasberry, and Robert J. Myers, *Advanced Business Communication* (Boston: PWS-Kent Publishing, 1989), p. 185.

7. Paul E. Resta, *The Research Report* (New York: American Book Company, 1972), p. 5.

8. Penrose et al., *Advanced Business Communication,* p. 185.

9. The following are drawn from J. Deese and R. A. Kaufman, "Serial Effects in Recall of Unorganized and Sequentially Organized Verbal Material," *Journal of Experimental Psychology* 54, no. 3 (1957), pp. 180–187; and B. B. Murdock Jr., "The Serial Position Effect of Free Recall," *Journal of Experimental Psychology* 64 (1962), pp. 482–488.

10. This list was developed with material from A. H. Monroe and D. Ehninger, *Principles and Types of Speech*, 6th ed. (Glenview, IL: Scott, Foresman and Co., 1967), pp. 264–265.

11. Donald R. Cooper, "An Experimental Study to Determine the Relative Effectiveness of the Motivated Sequence versus the Narrative Pattern of Organizational Development in a Persuasive Speech," Unpublished Master's Thesis, 1968.

12. Material in this section is developed from Rick Altman, *Why Most PowerPoint Presentations Suck: And How You Can Make Them Better* (Pleasanton, CA: Harvest Books Rick Altman: 2009), p. 31; and Edward Tufte, "PowerPoint Is Evil: Power Corrupts. PowerPoint Corrupts Absolutely," *Wired,* September 2003, downloaded February 6, 2010 (http://www.wired.com/wired/archive/11.09/ppt2.html).

13. The section on learning was developed from "What's Your Learning Style? The Learning Styles," EducationalPlanner.org, downloaded April 3, 2016 (http://www.educationplanner.org/students/self-assessments/learning-styles-styles.shtml); and "Kinesthetic Strategies," VARK, downloaded April 3, 2016 (http://vark-learn.com/strategies/kinesthetic-strategies/).

14. Aristotle's *Rhetoric, Stanford Encyclopedia of Philosophy*, first published May 2, 2002, downloaded December 29, 2009 (http://plato.stanford.edu/entries/aristotle-rhetoric/#4.4).

15. From the essay by Jeanne Fahnestock, "The Appeals: Ethos, Pathos, and Logos," downloaded January 7, 2010 (http://otal.umd.edu/~mikej/supplements/ethoslogospathos.html).

16. Aristotle's *Rhetoric, Stanford Encyclopedia of Philosophy.*

17. Guy Kawasaki, *The Macintosh Way* (New York: HarperCollins, 1990), p. 149.

18. The material in this section draws on Stephen M. Kosslyn, *Elements of Graph Design* (San Francisco: Freeman, 1993); DeltaPoint Inc., *DeltaGraph User's Guide 4.0* (Monterey, CA: DeltaPoint, 1996); Gene Zelazny, *Say It with Charts* (Homewood,IL: Business One Irwin, 1991); Jim Heid, "Graphs That Work," *MacWorld*, February 1994, pp. 155–56; and Penrose, Rasberry, and Myers, *Advanced Business Communication*, Chap. 3.

19. "How to Write Qualitative Marketing Research Reports," FocusGroups.com, downloaded March 30, 2016 (http://www.focusgrouptips.com/marketing-research-reports.html).

20. This section was developed using some of the principles presented by Stephen Kosslyn, *Clear and to the Point: 8 Principles for Compelling PowerPoint Presentations* (New York: Oxford Press, 2007), pp. 3–12.

21. Marilyn Stoll, "Charts Other Than Pie Are Appealing to the Eye," *PC Week,* March 25, 1986, pp. 138–139.

22. Stoll, "Charts Other Than Pie Are Appealing to the Eye."

23. Presentation by Dr. Olga Medvedkov and her research team to city leaders, Spring 2000. Due to client confidentiality, we can't release the city.

24. Material in this section was drawn from Garr Reynolds, *Presentation Zen: Simple Ideas on Presentation Design and Delivery* (Berkeley, CA: Pearson/New Riders, 2008), p. 33, p.117, and p. 97; Nancy Duarte, *slide: ology: The Art and Science of Creating Great Presentations* (Sebastopol, CA: O'Reilly Media, 2008), p. 92 and p. 152; Kosslyn, *Clear and to the Point,* pp. 52–59, 127–59; Altman, *Why Most PowerPoint Presentations Suck;* and Munter and Paradi, *Guide to PowerPoint,* pp. 6–12, 61–68.

25. Penrose et al., *Advanced Business Communication,* p. 89.

26. Stephen Few, *Information Dashboard Design: The Effective Visual Communication of Data* (Santa Rosa, CA: O'Reilly Media, January 1, 2006), p. 35.

27. "10 Tips for Marketing Research Reports That Get Read," *The Insider Blog*, Infosurv Research, March 24, 2015, downloaded March 30, 2016 (http://www.infosurv.com/tips-for-marketing-research-reports-that-get-read/).

28. Mark Smiciklas, "The Power of Infographics: Using Pictures to Communicate and Connect with Your Audiences," QUEPublishing.com, 2012, p. 4, downloaded June 27, 2017 (http://ptgmedia.pearsoncmg.com/images/9780789749499/samplepages/0789749491.pdf).

29. David McCandless, "The Beauty of Data Visualization," TED, November 23, 2012, downloaded June 25, 2017 (https://www.ted.com/talks/david_mccandless_the_beauty_of_data_visualization).

30. Smiciklas, "The Power of Infographics," p. 11.

31. Dominic Turnbull, "EPRA Real Economy Infographic," downloaded June 25, 2017 (www.epra.com/media/Real_estate_in_the_real_economy_-_EPRA_INREV_report_1353577808132.PDF).

32. A 2015 study by Microsoft documented a significant decrease in attention span, from 12 seconds in 2000, to 8 seconds in 2015.

It notes that "digital lifestyles deplete the ability to remain focused on a single task, particularly in non-digital environments." Alison Gausby, "Attention Spans," Microsoft Canada, Spring 2015, downloaded June 25, 2017 (microsoft-attention-spans-research-report .pdf).

33. Smiciklas, "The Power of Infographics," p. 11.

34. Jason Lankow, Josh Ritchie, and Ross Crooks, *Infographics: The Power of Visual Storytelling* (Hoboken, NJ: Wiley, 2012).

35. Jeffrey Heer, Michael Bostock, and Vadim Ogievetsky, "A Tour through the Visualization Zoo," *Communications of the ACM* 53, no. 6 (June 2010), pp. 59–67.

36. Malcolm Gladwell, *Outliers: The Story of Success* (New York: Little, Brown and Company, 2008).

*Exhibit 16–7 is adapted from Thomas Leech, *How to Prepare, Stage, and Deliver Winning Presentations* (New York: AMACOM, 2004), pp. 98–102; and "Supporting a Speech," Maui Community College, Speech Department, downloaded January, 2010 (http://www .hawaii.edu/mauispeech/html/suporting_materials.html).

References for Snapshots, PicProfiles, Captions, and Pull Quotes
Forester Research: Story Line

1. Mark Bunger, senior analyst, Forrester Research, interviewed January 22, 2004.

2. "Making Auto Retail Lean," TechStrategy report, Forrester Research, downloaded January 5, 2004 (http://www.forrester.com /ER/Research/Report/Summary/0,1338,32782,00.html).

Pixar

1. The lessons were developed using the insights provided by Emma Coats in her, "Pixars 22 Rules to Phenonomenal Storytelling," Slideshare, downloaded May 28, 2016 (http://www.slideshare.net/ powerfulpoint/pixar-22rulestophenomenalstorytellingpowerful-pointslideshare/24). The applications are the contribution of the author.

2. "About," Pixar, downloaded May 28, 2016 (http://www.pixar.com /about).

Pull quote

1. David McCandless, "The Beauty of Data Visualization," TED, November 23, 2012, downloaded June 25, 2017 (https://www.ted .com/talks/david_mccandless_the_beauty_of_data_visualization).

Schlesinger Associates: The Wall

1. "Announcing The Wall," Schlesinger Associates, April 25, 2016, downloaded May 18, 2016 (http://www.schlesingerassociates.com /whats_new/announcing_the_wall.aspx).

2. "Prysm Visual Workplace," Prysm, downloaded May 18, 2016 (http://www.prysm.com/).

3. Rob Ramirez, Executive Vice President, Strategic Development for Schlesinger Associates, phone interview, May 18, 2016, and email interview June 3, 2016.

4. "Wall Locations and Specs," Schlesinger Associates, downloaded May 18, 2016 (http://www.schlesingerassociates.com/qualitative _solutions/interactive_wall/wall_locations__spec.aspx).

Sisense Infographic

1. Shelby Blitz, "Infographic: Top 5 BI Trends you need to know right now," SISENSE.com, May 3, 2017, downloaded May 24, 2017 (https://www.sisense.com/blog/infographic-top-5-bi-trends -you-need-to-know-right-now/). Used with permission.

Appendix: Better Reports

1. This appendix was developed using some of the principles presented by Stephen Kosslyn, *Clear and to the Point: 8 Principles for Compelling PowerPoint Presentations* (New York: Oxford Press, 2007), pp. 3–12.

2. Carmine Gallo, *The Presentation Secrets of Steve Jobs: How to Be Insanely Great in Front of Any Audience* (New York: McGraw-Hill, 2010), p. 202.

3. This exhibit was created using the following sources: "Facts and Figures about the Olympic Park," accessed July 28, 2012 (http:// getset.london2012. com/en/the-games/about-london-2012/the -olympic-park/facts-and-figures-about-the-olympic-park); "How Many Countries Are Involved in the 2012 Olympics?" accessed July 28, 2012 (http://wiki.answers.com/Q/How_many_countries _are_involved_in_the_2012_Olympics); "London 2012 Olympic Athletes: The Full List," *The Guardian Datablog*, accessed July 28, 2012 (http://www.guardian.co.uk/sport/datablog/2012/jul/27 /london-olympic-athletes-full-list#data); and NBC news coverage of the Michael Phelps swimming events, August 4, 2012.

4. Max Mallet, Brett Nelson and Chris Steiner, "The Most Annoying, Pretentious and Useless Business Jargon," *Forbes*, January 26, 2012, accessed July 28, 2012 (http://www.forbes.com/sites /groupthink/2012/01/26/the-most-annoying-pretentious-and -useless-business-jargon/). Also visit BuzzWhack.com.

5. A. Mehrabian, *Silent Messages* (Belmont, CA: Wadsworth, 1971).

6. Mark L. Hickson, Don W. Stacks, and Nina-Jo Moore, *Nonverbal Communication: Studies and Applications*, 4th ed. (Boston, MA: Roxbury Publishing, 2004); and "Six Ways to Improve Your Nonverbal Communications," downloaded December 16, 2009 (http://wimvdd. blogspot.com/2006/12/six-ways-to-improve-your -nonverbal.html).

7. Andrew Dlugen, "Why Practice? Does Practice Make Perfect?" downloaded January 8, 2010 (http://sixminutes.dlugan.com /speech-preparation-8-practice-presentation/).

8. Blair Tindall, "Better Playing through Chemistry," *The New York Times,* October 17, 2004, downloaded January 8, 2010 (http:// www.nytimes. com/2004/10/17/arts/music/17tind.html?_r51 &ex51270785600& en537bef79604f97228&ei55090&partner5rs suserland).

9. J. J. Barrell, D. Medeiros, J. E. Barrell, and D. Price, "The Causes and Treatment of Performance Anxiety: An Experimental Approach," *Journal of Humanistic Psychology* 25, no. 2 (1985), pp. 106–122.

10. Ibid.

11. Nancy Duarte, *slide:ology: The Art and Science of Creating Great Presentations,* (Sebastopol, CA: O'Reilly Media, 2008).

12. Gallo, *The Presentation Secrets of Steve Jobs: How to Be Insanely Great in Front of Any Audience*, p. 83.

13. Diane Shand, Hina Shoeb, Flavia Bedran, Sophie Lin, Barbara Castellano, Bea Chiem, Peter DeLuca, Chris Johnson, Jerry Phelan, and Maxime Puget, "Industry Top Trends 2017," *S&P Global*, February 14, 2017, downloaded June 27, 2017 (https:// www.spratings.com/documents/20184/1481001/2017+ITT +Consumer+Products/aeba21e5-abb0-44ae-b7aa-6800bfbc9abb).

Chapter 17

1. *An Integrated Example* is a fictional account based on research conducted by Cooper Research Group for a manufacturer of laptop computers. The account has been modified to reflect current

research industry practices, as well as the teaching pedagogy of this text.

Pullquote

1. Frank Gehry. BrainyQuote.com, Xplore Inc, 2017, accessed August 1, 2017 (https://www.brainyquote.com/quotes/quotes/f /frankgehry412410.html).

Appendix A: Business Research Proposals and RFPs (with Sample RFP)

1. R. Lesikar and John Pettit, *Report Writing for Business*, 9th ed. (Burr Ridge, IL: Irwin, 1995).

2. Ibid., p. 51.

3. Charles T. Brusaw, Gerald J. Alred, and Walter E. Oliu, *Handbook of Technical Writing*, 4th ed. (New York: St. Martin's Press, 1992), p. 11.

4. Phillip V. Lewis and William H. Baker, *Business Report Writing* (Columbus, OH: Grid, 1978), p. 58.

5. Robert G. Murdick and Donald R. Cooper, *Business Research: Concepts and Guides* (Columbus, OH: Grid, 1982), p. 112.

6. William J. Roetzheim, *Proposal Writing for the Data Processing Consultant* (Englewood Cliffs, NJ: Prentice Hall, 1986), pp. 67–68.

7. Many texts cover project management and include details of scheduling and charting techniques such as Gantt charts and CPM charts, which are beyond the scope of this text. See for example, Don T. Philips, A. Ravindran, and James J. Solberg, *Operations Research: Principles and Practice* (New York: Wiley, 1976), Chap. 3; or K. Roscoe Davis and Patrick G. McKeon, *Quantitative Models of Management* (Boston: Kent, 1981), Chap. 6.

8. See, for example, Kate Turabian, *A Manual for Writers of Term Papers, Theses, and Dissertations* (Chicago: University of Chicago Press, 1996); Joseph Gibaldi, *MLA Handbook for Writers of Research Papers* (New York: Modern Language Association of America, 2003); and *Publication Manual of the American Psychological Association* (Washington, DC: APA, 2001).

9. The Covering Kids RFP was developed by Elaine Arkin, consultant to the Robert Wood Johnson Foundation (interviewed October 4, 2002) and Stuart Schear, senior communication officer, Robert Wood Johnson Foundation (interviewed July 23, 2002). The research contract was won by Wirthlin Worldwide; Maury Giles was the senior researcher (interviewed multiple times during 2002, 2003). This document is reprinted with permission.

3-D graphic a presentation technique that permits a graphical comparison of three or more variables; types include column, ribbon, wireframe, and surface line.

***a priori* contrasts** a special class of tests used in conjunction with the *F* test that is specifically designed to test the hypotheses of the experiment or study (in comparison to post hoc or unplanned tests).

acquiescence bias a tendency for participants to agree with an item or statement within a measurement question that asks for levels of agreement/disagreement; occurs when they have less knowledge on a topic; more a problem for less educated or less informed participants.

action research a methodology with brainstorming followed by sequential trial-and-error to discover the most effective solution to a problem; succeeding solutions are tried until the desired results are achieved; used with complex problems about which little is known.

actionable insights insights aligned with key business goals and strategic initiatives that are novel, unusual, or unexpected and that lead to recommendations for specific decisions.

administrative question a measurement question that identifies the participant, interviewer, interview location, and conditions; generates nominal data.

after-only design preexperimental design that takes one measurement of DV after manipulation of the IV.

alternative hypothesis (H_A) an assumption that a difference exists between the sample parameter and the population statistic to which it is compared; the logical opposite of the null hypothesis used in significance testing.

ambiguities and paradoxes a projective technique (imagination exercise) in which participants imagine a brand applied to a different product (e.g., a Tide dog food or Marlboro cereal), and then describe its attributes and position.

analogy a rhetorical device that compares two different things to highlight a point of similarity.

analysis of variance (ANOVA) tests the null hypothesis that the means of several independent populations are equal; test statistic is the *F* ratio; used when you need *k*-independent-samples tests.

anchoring bias an audience's tendency to rely on its first impressions.

area graph a graphical presentation that displays total frequency, group frequency, and time series data; a.k.a. *stratum chart* or *surface chart*.

area sampling a cluster sampling technique applied to a population with well-defined political or natural boundaries; population is divided into homogeneous clusters from which a single-stage or multistage sample is drawn.

artifact correlations occur when distinct subgroups in the data combine to give the impression of one.

assimilation effect question order that encourages more similarity in responses between the first and the second question.

asymmetrical relationship a relationship in which we postulate that change in one variable (IV) is responsible for change in another variable (DV).

attitude a learned, stable predisposition to respond to oneself, other persons, objects, or issues in a consistently favorable or unfavorable way.

attitude scaling process of assessing a person's disposition (from extremely favorable disposition to an extremely unfavorable one) toward an *object* or its *properties* using a number that represents a person's score on an attitudinal continuum range.

audience analysis an analysis of the expected audience for a research report.

audience-centric planning a research report orientation whose focus is on gaining the audience's embrace of data insights and recommendations; the resulting presentation is persuasive and tells a story employing statistics.

auditory learners audience members who learn through listening; represent about 20 to 30 percent of the audience; implies the need to include stories and examples in research presentations.

authority figure a projective technique (imagination exercise) in which participants are asked to imagine that the brand or product is an authority figure and to describe the attributes of the figure.

automatic interaction detection (AID) a data partitioning procedure that searches up to 300 variables for the single best predictor of a dependent variable.

balanced rating scale has an equal number of categories above and below the midpoint or an equal number of favorable/unfavorable response choices.

bar graph a graphical presentation technique that represents frequency data as horizontal or vertical bars; vertical bars are most often used for time series and quantitative classifications (histograms, stacked bar, and multiple-variable charts are specialized bar charts).

Bayesian statistics uses subjective probability estimates based on general experience rather than on data collected. (See "Decision Theory Problem" at the Online Learning Center.)

behavior cycle how much time is required for a behavior and between behavior events; used with behavior frequency in developing behavior-based measurement questions.

behavior frequency how often a participant executes a particular behavior; used with behavior cycle in developing behavior-based measurement questions.

behavior time frame a factor needed for every behavior measurement question; an appropriate length is determined by a participant's behavior cycle and behavior frequency.

bibliography (bibliographic database) a secondary source that helps locate a book, article, photograph, etc.

bivariate correlation analysis a statistical technique to assess the relationship of two continuous variables measured on an interval or ratio scale.

bivariate normal distribution data are from a random sample in which two variables are normally distributed in a joint manner.

blind when participants do not know if they are being exposed to the experimental treatment.

boxplot an EDA technique; a visual image of the variable's distribution location, spread, shape, tail length, and outliers; a.k.a. *box-and-whisker plot.*

branched question a measurement question sequence determined by the participant's previous answer(s); the answer to one question assumes other questions have been asked or answered and directs the participant to answer specific questions that follow and skip other questions; branched questions determine question sequencing.

brand mapping a projective technique (type of semantic mapping) where participants are presented with different brands and asked to talk about their perceptions, usually in relation to several criteria. They may also be asked to spatially place each brand on one or more semantic maps.

buffer question a neutral measurement question designed chiefly to establish rapport with the participant (usually nominal data).

business research a *systematic inquiry* that provides information to guide a specified managerial decision; it is a set of processes that include planning, acquiring, analyzing, and reporting relevant data, information, and insights to decision makers in ways that mobilize the organization to take appropriate actions

cartoons or empty balloons a projective technique in which participants are asked to write the dialog for a cartoonlike picture.

case a unit of the target population; possesses the information for one or more variables to be measured; the entity or thing the hypothesis talks about.

case study (case history) a methodology that combines individual and (sometimes) group interviews with record analysis and observation; used to understand events and their ramifications and processes; emphasizes the full contextual analysis of a few events or conditions and their interrelations for a single participant; a type of preexperimental design (one-shot case study).

categorization for this scale type, participants put themselves or property indicants in groups or categories; also, a process for grouping data for any variable into a limited number of categories.

causal hypothesis a speculation that an IV affects a DV in a specific way.

causal-explanatory study a study that is designed to determine whether one or more variables explain the causes or effects of one or more outcome (dependent) variables.

causal-predictive study a study that is designed to predict with regularity how one or more variables cause or affect one or more outcome (dependent) variables to occur.

causation situation where one variable leads to a specified effect on the other variable.

cell in a cross-tabulation, a subgroup of the data created by the value intersection of two (or more) variables; each cell contains the count of cases as well as the percentage of the joint classification.

census a count of all the elements in a target population.

checklist a measurement question that poses numerous alternatives and encourages multiple unordered responses; see *multiple-choice, multiple-response scale.*

chi-square (χ^2) test a test of significance used for nominal and ordinal measurements.

chi-square-based measures tests to detect the strength of the relationship between the variables tested with a chi-square test: phi, Cramer's V, and contingency coefficient C.

classical statistics an objective view of probability in which the hypothesis is rejected, or not, based on the sample data collected.

classification question a measurement question that provides demographic, economic, geographic, and sociological information about a participant; variables used for grouping participants' answers; provides nominal, ordinal, interval, or ratio data, depending on the scale used.

cluster sampling a sampling plan that involves dividing the population into subgroups and then draws a sample from each subgroup, a single-stage or multistage design.

coding scheme contains each variable in the study and specifies the application of *mapping rules* to the response codes of each variable.

coefficient of determination (r_2) the amount of common variance in X and Y, two variables in regression; the ratio of the line of best fit's error over that incurred by using the mean value of Y.

collage technique in which participants are asked to collect images (e.g., from personal photos, magazines, or the Internet) and use these to express their feelings on a topic or the feelings of others like them.

communication approach a study approach involving questioning or surveying people (by personal interview, telephone, mail, computer, or some combination of these) and recording their responses for analysis.

communication study the researcher questions the participants and collects their responses by personal or impersonal means.

comparative scale a scale in which the participant evaluates an object against a standard using a numerical, graphical, or verbal scale.

completion estimate the time estimate for a survey participant to complete the measurement instrument; usually determined during a pretest of the instrument.

completion/fill in the blank a projective technique in which participants are asked to complete a sentence related to a particular brand, product, event, user group, etc.

component sorts a projective technique in which participants are presented with flash cards containing component features and asked to create new combinations.

computer-administered telephone survey (CATS) a telephone survey via voice-synthesized computer questions; data are tallied continuously.

computer-assisted personal interview (CAPI) a personal, face-to-face interview (IDI) with computer-sequenced questions, employing visualization techniques where the interviewer has the ability to share their screen during the interview; real-time data entry possible.

computer-assisted self-interview (CASI) computer-delivered survey that is self-administered by the participant.

computer-assisted telephone interview (CATI) a telephone interview with computer-sequenced questions and real-time data entry; usually in a central location with interviewers in acoustically isolated interviewing carrels; data are tallied continuously.

concealment a technique in an observation study in which the observer is shielded from the participant to avoid error caused by observer's presence; this is accomplished by one-way mirrors, hidden cameras, hidden microphones, etc.

concept a bundle of meanings or characteristics associated with certain concrete, unambiguous events, objects, conditions, or situations.

conceptual scheme the interrelationships between concepts and constructs.

concordant pair when a participant that ranks higher on one ordinal variable also ranks higher on another variable, the pairs of variables are concordant.

confirmation bias an audience's tendency to seek information in a report that confirms what they already believe.

confirmatory data analysis (CFA) an analytical process guided by classical statistical inference in its use of significance and confidence.

conformity bias an audience's tendency to rely on groupthink, to not express or embrace conflicting ideas in order to maintain group harmony.

confounding variable (CFV) two or more variables that are confounded when their effects on a response variable cannot be distinguished from each other.

constant-sum scale the participant allocates points to more than one attribute or property indicant, such that they total to 100 or 10; a.k.a. *fixed-sum scale*.

construct an abstract idea specifically invented for a given research and/or theory-building purpose.

construct validity see **validity, construct**.

content analysis a systematic, objective approach used to code message characteristics so researchers can treat diverse textual or verbal content quantitatively as they look for patterns and draw inferences.

context units One of three types of data units in context analysis; refers to the content that directly relates to the objective of the research.

content validity see **validity, content**.

contingency coefficient C a measure of association for nominal, nonparametric variables; used with any size chi-square table, the upper limit varies with table sizes; does not provide direction of the association or reflect causation.

contingency table a cross-tabulation table constructed for statistical testing, with the test determining whether the classification variables are independent.

contrast effect the question order that encourages a greater difference in responses between the first and second question.

control the ability to replicate a scenario and dictate a particular outcome; the ability to exclude, isolate, or manipulate the influence of a variable in a study; a critical factor in inference from an experiment, implies that all factors, with the exception of the independent variable (IV), must be held constant and not confounded with another variable that is not part of the study.

control group a group of participants that is not exposed to the independent variable being studied but still generates a measure for the dependent variable.

control variable (CV) a variable introduced to help interpret the relationship between variables.

convenience sample nonprobability sample in which element selection is based on ease of accessibility.

convergent interviewing an IDI technique for interviewing a limited number of experts as participants in a sequential series of IDIs; after each successive interview, the researcher refines the questions, hoping to converge on the central issues in a topic area; sometimes called convergent and divergent interviewing.

correlational hypothesis a statement indicating that variables occur together in some specified manner without implying that one causes the other.

Cramer's V a measure of association for nominal, nonparametric variables; used with larger than 2×2 chi-square tables; does not provide direction of the association or reflect causation; ranges from zero to +1.0.

creative innovation role-play a qualitative exercise in which participants assume an innovation position (e.g., scientist), then create something (e.g., new product, package), and then explain it.

criterion-related validity see **validity, criterion-related**.

critical incident technique an IDI technique involving sequentially asked questions to reveal, in narrative form, what led up to an incident being studied; exactly what the observed party did or did not do that was especially effective or ineffective; the outcome or result of this action; and why this action was effective or what more effective action might have been expected.

critical value the dividing point(s) between the region of acceptance and the region of rejection; these values can be computed in terms of the standardized random variable due to the normal distribution of sample means.

cross-sectional study the study is conducted only once and reveals a snapshot of one point in time.

cross-tabulation technique for comparing data from two or more variables that results in a table.

cultural interview an IDI technique that asks a participant to relate his or her experiences with a culture or subculture, including the knowledge passed on by prior generations and the knowledge participants have or plan to pass on to future generations.

cumulative scale a scale development technique in which scale items are tested based on a scoring system, and agreement with one extreme scale item results also in endorsement of all other items that take a less extreme position.

custom-designed measurement questions measurement questions formulated specifically for a particular research project.

dashboard a data visualization tool that showcases current, as well as a period of prior, performance on each KPI metric; usually on one digital screen.

data raw, unprocessed facts in the form of numbers, text, pictures or video collected by either quantitative or qualitative means.

data analysis the process of editing and reducing accumulated data to a manageable size, developing summaries, looking for patterns, and applying statistical techniques.

data blending a process for combining data from separate data files and querying that composite data file to help make decisions.

data clarity visuals that meet the highest standard for providing an accurate visual impression of data and information, as well as being easily understood.

data collection the collective actions that field a measurement instrument.

data collection design the blueprint for collecting data; involves how, when, how often, and where data will be collected.

data entry the process of converting information gathered by secondary or primary methods to a medium for viewing and manipulation; usually done by keyboarding or optical scanning.

data field a single element of data from all participants in a study.

data file a set of data records (all responses from all participants in a study).

data missing at random (MAR) data from a participant that are not available for analysis for one or more variables of interest; a type of missing data characterized by a high probability that missing data for a particular variable are NOT dependent on the variable itself but ARE dependent on another variable in the data record.

data missing but not missing at random (NMAR) a type of missing data characterized by a high probability that missing data for a particular variable ARE dependent on the variable itself and ARE NOT dependent on other variables in the data record.

data missing completely at random (MCAR) a type of missing data characterized by a high probability that missing data for a particular variable are NOT dependent on the variable itself and are NOT dependent on another variable in the data record.

data preparation the processes that ensure the accuracy of data and their conversion from raw form into categories appropriate for analysis; includes postcollection coding of data and editing data.

data record a set of data fields from one case (all a participant's responses to all measurement questions).

data saturation the point at which no new information is forthcoming and no new insights seem feasible.

data validation a process that attempts to verify that research protocols that avoid data errors were followed and that data are real, by identifying fake or inaccurate data.

data warehouse electronic storehouse where vast arrays of collected integrated data are stored by categories to facilitate retrieval, interpretation, and sorting by data-mining techniques.

database a collection of data organized for computerized retrieval; defines data fields, data records, and data files.

data-centric planning a research report orientation whose focus is on delivering as much data and insights as was discovered; the resulting presentation is factual and statistical.

debriefing explanation, after the research, that the participant has been part of a research study; done to alleviate any possible harmful effects; may reveal the purpose of the study.

deception occurs when participants are told only part of the truth or the truth is fully compromised to prevent biasing participants or to protect sponsor confidentiality.

decision rule the criterion for judging the attractiveness of two or more alternatives when using a decision variable.

decision variable a quantifiable characteristic, attribute, or outcome on which a choice decision will be made.

deduction a form of reasoning in which the conclusion must necessarily follow from the reasons given; a deduction is valid if it is impossible for the conclusion to be false if the premises are true.

demonstration presentation support technique using a visual presentation aid to show how something works.

dependent variable (DV) the variable measured, predicted, or otherwise monitored by the researcher; expected to be affected by a manipulation of the independent variable; a.k.a. *criterion variable*.

descriptive hypothesis states the existence, size, form, or distribution of some variable.

descriptive study attempts to describe or define a subject, often by creating a profile of a group of problems, people, or events, through the collection of data and the tabulation of the frequencies on research variables or their interaction; the study reveals who, what, when, where, or how much; the study concerns a univariate question or hypothesis in which the research asks about or states something about the size, form, distribution, or existence of a variable.

desired audience effect what a researcher wants an audience to think, feel, and do as a result of the research report.

dichotomous question a measurement question built on a simple category scale; offers two mutually exclusive and exhaustive alternatives (nominal data);

dictionary secondary source that defines words, terms, or jargon unique to a discipline; may include information on people, events, or organizations that shape the discipline; an excellent source of acronyms.

direct observation occurs when the observer is physically present and personally monitors and records the behavior of the participant.

directory a reference source used to identify contact information (e.g., name, address, phone); many are free, but the most comprehensive are proprietary.

discordant pair when a subject that ranks higher on one ordinal variable ranks lower on another variable, the pairs of variables are discordant; as discordant pairs increase over concordant pairs, the association becomes negative.

discussion guide the list of topics to be discussed in an unstructured interview (e.g., focus group); a.k.a. *interview guide.*

disguised question a measurement question designed to conceal the question's and study's true purpose.

disposition-behavior a type of asymmetrical causal relationship where a disposition causes a specific behavior; e.g., attitude about a brand causes its purchase or rejection.

"don't know" (DK) response a response given when a participant has insufficient knowledge, direction, or willingness to answer a question; multiple reasons exist for DK responses.

double blind study design in which neither the researcher nor the participant knows when a subject is being exposed to the experimental treatment.

double sampling a procedure for selecting a subsample from a sample; a.k.a. *sequential sampling or multiphase sampling.*

double-barreled question a measurement question that includes two or more questions in one that the participant might need to answer differently; a question that requests so much content that it would be better if separate questions were asked.

"dummy" table displays data one expects to secure during data analysis; each dummy table is a cross-tabulation between two or more variables.

editing a process for verifying that variables have used the designated coding scheme and that all data collected is entered correctly; detects errors and omissions and corrects them when possible; certifies that minimum data standards are met.

encyclopedia a secondary source that provides background or historical information on a topic, including names or terms that can enhance your search results in other sources.

environmental control holding constant the physical environment of the experiment.

equivalence when an instrument secures consistent results with repeated measures by the same investigator or different samples.

error discrepancy between the sample value and the true population value that occurs when the participant fails to answer fully and accurately—either by choice or because of inaccurate or incomplete knowledge.

error of central tendency participant's tendency to choose the middle option; especially when they don't have a strong opinion on the issue or perceive that the correct answer among alternatives is likely to be placed in the middle position.

error of leniency when a participant ratings are consistently overly positive; see **leniency (error of)**.

error of strictness when a participant's ratings are consistently overly negative.

error term the deviations of the actual values of Y from the regression line (representing the mean value of Y for a particular value of X).

ethnography interviewer and participant collaborate in a fieldsetting participant observation and unstructured interview; typically takes place where the behavior being observed occurs (e.g., participant's home).

ethos how well the audience believes that the presenter is qualified to speak on the particular subject; determined by the perception of a presenter's character, his or her past experience, or the credibility and experience of those the presenter evokes.

event sampling the researcher records that a specific behavior or act occurs; the duration of the observation is determined by when the act begins and ends; may record the events antecedents and consequences.

ex post facto design after-the-fact report on what happened to the measured variable.

executive summary this document is written as the last element of a research report and either is a concise summary of the major findings, conclusions, and recommendations or is a report in miniature, covering all aspects in abbreviated form.

experiment (experimental study) study involving intervention (manipulation of one or more variables) by the researcher beyond that required for measurement to determine the effect on another variable.

experimental mortality a threat to the internal validity of an experiment caused by changes in the composition of the experimental group(s) during the experiment; usually caused by participants or subjects dropping out of the experimental group(s).

experimental treatment the manipulated independent variable.

expert group interview group interview consisting of individuals exceptionally knowledgeable about the issues or topics to be discussed.

expert interview a discussion with someone knowledgeable about the problem or its possible solutions.

exploration the process of collecting information to formulate or refine management, research, investigative, or measurement questions; loosely structured studies that discover future research tasks, including developing concepts, establishing priorities, developing operational definitions, and improving research design; a phase of a research project where the researcher expands understanding of the management dilemma, looks for ways others have addressed and/or solved problems similar to the management dilemma or management question, and gathers background information on the topic to refine the research question; a.k.a. *exploratory study* or *exploratory research*.

exploration strategy a process that defines what exploratory information sources will be used and what methods will be used to extract information from those sources.

exploratory data analysis (EDA) a process that explores—and reduces—the data using descriptive statistics and some graphical displays of data; patterns in the collected data guide the data analysis or suggest revisions to the preliminary data analysis plan.

exploratory research see **exploration**.

external validity occurs when an observed causal relationship can be generalized across persons, settings, and times.

extralinguistic behavior the vocal, temporal, interactive, and verbal stylistic behaviors of human participants.

extraneous variable (EV) variable to assume (because it has little effect or its impact is randomized) or exclude from a research study.

F **ratio** *F* test statistic comparing measurements of k independent samples.

fact a piece of information about a situation that exists or an event known to have occurred; it takes the form of a statement about verifiable data that support the presenter's argument.

field conditions measurement that occurs under the actual environmental conditions in which the dependent variable occurs.

field experiment a study of the dependent variable in actual environmental conditions.

filter question a question that determines whether a participant is asked one or more questions within a target question topic or excluded from answering; often leads to a branch question.

findings key patterns discovered by summarizing, reducing, and cross-tabulating data.

findings nondisclosure a type of confidentiality; the sponsor restricts the researcher from discussing the findings of the research project.

five-number summary the median, the upper and lower quartiles, and the largest and smallest observations of a variable's distribution.

focus group the simultaneous involvement of a small number of research participants (usually 8 to 10) who interact at the direction of a moderator in order to generate data on a particular issue or topic; widely used in exploratory studies; usually lasts 90 minutes to two hours; can be conducted in person or via phone or videoconference.

forced ranking scale a scale in which the participant orders several objects or properties of objects; faster than paired comparison to obtain a rank order.

forced-choice rating scale requires that participants select from available alternatives.

frequency table arrays category codes from lowest value to highest value, with columns for count, percent, valid percent, and cumulative percent.

gamma (γ) uses a preponderance of evidence of concordant pairs versus discordant pairs to predict association; the gamma value is the proportional reduction of error when prediction is done using preponderance of evidence (values from -1.0 to $+1.0$).

geograph uses a map to show regional variations in data.

goodness of fit a measure of how well the regression model is able to predict Y.

graph a diagram showing the relationship of various values from a single variable or between two or more variables.

graphic rating scale a scale in which the participant places his or her response along a line or continuum; the score or measurement is its distance in millimeters from either endpoint.

grounded theory an IDI technique in which analysis of the data takes place simultaneously with its collection, with the purpose of developing general concepts or theories with which to analyze the data.

group interview a data collection method using a single interviewer who simultaneously interviews more than one research participant.

group time series design quasi-experimental design using a multiple measurements of the DV, both before and after manipulation of the IV; the difference between the post-treatment measures is compared to determine effect, while differences between the pre-treatment measures reveals the possibility of any trend; can also use nonequivalent group design with multiple measures.

halo effect cognitive bias that influences the observer's impression of the person, object, event or act he or she is observing.

handbook a secondary source used to identify key terms, people, or events relevant to the management dilemma or management question.

heterogeneous group participant group consisting of individuals with a variety of opinions, backgrounds, and actions relative to a topic.

histogram a graphical bar chart that groups continuous data values into equal intervals with one bar for each interval; especially useful for revealing skewness, kurtosis, and modal pattern.

history a threat to internal validity of an experiment caused by the effect of intervening events on the subject or participant.

homogeneous group participant group consisting of individuals with similar opinions, backgrounds, and actions relative to a topic.

hypothesis unsubstantiated assumption about the relationship between concepts and constructs; it drives the research; a tentative descriptive statement that describes the relationship between two or more variables; formulated for significance testing.

hypothesis testing a process for proving that a hypothesis is valid, that a hypothesis about the relationship between two concepts/constructs/variables is true.

hypothetical construct construct inferred only from data; its presumption must be tested.

imaginary universe a projective technique (imagination exercise) in which participants are asked to assume that the brand and its users populate an entire universe; they then describe the features of this new world.

imagination exercises a projective technique in which participants are asked to relate the properties of one thing/person/brand to another.

independent variable (IV) the variable manipulated by the researcher, thereby causing an effect or change on the dependent variable.

index secondary data source that helps identify and locate a single book, journal article, author, etc., from among a large set.

indirect observation occurs when the recording of data is done by mechanical, photographic, or electronic means.

individual depth interview (IDI) a type of interview that encourages the participant to talk extensively, sharing as much information as possible; usually lasts one or more hours; three types: structured, semistructured, and unstructured. The structured IDI is used within survey via personal interview research design; semistructured and unstructured formats are used most in qualitative research.

induction (inductive reasoning) to draw a conclusion from one or more particular facts or pieces of evidence; the conclusion explains the facts.

inferential statistics includes the estimation of population values and the testing of statistical hypotheses.

infographic a visual display of the most important information needed to achieve one or more objectives, consolidated in a single digital image file; not linked to its data.

information processed data; created by aggregating and organizing data, applying rules of measurement, statistical summary and testing, and developing data visualizations.

informed consent participant gives full consent to participation after receiving full disclosure of the procedures of the proposed survey.

insights conclusions generated by *analyzing* information; formed by induction or deduction; uses all data—primary and secondary—collected during the projects, as well as an understanding of the organization.

instrument coverage one measure of a measurement instrument's completeness; measured by the number and breadth of questions within a target question's topic.

instrument disposition the procedure(s) by which the completed instrument is returned to the researcher.

instrument scope one measure of a measurement instrument's completeness; measured by the number and breadth of target question topics.

instrumentation a threat to the internal validity of an experiment caused by changes in the measurement instrument or observer during the experiment.

intercept (β_0) one of two regression coefficients; the value for the linear function when it crosses the Y axis or the estimate of Y when X is zero.

intercept interview a face-to-face communication that targets participants in a centralized location.

internal consistency characteristic of an instrument in which the items are homogeneous; measure of reliability.

internal validity the ability of a research instrument to measure what it is purported to measure; occurs when the conclusion(s) drawn about a demonstrated experimental relationship truly implies cause.

interquartile range (IQR) measures the distance between the first and third quartiles of a data distribution; a.k.a. *midspread*; the distance between the hinges in a boxplot.

inter-rater reliability a measure of the consistency of the application of a coding scheme by a single rater of content, across texts.

interval data data reveal classification, order, equal distance, but no natural origin.

interval scale scale with the properties of order and equal distance between points and with mutually exclusive and exhaustive categories; data that incorporate equality of interval (the distance between one measure and the next measure); e.g., temperature scale.

intervening variable (IVV) a factor that affects the observed phenomenon but cannot be seen, measured, or manipulated; thus its effect must be inferred from the effects of the independent and moderating variables on the dependent variable.

interview phone, in-person, or videoconference communication approach to collecting data.

interview guide see **discussion guide**.

interviewer error error that results from interviewer influence of the participant; includes problems with motivation, instructions, voice inflections, body language, question or response order, or cheating via falsification of one or more responses.

intra-rater reliability a measure of the consistency of the application of a coding scheme between raters of context, across texts, when multiple raters are used.

investigative questions questions the researcher must answer to satisfactorily answer the research question; what the manager feels he or she needs to know to arrive at a conclusion about the management dilemma.

jargon language unique to a profession or discipline; when unknown by the audience can reduce the clarity of the message.

judgment sampling a purposive sampling in which the researcher arbitrarily selects sample units to conform to some criterion.

key performance indicatiors (KPIs) metrics used to track current performance against prior performance and industry standards.

k-**independent-samples tests** significance tests in which measurements are taken from three or more samples (ANOVA for interval or ratio measures, Kruskal-Wallis for ordinal measures, chi-square for nominal measures).

kinesthetic learners people who learn by doing, moving, and touching.

k-**related-samples tests** compares measurements from more than two groups from the same sample or more than two measures from the same subject or participant (ANOVA for interval or ratio measures, Friedman for ordinal measures, Cochran Q for nominal measures).

laboratory conditions research where measurement occurs under staged or manipulated conditions.

laddering (benefit chain) a projective technique in which participants are asked to link functional features to their physical and psychological benefits, both real and ideal.

lambda (λ) a measure of how well the frequencies of one nominal variable predict the frequencies of another variable; values (vary between zero and 1.0) show the direction of the association.

language level determined by vocabulary and sentence structure.

leading question a measurement question whose wording suggests to the participant the desired answer (nominal, ordinal, interval, or ratio data).

level of significance the probability of rejecting a true null hypothesis.

life history an IDI technique that extracts from a single participant memories and experiences from childhood to the present day regarding a product or service category, brand, or firm.

Likert scale a variation of the summated rating scale, this scale asks a rater to agree or disagree with statements that express either favorable or unfavorable attitudes toward the object. The strength of attitude is reflected in the assigned score, and individual scores may be totaled for an overall attitude measure.

limitations significant methodology problems that affected data findings and how each has been handled.

line graph a statistical presentation technique used for time series and frequency distributions over time.

linearity an assumption of correlation analysis that the collection of data can be described by a straight line passing through the data array.

linguistic behavior the human verbal behavior during conversation, presentation, or interaction.

listwise deletion A type of corrective editing for missing data; any case with missing data on one variable is deleted from the sample for all analyses of that variable.

literature search a review of books, articles in journals or professional literature, research studies, and web-published materials that relate to the management dilemma, management question, or research question.

logos the logical argument; requires supporting evidence and analytical techniques that reveal and uphold the researcher's findings and conclusions.

longitudinal study the study includes repeated measures over an extended period of time, tracking changes in variables over time; includes panels or cohort groups.

loss-aversion bias an audience's tendency to favor ideas expressed positively rather than negatively.

management dilemma the problem or opportunity that requires a decision; a symptom of a problem or an early indication of an opportunity.

management question the management dilemma restated in question format; categorized as "choice of objectives," "generation and evaluation of solutions," or "troubleshooting or control of a situation."

management report a report written for the nontechnically oriented manager or client.

management–research question hierarchy process of sequential question formulation that leads a manager or researcher from management dilemma to measurement questions.

mapping rules a scheme for assigning numbers to aspects of an empirical event.

marginal(s) a term for the column and row totals in a cross-tabulation.

matching a process analogous to quota sampling for assigning participants to experimental and control groups by having participants match on every descriptive characteristic used in the research; used when random assignment is not possible; an attempt to eliminate the effect of confounding variables so that the confounding variable is present proportionally in each group.

maturation a threat to the internal validity of an experiment caused by changes that may occur within the participant or subject.

mean square the variance computed as an average or mean.

measurement assigning numbers to empirical events in compliance with a mapping rule.

measurement instrument a tool for collecting data on study variables; the primary tool used to extract information from a participant in a structured interview or observation; a sequenced list of measurement questions, using various scale options, complete with an invitation to participate, introduction, section transitions and skip directions, instructions, and conclusion; also called a *questionnaire* or *interview guide*, depending on the methodology in a communication-based study; called an *observation checklist* in observation research.

measurement questions the questions asked of the participants or the observations that must be recorded.

measurement scale the type of measurement question; includes rating (simple, multiple-choice, checklist, Likert, semantic differential, numerical, multiple-item, constant-sum, Stapel, graphical), ranking (paired comparison, forced ranking, comparative scale), sorting, and cumulative.

memory decay loss of detail about an event or prior behavior caused by passage of time or interfering events, such as learning.

metaphor a figure of speech in which an implicit comparison is made between two unlike things that actually have something important in common.

metaphor elicitation technique an individual depth interview that reveals participants' hidden or suppressed attitudes and perceptions by having them explain collected images and each image's relation to the topic being studied.

method of least squares a procedure for finding a regression line that keeps errors (deviations from actual value to the line value) to a minimum.

missing data data from a participant that is not available for analysis for one or more variables of interest; should be discovered and rectified during data preparation phase of analysis; e.g., miscoded data, out-of-range data, or extreme values.

model a representation of a system that is constructed to study some aspect of that system or the system as a whole.

moderating variable (MV) a second independent variable, believed to have a significant contributory or contingent effect on the originally stated IV–DV relationship.

moderator a trained interviewer used for group interviews such as focus groups.

monitoring study a study that inspects the activities of a subject or the nature of some material or activity and records the information from observations; the researcher does not attempt to elicit responses from anyone; includes record analysis.

multidimensional scale a scale that seeks to simultaneously measure more than one attribute of the participant or object.

multiple comparison tests compare group means following the finding of a statistically significant *F* test.

multiple rating list scale a single interval or ordinal numerical scale where raters respond to a series of objects; results facilitate visualization.

multiple-choice question a measurement question that offers more than two category responses but seeks a single answer.

multiple-choice, multiple-response scale a scale that offers the participant multiple options and solicits one or more answers (nominal or ordinal data); a.k.a. *checklist*.

multiple-choice question a measurement question developed using a multiple-choice, single-response scale.

multiple-choice, single-response scale a scale that poses more than two category responses but seeks a single answer, or one that seeks a single rating from a gradation of preference, interest, or agreement (nominal or ordinal data); a.k.a. *multiple-choice question*.

multiple-methodology design research design that employs more than one data collection method; can include both quantitative and qualitative research; often done in two or more stages, covering a longer time frame.

nominal data data that provide classification but no order, equal distance, or natural origin.

nominal scale scale with mutually exclusive and collectively exhaustive categories, but without the properties of order, distance, or unique origin.

noncontact rate the percent of potential contacts not reached.

nonequivalent control group design quasi-experimental design using a control group that takes four measurements of the DV: one for each group before and one for each group after the manipulation of the IV; the difference between the two pretest measures is compared to determine equivalence of the groups, while the difference between the two posttest measures determines the effect.

nonexpert group participants in a group interview who have at least some desired information but at an unknown level.

nonparametric tests significance tests for data derived from nominal and ordinal scales.

nonprobability sampling an arbitrary and subjective procedure in which each population element does not have a known nonzero chance of being included; no attempt is made to generate a statistically representative sample.

nonresistant statistics a statistical measure that is susceptible to the effects of extreme values; e.g., mean and standard deviation.

nonresponse error error that develops when an interviewer cannot locate the person with whom the study requires communication or when the targeted participant refuses to participate; especially troublesome in studies using probability sampling.

nonsampling error error not related to the sample but to all other decisions made in the research design.

nonverbal behavior human behaviors not related to conversation (e.g., body movement, facial expressions, exchanged glances, eyeblinks).

normal probability plot compares the observed values with those expected from a normal distribution.

null hypothesis (H_0) an assumption that no difference exists between the sample parameter and the population statistic.

numerical scale a scale in which equal intervals separate the numeric scale points, while verbal anchors serve as labels for the extreme points.

objects concepts defined by ordinary experience.

observation the full range of monitoring behavioral and nonbehavioral activities and conditions (including record analysis, physical condition analysis, physical process analysis, nonverbal analysis, linguistic analysis, extralinguistic analysis, and spatial analysis).

observation checklist a measurement instrument for recording data in an observation study; analogous to a questionnaire in a communication study.

observed significance level the probability value compared to the significance level (e.g., .05) chosen for testing and on this basis the null hypothesis is either rejected or not rejected.

observer drift gradual alterations over time in observation documentation; a source of decay that affects reliability or validity of the observations over time.

one-group pretest-posttest design preexperimental design that takes two measurements of DV after manipulation of the IV, one measurement before manipulation and one measurement after; the measurements are compared; no control group used.

one-sample tests tests that involve measures taken from a single sample compared to a specified population.

one-tailed test a test of a null hypothesis that assumes the sample parameter is not the same as the population statistic, but that the difference is in only one direction.

operational definition a definition for a variable stated in terms of specific testing criteria or operations, specifying what must be counted, measured, or gathered through our senses.

operationalized the process of transforming concepts and constructs into measurable variables suitable for testing.

option analysis process for choosing between two or more action decisions using decision variables, a decision rule, and estimated costs of alternative research designs.

oral history (narrative) an IDI technique that asks participants to relate their personal experiences and feelings related to historical events or past behavior.

ordinal data data provide classification and order but no equal distance or natural origin.

ordinal measures measures of association between variables generating ordinal data.

ordinal scale scale with mutually exclusive and collectively exhaustive categories, as well as the property of order, but not distance or unique origin; data capable of determining greater-than, equal-to, or less-than status of a property or an object.

outliers data points that exceed, by 1.5 times, the interquartile range (IQR).

p **value** probability of observing a sample value as extreme as, or more extreme than, the value actually observed, given that the null hypothesis is true.

paired-comparison scale the participant chooses a preferred object between several pairs of objects on some property; results in a rank ordering of objects.

pairwise deletion A type of corrective editing for missing data; editing replaces the missing data for a variable with an estimate based on all other cases on that variable.

panel a group of potential participants who have indicated a willingness to participate in research studies; often used for longitudinal communication studies; may be used for both qualitative and quantitative research.

parametric tests significance tests for data from interval and ratio scales.

Pareto diagram a graphical presentation that represents frequency data as a bar chart, ordered from most to least, overlaid with a line graph denoting the cumulative percentage at each variable level.

participant observation when the observer is physically involved in the research situation and interacts with the participant to influence some observation measures.

pathos an appeal to an audience's sense of identity, self-interest, and emotions, which relies on an emotional connection between the presenter and his or her audience.

Pearson correlation coefficient the *r* symbolizes the estimate of strength of linear association and its direction between interval and ratio variables; based on sampling data and varies over a range of +1 to −1; the prefix (+, −) indicates the direction of the relationship (positive or inverse), while the number represents the strength of the relationship (the closer to 1, the stronger the relationship; 0 = no relationship); and the *p* represents the population correlation.

performance anxiety (stage fright) a fear produced by the need to make a presentation in front of an audience or before a camera.

personification a projective technique (imagination exercise) in which participants are asked to imagine inanimate objects with the traits, characteristics and features, and personalities of humans.

phi (φ) a measure of association for nominal, nonparametric variables; ranges from zero to +1.0 and is used best with 2×2 chi-square tables; does not provide direction of the association or reflect causation.

physical condition analysis the recording of observations of current conditions resulting from prior decisions; includes inventory, signs, obstacles or hazards, cleanliness, etc.

physical presence bias a participant's conscious or subconscious response to the interviewer, often based on the interviewer's looks, body language, language, ethnicity, etc.

physical traces a type of observation that collects measures of wear data (erosion) and accretion data (deposit) rather than direct observation (e.g., a study of trash).

pictograph a bar chart using pictorial symbols rather than bars to represent frequency data; the symbol has an association with the subject of the statistical presentation and one symbol unit represents a specific count of that variable.

pie graph uses sections of a circle (slices of a pie) to represent 100 percent of a frequency distribution of the subject being graphed; not appropriate for changes over time.

population parameter a summary descriptor of a variable of interest in the population; e.g., incidence, mean, variance.

population proportion of incidence the number of category elements in the population, divided by the number of elements in the population.

posttest-only control group design a true experimental design using a control group that takes two measurements of the DV, one for each group after the manipulation of the IV; the difference between the two measures is compared to determine effect.

power of the test 1 minus the probability of committing a Type II error (1 minus the probability that we will correctly reject the false null hypothesis).

practical significance when a statistically significant difference has real importance to the decision maker.

practicality a characteristic of sound measurement concerned with a wide range of factors of economy, convenience, and interpretability.

precode assign variable codes to response categories during the instrument design stage; summarized in a coding scheme.

prediction and confidence bands bow-tie-shaped confidence intervals around a predictor; predictors farther from the mean have larger bandwidths in regression analysis.

predictive replacement A type of corrective editing for missing data; editing replaces the missing data for a variable with an estimate predicted from observed value on another variable.

predispositions the audience's attitudes and beliefs—formed by their experiences, knowledge, and values—about a report's research topics.

preliminary analysis plan the procedures the researcher plans for the data he collects; includes statistical summaries, cross-tabulations of variables to search for patterns, hypothesis tests, and measures of association, as well as graphical displays of data.

pretasking a variety of creative and mental exercises to prepare participants for individual or group interviews, such as an IDI or focus group; intended to increase understanding of participants' own thought processes and bring their ideas, opinions, and attitudes to the surface.

pretest the assessment of questions and instruments before the start of a study by surrogate participants or research colleagues; an established practice for discovering errors in questions, question sequencing, instructions, skip directions, etc.

pretest-posttest control group design a true experimental design with a control group that takes four measures of the DV, one pretest measure from the control and experimental groups and one posttest measure from each group following manipulation of the IV; the difference between the pretest measures is compared to the difference between the posttest measure to determine the effect.

primacy effect order bias in which the participant tends to choose the first alternative; a principle affecting presentation organization in which the first item in a list is initially distinguished as important and may be transferred to long-term memory; implies an important argument should be first in your presentation.

primary data data the researcher collects directly to address the specific problem at hand—the research question; raw and unprocessed.

primary sources original works of research or raw data without interpretation or pronouncements that represent an official opinion or position; include memos, letters, complete interviews or speeches, laws, regulations, court decisions, and most government data, including census, economic, and labor data; the most authoritative of all sources.

probability sampling a controlled, randomized procedure that ensures that each population element is given a known nonzero chance of selection; used to draw participants that are representative of a target population; necessary for projecting findings from the sample to the target population.

probe a questioning technique during an IDI where the interviewer asks the participant for clarification by asking prepared follow-up questions; in qualitative research, probes also are used to extract meaning and often follow tangents of a participant's thought by using spontaneous questions.

process (activity) analysis observation by a time study of stages in a process, evaluated on both effectiveness and efficiency; includes traffic flow within distribution centers and retailers, paperwork flow, customer complaint resolution, etc.

projective drawing a qualitative exercise in which participants are asked to draw a concept or create a model and are then asked to explain it.

projective techniques qualitative methods that encourage the participant to reveal hidden or suppressed attitudes, ideas, emotions, and motives; various techniques (e.g., sentence completion tests, cartoon or balloon tests, word association tests) used as part of an interview to disguise the study objective and allow the participant to transfer or project attitudes and behavior on sensitive subjects to third parties; the data collected via these techniques are often difficult to interpret (nominal, ordinal, or ratio data).

properties characteristics of objects that are measured; a person's properties are his or her weight, height, posture, hair color, etc.

property-behavior a type of asymmetrical causal relationship where an existing property causes a specific behavior; e.g., age and sports participation

property-disposition a type of asymmetrical causal relationship where an existing property causes a disposition; e.g., age and attitude about saving.

proportional reduction in error (PRE) measures of association used with contingency tables (a.k.a *cross-tabulations*) to predict frequencies.

Q-sort participant sorts a deck of cards (representing properties or objects) into piles that represent points along a continuum.

qualitative research interpretive techniques that seek to describe, decode, translate, and otherwise come to terms with the meaning, not the frequency, of certain phenomena; a fundamental approach of exploration, including individual depth interviews, group interviews, participant observation, videotaping of participants, projective techniques and psychological testing, case studies, street ethnography, elite interviewing, document analysis, and proxemics and kinesics; see also *content analysis*.

qualitative research nonquantitative data collection used to increase understanding of a topic.

quantitative research the precise count of some behavior, knowledge, opinion, or attitude.

quota matrix a means of visualizing the matching process.

quota sampling purposive sampling in which relevant characteristics are used to stratify the sample.

random assignment a process that uses a randomized sample frame for assigning sample units to test groups in an attempt to ensure that the groups are as comparable as possible with respect to the DV; each subject must have an equal chance for exposure to each level of the independent variable.

random dialing a computerized process that chooses phone exchanges or exchange blocks and generates numbers within these blocks for telephone surveys.

ranking question a measurement question that asks the participant to compare and order two or more objects or properties using a numeric scale; built on one of several types of ranking scales.

ranking scale a scale that scores an object or property by making a comparison and determining order among two or more objects or properties; uses a numeric scale and provides ordinal data; see also *ranking question*.

rapport a relationship characterized by agreement, mutual understanding, or empathy that makes communication possible or easy.

rating question a question that asks the participant to position each property or object on a verbal, numeric, or graphic continuum.

rating scale a scale that scores an object or property without making a direct comparison to another object or property; either verbal, numeric, or graphic; see also *rating question*.

ratio data data offer classification, order, equal distance, and natural origin.

ratio scale a scale with the properties of categorization, order, equal intervals, and unique origin; numbers used as measurements have numeric value; e.g., weight of an object.

reactivity response the phenomenon that occurs when participants alter their behavior due to the presence of the observer.

reasoning the basis of sound research, based on finding correct premises, testing connections between facts and assumptions, and making claims based on adequate evidence.

recency effect order bias occurs when the participant tends to choose the last alternative; in presentations, people remember what they hear at the end of the list of arguments in a speech, recalling those items best; implies an important argument should be the last in your presentation.

reciprocal relationship occurs when two variables mutually influence or reinforce each other.

recoding developing new mapping rules and assigning new codes based on the merging of initial variable categories; done during data preparation and examination; reduces the power of the original scale.

recommendation actions related to the research question that are empirically supported with findings and insights.

record analysis the extraction of data from current or historical records, either private or in the public domain; a technique of data mining.

recording units one of three types of data units in context analysis; refers to the ideas, topics, or themes embedded in the text; four types are syntactical units, referential units, propositional units, and thematic units.

recruitment screener semistructured or structured interview guide designed to ensure the interviewer that the prospect will be a good participant for the planned research.

refusal rate the percentage of contacted potential participants who decline the interview.

region of acceptance area between the two regions of rejection based on a chosen level of significance (two-tailed test) or the area above/below the region of rejection (one-tailed test).

region of rejection area beyond the region of acceptance set by the level of significance.

regression analysis uses simple and multiple predictions to predict Y from X values.

regression coefficients intercept and slope coefficients; the two association measures between X and Y variables.

regression toward the mean a threat to internal validity of an experiment caused when experimental groups are chosen for their extreme scores on IV; in subsequent measurements of the IV their scores tend to reveal *regression toward the mean*.

relational hypothesis describes a relationship between two or more concepts/constructs; each relationship is correlational or causal.

reliability a characteristic of measurement concerned with accuracy, precision, and consistency; a necessary but not sufficient condition for validity (if the measure is not reliable, it cannot be valid).

replication the process of repeating an experiment with different subject groups and conditions to determine the average effect of the IV across people, situations, and times.

report framework an organizational mechanism that influences not only content order but also type of support materials.

report structure combination of oral and written elements that comprise the research report; oral only, oral plus written, written only.

reporting study provides a summation of data, often recasting data to achieve a deeper understanding or to generate statistics for comparison.

research design the blueprint for fulfilling research objectives and answering questions.

research process a sequential process involving several clearly defined stages: clarify the research question, design the research, collect and prepare data, analyze and interpret data, and report insights and recommendations.

research questions the hypothesis that best states the objective of the research; often specifies a choice between action options; the answer to this question would provide the manager with the desired information necessary to make a decision with respect to the management dilemma.

residual the difference between the regression line value of Y and the real Y value; what remains after the regression line is fit.

resistant statistics statistical measures relatively unaffected by outliers within a data set; e.g., median and quartiles.

response error occurs when the participant fails to give a correct or complete answer.

right to confidentiality the participant's right to protect his or her identity and specific responses from being attached to his or her identity.

right to privacy the participant's right to refuse to be interviewed or to refuse to answer any questions in an interview.

right to quality the sponsor's right to appropriate, value-laden research design and data handling and reporting techniques.

right to safety the right of interviewers, surveyors, experimenters, observers, and participants to be protected from any threat of physical or psychological harm.

role-playing a qualitative exercise in which participants are asked to assume a role within the organization and respond to a situation as they think that individual would.

sample a group of cases (participants, events, or records) consisting of a portion of the target population, carefully selected to represent that population.

sample frame list of elements in the population from which the sample is actually drawn.

sample statistics descriptors of the relevant variables computed from sample data.

sampling the process of selecting some elements from a population to represent that population.

sampling design the process of determining the identity of who or what will be measured, and determining how to access or recruit that source.

sampling error error created by the sampling process; the error not accounted for by systematic variance; caused when estimates of a variable drawn from a sample differ from the true value of a population parameter.

sampling units one of three types of data units in context analysis; refers to what text elements the researcher will code (words, phrases, sentences, etc.).

scaling the assignment of numbers or symbols to an indicant of a property or objects to impart some of the characteristics of the numbers to the property; assigned according to value or magnitude.

scalogram analysis a procedure for determining whether a set of items forms a unidimensional scale; used to determine if an item is appropriate for scaling.

scatterplot a visual technique that depicts both the direction and the shape of a relationship between variables.

scientific method systematic, empirically based procedures for generating replicable research; includes direct observation of phenomena; clearly defined variables, methods, and procedures; empirically testable hypotheses; the ability to rule out rival hypotheses; and statistical rather than linguistic justification of conclusions.

scope a report's coverage of research variables among a defined target population.

screen question a question used to qualify the participant's knowledge or experiences relating to the the target questions in order to determine whether a participant has the requisite level of knowledge to participate in the survey.

secondary data data that contain at least one level of interpretation (e.g., results of studies done by others and for different purposes than the one for which the data are being reviewed).

secondary sources interpretations of primary data generally without new research.

selection a threat to interval validity of an experimental design caused by the nonequivalence of control and experimental groups; addressed by random assignment or by matching.

selective filtering (selective attention) due to sheer volume of information collected through our senses, we pay attention to only a small proportion of information we believe is critical.

self-administered survey a highly structured interview experience designed to be completed without an interviewer; it is usually in the form of a questionnaire delivered to the participant via personal (intercept) or nonpersonal (computer-delivered, mail-delivered) means.

semantic differential (SD) scale measures the psychological meanings of an attitude object and produces interval data; uses bipolar nouns, noun phrases, adjectives, or nonverbal stimuli such as visual sketches.

semantic mapping a projective technique in which participants are presented with a four-quadrant map in which different variables anchor the two different axes; they then spatially place brands, product components, or organizations within the four quadrants.

semistructured interview an IDI that starts with a few specific questions and then follows the individual's tangents of thought with interviewer probes; questions generally use an open-ended response strategy.

sensory sorts technique in which participants are presented with scents, textures, and sounds, usually verbalized on cards, and asked to arrange them by one or more criteria as they relate to a brand, product, event, etc.

separate sample pretest-posttest design quasi-experimental design using a separate sample control group that takes two measurements of the DV, a pretest measure of the control group and a posttest measurement of the experimental group; the difference between the two measures is compared to determine effect.

sequential interviewing an IDI technique in which the participant is asked questions formed around an anticipated series of activities that did happen or might have happened; used to stimulate recall within participants of both experiences and emotions; a.k.a. *chronologic interviewing.*

simple category scale a scale with two mutually exclusive response choices; a.k.a. *dichotomous scale.*

simple observation unstructured and exploratory observation of participants or objects.

simple prediction when we take the observed values of X to estimate or predict corresponding Y values; see also *regression analysis.*

simple random sample a probability sample in which each element has a known and equal chance of selection.

single-methodology design a research design that employs only one data collection method.

skip directions instructions that tell an interviewer or participant how to proceed in a measurement instrument, given a particular response to a given question.

skip interval interval between sample elements drawn from a sample frame in systematic sampling.

skip logic diagram a graphical presentation of measurement questions in a measurement instrument indicating the skip direction.

slope (β_1) the change in Y for a 1-unit change in X; one of two regression coefficients.

snowball sampling a nonprobability sampling procedure in which subsequent participants are referred by current sample elements; referrals may have characteristics, experiences, or attitudes similar to or different from those of the original sample element; commonly used in qualitative methodologies.

social desirability bias participants respond inaccurately to a question in order to present themselves in a positive light, respond as they perceive the researcher wants them to respond; a potential problem with sensitive topics.

Somers's *d* a measure of association for ordinal data that compensates for "tied" ranks and adjusts for direction of the independent variable.

sorting participants sort cards (representing concepts or constructs) into piles using criteria established by the researcher.

source evaluation the five-factor process for evaluating the quality and value of data from a secondary source; see also *purpose, scope, authority, audience,* and *format.*

spatial relationships study an observation study that records how humans physically relate to each other (see also *proxemics*).

Spearman's rho (ρ) correlates ranks between two ordered variables; an ordinal measure of association.

stability characteristic of a measurement scale if it provides consistent results with repeated measures of the same person with the same instrument.

Stapel scale a numerical scale with up to 10 categories (half positive, half negative) in which the central position is an attribute. The higher the positive number, the more accurately the attribute describes the object or its indicant.

static group comparison design preexperimental design that takes one posttest measurement of the DV after manipulation of the IV for two groups, one serving as the control; the posttest measurements are compared.

statistical significance an index of how meaningful the results of a statistical comparison are; the magnitude of difference between a sample value and its population value; the difference is statistically significant if it is unlikely to have occurred by chance (represent random sampling fluctuations).

statistical study a study that attempts to capture a population's characteristics by making inferences from a sample's characteristics; involves hypothesis testing and is more comprehensive than a case study.

statistics numerical summaries and calculations used in the collection, analysis, and interpretation of data, but also found in the data collection planning, measurement, and design; expected in research presentations; of several types including descriptive, inferential, Bayesian, classical, etc.

stem-and-leaf display an exploratory data analysis display for variables with continuous data that uses actual values to group data rather than equal intervals; each line or row is a stem; each item in the row is a leaf.

stimulus-response a type of asymmetrical causal relationship where an event or change in the IV results in a response in the DV.

story relates the particulars of a single act or occurrence or course of events to clarify a concept or construct or bring an insight to life; might relate the responses of an individual respondent via a quote, audio clip, or video clip; also describes the interwoven elements of a research report that uses the narrative organizational framework.

storytelling a qualitative exercise in which a scenario is described and participants are asked to tell a story related to the scenario.

stratified random sampling probability sampling that includes elements from each of the mutually exclusive strata within a population.

stratified sampling, disproportionate a probability sampling technique in which each stratum's size is not proportionate to the stratum's share of the population; allocation is usually based on variability of measures expected from the stratum, cost of sampling from a given stratum, and size of the various strata.

stratified sampling, proportionate a probability sampling technique in which each stratum's size is proportionate to the stratum's share of the population; higher statistical efficiency than a simple random sample.

structured interview an IDI that uses a detailed interview guide similar to a questionnaire, which specifies the questions and the order of the questions; permits probing for clarification (or in qualitative research, for meaning).

structured question a measurement question that presents the participant with a fixed set of choices; a.k.a *closed question*; generates nominal, ordinal, or interval data.

structured response participant's response is limited to specific alternatives provided by the researcher; a.k.a *closed response; this is typical of structured question.*

summated rating scale category of scales in which the participant agrees or disagrees with evaluative statements; the Likert scale is most known of this type of scale.

survey a measurement process using a highly structured interview; employs a measurement tool called a *questionnaire, measurement instrument*, or *interview schedule*.

survey activation the decision that launches the survey; it indicates the researcher has addressed all known measurement instrument problems and the process is as error-free as possible.

survey via personal interview a quantitative study using an individual depth interview between a trained interviewer and a single participant; a face-to-face structured interview that uses a measurement instrument similar to a questionnaire which specifies the questions and the order of the questions; gives the interviewer flexibility to probe the participant for clarification by asking prepared follow-up questions.

survivorship bias an audience's tendency to believe stories that resulted in success rather than failure.

symmetrical relationship occurs when two variables vary together but without causation.

systematic observation data collection through observation that employs standardized procedures, trained observers, schedules for recording, and other devices for the observer that mirror the scientific procedures of other primary data methods.

systematic sampling a probability sample drawn by applying a calculated skip interval to a sample frame; population (N) is divided by the desired sample (n) to obtain a skip interval (k). Using a random start between 1 and k, each kth element is chosen from the sample frame; usually treated as a simple random sample but statistically more efficient.

systematic variance the variation that causes measurements to skew in one direction or another.

***t* distribution** a normal distribution with more tail area than that in a Z normal distribution.

table a presentation of data or statistics in rows and columns built from cross-tabulated data; these data are related to each other and need to be presented together to facilitate comparison; two forms are summary tables (containing only a few key pieces of data) or general tables (tend to be large, complex, detailed, and contain many elements of data).

target population those people, events, or records that possess the desired information to answer the research question.

target question measurement question that addresses the core investigative questions of a specific study; these can be structured or unstructured questions.

tau (τ) a measure of association that uses table marginals to reduce prediction errors, with measures from 0 to 1.0 reflecting percentage of error estimates for prediction of one variable based on another variable.

tau *b* ($τ_b$) a refinement of gamma for ordinal data that considers "tied' pairs, not only discordant and concordant pairs (values from −1.0 to +1.0); used best on square tables (one of the most widely used measures for ordinal data).

tau *c* ($τ_c$) a refinement of gamma for ordinal data that considers "tied' pairs, not only discordant and concordant pairs (values from −1.0 to +1.0); useful for any size table (one of the most widely used measures for ordinal data).

technical report a report written for an audience of researchers.

telephone survey a structured interview conducted via telephone.

tertiary sources aids to discover primary or secondary sources, such as indexes, bibliographies, and Internet search engines; also may be an interpretation of a secondary source.

testimony (expert opinion) opinions of recognized experts who possess credibility for your audience on a topic; used as support or proof.

testing a threat to the internal validity of an experiment caused by changes that may occur within the participant as a result of learning from a pretest within the experimental design.

Thematic Apperception Test a projective technique in which participants are confronted with a picture (usually a photograph or drawing) and asked to describe how the person in the picture feels and thinks.

theory a set of systematically interrelated concepts, definitions, and propositions that are advanced to explain or predict phenomena (facts); the generalizations we make about variables and the relationships among variables.

third-party projection a qualitative exercise in which participants are asked to describe what others feel, believe, think, or do.

time sampling the process of selecting certain time points or time intervals to observe and record elements, acts, or conditions from a population of observable behaviors or conditions to represent the population as a whole; three types include time-point samples, time-interval samples, and continuous real-time samples.

tone a report's style or manner of expression; serious and professional is better than casual.

transition descriptive statement within a measurement instrument that is designed to alert the participant to a change in topic or a shift in question group.

treatment levels the arbitrary or natural groupings within the independent variable of an experiment.

trials repeated measures taken from the same subject or participant.

triangulation research design that combines several qualitative methods or qualitative with quantitative methods; most common are simultaneous QUAL/QUANT in single or multiple waves, sequential QUAL-QUANT or QUANT-QUAL, sequential QUAL-QUANT-QUAL.

t-test a parametric test to determine the statistical significance between a sample distribution mean and a population parameter; used when the population standard deviation is unknown and the sample standard deviation is used as a proxy.

two-independent-samples tests parametric and nonparametric tests used when the measurements are taken from two samples that are unrelated (Z test, t-test, chi-square, etc.).

two-related-samples tests parametric and nonparametric tests used when the measurements are taken from closely matched samples or the phenomena are measured twice from the same sample (t-test, McNemar test, etc).

two-tailed test a nondirectional test to reject the hypothesis that the sample statistic is either greater than or less than the population parameter.

Type I error (α) error that occurs when one rejects a true null hypothesis (there is no difference); the alpha (α) value, called the level of significance, is the probability of rejecting the true null hypothesis.

Type II error (β) error that occurs when one fails to reject a false null hypothesis; the beta (β) value is the probability of failing to reject the false null hypothesis; the power of the test ($1 - \beta$) is the probability that we will correctly reject the false null hypothesis.

unbalanced rating scale has an unequal number of favorable and unfavorable response choices.

unforced-choice rating scale provides participants with an opportunity to express no opinion when they are unable to make a choice among the alternatives offered.

unidimensional scale instrument scale that seeks to measure only one attribute of the participant or object.

unobtrusive measures a set of observational approaches that encourage creative and imaginative forms of indirect observation, archival searches, and variations on simple and contrived observation, including physical traces observation (erosion and accretion).

unstructured interview a customized IDI with no specific questions or order of topics to be discussed; usually starts with a participant narrative.

unstructured question a measurement question in which the participant chooses the words to frame the answer; a.k.a. *open-ended question, free-response question;* generates nominal, ordinal, or ratio data.

unstructured response participant's response is limited only by space, layout, instructions, or time; usually free-response or fill-in response strategies; structured questions may add an option for an unstructured response to cover alternatives that were not offered in the measurement question.

unsupported assumption question measurement question that assumes (right or wrong) an implied affirmative answer to an unasked question in order to answer the current question.

validity a characteristic of measurement concerned with the extent that a test measures what the researcher actually wishes to measure; ensures differences found with a measurement tool reflect true differences among participants drawn from a population.

variable (research variable) a characteristic, trait, or attribute that is measured; a symbol to which values are assigned; includes several different types: continuous, control, decision, dependent, dichotomous, discrete, dummy, extraneous, independent, intervening, and moderating variables.

visitor from another planet a projective technique (imagination exercise) in which participants are asked to assume that they are aliens and are confronting the product for the first time; they then describe their reactions, questions, and attitudes about purchase or retrial.

visual graphic rating scale A scale where participants mark their response at any point along a along a line between two response choices that are represented by images or symbols, rather than words; the measure is one of length from the end point; generates interval data.

visual learners people who learn through seeing; about 40 percent of the audience; implies the need to include visual imagery, including graphs, photographs, models, etc., in research presentations.

visualize the process of developing a report's textual, tabular, graphical, and audio support materials that help the audience share in the researcher's understanding of the data.

whitespace a design principle of leaving empty, uncluttered space surrounding important key visuals and text; permits audience to achieve a visual focus.

word or picture association a projective technique in which participants are asked to match images, experiences, emotions, products and services, and even people and places to whatever is being studied.

write a letter a qualitative exercise in which participants are asked to write a letter to a person empowered to make things happen (e.g., CEO, HR director, a parent, etc.).

Z **distribution** the normal distribution of measurements assumed for comparison.

Z **test** a parametric test to determine the statistical significance between a sample distribution mean and a population parameter; employs the Z distribution.

Note: locators with n indicate note.

A

Aczel, Amir D., 561n1, 571n14, 572n2, 573n3, 573n4, 573n11
Adamou, Betty, 197, 567n1, 567n2
Agresti, Alan, 573n8, 573n15
Akert, R., 569n14
Alpert, Geroffrey, 158
Allport, Gordon W., 569n14
Alreck, Pamela L., 569n17
Altman, Rick, 466, 574n12, 574n24
Alwin, Duane F., 569n26
Amoo, Taiwo, 569n6
Amram, Ron, 12
Anderson, Monica, 561n13, 562n3
Anderson, Tom H. C., 41, 134, 211, 274, 559n1, 561n1, 562n3, 563n1, 570n1, 571n1
Andrews, F. M., 572n7
Anscombe, F. J., 572n2
Aquino, Judith, 565n3
Archibald, Gregg, 35
Aristotle, 445–447, 574n14, 574n16
Aronson, E., 564n3, 569n14
Assael, Henry, 561n8

B

Babbie, Earl R., 565n9
Bailey, Kenneth D., 564n7, 565n8
Baldia, Sonia, 41
Bales, R., 564n4
Bales, Robert F., 159, 564n9
Bancroft, Gertrude, 570n10
Baron, Robert A., 569n15
Barrell, J. E., 575n9
Barrell, J. J., 575n9
Bauer, Martin, 563n23
Beatles, 459
Belk, Russel, 562n4
Benisch, Michael, 34, 559n2
Berenson, Conrad, 566n14, 566n15
Berger, Warren, 45, 52
Berggren, Kathy Lee, 43
Berkowitz, Eric N., 22, 558n16
Bezos, Jeff, 170, 397
Bierley, Calvin, 425, 573n2
Bigwood, Sally, 349, 350, 572n1
Blitz, Shelby, 575n1
Blumberg, Stephen J., 565n4, 567n3, 567n4, 567n5
Bolton, Brian, 15
Bostock, Michael, 575n35
Boyd, Harper W., Jr., 570n3, 572n21
Bramble, William J., 568n20, 573n4
Breese, Jennifer, 564n7
Broedling, L. A., 564n11
Brooks, William D., 560n3, 560n6
Broome, Jessica, 92, 93

Brown, Rex V., 559n13
Bruning, James L., 572n11, 572n12
Brusaw, Phillip V., 576n3
Bryan, Glenn L., 559n9
Bunger, Mark, 446, 575n1
Burke, Brian, 197
Buzzell, Robert D., 559n13
Byrne, Donn, 569n15

C

Cacioppo, John T., 569n14
Calhoun, Gia, 122
Campbell, Donald T., 564n10, 565n10, 564n11, 568n14
Cannell, Charles F., 566n35, 567, 569n30, 570n5
Cantril, Hadley, 290, 291, 570n12
Cape, Pete, 562n4, 567n1
Carson, David, 128, 135, 562n4, 562n7, 563n25, 563n27, 563n29
Cartwright, Dorwin, 569n3
Cascio, Wayne F., 568n17, 568n19
Case, Sean, 110, 562n1, 562n2
Castellan, N. J., Jr., 371, 572n13, 573n14
Cassidy, Richard, 8
Chambers, J., 571n20
Chatterjee, Samprit, 572n2
Chen, Jesse, 211
Christian, Brian, 375, 572n2
Churchill, G. A., 569n9
Clark, Cynthia, 5
Cleveland, W., 571n20
Coats, Emma, 448
Cochran, W. G., 556, 561n18, 561n24
Cohen, Morris R., 564n4
Cohen, Roger, 559n6
Conover, W. J., 572n9
Converse, Jean M., 569n31
Cook, Stuart W., 568n11, 568n12
Cook, Thomas D., 565n11, 568n14
Cooper, Donald R., 569n7, 572n1, 574n11, 575n1, 576n5
Covert, James, 559n1
Cox, Donald F., 559n13
Cox, Eli P., 569n10
Crooks, Ross, 575n34

D

Darley, J. M., 564n5
Davidson, T. N., 572n7
Day, Daniel D., 569n11
Daymon, Christine, 563n17
de Leeuw, Edith, 566n6, 566n8, 566n10
Dearing, Brian E., 571n9
Deese, J., 574n9
Degeling, D., 563n20
Deming, W. E., 94, 561n7
Denzin, Norman, 128, 135, 562n4
DePompe, B., 559n10

Dewey, John, 19, 558n14, 558n15
Diamantopoulus, A., 561n2
Dillman, Don A., 566n9, 566n11, 566n13
Dlugen, Andrew, 575n7
Doane, Seth, 176
Dobrenwend, Barbara Snell, 570n14
Drew, Nick, 70, 561n1
Duarte, Nancy, 470, 574n24, 575n11
Duboff, Robert, 567n5
Dunnette, Marvin D., 565n11, 568n14
Dykes, Brent, 434

E

Edwards, Allen L., 262
Ehninger, D., 574n10
Elliot, Stuart, 568nd, 573n2
Elliott, Nate, 564n8
Emerson, John D., 571n13, 571n14
Emmert, Philip, 560n3, 560n6
Enson, Dan, 260, 570n2, 570n3
Everitt, B. S., 572n8

F

Fahnestock, Jeanne, 574n15
Farley, James, 88
Few, Stephen, 574n26
Finlay, Barbara, 573n8, 573n15
Flick, Uwe, 563n30
Forsyth, Mark, 211
Fowler, Floyd J., Jr., 566n31, 566n34
Frey, J. H., Jr., 566n19
Friedman, H. H., 569n6, 569n10
Furtado, Bruno, 573n1

G

Gallo, Carmine, 575n2, 575n12
Gaskell, George, 563n23
Gates, Bill, 459
Geewax, Marilyn, 566n30
Genovese, Kitty, 565n5
Gibaldi, Joseph, 576n8
Gill, Sam, 570n1
Gilmore, Audrey, 128, 135, 562n4
Gillum, Gerald Earl, 85
Gladwell, Malcolm, 459, 567n3, 575n36
Glasser, G. J., 566n25
Goldberg, David, 194
Goodfellow, Pam, 338
Goode, William J., 564n2
Gopinath, Menaka, 571n2
Grimes, William, 564n12
Gronhaug, Kjell, 128, 135, 562n4, 562n7
Grove, J. B., 564n10
Groves, Robert M., 566n16, 566n29
Guba, E., 562n4
Guess, Andy, 43
Guilford, J. P., 569n5, 569n12
Guttman, Louis, 569n22

>company index

>subject index